OXFORD WORLD'S CLASSICS

MRS BEETON'S BOOK OF HOUSEHOLD MANAGEMENT

ISABELLA BEETON was born Isabella Mayson in the City of London in 1836, the daughter of a dry-goods trader. She spent most of her childhood in Epsom, living first at the home of her step-father, and then in the Grandstand on Epsom racecourse with her older siblings. In 1855, having attended schools in Islington and Germany, she married a young publisher, Samuel Beeton. She wrote columns on cooking and fashion for his *Englishwoman's Domestic Magazine*, and translated French novels for serialization. She began *Household Management* in 1857; it was published in parts between 1859 and 1861 and in volume form in 1861. She gave birth to four children, two of whom died in infancy. She died in 1865, at the age of 28, of an infection contracted during the delivery of her fourth child.

NICOLA HUMBLE is a Senior Lecturer in English at Roehampton Institute London. She is the co-author (with Kimberley Reynolds) of *Victorian Heroines* (Harvester, 1993), and has also published on Robert Browning, Jane Austen, children's literature, and cookery books. She is currently working on a study of middlebrow women writers of the first half of the twentieth century and a cultural history of cookery books.

OXFORD WORLD'S CLASSICS

*For almost 100 years Oxford World's Classics have brought
readers closer to the world's great literature. Now with over 700
titles—from the 4,000-year-old myths of Mesopotamia to the
twentieth century's greatest novels—the series makes available
lesser-known as well as celebrated writing.*

*The pocket-sized hardbacks of the early years contained
introductions by Virginia Woolf, T. S. Eliot, Graham Greene,
and other literary figures which enriched the experience of reading.
Today the series is recognized for its fine scholarship and
reliability in texts that span world literature, drama and poetry,
religion, philosophy and politics. Each edition includes perceptive
commentary and essential background information to meet the
changing needs of readers.*

OXFORD WORLD'S CLASSICS

MRS BEETON

Mrs Beeton's Book of Household Management

ABRIDGED EDITION

Edited with an Introduction and Notes by
NICOLA HUMBLE

OXFORD
UNIVERSITY PRESS

OXFORD
UNIVERSITY PRESS

Great Clarendon Street, Oxford OX2 6DP

Oxford University Press is a department of the University of Oxford.
It furthers the University's objective of excellence in research, scholarship,
and education by publishing worldwide in

Oxford New York

Athens Auckland Bangkok Bogotá Buenos Aires Calcutta
Cape Town Chennai Dar es Salaam Delhi Florence Hong Kong Istanbul
Karachi Kuala Lumpur Madrid Melbourne Mexico City Mumbai
Nairobi Paris São Paulo Singapore Taipei Tokyo Toronto Warsaw

with associated companies in Berlin Ibadan

Oxford is a registered trade mark of Oxford University Press
in the UK and in certain other countries

Published in the United States
by Oxford University Press Inc., New York

First published as an Oxford World's Classics paperback 2000

British Library Cataloguing in Publication Data

Data available

Library of Congress Cataloging in Publication Data

Data available

ISBN 0–19–283345–6

1 3 5 7 9 10 8 6 4 2

Typeset in Ehrhardt
by RefineCatch Limited, Bungay, Suffolk
Printed in Great Britain by
Cox & Wyman Ltd.
Reading, Berkshire

CONTENTS

INTRODUCTION

Mrs Beeton's Book of Household Management is the most famous English cookery book ever published. It stands four-square in the nation's imagination as a bastion of traditional English fare and solid Victorian values. It represents extravagance ('take 12 dozen eggs'), and a lost rural way of life ('first catch your hare'). We imagine Mrs Beeton as a sturdy matron (perhaps resembling Mrs Bridges of the 1970s television series *Upstairs, Downstairs*), ordering a well-regimented army of servants. Yet this popular perception of the book is false in every particular. Far from being traditional, *Household Management* was markedly innovative, introducing the newly expanded and self-consciously respectable Victorian middle class to the latest manufactured food products, to a wide range of foreign recipes, and to fashionably different modes of dining. Those famous lines about eggs and hares were never written by Beeton, but represent the persistent misinterpretation to which the book has been subject. Although it contains a smattering of extravagant recipes, if anything it errs on the side of frugality, with many pages devoted to plain family dinners and the use of left-overs (it was these which tended to be removed from later editions, encouraging the view of the book as extravagant). The rural economy in which most people produced their own food had long been lost by the time Beeton embarked on her book, and she is as nostalgic for that old connection to the land as we are today. Finally, Isabella Beeton was never the stately matron of our imaginings: she worked as a journalist throughout her married life, and died of an infection after giving birth to her fourth child, at the age of 28.

Household Management must rank as one of the great unread classics. Everyone has heard of it, a number of people own a copy (often an early twentieth-century edition, much expanded and bearing little relationship to Beeton's original text), but it is rarely considered as anything other than a culinary curiosity. Yet it was one of the major publishing success stories of the nineteenth century, selling over 60,000 copies in its first year of publication in 1861, and nearly two million by 1868. For the next century the names 'Mrs Beeton' and 'Household Management' were to continue to make enormous profits for Ward, Lock & Co., to whom Isabella's publisher husband Sam sold the rights in a disastrous deal soon after her death. A considerable amount of the book's success can be attributed to the assiduity and ingenuity with which its various publishers have exploited its title and its author's name as trademarks. Revised and abridged editions were issued constantly, both in Isabella Beeton's lifetime, when she and Sam made use of the book's phenomenal success to sell various spin-off projects, and ever since: even today we can buy books with titles as absurd as *Mrs Beeton's Caribbean Cooking* and *Microwaving with Mrs Beeton*, few of which contain a word written by their putative author.

  Household Management has long been seen as the quintessentially Victorian work, and its status has consequently risen and fallen with the shifting attitudes to that era. In the 1930s there was a brief wave of nostalgia for the nineteenth century, and it was at this time that Isabella's son, Sir Mayson Beeton, presented a painting of his mother to the National Portrait Gallery; the shadowy Mrs Beeton came into surprising focus as a fashionable young girl, and the accompanying postcard, giving the bare facts of her life, aroused new public interest in her and her book. By the time of the zenith of anti-Victorianism in the 1950s and early 1960s, however, Beeton had become a stock butt of comedians, and the subject of numerous comic representations—Guinness, for example, issued an elaborate parody in booklet form as an advertisement in 1956. As the wave of historical revivalism came round again in the 1970s, several facsimile editions of *Household Management* were published. In times of shortage it has proved particularly attractive: it was read by men on Scott's Antarctic expedition, and prisoners of war in Japanese camps later acclaimed it as their favourite escapist reading.

Isabella Beeton was an unlikely arbiter of middle-class tastes and manners. She was born in Cheapside in 1836, the eldest child of lower-middle-class parents: her father, John Mayson, was in the dry-goods trade, although his own father had ranked rather higher in the nineteenth-century taxonomy of class as a country parson; her mother, Elizabeth (née Jessam), was the daughter of a widow who kept a lodging-house. Isabella's father died when she was 5, and two years later her mother married again. Her new husband was a widower called Henry Dorling, who had inherited a prosperous printing business from his father, and enjoyed a stylish *nouveau riche* life-style in Epsom, where he had just been appointed Clerk of the Racecourse. Isabella and her three siblings moved with their mother to Epsom, where they joined Dorling's own four children in a grand house in the centre of the town. The Dorlings now lived a very different life from that of the Maysons in Cheapside: Henry was a significant figure in the small town, and the family was on visiting terms with the local aristocracy and gentry and hosted musical evenings and stately dinner parties. Having begun with a combined family of eight children, the Dorlings added to it assiduously and ended with twenty-one offspring—a startling number even by middle-class Victorian standards. The house in Epsom High Street was soon overflowing, and Isabella's mother hit on the ingenious, if cold-blooded, solution of sending the elder children to live on the racecourse, where Dorling had just acquired the lease of the huge Grandstand in his capacity as Clerk. So they moved into the rooms beneath the stands, sleeping in the committee rooms (except during Derby week, when they were farmed out to neighbouring families), eating in the saloon, and running wild in the enormous building and on the racecourse, looked after by 'Granny Jessam', helped by Isabella and the next eldest sister, Bessie. It was a highly unconventional childhood for a Victorian girl—one in which unwonted physical exercise and a lack of immediate parental authority were combined with early domestic responsibility, albeit of a rather ramshackle nature. Isabella was sent briefly to a boarding-school in Islington, which she found very boring, and then to a school in Heidelberg—notably not a finishing school—where she became fluent in French and German, became a promising pianist, and learnt to cook patisserie. In Germany, in contrast with England, it was considered entirely appropriate for middle-class girls to be trained in cookery—though only in the elaborate pastries that were the specialities of particular regions. When Isabella returned home she extended these studies in pastry-making at the local confectioner's—conduct, according to the later report of one of her sisters, that 'was supposed to be ultra-modern and not quite nice'.[1]

Shortly after her return Isabella became engaged to a young

---

[1] Nancy Spain, *Mrs Beeton and her Husband* (Collins: London, 1948), 62, quoting Isabella's younger sister, Lucy Smiles.

publisher, Samuel Beeton, who was the son of old friends of her
mother's from the Cheapside days. Since the age of 21 he had been a
partner in Clarke, Beeton & Co., whose successes in his time
included the first English edition of Harriet Beecher Stowe's *Uncle
Tom's Cabin*, which made Sam a fortune while he was still in his
twenties. Sam's particular contribution to the firm was the founding
of a number of extremely successful magazines, notably the *Boy's
Own Journal* (started 1855), and the *Englishwoman's Domestic Magazine* (started 1852). The latter was responsible for a number of
innovations that were to remain stalwart features of inexpensive
women's magazines for the next century: paper dress-patterns and
instructions for readers to make their own clothes, readers' essay
competitions, a problem page—known as 'Cupid's Letter Bag', a
medical column, and the distribution of prizes. A typical issue
(volume 7 of 1859) contained the following features: a historical
series, 'The Religions of the World', this issue's on Babylon; a story,
'The Tribune's Daughter'; an opinion article, 'Is Woman Superior to
Man?'; a poem, 'The Baby Dead'; an article in a series on 'What We
Used to Wear'; a historical article on 'Valentina Visconti, The First
Duchess of Orleans'; an article on the 'Management of Children',
which is identical to the introductory section of the chapter of that
name in *Household Management*; a reader's 'Letter on the Economy
of Dress', asking for cheaper fashions and for tips on the allocation
of one's dress allowance; a pattern and instructions for making a
jacket in 'The Fashions and Practical Dress Instructor'; an article on
'Cooking, Pickling and Preserving', which again was later to appear
in the same form in *Household Management*; instructions for a 'Collar
in Frivolite or Tatting' in a series called 'The Work Table'; and an
extract from a French novel called 'The Story of a Pin', by J. T. de St
Germain, almost certainly translated by Isabella, who worked on a
whole series of French novels for serialization in the magazine even
before she and Sam were married. The flavour and attitudes of the
Englishwoman's Domestic Magazine are apparent from this list of contents. Sam, who was a strong believer in women's independence and
education, concentrated on improving, serious articles, mixed with
sentimental verse and fiction, and practical advice on dress, health,
and running a home. The declared aim of the magazine, stated by
the editor in the first issue, was the fostering of successful domestic
life:

The Englishwoman's Domestic Magazine will doubtless be found an encouraging friend to those of our countrywomen already initiated in the secret of making 'home happy'; and to the uninitiated, who sometimes from carelessness but oftener from want of a guiding monitor have failed in this great particular, we shall offer hints and advice by which they may overcome every difficulty and acquire the art of rendering their efforts successful and their homes attractive.

The formula was immensely successful, and the magazine, priced at 2*d*. a month, rapidly attained a large circulation (50,000 by 1860) among the middle-class women at whom it was aimed.

Sam and Isabella were married in July 1856, when she was 20 and he 25; earlier the same year Sam had set himself up as an independent publisher, taking both his magazines with him. The couple moved into a new semi-detached suburban house in Pinner, the decoration of which Sam had scrupulously overseen in the course of the previous year. It was now that Isabella began to realize the rigours of both the publishing business and the business of running a house. The couple employed a cook, a kitchenmaid, a housemaid, and a gardener, all of whom Isabella had to supervise. Although she had some experience of managing a household, she initially found the task of running her own home fraught with difficulties, and, according to her sisters, frequently remarked 'Why has no one written a book—a good book for brides? To help them learn these things?'[2] It was in these early days of marriage that Isabella conceived the plan for the massive work that was to occupy her for the next three years. One of her major aims in *Household Management* was to reverse the trend of husbands eating both their midday and their evening meals in clubs or chop-houses. With the emphasis on business that characterized the new form of middle-class life, and the drift of the middle classes out to the suburbs of large towns, the home was becoming less central in its importance to men. Sam was a prime example—he often caught the last train back from London, and before his marriage had tended to eat in town. Isabella, though, insisted on keeping his meal warm for his return, and was to advise her readers in the Preface of *Household Management* that 'men are now so well served out of doors,—at their clubs, well-ordered taverns, and dining houses, that in order to compete with the attractions of these places,

[2] Spain, *Mrs Beeton and her Husband*, 62.

a mistress must be thoroughly acquainted with the theory and practice of cookery, as well as be perfectly conversant with all the other
arts of making and keeping a comfortable home'. It is no exagger-
ation to say that Isabella Beeton's preoccupation with getting her
husband to spend more time at home was in no small part responsible for the new cult of domesticity that was to play such a major
role in mid-Victorian life. Her significance in this regard was noted
by an academic writing at the time of the women's suffrage cam-
paigns in the early twentieth century, who remarked that 'Mrs Bee-
tonism has preserved the family as a social unit, and made social
reform a possibility'.[3]

In essence, Isabella Beeton was a journalist, contributing many
column inches to her husband's magazines, on fashion and cookery
as well as translations. This fact explains many of the most distinctive features of *Household Management*, and may account for some of
its success. The core of the book was the many thousands of recipes
contributed by readers of the *Englishwoman's Domestic Journal*,
which Isabella and her servants tested exhaustively in her kitchen in
Pinner. Isabella made no claims for herself as an originator of
recipes, and only a handful of the nearly two thousand the book
contains are presented as her own. Her skill was in clarity of language and the organization of a mass of information into easily
digestible nuggets. *Household Management* is encyclopaedic in its
range, and Isabella clearly found it hard to resist an interesting fact:
the notes that precede each recipe chapter are packed with information on history, myth, religion, agriculture, animal husbandry, science, sociology, and so on. These sections take the work far beyond
the conventional scope of a cookery book, and were envisaged by
Sam and Isabella as a key feature, emphasized at length in their
advertisements:

A new and important feature, which, it is felt, will form an invaluable
portion of *BEETON'S BOOK OF HOUSEHOLD MANAGEMENT*, is the history, description, properties, and uses, of every article directly or
indirectly connected with the Household. Thus, if in a recipe for a
Christmas plum-pudding, are named the various ingredients of raisins,
currants, candied oranges and lemon-peel, sugar, citron, bitter almonds

---

[3] See Graham Nown, *Mrs Beeton: 150 Years of Cookery and Household Management*
(Ward Lock: London, 1986), 60.

and brandy, BEETON'S BOOK OF HOUSEHOLD MANAGEMENT will give
ample information on questions such as these:-

*Where are Raisins grown, and how are they dried?—In what Countries do
Currants flourish most, and what Process do they undergo in order to be made
suitable for the English market?—How are Candied Orange and Lemon-peel
manufactured, and what are the characteristics of the growth of the Orange
and Lemon-trees? [. . .] What enters into the manufacture of Brandy, and
what are the names of the principal places it comes from?—Do we distil any in
this Country? &c.*[4]

That these questions resemble the schoolroom catechisms required
of Victorian girls is no accident: in its heterogenous and sometimes
seemingly random mix of disciplines and discourses, *Household
Management* belongs to an already-existing tradition of female education; one which, in the absence of professional careers for women,
offered learning with no object, and tended to exercise the memory
rather than the intellect. The often ludicrously piecemeal qualities of
this feminine education were admirably summarized by Elizabeth
Barrett-Browning in her long verse novel *Aurora Leigh*, as the
eponymous heroine complains at the academic instruction arranged
for her by her aunt:

> I learnt a little algebra, a little
> Of the mathematics,—brushed with extreme flounce
> The circle of the sciences, because
> She misliked women who are frivolous.
> I learnt the royal genealogies
> Of Oviedo, the internal laws
> Of the Burmese empire,—by how many feet
> Mount Chimaborazo outsoars Teneriffe.
> What navigable river joins itself
> To Lara, and what census of the year five
> Was taken at Klagenfurt,—because she liked
> A general insight into useful facts.
>
> (*Aurora Leigh* (1857), i. 403–14)

Although the curriculum offered by *Household Management*, with
its similar preoccupation with useful facts, was not in itself particularly radical, it did at least offer a systematic body of knowledge
connected with the domestic lives lived by its readers. It was also

[4] Advertisement in the second volume of the 24-vol. part work of *Household
Management*, published between 1859 and 1861.

highly unusual in its assumption of the intellectual curiosity of those female readers, crediting them with enquiring minds and a desire for self-improvement. Sometimes, though, Isabella assumes too much, and loses the logic of her primary endeavour in a welter of secondary concerns: she begins the chapter on vegetable cooking, for example, with an abstruse discussion of the ultimate scientific impossibility of drawing a firm dividing line between plants and animals, and follows it with a lengthy disquisition on the natural and economic history of lichens—not something that many readers would have expected or required when they turned to the section for a new recipe for cabbage.

In the recipe sections which formed the bulk of the book, Beeton retained her journalistic perspective, approaching each dish as a novice rather than an expert, and painstakingly describing every stage in its construction. Her style is matter-of-fact, and determinedly impersonal: there are very few anecdotes and asides, no glimpses of her own kitchen, or hints as to her preferences. Instead, she tries to put cooking on a logical, scientific basis. The form in which the recipes are given is one invented by the earlier food writer Eliza Acton (1799–1859), who was the first writer to list ingredients, quantities, and times separately from method. Beeton elaborated on Acton's approach by giving the ingredients list logically at the start of the recipe, rather than at the end, and also in giving the number of people each dish would serve, and an estimate of its cost. She also devoted a great deal of attention to perfecting her descriptions of methods to make them clear, logical, and unambiguous. In this respect she differs markedly from the style and approach of her immediate culinary predecessors. The most important food writers just prior to Beeton were Eliza Acton and Alexis Soyer. Acton's *Modern Cookery for Private Families* of 1845 was one of the first books to address itself centrally to the culinary needs of the middle classes. Written in response to a publisher's half-joking suggestion that she write a cookery book instead of the volume of verse she was trying to sell him, Acton's book was in many ways the antithesis of Beeton's. Where Beeton gives clear, impersonal instructions, Acton (despite her rationalist innovations in the way of recipe lay-out) offers discussion, explanation, and the quirky, confident perspective of the expert. Beeton, in contrast, habitually omits explanation in the recipes themselves, with sometimes frustrating results (she gives a recipe, for instance, for 'asparagus peas', in which the asparagus is laboriously cut into pea-sized segments, with no indication of why anyone would wish to make one luxury vegetable resemble another; we have to turn to Acton for the information that the process is used for very young asparagus, when the stems are too small to make a good appearance whole). In essence, Acton was the Elizabeth David of her day, while the reassuringly plodding Beeton was the Delia Smith—less stylish, but reaching a far wider range of the population, and decisively affecting the eating habits of the nation. To continue the analogy, Alexis Soyer (1809–58), the flamboyant chef of the famous Reform Club, was the equivalent of the modern television chef, with a strong media profile, and a finger in every available pie. Soyer was the first to establish soup kitchens for the poor, and took the idea to Ireland during the potato famine; he visited the troops in the Crimean war, and reorganized their mess arrangements in the interests of improved nutrition. He was the author of a number of very successful cookery books, including *The Gastronomic Regenerator* of 1846, in which he proposed a new and simplified culinary system; the *Modern Housewife* of 1850, which presents its culinary and domestic advice in the form of letters exchanged between two fictional women friends; and *The Pantropheon* (1853), a scholarly history of food from 'the earliest ages of the world' to the present.

Isabella Beeton borrowed largely and unashamedly from the publications of both Acton and Soyer, with random and scanty acknowledgement. In fact, there is very little that is original in *Household Management*—but it does not claim otherwise. Rather than being a unified culinary system, it is a huge hotch-potch of dishes from different nations, regions, classes, and periods. It was perhaps because of its inclusivity that the book spoke so widely to the needs of so many readers—but to understand exactly what *Household Management* was saying to the Victorian middle classes, we need to look beneath its cool, factual surface for the ideologies and subtexts bubbling underneath.

It is precisely because they are an ephemeral, market-led form of writing that cookery books reveal so much about the features of a particular historical moment. We must remember, though, that like any other text they consist of constructed discourses, and can never be clear windows onto the kitchens of the past. *Household Management* does not reveal in any straightforward way what middle-class people actually ate in the middle years of the nineteenth century, but—perhaps more interestingly—it offers us the recipes which (in the case of readers' contributions) they chose to represent themselves, and the dishes which one woman collected because she considered them desirable, stylish, or nutritious. Cookery books are always interventions in the nation's diet, rather than accurate reflections of its current state: they represent an attempt to popularize new foods, new methods, fresh attitudes. They tell us more about the fantasies and fears associated with foods than about what people actually had for dinner at a particular date.

Read analytically and against the grain, *Household Management* reveals a concern with new constructions of class, revised gender roles and relations, regional and national identities, history, economics, and the momentous cultural clash between science and religion. Among its lesser themes are violence and cruelty, illness and death, the birth and rearing of children, poison and the adulteration of food, factory farming, industrial food production, poverty, and charity. To fully comprehend the book, we need to take into account the multiple and hybrid discourses it employs—ranging from classical quotation to quaint old proverbs, religious exhortation to scientific analysis, humorous anecdotes to furious diatribes. We need also to consider how its shifting modes of address, its alternations between extravagance and frugality, and its construction of its imagined readers relate to the fantasies and anxieties of the new urban middle class it was addressing.

Considering how deeply *Household Management* is associated with the name of its author, with the one often substituting for the other, it is a surprisingly polyphonic text. Its recipes were almost all supplied by readers of the *Englishwoman's Domestic Magazine*; its last three chapters, 'The Rearing and Management of Children', 'The Doctor', and 'Legal Memoranda', were written by a doctor and a solicitor; and there has long been a question mark about just how much Sam contributed to the book, particularly those encyclopaedic sections that overlap with his own *Dictionary of Universal Information*. The copious borrowings from other sources have already been noted, and careless editing—as in the section on the groom in the 'Domestic Servants' chapter, where the writer is repeatedly referred to as 'he'—increases the multi-vocal effect. These various voices do not always mesh well together: the writer in the legal section tends to assume that his reader is male, in direct contrast to Beeton's own assumption throughout the main body of the book, while 'the Doctor' employs a bluff, masculine tone, with notes of rather gruesome humour, that is at odds with Beeton's air of measured good sense. These conflicting voices echo a deeper level of conflict within the book: *Household Management* is an exemplary case of the dialogic text. 'Dialogism' is the term employed by the Russian theorist Mikhail Bakhtin to describe a state in which different discourses battle for primacy.[5] For Bakhtin, the novel is the essentially dialogic form, but his theory allows us to make sense of the many conflicts and contradictions in Beeton's text. Some of the many different discourses Beeton employs have already been listed: religious, scientific, industrial, agricultural, literary, sentimental, and polemical utterances jostle each other in her pages. There is no attempt to merge them into a seamless authorial position; rather, the reader is left to adjudicate between the competing discourses.

Perhaps the most obvious competition, and one that dominated Victorian cultural life in general, is that between science and religion. Momentous scientific theories and discoveries in the course of the eighteenth and nineteenth centuries had systematically displaced religious certainties; most recently, the work of the geologist Charles Lyell had suggested that the earth was much older than the Bible claimed, and that of Charles Darwin had set the model of evolving species against the biblical account of God's creation.[6] Writing in the immediate aftermath of the furore following the publication in 1859 of Darwin's *Origin of Species*, Beeton shows a strong awareness of this conflict of world views, tempering her evident enthusiasm for science by juxtaposing it with a language of religious awe, particularly when discussing issues of natural history. Thus, a detailed analysis of the physical form, social behaviour, and breeding habits of fish is followed by determined lip-service to the religious perspective: 'fish . . . whether considered in their solitary or

[5] See *The Dialogic Imagination*, translated by Caryl Emerson and Michael Holquist (Austin: University of Texas Press, 1981).

[6] Charles Lyell (1797–1875) expounded his theories in *The Principles of Geology* (1830–3); Charles Darwin (1809–82) published *On the Origin of Species by Means of Natural Selection or the Preservation of Favoured Races in the Struggle for Life* in 1859.

gregarious capacity ... are alike wonderful to all who look through Nature up to Nature's God, and consider, with due humility, yet exalted admiration, the sublime variety, beauty, power, and grandeur of His productions, as manifested in the Creation' (p. 98). Such language is an active assertion of the possibility of combining biological science and a Creationist faith, but the jarring incompatibility of the two discourses within the text tells a different story.

Another authoritative discourse in the mid-nineteenth century was that of industrialism. By the 1850s the growing-pains of the industrial revolution had been largely overcome, and industrial interests held sway economically, politically, and—increasingly— socially. In his 1829 essay 'Signs of the Times', the historian Thomas Carlyle had anticipated these developments, calling the nineteenth century the Age of Machinery, and complaining that a mechanistic emphasis was beginning to dominate every aspect of contemporary life: 'not the external and physical alone is now managed by machinery, but the internal and spiritual also.' We find many examples of this mechanistic consciousness in *Household Management*: so the tail movements of certain fish are compared to the actions of the screw propellers of steamships (p. 97), and new items of kitchen equipment—particularly the latest cookers—are brooded over lasciviously in the chapter on 'The Arrangement and Economy of the Kitchen', with pictures, prices, and names of suppliers copiously provided. Industrially produced food products are welcomed with open arms, with recommendations of the quality of bottled sauces and relishes in Chapter IX, and an enthusiastic fanfare for the advent of aerated bread in Chapter XXXIV. More than this, the entire structure of *Household Management* is industrial in conception. Its declared purpose is to offer guidance in the efficient organization of the home; its methods—including the scientific approach to food preparation, and the elaborate classification, on a virtually hour-by-hour basis, of every servant's tasks—are those of the factory, in which work is broken down mechanistically into stages, and the time and labour of each employee is meticulously costed.

The world view displaced by the industrial perspective was agricultural. The eighteenth-century enclosures movement and the industrial revolution had initiated a widespread shift of population from the countryside to the towns, and cut off the average person from a centuries-old connection to the land. *Household Management* reflects a powerful contemporary nostalgia for a rural way of life in its descriptions of the seasonal round of food husbandry and preservation detailed particularly in the 'Housekeeper' chapter and in the chapters on meat, bread, and dairy products. Beeton reaches heights of lyricism in her descriptions of various breeds of farm animals and their care—she is particularly powerful on pigs, on the subject of whom she expresses, as someone once remarked, a 'grandiose pathos'.[7] A powerful advocate for the pleasures of meat (her chapters on the subject far outnumber any other type of food discussed), Beeton is also strong in her opposition to cruelty to animals— castigating the ancient practice of putting rings through pigs' noses to lead them, and furious at the emerging battery farming of hens and the increasing mechanization of veal production. This dual emphasis leads to curious tensions in her discussions of animal husbandry, with poetic accounts of the beauty and intelligence of particular animals, and sentimental pictures of large-eyed cows and noble pigs, immediately juxtaposed with gruesome descriptions of the best methods of slaughter and diagrams of sides of meat marked up for the butcher's cuts. In tension with the modernistic pull towards the industrial, urban world, there is a powerful nostalgia for a time in which a frothy syllabub could be made by milking the cow straight into the mixing bowl (p. 298), or when every family kept a pig and cured the hams and bacon themselves (see the Explanatory Note to p. 184). In many ways, however, these positions represent two sides of the same coin: Beeton's humanitarian opposition to animal cruelty and her sentimentalization of rural life are the responses of the urbanite to a world whose harshness and pragmatism she does not understand.

This rural nostalgia is at one with the powerful historical impulse which dominated so much of nineteenth-century culture, and manifested itself in the Gothic revival in architecture, the medievalism of the Pre-Raphaelites, and the historicism of numerous poets and novelists: an obsessive comparison of the present with the past which John Stuart Mill described as the dominant spirit of the age. Caught up in a time of rapid change and shifting values, Victorian culture took refuge in its constructions of various

[7] See Nown, *Mrs Beeton*, 63.

past golden ages, valuing the past as the source of moral and social stability. Although in most respects Beeton was a whole-hearted enthusiast for her century's advances (and died, notably, before the disillusionment of the latter part of the century), she is not free of this dominant historicist impulse. She delves at length into the culinary tastes and habits of the past, and expresses the unthinking reverence at the mere fact of antiquity that is such a significant feature of her cultural moment: elaborating with awe, for instance, on ciphers cut into oak trees, showing them to have been growing in the reigns of particular monarchs (pp. 241–2). Historical knowledge is treated as a highly desirable commodity, with serious attention given to the intricacies of Egyptian attitudes to the cabbage (p. 81) and the practices at Roman banquets (p. 99, for example). Tantalizingly oblique references to Herodotus (p. 271), and the St Bartholomew's Day Massacre (p. 305) flatteringly assume a high level of knowledge in the reader. Literary and classical quotation is used to similar effect, particularly in the more high-flown of the chapters ('The Mistress', and 'Dinners and Dining') addressed principally to the lady of the house. A shared literary background is assumed, and quotations from Dr Johnson, William Cowper, Joseph Addison, Francis Bacon, and other acknowledged stylists, are given with scant explanation. The effect is to create an atmosphere of cultured appreciation in the discussion of food and its preparation. Those chapters addressed to the housekeeper or cook, in contrast, convey a sense of sturdy, time-honoured wisdom through their use of proverbs and aphorisms (several of which— for instance 'a place for everything and everything in its place'— were coined by Beeton herself, although presented as ancient saws).

All of the hybrid and conflicting discourses represented in *Household Management* place it in the category of another, governing, discourse—that of Self-Help. The phrase derives from the title of another best-selling book of the period, by Samuel Smiles (a friend, incidentally, of the Dorling family, whose son was later to marry Isabella's younger sister Lucy). Smiles's *Self-Help* (1859) was a compilation of practical advice and inspirational life-stories, directed at young men of the working and lower-middle classes, to enable them to educate themselves and achieve social and financial success. What Beeton's book did for women, Smiles's did for men. Like

Household Management, *Self-Help* was a textbook of the new bourgeois ideology of industriousness, placing a similar emphasis on organized, dutiful living, education, and will-power. They are the establishing texts of the discourse of Self-Help, which promised, in exchange for virtuous diligence, to secure the precarious middle-class status of their readers.

The middle class for whom Beeton was writing was growing at immense speed: in the twenty years between 1851 and 1871 it tripled in size.[8] Those who had newly acquired middle-class status were anxious to do nothing to jeopardize their position, while those longer established were equally anxious to draw a firm distinction between themselves and the *arrivistes*, and worked hard to ally themselves instead with the gentry and aristocracy. It was a time of rapid class mobility, with many opportunities to both make and lose fortunes, and there was a nagging awareness that a fall in status was as possible as a rise. As a number of historians have noted, the middle class has in fact been rising for the past 500 years, but the Victorian middle-class expansion was unique because it was taking place at the same time as a massive process of industrialization and urbanization. New jobs in industry and trade created a distinctly different middle class whose interests and identity were often at odds with those of the old professional class—a tension which is reflected in many novels of the period.[9] Active snobbery about those in trade was one of the ways in which members of the older middle class could feel more secure about their own position, and Beeton is certainly not free of these prejudices—despite, or perhaps because of, her own father's choice of a career in trade. When discussing the hard life of the maid of all work, for instance, she draws a distinction between 'some small tradesman' and a 'respectable tradesman', imputing much of the hardship of the sole maid to the fact that she usually begins her career working for the wife of the former, who is 'just a step above her in the social scale'. Beeton softens the blow by declaring that 'many excellent . . . women' are to be found in this class, but clearly sees her main readership as belonging to a rather more elevated class position. An entertaining glimpse of how Beeton saw her

[8] The 1851 census recorded 272,000 professional workers; that in 1871 showed three times as many.

[9] Elizabeth Gaskell's *North and South* (1854–5), Dickens's *Dombey and Son* (1847–8), and, George Eliot's *The Mill on the Floss* (1860) are just a few examples.

readers is given in her account of the relatively new innovation of the Christmas turkey:

A noble dish is a turkey, roast or boiled. A Christmas dinner, with the middle classes of this empire, would scarcely be a Christmas dinner without its turkey; and we can hardly imagine an object of greater envy than is presented by a respectable portly paterfamilias carving, at the season devoted to good cheer and genial charity, his own fat turkey, and carving it well. (pp. 225–6)

To address the issue of class in such naked terms is typical of Beeton—her work is unusually free of genteel circumlocutions. Particularly interesting is her sense of the prosperous middle classes as objects of envy—and her assumption that this is an image of themselves that her readers will appreciate.

Anxious, snobbish, and always looking over their shoulders, the middle classes Beeton wrote for often lived lives that veered schizophrenically between economy and rampant extravagance. In the bills of fare section of the chapter 'Dinners and Dining', she provides recipes for grand dinner parties with up to eighteen guests and lavish ball suppers and banquets, but these are balanced by modest week-by-week plans for 'Plain Family Dinners', with three basic courses and careful thought given to the employment of left-overs. These different sorts of meals were not intended for different readerships: guided by books like Beeton's, the average middle-class family devoted a sizeable proportion of its income to entertaining on a lavish scale, usually on a monthly basis.

Despite the eagerness of many of her readers to maintain a high standard of living, there are recipes given by Beeton that would have been beyond the means of any of them. Three pages are devoted to an elaborate recipe for turtle soup, a dish so expensive and complicated that it formed the centre-piece of the annual Lord Mayor's banquet, and was quite beyond the scope of a domestic kitchen. We are also told how 'to dress truffles with champagne', a dish for which Beeton refrains from giving a price, merely remarking that 'truffles are not often bought in this country'. These are essentially fantasy recipes, included to give aspirational readers something to aim for—talismans of the pleasures that await them at the top of the social tree. There is also fantasy present in the lengthy list of servants and the carefully calculated systems of their daily tasks: most Victorians of the class Beeton was addressing kept a cook, one or two maids, and perhaps a man-of-all-work or a part-time gardener. The idea of worrying about the relative status of a footman and a coachman, or how a butler should handle his cellar duties, was only a pleasant pipe dream for most of them.

Beeton gives such detailed instructions on every aspect of contemporary middle-class life because many of her readers were in need of such guidance. In particular, many middle-class women found themselves living completely different lives from those of their mothers and grandmothers, in tall, narrow townhouses, where industrial soot and grime necessitated extra cleaning, where food was not produced locally but supplied by numerous potentially unreliable tradespeople, and where neighbours were unknown to each other unless an elaborate system of calls was initiated. Large numbers of manufactured goods were now available, and the housewife needed to choose between different styles of furniture, clothing, kitchen equipment, and foodstuffs, including many imports from the colonies. Husbands, as noted earlier, increasingly travelled into the centre of London and other large cities to work, and took their midday and often their evening meal in town. Consequently, meal times shifted, with the midday dinner moving into the evening, and a light luncheon replacing it in the daytime. Wives would often eat this meal with their children in the nursery. When they held their weekly 'at home' gatherings, they would serve the relatively new afternoon tea, with elegantly cut sandwiches and cakes. These women had increasingly complex lives, and *Household Management* offered guidance on virtually every aspect of their domestic existence. As well as recipes for and information on an enormous variety of foodstuffs, there is advice on the principles of cookery, the organization and planning of a kitchen, invalid food, the etiquette of dining, domestic servants, children, and medical and legal matters. The role of the mistress and that of the housekeeper are dealt with in consecutive chapters at the beginning of the work—a masterly piece of tact given that in most middle-class households they were the same person.

In her first chapter, 'The Mistress', Beeton sets out the key aspects of the ideology of female domesticity that she espouses. From the very beginning she outlines the mode of femininity she is interested in as one distinct from other contemporary constructions, quoting *The Vicar of Wakefield* to support modesty, prudence, and carefulness—serviceable virtues—against alternative models of bluestockings, 'blustering heroines, or virago queens'. In actively rejecting these more assertive models of femininity, Beeton's might appear a reactionary philosophy, but within the limitations she sets herself, she offers an image of an active, powerful femininity. In her opening sentence she employs a daring analogy, comparing the housewife to the commander of an army, responsible for a weighty organization. Although her work fits neatly into the contemporary ideology of 'separate spheres', which assigns each sex its proper and distinct place in the world, she expands considerably the notion of what the domestic sphere consists of, greatly enhancing the significance of the woman's role. The Beeton woman is instructed about what time to get up (early), how to manage her finances, how to choose friends and acquaintances and how to act towards them, what subjects to broach in conversation, how to govern her temper, how to dress and shop, how to offer charity, and—most fully—how to hire, fire, and manage servants. One reason for the elaborate detail in this latter respect is that many of the women addressed may have been the first in their families to have servants; the first not to work at something other than keeping a house. The keeping of servants increased dramatically in the course of the nineteenth century, as did the practice of middle-class women being economically non-productive. It is not just because many more people were becoming middle class that the rules needed spelling out: it was because the meaning of being middle class was changing.

Household Management is full of ambivalence on the issue of servants—reflecting the general unease the middle class felt about these intruders in the home. It is a paranoia strikingly represented by sensation novelist Mary Elizabeth Braddon in a novel published two years after *Household Management* appeared in volume form:

Your servants listen at your doors, and repeat your spiteful speeches in the kitchen, and watch you while they wait at table, and understand every sarcasm, every innuendo, every look, as well as those at whom the cruel glances and stinging words are aimed. They understand your sulky silence, your studied and over-acted politeness. The most polished form your hate and anger can take is as transparent to those household spies as if you threw knives at each other, or pelted your enemy with the side-dishes and vegetables, after the fashion of disputants in a pantomime.

Nothing that is done in the parlour is lost upon these quiet, well-behaved watchers from the kitchen.[10]

While Beeton's householders are much better behaved than Braddon's, the worry about servants as spies and commentators on the lives of their employers is common to both. The chapter on servants contains many anecdotes (mostly presented as humorous) about servants reading their employers' letters, advising them on their hands of cards, and pointing out their *faux pas* in public. The point of the humour relies on a sense of servants as intrinsically comic in a childlike manner—an idea with a very long literary heritage. This sense of servants as not fully adult or independent beings can result in some attitudes that seem repugnant today, as in the suggestion that the keeping of men servants is advantageous because

Families accustomed to such attendants have always about them humble dependents, whose children have no other prospect than domestic service to look forward to; to them it presents no degradation, but the reverse, to be so employed; they are initiated step by step into the mysteries of the household, with the prospect of rising in the service, if it is a house admitting of promotion,—to the respectable position of butler or house-steward. In families of humbler pretensions, where they must look for promotion elsewhere, they know that can only be attained by acquiring the good-will of their employers. Can there be any stronger security for their good conduct . . .? (p. 393)

No doubt seen by Beeton as offering a benign picture of domestic harmony, this passage carries unfortunate overtones, for the modern reader, of the attitudes of slave-owners. Such unwittingly contemptuous statements are balanced, though, by the opening of the chapter, where the habit of the aristocracy and gentry (or '"Society"' as Beeton puts it, with some irony) of abusing their servants as a matter of course is condemned, and the point made that good servants are produced by good employers. Beeton alternates between these positions throughout the book; the iniquities of shirking and incompetent servants are castigated, but there is an insistence on the need to treat servants well, and remember that they are dependants. The ambivalence is heightened by the fact that Beeton derives much of her material on the duties of servants from *The Complete Servant*

[10] *Aurora Floyd* (1863; Oxford World's Classics edn., 1996), 177–8.

(1825) by Samuel and Sarah Adams. The Adamses describe themselves as servants, and give a brief biographical account of their rise
up the ladder of domestic service. Their book therefore functions as
a guide to social advancement for the ambitious servant, rather than
simply a description of duties. Though this self-improving pair may
simply have been a publisher's invention, their book did address
servants as rational beings, and assume that they had their own
agenda in life, rather than being motivated simply out of devotion to
their employers. Little of this radical subtext survives in Beeton's
use of the Adamses' material, but there is a trace in those moments
when she adopts the servants' perspective.

The ambivalence about servants is also reflected in the modes of
address Beeton employs. A cookery book in the middle years of the
nineteenth century inevitably addressed itself simultaneously to several different readerships: the mistress would read it to decide on the
day's meals, and then pass it to her cook to follow the detailed
instructions for individual dishes. Since Beeton's book so com-
prehensively covers the affairs of the house at large as well as the
kitchen, she could also have expected the husband to consult the
legal and perhaps the medical sections, and upper servants to read
the chapter on servants' duties in their managerial capacity. Beeton,
as already discussed, adjusts her mode of address accordingly,
employing high-flown classical quotations in the 'Mistress' chapter,
and homely proverbs in that on the housekeeper. Her separation of
the encyclopaedic chapters on foods from the recipe chapters is also
perhaps a nod towards the different requirements of mistress and
cook. It is notable that although the mode of address throughout
privileges the mistress, the arrangement of dishes in particular chapters is suited instead to the needs of the cook: puddings, sweet and
savoury, are grouped together, and dishes with similar methods and
ingredients appear in the same place, rather than in categories
reflecting their place in the meal, which would have been more help-
ful for the mistress ordering the day's food.

In fact, the roles of mistress and servant could not be absolutely
distinguished from each other. As noted earlier, mistress and housekeeper were very often one and the same, and in many households
(including Beeton's own), the mistress took charge of a considerable
proportion of the cooking. Beeton maintains the polite fiction that
middle-class women need not soil their hands with physical work,

while actually providing them with copious instructions for how to do such work well. Because, therefore, it is never quite clear whom she is really instructing in a particular chapter, her modes of address often become confused, and her focus will shift abruptly from the mistress to the maid, often in the course of a single paragraph. In the 'Domestic Servants' chapter, particularly, she will often alternate between the descriptive and the imperative moods: 'the footman is expected to rise early, in order to get through all his dirty work before the family are stirring . . . when knives are so cleaned, see that they are carefully polished.' On the whole she maintains the distinction between servant and employer by addressing the former in a smaller typeface, but this nicety is not consistently observed. In fact, Beeton's book is a useful guide to the problems the Victorian middle classes faced in maintaining appropriate distinctions of status between themselves and their servants, and the energy they put into the process. The literature of the period is full of overweening servants (Sam Weller in *Pickwick Papers*, the many contemptuous inn-servants and waiters who best the young David Copperfield, the bossy Bessie in *Jane Eyre*, the bumptious Phoebe in Mary Elizabeth Braddon's *Lady Audley's Secret*, and so on), suggesting both a difficulty in keeping servants in their place, and a deep anxiety about the fact. If we read between the lines, in laying down such detailed prescriptions of the qualities to be expected in a servant, Beeton is tacitly acknowledging that these expectations are usually not fulfilled—the respectful reserve, modest demeanour and polite manner required of a valet or lady's-maid, for instance, is particularly over-stressed, suggesting that these desirable qualities were not often to be met with. In places, Beeton is unusually honest about the anxiety of her class to bolster up the wall between themselves and their servants: in detailing the duties of the lady's-maid, she remarks that 'the *Chausserie*, or foot-gear of a lady, is one of the few things left to mark her station, and requires special care'. This was because cheaply manufactured silks and cottons enabled the working classes—and even servants—to dress in much the same style as their social superiors, leaving points of class distinction to be signalled in much more subtle—but no less crucial—ways.

Middle-class identity was absolutely dependent on the ability to draw a firm line between themselves and the working classes. The first half of the nineteenth century had been marked by extreme poverty and political agitation on the part of the workers, and an ambivalent response of fear and pity from the middle classes. With the new economic security of the middle years of the century, and a gradual improvement in the material conditions of the poor, this class antagonism died down, but there were new problems for the middle classes in that the social chasm separating them from the working classes was increasingly bridgeable. Like many other texts of the mid-century, *Household Management* deals with the issue by adopting an attitude of benevolent disdain towards social inferiors, so the mistress is advised that 'great advantages may result from visits paid to the poor; for there being, unfortunately, much ignorance, generally, amongst them with respect to all household knowledge, there will be opportunities for advising and instructing them, in a pleasant and unobtrusive manner, in cleanliness, industry, cookery, and good management' (p. 13), and the writer of the medical chapter comments with repulsed amazement on the fact that 'children, reared in the reeking dens of squalor and poverty' often survive when those with material advantages fall ill and die (p. 479). In the opposite direction, there is also an impulse to draw a distinction between the frivolity of the aristocracy and gentry, and the solid domestic virtues presented as typical of the middle class: there are frequent snide asides about the excesses of the fashionable world, as when the taste of 'some connoisseurs' for carving a leg of mutton upside down, so as to get at the fine-grained meat at the bottom, is condemned as 'an extravagant fashion, and one that will hardly find favour in the eyes of many economical British housewives and housekeepers' (p. 184).

Here, and elsewhere, Beeton claims to be writing for a British readership, but in fact her emphasis is on the cookery of England rather than Britain as a whole. The food of the other nations of the United Kingdom is represented by a few classics like Cock-a-Leekie and Irish Stew, and—with unconscious irony—by a number of those old dishes named by the English with insulting implications of the poverty of their neighbours, such as Welsh Rabbit and Scotch Woodcock. As with so many of its concerns, *Household Management* is curiously schizoid in the culinary traditions it represents. As remarked at the start, Mrs Beeton is popularly thought to stand for traditional English food, and her round suet puddings, boiled for many hours, her spit-roasted haunches of meat, and raised game pies certainly do belong to a central tradition of English cooking that dates back to the Middle Ages. These sit side by side, however, with many recipes for dishes of foreign extraction. Some of these, such as blancmange and fritters, can be traced to the Norman influence in the Middle Ages. A large number of other French dishes Beeton includes were imported in the eighteenth century, when French chefs and recipes became very fashionable in England. She also includes a considerable number of recipes from less familiar cuisines, notably Italian, German, Belgian, Dutch, and Portuguese. A few foreign recipes are quite new, like the 'Soup a la Solferino', which she got from an English gentleman who had it from Italian troops at the famous battle—notably, though, she reports with approval that the gentleman in question had Anglicized the recipe and therefore much improved it. Another significant body of recipes comes from India: mulligatawny, various curries, kedgeree, and a number of chutneys are all included, with the assumption that they will already be fairly familiar to the reader. Until the 1870s there was little attempt made to introduce European food into the homes of British officials in India—Indian cooks tended to be left to their own devices, and produced a series of curries. Those foods particularly enjoyed by the British were passed around as recipes both in India and at home, and in the process of translation and transmission gradually mutated—the development of kedgeree from a vegetarian dish of rice and lentils to one containing smoked fish and eggs is a notable example. It is a remarkable fact (and tells us much about the constituents of national identity in the nineteenth century) that there are roughly as many recipes in the book from India as from Wales, Scotland, and Ireland put together.

Ultimately, *Household Management* tells a story of a culture caught between the old world and the new, poised between modernity and nostalgia. It tells of kitchens in which meat is still roasted on spits over open fires, but where many of the bottled sauces and condiments we take for granted today were already available. Its medical chapters describe the significance of vaccination while also offering advice on the use of leeches for bloodletting. The book offers markedly advanced advice on the bearing and rearing of children— warning parents of the dangers of drunken or incompetent nurses, castigating the common practices of binding small babies tightly with wrappers and dosing children with alcohol or laudanum to get them to sleep, and calling for the invention of nappies without pins and elastic baby clothes. These anticipations of modern thinking on the subject are made heavily ironic by the fact that the author of the book in which they appear suffered repeated miscarriages, lost two children in infancy, and died—along with tens of thousands of her contemporaries—as the result of an avoidable infection contracted in childbirth.

This tension between old and new is matched by all those other contradictions: the eccentrically raised woman-journalist devoting herself to the promotion of domestic conformity; the attempt to expand women's social roles through an increase in their domestic responsibilities; and the shifting of sympathy and modes of address between mistress and servant. It is precisely because *Household Management* maintains its dialogic stance throughout, with no attempt made to unify different positions, that it is such a useful document of a multifarious, contradictory, and rapidly changing society.

NOTE ON THE TEXT

Mrs Beeton's Book of Household Management was first published in a single volume in October 1861, by the firm of S. O. Beeton, owned and run by Isabella's husband, Samuel Orchart. Priced at 7s. 6d., and nearly as thick as it was high, it achieved a steady success, selling over 60,000 copies in the first year. This was not, though, its first appearance in print. Between 1859 and 1861 it had been issued in 24 monthly parts (the original plan was for 15–18), as an offshoot of Sam's *Englishwoman's Domestic Magazine*. Each part was priced at 3d., and the setting of the type was identical to that of the later volume publication, except that the endpapers of the part work carried advertisements for booksellers, chemists and jewellers, and for Beeton's other publications. Much of the text of *Household Management* had appeared even earlier as columns on 'Cooking, Pickling and Preserving', 'The Management of Children', and so on, in the *Englishwoman's Domestic Magazine*, to which Isabella had begun contributing after their marriage in 1856. Samuel, an expert at the efficient exploitation of his publications, later re-issued portions of *Household Management* in forms suited for different markets: the 1s. *Englishwoman's Cookery Book* of 1864 offered 'to help Plain Cooks and Maids-of-all-Work to a knowledge of some of their duties, and to assist them in the important task of dressing and serving daily food'; the *Dictionary of Cookery* in the 'Beeton's All About It Books' series was sold at the middling price of 3s. 6d. and achieved even greater success than its monumental predecessor. Isabella revised both books, but the *Dictionary* was published posthumously, and contained a moving afterword from Sam, praising his wife's virtues and talents.

Household Management and its offshoots were the stars of Sam's list, which consisted mainly of self-help and reference books such as *Beeton's Book of Anecdote, Wit and Humour* (1865), *Beeton's Book of Birds, showing how to manage them in sickness and health* (1864), *Beeton's Book of Songs* (1865), *Beeton's Historian* (1858), and *Beeton's Dictionary of Universal Information* (1858–62). Sam had joined the firm of Clarke, Beeton & Co. as a partner in 1852; among their major successes was the first English publication of Harriet Beecher

Stowe's *Uncle Tom's Cabin* (in 1852). While with the firm, Beeton instituted his two very successful magazines, the *Englishwoman's Domestic Magazine* in 1852, and the *Boy's Own Journal* in 1855. Shortly after founding the latter he left the firm to set up on his own account, taking his magazines with him. He had considerable financial success until May 1866 (the year after Isabella's death), when the failure of the great banking house Overend, Gurney & Co. threatened to pitch Beeton, along with numerous other small firms, into bankruptcy. The large publishers Ward, Lock & Co. offered to buy up his copyrights and provide him with a salaried post as literary adviser. In order to pay his debts he accepted the far from generous offer of £400 a year and an initial one-sixth of the profits from his publications. After a legal dispute with Ward, Lock in 1874 (about the contents of the *Beeton's Christmas Annual*, in which Sam, a life-long Radical, wanted to publish a parody of the Prince of Wales and his social set, called 'The Silead'), the contract of employment was dissolved. Sam died three years later on 6 June 1877. Ward Lock continued the principle of exploitation Sam had started, bringing out numerous abridged and enlarged versions of *Household Management* throughout the nineteenth and twentieth centuries. Subsequent editions included information on new cooking equipment such as gas and electrical stoves and refrigerators, and gradually moved further and further away from the text of the original. Even today, a weight of historical credence is lent to a whole range of cookery books through the use of the words 'Mrs Beeton' and 'Household Management', which have become the ultimate in culinary brand names.

The present text is abridged from the first volume edition, with the aim of keeping those sections of the text most significant from cultural, historical, and social perspectives, and in consequence much of the discursive matter from the original remains. About one-fifth of the recipes have been retained, selected both for their representative qualities and for the points of particular interest they raise. The editor's explanatory notes, which also give information on what has been omitted, range widely across areas of culinary, literary, social, historical, and scientific interest.

SELECT BIBLIOGRAPHY

Primary Texts

Eliza Acton, *Modern Cookery for Private Families*, first published 1845 (Southover Press: Lewes, 1993).

Samuel and Sarah Adams, *The Complete Servant*, first published 1825 (Southover Press: Lewes, 1989).

Isabella Beeton, *Beeton's Book of Household Management*, a part-work (S. O. Beeton: London, 1859–61).

—— *Beeton's Book of Household Management* (S. O. Beeton: London, 1861).

—— *Beeton's Book of Household Management*, a facsimile edition (Chancellor Press: London, 1982).

Beeton's Medical Dictionary (Ward, Lock & Tyler: London, 1871).

Beeton's Dictionary of Universal Information (S. O. Beeton: London, 1858–62).

Jean-Anthelme Brillat-Savarin, *The Philosopher in the Kitchen*, a translation of *La Physiologie du goût*, first published 1825 (Penguin: Harmondsworth, 1970, repr. 1988).

Englishwoman's Domestic Magazine, 1852–65.

Alexis Soyer, *The Gastronomic Regenerator* (Simpkin, Marshall & Co.: London, 1846).

—— *The Modern Housewife, or Ménagère* (Simpkin, Marshall & Co.: London, 1850).

—— *The Pantropheon, or History of Food and Its Preparation, from the Earliest Ages of the World* (Simpkin, Marshall & Co.: London, 1853).

Biographies

Sarah Freeman, *Isabella and Sam: The Story of Mrs Beeton* (Victor Gollancz Ltd.: London, 1977).

H. Montgomery Hyde, *Mr and Mrs Beeton* (Harrap & Co. Ltd.: London, 1951).

Nancy Spain, *Mrs Beeton and her Husband* (London: Collins, 1948).

Secondary Texts

Dena Attar, *A Bibliography of Household Books Published in Britain 1800–1914* (Prospect Books: London, 1987).

Elisabeth Ayrton, *The Cookery of England*, first published 1974 (Penguin: Harmondsworth, 1977).

Asa Briggs, *Victorian Things* (Batsford: London, 1988).

Elizabeth David, *English Bread and Yeast Cookery*, first published 1977 (Penguin: Harmondsworth, 1979).

Jane Grigson, *English Food* (Purnell Book Services: London, 1974).

Dorothy Hartley, *Food in England*, first published 1954 (Little, Brown & Co., 1996).

E. J. Hobsbawm, *Industry and Empire*, first published 1968 (Penguin: Harmondsworth, 1982).

Harold McGee, *On Food and Cooking: The Science and Lore of the Kitchen* (George Allen & Unwin: London, 1986).

Graham Nown, *Mrs Beeton: 150 Years of Cookery and Household Management* (London: Ward Lock, 1986).

Arnold Palmer, *Movable Feasts: Changes in English Eating Habits*, first published 1952 (Oxford University Press: Oxford, 1984).

Roy Porter, *The Greatest Benefit to Mankind: A Medical History of Humanity from Antiquity to the Present* (HarperCollins: London, 1997).

Phillipa Pullar, *Consuming Passions: A History of English Food and Appetite* (Hamish Hamilton: London, 1970).

Margaret Visser, *The Rituals of Dinner: The Origins, Evolution, Eccentricities and Meaning of Table Manners* (Viking: London, 1992).

Florence White, *Good Things in England: A Book of Real English Cookery* (Jonathan Cape: London, 1932).

Further Reading in Oxford World's Classics

Mary Elizabeth Braddon, *Aurora Floyd*, ed. P. D. Edwards.

Elizabeth Barrett Browning, *Aurora Leigh*, ed. Kerry McSweeney.

Charles Darwin, *The Origin of Species*, ed. Gillian Beer.

A CHRONOLOGY OF ISABELLA BEETON

Life	*Historical and Cultural Background*
Islington and then school in Heidelberg, Germany, where she learns fluent French and German, becomes a promising pianist, and learns to cook patisserie.	
1848	Ignaz Semmelweiss, an Austrian obstetrician, demonstrates that puerperal fever is contagious and succeeds in reducing it in the Vienna hospital by requiring physicians to wash their hands in chlorinated water. Elizabeth Gaskell, *Mary Barton* William Makepeace Thackeray, *Vanity Fair*
1849	Cholera epidemic in London.
1850	Britain embraces free trade principles and begins to import more food than it exports. Food prices rise less swiftly than other prices and wages increases more than keep pace with price rises. Salmon is taken from the Thames for the last time; due to pollution it will not be seen again for 120 years. Charles Dickens, *David Copperfield* Alfred Tennyson, *In Memoriam*
1851	The Great Exhibition held in London, demonstrating works of industry of all nations.
1853	Elizabeth Gaskell, *Cranford*
1854	The Crimean War begins. Florence Nightingale goes to nurse patients of the typhus, which was epidemic in the British, French, and Russian armies.
1855 Isabella becomes engaged to Samuel Beeton, a young publisher, among whose publications are the *Englishwoman's Domestic Magazine*, the *Boy's Own Journal*, and the first English edition of Harriet Beecher Stowe's *Uncle Tom's Cabin*. Isabella begins to translate French novels for the *EDM*.	*Food and its Adulterations* by chemist Arthur Hill Hassall scandalizes Britain with its reports that all but the most costly beer, bread, butter, coffee, pepper, and tea contain trace amounts of arsenic, copper, lead, or mercury.

Life	*Historical and Cultural Background*
1856 Isabella and Sam marry in July, and move to a new semi-detached suburban house: 2 Chandos Villas, Pinner.	End of the Crimean War.
1857 Their first child, Samuel Orchart Beeton, born in May; dies in August. Isabella contributes recipe and fashion columns to the *Englishwoman's Domestic Magazine*. She begins to plan a cookery book and Sam advertises for recipe contributions in the magazine.	
1859 Their second child, Samuel Orchart Beeton junior, born in September. *Household Management* begins to appear in monthly parts.	Charles Darwin, *Origin of Species* J. S. Mill, *On Liberty*
1860 Isabella and Sam take a trip to Paris in March to hire a French nursery maid for their child, and to bring back French fashion plates for the *EDM*. Innovation of dress patterns for crinolines offered to readers of the *EDM*; Isabella writes a regular column on the French fashions.	Wilkie Collins, *The Woman in White* George Eliot, *The Mill on the Floss*
1861 *Household Management* published in volume form.	
1862 Samuel Orchart ('Orchy') dies on New Year's Eve, possibly of scarlet fever, aged 3.	
1863 Their third child, Orchart, born in December. He lives to be 83 (dying in January 1947).	The first underground railway line (the Metropolitan line) opens in London.
1864	Britain's first fish-and-chip shop opens, as steam trawlers are developed that can carry deep-sea fish packed in ice.
1865 On 29 January, their fourth child, Mayson, born (he also lives until 1947). Isabella dies seven days later, on 6 February, from puerperal fever, almost certainly caused by a neglect of hygiene on the part of the doctor and midwife.	London dispensary for women opens, under the direction of local physician Elizabeth Garrett Anderson, who pioneers admission of women to the professions. Lewis Carroll, *Alice in Wonderland*

MRS BEETON'S BOOK

OF

HOUSEHOLD MANAGEMENT

Comprising Information for the

MISTRESS,	COACHMAN,	LAUNDRY-MAID,
HOUSEKEEPER,	VALET,	NURSE AND NURSE-
COOK,	UPPER AND UNDER	MAID,
KITCHEN-MAID,	HOUSE-MAIDS,	MONTHLY, WET, AND
BUTLER,	LADY'S-MAID,	SICK NURSES,
FOOTMAN,	MAID-OF-ALL-WORK,	ETC. ETC.

ALSO, SANITARY, MEDICAL, & LEGAL MEMORANDA;

WITH A HISTORY OF THE ORIGIN, PROPERTIES, AND USES OF ALL THINGS
CONNECTED WITH HOME LIFE AND COMFORT.

BY MRS ISABELLA BEETON.

Nothing lovelier can be found
In Woman, than to study household good.—MILTON*

PREFACE

I MUST frankly own, that if I had known, beforehand, that this book would have cost me the labour which it has, I should never have been courageous enough to commence it. What moved me, in the first instance, to attempt a work like this, was the discomfort and suffering which I had seen brought upon men and women by household mismanagement. I have always thought that there is no more fruitful source of family discontent than a housewife's badly-cooked dinners and untidy ways. Men are now so well served out of doors,—at their clubs, well-ordered taverns, and dining-houses, that in order to compete with the attractions of these places, a mistress must be thoroughly acquainted with the theory and practice of cookery, as well as be perfectly conversant with all the other arts of making and keeping a comfortable home.

In this book I have attempted to give, under the chapters devoted to cookery, an intelligible arrangement to every recipe, a list of the *ingredients*, a plain statement of the *mode* of preparing each dish, and a careful estimate of its *cost*, the *number of people* for whom it is *sufficient*, and the time when it is *seasonable*. For the matter of the recipes, I am indebted, in some measure, to many correspondents of the 'Englishwoman's Domestic Magazine,'* who have obligingly placed at my disposal their formulae for many original preparations. A large private circle has also rendered me considerable service. A diligent study of the works of the best modern writers on cookery* was also necessary to the faithful fulfilment of my task. Friends in England, Scotland, Ireland, France, and Germany, have also very materially aided me. I have paid great attention to those recipes which come under the head of 'COLD MEAT COOKERY.' But in the department belonging to the Cook I have striven, too, to make my work something more than a Cookery Book, and have, therefore, on the best authority that I could obtain, given an account of the natural history of the animals and vegetables which we use as food. I have followed the animal from his birth to his appearance on the table; have described the manner of feeding him, and of slaying him, the position of his various joints, and, after giving the recipes, have described the modes of carving Meat, Poultry, and Game. Skilful artists have designed the numerous drawings which appear in this work, and which illustrate, better than any description, many important and interesting items. The coloured plates* are a novelty not without value.

Besides the great portion of the book which has especial reference to the cook's department, there are chapters devoted to those of the other servants of the household, who have all, I trust, their duties clearly assigned to them.

Towards the end of the work will be found valuable chapters on the 'Management of Children'—'The Doctor,' the latter principally referring to accidents and emergencies, some of which are certain to occur in the experience of every one of us; and the last chapter contains 'Legal Memoranda,' which will be serviceable in cases of doubt as to the proper course to be adopted in the relations between Landlord and Tenant, Tax-gatherer and Tax-payer, and Tradesman and Customer.

These chapters have been contributed by gentlemen fully entitled to confidence; those on medical subjects by an experienced surgeon, and the legal matter by a solicitor.

I wish here to acknowledge the kind letters and congratulations I have received during the progress of this work, and have only further to add, that I trust the result of the four years' incessant labour which I have expended will not be altogether unacceptable to some of my countrymen and countrywomen.

ISABELLA BEETON

GENERAL CONTENTS

THE BOOK OF
HOUSEHOLD MANAGEMENT

CHAPTER I

THE MISTRESS

'Strength and honour are her clothing; and she shall rejoice in
time to come. She openeth her mouth with wisdom; and in her
tongue is the law of kindness. She looketh well to the ways of her
household; and eateth not the bread of idleness. Her children arise
up, and call her blessed; her husband also, and he praiseth her.'

—*Proverbs*, xxxi. 25–28.

As with the COMMANDER OF AN ARMY, or the leader of any enterprise, so is it with the mistress of a house. Her spirit will be seen
through the whole establishment; and just in proportion as she performs her duties intelligently and thoroughly, so will her domestics
follow in her path. Of all those acquirements, which more particularly belong to the feminine character, there are none which take a
higher rank, in our estimation, than such as enter into a knowledge
of household duties; for on these are perpetually dependent the
happiness, comfort, and well-being of a family. In this opinion we are
borne out by the author of 'The Vicar of Wakefield',* who says: 'The
modest virgin, the prudent wife, and the careful matron, are much
more serviceable in life than petticoated philosophers, blustering
heroines, or virago queens. She who makes her husband and her
children happy, who reclaims the one from vice and trains up the
other to virtue, is a much greater character than ladies described in
romances, whose whole occupation is to murder mankind with shafts
from their quiver, or their eyes.'

Pursuing the picture, we may add, that to be a good housewife
does not necessarily imply an abandonment of proper pleasures or
amusing recreation; and we think it the more necessary to express
this, as the performance of the duties of a mistress may, to some

minds, perhaps seem to be incompatible with the enjoyment of life. Let us, however, now proceed to describe some of those home qualities and virtues which are necessary to the proper management of a Household, and then point out the plan which may be the most profitably pursued for the daily regulation of its affairs.

EARLY RISING is one of the most essential qualities which enter into good Household Management, as it is not only the parent of health, but of innumerable other advantages. Indeed, when a mistress is an early riser, it is almost certain that her house will be orderly and well-managed. On the contrary, if she remain in bed till a late hour, then the domestics, who, as we have before observed, invariably partake somewhat of their mistress's character, will surely become sluggards. To self-indulgence all are more or less disposed, and it is not to be expected that servants are freer from this fault than the heads of houses. The great Lord Chatham* thus gave his advice in reference to this subject:—'I would have inscribed on the curtains of your bed, and the walls of your chamber, "If you do not rise early, you can make progress in nothing." '

CLEANLINESS is also indispensable to health, and must be studied both in regard to the person and the house, and all that it contains. Cold or tepid baths should be employed every morning, unless, on account of illness or other circumstances, they should be deemed objectionable. The bathing of *children* will be treated of under the head of 'MANAGEMENT OF CHILDREN.'

FRUGALITY AND ECONOMY are home virtues, without which no household can prosper. Dr Johnson* says: 'Frugality may be termed the daughter of Prudence, the sister of Temperance, and the parent of Liberty. He that is extravagant will quickly become poor, and poverty will enforce dependence and invite corruption.' The necessity of practising economy should be evident to every one, whether in the possession of an income no more than sufficient for a family's requirements, or of a large fortune, which puts financial adversity out of the question. We must always remember that it is a great merit in housekeeping to manage a little well. 'He is a good waggoner,' says Bishop Hall,* that can turn in a little room. To live well in abundance is the praise of the estate, not of the person. I will study more how to give a good account of my little, than how to make it more.' In this there is true wisdom, and it may be added, that those who can manage a little well, are most likely to succeed in their management of larger matters. Economy and frugality must never, however, be allowed to degenerate into parsimony and meanness.

The choice of ACQUAINTANCES is very important to the happiness of a mistress and her family. A gossiping acquaintance, who indulges in the scandal and ridicule of her neighbours, should be avoided as a pestilence. It is likewise all-necessary to beware, as Thomson* sings,

> 'The whisper'd tale,
> That, like the fabling Nile, no fountain knows;—
> Fair-faced Deceit, whose wily, conscious eye
> Ne'er looks direct; the tongue that licks the dust
> But, when it safely dares, as prompt to sting.'

If the duties of a family do not sufficiently occupy the time of a mistress, society should be formed of such a kind as will tend to the mutual interchange of general and interesting information.

FRIENDSHIPS should not be hastily formed, nor the heart given, at once, to every new-comer. There are ladies who uniformly smile at, and approve everything and everybody, and who possess neither the courage to reprehend vice, nor the generous warmth to defend virtue. The friendship of such persons is without attachment, and their love without affection or even preference. They imagine that every one who has any penetration is ill-natured, and look coldly on a discriminating judgment. It should be remembered, however, that this discernment does not always proceed from an uncharitable temper, but that those who possess a long experience and thorough knowledge of the world, scrutinize the conduct and dispositions of people before they trust themselves to the first fair appearances. Addison,* who was not deficient in a knowledge of mankind, observes that 'a friendship, which makes the least noise, is very often the most useful; for which reason, I should prefer a prudent friend to a zealous one.' And Joanna Baillie* tells us that

> 'Friendship is no plant of hasty growth,
> Though planted in esteem's deep-fixèd soil,
> The gradual culture of kind intercourse
> Must bring it to perfection.'

HOSPITALITY is a most excellent virtue; but care must be taken that the love of company, for its own sake, does not become a prevailing passion; for then the habit is no longer hospitality, but dissipation. Reality and truthfulness in this, as in all other duties of life, are the points to be studied; for, as Washington Irving* well says, 'There is an emanation from the heart in genuine hospitality, which cannot be described, but is immediately felt, and puts the stranger at once at his ease.' With respect to the continuance of friendships, however, it may be found necessary, in some cases, for a mistress to relinquish, on assuming the responsibility of a household, many of those commenced in the earlier part of her life. This will be the more requisite, if the number still retained be quite equal to her means and opportunities.

IN CONVERSATION, trifling occurrences, such as small disappointments, petty annoyances, and other every-day incidents, should never be mentioned to your friends. The extreme injudiciousness of repeating these will be at once apparent, when we reflect on the unsatisfactory discussions which they too frequently occasion, and on the load of advice which they are the cause of being tendered, and which is, too often, of a kind neither to be useful nor agreeable. Greater events, whether of joy or sorrow, should be communicated to friends; and, on such occasions, their sympathy gratifies and comforts. If the mistress be a wife, never let an account of her husband's failings pass her lips; and in cultivating the power of conversation, she should keep the versified advice of Cowper* continually in her memory, that it

> 'Should flow like water after summer showers,
> Not as if raised by mere mechanic powers.'

In reference to its style, Dr Johnson, who was himself greatly distinguished for his colloquial abilities, says that 'no style is more extensively acceptable than the narrative, because this does not carry an air of superiority over the rest of the company; and, therefore, is most likely to please them. For this purpose we should store our memory with short anecdotes and entertaining pieces of history. Almost every one listens with eagerness to extemporary history. Vanity often co-operates with curiosity; for he that is a hearer in one place wishes to qualify himself to be a principal speaker in some inferior company; and therefore more attention is given to narrations than anything else in conversation. It is true, indeed, that sallies of wit and quick replies are very pleasing in conversation; but they frequently tend to raise envy in some of the company: but the narrative way neither raises this, nor any other evil passion, but keeps all the company nearly upon an equality, and, if judiciously managed, will at once entertain and improve them all.'*

GOOD TEMPER should be cultivated by every mistress, as upon it the welfare of the household may be said to turn; indeed, its influence can hardly be over-estimated, as it has the effect of moulding the characters of those around her, and of acting most beneficially on the happiness of the domestic circle. Every head of a household should strive to be cheerful, and should never fail to show a deep interest in all that appertains to the well-being of those who claim the protection of her roof. Gentleness, not partial and temporary, but universal and regular, should pervade her conduct; for where such a spirit is habitually manifested, it not only delights her children, but makes her domestics attentive and respectful; her visitors are also pleased by it, and their happiness is increased.

On the important subject of DRESS and FASHION we cannot do better than quote an opinion from the eighth volume of the 'Englishwoman's Domestic Magazine.' The writer* there says, 'Let people write, talk, lecture, satirize, as they may, it cannot be denied that, whatever is the prevailing mode in attire, let it intrinsically be ever so absurd, it will never *look* as ridiculous as another, or as any other, which, however convenient, comfortable, or even becoming, is totally opposite in style to that generally worn.'

In PURCHASING articles of wearing apparel, whether it be a silk dress, a bonnet, shawl, or riband, it is well for the buyer to consider three things: I. That it be not too expensive for her purse. II. That its colour harmonize with her complexion, and its size and pattern with her figure. III. That its tint allow of its being worn with the other garments she possesses. The quaint Fuller* observes, that the good wife is none of our dainty dames, who love to appear in a variety of suits every day new, as if a gown, like a stratagem in war, were to be used but once. But our good wife sets up a sail according to the keel of her husband's estate; and, if of high parentage, she doth not so remember what she was by birth, that she forgets what she is by match.

To *Brunettes*, or those ladies having dark complexions, silks of a grave hue are adapted. For *Blondes*, or those having fair complexions, lighter colours are preferable, as the richer, deeper hues are too overpowering for the latter. The colours which go best together are green with violet, gold-colour with dark crimson or lilac; pale blue with scarlet; pink with black or white; and gray with scarlet or pink. A cold colour generally requires a warm tint to give life to it. Gray and pale blue, for instance, do not combine well, both being cold colours.

The DRESS of the mistress should always be adapted to her circumstances, and be varied with different occasions. Thus, at breakfast she should be attired in a very neat and simple manner, wearing no ornaments. If this dress should decidedly pertain only to the breakfast-hour, and be specially suited for such domestic occupations as usually follow that meal, then it would be well to exchange it before the time for receiving visitors, if the mistress be in the habit of doing so. It is still to be remembered, however, that, in changing the dress, jewellery and ornaments are not to be worn until the full dress for dinner is assumed. Further information and hints on the subject of the toilet will appear under the department of the 'LADY'S-MAID.'

The advice of Polonius to his son Laertes, in Shakspeare's tragedy of 'Hamlet,' is most excellent; and although given to one of the male sex, will equally apply to a 'fayre ladye:'—

> 'Costly thy habit as thy purse can buy,
> But not express'd in fancy; rich, not gaudy;
> For the apparel oft proclaims the man.'

CHARITY and BENEVOLENCE are duties which a mistress owes to herself as well as to her fellow-creatures; and there is scarcely any income so small, but something may be spared from it, even if it be but 'the widow's mite.' It is to be always remembered, however, that it is the *spirit* of charity which imparts to the gift a value far beyond its actual amount, and is by far its better part.

> True Charity, a plant divinely nursed,
> Fed by the love from which it rose at first,
> Thrives against hope, and, in the rudest scene,
> Storms but enliven its unfading green;
> Exub'rant is the shadow it supplies,
> Its fruit on earth, its growth above the skies.*

Visiting the houses of the poor is the only practical way really to understand the actual state of each family; and although there may be difficulties in following out this plan in the metropolis and other large cities, yet in country towns and rural districts these objections do not obtain. Great advantages may result from visits paid to the poor; for there being, unfortunately, much ignorance, generally, amongst them with respect to all household knowledge, there will be opportunities for advising and instructing them, in a pleasant and unobtrusive manner, in cleanliness, industry, cookery, and good management.

In MARKETING, that the best articles are the cheapest, may be laid down as a rule; and it is desirable, unless an experienced and confidential housekeeper be kept, that the mistress should herself purchase all provisions and stores needed for the house. If the mistress be a young wife, and not accustomed to order 'things for the house,' a little practice and experience will soon teach her who are the best tradespeople to deal with, and what are the best provisions to buy. Under each particular head of FISH, MEAT, POULTRY, GAME, &c., will be described the proper means of ascertaining the quality of these comestibles.

A HOUSEKEEPING ACCOUNT-BOOK should invariably be kept, and kept punctually and precisely. The plan for keeping household accounts, which we should recommend, would be to make an entry, that is, write down into a daily diary every amount paid on that particular day, be it ever so small; then, at the end of the month, let these various payments be ranged under their specific heads of Butcher, Baker, &c.; and thus will be seen the proportions paid to each tradesman, and any one month's expenses may be contrasted with another. The housekeeping accounts should be balanced not less than once a month; so that you may see that the money you have in hand tallies with your account of it in your diary. Judge Haliburton* never wrote truer words than when he said, 'No man is rich whose expenditure exceeds his means, and no one is poor whose incomings exceed his outgoings.'

When, in a large establishment, a housekeeper is kept, it will be advisable for the mistress to examine her accounts regularly. Then any increase of expenditure which may be apparent, can easily be explained, and the housekeeper will have the satisfaction of knowing whether her efforts to manage her department well and economically, have been successful.

ENGAGING DOMESTICS is one of those duties in which the

judgment of the mistress must be keenly exercised. There are some respectable registry-offices, where good servants may sometimes be hired; but the plan rather to be recommended is, for the mistress to make inquiry amongst her circle of friends and acquaintances, and her tradespeople. The latter generally know those in their neighbourhood, who are wanting situations, and will communicate with them, when a personal interview with some of them will enable the mistress to form some idea of the characters of the applicants, and to suit herself accordingly.

We would here point out an error—and a grave one it is—into which some mistresses fall. They do not, when engaging a servant, expressly tell her all the duties which she will be expected to perform. This is an act of omission severely to be reprehended. Every portion of work which the maid will have to do, should be plainly stated by the mistress, and understood by the servant. If this plan is not carefully adhered to, domestic contention is almost certain to ensue, and this may not be easily settled; so that a change of servants, which is so much to be deprecated, is continually occurring.

In obtaining a SERVANT'S CHARACTER, it is not well to be guided by a written one from some unknown quarter; but it is better to have an interview, if at all possible, with the former mistress. By this means you will be assisted in your decision of the suitableness of the servant for your place, from the appearance of the lady and the state of her house. Negligence and want of cleanliness in her and her household generally, will naturally lead you to the conclusion, that her servant has suffered from the influence of the bad example.

The proper course to pursue in order to obtain a personal interview with the lady is this:—The servant in search of the situation must be desired to see her former mistress, and ask her to be kind enough to appoint a time, convenient to herself, when you may call on her; this proper observance of courtesy being necessary to prevent any unseasonable intrusion on the part of a stranger. Your first questions should be relative to the honesty and general morality of her former servant; and if no objection is stated in that respect, her other qualifications are then to be ascertained. Inquiries should be very minute, so that you may avoid disappointment and trouble, by knowing the weak points of your domestic.

The TREATMENT OF SERVANTS is of the highest possible moment, as well to the mistress as to the domestics themselves. On the head of the house the latter will naturally fix their attention; and if they perceive that the mistress's conduct is regulated by high and correct principles, they will not fail to respect her. If, also, a benevolent desire is shown to promote their comfort, at the same time that a steady performance of their duty is exacted, then their respect will not be unmingled with affection, and they will be still more solicitous to continue to deserve her favour.

In giving a CHARACTER, it is scarcely necessary to say that the mistress should be guided by a sense of strict justice. It is not fair for one lady to recommend to another, a servant she would not keep herself. The benefit, too, to the servant herself is of small advantage; for the failings which she possesses will increase if suffered to be indulged with impunity. It is hardly necessary to remark, on the other hand, that no angry feelings on the part of a mistress towards her late servant, should ever be allowed, in the slightest degree, to influence her, so far as to induce her to disparage her maid's character.

The following table* [p. 16] of the AVERAGE YEARLY WAGES paid to domestics, with the various members of the household placed in the order in which they are usually ranked, will serve as a guide to regulate the expenditure of an establishment.

Having thus indicated some of the more general duties of the mistress, relative to the moral government of her household, we will now give a few specific instructions on matters having a more practical relation to the position which she is supposed to occupy in the eye of the world. To do this the more clearly, we will begin with her earliest duties, and take her completely through the occupations of a day.

Having risen early, as we have already advised, and having given due attention to the bath, and made a careful toilet, it will be well at once to see that the children have received their proper ablutions, and are in every way clean and comfortable. The first meal of the day, breakfast, will then be served, at which all the family should be punctually present, unless illness, or other circumstances, prevent.

After breakfast is over, it will be well for the mistress to make a round of the kitchen and other offices, to see that all are in order, and that the morning's work has been properly performed by the various domestics. The orders for the day should then be given, and any

	When not found in Livery	When found in Livery
The House Steward	From £40 to £80	—
The Valet	From £25 to £50	From £20 to £30
The Butler	From £25 to £50	—
The Cook	From £20 to £40	—
The Gardener	From £20 to £40	—
The Footman	From £20 to £40	From £15 to £25
The Under Butler	From £15 to £30	From £15 to £25
The Coachman	—	From £20 to £35
The Groom	From £15 to £30	From £12 to £20
The Under Footman	—	From £12 to £20
The Page or Footboy	From £8 to £18	From £6 to £14
The Stableboy	From £6 to £12	—

	When no extra allowance is made for Tea, Sugar, and Beer	When an extra allowance is made for Tea, Sugar, and Beer
The Housekeeper	From £20 to £45	From £18 to £40
The Lady's-maid	From £12 to £25	From £10 to £20
The Head Nurse	From £15 to £30	From £13 to £26
The Cook	From £14 to £30	From £12 to £26
The Upper Housemaid	From £12 to £20	From £10 to £17
The Upper Laundry-maid	From £12 to £18	From £10 to £15
The Maid-of-all-work	From £9 to £14	From £7½ to £11
The Under Housemaid	From £8 to £12	From £6½ to £10
The Still-room Maid	From £9 to £14	From £8 to £12
The Nursemaid	From £8 to £12	From £5 to £10
The Under Laundry-maid	From £9 to £14	From £8 to £12
The Kitchen-maid	From £9 to £14	From £8 to £12
The Scullery-maid	From £5 to £9	From £4 to £8

These quotations of wages are those usually given in or near the metropolis; but, of course, there are many circumstances connected with locality, and also having reference to the long service on the one hand, or the inexperience on the other, of domestics, which may render the wages still higher or lower than those named above. All the domestics mentioned in the above table would enter into the establishment of a wealthy nobleman. The number of servants, of course, would become smaller in proportion to the lesser size of the establishment; and we may here enumerate a scale of servants suited to various incomes, commencing with—

About £1,000 a year—A cook, upper housemaid, nursemaid, under housemaid, and a man servant.

About £750 a year—A cook, housemaid, nursemaid, and footboy.

About £500 a year—A cook, housemaid, and nursemaid.

About £300 a year—A maid-of-all-work and nursemaid.

About £200 or £150 a year—A maid-of-all-work (and girl occasionally).

questions which the domestics desire to ask, respecting their several departments, should be answered, and any special articles they may require, handed to them from the store-closet.

In those establishments where there is a housekeeper, it will not be so necessary for the mistress, personally, to perform the above-named duties.

After this general superintendence of her servants, the mistress, if a mother of a young family, may devote herself to the instruction of some of its younger members, or to the examination of the state of their wardrobe, leaving the later portion of the morning for reading, or for some amusing recreation. 'Recreation,' says Bishop Hall, 'is intended to the mind as whetting is to the scythe, to sharpen the edge of it, which would otherwise grow dull and blunt. He, therefore, that spends his whole time in recreation is ever whetting, never mowing; his grass may grow and his steed starve; as, contrarily, he that always toils and never recreates, is ever mowing, never whetting, labouring much to little purpose. As good no scythe as no edge. Then only doth the work go forward, when the scythe is so seasonably and moderately whetted that it may cut, and so cut, that it may have the help of sharpening.'*

Unless the means of the mistress be very circumscribed, and she be obliged to devote a great deal of her time to the making of her children's clothes, and other economical pursuits, it is right that she should give some time to the pleasures of literature, the innocent delights of the garden, and to the improvement of any special abilities for music, painting, and other elegant arts, which she may, happily, possess.

These duties and pleasures being performed and enjoyed, the hour of luncheon will have arrived. This is a very necessary meal between an early breakfast and a late dinner, as a healthy person, with good exercise, should have a fresh supply of food once in four hours. It should be a light meal; but its solidity must, of course, be, in some degree, proportionate to the time it is intended to enable you to wait for your dinner, and the amount of exercise you take in the mean time. At this time, also, the servants' dinner will be served.

In those establishments where an early dinner is served, that will, of course, take the place of the luncheon. In many houses, where a nursery dinner is provided for the children at about one o'clock, the mistress and the elder portion of the family make their luncheon at the same time from the same joint, or whatever may be provided. A mistress will arrange, according to circumstances, the serving of the meal; but the more usual plan is for the lady of the house to have the joint brought to her table, and afterwards carried to the nursery.

After luncheon, MORNING CALLS* AND VISITS may be made and received. These may be divided under three heads: those of ceremony, friendship, and congratulation or condolence. Visits of ceremony, or courtesy, which occasionally merge into those of friendship, are to be paid under various circumstances. Thus, they are uniformly required after dining at a friend's house, or after a ball, picnic, or any other party. These visits should be short, a stay of from fifteen to twenty minutes being quite sufficient. A lady paying a visit may remove her boa or neckerchief; but neither her shawl nor bonnet.

When other visitors are announced, it is well to retire as soon as possible, taking care to let it appear that their arrival is not the cause. When they are quietly seated, and the bustle of their entrance is over, rise from your chair, taking a kind leave of the hostess, and bowing politely to the guests. Should you call at an inconvenient time, not having ascertained the luncheon hour, or from any other inadvertence, retire as soon as possible, without, however, showing that you feel yourself an intruder. It is not difficult for any well-bred or even good-tempered person, to know what to say on such an occasion, and, on politely withdrawing, a promise can be made to call again, if the lady you have called on, appear really disappointed.

In paying VISITS OF FRIENDSHIP, it will not be so necessary to be guided by etiquette as in paying visits of ceremony; and if a lady be pressed by her friend to remove her shawl and bonnet, it can be done if it will not interfere with her subsequent arrangements. It is, however, requisite to call at suitable times, and to avoid staying too long, if your friend is engaged. The courtesies of society should ever be maintained, even in the domestic circle, and amongst the nearest friends. During these visits, the manners should be easy and cheerful, and the subjects of conversation such as may be readily terminated. Serious discussions or arguments are to be altogether avoided, and there is much danger and impropriety in expressing opinions of those persons and characters with whom, perhaps, there is but a slight acquaintance. (*See* pp. 9–11.)

It is not advisable, at any time, to take favourite dogs into another lady's drawing-room, for many persons have an absolute dislike to such animals; and besides this, there is always a chance of a breakage of some article occurring, through their leaping and bounding here and there, sometimes very much to the fear and annoyance of the hostess. Her children, also, unless they are particularly well-trained and orderly, and she is on exceedingly friendly terms with the hostess, should not accompany a lady in making morning calls. Where a lady, however, pays her visits in a carriage, the children can be taken in the vehicle, and remain in it until the visit is over.

For MORNING CALLS, it is well to be neatly attired; for a costume very different to that you generally wear, or anything approaching an evening dress, will be very much out of place. As a general rule, it may be said, both in reference to this and all other occasions, it is better to be under-dressed than over-dressed.

A strict account should be kept of ceremonial visits, and notice how soon your visits have been returned. An opinion may thus be formed as to whether your frequent visits are, or are not, desirable. There are, naturally, instances when the circumstances of old age or ill health will preclude any return of a call; but when this is the case, it must not interrupt the discharge of the duty.

In Paying VISITS OF CONDOLENCE, it is to be remembered that they should be paid within a week after the event which occasions them. If the acquaintance, however, is but slight, then immediately after the family has appeared at public worship. A lady should send in her card, and if her friends be able to receive her, the visitor's manner and conversation should be subdued and in harmony with the character of her visit. Courtesy would dictate that a mourning card should be used, and that visitors, in paying condoling visits, should be dressed in black, either silk or plain-coloured apparel. Sympathy with the affliction of the family, is thus expressed, and these attentions are, in such cases, pleasing and soothing.

In all these visits, if your acquaintance or friend be not at home, a card should be left. If in a carriage, the servant will answer your inquiry and receive your card; if paying your visits on foot, give your card to the servant in the hall, but leave to go in and rest should on no account be asked. The form of words, 'Not at home,' may be understood in different senses; but the only courteous way is to receive them as being perfectly true. You may imagine that the lady of the house is really at home, and that she would make an exception in your favour, or you may think that your acquaintance is not desired; but, in either case, not the slightest word is to escape you, which would suggest, on your part, such an impression.

In receiving MORNING CALLS, the foregoing description of the etiquette to be observed in paying them, will be of considerable service. It is to be added, however, that the occupations of drawing, music, or reading should be suspended on the entrance of morning visitors. If a lady, however, be engaged with light needlework, and none other is appropriate in the drawing-room, it may not be, under some circumstances, inconsistent with good breeding to quietly continue it during conversation, particularly if the visit be protracted, or the visitors be gentlemen.

Formerly the custom was to accompany all visitors quitting the house to the door, and there take leave of them; but modern society which has thrown off a great deal of this kind of ceremony, now merely requires that the lady of the house should rise from her seat, shake hands, or courtesy, in accordance with the intimacy she has with her guests, and ring the bell to summon the servant to attend them and open the door. In making a first call, either upon a newly-married couple, or persons newly arrived in the neighbourhood, a lady should leave her husband's card together with her own, at the same time, stating that the profession or business in which he is engaged has prevented him from having the pleasure of paying the visit with her. It is a custom with many ladies, when on the eve of an absence from their neighbourhood, to leave or send their own and husband's cards, with the letters P. P. C. in the right-hand corner. These letters are the initials of the French words, '*Pour prendre congé*,' meaning, 'To take leave.'

The MORNING CALLS being paid or received, and their etiquette properly attended to, the next great event of the day in most establishments is 'The Dinner;' and we only propose here to make a few general remarks on this important topic, as, in future pages, the whole 'Art of Dining' will be thoroughly considered, with reference to its economy, comfort, and enjoyment.

In giving or accepting an INVITATION FOR DINNER, the following is the form of words generally made use of. They, however, can be varied in proportion to the intimacy or position of the hosts and guests:—

Mr and Mrs A—— present their compliments to Mr and Mrs B——, and request the honour, [or hope to have the pleasure] of their company to dinner on Wednesday, the 6th of December next.

A—— STREET,
November 13*th*, 1859.   *R. S. V. P.*

The letters in the corner imply '*Répondez, s'il vous plaît*;' meaning, 'an answer will oblige.' The reply, accepting the invitation; is couched in the following terms:—

Mr and Mrs B—— present their compliments to Mr and Mrs A——, and will do themselves the honour of, [or will have much pleasure in] accepting their kind invitation to dinner on the 6th of December next.

B—— SQUARE,
November 18th, 1859.

Cards, or invitations for a dinner-party, should be issued a fortnight or three weeks (sometimes even a month) beforehand, and care should be taken by the hostess, in the selection of the invited guests, that they should be suited to each other. Much also of the pleasure of a dinner-party will depend on the arrangement of the guests at table, so as to form a due admixture of talkers and listeners, the grave and the gay. If an invitation to dinner is accepted, the guests should be punctual, and the mistress ready in her drawing-room to receive them. At some periods it has been considered fashionable to come late to dinner, but lately *nous avons changé tout cela.**

The HALF-HOUR BEFORE DINNER has always been considered as the great ordeal through which the mistress, in giving a dinner-party, will either pass with flying colours, or, lose many of her laurels. The anxiety to receive her guests,—her hope that all will be present in due time,—her trust in the skill of her cook, and the attention of the other domestics, all tend to make these few minutes a trying time. The mistress, however, must display no kind of agitation, but show her tact in suggesting light and cheerful subjects of conversation, which will be much aided by the introduction of any particular new book, curiosity of art, or article of vertu, which may pleasantly engage the attention of the company. 'Waiting for Dinner,' however, is a trying time, and there are few who have not felt—

> 'How sad it is to sit and pine,
> The long *half-hour* before we dine!
> Upon our watches oft to look,
> Then wonder at the clock and cook
>
> .   .   .   .
>
> And strive to laugh in spite of Fate!
> But laughter forced soon quits the room,
> And leaves it in its former gloom.

But lo! the dinner now appears,
The object of our hopes and fears,
The end of all our pain!'*

In giving an entertainment of this kind, the mistress should remember that it is her duty to make her guests feel happy, comfortable, and quite at their ease; and the guests should also consider that they have come to the house of their hostess to be happy. Thus an opportunity is given to all for innocent enjoyment and intellectual improvement, when also acquaintances may be formed that may prove invaluable through life, and information gained that will enlarge the mind. Many celebrated men and women have been great talkers; and, amongst others, the genial Sir Walter Scott, who spoke freely to every one, and a favourite remark of whom it was, that he never did so without learning something he didn't know before.

DINNER being announced, the host offers his arm to, and places on his right hand at the dinner-table, the lady to whom he desires to pay most respect either on account of her age, position, or from her being the greatest stranger in the party. If this lady be married and her husband present, the latter takes the hostess to her place at table, and seats himself at her right hand. The rest of the company follow in couples, as specified by the master and mistress of the house, arranging the party according to their rank and other circumstances which may be known to the host and hostess.

It will be found of great assistance to the placing of a party at the dinner-table, to have the names of the guests neatly (and correctly) written on small cards, and placed at that part of the table where it is desired they should sit. With respect to the number of guests, it has often been said, that a private dinner-party should consist of not less than the number of the Graces, or more than that of the Muses.* A party of ten or twelve is, perhaps, in a general way, sufficient to enjoy themselves and be enjoyed. White kid gloves are worn by ladies at dinner-parties, but should be taken off before the business of dining commences.

The GUESTS being seated at the dinner-table, the lady begins to help the soup, which is handed round, commencing with the gentleman on her right and on her left, and continuing in the same order till all are served. It is generally established as a rule, not to ask for soup or fish twice, as, in so doing, part of the company may be kept waiting too long for the second course, when, perhaps, a little revenge is taken by looking at the awkward consumer of a second portion. This rule, however, may, under various circumstances, not be considered as binding.

It is not usual, where taking wine is *en règle*,* for a gentleman to ask a lady to take wine until the fish is finished, and then the gentleman honoured by sitting on the right of the hostess, may politely inquire if she will do him the honour of taking wine with him. This will act as a signal to the rest of the company, the gentleman of the house most probably requesting the same pleasure of the ladies at his right and left. At many tables, however, the custom or fashion of drinking wine in this manner, is abolished, and the servant fills the glasses of the guests with the various wines suited to the course which is in progress.

When dinner is finished, the DESSERT is placed on the table, accompanied with finger-glasses. It is the custom of some gentlemen to wet a corner of the napkin but the hostess, whose behaviour will set the tone to all the ladies present, will merely wet the tips of her fingers, which will serve all the purposes required. The French and other continentals have a habit of gargling the mouth; but it is a custom which no English gentlewoman should, in the slightest degree, imitate.

When FRUIT has been taken, and a glass or two of wine passed round, the time will have arrived when the hostess will rise, and thus give the signal for the ladies to leave the gentlemen, and retire to the drawing-room. The gentlemen of the party will rise at the same time, and he who is nearest the door, will open it for the ladies, all remaining courteously standing until the last lady has withdrawn. Dr Johnson has a curious paragraph on the effects of a dinner on men. 'Before dinner,' he says, 'men meet with great inequality of understanding; and those who are conscious of their inferiority have the modesty not to talk. When they have drunk wine, every man feels himself happy, and loses that modesty, and grows impudent and vociferous; but he is not improved, he is only not sensible of his defects.'* This is rather severe, but there may be truth in it.

In former times, when the bottle circulated freely amongst the guests, it was necessary for the ladies to retire earlier than they do at present, for the gentlemen of the company soon became unfit to conduct themselves with that decorum which is essential in the presence of ladies. Thanks, however, to the improvements in modern society, and the high example shown to the nation by its most illustrious personages, temperance is, in these happy days, a striking feature in the character of a gentleman. Delicacy of conduct towards the female sex has increased with the esteem in which they are now universally held, and thus, the very early withdrawing of the ladies from the dining-room is to be deprecated. A lull in the conversation will seasonably indicate the moment for the ladies' departure.

AFTER-DINNER INVITATIONS may be given; by which we wish to be understood, invitations for the evening. The time of the arrival of these visitors will vary according to their engagements, or sometimes will be varied in obedience to the caprices of fashion. Guests invited for the evening are, however, generally considered at liberty to arrive whenever it will best suit themselves,—usually between nine and twelve, unless earlier hours are specifically named. By this arrangement, many fashionable people and others, who have numerous engagements to fulfil, often contrive to make their appearance at two or three parties in the course of one evening.

The etiquette of the DINNER-PARTY TABLE being disposed of, let us now enter slightly into that of an evening party or ball. The invitations issued and accepted for either of these, will be written in the same style as those already described for a dinner-party. They should be sent out *at least* three weeks before the day fixed for the event, and should be replied to within a week of their receipt. By attending to these courtesies, the guests will have time to consider their engagements and prepare their dresses, and the hostess will, also, know what will be the number of her party.

If the entertainment is to be simply an evening party, this must be specified on the card or note of invitation. Short or verbal invitations, except where persons are exceedingly intimate, or are very near relations, are very far from proper, although, of course, in this respect and in many other respects, very much always depends on the manner in which the invitation is given. True politeness, however, should be studied even amongst the nearest friends and relations; for the mechanical forms of good breeding are of great consequence, and too much familiarity may have, for its effect, the destruction of friendship.

As the LADIES AND GENTLEMEN arrive, each should be shown to a room exclusively provided for their reception; and in that set apart for the ladies, attendants should be in waiting to assist in uncloaking, and helping to arrange the hair and toilet of those who require it. It will be found convenient, in those cases where the number of guests is large, to provide numbered tickets, so that they can be attached to the cloaks and shawls of each lady, a duplicate of which should be handed to the guest. Coffee is sometimes provided in this, or an ante-room, for those who would like to partake of it.

As the VISITORS are announced by the servant, it is not necessary for the lady of the house to advance each time towards the door, but merely to rise from her seat to receive their courtesies and congratulations. If, indeed, the hostess wishes to show particular favour to some peculiarly honoured guests, she may introduce them to others, whose acquaintance she may imagine will be especially suitable and agreeable. It is very often the practice of the master of the house to introduce one gentleman to another, but occasionally the lady performs this office; when it will, of course, be polite for the persons thus introduced to take their seats together for the time being.

The custom of non-introduction is very much in vogue in many houses, and guests are thus left to discover for themselves the position and qualities of the people around them. The servant, indeed, calls out the names of all the visitors as they arrive, but, in many instances, mispronounces them; so that it will not be well to follow this information, as if it were an unerring guide. In our opinion, it is a cheerless and depressing custom, although, in thus speaking, we do not allude to the large assemblies of the aristocracy, but to the smaller parties of the middle classes.

A separate room or CONVENIENT BUFFET should be appropriated for refreshments, and to which the dancers may retire; and cakes and biscuits, with wine negus,* lemonade, and ices, handed round. A supper is also mostly provided at the private parties of the middle classes; and this requires, on the part of the hostess, a great deal of attention and supervision. It usually takes place between the first and second parts of the programme of the dances, of which there should be several prettily written or printed copies distributed about the ball-room.

In private parties, a lady is not to refuse the invitation of a gentleman to dance, unless she be previously engaged. The hostess must be supposed to have asked to her house only those persons whom she knows to be perfectly respectable and of unblemished character, as well as pretty equal in position; and thus, to decline the offer of any gentleman present, would be a tacit reflection on the master and mistress of the house. It may be mentioned here, more especially for the young who will read this book, that introductions at balls or evening parties, cease with the occasion that calls them forth, no introduction, at these times, giving a gentleman a right to address afterwards, a lady. She is, consequently, free next morning, to pass her partner at a ball of the previous evening without the slightest recognition.

The BALL is generally opened, that is, the first place in the first quadrille is occupied, by the lady of the house. When anything prevents this, the host will usually lead off the dance with the lady who is either the highest in rank, or the greatest stranger. It will be well for the hostess, even if she be very partial to the amusement, and a graceful dancer, not to participate in it to any great extent, lest her lady guests should have occasion to complain of her monopoly of the gentlemen, and other causes of neglect. A few dances will suffice to show her interest in the entertainment, without unduly trenching on the attention due to her guests. In all its parts a ball should be perfect,—

> 'The music, and the banquet, and the wine;
> The garlands, the rose-odours, and the flowers.'

The hostess or host, during the progress of a ball, will courteously accost and chat with their friends, and take care that the ladies are furnished with seats, and that those who wish to dance are provided with partners. A gentle hint from the hostess, conveyed in a quiet ladylike manner, that certain ladies have remained unengaged during several dances, is sure not to be neglected by any gentleman. Thus will be studied the comfort and enjoyment of the guests, and no lady, in leaving the house, will be able to feel the chagrin and disappointment of not having been invited to 'stand up' in a dance during the whole of the evening.

When any of the CARRIAGES OF THE GUESTS are announced, or the time for their departure arrived, they should make a slight intimation to the hostess, without, however, exciting any observation, that they are about to depart. If this cannot be done, however, without creating too much bustle, it will be better for the visitors to retire quietly without taking their leave. During the course of the week, the hostess will expect to receive from every guest a call, where it is possible, or cards expressing the gratification experienced from her entertainment. This attention is due to every lady for the pains and trouble she has been at, and tends to promote social, kindly feelings.

Having thus discoursed of parties of pleasure, it will be an interesting change to return to the more domestic business of the house, although all the details we have been giving of dinner-parties, balls, and the like, appertain to the department of the mistress. Without a knowledge of the etiquette to be observed on these occasions, a mistress would be unable to enjoy and appreciate those friendly pleasant meetings which give, as it were, a fillip to life, and make the quiet happy home of an English gentlewoman appear the more delightful and enjoyable. In their proper places, all that is necessary to be known respecting the dishes and appearance of the breakfast, dinner, tea, and supper tables, will be set forth in this work.

A FAMILY DINNER at home, compared with either giving or going to a dinner-party, is, of course, of much more frequent occurrence, and many will say, of much greater importance. Both, however, have to be considered with a view to their nicety and enjoyment; and the latter more particularly with reference to economy. These points will be especially noted in the following pages on 'Household Cookery.' Here we will only say, that for both mistress and servants, as well in large as small households, it will be found, by far, the better plan, to cook, and serve the dinner, and to lay the tablecloth and the side-board, with the same cleanliness, neatness, and scrupulous exactness, whether it be for the mistress herself alone, a small family, or for 'company.' If this rule be strictly adhered to, all will find themselves increase in managing skill; whilst a knowledge of their daily duties will become familiar, and enable them to meet difficult occasions with ease, and overcome any amount of obstacles.

Of the manner of passing EVENINGS AT HOME, there is none pleasanter than in such recreative enjoyments as those which relax the mind from its severer duties, whilst they stimulate it with a gentle delight. Where there are young people forming a part of the evening circle, interesting and agreeable pastime should especially be promoted. It is of incalculable benefit to them that their homes should possess all the attractions of healthful amusement, comfort, and happiness; for if they do not find pleasure there, they will seek it elsewhere. It ought, therefore, to enter into the domestic policy of every parent, to make her children feel that home is the happiest place in the world; that to imbue them with this delicious home-feeling is one of the choicest gifts a parent can bestow.

Light or fancy needlework often forms a portion of the evening's recreation for the ladies of the household, and this may be varied by an occasional game at chess or backgammon. It has often been remarked, too, that nothing is more delightful to the feminine members of a family, than the reading aloud of some good standard work or amusing publication. A knowledge of polite literature may be thus obtained by the whole family, especially if the reader is able and willing to explain the more difficult passages of the book, and expatiate on the wisdom and beauties it may contain. This plan, in a great measure, realizes the advice of Lord Bacon,* who says, 'Read not to contradict and refute, nor to believe and take for granted, nor to find talk and discourse, but to weigh and consider.'

In RETIRING for the night, it is well to remember that early rising is almost impossible, if late going to bed be the order, or rather disorder, of the house. The younger members of a family should go early and at regular hours to their beds, and the domestics as soon as possible after a reasonably appointed hour. Either the master or the mistress of a house should, after all have gone to their separate rooms, see that all is right with respect to the lights and fires below; and no servants should, on any account, be allowed to remain up after the heads of the house have retired.

Having thus gone from early rising to early retiring, there remain only now to be considered a few special positions respecting which the mistress of the house will be glad to receive some specific information.

When a mistress takes a house in a new locality, it will be etiquette for her to wait until the older inhabitants of the neighbourhood call upon her; thus evincing a desire, on their part, to become acquainted with the new comer. It may be, that the mistress will desire an intimate acquaintance with but few of her neighbours; but it is to be specially borne in mind that all visits, whether of ceremony, friendship, or condolence, should be punctiliously returned.

You may perhaps have been favoured with letters of introduction from some of your friends, to persons living in the neighbourhood to which you have just come. In this case inclose the letter of introduction in an envelope with your card. Then, if the person, to whom it is addressed, calls in the course of a few days, the visit should be returned by you within the week, if possible. Any breach of etiquette, in this respect, will not readily be excused.

In the event of your being invited to dinner under the above circumstances, nothing but necessity should prevent you from accepting the invitation. If, however, there is some distinct reason why you cannot accept, let it be stated frankly and plainly, for politeness and truthfulness should be ever allied. An opportunity should, also, be taken to call in the course of a day or two, in order to politely express your regret and disappointment at not having been able to avail yourself of their kindness.

In giving a LETTER OF INTRODUCTION, it should always be handed to your friend, unsealed. Courtesy dictates this, as the person whom you are introducing would, perhaps, wish to know in what manner he or she was spoken of. Should you *receive* a letter from a friend, introducing to you any person known to and esteemed by the writer, the letter should be immediately acknowledged, and your willingness expressed to do all in your power to carry out his or her wishes.

Such are the onerous duties which enter into the position of the mistress of a house, and such are, happily, with a slight but continued attention, of by no means difficult performance. She ought always to remember that she is the first and the last, the Alpha and the Omega in the government of her establishment; and that it is by her conduct that its whole internal policy is regulated. She is, therefore, a person of far more importance in a community than she usually thinks she is. On her pattern her daughters model themselves; by her counsels they are directed; through her virtues all are honoured;—'her children rise up and call her blessed; her husband, also, and he praiseth her.'* Therefore, let each mistress always remember her responsible position, never approving a mean action, nor speaking an unrefined word. Let her conduct be such that her inferiors may respect her, and such as an honourable and right-minded man may look for in his wife and the mother of his children. Let her think of the many compliments and the sincere homage that have been paid to her sex by the greatest philosophers and writers, both in ancient and modern times. Let her not forget that she has to show herself worthy of Campbell's* compliment when he said,—

> 'The world was sad! the garden was a wild!
> And man the hermit sigh'd, till *woman* smiled.'

Let her prove herself, then, the happy companion of man, and able to take unto herself the praises of the pious prelate, Jeremy Taylor,*

who says,—'A good wife is Heaven's last best gift to man,—his angel
and minister of graces innumerable,—his gem of many virtues,—his
casket of jewels—her voice is sweet music—her smiles his brightest
day;—her kiss, the guardian of his innocence;—her arms, the pale of
his safety, the balm of his health, the balsam of his life;—her industry, his surest wealth;—her economy, his safest steward;—her lips,
his faithful counsellors;—her bosom, the softest pillow of his cares;
and her prayers, the ablest advocates of Heaven's blessings on his
head.'

Cherishing, then, in her breast the respected utterances of the
good and the great, let the mistress of every house rise to the
responsibility of its management; so that, in doing her duty to all
around her, she may receive the genuine reward of respect, love, and
affection!

Note.—Many mistresses have experienced the horrors of house-
hunting, and it is well known that 'three removes are as good (or bad,
rather) as a fire'.* Nevertheless, it being quite evident that we must, in
these days at least, live in houses, and are sometimes obliged to
change our residences, it is well to consider some of the conditions
which will add to, or diminish, the convenience and comfort of our
homes.

Although the choice of a house must be dependent on so many
different circumstances with different people, that to give any specific directions on this head would be impossible and useless; yet it
will be advantageous, perhaps, to many, if we point out some of those
general features as to locality, soil, aspect, &c., to which the attention
of all house-takers should be carefully directed.

Regarding the locality, we may say, speaking now more particularly of a town house, that it is very important to the health and
comfort of a family, that the neighbourhood of all factories of any
kind, producing unwholesome effluvia or smells, should be strictly
avoided. Neither is it well to take a house in the immediate vicinity of
where a noisy trade is carried on, as it is unpleasant to the feelings,
and tends to increase any existing irritation of the system.

Referring to soils; it is held as a rule, that a gravel soil is superior
to any other, as the rain drains through it very quickly, and it is

consequently drier and less damp than clay, upon which water rests a far longer time. A clay country, too, is not so pleasant for walking exercise as one in which gravel predominates.

The aspect of the house should be well considered, and it should be borne in mind that the more sunlight that comes into the house, the healthier is the habitation. The close, fetid smell which assails one on entering a narrow court, or street, in towns, is to be assigned to the want of light, and, consequently, air. A house with a south or south-west aspect, is lighter, warmer, drier, and consequently more healthy, than one facing the north or north-east.

Great advances have been made, during the last few years, in the principles of sanitary knowledge, and one most essential point to be observed in reference to a house, is its 'drainage,' as it has been proved in an endless number of cases, that bad or defective drainage is as certain to destroy health as the taking of poisons. This arises from its injuriously affecting the atmosphere; thus rendering the air we breathe unwholesome and deleterious. Let it be borne in mind, then, that unless a house is effectually drained, the health of its inhabitants is sure to suffer; and they will be susceptible of ague, rheumatism, diarrhoea, fevers, and cholera.

We now come to an all-important point,—that of the water supply. The value of this necessary article has also been lately more and more recognized in connection with the question of health and life; and most houses are well supplied with every convenience connected with water. Let it, however, be well understood, that no house, however suitable in other respects, can be desirable, if this grand means of health and comfort is, in the slightest degree, scarce or impure. No caution can be too great to see that it is pure and good, as well as plentiful; for, knowing, as we do, that not a single part of our daily food is prepared without it, the importance of its influence on the health of the inmates of a house cannot be over-rated.

Ventilation is another feature which must not be overlooked. In a general way, enough of air is admitted by the cracks round the doors and windows; but if this be not the case, the chimney will smoke; and other plans, such as the placing of a plate of finely-perforated zinc in the upper part of the window, must be used. Cold air should never be admitted under the doors, or at the bottom of a room, unless it be close to the fire or stove; for it will flow along the floor towards the fireplace, and thus leave the foul air in the upper part of the room, unpurified, cooling, at the same time, unpleasantly and injuriously, the feet and legs of the inmates.

The rent of a house, it has been said, should not exceed one-eighth of the whole income of its occupier; and, as a general rule, we are disposed to assent to this estimate, although there may be many circumstances which would not admit of its being considered infallible.

CHAPTER II

THE HOUSEKEEPER

As Second in Command in the house, except in large establish-ments, where there is a house steward, the housekeeper must con-sider herself as the immediate representative of her mistress, and bring, to the management of the household, all those qualities of honesty, industry, and vigilance, in the same degree as if she were at the head of *her own* family. Constantly on the watch to detect any wrong-doing on the part of any of the domestics, she will overlook all that goes on in the house, and will see that every department is thoroughly attended to, and that the servants are comfortable, at the same time that their various duties are properly performed.

Cleanliness, punctuality, order, and method, are essentials in the character of a good housekeeper. Without the first, no household can be said to be well managed. The second is equally all-important; for those who are under the housekeeper will take their 'cue' from her; and in the same proportion as punctuality governs her movements, so will it theirs. Order, again, is indispensable; for by it we wish to be understood that 'there should be a place for everything, and everything in its place.'* Method, too, is most necessary; for when the work is properly contrived, and each part arranged in regular succession, it will be done more quickly and more effectually.

A necessary qualification for a housekeeper is, that she should be thoroughly able to understand accounts. She will have to write in her books an accurate registry of all sums paid for any and every pur-pose, all the current expenses of the house, tradesmen's bills, and other extraneous matter. As we have mentioned under the head of the Mistress (*see* p. 13), a housekeeper's accounts should be periodic-ally balanced, and examined by the head of the house. Nothing tends more to the satisfaction of both employer and employed, than this arrangement. 'Short reckonings make long friends,'* stands good in this case, as in others.

It will be found an excellent plan to take an account of every article which comes into the house connected with housekeeping, and is not paid for at the time. The book containing these entries can then be compared with the bills sent in by the various tradesmen, so that any discrepancy can be inquired into and set right. An intelligent housekeeper will, by this means, too, be better able to judge of the average consumption of each article by the household, and if that quantity be, at any time, exceeded, the cause may be discovered and rectified, if it proceed from waste or carelessness.

Although in the department of the COOK, the housekeeper does not generally much interfere, yet it is necessary that she should possess a good knowledge of the culinary art, as, in many instances, it may be requisite for her to take the superintendence of the kitchen. As a rule, it may be stated, that the housekeeper, in those establishments where there is no house steward or man cook, undertakes the preparation of the confectionary, attends to the preserving and pickling of fruits and vegetables; and, in a general way, to the more difficult branches of the art of cookery.

Much of these arrangements will depend, however, on the qualifications of the cook; for instance, if she be an able artiste, there will be but little necessity for the housekeeper to interfere, except in the already noticed articles of confectionary, &c. On the contrary, if the cook be not so clever an adept in her art, then it will be requisite for the housekeeper to give more of her attention to the business of the kitchen, than in the former case. It will be one of the duties of the housekeeper to attend to the marketing; in the absence of either a house steward or man cook.

The DAILY DUTIES of a housekeeper are regulated, in a great measure, by the extent of the establishment she superintends. She should, however, rise early, and see that all the domestics are duly performing their work, and that everything is progressing satisfactorily for the preparation of the breakfast for the household and family. After breakfast, which, in large establishments, she will take in the 'housekeeper's room' with the lady's-maid, butler, and valet, and where they will be waited on by the still-room maid, she will, on various days set apart for each purpose, carefully examine the household linen, with a view to its being repaired, or to a further quantity being put in hand to be made; she will also see that the furniture throughout the house is well rubbed and polished; and will, besides, attend to all the necessary details of marketing and ordering goods from the tradesmen.

The housekeeper's room is generally made use of by the lady's-maid, butler, and valet, who take there their breakfast, tea, and supper. The lady's-maid will also use this apartment as a sitting-room, when not engaged with her lady, or with some other duties, which would call her elsewhere. In different establishments, according to their size and the rank of the family, different rules of course prevail. For instance, in the mansions of those of very high rank, and where there is a house steward, there are two distinct tables kept, one in the steward's room for the principal members of the household, the other in the servants' hall, for the other domestics. At the steward's dinner-table, the steward and housekeeper preside; and here, also, are present the lady's-maid, butler, valet, and head gardener. Should any visitors be staying with the family, their servants, generally the valet and lady's-maid, will be admitted to the steward's table.

After dinner, the housekeeper, having seen that all the members of the establishment have regularly returned to their various duties, and that all the departments of the household are in proper working order, will have many important matters claiming her attention. She will, possibly, have to give the finishing touch to some article of confectionary, or be occupied with some of the more elaborate processes of the still-room. There may also be the dessert to arrange, ice-creams to make; and all these employments call for no ordinary degree of care, taste, and attention.

The still-room was formerly much more in vogue than at present; for in days of 'auld lang syne,' the still was in constant requisition for the supply of sweet-flavoured waters for the purposes of cookery, scents and aromatic substances used in the preparation of the toilet, and cordials in cases of accidents and illness. There are some establishments, however, in which distillation is still carried on, and in these, the still-room maid has her old duties to perform. In a general way, however, this domestic is immediately concerned with the housekeeper. For the latter she lights the fire, dusts her room, prepares the breakfast-table, and waits at the different meals taken in the housekeeper's room. A still-room maid may learn a very great deal of useful knowledge from her intimate connection with the house-keeper, and if she be active and intelligent, may soon fit herself for a better position in the household.

In the evening, the housekeeper will often busy herself with the necessary preparations for the next day's duties. Numberless small, but still important arrangements, will have to be made, so that everything may move smoothly. At times, perhaps, attention will have to be paid to the breaking of lump-sugar, the stoning of raisins, the washing, cleansing, and drying of currants, &c. The evening, too, is the best time for setting right her account of the expenditure, and duly writing a statement of moneys received and paid, and also for making memoranda of any articles she may require for her store-room or other departments.

Periodically, at some convenient time,—for instance, quarterly or half-yearly, it is a good plan for the housekeeper to make an inventory of everything she has under her care, and compare this with the lists of a former period; she will then be able to furnish a statement, if necessary, of the articles which, on account of time, breakage, loss, or other causes, it has been necessary to replace or replenish.

In concluding these remarks on the duties of the housekeeper, we will briefly refer to the very great responsibility which attaches to her position. Like 'Caesar's wife,' she should be 'above suspicion,'* and her honesty and sobriety unquestionable; for there are many temptations to which she is exposed. In a physical point of view, a housekeeper should be healthy and strong, and be particularly clean in her person, and her hands, although they may show a degree of roughness, from the nature of some of her employments, yet should have a nice inviting appearance. In her dealings with the various tradesmen, and in her behaviour to the domestics under her, the demeanour and conduct of the housekeeper should be such as, in neither case, to diminish, by an undue familiarity, her authority or influence.

*Note.**—It will be useful for the mistress and housekeeper to know the best seasons for various occupations connected with Household Management; and we, accordingly, subjoin a few hints which we think will prove valuable.

As, in the winter months, servants have much more to do in consequence of the necessity there is to attend to the number of fires throughout the household, not much more than the ordinary every-day work can be attempted.

In the summer, and when the absence of fires gives the domestics more leisure, then any extra work that is required, can be more easily performed.

The spring is the usual period set apart for house-cleaning, and removing all the dust and dirt, which will necessarily, with the best of housewives, accumulate during the winter months, from the smoke of the coal, oil, gas, &c. This season is also well adapted for washing and bleaching linen, &c., as, the weather, not being then too hot for the exertions necessary in washing counterpanes, blankets, and heavy things in general, the work is better and more easily done than in the intense heats of July, which month some recommend for these purposes. Winter curtains should be taken down, and replaced by the summer white ones; and furs and woollen cloths also carefully laid by. The former should be well shaken and brushed, and then pinned upon paper or linen, with camphor to preserve them from the moths. Furs, &c., will be preserved in the same way. Included, under the general description of house-cleaning, must be understood, turning out all the nooks and corners of drawers, cupboards, lumber-rooms, lofts, &c., with a view of getting rid of all unnecessary articles, which only create dirt and attract vermin; sweeping of chimneys, taking up carpets, painting and whitewashing the kitchen and offices, papering rooms, when needed, and, generally speaking, the house putting on, with the approaching summer, a bright appearance, and a new face, in unison with nature. Oranges now should be preserved, and orange wine made.

The summer will be found, as we have mentioned above, in consequence of the diminution of labour for the domestics, the best period for examining and repairing household linen, and for 'putting to rights' all those articles which have received a large share of wear and tear during the dark winter days. In direct reference to this matter, we may here remark, that sheets should be turned 'sides to middle' before they are allowed to get very thin.* Otherwise, patching, which is uneconomical from the time it consumes, and is unsightly in point of appearance, will have to be resorted to. In June and July, gooseberries, currants, raspberries, strawberries, and other summer fruits, should be preserved, and jams and jellies made. In July, too, the making of walnut ketchup should be attended to, as the green walnuts will be approaching perfection for this purpose. Mixed pickles may also be now made, and it will be found a good plan to have ready a jar of pickle-juice (for the making of which all information will be given in future pages), into which to put occasionally some young French beans, cauliflowers, &c.

In the early autumn, plums of various kinds are to be bottled and preserved, and jams and jellies made. A little later, tomato sauce, a most useful article to have by you, may be prepared; a supply of apples laid in, if you have a place to keep them, as also a few keeping pears and filberts. Endeavour to keep also a large vegetable marrow,—it will be found delicious in the winter.

In October and November, it will he necessary to prepare for the cold weather, and get ready the winter clothing for the various members of the family. The white summer curtains will now be carefully put away, the fireplaces, grates, and chimneys looked to, and the house put in a thorough state of repair, so that no 'loose tile' may, at a future day, interfere with your comfort, and extract something considerable from your pocket.

In December, the principal household duty lies in preparing for the creature comforts of those near and dear to us, so as to meet old Christmas with a happy face, a contented mind, and a full larder; and in stoning the plums, washing the currants, cutting the citron, beating the eggs, and MIXING THE PUDDING, a housewife is not unworthily greeting the genial season of all good things.

CHAPTER III

ARRANGEMENT AND ECONOMY
OF THE KITCHEN

'The distribution of a kitchen,' says Count Rumford, the celebrated philosopher and physician, who wrote so learnedly on all subjects connected with domestic economy and architecture, 'must always depend so much on local circumstances, that general rules can hardly be given respecting it; the principles, however, on which this distribution ought, in all cases, to be made, are simple and easy to be understood,' and, in his estimation, these resolve themselves into symmetry of proportion in the building and convenience to the cook. The requisites of a good kitchen, however, demand something more special than is here pointed out. It must be remembered that it is the great laboratory of every household, and that much of the 'weal or woe,' as far as regards bodily health, depends upon the nature of the preparations concocted within its walls. A good kitchen, therefore, should be erected with a view to the following particulars. 1. Convenience of distribution in its parts, with largeness of dimension. 2. Excellence of light, height of ceiling, and good ventilation. 3. Easiness of access, without passing through the house. 4. Sufficiently remote from the principal apartments of the house, that the members, visitors, or guests of the family, may not perceive the odour incident to cooking, or hear the noise of culinary operations. 5. Plenty of fuel and water, which, with the scullery, pantry, and storeroom, should be so near it, as to offer the smallest possible trouble in reaching them.

The kitchens of the Middle Ages in England, are said to have been constructed after the fashion of those of the Romans. They were generally octagonal, with several fireplaces, but no chimneys; neither was there any wood admitted into the building. The accompanying cut, fig. 1, represents the turret which was erected on the top of the conical roof of the kitchen at Glastonbury Abbey, and which was perforated with holes to allow the smoke of the fire, as well as the steam from cooking, to escape. Some kitchens had funnels or vents below the eaves to let out the steam, which was sometimes considerable, as the Anglo-Saxons used their meat chiefly in a boiled state. From this circumstance, some of their large

Fig. 1

kitchens had four ranges, comprising a boiling-place for small boiled meats, and a boiling-house for the great boiler. In private houses the culinary arrangements were no doubt different; for Du Cange mentions a little kitchen with a chamber, even in a solarium, or upper-floor.

The simplicity of the primitive ages has frequently been an object of poetical admiration, and it delights the imagination to picture men living upon such fruits as spring spontaneously from the earth, and desiring no other beverages to slake their thirst, but such as fountains and rivers supply. Thus we are told,* that the ancient inhabitants of Argos lived principally on pears; that the Arcadians revelled in acorns, and the Athenians in figs. This, of course, was in the golden age, before ploughing began, and when mankind enjoyed all kinds of plenty without having to earn their bread 'by the sweat of their brow.' This delightful period, however, could not last for ever, and the earth became barren, and continued unfruitful till Ceres came and taught the art of sowing, with several other useful inventions. The first whom she taught to till the ground was Triptolemus, who communicated his instructions to his countrymen the Athenians. Thence the art was carried into Achaia, and thence into Arcadia. Barley was the first grain that was used, and the invention of bread-making is ascribed to Pan.

The use of fire, as an instrument of cookery, must have been coeval with this invention of bread, which, being the most necessary of all kinds of food, was frequently used in a sense so comprehensive as to include both meat and drink. It was, by the Greeks, baked under the ashes.

In the primary ages it was deemed unlawful to eat flesh, and when mankind began to depart from their primitive habits, the flesh of swine was the first that was eaten. For several ages, it was pronounced unlawful to slaughter oxen, from an estimate of their great value in assisting men to cultivate the ground; nor was it usual to kill young animals, from a sentiment which considered it cruel to take away the life of those that had scarcely tasted the joys of existence.

At this period no cooks were kept, and we know from Homer that his ancient heroes prepared and dressed their victuals with their own hands. Ulysses, for example, we are told, like a modern charwoman, excelled at lighting a fire, whilst Achilles was an adept at turning a spit. Subsequently, heralds, employed in civil and military affairs, filled the office of cooks, and managed marriage feasts; but this, no doubt, was after mankind had advanced in the art of living, a step further than *roasting*, which, in all places, was the ancient manner of dressing meat.

The age of roasting we may consider as that in which the use of the metals would be introduced as adjuncts to the culinary art; and amongst these, iron, the most useful of them all, would necessarily take a prominent place. This metal is easily oxidized, but to bring it to a state of fusibility, it requires a most intense heat. Of all the metals, it is the widest diffused and most abundant; and few stones or mineral bodies are without an admixture of it. It possesses the valuable property of being welded by hammering; and hence its adaptation to the numerous purposes of civilized life.

Metallic grains of iron have been found in strawberries, and a twelfth of the weight of the wood of dried oak is said to consist of this metal. Blood owes its colour of redness to the quantity of iron it contains, and rain and snow are seldom perfectly free from it. In the arts it is employed in three states,—as *cast* iron, *wrought* iron, and *steel*. In each of these it largely enters into the domestic economy, and stoves, grates, and the general implements of cookery, are usually composed of it. In antiquity, its employment was, comparatively speaking, equally universal. The excavations made at Pompeii have proved this. The accompanying cuts present us with specimens of stoves, both ancient and modern. Fig. 2 is the remains of a kitchen stove found in the house of Pansa, at Pompeii, and would seem, in its perfect state, not to have been materially different from such as are in use at the present day. Fig. 3 is a self-acting, simple open range in modern use, and may be had of two qualities, ranging, according to their dimensions, from £3. 10s. and £3. 18s. respectively, up to £4. 10s. and £7. 5s. They are completely fitted up with oven, boiler, sliding cheek, wrought-iron bars, revolving shelves, and brass tap. Fig. 4 is called the Improved Leamington Kitchener, and is said to surpass any other range in use, for easy cooking by one fire. It has a hot plate, which is well calculated for an ironing-stove, and on which as many vessels as will stand upon it, may be kept boiling, without being either soiled or injured. Besides, it has a perfectly ventilated and spacious wrought-iron roaster, with movable shelves, draw-out stand, double dripping-pan, and meat-stand. The roaster can be converted into an oven by closing the valves, when bread and pastry can be baked in it in a superior manner. It also has a large iron boiler with brass tap and steam-pipe, round and square gridirons for

Fig. 2

Fig. 3

Fig. 4

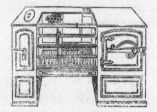

Fig. 5

chops and steaks, ash-pan, open fire for roasting, and a set of ornamental covings with plate-warmer attached. It took a first-class prize and medal in the Great Exhibition of 1851, and was also exhibited, with all the recent improvements, at the Dublin Exhibition in 1853. Fig. 5 is another kitchener, adapted for large families. It has on the one side, a large venti- lated oven; and on the other, the fire and roaster. The hot plate is over all, and there is a back boiler, made of wrought iron, with brass tap and steam- pipe. In other respects it resembles Fig. 4, with which it possesses similar advantages of construction. Either may be had at varying prices, according to size, from £5. 15s. up to £23. 10s. They are supplied by Messrs Richard & John Slack, 336, Strand, London.

From kitchen ranges to the implements used in cookery is but a step. With these, every kitchen should be well supplied, otherwise the cook must not be expected to 'perform her office' in a satisfactory manner. Of the culinary utensils of the ancients, our knowledge is very limited; but as the art of living, in every civilized country, is pretty much the same, the instruments for cooking must, in a great degree, bear a striking resemblance to each other. On referring to classical antiquities, we find mentioned, among household utensils, leather bags, baskets constructed of twigs, reeds, and rushes; boxes, basins, and bellows; bread-moulds,* brooms, and brushes; caldrons, colanders, cisterns, and chafing-dishes; cheese-rasps,* knives, and ovens of the Dutch kind;* funnels and frying-pans; handmills, soup-ladles, milk-pails, and oil-jars; presses,* scales, and sieves; spits of different sizes, but some of them large enough to roast an ox; spoons, fire-tongs, trays, trenchers,* and drinking-vessels; with others for carrying food, preserving milk, and holding cheese. This enumeration, if it does nothing else, will, to some extent, indicate the state of the simpler kinds of mechanical arts among the ancients.

In so far as regards the shape and construction of many of the kitchen utensils enumerated above, they bore a great resemblance to our own. This will be seen by the accompanying cuts. Fig. 6 is an ancient stock-pot in bronze, which seems to have been made to hang over the fire, and was found in the buried city of Pompeii. Fig. 7 is one of modern make, and may be obtained either of copper or wrought iron, tinned inside. Fig. 8 is another of antiquity, with a large ladle and colander, with holes attached. It is taken from the column of Trajan. The modern ones can be obtained at all prices, according to size, from 13s. 6d. up to £1. 1s.

Fig. 6   Fig. 7   Fig. 8

In the manufacture of these utensils, bronze metal seems to have been much in favour with the ancients. It was chosen not only for their domestic vessels, but it was also much used for their public sculptures and medals. It is a compound, composed of from six to twelve parts of tin to one hundred of copper. It gives its name to figures and all pieces of sculpture made of it. Brass was another favourite metal, which is composed of copper and zinc. It is more fusible than copper, and not so apt to tarnish. In a pure state it is not malleable, unless when hot, and after it has been melted twice it will not bear the hammer. To render it capable of being wrought, it requires 7 lb. of lead to be put to 1 cwt. of its own material.

The Corinthian brass of antiquity was a mixture of silver, gold, and copper. A fine kind of brass, supposed to be made by the cementation of copper plates with calamine, is, in Germany, hammered out into leaves, and is called Dutch metal in this country. It is employed in the same way as gold leaf. Brass is much used for watchworks, as well as for wire.

The braziers,* ladles, stewpans, saucepans, gridirons,* and colanders of antiquity might generally pass for those of the English manufacture of the present day, in so far as shape is concerned. In proof of this we have placed together the following similar articles of ancient and modern pattern, in order that the reader may, at a single view, see wherein any difference that is between them, consists.

Fig. 9 Modern

Fig. 11 Modern

Fig. 13 Modern

Fig. 10 Ancient

Fig. 12 Ancient

Fig. 14 Ancient

Fig. 15 Modern   Fig. 16 Modern   Fig. 17 Ancient   Fig. 18 Ancient

Figs. 9 and 10 are flat sauce or *sauté* pans, the ancient one being fluted in the handle, and having at the end a ram's head. Figs. 11 and 12 are colanders, the handle of the ancient one being adorned in the original, with carved representations of a cornucopia, a satyr, a goat, pigs, and other animals. Any display of taste in the adornment of such utensils, might seem to be useless; but when we remember how much more natural it is for us all to be careful of the beautiful and costly, than of the plain and cheap, it may even become a question in the economy of a kitchen, whether it would not, in the long run, be cheaper to have articles which displayed some tasteful ingenuity in their manufacture, than such as are so perfectly plain as to have no attractions whatever beyond their mere suitableness to the purposes for which they are made. Figs. 13 and 14 are saucepans, the ancient one being of bronze, originally copied from the cabinet of M. l'Abbé Charlet, and engraved in the Antiquities of Montfaucon. Figs. 15 and 17 are gridirons, and 16 and 18 dripping-pans. In all these utensils the resemblance between such as were in use 2,000 years ago, and those in use at the present day, is strikingly manifest.

Some of the ancient utensils represented in the above cuts, are copied from those found amid the ruins of Herculaneum and Pompeii. These Roman cities were, in the first century, buried beneath the lava of an eruption of Vesuvius, and continued to be lost to the world till the beginning of the last century, when a peasant, in digging for a well, gradually discovered a small temple with some statues. Little notice, however, was taken of this circumstance till 1736, when the king of Naples, desiring to erect a palace at Portici, caused extensive excavations to be made, when the city of Herculaneum was slowly unfolded to view. Pompeii was discovered about 1750, and being easier cleared from the lava in which it had so long been entombed, disclosed itself as it existed immediately before the catastrophe which overwhelmed it, nearly two thousand years ago. It presented, to the modern world, the perfect picture of the form and structure of an ancient Roman city. The interior of its habitations, shops, baths, theatres, and temples, were all disclosed, with many of the implements used by the workmen in their various trades, and the materials on which they were employed, when the doomed city was covered with the lavian stream.

Amongst the most essential requirements of the kitchen are scales or weighing-machines for family use. These are found to have existed among the ancients, and must, at a very early age, have been both publicly and privately employed for the regulation of quantities. The modern English weights were adjusted by the 27th chapter of Magna Charta, or the great charter forced, by the barons, from King John at Runnymede, in Surrey. Therein it is declared that the weights, all over England, shall be the same, although for different commodities there were two different kinds, Troy and Avoirdupois. The origin of both is taken from a grain of wheat gathered in the middle of an ear. The standard of measures was originally kept at Winchester, and by a law of King Edgar was ordained to be observed throughout the kingdom.

Fig. 19 is an ancient pair of common scales, with two basins and a movable weight, which is made in the form of a head, covered with the pileus, because Mercury had the weights and measures under his superintendence. It is engraved on a stone in the gallery of Florence. Fig. 20 represents a modern weighing-machine, of great convenience, and generally in use in those establishments where a great deal of cooking is carried on.

Fig. 19   *Fig.* 20

Accompanying the scales, or weighing-machines, there should be spice boxes, and sugar and biscuit-canisters of either white or japanned tin. The covers of these should fit tightly, in order to exclude the air, and if necessary, be lettered in front, to distinguish them. The white metal of which they are usually composed, loses its colour when exposed to the air, but undergoes no further change. It enters largely into the composition of culinary utensils, many of them being entirely composed of tinned sheet-iron; the inside of copper and iron vessels also, being usually what is called *tinned*. This art consists of covering any metal with a thin coating of tin; and it requires the metal to be covered, to be perfectly clean and free from rust, and also that the tin, itself, be purely metallic, and entirely cleared from all ashes or refuse. Copper boilers, saucepans, and other kitchen utensils, are tinned after they are manufactured, by being first made hot and the tin rubbed on with resin. In this process, nothing ought to be used but pure grain-tin. Lead, however, is sometimes mixed with that metal, not only to make it lie more easily, but to adulterate it—a pernicious practice, which in every article connected with the cooking and preparation of food, cannot be too severely reprobated.—The following list, supplied by Messrs Richard & John Slack, 336, Strand, will show the articles required for the kitchen of a family in the middle class of life, although it does not contain all the things that may be deemed necessary for some families, and may contain more than are required for others. As Messrs Slack themselves, however, publish a useful illustrated catalogue, which may be had at their establishment *gratis*, and which it will be found advantageous to consult by those about to furnish, it supersedes the necessity of our enlarging that which we give:—

		s.	d.			s.	d.
1	Tea-kettle	6	6	1	Dripping-pan and		
1	Toasting-fork	1	0		Stand	6	6
1	Bread-grater	1	0	1	Dustpan	1	0
1	Pair of Brass			1	Fish and Egg-slice	1	9
	Candlesticks	3	6	2	Fish-kettles	10	0
1	Teapot and Tray	6	6	1	Flour-box	1	0
1	Bottle-jack	9	6	3	Flat-irons	3	6
6	Spoons	1	6	2	Frying-pans	4	0
2	Candlesticks	2	6	1	Gridiron	2	0
1	Candle-box	1	4	1	Mustard-pot	1	0
6	Knives and Forks	5	3	1	Salt-cellar	0	8
2	Sets of Skewers	1	0	1	Pepper-box	0	6
1	Meat-chopper	1	9	1	Pair of Bellows	2	0
1	Cinder-shifter	1	3	3	Jelly-moulds	8	0
1	Coffee-pot	2	3	1	Plate-basket	5	6
1	Colander	1	6	1	Cheese-toaster	1	10
3	Block-tin Saucepans	5	9	1	Coal-shovel	2	6
5	Iron Saucepans	12	0	1	Wood Meat-screen	30	0
1	Ditto and Steamer	6	6				
1	Large Boiling-pot	10	0		The Set	£8 11	1
4	Iron Stewpans	8	9				

As not only health but life may be said to depend on the cleanliness of culinary utensils, great attention must be paid to their condition generally, but more especially to that of the saucepans, stewpans, and boilers. Inside they should be kept perfectly clean, and where an open fire is used, the outside as clean as possible. With a Leamington range,* saucepans, stewpans, &c., can be kept entirely free from smoke and soot on the outside, which is an immense saving of labour to the cook or scullery-maid. Care should be taken that the lids fit tight and close, so that soups or gravies may not be suffered to waste by evaporation. They should be made to keep the steam in and the smoke out, and should always be bright on the upper rim, where they do not immediately come in contact with the fire. Soup-pots and kettles should be washed immediately after being used, and dried before the fire, and they should be kept in a dry place, in order that they may escape the deteriorating influence of rust, and, thereby, be destroyed. Copper utensils should never be used in the kitchen unless tinned, and the utmost care should be taken, not to let the tin be rubbed off. If by chance this should occur, have it replaced before the vessel is again brought into use. Neither soup nor gravy should, at any time, be suffered to remain in them longer than is absolutely necessary, as any fat or acid that is in them, may affect the metal, so as to impregnate with poison what is intended to be eaten. Stone and earthenware vessels should be provided for soups and gravies not intended for immediate use, and, also, plenty of common dishes for the larder, that the table-set may not be used for such purposes. It is the nature of vegetables soon to turn sour, when they are apt to corrode glazed red-ware, and even metals, and frequently, thereby, to become impregnated with poisonous particles. The vinegar also in pickles, by its acidity, does the same. Consideration, therefore, should be given to these facts, and great care also taken that all *sieves, jelly-bags*, and tapes for collared articles, be well scalded and kept dry, or they will impart an unpleasant flavour when next used. To all these directions the cook should pay great attention, nor should they, by any means, be neglected by the *mistress of the household*, who ought to remember that cleanliness in the kitchen gives health and happiness to home, whilst economy will immeasurably assist in preserving them.

Without fuel, a kitchen might be pronounced to be of little use; therefore, to discover and invent materials for supplying us with the means of domestic heat and comfort, has exercised the ingenuity of man. Those now known have been divided into five classes; the first comprehending the fluid inflammable bodies; the second, peat or turf; the third, charcoal of wood; the fourth, pit-coal charred; and the fifth, wood or pit-coal in a crude state, with the capacity of yielding a copious and bright flame. The first may be said seldom to be employed for the purposes of cookery; but *peat*, especially amongst rural populations, has, in all ages, been regarded as an excellent fuel. It is one of the most important productions of an alluvial soil, and belongs to the vegetable rather than the mineral kingdom. It may be described as composed of wet, spongy black earth, held together by decayed vegetables. Formerly it covered extensive tracts in England, but has greatly disappeared before the genius of agricultural improvement. *Charcoal* is a kind of artificial coal, used principally where a strong and clear fire is desired. It is a black, brittle, insoluble, inodorous, tasteless substance, and, when newly-made, possesses the remarkable property of absorbing certain quantities of the different gases. Its dust, when used as a polishing powder, gives great brilliancy to metals. It consists of wood half-burned, and is manufactured by cutting pieces of timber into nearly the same size, then disposing them in heaps, and covering them with earth, so as to prevent communication with the air, except when necessary to make them burn. When they have been sufficiently charred, the fire is extinguished by stopping the vents through which the air is admitted. Of *coal* there are various species; as, pit, culm, slate, cannel, Kilkenny, sulphurous, bovey, jet, &c. These have all their specific differences, and are employed for various purposes; but are all, more or less, used as fuel.

The use of coal for burning purposes was not known to the Romans. In Britain it was discovered about fifty years before the birth of Christ, in Lancashire, not far from where Manchester now stands; but for ages after its discovery, so long as forests abounded, wood continued to be the fuel used for firing. The first public notice of coal is in the reign of Henry III, who, in 1272, granted a charter to the town of Newcastle, permitting the inhabitants to dig for coal. It took some centuries more, however, to bring it into common use, as this

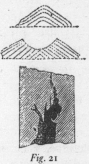

Fig. 21

did not take place till about the first quarter of the seventeenth century, in the time of Charles I. A few years after the Restoration, we find that about 200,000 chaldrons were consumed in London. Although several countries possess mines of coal, the quality of their mineral is, in general, greatly inferior to that of Great Britain, where it is found mostly in undulating districts abounding with valleys, and interspersed with plains of considerable extent. It lies usually between the *strata* of other substances, and rarely in an horizontal position, but with a *dip* or inclination to one side. Our cut, Fig. 21, represents a section of coal as it is found in the stratum.

To be acquainted with the periods when things are in season, is one of the most essential pieces of knowledge which enter into the 'Art of Cookery.' We have, therefore, compiled the following list, which will serve to show for every month in the year the

TIMES WHEN THINGS ARE IN SEASON

January

FISH.—Barbel, brill, carp, cod, crabs, crayfish, dace, eels, flounders, haddocks, herrings, lampreys, lobsters, mussels, oysters, perch, pike, plaice, prawns, shrimps, skate, smelts, soles, sprats, sturgeon, tench, thornback, turbot, whitings.

MEAT.—Beef, house lamb,* mutton, pork, veal, venison.

POULTRY.—Capons,* fowls, tame pigeons, pullets,* rabbits, turkeys.

GAME.—Grouse, hares, partridges, pheasants, snipe, wild-fowl,* woodcock.

VEGETABLES.—Beetroot, broccoli, cabbages, carrots, celery, chervil, cresses, cucumbers (forced), endive, lettuces, parsnips, potatoes, savoys,* spinach, turnips,—various herbs.

FRUIT.—Apples, grapes, medlars,* nuts, oranges, pears, walnuts, crystallized preserves (foreign), dried fruits, such as almonds and raisins; French and Spanish plums; prunes, figs, dates.

February

FISH.—Barbel, brill, carp, cod may be bought, but is not so good as in January, crabs, crayfish, dace, eels, flounders, haddocks, herrings, lampreys, lobsters, mussels, oysters, perch, pike, plaice, prawns, shrimps, skate, smelts, soles, sprats, sturgeon, tench, thornback, turbot, whiting.

MEAT.—Beef, house lamb, mutton, pork, veal.

POULTRY.—Capons, chickens, ducklings, tame and wild pigeons, pullets with eggs, turkeys, wild-fowl, though now not in full season.

GAME.—Grouse, hares, partridges, pheasants, snipes, woodcock.

VEGETABLES.—Beetroot, broccoli (purple and white), Brussels sprouts, cabbages, carrots, celery, chervil, cresses, cucumbers (forced), endive, kidney-beans, lettuces, parsnips, potatoes, savoys, spinach, turnips,—various herbs.

FRUIT.—Apples (golden and Dutch pippins), grapes, medlars, nuts, oranges, pears (Bon Chrétien), walnuts, dried fruits (foreign), such as almonds and raisins; French and Spanish plums; prunes, figs, dates, crystallized preserves.

March

FISH.—Barbel, brill, carp, crabs, crayfish, dace, eels, flounders, haddocks, herrings, lampreys, lobsters, mussels, oysters, perch, pike, plaice, prawns, shrimps, skate, smelts, soles, sprats, sturgeon, tench, thornback, turbot, whiting.

MEAT.—Beef, house lamb, mutton, pork, veal.

POULTRY.—Capons, chickens, ducklings, tame and wild pigeons, pullets with eggs, turkeys, wild-fowl, though now not in full season.

GAME.—Grouse, hares, partridges, pheasants, snipes, woodcock.

VEGETABLES.—Beetroot, broccoli (purple and white), Brussels sprouts, cabbages, carrots, celery, chervil, cresses, cucumbers (forced), endive, kidney-beans, lettuces, parsnips, potatoes, savoys, sea-kale,* spinach, turnips,—various herbs.

FRUIT.—Apples (golden and Dutch pippins), grapes, medlars, nuts, oranges, pears (Bon Chrétien), walnuts, dried fruits (foreign), such as almonds and raisins; French and Spanish plums; prunes, figs, dates, crystallized preserves.

April

FISH.—Brill, carp, cockles, crabs, dory, flounders, ling, lobsters, red and gray mullet, mussels, oysters, perch, prawns, salmon (but rather scarce and expensive), shad, shrimps, skate, smelts, soles, tench, turbot, whitings.

MEAT.—Beef, lamb, mutton, veal.

POULTRY.—Chickens, ducklings, fowls, leverets,* pigeons, pullets, rabbits.

GAME.—Hares.

VEGETABLES.—Broccoli, celery, lettuces, young onions, parsnips, radishes, small salad, sea-kale, spinach, sprouts,—various herbs.

FRUIT.—Apples, nuts, pears, forced cherries, &c. for tarts, rhubarb, dried fruits, crystallized preserves.

May

FISH.—Carp, chub, crabs, crayfish, dory, herrings, lobsters, mackerel, red and gray mullet, prawns, salmon, shad, smelts, soles, trout, turbot.

MEAT.—Beef, lamb, mutton, veal.

POULTRY.—Chickens, ducklings, fowls, green geese,* leverets, pullets, rabbits.

VEGETABLES.—Asparagus, beans, early cabbages, carrots, cauliflowers, cresses, cucumbers, lettuces, pease,* early potatoes, salads, sea-kale,—various herbs.

FRUIT.—Apples, green apricots, cherries, currants for tarts, gooseberries, melons, pears, rhubarb, strawberries.

June

FISH.—Carp, crayfish, herrings, lobsters, mackerel, mullet, pike, prawns, salmon, soles, tench, trout, turbot.

MEAT.—Beef, lamb, mutton, veal, buck venison.

POULTRY.—Chickens, ducklings, fowls, green geese, leverets, plovers,* pullets, rabbits, turkey poults,* wheatears.*

VEGETABLES.—Artichokes, asparagus, beans, cabbages, carrots, cucumbers, lettuces, onions, parsnips, pease, potatoes, radishes, small salads, sea-kale, spinach,—various herbs.

FRUIT.—Apricots, cherries, currants, gooseberries, melons, nectarines, peaches, pears, pineapples, raspberries, rhubarb, strawberries.

July

FISH.—Carp, crayfish, dory, flounders, haddocks, herrings, lobsters, mackerel, mullet, pike, plaice, prawns, salmon, shrimps, soles, sturgeon, tench, thornback.

MEAT.—Beef, lamb, mutton, veal, buck venison.

POULTRY.—Chickens, ducklings, fowls, green geese, leverets, plovers, pullets, rabbits, turkey poults, wheatears, wild ducks (called flappers).

VEGETABLES.—Artichokes, asparagus, beans, cabbages, carrots, cauliflowers, celery, cresses, endive, lettuces, mushrooms, onions, pease, radishes, small salading,* sea-kale, sprouts, turnips, vegetable marrow,—various herbs.

FRUIT.—Apricots, cherries, currants, figs, gooseberries, melons, nectarines, pears, pineapples, plums, raspberries, strawberries, walnuts in high season,* and pickled.

August

FISH.—Brill, carp, chub, crayfish, crabs, dory, eels, flounders, grigs, herrings, lobsters, mullet, pike, prawns, salmon, shrimps, skate, soles, sturgeon, thornback, trout, turbot.

MEAT.—Beef, lamb, mutton, veal, buck venison.

POULTRY.—Chickens, ducklings, fowls, green geese, pigeons, plovers, pullets, rabbits, turkey poults, wheatears, wild ducks.

GAME.—Leverets, grouse, blackcock.*

VEGETABLES.—Artichokes, asparagus, beans, carrots, cabbages, cauliflowers, celery, cresses, endive, lettuces, mushrooms, onions, pease, potatoes, radishes, sea-kale, small salading, sprouts, turnips, various kitchen herbs, vegetable marrows.

FRUIT.—Currants, figs, filberts,* gooseberries, grapes, melons, mulberries, nectarines, peaches, pears, pineapples, plums, raspberries, walnuts.

September

FISH.—Brill, carp, cod, eels, flounders, lobsters, mullet, oysters, plaice, prawns, skate, soles, turbot, whiting, whitebait.

MEAT.—Beef, lamb, mutton, pork, veal.

POULTRY.—Chickens, ducks, fowls, geese, larks, pigeons, pullets, rabbits, teal, turkeys.

GAME.—Blackcock, buck venison, grouse, hares, partridges, pheasants.

VEGETABLES.—Artichokes, asparagus, beans, cabbage sprouts, carrots, celery, lettuces, mushrooms, onions, pease, potatoes, salading, sea-kale, sprouts, tomatoes, turnips, vegetable marrows,—various herbs.

FRUIT.—Bullaces,* damsons, figs, filberts, grapes, melons, morella-cherries, mulberries, nectarines, peaches, pears, plums, quinces, walnuts.

October

FISH.—Barbel, brill, cod, crabs, eels, flounders, gudgeons, haddocks, lobsters, mullet, oysters, plaice, prawns, skate, soles, tench, turbot, whiting.

MEAT.—Beef, mutton, pork, veal, venison.

POULTRY.—Chickens, fowls, geese, larks, pigeons, pullets, rabbits, teal, turkeys, widgeons, wild ducks.

GAME.—Blackcock, grouse, hares, partridges, pheasants, snipes, woodcocks, doe venison.

VEGETABLES.—Artichokes, beets, cabbages, cauliflowers, carrots, celery, lettuces, mushrooms, onions, potatoes, sprouts, tomatoes, turnips, vegetable marrows,—various herbs.

FRUIT.—Apples, black and white bullaces, damsons, figs, filberts, grapes, pears, quinces, walnuts.

November

FISH.—Brill, carp, cod, crabs, eels, gudgeons, haddocks, oysters, pike, soles, tench, turbot, whiting.

MEAT.—Beef, mutton, veal, doe venison.

POULTRY.—Chickens, fowls, geese, larks, pigeons, pullets, rabbits, teal, turkeys, widgeons, wild duck.

GAME.—Hares, partridges, pheasants, snipes, woodcocks.

VEGETABLES.—Beetroot, cabbages, carrots, celery, lettuces, late cucumbers, onions, potatoes, salading, spinach, sprouts,—various herbs.

FRUIT.—Apples, bullaces, chestnuts, filberts, grapes, pears, walnuts.

December

FISH.—Barbel, brill, carp, cod, crabs, eels, dace, gudgeons, haddocks, herrings, lobsters, oysters, perch, pike, shrimps, skate, sprats, soles, tench, thornback, turbot, whiting.

MEAT.—Beef, house lamb, mutton, pork, venison.

POULTRY.—Capons, chickens, fowls, geese, pigeons, pullets, rabbits, teal, turkeys, widgeons, wild ducks.

GAME.—Hares, partridges, pheasants, snipes, woodcocks.

VEGETABLES.—Broccoli, cabbages, carrots, celery, leeks, onions, potatoes, parsnips, Scotch kale, turnips, winter spinach.

FRUIT.—Apples, chestnuts, filberts, grapes, medlars, oranges, pears, walnuts, dried fruits, such as almonds and raisins, figs, dates, &c.,—crystallized preserves.

When fuel and food are procured, the next consideration is, how the latter may be best preserved, with a view to its being suitably dressed. More waste is often occasioned by the want of judgment, or of necessary care in this particular, than by any other cause. In the absence of proper places for keeping provisions, a hanging safe, suspended in an airy situation, is the best substitute. A well-ventilated larder, dry and shady, is better for meat and poultry, which require to be kept for some time; and the utmost skill in the culinary art will not compensate for the want of proper attention to this particular. Though it is advisable that animal food should be hung up in the open air till its fibres have lost some degree of their toughness, yet, if it is kept till it loses its natural sweetness, its flavour has become deteriorated, and, as a wholesome comestible, it has lost many of its qualities conducive to health. As soon, therefore, as the slightest trace of putrescence is detected, it has reached its highest degree of tenderness, and should be dressed immediately. During the sultry summer months, it is difficult to procure meat that is not either tough or tainted. It should, therefore, be well examined when it comes in, and if flies have touched it, the part must be cut off, and the remainder well washed. In very cold weather, meat and vegetables touched by the frost, should be brought into the kitchen early in the morning, and soaked in cold water. In loins of meat, the long pipe that runs by the bone should be taken out, as it is apt to taint; as also the kernels of beef. Rumps and edgebones of beef, when bruised, should not be purchased. All these things ought to enter into the consideration of every household manager, and great care should be taken that nothing is thrown away, or suffered to be wasted in the kitchen, which might, by proper management, be turned to a good account. The shank-bones of mutton, so little esteemed in general, give richness to soups or gravies, if well soaked and brushed before they are added to the boiling. They are also particularly nourishing for sick persons. Roast-beef bones, or shank-bones of ham, make excellent stock for pea-soup.—When the whites of eggs are used for jelly, confectionary, or other purposes, a pudding or a custard should be made, that the yolks may be used. All things likely to be wanted should be in readiness: sugars of different sorts; currants washed, picked, and perfectly dry; spices pounded, and kept in very small bottles closely corked, or in canisters, as we have already directed. Not more of these should be purchased at a time than are likely to be used in the course of a month. Much waste is always prevented by keeping every article in the place best suited to it. Vegetables keep best on a stone floor, if the air be excluded; meat, in a cold dry place; as also salt, sugar, sweetmeats, candles, dried meats, and hams. Rice, and all sorts of seed for puddings, should be closely covered to preserve them from insects; but even this will not prevent them from being affected by these destroyers, if they are long and carelessly kept.

CHAPTER IV

INTRODUCTION TO COOKERY

As in the fine arts, the progress of mankind from barbarism to civilization is marked by a gradual succession of triumphs over the rude materialities of nature, so in the art of cookery is the progress gradual from the earliest and simplest modes, to those of the most complicated and refined. Plain or rudely-carved stones, tumuli, or mounds of earth, are the monuments by which barbarous tribes denote the events of their history, to be succeeded, only in the long course of a series of ages, by beautifully-proportioned columns, gracefully-sculptured statues, triumphal arches, coins, medals, and the higher efforts of the pencil and the pen, as man advances by culture and observation to the perfection of his faculties. So is it with the art of cookery. Man, in his primitive state, lives upon roots and the fruits of the earth, until, by degrees, he is driven to seek for new means, by which his wants may be supplied and enlarged. He then becomes a hunter and a fisher. As his species increases, greater necessities come upon him, when he gradually abandons the roving life of the savage for the more stationary pursuits of the herdsman. These beget still more settled habits, when he begins the practice of agriculture, forms ideas of the rights of property, and has his own, both defined and secured. The forest, the stream, and the sea are now no longer his only resources for food. He sows and he reaps, pastures and breeds cattle, lives on the cultivated produce of his fields, and revels in the luxuries of the dairy; raises flocks for cloth-ing, and assumes, to all intents and purposes, the habits of perman-ent life and the comfortable condition of a farmer. This is the fourth stage of social progress, up to which the useful or mechanical arts have been incidentally developing themselves, when trade and com-merce begin. Through these various phases, *only to live* has been the great object of mankind; but, by-and-by, comforts are multiplied, and accumulating riches create new wants. The object, then, is not only to *live*, but to live economically, agreeably, tastefully, and well. Accordingly, the art of cookery commences; and although the fruits of the earth, the fowls of the air, the beasts of the field, and the fish of the sea, are still the only food of mankind, yet these are so prepared, improved, and dressed by skill and ingenuity, that they are the means of immeasurably extending the boundaries of human enjoyments. Everything that is edible, and passes under the hands of the cook, is more or less changed, and assumes new forms. Hence the influence of that functionary is immense upon the happiness of a household.

In order that the duties of the Cook may be properly performed, and that he may be able to reproduce esteemed dishes with certainty, all terms of indecision should be banished from his art. Accordingly, what is known only to him, will, in these pages, be made known to others. In them all those indecisive terms expressed by a bit of this, some of that, a small piece of that, and a handful of the other, shall never be made use of, but all quantities be precisely and explicitly stated. With a desire, also, that all ignorance on this most essential part of the culinary art should disappear, and that a uniform system of weights and measures should be adopted, we give an account of the weights which answer to certain measures.

A TABLE-SPOONFUL is frequently mentioned in a recipe, in the prescriptions of medical men, and also in medical, chemical, and gastronomical works. By it is generally meant and understood a measure or bulk equal to that which would be produced by *half an ounce* of water.

A DESSERT-SPOONFUL is the half of a table-spoonful; that is to say, by it is meant a measure or bulk equal to a *quarter of an ounce* of water.

A TEA-SPOONFUL is equal in quantity to a *drachm* of water.

A DROP.—This is the name of a vague kind of measure, and is so called on account of the liquid being *dropped* from the mouth of a bottle. Its quantity, however, will vary, either from the consistency of the liquid or the size and shape of the mouth of the bottle. The College of Physicians determined the quantity of a drop to be *one grain*, 60 drops making one fluid drachm. Their drop, or sixtieth part of a fluid drachm, is called a *minim*.

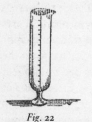

Fig. 22

Graduated glass measures can be obtained at any chemist's, and they save much trouble. One of these, containing a wine pint, is divided into 16 oz., and the oz. into 8 drachms of water; by which any certain weight mentioned in a recipe can be accurately measured out. Home-made measures of this kind can readily be formed by weighing the water contained in any given measure, and marking on any tall glass the space it occupies. This mark can easily be made with a file. It will be interesting to many readers to know the basis on which the French found their system of weights and measures, for it certainly possesses the grandeur of simplicity. The mètre, which is the basis of the whole system of French weights and measures, is the exact measurement of one forty-millionth part of a meridian of the earth.

Excellence in the art of cookery, as in all other things, is only attainable by practice and experience. In proportion, therefore, to the opportunities which a cook has had of these, so will be his excellence in the art. It is in the large establishments of princes, noblemen, and very affluent families alone, that the man cook is found in this country. He, also, superintends the kitchens of large hotels, clubs, and public institutions, where he, usually, makes out the bills of fare, which are generally submitted to the principal for approval. To be able to do this, therefore, it is absolutely necessary that he should be a judge of the season of every dish, as well as know perfectly the state of every article he undertakes to prepare. He must also be a judge of every article he buys; for no skill, however great it may be, will enable him to make that good which is really bad. On him rests the responsibility of the cooking generally, whilst a speciality of his department, is to prepare the rich soups, stews, ragouts, and such dishes as enter into the more refined and complicated portions of his art, and such as are not usually understood by ordinary professors. He, therefore, holds a high position in a household, being inferior in rank, as already shown (*see* p. 16), only to the house steward, the valet, and the butler.

In the luxurious ages of Grecian antiquity, Sicilian cooks were the most esteemed, and received high rewards for their services. Among them, one called Trimalcio was such an adept in his art, that he could impart to common fish both the form and flavour of the most esteemed of the piscatory tribes. A chief cook in the palmy days of Roman voluptuousness had about £800 a year, and Antony rewarded the one that cooked the supper which pleased Cleopatra, with the present of a city. With the fall of the empire, the culinary art sank into less consideration. In the middle ages, cooks laboured to acquire a reputation for their sauces, which they composed of strange combinations, for the sake of novelty, as well as singularity.

The duties of the cook, the kitchen and the scullery maids, are so intimately associated, that they can hardly be treated of separately. The cook, however, is at the head of the kitchen; and in proportion to her possession of the qualities of cleanliness, neatness, order, regularity, and celerity of action, so will her influence appear in the conduct of those who are under her; as it is upon her that the whole responsibility of the business of the kitchen rests, whilst the others must lend her, both a ready and a willing assistance, and be especially tidy in their appearance, and active in their movements.

In the larger establishments of the middle ages, cooks, with the authority of feudal chiefs, gave their orders from a high chair in which they ensconced themselves, and commanded a view of all that was going on throughout their several domains. Each held a long wooden spoon with which he tasted, without leaving his seat, the various comestibles that were cooking on the stoves, and which he frequently used as a rod of punishment on the backs of those whose idleness and gluttony too largely predominated over their diligence and temperance.

If, as we have said, the quality of early rising be of the first importance to the mistress, what must it be to the servant! Let it, therefore, be taken as a long-proved truism, that without it, in every domestic, the effect of all things else, so far as *work* is concerned may, in a great measure, be neutralized. In a cook, this quality is most essential, for an hour lost in the morning, will keep her toiling, absolutely toiling, all day, to overtake that which might otherwise have been achieved with ease. In large establishments, six is a good hour to rise in the summer, and seven in the winter.

Her first duty, in large establishments and where it is requisite, should be to set her dough for the breakfast rolls, provided this has not been done on the previous night, and then to engage herself with those numerous little preliminary occupations which may not inappropriately be termed laying out her duties for the day. This will bring in the breakfast hour of eight, after which, directions must be given, and preparations made, for the different dinners of the household and family.

In those numerous households where a cook and housemaid are only kept, the general custom is, that the cook should have the charge of the dining-room. The hall, the lamps, and the doorstep are also committed to her care, and any other work there may be on the outside of the house. In establishments of this kind, the cook will, after having lighted her kitchen fire, carefully brushed the range, and cleaned the hearth, proceed to prepare for breakfast. She will thoroughly rinse the kettle, and, filling it with fresh water, will put it on the fire to boil. She will then go to the breakfast-room, or parlour, and there make all things ready for the breakfast of the family. Her attention will next be directed to the hall, which she will sweep and wipe, the kitchen stairs, if there be any, will now be swept; and the hall mats, which have been removed and shaken, will be again put in their places.

The cleaning of the kitchen, pantry, passages, and kitchen stairs must always be over before breakfast, so that it may not interfere with the other business of the day. Everything should be ready, and the whole house should wear a comfortable aspect when the heads of the house and members of the family make their appearance. Nothing, it may be depended on, will so please the mistress of an establishment, as to notice that, although she has not been present to see that the work was done, attention to smaller matters has been carefully paid, with a view to giving her satisfaction and increasing her comfort.

By the time that the cook has performed the duties mentioned above, and well swept, brushed, and dusted her kitchen, the breakfast-bell will most likely summon her to the parlour, to 'bring in' the breakfast. It is the cook's department, generally, in the smaller establishments, to wait at breakfast, as the housemaid, by this time, has gone up-stairs into the bedrooms, and has there applied herself to her various duties. The cook usually answers the bells and single knocks at the door in the early part of the morning, as the tradesmen, with whom it is her more special business to speak, call at these hours.

It is in her preparation of the dinner that the cook begins to feel the weight and responsibility of her situation, as she must take upon herself all the dressing and the serving of the principal dishes, which her skill and ingenuity have mostly prepared. Whilst these, however, are cooking, she must be busy with her pastry, soups, gravies, rag-outs, &c. Stock, or what the French call *consommé*, being the basis of most made dishes, must be always at hand, in conjunction with her sweet herbs and spices for seasoning. 'A place for everything, and everything in its place,' must be her rule, in order that time may not be wasted in looking for things when they are wanted, and in order that the whole apparatus of cooking may move with the regularity and precision of a well-adjusted machine;—all must go on simultaneously. The vegetables and sauces must be ready with the dishes they are to accompany, and in order that they may be suitable, the smallest oversight must not be made in their preparation. When the dinner-hour has arrived, it is the duty of the cook to dish-up such dishes as may, without injury, stand, for some time, covered on the hot plate or in the hot closet; but such as are of a more important or *recherché** kind, must be delayed until the order 'to serve' is given from the drawing-room. Then comes haste; but there must be no hurry,— all must work with order. The cook takes charge of the fish, soups, and poultry; and the kitchen-maid of the vegetables, sauces, and gravies. These she puts into their appropriate dishes, whilst the scullery-maid waits on and assists the cook. Everything must be timed so as to prevent its getting cold, whilst great care should be taken, that, between the first and second courses, no more time is allowed to elapse than is necessary, for fear that the company in the dining-room lose all relish for what has yet to come of the dinner. When the dinner has been served, the most important feature in the daily life of the cook is at an end. She must, however, now begin to look to the contents of her larder, taking care to keep everything sweet and clean, so that no disagreeable smells may arise from the gravies, milk, or meat that may be there. These are the principal duties of a cook in a first-rate establishment.

In smaller establishments, the housekeeper often conducts the higher department of cooking (*see* pp. 34–5), and the cook, with the assistance of a scullery-maid, performs some of the subordinate duties of the kitchen-maid.

When circumstances render it necessary, the cook engages to perform the whole of the work of the kitchen, and, in some places, a portion of the house-work also.

Whilst the cook is engaged with her morning duties, the kitchen-maid is also occupied with hers. Her first duty, after the fire is lighted, is to sweep and clean the kitchen, and the various offices belonging to it. This she does every morning, besides cleaning the stone steps at the entrance of the house, the halls, the passages, and the stairs which lead to the kitchen. Her general duties, besides these, are to wash and scour all these places twice a week, with the tables, shelves, and cupboards. She has also to dress the nursery and servants'-hall dinners, to prepare all fish, poultry, and vegetables, trim meat joints and cutlets, and do all such duties as may be considered to enter into the cook's department in a subordinate degree.

The duties of the scullery-maid are to assist the cook; to keep the scullery clean, and all the metallic as well as earthenware kitchen utensils.

The position of scullery-maid is not, of course, one of high rank, nor is the payment for her services large. But if she be fortunate enough to have over her a good kitchen-maid and clever cook, she may very soon learn to perform various little duties connected with cooking operations, which may be of considerable service in fitting her for a more responsible place. Now, it will be doubtless thought by the majority of our readers, that the fascinations connected with the position of the scullery-maid, are not so great as to induce many people to leave a comfortable home in order to work in a scullery. But we are acquainted with one instance in which the desire, on the part of a young girl, was so strong to become connected with the kitchen and cookery, that she absolutely left her parents, and engaged herself as a scullery-maid in a gentleman's house. Here she showed herself so active and intelligent, that she very quickly rose to the rank of kitchen-maid; and from this, so great was her gastronomical genius, she became, in a short space of time, one of the best women-cooks in England. After this, we think, it must be allowed, that a cook, like a poet, *nascitur, non fit.**

Modern cookery stands so greatly indebted to the gastronomic propensities of our French neighbours, that many of their terms are adopted and applied by English artists to the same as well as similar preparations of their own. A vocabulary of these is, therefore, indispensable in a work of this kind. Accordingly, the following will be found sufficiently complete for all ordinary purposes:—

EXPLANATION OF FRENCH TERMS USED IN MODERN HOUSEHOLD COOKERY*

ASPIC.—A savoury jelly, used as an exterior moulding for cold game, poultry, fish, &c. This, being of a transparent nature, allows the bird which it covers to be seen through it. This may also be used for decorating or garnishing.

ASSIETTE (plate).—*Assiettes* are the small *entrées* and *hors-d'œuvres*, the quantity of which does not exceed what a plate will hold. At dessert, fruits, cheese, chestnuts, biscuits, &c., if served upon a plate, are termed *assiettes*.—ASSIETTE VOLANTE is a dish which a servant hands round to the guests, but is not placed upon the table. Small cheese soufflés and different dishes, which ought to be served very hot, are frequently made *assiettes volanetes*.

AU-BLEU.—Fish dressed in such a manner as to have a *bluish* appearance.*

BAIN-MARIE.—An open saucepan or kettle* of nearly boiling water, in which a smaller vessel can be set for cooking and warming. This is very useful for keeping articles hot, without altering their quantity or quality. If you keep sauce, broth, or soup by the fireside, the soup reduces and becomes too strong, and the sauce thickens as well as reduces; but this is prevented by using the *bain-marie*, in which the water should be very hot, but not boiling.

BÉCHAMEL.—French white sauce, now frequently used in English cookery.

BLANCH.—To whiten poultry, vegetables, fruit, &., by plunging them into boiling water for a short time, and afterwards plunging them into cold water, there to remain until they are cold.

BLANQUETTE.—A sort of fricassee.*

BOUILLI.—Beef or other meat boiled; but, generally speaking, boiled beef is understood by the term.

BOUILLIE.—A French dish resembling hasty-pudding.*

BOUILLON.—A thin broth or soup.

BRAISE.—To stew meat with fat bacon until it is tender, it having previously been blanched.

BRAISIÈRE.—A saucepan having a lid with ledges, to put fire on the top.

BRIDER.—To pass a packthread through poultry, game, &c., to keep together their members.

CARAMEL (burnt sugar).—This is made with a piece of sugar, of the size of a nut, browned in the bottom of a saucepan; upon which a cupful of stock is gradually poured, stirring all the time a glass of broth, little by little. It may be used with the feather of a quill, to colour meats, such as the upper part of fricandeaux; and to impart colour to sauces. Caramel made with water instead of stock may be used to colour *compôtes* and other *entremets*.

CASSEROLE.—A crust of rice, which, after having been moulded into the form of a pie, is baked, and then filled with a fricassee of white meat or a purée of game.

COMPOTE.—A stew, as of fruit or pigeons.

CONSOMMÉ.—Rich stock, or gravy.

CROQUETTE.—Ball of fried rice or potatoes.

CROUTONS.—Sippets of bread.

DAUBIÈRE.—An oval stewpan, in which *daubes* are cooked; *daubes* being meat or fowl stewed in sauce.

DÉSOSSER.—To *bone*, or take out the bones from poultry, game, or fish. This is an operation requiring considerable experience.

ENTRÉES.*—Small side or corner dishes, served with the first course.

ENTREMETS.—Small side or corner dishes, served with the second course.

ESCALOPES.—Collops; small, round, thin pieces of tender meat, or of fish, beaten with the handle of a strong knife to make them tender.

FEUILLETAGE.—Puff-paste.

FLAMBER.—To singe fowl or game, after they have been picked.

FONCER.—To put in the bottom of a saucepan slices of ham, veal, or thin broad slices of bacon.

GALETTE.—A broad thin cake.

GÂTEAU.—A cake, correctly speaking; but used sometimes to denote a pudding and a kind of tart.

GLACER.—To glaze, or spread upon hot meats, or larded fowl, a thick and rich sauce or gravy, called *glaze*. This is laid on with a feather or brush, and in confectionary the term means to ice fruits and pastry with sugar, which glistens on hardening.

HORS-D'ŒUVRES.—Small dishes, or *assiettes volantes* of sardines, anchovies, and other relishes of this kind, served to the guests during the first course. (*See* ASSIETTES VOLANTES.)

LIT.—A bed or layer; articles in thin slices are placed in layers, other articles, or seasoning, being laid between them.

MAIGRE.—Broth, soup, or gravy, made without meat.

MATELOTE.—A rich fish-stew, which is generally composed of carp, eels, trout, or barbel. It is made with wine.

MAYONNAISE.—Cold sauce, or salad dressing.

MENU.—The bill of fare.

MERINGUE.—A kind of icing, made of whites of eggs and sugar, well beaten.

MIROTON.—Larger slices of meat than collops; such as slices of beef for a vinaigrette, or ragout or stew of onions.

MOUILLER.—To add water, broth, or other liquid, during the cooking.

PANER.—To cover over with very fine crumbs of bread, meats, or any other articles to be cooked on the gridiron, in the oven, or frying-pan.

PIQUER.—To lard with strips of fat bacon, poultry, game, meat, &c. This should always be done according to the vein of the meat, so that in carving you slice the bacon across as well as the meat.

POÊLÉE.—Stock used instead of water for boiling turkeys, sweet-breads, fowls, and vegetables, to render them less insipid. This is rather an expensive preparation.

PURÉE.—Vegetables, or meat reduced to a very smooth pulp, which is afterwards mixed with enough liquid to make it of the consistency of very thick soup.

RAGOUT.—Stew or hash.

REMOULADE.—Salad dressing.

RISSOLES.—Pastry, made of light puff-paste, and cut into various forms, and fried. They may be filled with fish, meat, or sweets.

ROUX.—Brown and white; French thickening.

SALMI.—Ragout of game previously roasted.

SAUCE PIQUANTE.—A sharp sauce, in which somewhat of a vinegar flavour predominates.

SAUTER.—To dress with sauce in a saucepan, repeatedly moving it about.

TAMIS.—Tammy, a sort of open cloth or sieve through which to strain broth and sauces, so as to rid them of small bones, froth, &c.

TOURTE.—Tart. Fruit pie.

TROUSSER.—To truss a bird; to put together the body and tie the wings and thighs, in order to round it for roasting or boiling, each being tied then with packthread, to keep it in the required form.

VOL-AU-VENT.—A rich crust of very fine puff-paste, which may be filled with various delicate ragouts or fricassees, of fish, flesh, or fowl. Fruit may also be inclosed in a *vol-au-vent*.

SOUPS

CHAPTER V
GENERAL DIRECTIONS FOR MAKING SOUPS

LEAN, JUICY BEEF, MUTTON, AND VEAL, form the basis of all good soups; therefore it is advisable to procure those pieces which afford the richest succulence, and such as are fresh-killed. Stale meat renders them bad, and fat is not so well adapted for making them. The principal art in composing good rich soup, is so to proportion the several ingredients that the flavour of one shall not predominate over another, and that all the articles of which it is composed, shall form an agreeable whole. To accomplish this, care must be taken that the roots and herbs are perfectly well cleaned, and that the water is proportioned to the quantity of meat and other ingredients. Generally a quart of water may be allowed to a pound of meat for soups, and half the quantity for gravies. In making soups or gravies, gentle stewing or simmering is incomparably the best. It may be remarked, however, that a really good soup can never be made but in a well-closed vessel, although, perhaps, greater wholesomeness is obtained by an occasional exposure to the air. Soups will, in general, take from three to six hours doing, and are much better prepared the day before they are wanted. When the soup is cold, the fat may be much more easily and completely removed; and when it is poured off; care must be taken not to disturb the settlings at the bottom of the vessel, which are so fine that they will escape through a sieve. A tamis is the best strainer, and if the soup is strained while it is hot, let the tamis or cloth be previously soaked in cold water. Clear soups must be perfectly transparent, and thickened soups about the consistence of cream. To thicken and give body to soups and gravies, potato-mucilage, arrow-root, bread-raspings,* isinglass,* flour and butter, barley, rice, or oatmeal, in a little water rubbed well together, are used. A piece of boiled beef pounded to a pulp, with a bit of butter and flour, and rubbed through a sieve, and gradually incorporated with the soup, will be found an excellent addition. When the soup appears to be *too thin* or *too weak*, the cover of the boiler should be taken off, and the contents allowed to boil till some of the watery parts have evaporated; or some of the thickening materials, above mentioned, should be added. When soups and gravies are kept from day to day in hot weather, they should be warmed up every day, and put into fresh scalded pans or tureens, and placed in a cool cellar. In temperate weather, every other day may be sufficient.

For the seasoning of soups, bay-leaves, tomato, tarragon, chervil, burnet, allspice, cinnamon, ginger, nutmeg, clove, mace, black and white pepper, essence of anchovy, lemon-peel, and juice, and Seville orange-juice, are all taken. The latter imparts a finer flavour than the lemon, and the acid is much milder. These materials, with wine, mushroom ketchup, Harvey's sauce, tomato sauce, combined in various proportions, are, with other ingredients, manipulated into an almost endless variety of excellent soups and gravies. Soups, which are intended to constitute the principal part of a meal, certainly ought not to be flavoured like sauces, which are only designed to give a relish to some particular dish.

SOUP, BROTH, AND BOUILLON

It has been asserted, that English cookery is, nationally speaking, far from being the best in the world. More than this, we have been frequently told by brilliant foreign writers, half philosophers, half *chefs*, that we are the *worst* cooks on the face of the earth, and that the proverb which alludes to the divine origin of food, and the precisely opposite origin of its preparers is peculiarly applicable to us islanders.* Not, however, to the inhabitants of the whole island; for, it is stated in a work which treats of culinary operations, north of the Tweed, that the 'broth' of Scotland claims, for excellence and whole-someness, a very close second place to the *bouillon*, or common soup of France. '*Three* hot meals of broth and meat, for about the price of ONE roasting joint,' our Scottish brothers and sisters get, they say; and we hasten to assent to what we think is now a very well-ascertained fact. We are glad to note, however, that soups of vege-tables, fish, meat, and game, are now very frequently found in the homes of the English middle classes, as well as in the mansions of the wealthier and more aristocratic; and we take this to be one evidence, that we are on the right road to an improvement in our system of cookery. One great cause of many of the spoilt dishes and badly-cooked meats which are brought to our tables, arises, we think, and most will agree with us, from a non-acquaintance with 'common, every-day things.' Entertaining this view, we intend to preface the chapters of this work with a simple scientific *résumé* of all those causes and circumstances which relate to the food we have to prepare, and the theory and chemistry of the various culinary operations. Accordingly, this is the proper place to treat of the quality of the flesh of animals, and describe some of the circumstances which influence it for good or bad. We will, therefore, commence with the circumstance of *age*, and examine how far this affects the quality of meat.

During the period between the birth and maturity of animals, their flesh undergoes very considerable changes. For instance, when the animal is young, the fluids which the tissues of the muscles contain, possess a large proportion of what is called *albu-men*. This albumen, which is also the chief component of the white of eggs, possesses the peculiarity of coagulating or hardening at a certain temperature, like the white of a boiled egg, into a soft, white fluid, no longer soluble, or capable of being dissolved in water. As animals grow older, this peculiar animal matter gradually decreases, in proportion to the other constituents of the juice of the flesh. Thus, the reason why veal, lamb, and young pork are *white, and without gravy* when cooked, is, that the large quantity of albumen they contain hardens, or becomes coagulated. On the other hand, the reason why beef and mutton are *brown, and have gravy*, is, that the proportion of albumen they contain, is small, in comparison with their greater quantity of fluid which is soluble, and not coagulable.*

The quality of the flesh of an animal is considerably influenced by the nature of the *food on which it has been fed*; for the food supplies the material which produces the flesh. If the food be not suitable and good, the meat cannot be good either; just as the paper on which these words are printed, could not be good, if the rags from which it is made, were not of a fine quality. To the experienced in this matter, it is well known that the flesh of animals fed on farinaceous produce, such as corn, pulse, &c., is firm, well-flavoured, and also economical in the cooking; that the flesh of those fed on succulent and pulpy substances, such as roots, possesses these qualities in a somewhat less degree; whilst the flesh of those whose food contains fixed oil, as linseed, is greasy, high coloured, and gross in the fat, and if the food has been used in large quantities, possessed of a rank flavour.

It is indispensable to the good quality of meat, that the animal should be *perfectly healthy* at the time of its slaughter. However slight the disease in an animal may be, inferiority in the quality of its flesh, as food, is certain to be produced. In most cases, indeed, as the flesh of diseased animals has a tendency to very rapid putrefaction, it becomes not only unwholesome, but absolutely poisonous, on account of the absorption of the *virus* of the unsound meat into the systems of those who partake of it. The external indications of good and bad meat will be described under its own particular head, but we may here premise that the lyer* of all wholesome meat, when freshly killed, adheres firmly to the bone.

Another circumstance greatly affecting the quality of meat, is the animal's treatment *before it is slaughtered*. This influences its value and wholesomeness in no inconsiderable degree. It will be easy to understand this, when we reflect on those leading principles by which the life of an animal is supported and maintained. These are, the digestion of its food, and the assimilation of that food into its substance. Nature, in effecting this process, first reduces the food in the stomach to a state of pulp, under the name of chyme, which passes into the intestines, and is there divided into two principles, each distinct from the other. One, a milk-white fluid,—the nutritive portion,—is absorbed by innumerable vessels which open upon the mucous membrane, or inner coat of the intestines. These vessels, or absorbents, discharge the fluid into a common duct, or road, along which it is conveyed to the large veins in the neighbourhood of the heart. Here it is mixed with the venous blood (which is black and impure) returning from every part of the body, and then it supplies the waste which is occasioned in the circulating stream by the arterial (or pure) blood having furnished matter for the substance of the animal. The blood of the animal having completed its course through all parts, and having had its waste recruited by the digested food, is now received into the heart, and by the action of that organ it is urged through the lungs, there to receive its purification from the air which the animal inhales. Again returning to the heart, it is forced through the arteries, and thence distributed, by innumerable ramifications, called capillaries, bestowing to every part of the animal, life and nutriment. The other principle—the innutritive portion—passes from the intestines, and is thus got rid of. It will now be readily understood how flesh is affected for bad, if an animal is slaughtered when the circulation of its blood has been increased by over-driving, ill-usage, or other causes of excitement, to such a degree of rapidity as to be too great for the capillaries to perform their functions, and causing the blood to be congealed in its minuter vessels. Where this has been the case, the meat will be dark-coloured, and become rapidly putrid; so that self-interest and humanity alike dictate kind and gentle treatment of all animals destined to serve as food for man.*

THE CHEMISTRY AND ECONOMY OF SOUP-MAKING

Stock being the basis of all meat soups, and, also, of all the principal sauces, it is essential to the success of these culinary operations, to know the most complete and economical method of extracting, from a certain quantity of meat, the best possible stock or broth. The theory and philosophy of this process we will, therefore, explain, and then proceed to show the practical course to be adopted.

As all meat is principally composed of fibres, fat, gelatine, osmazome,* and albumen, it is requisite to know that the FIBRES are inseparable, constituting almost all that remains of the meat after it has undergone a long boiling.

FAT is dissolved by boiling; but as it is contained in cells covered by a very fine membrane, which never dissolves, a portion of it always adheres to the fibres. The other portion rises to the surface of the stock, and is that which has escaped from the cells which were not whole, or which have burst by boiling.

GELATINE is soluble: it is the basis and the nutritious portion of the stock. When there is an abundance of it, it causes the stock, when cold, to become a jelly.

OSMAZOME is soluble even when cold, and is that part of the meat which gives flavour and perfume to the stock. The flesh of old animals contains more *osmazome* than that of young ones. Brown meats contain more than white, and the former make the stock more fragrant. By roasting meat, the osmazome appears to acquire higher properties; so, by putting the remains of roast meats into your stock-pot, you obtain a better flavour.

ALBUMEN is of the nature of the white of eggs; it can be dissolved in cold or tepid water, but coagulates when it is put into water not quite at the boiling-point. From this property in albumen, it is evident that if the meat is put into the stock-pot when the water boils, or after this is made to boil up quickly, the albumen, in both cases, hardens. In the first it rises to the surface, in the second it remains in the meat, but in both it prevents the gelatine and osmazome from dissolving; and hence a thin and tasteless stock will be obtained. It ought to be known, too, that the coagulation of the albumen in the meat, always takes place, more or less, according to the size of the piece, as the parts farthest from the surface always acquire *that degree* of heat which congeals it before entirely dissolving it.

BONES ought always to form a component part of the stock-pot. They are composed of an earthy substance,—to which they owe their solidity,—of gelatine, and a fatty fluid, something like marrow. *Two ounces* of them contain as much gelatine as *one pound* of meat; but in them, this is so incased in the earthy substance, that boiling water can dissolve only the surface of whole bones. By breaking them, however, you can dissolve more, because you multiply their surfaces; and by reducing them to powder or paste, you can dissolve them entirely; but you must not grind them dry. We have said that gelatine forms the basis of stock; but this, though very nourishing, is entirely without taste; and to make the stock savoury, it must contain *osmazone*. Of this, bones do not contain a particle; and that is the reason why stock made entirely of them, is not liked; but when you add meat to the broken or pulverized bones, the osmazome contained in it makes the stock sufficiently savoury.

In concluding this part of our subject, the following condensed hints and directions should be attended to in the economy of soup-making:—

I. BEEF makes the best stock; veal stock has less colour and taste; whilst mutton sometimes gives it a tallowy smell, far from agreeable, unless the meat has been previously roasted or broiled. Fowls add very little to the flavour of stock, unless they be old and fat. Pigeons, when they are old, add the most flavour to it; and a rabbit or partridge is also a great improvement. From the freshest meat the best stock is obtained.

II. If the meat be boiled solely to make stock, it must be cut up into the smallest possible pieces; but, generally speaking, if it is desired to have good stock and a piece of savoury meat as well, it is necessary to put a rather large piece into the stock-pot, say sufficient for two or three days, during which time the stock will keep well in all weathers. Choose the freshest meat, and have it cut as thick as possible; for if it is a thin, flat piece, it will not look well, and will be very soon spoiled by the boiling.

III. Never wash meat, as it deprives its surface of all its juices; separate it from the bones, and tie it round with tape, so that its shape may be preserved, then put it into the stock-pot, and for each pound of meat, let there be one pint of water; press it down with the hand, to allow the air, which it contains, to escape, and which often raises it to the top of the water.

IV. Put the stock-pot on a gentle fire, so that it may heat gradually. The albumen will first dissolve, afterwards coagulate; and as it is in this state lighter than the liquid, it will rise to the surface; bringing with it all its impurities. It is this which makes *the scum*.

The rising of the hardened albumen has the same effect in clarifying stock as the white of eggs; and, as a rule, it may be said that the more scum there is, the clearer will be the stock. Always take care that the fire is very regular.

V. Remove the scum when it rises thickly, and do not let the stock boil, because then one portion of the scum will be dissolved, and the other go to the bottom of the pot; thus rendering it very difficult to obtain a clear broth. If the fire is regular, it will not be necessary to add cold water in order to make the scum rise; but if the fire is too large at first, it will then be necessary to do so.

When the stock is well skimmed, and begins to boil, put in salt and vegetables, which may be two or three carrots, two turnips, one parsnip, a bunch of leeks and celery tied together. You can add, according to taste, a piece of cabbage, two or three cloves stuck in an onion, and a tomato. The latter gives a very agreeable flavour to the stock. If fried onion be added, it ought, according to the advice of a famous French *chef*, to be tied in a little bag: without this precaution, the colour of the stock is liable to be clouded.

VII. By this time we will now suppose that you have chopped the bones which were separated from the meat, and those which were left from the roast meat of the day before. Remember, as was before pointed out, that the more these are broken, the more gelatine you will have. The best way to break them up is to pound them roughly in an iron mortar, adding, from time to time, a little water, to prevent them getting heated. It is a great saving thus to make use of the bones of meat, which, in too many English families, we fear, are entirely wasted; for it is certain, as previously stated, that two ounces of bone contain as much gelatine (which is the nutritive portion of stock) as one pound of meat. In their broken state tie them up in a bag, and put them in the stock-pot; adding the gristly parts of cold meat and trimmings, which can be used for no other purpose. If, to make up the weight, you have received from the butcher a piece of mutton or veal, broil it slightly over a clear fire before putting it in the stock-pot, and be very careful that it does not contract the least taste of being smoked or burnt.

VIII. Add now the vegetables, which, to a certain extent, will stop the boiling of the stock. Wait, therefore, till it simmers well up again, then draw it to the side of the fire, and keep it gently simmering till it is served, preserving, as before said, your fire always the same. Cover the stock-pot well, to prevent evaporation; do not fill it up, even if you take out a little stock, unless the meat is exposed; in which case a little boiling water may be added, but only enough to cover it. After six hours' slow and gentle simmering, the stock is done; and it should not be continued on the fire, longer than is necessary, or it will tend to insipidity.

Note.—It is on a good stock, or first good broth and sauce, that excellence in cookery depends. If the preparation of this basis of the culinary art is intrusted to negligent or ignorant persons, and the stock is not well skimmed, but indifferent results will be obtained. The stock will never be clear; and when it is obliged to be clarified, it is deteriorated both in quality and flavour. In the proper management of the stock-pot an immense deal of trouble is saved, inasmuch as one stock, in a small dinner, serves for all purposes. Above all things, the greatest economy, consistent with excellence, should be practised, and the price of everything which enters the kitchen correctly ascertained.* The *theory* of this part of Household Management may appear trifling; but its practice is extensive, and therefore it requires the best attention.

CHAPTER VI

RECIPES*

FRUIT AND VEGETABLE SOUPS

It will be seen, by reference to the following Recipes, that an entirely original and most intelligible system has been pursued in explaining the preparation of each dish. We would recommend the young housekeeper, cook, or whoever may be engaged in the important task of 'getting ready' the dinner, or other meal, to follow precisely the order in which the recipes are given. Thus, let them first place on their table all the INGREDIENTS *necessary; then the* modus operandi, *or* MODE *of preparation, will be easily managed. By a careful reading, too, of the recipes, there will not be the slightest difficulty in arranging a repast for any number of persons, and an accurate notion will be gained of the* TIME *the cooking of each dish will occupy, of the periods at which it is* SEASONABLE, *as also of its* AVERAGE COST.

The addition of the natural history, and the description of the various properties of the edible articles in common use in every family, will be serviceable both in a practical and an educational point of view.

Speaking specially of the Recipes for Soups, it may be added, that by the employment of the BEST, MEDIUM, *or* COMMON STOCK, *the quality of the Soups and their cost may be proportionately increased or lessened.**

STOCKS FOR ALL KINDS OF SOUPS

Rich Strong Stock

INGREDIENTS.—4 lbs. of shin of beef, 4 lbs. of knuckle of veal, ¾ lb. of good lean ham; any poultry trimmings; 3 small onions, 3 small carrots, 3 turnips (the latter should be omitted in summer, lest they ferment), 1 head of celery, a few chopped mushrooms, when obtainable; 1 tomato, a bunch of savoury herbs, not forgetting parsley; 1½ oz. of salt, 12 white peppercorns, 6 cloves, 3 small blades of mace, 4 quarts of water.

Mode.—Line a delicately clean stewpan with the ham cut in thin broad slices, carefully trimming off all its rusty fat; cut up the beef and veal in pieces about 3 inches square, and lay them on the ham; set it on the stove, and draw it down, and stir frequently. When the meat is equally browned, put in the beef and veal bones, the poultry trimmings, and pour in the cold water. Skim well, and occasionally add a little cold water, to stop its boiling, until it becomes quite clear; then put in all the other ingredients, and simmer very slowly for 5 hours. Do not let it come to a brisk boil, that the stock be not wasted, and that its colour may be preserved. Strain through a very fine hair sieve, or tammy, and it will be fit for use.

Time.—5 hours. *Average cost*, 1s. 3d. per quart.

Medium Stock

INGREDIENTS.—4 lbs. of shin of beef, or 4 lbs. of knuckle of veal, or 2 lbs. of each; any bones, trimmings of poultry, or fresh meat, ½ a lb. of lean bacon or ham, 2 oz. of butter, 2 large onions, each stuck with 3 cloves; 1 turnip, 3 carrots, ½ a leek, 1 head of celery, 2 oz. of salt, ½ a teaspoonful of whole pepper, 1 large blade of mace, 1 small bunch of savoury herbs, 4 quarts and ½ pint of cold water.

Mode.—Cut up the meat and bacon or ham into pieces about 3 inches square; rub the butter on the bottom of the stewpan; put in ½ a pint of water, the meat, and all the other ingredients. Cover the stewpan, and place it on a sharp fire, occasionally stirring its contents. When the bottom of the pan becomes covered with a pale, jelly-like substance, add 4 quarts of cold water, and simmer very gently for 5 hours. As we have said before, do not let it boil quickly. Skim off every particle of grease whilst it is doing, and strain it through a fine hair sieve.

This is the basis of many of the soups afterwards mentioned, and will be found quite strong enough for ordinary purposes.

Time.—5½ hours. *Average cost*, 9d. per quart.

Economical Stock

INGREDIENTS.—The liquor in which a joint of meat has been boiled, say 4 quarts; trimmings of fresh meat or poultry, shank-bones, &c., roast-beef bones, any pieces the larder may furnish; vegetables, spices, and the same seasoning as in the foregoing recipe.

Mode.—Let all the ingredients simmer gently for 6 hours, taking care to skim carefully at first. Strain it off, and put by for use.

Time.—6 hours.   *Average cost*, 3*d.* per quart.

Apple Soup*

INGREDIENTS.—2 lbs. of good boiling apples, ¾ teaspoonful of white pepper, 6 cloves, cayenne or ginger to taste, 3 quarts of medium stock.

Mode.—Peel and quarter the apples, taking out their cores; put them into the stock, stew them gently till tender. Rub the whole through a strainer, add the seasoning, give it one boil up, and serve.

Time.—1 hour.   *Average cost* per quart, 1*s.*

Seasonable from September to December.

Sufficient for 10 persons.

THE APPLE.—This useful fruit is mentioned in Holy Writ; and Homer describes it as valuable in his time. It was brought from the East by the Romans, who held it in the highest estimation. Indeed, some of the citizens of the 'Eternal city' distinguished certain favourite apples by their names. Thus the Manlians were called after Manlius, the Claudians after Claudius, and the Appians after Appius. Others were designated after the country whence they were brought; as the Sidonians, the Epirotes, and the Greeks. The best varieties are natives of Asia, and have, by grafting them upon others, been introduced into Europe. The crab, found in our hedges, is the only variety indigenous to Britain; therefore, for the introduction of other kinds we are, no doubt, indebted to the Romans. In the time of the Saxon heptarchy, both Devon and Somerset were distinguished as *the apple country*; and there are still existing in Herefordshire some trees said to have been planted in the time of William the Conqueror. From that time to this, the varieties of this precious fruit have

Apple and Blossom

gone on increasing, and are now said to number upwards of 1,500. It is peculiar to the temperate zone, being found neither in Lapland, nor within the tropics. The best baking apples for early use are the Colvilles; the best for autumn are the rennets and pearmains; and the best for winter and spring are russets. The best table, or eating apples, are the Margarets for early use; the Kentish codlin and summer pearmain for summer; and for autumn, winter, or spring, the Dowton, golden, and other pippins, as the ribstone, with small russets. As a food, the apple cannot be considered to rank high, as more than the half of it consists of water, and the rest of its properties are not the most nourishing. It is, however, a useful adjunct to other kinds of food, and, when cooked, is esteemed as slightly laxative.

Artichoke (Jerusalem) Soup*
(*A White Soup*)

INGREDIENTS.—3 slices of lean bacon or ham, ½ a head of celery, 1 turnip, 1 onion, 3 oz. of butter, 4 lbs. of artichokes, 1 pint of boiling milk, or ½ pint of boiling cream, salt and cayenne to taste, 2 lumps of sugar, 2½ quarts of white stock.

Mode.—Put the bacon and vegetables, which should be cut into thin slices, into the stewpan with the butter. Braise these for ¼ of an hour, keeping them well stirred. Wash and pare the artichokes, and after cutting them into thin slices, add them, with a pint of stock, to the other ingredients. When these have gently stewed down to a smooth pulp, put in the remainder of the stock. Stir it well, adding the seasoning, and when it has simmered for five minutes, pass it through a strainer. Now pour it back into the stewpan, let it again simmer five minutes, taking care to skim it well, and stir it to the boiling milk or cream. Serve with small sippets of bread fried in butter.

Time.—1 hour.   *Average cost* per quart, 1s. 2d.

Seasonable from June to October.

Sufficient for 8 persons.

Bread Soup*
(*Economical*)

INGREDIENTS.—1 lb. of bread crusts, 2 oz. butter, 1 quart of common stock.

Mode.—Boil the bread crusts in the stock with the butter; beat the whole with a spoon, and keep it boiling till the bread and stock are well mixed. Season with a little salt.

Time.—Half an hour.   *Average cost* per quart, 4d.

Seasonable at any time.

Sufficient for 4 persons.

Note.—This is a cheap recipe, and will be found useful where extreme economy is an object.

Cabbage Soup

INGREDIENTS.—1 large cabbage, 3 carrots, 2 onions, 4 or 5 slices of lean bacon, salt and pepper to taste, 2 quarts of medium stock.

Mode.—Scald the cabbage, cut it up and drain it. Line the stewpan with the bacon, put in the cabbage, carrots, and onions; moisten with skimmings from the stock, and simmer very gently, till the cabbage is tender; add the stock, stew softly for half an hour, and carefully skim off every particle of fat. Season and serve.

Time.—1½ hour.   *Average cost*, 1s. per quart.

Seasonable in winter.

Sufficient for 8 persons.

THE CABBAGE.—It is remarkable, that although there is no country in the world now more plentifully supplied with fruits and vegetables than Great Britain, yet the greater number of these had no existence in it before the time of Henry VIII. Anderson, writing under the date of 1548, says, 'The English cultivated scarcely any vegetables before the last two centuries. At the commencement of the reign of Henry VIII, neither salad, nor carrots, nor cabbages, nor radishes, nor any other comestibles of a like nature, were grown in any part of the kingdom; they came from Holland and Flanders.' The original of all the cabbage tribe is the wild plant *sea-colewort*, which is to be found *wasting* whatever sweetness it may have on the desert air, on many of the cliffs of the south coast of England. In this state, it scarcely weighs more than half an ounce, yet, in a cultivated state, to what dimensions can it be made to grow! However greatly the whole of the tribe is esteemed among the moderns, by the ancients they were held in yet higher estimation. The Egyptians adored and raised altars to them, and the Greeks and Romans ascribed many of the most exalted virtues to them. Cato affirmed, that the cabbage cured all diseases, and declared, that it was to its use that the Romans were enabled to live in health and without the assistance of physicians for 600 years. It was introduced by that people into Germany, Gaul, and, no doubt, Britain; although, in this last, it may have been suffered to pass into desuetude for some centuries. The whole tribe is in general wholesome and nutritive, and forms a valuable adjunct to animal food.

Soup à la Cantatrice*

(*An Excellent Soup, very Beneficial for the Voice*)

INGREDIENTS.—3 oz. of sago, ½ pint of cream, the yolks of 3 eggs, 1 lump of sugar, and seasoning to taste, 1 bay-leaf (if liked), 2 quarts of medium stock.

Mode.—Having washed the sago in boiling water, let it be gradually added to the nearly boiling stock. Simmer for ½ an hour, when it should be well dissolved. Beat up the yolks of the eggs, add to them the boiling cream; stir these quickly in the soup, and serve immediately. Do not let the soup boil, or the eggs will curdle.

Time.—40 minutes.   *Average cost*, 1s. 6d. per quart.

Seasonable all the year.

Sufficient for 8 persons.

Note.—This is a soup, the principal ingredients of which, sago and eggs, have always been deemed very beneficial to the chest and throat. In various quantities, and in different preparations, these have been partaken of by the principal singers of the day, including the celebrated Swedish Nightingale, Jenny Lind, and, as they have always avowed, with considerable advantage to the voice, in singing.

Celery Soup

INGREDIENTS.—9 heads of celery, 1 teaspoonful of salt, nutmeg to taste, 1 lump of sugar, ½ pint of strong stock, a pint of cream, and 2 quarts of boiling water.

Mode.—Cut the celery into small pieces; throw it into the water, seasoned with the nutmeg, salt, and sugar. Boil it till sufficiently tender; pass it through a sieve, add the stock, and simmer it for half an hour. Now put in the cream, bring it to the boiling point, and serve immediately.

Time.—1 hour.   *Average cost*, 1s. per quart.

Seasonable from September to March.

Sufficient for 10 persons.

Note.—This soup can be made brown, instead of white, by omitting the cream, and colouring it a little.* When celery cannot be procured, half a drachm* of the seed, finely pounded, will give a flavour to the soup, if put in a quarter of an hour before it is done. A little of the essence of celery will answer the same purpose.

CELERY.—This plant is indigenous to Britain, and, in its wild state, grows by the side of ditches and along some parts of the seacoast. In this state it is called *smallage*, and, to some extent, is a dangerous narcotic. By cultivation, however, it has been brought to the fine flavour which the garden plant possesses. In the vicinity of Manchester it is raised to an enormous size. When our natural observation is assisted by the accurate results ascertained by the light of science, how infinitely does it enhance our delight in contemplating the products of nature! To know, for example, that the endless variety of colour which we see in plants is developed only by the rays of the sun, is to know a truism sublime by its very comprehensiveness. The cause of the whiteness of celery is nothing more than the want of light in its vegetation, and in order that this effect may be produced, the plant is almost wholly covered with earth; the tops of the leaves alone being suffered to appear above the ground.*

Chestnut (Spanish) Soup*

INGREDIENTS.—¾ lb. of Spanish chestnuts, ¼ pint of cream; seasoning to taste of salt, cayenne, and mace; 1 quart of [medium] stock.

Mode.—Take the outer rind from the chestnuts, and put them into a large pan of warm water. As soon as this becomes too hot for the fingers to remain in it, take out the chestnuts, peel them quickly, and immerse them in cold water, and wipe and weigh them. Now cover them with good stock, and stew them gently for rather more than ¾ of an hour, or until they break when touched with a fork; then drain, pound, and rub them through a fine sieve reversed; add sufficient stock, mace, cayenne, and salt, and stir it often until it boils, and put in the cream. The stock in which the chestnuts are boiled can be used for the soup, when its sweetness is not objected to, or it may, in part, be added to it; and the rule is, that ¾ lb. of chestnuts should be given to each quart of soup.

Time.—Rather more than 1 hour.   *Average cost* per quart, 1*s*. 6*d*.

Seasonable from October to February.

Sufficient for 4 persons.

THE CHESTNUT.—This fruit is said, by some, to have originally come from Sardis, in Lydia; and by others, from Castanea, a city of Thessaly, from which it takes its name. By the ancients it was much used as a food, and is still common in France and Italy, to which countries it is, by some, considered indigenous. In the southern part of the European continent, it is eaten both raw and roasted. The tree was introduced into Britain by the Romans; but it only flourishes in the warmer parts of the island, the fruit rarely arriving at maturity in Scotland. It attains a great age, as well as an

immense size. As a food, it is the least oily and most farinaceous of all the nuts, and, therefore, the easiest of digestion. The tree called the *horse chestnut* is very different, although its fruit very much resembles that of the other. Its 'nuts,' though eaten by horses and some other animals, are unsuitable for human food.

Chestnut

Soup à la Flamande (Flemish)*

INGREDIENTS.—1 turnip, 1 small carrot, ½ head of celery, 6 green onions shred very fine, 1 lettuce cut small, chervil, ¼ pint of asparagus cut small, ¼ pint of peas, 2 oz. butter, the yolks of 4 eggs, ½ pint of cream, salt to taste, 1 lump of sugar, 2 quarts of [medium] stock.

Mode.—Put the vegetables in the butter to stew gently for an hour with a teacupful of stock; then add the remainder of the stock, and simmer for another hour. Now beat the yolks of the eggs well, mix with the cream (previously boiled), and strain through a hair sieve. Take the soup off the fire, put the eggs, &c. to it, and keep stirring it well. Bring it to a boil, but do not leave off stirring, or the eggs will curdle. Season with salt, and add the sugar.

Time.—2½ hours.   *Average cost,* 1s. 9d. per quart.

Seasonable from May to August.

Sufficient for 8 persons.

CHERVIL.—Although the roots of this plant are poisonous, its leaves are tender, and are used in salads. In antiquity it made a relishing dish, when prepared with oil, wine, and gravy. It is a native of various parts of Europe; and the species cultivated in the gardens of Paris, has beautifully frizzled leaves.

Kale Brose (a Scotch Recipe)*

INGREDIENTS.—Half an ox-head or cow-heel, a teacupful of toasted oatmeal, salt to taste, 2 handfuls of greens, 3 quarts of water.

Mode.—Make a broth of the ox-head or cow-heel, and boil it till oil floats on the top of the liquor, then boil the greens, shred, in it. Put the oatmeal, with a little salt, into a basin, and mix with it quickly a teacupful of the fat broth: it should not run into one doughy mass, but form knots. Stir it into the whole, give one boil, and serve very hot.

Time.—4 hours.   *Average cost*, 8*d*. per quart.

Seasonable all the year, but more suitable in winter.

Sufficient for 10 persons.

Leek Soup, Commonly Called Cock-A-Leekie

INGREDIENTS.—A capon or large fowl (sometimes an old cock, from which the recipe takes its name, is used), which should be trussed as for boiling; 2 or 3 bunches of fine leeks, 5 quarts of [medium] stock, pepper and salt to taste.

Mode.—Well wash the leeks (and, if old, scald them in boiling water for a few minutes), taking off the roots and part of the heads, and cut them into lengths of about an inch. Put the fowl into the stock, with, at first, one half of the leeks, and allow it to simmer gently. In half an hour add the remaining leeks, and then it may simmer for 3 or 4 hours longer. It should be carefully skimmed, and can be seasoned to taste. In serving, take out the fowl, and carve it neatly, placing the pieces in a tureen, and pouring over them the soup, which should be very thick of leeks (a *purée* of leeks the French would call it).

Time.—4 hours.   Average cost, 1*s*. 6*d*. per quart; or, with [economical] stock, 1*s*.

Seasonable in winter.

Sufficient for 10 persons.

Note.—Without the fowl, the above, which would then be merely called leek soup, is very good, and also economical. Cock-a-leekie was largely consumed at the Burns Centenary Festival at the Crystal Palace, Sydenham, in 1859.

THE LEEK.—As in the case of the cucumber, this vegetable was bewailed by the Israelites in their journey through the desert.* It is one of the alliaceous tribe, which consists of the onion, garlic, chive, shalot, and leek. These, as articles of food, are perhaps more widely diffused over the face of the earth than any other *genus* of edible plants. It is the national badge of the Welsh, and tradition ascribes its introduction to that part of

Soups

Britain, to St David. The origin of the wearing of the leek on St David's day, among that people, is thus given in 'BEETON'S DICTIONARY OF UNIVERSAL INFORMATION:'*—'It probably originated from the custom of *Cymhortha*, or the friendly aid, practised among farmers. In some districts of South Wales, all the neighbours of a small farmer were wont to appoint a day when they attended to plough his land, and the like; and, at such time, it was the custom for each to bring his portion of leeks with him for making the broth or soup.' (*See* ST DAVID.) Others derive the origin of the custom from the battle of Cressy. The plant, when grown in Wales and Scotland, is sharper than it is in England, and its flavour is preferred by many to that of the onion in broth. It is very wholesome, and, to prevent its tainting the breath, should be well boiled.

Leeks

Pan Kail

INGREDIENTS.—2 lbs. of cabbage, or Savoy greens; ¼ lb. of butter or dripping, salt and pepper to taste, oatmeal for thickening, 2 quarts of water.

Mode.—Chop the cabbage very fine, thicken the water with oatmeal, put in the cabbage and butter, or dripping; season and simmer for 1½ hour. It can be made sooner by blanching and mashing the greens, adding any good liquor that a joint has been boiled in, and then further thicken with bread or pounded biscuit.

Time.—1½ hour.   *Average cost,* 1½ *d.* per quart.

Seasonable all the year, but more suitable in winter.

Sufficient for 8 persons.

THE SAVOY.—This is a close-hearted wrinkle-leaved cabbage, sweet and tender, especially the middle leaves, and in season from November to spring. The yellow species bears hard weather without injury, whilst the *dwarf* kind are improved and rendered more tender by frost.

Prince of Wales's Soup

INGREDIENTS.—12 turnips, 1 lump of sugar, 2 spoonfuls of strong veal stock, salt and white pepper to taste, 2 quarts of very bright [medium] stock.

Mode.—Peel the turnips, and with a cutter cut them in balls as round as possible, but very small. Put them in the stock, which must be very bright, and simmer till tender. Add the veal stock and seasoning. Have little pieces of bread cut round, about the size of a shilling; moisten them with stock; put them into a tureen and pour the soup over without shaking, for fear of crumbling the bread, which would spoil the appearance of the soup, and make it look thick.

Time.—2 hours.

Seasonable in the winter.

Sufficient for 8 persons.

THE PRINCE OF WALES.*—This soup was invented by a philanthropic friend of the Editress, to be distributed among the poor of a considerable village, when the Prince of Wales attained his majority, on the 9th November, 1859. Accompanying this fact, the following notice, which appears in 'BEETON'S DICTIONARY OF UNIVERSAL INFORMATION,' may appropriately be introduced, premising that British princes attain their majority in their 18th year, whilst mortals of ordinary rank do not arrive at that period till their 21st.—'ALBERT EDWARD, Prince of Wales, and heir to the British throne, merits a place in this work on account of the high responsibilities which he is, in all probability, destined to fulfil as sovereign of the British empire. On the 10th of November, 1858, he was gazetted as having been invested with the rank of a colonel in the army. Speaking of this circumstance, the *Times* said,—"The significance of this event is, that it marks the period when the heir to the British throne is about to take rank among men, and to enter formally upon a career, which every loyal subject of the queen will pray may be a long and a happy one, for his own sake and for the sake of the vast empire which, in the course of nature, he will one day be called to govern. The best wish that we can offer for the young prince is, that in his own path he may ever keep before him the bright example of his royal mother, and show himself worthy of her name." There are few in these realms who will not give a fervent response to these sentiments. B. November 9th, 1841.'

Soup à la Solferino* (Sardinian Recipe)

INGREDIENTS.—4 eggs, ½ pint of cream, 2 oz. of fresh butter, salt and pepper to taste, a little flour to thicken, 2 quarts of bouillon [medium stock].

Mode.—Beat the eggs, put them into a stewpan, and add the cream, butter, and seasoning; stir in as much flour as will bring it to the consistency of dough; make it into balls, either round or egg-shaped, and fry them in butter; put them in the tureen, and pour the boiling bouillon over them.

Time.—1 hour.   *Average cost*, 1s. 3d. per quart.

Seasonable all the year.

Sufficient for 8 persons.

Note.—This recipe was communicated to the Editress by an English gentleman, who was present at the battle of Solferino, on June 24, 1859, and who was requested by some of Victor Emmanuel's troops, on the day before the battle, to partake of a portion of their *potage*. He willingly enough consented, and found that these clever campaigners had made a most palatable dish from very easily-procured materials. In sending the recipe for insertion in this work, he has, however, Anglicized, and somewhat, he thinks, improved it.

Useful Soup for Benevolent Purposes*

INGREDIENTS.—An ox-cheek, any pieces of trimmings of beef, which may be bought very cheaply (say 4 lbs.), a few bones, any pot-liquor the larder may furnish, ¼ peck of onions, 6 leeks, a large bunch of herbs, ½ lb. of celery (the outside pieces, or green tops, do very well); ½ lb. of carrots, ½ lb. of turnips, ½ lb. of coarse brown sugar, ½ a pint of beer, 4 lbs. of common rice, or pearl barley; ½ lb. of salt, 1 oz. of black pepper, a few raspings, 10 gallons of water.

Mode.—Cut up the meat in small pieces, break the bones, put them in a copper, with the 10 gallons of water, and stew for ½ an hour. Cut up the vegetables, put them in with the sugar and beer, and boil for 4 hours. Two hours before the soup is wanted, add the rice and raspings, and keep stirring till it is well mixed in the soup, which simmer gently. If the liquor reduces too much, fill up with water.

Time.—6½ hours.   *Average cost*, 1½d. per quart.

Note.—The above recipe was used in the winter of 1858 by the Editress, who made, each week, in her copper, 8 or 9 gallons of this soup, for distribution amongst about a dozen families of the village near which she lives. The cost, as will be seen, was not great; but she has reason to believe that it was very much liked, and gave to the members of those families, a dish of warm, comforting food, in place of the cold meat and piece of bread which form, with too many cottagers, their usual meal, when, with a little more knowledge of the 'cooking' art, they might have, for less expense, a warm dish every day.

MEAT, POULTRY, AND GAME SOUPS

Mock Turtle*

INGREDIENTS.—½ a calf's head, ¼ lb. of butter, ¼ lb. of lean ham, 2 tablespoonfuls of minced parsley, a little minced lemon thyme, sweet marjoram, basil, 2 onions, a few chopped mushrooms (when obtainable), 2 shalots, 2 tablespoonfuls of flour, ¼ bottle of Madeira or sherry, force-meat balls, cayenne, salt and mace to taste, the juice of 1 lemon and 1 Seville orange, 1 dessert-spoonful of pounded sugar, 3 quarts of best stock (p. 77).

Mode.—Scald the head with the skin on, remove the brain, tie the head up in a cloth, and let it boil for 1 hour. Then take the meat from the bones, cut it into small square pieces, and throw them into cold water. Now take the meat, put it into a stewpan, and cover with stock; let it boil gently for an hour, or rather more, if not quite tender, and set it on one side. Melt the butter in another stewpan, and add the ham, cut small, with the herbs, parsley, onions, shalots, mushrooms, and nearly a pint of stock; let these simmer slowly for 2 hours, and then dredge in as much flour as will dry up the butter. Fill up with the remainder of the stock, add the wine, let it stew gently for 10 minutes, rub it through a tammy, and put it to the calf's head; season with cayenne, and, if required, a little salt; add the juice of the orange and lemon; and when liked, ¼ teaspoonful of pounded mace, and the sugar. Put in the force-meat balls, simmer 5 minutes, and serve very hot.

Time.—4½ hours. *Average cost,* 3s. 6d. per quart, or 2s. 6d. without wine or force-meat balls.

Seasonable in winter.

Sufficient for 10 persons.

Note.—The bones of the head should be well stewed in the liquor it was first boiled in, and will make good white stock, flavoured with vegetables, &c.

Mullagatawny Soup*

INGREDIENTS.—2 tablespoonfuls of curry powder, 6 onions, 1 clove of garlic, 1 oz. of pounded almonds, a little lemon-pickle, or mango-juice, to taste; 1 fowl or rabbit, 4 slices of lean bacon; 2 quarts of medium stock, or, if wanted very good, best stock.

Mode.—Slice and fry the onions of a nice colour; line the stewpan with the bacon; cut up the rabbit or fowl into small joints, and slightly brown them; put in the fried onions, the garlic, and stock, and simmer gently till the meat is tender; skim very carefully, and when the meat is done, rub the curry powder to a smooth batter; add it to the soup with the almonds, which must be first pounded with a little of the stock. Put in seasoning and lemon-pickle or mango-juice to taste, and serve boiled rice with it.

Time.—2 hours.   *Average cost,* 1s. 6d. per quart, with [medium] stock.

Seasonable in winter.

Sufficient for 8 persons.

Note.—This soup can also be made with breast of veal, or calf's head. Vegetable Mullagatawny is made with veal stock, by boiling and pulping chopped vegetable marrow, cucumbers, onions, and tomatoes, and seasoning with curry powder and cayenne. Nice pieces of meat, good curry powder, and strong stock, are necessary to make this soup good.

Turtle Soup* (founded on M. Ude's Recipe)

INGREDIENTS.—A turtle, 6 slices of ham, 2 knuckles of veal, 1 large bunch of sweet herbs, 3 bay-leaves, parsley, green onions, 1 onion, 6 cloves, 4 blades of mace, ¼ lb. of fresh butter, 1 bottle of Madeira, 1 lump of sugar. For the *Quenelles à Tortue*, 1 lb. of veal, 1 lb. of bread crumbs, milk, 7 eggs, cayenne, salt, spices, chopped parsley, the juice of 2 lemons.

Mode.—To make this soup with less difficulty, cut off the head of the turtle the preceding day. In the morning open the turtle by leaning heavily with a knife on the shell of the animal's back, whilst you cut this off all round. Turn it upright on its end, that all the water, &c. may run out, when the flesh should be cut off along the spine, with the knife sloping towards the bones, for fear of touching the gall, which sometimes might escape the eye. When all the flesh about the members is obtained, wash these clean, and let them drain. Have ready, on the fire, a large vessel full of boiling water, into which put the shells; and when you perceive that they come easily off, take them out of the water, and prick them all, with those of the back, belly, fins, head, &c. Boil the back and belly till the bones can be taken off, without, however, allowing the softer parts to be sufficiently done, as they will be boiled again in the soup. When these latter come off easily, lay them on earthen dishes singly, for fear they should stick together, and put them to cool. Keep the liquor in which you have blanched the softer parts, and let the bones stew thoroughly in it, as this liquor must be used to moisten all the sauces.

All the flesh of the interior parts, the four legs and head, must be drawn down in the following manner:—Lay the slices of ham on the bottom of a very large stewpan, over them the knuckles of veal, according to the size of the turtle; then the inside flesh of the turtle, and over the whole the members. Now moisten with the water in which you are boiling the shell, and draw it down thoroughly. It may now be ascertained if it be thoroughly done by thrusting a knife into the fleshy part of the meat. If no blood appears, it is time to moisten it again with the liquor in which the bones, &c. have been boiling. Put in a large bunch of all such sweet herbs as are used in the cooking of a turtle,—sweet basil, sweet marjoram, lemon thyme, winter savory, 2 or 3 bay-leaves, common thyme, a handful of parsley and green onions, and a large onion stuck with 6 cloves. Let the whole be thoroughly done. With respect to the members, probe them, to see whether they are done, and if so, drain and send them to the larder, as they are to make their appearance only when the soup is absolutely completed. When the flesh is also completely done, strain it through a silk sieve, and make a very thin white *roux*; for turtle soup must not be much thickened. When the flour is sufficiently done on a slow fire, and has a good colour, moisten it with the liquor, keeping it over the fire till it boils. Ascertain that the sauce is neither too thick nor too thin; then draw the stewpan on the side of the stove, to skim off the white scum, and all the fat and oil that rise to the surface of the sauce. By this time all the softer parts will be sufficiently cold; when they must be cut to about the size of one or two inches square, and thrown into the soup, which must now be left to simmer gently. When done, skim off all the fat and froth. Take all the leaves of the herbs from the stock,—sweet basil, sweet marjoram, lemon thyme, winter savory, 2 or 3 bay-leaves, common thyme, a handful of parsley and green onions, and a large onion cut in four pieces, with a few blades of mace. Put these in a stewpan, with about ¼ lb. of fresh butter, and let it simmer on a slow fire till quite melted, when pour in 1 bottle of good Madeira, adding a small bit of sugar, and let it boil gently for 1 hour. When done, rub it through a tammy, and add it to the soup. Let this boil, till no white scum rises; then take with a skimmer all the bits of turtle out of the sauce, and put them in a clean stewpan: when you have all out, pour the soup over the bits of turtle, through a tammy, and proceed as follows:—

QUENELLES A TORTUE.—Make some *quenelles à tortue*, which being substitutes for eggs, do not require to be very delicate. Take out the fleshy part of a leg of veal, about 1 lb., scrape off all the meat, without leaving any sinews or fat, and soak in milk about the same quantity of crumbs of bread. When the bread is well soaked, squeeze it, and put it into a mortar, with the veal, a small quantity of calf's udder, a little butter, the yolks of 4 eggs, boiled hard, a little cayenne pepper, salt, and spices, and pound the whole very fine; then thicken the mixture with 2 whole eggs, and the yolk of another. Next try this *farce* or stuffing in boiling-hot water, to ascertain its consistency: if it is too thin, add the yolk of an egg. When the *farce* is perfected, take half of it, and put into it some chopped parsley. Let the whole cool, in order to roll it of the size of the yolk of an egg; poach it in salt and boiling water, and when very hard, drain on a sieve, and put it into the turtle. Before you send up, squeeze the juice of 2 or 3 lemons, with a little cayenne pepper, and pour that into the soup. THE FINS may be served as a *plat d'entrée* with a little turtle sauce; if not, on the following day you may warm the turtle *au bain marie*, and serve the members entire, with a *matelote* sauce, garnished with mushrooms, cocks' combs, *quenelles*, &c. When either lemon-juice or cayenne pepper has been introduced, no boiling must take place.

Note.—It is necessary to observe, that the turtle prepared a day before it is used, is generally preferable, the flavour being more uniform. Be particular, when you dress a very large turtle, to preserve the green fat (be cautious not to study a very brown colour,—the natural green of the fish is preferred by every epicure and true connoisseur) in a separate stewpan, and likewise when the turtle is entirely done, to have as many tureens as you mean to serve each time. You cannot put the whole in a large vessel, for many reasons: first, it will be long in cooling; secondly, when you take some out, it will break all the rest into rags. If you warm in a *bain marie*, the turtle will always retain the same taste; but if you boil it often, it becomes strong, and loses the delicacy of its flavour.

The Cost of Turtle Soup.—This is the most expensive soup brought to table. It is sold by the quart,—one guinea being the standard price for that quantity. The price of live turtle ranges from 8*d.* to 2*s.* per lb., according to supply and demand. When live turtle is dear, many cooks use the tinned turtle, which is killed when caught, and preserved by being put in hermetically-sealed canisters, and so sent over to England. The cost of a tin, containing 2 quarts, or 4 lbs., is about £2, and for a small one, containing the green fat, 7*s.* 6*d.* From these about 6 quarts of good soup may be made.

THE GREEN TURTLE.—This reptile is found in large numbers on the coasts of all the islands and continents within the tropics, in both the old and new worlds. Their length is often five feet and upwards, and they range in weight from 50 to 500 or 600 lbs. As turtles find a constant supply of food on the coasts which they frequent, they are not of a quarrelsome disposition, as the submarine meadows in which they pasture, yield plenty for them all. Like other species of amphibia, too, they have the power of living many months without

The Turtle

food; so that they live harmlessly and peaceably together, notwithstanding that they seem to have no common bond of association, but merely assemble in the same places as if entirely by accident. England is mostly supplied with them from the West Indies, whence they are brought alive and in tolerable health. The green turtle is highly prized on account of the delicious quality of its flesh, the fat of the upper and lower shields of the animal being esteemed the richest and most delicate parts. The soup, however, is apt to disagree with weak stomachs. As an article of luxury, the turtle has only come into fashion within the last 100 years, and some hundreds of tureens of turtle soup are served annually at the lord mayor's dinner in Guildhall.

Hodge-Podge*

INGREDIENTS.—2 lbs. of shin of beef, 3 quarts of water, 1 pint of table-beer, 2 onions, 2 carrots, 2 turnips, 1 head of celery; pepper and salt to taste; thickening of butter and flour.

Mode.—Put the meat, beer, and water in a stewpan; simmer for a few minutes, and skim carefully. Add the vegetables and seasoning; stew gently till the meat is tender. Thicken with the butter and flour, and serve with turnips and carrots, or spinach and celery.

Time.—3 hours, or rather more.   *Average cost*, 3*d*. per quart.

Seasonable at any time.

Sufficient for 12 persons.

TABLE BEER.—This is nothing more than a weak ale, and is not made so much with a view to strength, as to transparency of colour and an agreeable bitterness of taste. It is, or ought to be, manufactured by the London professional brewers, from the best pale malt, or amber and malt. Six barrels are usually drawn from one quarter of malt, with which are mixed 4 or 5 lbs. of hops. As a beverage, it is agreeable when fresh; but it is not adapted to keep long.

FISH SOUPS

Lobster Soup

INGREDIENTS.—3 large lobsters, or 6 small ones; the crumb of a French roll, 2 anchovies, 1 onion, 1 small bunch of sweet herbs, 1 strip of lemon-peel, 2 oz. of butter, a little nutmeg, 1 teaspoonful of flour, 1 pint of cream, 1 pint of milk; forcemeat balls, mace, salt and pepper to taste, bread crumbs, 1 egg, 2 quarts of water.

Mode.—Pick the meat from the lobsters, and beat the fins, chine, and small claws in a mortar, previously taking away the brown fin and the bag in the head. Put it in a stewpan, with the crumb of the roll, anchovies, onions, herbs, lemon-peel, and the water; simmer gently till all the goodness is extracted, and strain it off. Pound the spawn in a mortar, with the butter, nutmeg, and flour, and mix with it the cream and milk. Give one boil up, at the same time adding the tails cut in pieces. Make the forcemeat balls with the remainder of the lobster, seasoned with mace, pepper, and salt, adding a little flour, and a few bread crumbs; moisten them with the egg, heat them in the soup, and serve.

Time.—2 hours, or rather more.   *Average cost*, 3*s*. 6*d*. per quart.

Seasonable from April to October.

Sufficient for 8 persons.

FISH

CHAPTER VII

THE NATURAL HISTORY OF FISHES*

In natural history, fishes form the fourth class in the system of
Linnaeus, and are described as having long under-jaws, eggs without
white, organs of sense, fins for supporters, bodies covered with concave scales, gills to supply the place of lungs for respiration, and
water for the natural element of their existence. Had mankind no
other knowledge of animals than of such as inhabit the land and
breathe their own atmosphere, they would listen with incredulous
wonder, if told that there were other kinds of beings which existed
only in the waters, and which would die almost as soon as they were
taken from them. However strongly these facts might be attested,
they would hardly believe them, without the operation of their
own senses, as they would recollect the effect produced on their own
bodies when immersed in water, and the impossibility of their
sustaining life in it for any lengthened period of time. Experience,
however, has taught them, that the 'great deep' is crowded with
inhabitants of various sizes, and of vastly different constructions,

with modes of life entirely distinct from those which belong to the animals of the land, and with peculiarities of design, equally wonderful with those of any other works which have come from the hand of the Creator. The history of these races, however, must remain for ever, more or less, in a state of darkness, since the depths in which they live, are beyond the power of human exploration, and since the illimitable expansion of their domain places them almost entirely out of the reach of human accessibility.*

In studying the conformation of fishes, we naturally conclude that they are, in every respect, well adapted to the element in which they have their existence. Their shape has a striking resemblance to the lower part of a ship; and there is no doubt that the form of the fish originally suggested the form of the ship. The body is in general slender, gradually diminishing towards each of its extremities, and flattened on each of its sides. This is precisely the form of the lower part of the hull of a ship; and it enables both the animal and the vessel, with comparative ease, to penetrate and divide the resisting medium for which they have been adapted. The velocity of a ship, however, in sailing before the wind, is by no means to be compared to that of a fish. It is well known that the largest fishes will, with the greatest ease, overtake a ship in full sail, play round it without effort, and shoot ahead of it at pleasure. This arises from their great flexibility, which, to compete with mocks the labours of art, and enables them to migrate thousands of miles in a season, without the slightest indications of languor or fatigue.

The principal instruments employed by fishes to accelerate their motion, are their air-bladder, fins, and tail. By means of the air-bladder they enlarge or diminish the specific gravity of their bodies. When they wish to sink, they compress the muscles of the abdomen, and eject the air contained in it; by which, their weight, compared with that of the water, is increased, and they consequently descend. On the other hand, when they wish to rise, they relax the compression of the abdominal muscles, when the air-bladder fills and distends, and the body immediately ascends to the surface. How simply, yet how wonderfully, has the Supreme Being adapted certain means to the attainment of certain ends! Those fishes which are destitute of the air-bladder are heavy in the water, and have no great 'alacrity' in rising. The larger proportion of them remain at the bottom, unless they are so formed as to be able to strike their native element downwards with sufficient force to enable them to ascend. When the air-bladder of a fish is burst, its power of ascending to the surface has for ever passed away. From a knowledge of this fact, the fishermen of cod are enabled to preserve them alive for a considerable time in their well-boats. The means they adopt to accomplish this, is to perforate the sound, or air-bladder, with a needle, which disengages the air, when the fishes immediately descend to the bottom of the well, into which they are thrown. Without this operation, it would be impossible to keep the cod under water whilst they had life. In swimming, the *fins* enable fishes to preserve their upright position, especially those of the belly, which act like two feet. Without these, they would swim with their bellies upward, as it is in their backs that the centre of gravity lies. In ascending and descending, these are likewise of great assistance, as they contract and expand accordingly. The *tail* is an instrument of great muscular force, and largely assists the fish in all its motions. In some instances it acts like the rudder of a ship, and enables it to turn sideways; and when moved from side to side with a quick vibratory motion, fishes are made, in the same manner as the 'screw' propeller makes a steamship, to dart forward with a celerity proportioned to the muscular force with which it is employed.*

With respect to the food of fishes, this is almost universally found in their own element. They are mostly carnivorous, though they seize upon almost anything that comes in their way: they even devour their own offspring, and manifest a particular predilection for all living creatures. Those, to which Nature has meted out mouths of the greatest capacity, would seem to pursue everything with life, and frequently engage in fierce conflicts with their prey. The animal with the largest mouth is usually the victor; and he has no sooner conquered his foe than he devours him. Innumerable shoals of one species pursue those of another, with a ferocity which draws them from the pole to the equator, through all the varying temperatures and depths of their boundless domain.* In these pursuits a scene of universal violence is the result; and many species must have become extinct, had not Nature accurately proportioned the means of escape, the production, and the numbers, to the extent and variety of the danger to which they are exposed. Hence the smaller species are not only more numerous, but more productive than the larger; whilst their instinct leads them in search of food and safety near the shores, where, from the shallowness of the waters, many of their foes are unable to follow them.

Fishes are either solitary or gregarious, and some of them migrate to great distances, and into certain rivers, to deposit their spawn. Of sea-fishes, the cod, herring, mackerel, and many others, assemble in immense shoals, and migrate through different tracts of the ocean; but, whether considered in their solitary or gregarious capacity, they are alike wonderful to all who look through Nature up to Nature's God, and consider, with due humility, yet exalted admiration, the sublime variety, beauty, power, and grandeur of His productions, as manifested in the Creation.*

FISH AS AN ARTICLE OF HUMAN FOOD*

As the nutritive properties of fish are deemed inferior to those of what is called butchers' meat, it would appear, from all we can learn, that, in all ages, it has held only a secondary place in the estimation of those who have considered the science of gastronomy as a large element in the happiness of mankind. Among the Jews of old it was very little used, although it seems not to have been entirely inter-dicted, as Moses prohibited only the use of such as had neither scales nor fins. The Egyptians, however, made fish an article of diet, not-withstanding that it was rejected by their priests. Egypt, however, is not a country favourable to the production of fish, although we read of the people, when hungry, eating it raw; of epicures among them having dried it in the sun; and of its being salted and preserved, to serve as a repast on days of great solemnity.

The modern Egyptians are, in general, extremely temperate in regard to food. Even the richest among them take little pride, and, perhaps, experience as little delight, in the luxuries of the table. Their dishes mostly consist of pilaus, soups, and stews, prepared principally of onions, cucumbers, and other cold vegetables, mixed with a little meat cut into small pieces. On special occasions, however, a whole sheep is placed on the festive board; but during several of the hottest months of the year, the richest restrict themselves entirely to a vegetable diet. The poor are contented with a little oil or sour milk, in which they may dip their bread.

Passing from Africa to Europe, we come amongst a people who have, almost from time immemorial, occupied a high place in the estimation of every civilized country; yet the Greeks, in their earlier ages, made very little use of fish as an article of diet. In the eyes of the heroes of Homer it had little favour; for Menelaus complained that 'hunger pressed their digestive organs,' and they had been obliged to live upon fish. Subsequently, however, fish became one of the principal articles of diet amongst the Hellenes; and both Aristophanes and Athenaeus allude to it, and even satirize their countrymen for their excessive partiality to the turbot and mullet.

So infatuated were many of the Greek gastronomes with the love of fish, that some of them would have preferred death from indigestion to the relinquishment of the precious dainties with which a few of the species supplied them. Philoxenes of Cythera was one of these. On being informed by his physician that he was going to die of indigestion, on account of the quantity he was consuming of a delicious fish, 'Be it so,' he calmly observed; 'but before I die, let me finish the remainder?'

As the Romans, in a great measure, took their taste in the fine arts from the Greeks, so did they, in some measure, their piscine appetites. The eel-pout and the lotas's liver were the favourite fish dishes of the Roman epicures; whilst the red mullet was esteemed as one of the most delicate fishes that could be brought to the table.

With all the elegance, taste, and refinement of Roman luxury, it was sometimes promoted or accompanied by acts of great barbarity. In proof of this, the mention of the red mullet suggests the mode in which it was sometimes treated for the, to us, *horrible* entertainment of the *fashionable* in Roman circles. It may be premised, that as England has, Rome, in her palmy days, had, her fops, who had, no doubt, through the medium of their cooks, discovered that when the scales of the red mullet were removed, the flesh presented a fine pink-colour. Having discovered this, it was further observed that at the death of the animal, this colour passed through a succession of beautiful shades, and, in order that these might be witnessed and enjoyed in their fullest perfection, the poor mullet was served alive in a glass vessel.*

The love of fish among the ancient Romans rose to a real mania. Apicius offered a prize to any one who could invent a new brine compounded of the liver of red mullets; and Lucullus had a canal cut through a mountain, in the neighbourhood of Naples, that fish might be the more easily transported to the gardens of his villa. Hortensius, the orator, wept over the death of a turbot which he had fed with his own hands; and the daughter of Druses adorned one that she had, with rings of gold. These were, surely, instances of misplaced affection; but there is no accounting for tastes. It was but the other day that we read in the '*Times*' of a wealthy *living* English hermit, who delights in the companionship of rats!

The modern Romans are merged in the general name of Italians, who, with the exception of macaroni, have no specially characteristic article of food.

The general use of fish, as an article of human food among civilized nations, we have thus sufficiently shown, and will conclude this portion of our subject with the following hints, which ought to be remembered by all those who are fond of occasionally varying their dietary with a piscine dish:—*

I.   Fish shortly before they spawn are, in general, best in condition. When the spawning is just over, they are out of season, and unfit for human food.

II.   When fish is out of season, it has a transparent, bluish tinge, however much it may be boiled; when it is in season, its muscles are firm, and boil white and curdy.

III.   As food for invalids, white fish, such as the ling, cod, haddock, coal-fish, and whiting, are the best; flat fish, as soles, skate, turbot, and flounders, are also good.

IV.   Salmon, mackerel, herrings, and trout soon spoil or decompose after they are killed; therefore, to be in perfection, they should be prepared for the table on the day they are caught. With flat fish, this is not of such consequence, as they will keep longer. The turbot, for example, is improved by being kept a day or two.

GENERAL DIRECTIONS FOR DRESSING FISH

In garnishing fish, great attention is required, and plenty of parsley, horseradish, and lemon should be used. If fried parsley be used, it must be washed and picked, and thrown into fresh water. When the lard or dripping boils, throw the parsley into it immediately from the water, and instantly it will be green and crisp, and must be taken up with a slice. When well done, and with very good sauce, fish is more appreciated than almost any other dish. The liver and roe, in some instances, should be placed on the dish, in order that they may be distributed in the course of serving; but to each recipe will be appended the proper mode of serving and garnishing.

In choosing fish, it is well to remember that it is possible it may be *fresh*, and yet not *good*. Under the head of each particular fish in this work, are appended rules for its choice and the months when it is in season. Nothing can be of greater consequence to a cook than to have the fish good; as if this important course in a dinner does not give satisfaction, it is rarely that the repast goes off well.

CHAPTER VIII

RECIPES*

FISH

Nothing is more difficult than to give the average prices of Fish, inasmuch as a few hours of bad weather at sea will, in the space of one day, cause such a difference in its supply, that the same fish—a turbot for instance—which may be bought to-day for six or seven shillings, will, to-morrow, be, in the London markets, worth, perhaps, almost as many pounds. The average costs, therefore, which will be found appended to each recipe, must be understood as about the average price for the different kinds of fish, when the market is supplied upon an average, and when the various sorts are of an average size and quality.

GENERAL RULE IN CHOOSING FISH.—*A proof of freshness and goodness in most fishes, is their being covered with scales; for, if deficient in this respect, it is a sign of their being stale, or having been ill-used.*

Anchovy Butter or Paste*

INGREDIENTS.—2 dozen anchovies, ½ lb. of fresh butter.

Mode.—Wash the anchovies thoroughly; bone and dry them, and pound them in a mortar to a paste. Mix the butter gradually with them, and rub the whole through a sieve. Put it by in small pots for use, and carefully exclude the air with a bladder, as it soon changes the colour of anchovies, besides spoiling them.

Average cost for this quantity, 2s.

ANCHOVY PASTE.—'When some delicate zest,' says a work just issued on the adulterations of trade, 'is required to make the plain English breakfast more palatable, many people are in the habit of indulging in what they imagine to be anchovies. These fish are preserved in a kind of pickling-bottle, carefully corked down, and surrounded by a red-looking liquor, resembling in appearance diluted clay. The price is moderate, one shilling only being demanded for the luxury. When these anchovies are what is termed potted, it implies that the fish have been pounded into the consist-ency of a paste, and then placed in flat pots, somewhat similar in shape to those used for pomatum. This paste is usually eaten spread upon toast, and is said to form an excellent *bonne bouche*, which enables gentlemen at wine-parties to enjoy their port with redoubled gusto. Unfortunately, in six cases out of ten, the only portion of these preserved delicacies, that contains anything indicative of anchovies, is the paper label pasted on the bottle or pot, on which the word itself is printed. . . . All the samples of anchovy paste, analyzed by different medical men, have been found to be highly and vividly coloured with very large quantities of bole Armenian.' The anchovy itself, when imported, is of a dark dead colour, and it is to make it a bright 'handsome-looking sauce' that this red earth is used.

Codfish

Cod may be boiled whole; but a large head and shoulders are quite sufficient for a dish, and contain all that is usually helped, because, when the thick part is done, the tail is insipid and overdone. The latter, cut in slices, makes a very good dish for frying; or it may be salted down and served with egg sauce and parsnips. Cod, when boiled quite fresh, is watery; salting a little, renders it firmer.

THE COD TRIBE.—The Jugular, characterized by bony gills, and ventral fins before the pectoral ones, commences the second of the Linnaen orders of fishes, and is a numerous tribe, inhabiting only the depths of the ocean, and seldom visiting the fresh waters. They have a smooth head, and the gill mem-

The Cod

brane has seven rays. The body is oblong, and covered with deciduous scales. The fins are all inclosed in skin, whilst their rays are unarmed. The ventral fins are slender, and terminate in a point. Their habits are gregarious, and they feed on smaller fish and other marine animals.

Salt Cod, Commonly Called 'Salt-Fish'*

INGREDIENTS.—Sufficient water to cover the fish.

Mode.—Wash the fish, and lay it all night in water, with a ¼ pint of vinegar. When thoroughly soaked, take it out, see that it is perfectly clean, and put it in the fish-kettle with sufficient cold water to cover it. Heat it gradually, but do not let it boil much, or the fish will be hard. Skim well, and when done, drain the fish and put it on a napkin garnished with hard-boiled eggs cut in rings.

Time.—About 1 hour.   *Average cost*, 6*d* per lb.

Seasonable in the spring.

Sufficient for each person, ¼ lb.

Note.—Serve with egg sauce and parsnips. This is an especial dish on Ash-Wednesday.

PRESERVING COD.—Immediately as the cod are caught, their heads are cut off. They are then opened, cleaned, and salted, when they are stowed away in the hold of the vessel, in beds of five or six yards square, head to tail, with a layer of salt to each layer of fish. When they have lain in this state three or four days, in order that the water may drain from them, they are shifted into a different part of the vessel, and again salted. Here they remain till the vessel is loaded, when they are sometimes cut into thick pieces and packed in barrels for the greater convenience of carriage.

Cod à la Béchamel*

INGREDIENTS.—Any remains of cold cod, 4 tablespoonfuls of béchamel (*see* SAUCES), 2 oz. butter; seasoning to taste of pepper and salt; fried bread, a few bread crumbs.

Mode.—Flake the cod carefully, leaving out all skin and bone; put the béchamel in a stewpan with the butter, and stir it over the fire till the latter is melted; add seasoning, put in the fish, and mix it well with the sauce. Make a border of fried bread round the dish, lay in the fish, sprinkle over with bread crumbs, and baste with butter. Brown either before the fire or with a salamander, and garnish with toasted bread cut in fanciful shapes.

Time.— ½ hour.

Average cost, exclusive of the fish, 6*d*.

Baked Carp*

INGREDIENTS.—1 carp, forcemeat, bread crumbs, 1 oz. butter, ½ pint of [medium] stock, ½ pint of port wine, 6 anchovies, 2 onions sliced, 1 bay-leaf, a faggot of sweet herbs, flour to thicken, the juice of 1 lemon; cayenne and salt to taste; ½ teaspoonful of powdered sugar.

Mode.—Stuff the carp with a delicate forcemeat, after thoroughly cleansing it, and sew it up, to prevent the stuffing from falling out. Rub it over with an egg, and sprinkle it with bread crumbs, lay it in a deep earthen dish, and drop the butter, oiled, over the bread crumbs. Add the stock, onions, bay-leaf, herbs, wine, and anchovies, and bake for 1 hour. Put 1 oz. of butter into a stewpan, melt it, and dredge in sufficient flour to dry it up; put in the strained liquor from the carp, stir frequently, and when it has boiled, add the lemon-juice and seasoning. Serve the carp on a dish garnished with parsley and cut lemon, and the sauce in a boat.

Time.—1¼ hour.   *Average cost.* Seldom bought.

Seasonable from March to October.

Sufficient for 1 or 2 persons

THE CARP.—This species of fish inhabit the fresh waters, where they feed on worms, insects, aquatic plants, small fish, clay, or mould. Some of them are migratory. They have very small mouths and no teeth, and the gill membrane has three rays. The

The Carp

body is smooth, and generally whitish. The carp both grows and increases very fast, and is accounted the most valuable of all fish for the stocking of ponds. It has been pronounced the queen of river-fish, and was first introduced to this country about three hundred years ago. Of its sound, or air-bladder, a kind of glue is made, and a green paint of its gall.

Hot Crab

INGREDIENTS.—1 crab, nutmeg, salt and pepper to taste, 3 oz. of butter, ¼ lb. of bread crumbs, 3 tablespoonfuls of vinegar.

Mode.—After having boiled the crab, pick the meat out from the shells, and mix with it the nutmeg and seasoning. Cut up the butter in small pieces, and add the bread crumbs and vinegar. Mix altogether, put the whole in the large shell, and brown before the fire or with a salamander.

Time.—1 hour.   *Average cost*, from 10*d.* to 2*s.*

Seasonable all the year; but not so good in May, June, and July.

Sufficient for 3 persons.

THE CRAB TRIBE.—The whole of this tribe of animals have the body covered with a hard and strong shell, and they live chiefly in the sea. Some, however, inhabit fresh waters, and a few live upon land. They feed variously, on aquatic or marine plants, small fish, molluscae, or dead bodies.

The *black-clawed* species is found on the rocky coasts of both Europe and India, and is the same that is introduced to our tables, being much more highly esteemed as a food than many others of the tribe. The most remarkable feature in their history, is the changing of their shells, and the

reproduction of their broken claws. The former occurs once a year, usually between Christmas and Easter, when the crabs retire to cavities in the rocks, or conceal themselves under great stones. Fishermen say that they will live confined in a pot or basket for several months together, without any other food than what is collected from the sea-water; and that, even in

The Crab

this situation, they will not decrease in weight. The *hermit* crab is another of the species, and has the peculiarity of taking possession of the deserted shell of some other animal, as it has none of its own. This circumstance was known to the ancients, and is alluded to in the following lines from Oppian:—

> The hermit fish, unarm'd by Nature, left
> Helpless and weak, grow strong by harmless theft.
> Fearful, they stroll, and look with panting wish
> For the cast crust of some new-cover'd fish;
> Or such as empty lie, and deck the shore,
> Whose first and rightful owners are no more.
> They make glad seizure of the vacant room,
> And count the borrow'd shell their native home;
> Screw their soft limbs to fit the winding case,
> And boldly herd with the crustaceous race.

Eel Pie*

INGREDIENTS.—1 lb. of eels, a little chopped parsley, 1 shalot; grated nutmeg; pepper and salt to taste; the juice of ½ a lemon, small quantity of forcemeat, ¼ pint of béchamel (*see* SAUCES); puff paste.

Mode.—Skin and wash the eels, cut them into pieces 2 inches long, and line the bottom of the pie-dish with forcemeat. Put in the eels, and sprinkle them with the parsley, shalots, nutmeg, seasoning, and lemon-juice, and cover with puff-paste. Bake for 1 hour, or rather more; make the béchamel hot, and pour it into the pie.

Time.—Rather more than 1 hour.

Seasonable from August to March.

Eels en Matelote

INGREDIENTS.—5 or 6 young onions, a few mushrooms, when obtainable; salt, pepper, and nutmeg to taste; 1 laurel-leaf, ½ pint of port wine, ½ pint of medium stock; butter and flour to thicken; 2 lbs. of eels.

Mode.—Rub the stewpan with butter, dredge in a little flour, add the onions cut very small, slightly brown them, and put in all the other ingredients. Wash, and cut up the eels into pieces 3 inches long; put them in the stewpan, and simmer for ½ hour. Make round the dish, a border of croûtons, or pieces of toasted bread; arrange the eels in a pyramid in the centre, and pour over the sauce. Serve very hot.

Time.—¾ hour.   *Average cost*, 1s. 9d. for this quantity.

Seasonable from August to March.

Sufficient for 5 or 6 persons.

TENACITY OF LIFE IN THE EEL.—There is no fish so tenacious of life as this. After it is skinned and cut in pieces, the parts will continue to move for a considerable time, and no fish will live so long out of water.

VORACITY OF THE EEL.—We find in a note upon Isaac Walton, by Sir John Hawkins, that he knew of eels, when kept in ponds, frequently destroying ducks. From a canal near his house at Twickenham he himself missed many young ducks; and on draining, in order to clean it, great numbers of large eels were caught in

The Lamprey

the mud. When some of these were opened, there were found in their stomachs the undigested heads of the quacking tribe which had become their victims.

Fish Cake

INGREDIENTS.—The remains of any cold fish, 1 onion, 1 faggot of sweet herbs; salt and pepper to taste, 1 pint of water, equal quantities of bread crumbs and cold potatoes, ½ teaspoonful of parsley, 1 egg, bread crumbs.

Mode.—Pick the meat from the bones of the fish, which latter put, with the head and fins, into a stewpan with the water; add pepper and salt, the onion and herbs, and stew slowly for gravy about

2 hours; chop the fish fine, and mix it well with bread crumbs and cold potatoes, adding the parsley and seasoning; make the whole into a cake with the white of an egg, brush it over with egg, cover with bread crumbs, and fry of a light brown; strain the gravy, pour it over, and stew gently for ¼ hour, stirring it carefully once or twice. Serve hot, and garnish with slices of lemon and parsley.

Time.—½ hour, after the gravy is made.

Red Herrings, or Yarmouth Bloaters*

The best way to cook these is to make incisions in the skin across the fish, because they do not then require to be so long on the fire, and will be far better than when cut open. The hard roe makes a nice relish by pounding it in a mortar, with a little anchovy, and spreading it on toast. If very dry, soak in warm water 1 hour before dressing.

THE RED HERRING.—*Red* herrings lie twenty-four hours in the brine, when they are taken out and hung up in a smoking-house formed to receive them. A brushwood fire is then kindled beneath them, and when they are sufficiently smoked and dried, they are put into barrels for carriage.

To Boil Lobsters*

INGREDIENTS.—¼ lb of salt to each gallon of water.

Mode.—Buy the lobsters alive, and choose those that are heavy and full of motion, which is an indication of their freshness. When the shell is incrusted, it is a sign they are old: medium-sized lobsters are the best. Have ready a stewpan of boiling water, salted in the above proportion; put in the lobster, and keep it boiling quickly from 20 minutes to ¾ hour, according to its size, and do not forget to skim well. If it boils too long, the meat becomes thready, and if not done enough, the spawn is not red: this must be obviated by great attention. Rub the shell over with a little butter or sweet oil, which wipe off again.

Time.—Small lobster, 20 minutes to ½ hour; large ditto, ½ to ¾ hour.

Average cost, medium size, 1s. 6d. to 2s. 6d.

Seasonable all the year, but best from March to October.

To Choose Lobsters.—This shell-fish, if it has been cooked alive, as it ought to have been, will have a stiffness in the tail, which, if gently raised, will return with a spring. Care, however, must be taken in thus proving it; for if the tail is pulled straight out, it will not return; when the fish might be pronounced inferior, which, in reality, may not be the case. In order to be good, lobsters should be weighty for their bulk; if light, they will be watery; and those of the medium size, are always the best. Small-sized lobsters are cheapest, and answer very well for sauce. In boiling lobsters, the appearance of the shell will be much improved by rubbing over it a little butter or salad-oil on being immediately taken from the pot.

THE LOBSTER.—This is one of the crab tribe, and is found on most of the rocky coasts of Great Britain. Some are caught with the hand, but the larger number in pots, which serve all the purposes of a trap, being made of osiers, and baited with garbage. They are shaped like a wire mousetrap; so that when the lobsters once enter them, they cannot get out again. They are fastened to a cord and sunk in the sea, and their place marked by a buoy. The fish is very prolific, and deposits its eggs in the

The Lobster

sand, where they are soon hatched. On the coast of Norway, they are very abundant, and it is from there that the English metropolis is mostly supplied. They are rather indigestible, and, as a food, not so nutritive as they are generally supposed to be.

Lobster (à la Mode Française)

INGREDIENTS.— 1 lobster, 4 tablespoonfuls of white stock, 2 table-spoonfuls of cream, pounded mace, and cayenne to taste; bread crumbs.

Mode.—Pick the meat from the shell, and cut it up into small square pieces; put the stock, cream, and seasoning into a stewpan, add the lobster, and let it simmer gently for 6 minutes. Serve it in the shell, which must be nicely cleaned, and have a border of puff-paste; cover it with bread crumbs, place small pieces of butter over, and brown before the fire, or with a salamander.

Time.—¼ hour.   *Average cost,* 2s. 6d.

Seasonable at any time.

CELEBRITY OF THE LOBSTER.—In its element, the lobster is able to run with great speed upon its legs, or small claws, and, if alarmed, to spring, tail foremost, to a considerable distance, 'even,' it is said, 'with the swiftness of a bird flying.' Fishermen have seen some of them pass about thirty feet with a wonderful degree of swiftness. When frightened, they will take their spring, and, like a chamois of the Alps, plant themselves upon the very spot upon which they designed to hold themselves.

Broiled Mackerel

INGREDIENTS.—Pepper and salt to taste, a small quantity of oil.

Mode.—Mackerel should never be washed when intended to be broiled, but merely wiped very clean and dry, after taking out the gills and insides. Open the back, and put in a little pepper, salt, and oil; broil it over a clear fire, turn it over on both sides, and also on the back. When sufficiently cooked, the flesh can be detached from the bone, which will be in about 15 minutes for a small mackerel. Chop a little parsley, work it up in the butter, with pepper and salt to taste, and a squeeze of lemon-juice, and put it in the back. Serve before the butter is quite melted, with a *maître d'hôtel* sauce in a tureen.

Time.—Small mackerel 15 minutes.

Average cost, from 4*d*.

Seasonable from April to July.

The Mackerel

THE MACKEREL.—This is not only one of the most elegantly-formed, but one of the most beautifully-coloured fishes, when taken out of the sea, that we have. Death, in some degree, impairs the vivid splendour of its colours; but it does not entirely obliterate them. It visits the shores of Great Britain in countless shoals, appearing about March, off the Land's End; in the bays of Devonshire, about April; off Brighton in the beginning of May; and on the coast of Suffolk about the beginning of June. In the Orkneys they are seen till August; but the greatest fishery is on the west coasts of England.

To choose mackerel.—In choosing this fish, purchasers should, to a great extent, be regulated by the brightness of its appearance. If it have a transparent, silvery hue, the flesh is good; but if it be red about the head, it is stale.

Scalloped Oysters*

INGREDIENTS.—Oysters, say 1 pint, 1 oz. butter, flour, 2 table-spoonfuls of white stock, 2 tablespoonfuls of cream; pepper and salt to taste; bread crumbs, oiled butter.

Mode.—Scald the oysters in their own liquor, take them out, beard them, and strain the liquor free from grit. Put 1 oz. of butter into a stewpan; when melted, dredge in sufficient flour to dry it up; add the stock, cream, and strained liquor, and give one boil. Put in the oysters and seasoning; let them gradually heat through, but not boil. Have ready the scallop-shells buttered; lay in the oysters, and as much of the liquid as they will hold; cover them over with bread crumbs, over which drop a little oiled butter. Brown them in the oven, or before the fire, and serve quickly, and very hot.

Time.—Altogether, ¼ hour.

Average cost for this quantity, 3s. 6d.

Sufficient for 5 or 6 persons.

Salmon and Caper Sauce*

INGREDIENTS.—2 slices of salmon, ¼ lb. butter, ½ teaspoonful of chopped parsley, 1 shalot; salt, pepper, and grated nutmeg to taste.

Mode.—Lay the salmon in a baking-dish, place pieces of butter over it, and add the other ingredients, rubbing a little of the season-ing into the fish; baste it frequently; when done, take it out and drain for a minute or two; lay it in a dish, pour caper sauce over it, and serve. Salmon dressed in this way, with tomato sauce, is very delicious.

Time.—About ¾ hour.   *Average cost*, 1s. 3d. per lb.

Seasonable from April to August.

Sufficient for 4 or 5 persons.

THE MIGRATORY HABITS OF THE SALMON.—The instinct with which the salmon revisits its native river, is one of the most curious circumstances in its natural history. As the swallow returns annually to its nest, so it returns to the same spot to deposit its ova. This fact would seem to have been repeatedly proved. M. De Lande fastened a copper ring round a salmon's tail, and found that, for three successive seasons, it returned to the same place. Dr Bloch states that gold and silver rings have been attached by eastern princes to salmon, to prove that a communica-tion existed between the Persian Gulf and the Caspian and Northern Seas, and that the experiment succeeded.

Potted Shrimps*

INGREDIENTS.—1 pint of shelled shrimps, ¼ lb. of fresh butter,
1 blade of pounded mace, cayenne to taste; when liked, a little nutmeg.

Mode.—Have ready a pint of picked shrimps, and put them, with
the other ingredients, into a stewpan; let them heat gradually in the
butter, but do not let it boil. Pour into small pots, and when cold,
cover with melted butter, and carefully exclude the air.

Time.—¼ hour to soak in the butter.

Average cost for this quantity, 1s. 3d.

Crimped Skate*

INGREDIENTS.—½ lb. of salt to each gallon of water.

Mode.—Clean, skin, and cut the fish into slices, which roll and tie
round with string. Have ready some water highly salted, put in the
fish, and boil till it is done. Drain well, remove the string, dish on
a hot napkin, and serve with shrimp, lobster, or caper sauce. Skate
should never be eaten out of season, as it is liable to produce
diarrhoea and other diseases. It may be dished without a napkin, and
the sauce poured over.

Time.—About 20 minutes.   *Average cost,* 4d. per lb.

Seasonable from August to April.

To choose Skate.—This fish should be chosen for its firmness,
breadth, and thickness, and should have a creamy appearance. When
crimped, it should not be kept longer than a day or two, as all kinds
of crimped fish soon become sour.

Thornback Skate

THE SKATE.—This is one of the
ray tribe, and is extremely abundant
and cheap in the fishing towns of England. The flesh is white, thick, and
nourishing; but, we suppose, from its
being so plentiful, it is esteemed less
than it ought to be on account of its
nutritive properties, and the ease with
which it is digested. It is much
improved by crimping; in which state
it is usually sold in London. The THORNBACK differs from the true skate
by having large spines in its back, of which the other is destitute. It is
taken in great abundance during the spring and summer months, but its

flesh is not so good as it is in November. It is, in regard to quality, inferior to that of the true skate.

Soles with Cream Sauce*

INGREDIENTS.—2 soles; salt, cayenne, and pounded mace to taste; the juice of ½ lemon, salt and water, ½ pint of cream.

Mode.—Skin, wash, and fillet the soles, and divide each fillet in 2 pieces; lay them in cold salt and water, which bring gradually to a boil. When the water boils, take out the fish, lay it in a delicately clean stewpan, and cover with the cream. Add the seasoning, simmer very gently for ten minutes, and, just before serving, put in the lemon-juice. The fillets may be rolled, and secured by means of a skewer; but this is not so economical a way of dressing them, as double the quantity of cream is required.

Time.—10 minutes in the cream.

Average cost, from 1s. to 2s. per pair.

Seasonable at any time.

Sufficient for 4 or 5 persons.

This will be found a most delicate and delicious dish.

THE SOLE, A FAVOURITE WITH THE ANCIENT GREEKS.—This fish was much sought after by the ancient Greeks on account of its light and nourishing qualities. The brill, the flounder, the diamond and Dutch plaice, which, with the sole, were known under the general name of *passeres*, were all equally esteemed, and had generally the same qualities attributed to them.

Fricasseed Soles

INGREDIENTS.—2 middling-sized soles, 1 small one, ½ teaspoonful of chopped lemon-peel, 1 teaspoonful of chopped parsley, a little grated bread; salt, pepper, and nutmeg to taste; 1 egg, 2 oz. butter, ½ pint of good gravy, 2 tablespoonfuls of port wine, cayenne and lemon-juice to taste.

Mode.—Fry the soles of a nice brown, and drain them well from fat. Take all the meat from the small sole, chop it fine, and mix with it the lemon-peel, parsley, bread, and seasoning; work altogether, with the yolk of an egg and the butter; make this into small balls, and fry them. Thicken the gravy with a dessert-spoonful of flour, add the port wine, cayenne, and lemon-juice; lay in the 2 soles and balls; let them simmer gently for 5 minutes; serve hot, and garnish with cut lemon.

Time.—10 minutes to fry the soles.

Average cost for this quantity, 3s.

Seasonable at any time.   *Sufficient* for 4 or 5 persons.

HOW SOLES ARE CAUGHT.—The instrument usually employed is a trawl net, which is shaped like a pocket, of from sixty to eighty feet long, and open at the mouth from thirty-two to forty feet, and three deep. This is dragged along the ground by the vessel, and on the art of the fisherman in its employment, in a great measure depends the quality of the fish he catches. If, for example, he drags the net too quickly, all that are caught are swept rapidly to the end of the net, where they are smothered, and sometimes destroyed. A medium has to be observed, in order that as few as possible escape being caught in the net, and as many as possible preserved alive in it.

Roast Sturgeon*

INGREDIENTS.—Veal stuffing, buttered paper, the tail-end of a sturgeon.

Mode.—Cleanse the fish, bone and skin it; make a nice veal stuffing (*see* FORCEMEATS), and fill it with the part where the bones came from; roll it in buttered paper, bind it up firmly with tape, like a fillet of veal, and roast it in a Dutch oven before a clear fire. Serve with good brown gravy, or plain melted butter.

Time.—About 1 hour.   *Average cost*, 1s. to 1s. 6d. per lb.

Seasonable from August to March.

Note.—Sturgeon may be plain-boiled, and served with Dutch sauce. The fish is very firm, and requires long boiling.

ESTIMATE OF THE STURGEON BY THE ANCIENTS.—By the ancients, the flesh of this fish was compared to the ambrosia of the immortals. The poet Martial passes a high eulogium upon it, and assigns it a place on the luxurious tables of the Palatine Mount. If we may credit a modern traveller in China, the people of that country generally entirely abstain from it, and the sovereign of the Celestial Empire confines it to his own kitchen, or dispenses it to only a few of his greatest favourites.

Boiled Turbot

INGREDIENTS.—6 oz. of salt to each gallon of water.

Mode.—Choose a middling-sized turbot; for they are invariably the most valuable: if very large, the meat will be tough and thready. Three or four hours before dressing, soak the fish in salt and water to take off the slime; then thoroughly cleanse it, and with a knife make an incision down the middle of the back, to prevent the skin of the belly from cracking. Rub it over with lemon, and be particular not to cut off the fins. Lay the fish in a very clean turbot-kettle, with sufficient cold water to cover it, and salt in the above proportion. Let it gradually come to a boil, and skim very carefully; keep it gently simmering, and on no account let it boil fast, as the fish would have a very unsightly appearance. When the meat separates easily from the bone, it is done; then take it out, let it drain well, and dish it on a hot napkin. Rub a little lobster spawn through a sieve, sprinkle it over the fish, and garnish with tufts of parsley and cut lemon. Lobster or shrimp sauce, and plain melted butter, should be sent to table with it.

Time.—After the water boils, about ½ hour for a large turbot; middling size, about 20 minutes.

Average cost,—large turbot, from 10s. to 12s.; middling size, from 12s. to 15s.

Seasonable at any time.

Sufficient, 1 middling-sized turbot for 8 persons.

Note.—An amusing anecdote is related, by Miss Edgeworth, of a bishop, who, descending to his kitchen to superintend the dressing of a turbot, and discovering that his cook had stupidly cut off the fins, immediately commenced sewing them on again with his own episcopal fingers. This dignitary knew the value of a turbot's gelatinous appendages.*

Fried Whiting

INGREDIENTS.—Egg and bread crumbs, a little flour, hot lard or clarified dripping.

Mode.—Take off the skin, clean, and thoroughly wipe the fish free from all moisture, as this is most essential, in order that the egg and bread crumbs may properly adhere. Fasten the tail in the mouth by means of a small skewer,* brush the fish over with egg, dredge with a little flour, and cover with bread crumbs. Fry them in hot lard or clarified dripping of a nice colour, and serve them on a napkin, garnished with fried parsley. Send them to table with shrimp sauce and plain melted butter.

Time.—About 6 minutes.   *Average cost,* 4d. each.

Seasonable all the year, but best from October to March.

Sufficient, 1 small whiting for each person.

Note.—Large whitings may be filleted, rolled, and served as fried filleted soles. Small fried whitings are frequently used for garnishing large boiled fish, such as turbot, cod, &c.

Water Souchy*

Perch, tench, soles, eels, and flounders are considered the best fish for this dish. For the souchy, put some water into a stewpan with a bunch of chopped parsley, some roots, and sufficient salt to make it brackish. Let these simmer for 1 hour, and then stew the fish in this water. When they are done, take them out to drain, have ready some finely-chopped parsley, and a few roots cut into slices of about one inch thick and an inch in length. Put the fish in a tureen or deep dish, strain the liquor over them, and add the minced parsley and roots. Serve with brown bread and butter.

FISH CARVING

General Directions for Carving Fish*

In carving fish, care should be taken to help it in perfect flakes, as, if these are broken, the beauty of the fish is lost. The carver should be acquainted, too, with the choicest parts and morsels; and to give each guest an equal share of these *titbits* should be his maxim. Steel knives and forks should on no account be used in helping fish, as these are liable to impart to it a very disagreeable flavour. Where silver fish-carvers are considered too dear to be bought, good electro-plated ones answer very well, and are inexpensive. The prices set down for them by Messrs Slack, of the Strand, are from a guinea upwards.

Cod's Head and Shoulders

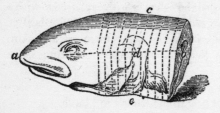

First run the knife along the centre of the side of the fish, namely, from *d* to *b*, down to the bone; then carve it in unbroken slices downwards from *d* to *e*, or upwards from *d* to *c*, as shown in the engraving. The carver should ask the guests if they would like a portion of the roe and liver.

Note.—Of this fish, the parts about the backbone and shoulders are the firmest, and most esteemed by connoisseurs. The sound, which lines the fish beneath the backbone, is considered a delicacy, as are also the gelatinous parts about the head and neck.

Turbot
(For recipe, see p. 114.)

First run the fish-slice down the thickest part of the fish, quite through to the bone, from *a* to *b*, and then cut handsome and regular slices in the direction of the lines downwards, from *c* to *e*, and upwards from *c* to *d*, as shown in the engraving. When the carver has removed all the meat from the upper side of the fish, the backbone should be raised, put on one side of the dish, and the under side helped as the upper.

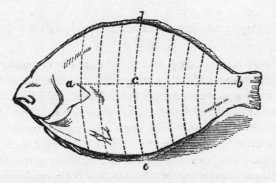

A Brill and John Dory are carved in the same manner as a Turbot.

Note.—The thick parts of the middle of the back are the best slices in a turbot; and the rich gelatinous skin covering the fish, as well as a little of the thick part of the fins, are dainty morsels, and should be placed on each plate.

CHAPTER IX

SAUCES, PICKLES, GRAVIES, AND
FORCEMEATS: GENERAL REMARKS

An anecdote* is told of the prince de Soubise, who, intending to give an entertainment, asked for the bill of fare. His *chef* came, presenting a list adorned with vignettes, and the first article of which, that met the prince's eye, was 'fifty hams.' 'Bertrand,' said the prince, 'I think you must be extravagant; Fifty hams! do you intend to feast my whole regiment?' 'No, Prince, there will be but one on the table, and the surplus I need for my Espagnole, blondes, garnitures, &c.' 'Bertrand, you are robbing me: this item will not do.' 'Monseigneur,' said the *artiste*, 'you do not appreciate me. Give me the order, and I will put those fifty hams in a crystal flask no longer than my thumb.' The prince smiled, and the hams were passed. This was all very well for the prince de Soubise; but as we do not write for princes and nobles alone, but that our British sisters may make the best dishes out of the least expensive ingredients, we will also pass the hams, and give a few general directions concerning Sauces, &c.

The preparation and appearance of sauces and gravies are of the highest consequence, and in nothing does the talent and taste of the cook more display itself. Their special adaptability to the various viands they are to accompany cannot be too much studied, in order that they may harmonize and blend with them as perfectly, so to speak, as does a pianoforte accompaniment with the voice of the singer.

The general basis of most gravies and some sauces is the same stock as that used for soups (*see* pp. 77–9); and, by the employment of these, with, perhaps, an additional slice of ham, a little spice, a few herbs, and a slight flavouring from some cold sauce or ketchup, very nice gravies may be made for a very small expenditure. A milt* (either of a bullock or sheep), the shank-end of mutton that has already been dressed, and the necks and feet of poultry, may all be advantageously used for gravy, where much is not required. It may, then, be established as a rule, that there exists no necessity for good gravies to be expensive, and that there is no occasion, as many would have the world believe, to buy ever so many pounds of fresh meat, in order to furnish an ever so little quantity of gravy.

Brown sauces, generally speaking, should scarcely be so thick as white sauces; and it is well to bear in mind, that all those which are intended to mask the various dishes of poultry or meat, should be of a sufficient consistency to slightly adhere to the fowls or joints over which they are poured. For browning and thickening sauces, &c., browned flour may be properly employed.

Sauces should possess a decided character; and whether sharp or sweet, savoury or plain, they should carry out their names in a distinct manner, although, of course, not so much flavoured as to make them too piquant on the one hand, or too mawkish on the other.

Gravies and sauces should be sent to table very hot; and there is all the more necessity for the cook to see to this point, as, from their being usually served in small quantities, they are more liable to cool quickly than if they were in a larger body. Those sauces, of which cream or eggs form a component part, should be well stirred, as soon as these ingredients are added to them, and must never be allowed to boil; as, in that case, they would instantly curdle.

Although pickles may be purchased at shops at as low a rate as they can usually be made for at home, or perhaps even for less, yet we would advise all housewives, who have sufficient time and convenience, to prepare their own. The only general rules, perhaps, worth stating here,—as in the recipes all necessary details will be explained, are, that the vegetables and fruits used should be sound, and not over ripe, and that the very best vinegar should be employed.

For forcemeats, special attention is necessary. The points which cooks should, in this branch of cookery, more particularly observe, are the thorough chopping of the suet, the complete mincing of the herbs, the careful grating of the bread-crumbs, and the perfect mixing of the whole. These are the three principal ingredients of forcemeats, and they can scarcely be cut too small, as nothing like a lump or fibre should be anywhere perceptible. To conclude, the flavour of no one spice or herb should be permitted to predominate.

CHAPTER X

RECIPES*

Apple Sauce for Geese, Pork, &c.*

INGREDIENTS.—6 good-sized apples, sifted sugar to taste, a piece of butter the size of a walnut, water.

Mode.—Pare, core, and quarter the apples, and throw them into cold water to preserve their whiteness. Put them in a saucepan, with sufficient water to moisten them, and boil till soft enough to pulp. Beat them up, adding sugar to taste, and a small piece of butter. This quantity is sufficient for a good-sized tureen.

Time.—According to the apples, about ¾ hour.

Average cost, 4*d*.

Sufficient, this quantity, for a goose or couple of ducks.

Aspic, or Ornamental Savoury Jelly*

INGREDIENTS.—4 lbs. of knuckle of veal, 1 cow-heel, 3 or 4 slices of ham, any poultry trimmings, 2 carrots, 1 onion, 1 faggot of savoury herbs, 1 glass of sherry, 3 quarts of water; seasoning to taste of salt and whole white pepper; 3 eggs.

Mode.—Lay the ham on the bottom of a stewpan, cut up the veal and cow-heel into small pieces, and lay them on the ham; add the poultry trimmings, vegetables, herbs, sherry, and water, and let the whole simmer very gently for 4 hours, carefully taking away all scum that may rise to the surface; strain through a fine sieve, and pour into an earthen pan to get cold. Have ready a clean stewpan, put in the jelly, and be particular to leave the sediment behind, or it will not be clear. Add the whites of 3 eggs, with salt and pepper, to clarify; keep stirring over the fire, till the whole becomes very white; then draw it to the side, and let it stand till clear. When this is the case, strain it through a cloth or jelly-bag, and use it for moulding poultry, &c. (*See* EXPLANATION OF FRENCH TERMS, p. 63.) Tarragon vinegar may be added to give an additional flavour.

Time.—Altogether 4½ hours.

Average cost for this quantity, 4*s*.

Béchamel, or French White Sauce*

INGREDIENTS.—1 small bunch of parsley, 2 cloves, ½ bay-leaf, 1 small faggot of savoury herbs, salt to taste; 3 or 4 mushrooms, when obtainable; 2 pints of white stock,* 1 pint of cream, 1 tablespoonful of arrowroot.

Mode.—Put the stock into a stewpan, with the parsley, cloves, bay-leaf, herbs, and mushrooms; add a seasoning of salt, but no pepper, as that would give the sauce a dusty appearance, and should be avoided. When it has boiled long enough to extract the flavour of the herbs, &c., strain it, and boil it up quickly again, until it is nearly half-reduced. Now mix the arrowroot smoothly with the cream, and let it simmer very gently for 5 minutes over a slow fire; pour to it the reduced stock, and continue to simmer slowly for 10 minutes, if the sauce be thick. If, on the contrary, it be too thin, it must be stirred over a sharp fire till it thickens. This is the foundation of many kinds of sauces, especially white sauces. Always make it thick, as you can easily thin it with cream, milk, or white stock.

Time.—Altogether, 2 hours.   *Average cost*, 1s. per pint.

Bread Sauce (to serve with Roast Turkey, Fowl, Game, &c.)

INGREDIENTS.—1 pint of milk, ¾ lb. of the crumb of a stale loaf, 1 onion; pounded mace, cayenne, and salt to taste; 1 oz. of butter.

Mode.—Peel and quarter the onion, and simmer it in the milk till perfectly tender. Break the bread, which should be stale, into small pieces, carefully picking out any hard outside pieces; put it in a very clean saucepan, strain the milk over it, cover it up, and let it remain for an hour to soak. Now beat it up with a fork very smoothly, add a seasoning of pounded mace, cayenne, and salt, with 1 oz. of butter; give the whole one boil, and serve. To enrich this sauce, a small quantity of cream may be added just before sending it to table.

Mace

Time.—Altogether, 1¾ hour.

Average cost for this quantity, 4d.

Sufficient to serve with a turkey, pair of fowls, or brace of partridges.

MACE.—This is the membrane which surrounds the shell of the nutmeg. Its general qualities are the same as those of the nutmeg, producing an agreeable aromatic odour, with a hot and acrid taste. It is of an oleaginous nature, is yellowish in its hue, and is used largely as a condiment. In 'Beeton's Dictionary'* we find that the four largest of the Banda Islands produce 150,000 lbs. of it annually, which, with nutmegs, are their principal articles of export.

Beurre Noir, or Browned Butter (a French Sauce)

INGREDIENTS.—¼ lb. of butter, 1 tablespoonful of minced parsley, 3 tablespoonfuls of vinegar, salt and pepper to taste.

Mode.—Put the butter into a frying-pan over a nice clear fire, and when it smokes, throw in the parsley, and add the vinegar and seasoning. Let the whole simmer for a minute or two, when it is ready to serve. This is a very good sauce for skate.

Time.—¼ hour.

Caper Sauce for Boiled Mutton

INGREDIENTS.—½ pint of melted butter,* 3 tablespoonfuls of capers or nasturtiums, 1 tablespoonful of their liquor.

Mode.—Chop the capers twice or thrice, and add them, with their liquor, to ½ pint of melted butter, made very smoothly; keep stirring well; let the sauce just simmer, and serve in a tureen. Pickled nasturtium-pods are fine-flavoured, and by many are eaten in preference to capers. They make an excellent sauce.

Time.—2 minutes to simmer.   *Average cost* for this quantity, 8*d*.

Sufficient to serve with a leg of mutton.

Chestnut Sauce for Fowls or Turkey

INGREDIENTS.—½ lb. of chestnuts, ½ pint of white stock, 2 strips of lemon-peel, cayenne to taste, ¼ pint of cream or milk.

Mode.—Peel off the outside skin of the chestnuts, and put them into boiling water for a few minutes; take off the thin inside peel, and put them into a saucepan, with the white stock and lemon-peel, and let them simmer for 1½ hour, or until the chestnuts are quite tender. Rub the whole through a hair-sieve with a wooden spoon; add seasoning and the cream; let it just simmer, but not boil, and keep stirring all the time. Serve very hot, and quickly. If milk is used instead of cream, a very small quantity of thickening may be required: that, of course, the cook will determine.

Time.—Altogether nearly two hours.   *Average cost*, 8*d.*
Sufficient, this quantity, for a turkey.

Bengal Recipe for Making Mango Chetney*

INGREDIENTS.—1½ lbs. of moist sugar, ¾ lb. of salt, ¼ lb. of garlic, ¼ lb. of onions, ¾ lb. of powdered ginger, ¼ lb. of dried chilies, ¾ lb. of mustard-seed, ¾ lb. of stoned raisins, 2 bottles of best vinegar, 30 large unripe sour apples.

Mode.—The sugar must be made into syrup; the garlic, onions, and ginger be finely pounded in a mortar; the mustard-seed be washed in cold vinegar, and dried in the sun; the apples be peeled, cored, and sliced, and boiled in a bottle, and a half of the vinegar. When all this is done, and the apples are quite cold, put them into a large pan, and gradually mix the whole of the rest of the ingredients, including the remaining half-bottle of vinegar. It must be well stirred until the whole is thoroughly blended, and then put into bottles for use. Tie a piece of wet bladder over the mouths of the bottles, after they are well corked. This chetney is very superior to any which can be bought, and one trial will prove it to be delicious.

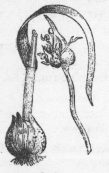

Garlic

Note.—This recipe was given by a native to an English lady, who had long been a resident in India, and who, since her return to her native country, has become quite celebrated amongst her friends for the excellence of this Eastern relish.

GARLIC.—The smell of this plant is generally considered offensive, and it is the most acrimonious in its taste of the whole of the alliaceous tribe. In 1548 it was introduced to England from the shores of the Mediterranean, where it is abundant, and in Sicily it grows naturally. It was in greater repute with our ancestors than it is with ourselves, although it is still used as a seasoning herb. On the continent, especially in Italy, it is much used, and the French consider it an essential in many made dishes.

Chili Vinegar*

INGREDIENTS.—50 fresh red English chilies, 1 pint of vinegar.

Mode.—Pound or cut the chilies in half, and infuse them in the vinegar for a fortnight, when it will be fit for use. This will be found an agreeable relish to fish, as many people cannot eat it without the addition of an acid and cayenne pepper.

An Excellent Way of Preserving Cucumbers*

INGREDIENTS.—Salt and water; 1 lb. of lump sugar, the rind of 1 lemon, 1 oz. of ginger, cucumbers.

Mode.—Choose the greenest cucumbers, and those that are most free from seeds; put them in strong salt and water, with a cabbage-leaf to keep them down; tie a paper over them, and put them in a warm place till they are yellow; then wash them and set them over the fire in fresh water, with a very little salt, and another cabbage-leaf over them; cover very closely, but take care they do not boil. If they are not a fine green, change the water again, cover them as before, and make them hot. When they are a good colour, take them off the fire and let them cool; cut them in quarters, take out the seeds and pulp, and put them into cold water. Let them remain for 2 days, changing the water twice each day, to draw out the salt. Put the sugar, with ½ pint of water, in a saucepan over the fire; remove the scum as it rises, and add the lemon-peel and ginger with the outside scraped off; when the syrup is tolerably thick, take it off the fire, and when *cold*, wipe the cucumbers *dry*, and put them in. Boil the syrup once in 2 or 3 days for 3 weeks; strengthen it if required, and let it be quite cold before the cucumbers are put in. Great attention must be paid to the directions in the commencement of this recipe, as, if these are not properly carried out, the result will be far from satisfactory.

Seasonable.—This recipe should be used in June, July, or August.

COMMON SALT.—By this we mean salt used for cooking purposes, which is found in great abundance both on land and in the waters of the ocean. Sea or salt water, as it is often called, contains, it has been discovered, about three per cent of salt on an average. Solid rocks of salt are also found in various parts of the world, and the county of Chester contains many of these mines, and it is from there that much of our salt comes. Some springs are so highly impregnated with salt, as to have received the name of 'brine' springs, and are supposed to have become so by passing through the salt rocks below ground, and thus dissolving a portion of this mineral substance. [There is a] salt-mine at Northwich, Cheshire, where both salt-mines and brine-springs are exceedingly productive, and are believed to have been wrought so far back as during the occupation of Britain by the Romans.

Custard Sauce for Sweet Puddings or Tarts

INGREDIENTS.—1 pint of milk, 2 eggs, 3 oz. of pounded sugar, 1 tablespoonful of brandy.

Mode.—Put the milk in a very clean saucepan, and let it boil. Beat the eggs, stir to them the milk and pounded sugar, and put the mixture into a jug. Place the jug in a saucepan of boiling water; keep stirring well until it thickens, but do not allow it to boil, or it will curdle. Serve the sauce in a tureen, stir in the brandy, and grate a little nutmeg over the top. This sauce may be made very much nicer by using cream instead of milk; but the above recipe will be found quite good enough for ordinary purposes.

Average cost, 6*d*. per pint.

Sufficient, this quantity, for 2 fruit tarts, or 1 pudding.

Dutch Sauce for Fish*

INGREDIENTS.—½ teaspoonful of flour, 2 oz. of butter, 4 table-spoonfuls of vinegar, the yolks of 2 eggs, the juice of ½ lemon; salt to taste.

Mode.—Put all the ingredients, except the lemon-juice, into a stewpan; set it over the fire, and keep continually stirring. When it is sufficiently thick, take it off, as it should not boil. If, however, it happens to curdle, strain the sauce through a tammy, add the lemon-juice, and serve. Tarragon vinegar may be used instead of plain, and, by many, is considered far preferable.

Average cost, 6*d*.

Note.—This sauce may be poured hot over salad and left to get quite cold, when it should be thick, smooth, and somewhat stiff. Excellent salads may be made of hard eggs, or the remains of salt fish flaked nicely from the bone, by pouring over a little of the above mixture when hot, and allowing it to cool.

THE LEMON.—This fruit is a native of Asia, and is mentioned by Virgil as an antidote to poison. It is hardier than the orange, and, as one of the citron tribe, was brought into Europe by the Arabians. The lemon was first cultivated in England in the beginning of the 17th century, and is now often to be found in

The Lemon

our greenhouses. The kind commonly sold, however, is imported from Portugal, Spain, and the Azores. Some also come from St Helena; but those from Spain are esteemed the best. Its juice is now an essential for culinary purposes; but as an antiscorbutic its value is still greater. This juice, which is called *citric acid*, may be preserved in bottles for a considerable time, by covering it with a thin stratum of oil. *Shrub* is made from it with rum and sugar.

To Pickle Eggs

INGREDIENTS.—16 eggs, 1 quart of vinegar, ½ oz. of black pepper, ½ oz. of Jamaica pepper, ½ oz. of ginger.

Mode.—Boil the eggs for 12 minutes, then dip them into cold water, and take off the shells. Put the vinegar, with the pepper and ginger, into a stewpan, and let it simmer for 10 minutes. Now place the eggs in a jar, pour over them the vinegar, &c, boiling hot, and, when cold, tie them down with bladder to exclude the air. This pickle will be ready for use in a month.

Average cost, for this quantity, 1s. 9d.

Seasonable.—This should be made about Easter, as at this time eggs are plentiful and cheap. A store of pickled eggs will be found very useful and ornamental in serving with many first and second course dishes.

Egg Sauce for Salt Fish

INGREDIENTS.—4 eggs, ½ pint of melted butter; when liked, a very little lemon-juice.

Mode.—Boil the eggs until quite hard, which will be in about 20 minutes, and put them into cold water for ½ hour. Strip off the shells, chop the eggs into small pieces, not, however, too fine. Make the melted butter very smoothly,* and, when boiling, stir in the eggs, and serve very hot. Lemon-juice may be added at pleasure.

Time.—20 minutes to boil the eggs.   *Average cost*, 8d.

Sufficient.—This quantity for 3 or 4 lbs. of fish.

Note.—When a thicker sauce is required, use one or two more eggs to the same quantity of melted butter.

Espagnole, or Brown Spanish Sauce

INGREDIENTS.—2 slices of lean ham, 1 lb. of veal, 1½ pint of white stock; 2 or 3 sprigs of parsley, ½ a bay-leaf, 2 or 3 sprigs of savoury herbs, 6 green onions, 3 shalots, 2 cloves, 1 blade of mace, 2 glasses of sherry or Madeira, thickening of butter and flour.

Mode.—Cut up the ham and veal into small square pieces, and put them into a stewpan. Moisten these with ½ pint of the stock, and simmer till the bottom of the stewpan is covered with a nicely-coloured glaze, when put in a few more spoonfuls to detach it. Add the remainder of the stock, with the spices, herbs, shalots, and onions, and simmer very gently for 1 hour. Strain and skim off every particle of fat, and when required for use, thicken with butter and flour, or with a little roux. Add the wine, and, if necessary, a seasoning of cayenne; when it will be ready to serve.

Time.—1½ hour.   *Average cost*, 2s. per pint.

Note.—The wine in this sauce may be omitted, and an onion sliced and fried of a nice brown substituted for it. This sauce or gravy is used for many dishes, and with most people is a general favourite.

Forcemeat Balls for Fish Soups*

INGREDIENTS.—1 middling-sized lobster, ½ an anchovy, 1 head of boiled celery, the yolk of a hard-boiled egg; salt, cayenne, and mace to taste; 4 tablespoonfuls of bread crumbs, 2 oz. of butter, 2 eggs.

Mode.—Pick the meat from the shell of the lobster, and pound it, with the soft parts, in a mortar; add the celery, the yolk of the hard-boiled egg, seasoning, and bread crumbs. Continue pounding till the whole is nicely amalgamated. Warm the butter till it is in a liquid state; well whisk the eggs, and work these up with the pounded lobster-meat. Make into balls of about an inch in diameter, and fry of a nice pale brown.

Sufficient, from 18 to 20 balls for 1 tureen of soup.

Forcemeat for Veal, Turkeys, Fowls, Hare, &c.

INGREDIENTS.—2 oz. of ham or lean bacon, ¼ lb. of suet, the rind of half a lemon, 1 teaspoonful of minced parsley, 1 teaspoonful of minced sweet herbs; salt, cayenne, and pounded mace to taste; 6 oz. of bread crumbs, 2 eggs.

Mode.—Shred the ham or bacon, chop the suet, lemon-peel, and herbs, taking particular care that all be very finely minced; add a seasoning to taste, of salt, cayenne, and mace, and blend all thoroughly together with the bread crumbs, before wetting. Now beat and strain the eggs, work these up with the other ingredients, and the forcemeat will be ready for use. When it is made into balls, fry of a nice brown, in boiling lard, or put them on a tin and bake for ½ hour in a moderate oven. As we have stated before, no one flavour should predominate greatly, and the forcemeat should be of sufficient body to cut with a knife, and yet not dry and heavy. For very delicate forcemeat, it is advisable to pound the ingredients together before binding with the egg; but for ordinary cooking, mincing very finely answers the purpose.

Average cost, 8*d.*

Sufficient for a turkey, a moderate-sized fillet of veal, or a hare.

Note.—In forcemeat for HARE, the liver of the animal is sometimes added. Boil for 5 minutes, mince it very small, and mix it with the other ingredients. If it should be in an unsound state, it must be on no account made use of.

SWEET HERBS.—Those most usually employed for purposes of cooking, such as the flavouring of soups, sauces, forcemeats, &c., are thyme, sage, mint, marjoram, savory, and basil. Other sweet herbs are cultivated for purposes of medicine and perfumery: they are most grateful both to the organs of taste and smelling; and to the aroma derived from them is due, in a great measure, the sweet and exhilarating fragrance of our 'flowery meads.' In town, sweet herbs have to be procured at the green-

Basil

grocers' or herbalists', whilst, in the country, the garden should furnish all that are wanted, the cook taking great care to have some dried in the autumn for her use throughout the winter months.

Pickled Gherkins

INGREDIENTS.—Salt and water, 1 oz. of bruised ginger, ½ oz of whole black pepper, ¼ oz. of whole allspice, 4 cloves, 2 blades of mace, a little horseradish. This proportion of pepper, spices, &c., for 1 quart of vinegar.

Mode.—Let the gherkins remain in salt and water for 3 or 4 days, when take them out, wipe perfectly dry, and put them into a stone jar. Boil sufficient vinegar to cover them, with spices and pepper, &c., in the above proportion, for 10 minutes; pour it, quite boiling, over the gherkins, cover the jar with vine-leaves, and put over them a plate, setting them near the fire, where they must remain all night. Next day drain off the vinegar, boil it up again, and pour it hot over them. Cover up with fresh leaves, and let the whole remain till quite cold. Now tie down closely with bladder to exclude the air, and in a month or two, they will be fit for use.

Time.—4 days.

Seasonable from the middle of July to the end of August.

GHERKINS.—Gherkins are young cucumbers; and the only way in which they are used for cooking purposes is pickling them, as by the recipe here given. Not having arrived at maturity, they have not, of course, so strongly a developed flavour as cucumbers, and, as a pickle, they are very general favourites.

Gherkins

Gooseberry Sauce for Boiled Mackerel

INGREDIENTS.—1 pint of green gooseberries, 3 tablespoonfuls of Béchamel, p. 122 (veal gravy may be substituted for this), 2 oz. of fresh butter; seasoning to taste of salt, pepper, and grated nutmeg.

Mode.—Boil the gooseberries in water until quite tender; strain them, and rub them through a sieve. Put into a saucepan the Béchamel or gravy, with the butter and seasoning; add the pulp from the gooseberries, mix all well together, and heat gradually through. A little pounded sugar added to this sauce is by many persons considered an improvement, as the saccharine matter takes off the extreme acidity of the unripe fruit.

Time.—Boil the gooseberries from 20 minutes to ½ hour.

Sufficient, this quantity, for a large dish of mackerel.

Seasonable from May to July.

General Stock for Gravies

Either of the stocks [rich strong stock, medium stock, white stock]* will be found to answer very well for the basis of many gravies, unless these are wanted very rich indeed. By the addition of various store sauces, thickening and flavouring, the stocks here referred to may be converted into very good gravies. It should be borne in mind, however, that the goodness and strength of spices, wines, flavourings, &c., evaporate, and that they lose a great deal of their fragrance, if added to the gravy a long time before they are wanted. If this point is attended to, a saving of one half the quantity of these ingredients will be effected, as, with long boiling, the flavour almost entirely passes away. The shank-bones of mutton, previously well soaked, will be found a great assistance in enriching gravies; a kidney or melt, beef skirt, trimmings of meat, &c. &c., answer very well when only a small quantity is wanted, and, as we have before observed, a good gravy need not necessarily be so very expensive; for economically-prepared dishes are oftentimes found as savoury and wholesome as dearer ones. The cook should also remember that the fragrance of gravies should not be overpowered by too much spice, or any strong essences, and that they should always be warmed in a *bain-marie*, after they are flavoured, or else in a jar or jug placed in a saucepan full of boiling water. The remains of roast-meat gravy should always be saved; as, when no meat is at hand, a very nice gravy in haste may be made from it, and when added to hashes, ragoûts, &c., is a great improvement.

GRAVY-KETTLE.—This is a utensil which will not be found in every kitchen; but it is a useful one where it is necessary to keep gravies hot for the purpose of pouring over various

Gravy-Kettle

dishes as they are cooking. It is made of copper, and should, consequently, be heated over the hot plate, if there be one, or a charcoal stove. The price at which it can be purchased is set down by Messrs Slack at 14*s*.

A Good Beef Gravy for Poultry, Game, &c.

INGREDIENTS.—½ lb. of lean beef, ½ pint of cold water, 1 shalot or small onion, ½ a teaspoonful of salt, a little pepper, 1 tablespoonful of Harvey's sauce or mushroom ketchup, ½ a teaspoonful of arrowroot.

Mode.—Cut up the beef into small pieces, and put it, with the water, into a stewpan. Add the shalot and seasoning, and simmer gently for 3 hours, taking care that it does not boil fast. A short time before it is required, take the arrowroot, and having mixed it with a little cold water, pour it into the gravy, which keep stirring, adding the Harvey's sauce, and just letting it boil. Strain off the gravy in a tureen, and serve very hot.

Time.—3 hours.   *Average cost*, 8*d*. per pint.

Horseradish Sauce, to serve with Roast Beef

INGREDIENTS.—4 tablespoonfuls of grated horseradish, 1 teaspoonful of pounded sugar, 1 teaspoonful of salt, ½ teaspoonful of pepper, 2 teaspoonfuls of made mustard; vinegar.

Mode.—Grate the horseradish, and mix it well with the sugar, salt, pepper, and mustard; moisten it with sufficient vinegar to give it the consistency of cream, and serve in a tureen: 3 or 4 tablespoonfuls of cream added to the above, very much improve the appearance and flavour of this sauce. To heat it to serve with hot roast beef, put it in a bain-marie or a jar, which place in a saucepan of boiling water; make it hot, but do not allow it to boil, or it will curdle.

Note.—This sauce is a great improvement on the old-fashioned way of serving cold-scraped horseradish with hot roast beef. The mixing of the cold vinegar with the warm gravy cools and spoils everything on the plate. Of course, with cold meat, the sauce should be served cold.

The Horseradish

THE HORSERADISH.—This has been, for many years, a favourite accompaniment of roast beef, and is a native of England. It grows wild in wet ground, but has long been cultivated in the garden, and is, occasionally, used in winter salads and in sauces. On account of the great volatility of its oil, it should never be preserved by drying, but should be kept moist by being buried in sand. So rapidly does its volatile oil evaporate, that even when scraped for the table, it almost immediately spoils by exposure to the air.

Indian Curry-Powder, founded on Dr Kitchener's* Recipe

INGREDIENTS.—¼ lb. of coriander-seed, ¼ lb. of turmeric, 2 oz. of cinnamon-seed, ½ oz. of cayenne, 1 oz. of mustard, 1 oz. of ground ginger, ½ ounce of allspice, 2 oz. of fenugreek-seed.

Mode.—Put all the ingredients in a cool oven, where they should remain one night; then pound them in a mortar, rub them through a sieve, and mix thoroughly together; keep the powder in a bottle, from which the air should be completely excluded.

Note.—We have given this recipe for curry-powder, as some persons prefer to make it at home; but that purchased at any respectable shop is, generally speaking, far superior, and, taking all things into consideration, very frequently more economical.

To Pickle Lemons with the Peel on*

INGREDIENTS.—6 lemons, 2 quarts of boiling water; to each quart of vinegar allow ½ oz. of cloves, ½ oz. of white pepper, 1 oz. of bruised ginger, ¼ oz. of mace and chilies, 1 oz. of mustard-seed, ½ stick of sliced horseradish, a few cloves of garlic.

Mode.—Put the lemons into a brine that will bear an egg; let them remain in it 6 days, stirring them every day; have ready 2 quarts of boiling water, put in the lemons, and allow them to boil for ¼ hour; take them out, and let them lie in a cloth until perfectly dry and cold. Boil up sufficient vinegar to cover the lemons, with all the above ingredients, allowing the same proportion as stated to each quart of vinegar. Pack the lemons in a jar, pour over the vinegar, &c. boiling hot, and tie down with a bladder. They will be fit for use in about 12 months, or rather sooner.

Seasonable.—This should be made from November to April.

Liver and Lemon Sauce for Poultry*

INGREDIENTS.—The liver of a fowl, one lemon, salt to taste, ½ pint of melted butter.

Mode.—Wash the liver, and let it boil for a few minutes; peel the lemon very thin, remove the white part and pips, and cut it into very small dice; mince the liver and a small quantity of the lemon rind very fine; add these ingredients to ½ pint of smoothly-made melted butter; season with a little salt, put in the cut lemon, heat it gradually, but do not allow it to boil, lest the butter should oil.

Time.—1 minute to simmer.

Sufficient to serve with a pair of small fowls.

Maître d'Hôtel Butter, for putting into Broiled Fish
just before it is sent to Table

INGREDIENTS.—¼ lb. of butter, 2 dessertspoonfuls of minced parsley, salt and pepper to taste, the juice of 1 large lemon.

Mode.—Work the above ingredients well together, and let them be thoroughly mixed with a wooden spoon. If this is used as a sauce, it may be poured either under or over the meat or fish it is intended to be served with.

Average cost, for this quantity, 5*d.*

Note.—4 tablespoonfuls of Béchamel, 2 do. of white stock, with 2 oz. of the above maître d'hôtel butter stirred into it, and just allowed to simmer for 1 minute, will be found an excellent hot maître d'hôtel sauce.

THE MAÎTRE D'HÔTEL.—The house-steward of England is synonymous with the maître d'hôtel of France; and, in ancient times, amongst the Latins, he was called procurator, or major-domo. In Rome, the slaves, after they had procured the various articles necessary for the repasts of the day, would return to the spacious kitchen laden with meat, game, sea-fish, vegetables, fruit, &c. Each one would then lay his basket at the feet of the major-domo, who would examine its contents and register them on his tablets, placing in the pantry contiguous to the dining-room, those of the provisions which need no preparation, and consigning the others to the more immediate care of the cooks.

Mayonnaise,* a Sauce or Salad-Dressing for cold
Chicken, Meat, and other cold Dishes

INGREDIENTS.—The yolks of 2 eggs, 6 tablespoonfuls of salad-oil, 4 tablespoonfuls of vinegar, salt and white pepper to taste, 1 tablespoonful of white stock, 2 tablespoonfuls of cream.

Mode.—Put the yolks of the eggs into a basin, with a seasoning of pepper and salt; have ready the above quantities of oil and vinegar, in separate vessels; add them *very gradually* to the eggs; continue stirring and rubbing the mixture with a wooden spoon, as herein consists the secret of having a nice smooth sauce. It cannot be stirred too frequently, and it should be made in a very cool place, or, if ice is at hand, it should be mixed over it. When the vinegar and oil are well incorporated with the eggs, add the stock and cream, stirring all the time, and it will then be ready for use.

For a fish Mayonnaise, this sauce may be coloured with lobster-spawn, pounded; and for poultry or meat, where variety is desired, a little parsley-juice may be used to add to its appearance. Cucumber, Tarragon, or any other flavoured vinegar, may be substituted for plain, where they are liked.

Average cost, for this quantity, 7*d*.

Sufficient for a small salad.

Note.—In mixing the oil and vinegar with the eggs, put in first a few drops of oil, and then a few drops of vinegar, never adding a large quantity of either at one time. By this means, you can be more certain of the sauce not curdling. Patience and practice, let us add, are two essentials for making this sauce good.

Mint Sauce, to serve with Roast Lamb

INGREDIENTS.—4 dessertspoonfuls of chopped mint, 2 dessert-spoonfuls of pounded white sugar, ¼ pint of vinegar.

Mode.—Wash the mint, which should be young and fresh-gathered, free from grit; pick the leaves from the stalks, mince them very fine, and put them into a tureen; add the sugar and vinegar, and stir till the former is dissolved. This sauce is better by being made 2 or 3 hours before wanted for table, as the vinegar then becomes impregnated with the flavour of the mint. By many persons, the above proportion of sugar would not be considered sufficient; but as tastes vary, we have given the quantity which we have found to suit the general palate.

Average cost, 3*d*.

Sufficient to serve with a middling-sized joint of lamb.

Note.—Where green mint is scarce and not obtainable, mint vinegar may be substituted for it, and will be found very acceptable in early spring.

Mint

MINT.—The common mint cultivated in our gardens is known as the *Mentha viridis*, and is employed in different culinary processes, being sometimes boiled with certain dishes, and afterwards withdrawn. It has an agreeable aromatic flavour, and forms an ingredient in soups, and sometimes is used in spring salads. It is valuable as a stomachic and antispasmodic; on which account it is generally served at table with pea-soup. Several of its species grow wild in low situations in the country.

Mushroom Ketchup*

INGREDIENTS.—To each peck of mushrooms ½ lb. of salt; to each quart of mushroom-liquor ¼ oz. of cayenne, ½ oz. of allspice, ½ oz. of ginger, 2 blades of pounded mace.

Mode.—Choose full-grown mushroom-flaps, and take care they are perfectly *fresh-gathered* when the weather is tolerably dry; for, if they are picked during very heavy rain, the ketchup from which they are made is liable to get musty, and will not keep long. Put a layer of them in a deep pan, sprinkle salt over them, and then another layer of mushrooms, and so on alternately. Let them remain for a few hours, when break them up with the hand; put them in a nice cool place for 3 days, occasionally stirring and mashing them well, to extract from them as much juice as possible. Now measure the quantity of liquor without straining, and to each quart allow the above proportion of spices, &c. Put all into a stone jar, cover it up very closely, put it in a saucepan of boiling water, set it over the fire, and let it boil for 3 hours. Have ready a nice clean stewpan; turn into it the contents of the jar, and let the whole simmer very gently for ½ hour; pour it into a jug, where it should stand in a cool place till the next day; then pour it off into another jug, and strain it into very dry clean bottles, and do not squeeze the mushrooms. To each pint of ketchup add a few drops of brandy. Be careful not to shake the contents, but leave all the sediment behind in the jug; cork well, and either seal or rosin the cork, so as perfectly to exclude the air. When a very clear bright ketchup is wanted, the liquor must be strained through a very fine hair-sieve, or flannel bag, *after* it has been very gently poured off; if the operation is not successful, it must be repeated until you have quite a clear liquor. It should be examined occasionally, and if it is spoiling, should be reboiled with a few peppercorns.

Seasonable from the beginning of September to the middle of October, when this ketchup should be made.

Note.—This flavouring ingredient, if genuine and well prepared, is one of the most useful store sauces to the experienced cook, and no trouble should be spared in its preparation. Double ketchup is made by reducing the liquor to half the quantity; for example, 1 quart must be boiled down to 1 pint. This goes farther than ordinary ketchup, as so little is required to flavour a good quantity of gravy. The sediment may also be bottled for immediate use, and will be found to answer for flavouring thick soups or gravies.

HOW TO DISTINGUISH MUSHROOMS FROM TOADSTOOLS.—The cultivated mushroom, known as *Agaricus campestris*, may be distinguished from other poisonous kinds of fungi by its having pink or flesh-coloured gills, or under-side, and by its invariably having an agreeable smell, which the toadstool has not. When young, mushrooms are like a small round button, both the stalk and head being white. As they grow larger, they expand their heads by degrees into a flat form, the gills underneath being at first of a pale flesh-colour, but becoming, as they stand longer, dark brown or blackish. Nearly all the poisonous kinds are brown, and have in general a rank and putrid smell. Edible mushrooms are found in closely-fed pastures, but seldom grow in woods, where most of the poisonous sorts are to be found.

Pickled Onions (a very Simple Method, and exceedingly Good)

INGREDIENTS.—Pickling onions; to each quart of vinegar, 2 teaspoonfuls of allspice, 2 teaspoonfuls of whole black pepper.

Mode.—Have the onions gathered when quite dry and ripe, and, with the fingers, take off the thin outside skin; then, with a silver knife (steel should not be used, as it spoils the colour of the onions), remove one more skin, when the onion will look quite clear. Have ready some very dry bottles or jars, and as fast as they are peeled, put them in. Pour over sufficient cold vinegar to cover them, with pepper and allspice in the above proportions, taking care that each jar has its share of the latter ingredients. Tie down with bladder, and put them in a dry place, and in a fortnight they will be fit for use. This is a most simple recipe and very delicious, the onions being nice and crisp. They should be eaten within 6 or 8 months after being done, as the onions are liable to become soft.

Seasonable from the middle of July to the end of August.

Oyster Ketchup

INGREDIENTS.—Sufficient oysters to fill a pint measure, 1 pint of sherry, 3 oz. of salt, 1 drachm of cayenne, 2 drachms of pounded mace.

Mode.—Procure the oysters very fresh, and open sufficient to fill a pint measure; save the liquor, and scald the oysters in it with the sherry; strain the oysters, and put them in a mortar with the salt, cayenne, and mace; pound the whole until reduced to a pulp, then add it to the liquor in which they were scalded; boil it again five minutes, and skim well; rub the whole through a sieve, and, when cold, bottle and cork closely. The corks should be sealed.

Seasonable from September to April.

Note.—Cider may be substituted for the sherry.

Plum-Pudding Sauce*

INGREDIENTS.—1 wineglassful of brandy, 2 oz. of very fresh butter, 1 glass of Madeira, pounded sugar to taste.

Mode.—Put the pounded sugar in a basin, with part of the brandy and the butter; let it stand by the side of the fire until it is warm and the sugar and butter are dissolved; then add the rest of the brandy, with the Madeira. Either pour it over the pudding, or serve in a tureen. This is a very rich and excellent sauce.

Average cost, 1s. 3d. for this quantity.

Sufficient for a pudding made for 6 persons.

Sage-and-Onion Stuffing, for Geese, Ducks, and Pork

INGREDIENTS.—4 large onions, 10 sage-leaves, ¼ lb. of bread crumbs, 1½ oz. of butter, salt and pepper to taste, 1 egg.

Mode.—Peel the onions, put them into boiling water, let them simmer for 5 minutes or rather longer, and, just before they are taken out, put in the sage-leaves for a minute or two to take off their rawness. Chop both these very fine, add the bread, seasoning, and butter, and work the whole together with the yolk of an egg, when the stuffing will be ready for use. It should be rather highly seasoned, and the sage-leaves should be very finely chopped. Many cooks do not parboil the onions in the manner just stated, but merely use them raw. The stuffing then, however, is not nearly so mild, and, to many tastes, its strong flavour would be very objectionable. When made for goose, a portion of the liver of the bird, simmered for a few minutes and very finely minced, is frequently added to this stuffing; and where economy is studied, the egg may be dispensed with.

Time.—Rather more than 5 minutes to simmer the onions.

Average cost, for this quantity, 4*d*.

Sufficient for 1 goose, or a pair of ducks.

SOYER'S RECIPE FOR GOOSE STUFFING.—Take 4 apples, peeled and cored, 4 onions, 4 leaves of sage, and 4 leaves of lemon thyme not broken, and boil them in a stewpan with sufficient water to cover them; when done, pulp them through a sieve, removing the sage and thyme; then add sufficient pulp of mealy potatoes to cause it to be sufficiently dry without sticking to the hand; add pepper and salt, and stuff the bird.

Salad Dressing (Excellent)*

INGREDIENTS.—4 eggs, 1 teaspoonful of mixed mustard, ¼ tea-spoonful of white pepper, half that quantity of cayenne, salt to taste, 4 tablespoonfuls of cream, vinegar.

Mode.—Boil the eggs until hard, which will be in about ¼ hour or 20 minutes; put them into cold water, take off the shells, and pound the yolks in a mortar to a smooth paste. Then add all the other ingredients, except the vinegar, and stir them well until the whole are thoroughly incorporated one with the other. Pour in sufficient vinegar to make it of the consistency of cream, taking care to add but little at a time. The mixture will then be ready for use.

Average cost, for this quantity, 7*d*.

Sufficient for a moderate-sized salad.

Note.—The whites of the eggs, cut into rings, will serve very well as a garnishing to the salad.

THE OLIVE AND OLIVE OIL.—This tree assumes a high degree of interest from the historical circumstances with which it is connected. A leaf of it was brought into the ark by the dove, when that vessel was still floating on the waters of the great deep, and gave the first token that the deluge was sub-siding. Among the Greeks, the prize of the victor in the Olympic games was a wreath of wild olive; and the 'Mount of Olives' is rendered familiar to our ears by its being

The Olive

mentioned in the Scriptures as near to Jerusalem. The tree is indigenous in the north of Africa, Syria, and Greece; and the Romans introduced it to Italy. In Spain and the south of France it is now cultivated; and although it grows in England, its fruit does not ripen in the open air. Both in Greece and Portugal the fruit is eaten in its ripe state; but its taste is not agreeable to many palates. To the Italian shepherd, bread and olives, with a little wine, form a nourishing diet; but in England, olives are usually only introduced by way of dessert, to destroy the taste of the viands which have been previously eaten, that the flavour of the wine may be the better enjoyed. There are three kinds of olives imported to London,—the French, Spanish, and Italian: the first are from Provence, and are generally accounted excellent; the second are larger, but more bitter; and the last are from Lucca, and are esteemed the best. The oil extracted from olives, called olive oil, or salad oil, is, with the continentals, in continual request, more dishes being prepared with than without it, we should imagine. With us, it is principally used in mixing a salad, and when thus employed, it tends to prevent fermentation, and is an antidote against flatulency.

Sauce Aristocratique (a Store Sauce)

INGREDIENTS.—Green walnuts. To every pint of juice, 1 lb. of anchovies, 1 drachm of cloves, 1 drachm of mace, 1 drachm of Jamaica ginger bruised, 8 shalots. To every pint of the boiled liquor, ½ pint of vinegar, ¼ pint of port wine, 2 tablespoonfuls of soy.

Mode.—Pound the walnuts in a mortar, squeeze out the juice through a strainer, and let it stand to settle. Pour off the clear juice, and to every pint of it, add anchovies, spices, and cloves in the above proportion. Boil all these together till the anchovies are dissolved, then strain the juice again, put in the shalots (8 to every pint), and boil again. To every pint of the boiled liquor add vinegar, wine, and soy, in the above quantities, and bottle off for use. Cork well, and seal the corks.

Seasonable.—Make this sauce from the beginning to the middle of July, when walnuts are in perfection for sauces and pickling.

Average cost, 3s 6d. for a quart.

MANUFACTURE OF SAUCES.—In France, during the reign of Louis XII., at the latter end of the 14th century, there was formed a company of sauce-manufacturers, who obtained, in those days of monopolies, the exclusive privilege of making sauces. The statutes drawn up by this company inform us that the famous sauce à la cameline, sold by them, was to be composed of 'good cinnamon, good ginger, good cloves, good grains of paradise, good bread, and good vinegar.' The sauce Tence, was to be made of 'good sound almonds, good ginger, good wine, and good verjuice.' May we respectfully express a hope—not that we desire to doubt it in the least—that the English sauce-manufacturers of the 19th century are equally considerate and careful in choosing their ingredients for their various well-known preparations.

A Good Sauce for Various Boiled Puddings

INGREDIENTS.—¼ lb. of butter, ¼ lb. of pounded sugar, a wine-glassful of brandy or rum.

Mode.—Beat the butter to a cream, until no lumps remain; add the pounded sugar, and brandy or rum; stir once or twice until the whole is thoroughly mixed, and serve. This sauce may either be poured round the pudding or served in a tureen, according to the taste or fancy of the cook or mistress.

Average cost, 8*d*. for this quantity.

Sufficient for a pudding.

Sauce Robert,* for Steaks, &c.

INGREDIENTS.—2 oz. of butter, 3 onions, 1 teaspoonful of flour, 4 tablespoonfuls of gravy, or stock, salt and pepper to taste, 1 teaspoonful of made mustard, 1 teaspoonful of vinegar, the juice of ½ lemon.

Mode.—Put the butter into a stewpan, set it on the fire, and, when browning, throw in the onions, which must be cut into small slices. Fry them brown, but do not burn them; add the flour, shake the onions in it, and give the whole another fry. Put in the gravy and seasoning, and boil it gently for 10 minutes; skim off the fat, add the mustard, vinegar, and lemon-juice; give it one boil, and pour round the steaks, or whatever dish the sauce has been prepared for.

Time.—Altogether ½ hour.   *Average cost*, for this quantity, 6*d*.

Seasonable at any time.

Sufficient for about 2 lbs. of steak.

Note.—This sauce will be found an excellent accompaniment to roast goose, pork, mutton cutlets, and various other dishes.

Sausage-Meat Stuffing, for Turkey

INGREDIENTS.—6 oz. of lean pork, 6 oz. of fat pork, both weighed after being chopped (beef suet may be substituted for the latter), 2 oz. of bread crumbs, 1 small tablespoonful of minced sage, 1 blade of pounded mace, salt and pepper to taste, 1 egg.

Mode.—Chop the meat and fat very finely, mix with them the other ingredients, taking care that the whole is thoroughly incorporated. Moisten with the egg, and the stuffing will be ready for use. Equal quantities of this stuffing and forcemeat (*see* p. 128) will be found to answer very well, as the herbs, lemon-peel, &c. in the latter, impart a very delicious flavour to the sausage-meat. As preparations, however, like stuffings and forcemeats, are matters to be decided by individual tastes, they must be left, to a great extent, to the discrimination of the cook, who should study her employer's taste in this, as in every other respect.

Average cost, 9d.

Sufficient for a small turkey.

Spinach Green for Colouring Various Dishes*

INGREDIENTS.—2 handfuls of spinach.

Mode.—Pick and wash the spinach free from dirt, and pound the leaves in a mortar to extract the juice; then press it through a hair sieve, and put the juice into a small stewpan or jar. Place this in a bainmarie, or saucepan of boiling water, and let it set. Watch it closely, as it should not boil; and, as soon as it is done, lay it in a sieve, so that all the water may drain from it, and the green will then be ready for colouring. If made according to this recipe, the spinach-green will be found far superior to that boiled in the ordinary way.

Store Sauce, or Cherokee*

INGREDIENTS.— ½ oz. of cayenne pepper, 5 cloves of garlic, [?] tablespoonfuls of soy, 1 tablespoonful of walnut ketchup, 1 pint of vinegar.

Mode.—Boil all the ingredients *gently* for about ½ hour; strain the liquor, and bottle off for use.

Time.— ½ hour.

Seasonable.—This sauce can be made at any time.

Universal Pickle

INGREDIENTS.—To 6 quarts of vinegar allow 1 lb. of salt, ¼ lb. of ginger, 1 oz. of mace, ½ lb. of shalots, 1 tablespoonful of cayenne, [½] oz. of mustard-seed, 1½ oz. of turmeric.

Mode.—Boil all the ingredients together for about 20 minutes; when cold, put them into a jar with whatever vegetables you choose, such as radish-pods, French beans, cauliflowers, gherkins, &c. &c., as these come into season; put them in fresh as you gather them, having previously wiped them perfectly free from moisture and grit. This pickle will be fit for use in about 8 or 9 months.

Time.—20 minutes.

Seasonable.—Make the pickle in May or June, to be ready for the various vegetables.

Note.—As this pickle takes 2 or 3 months to make,—that is to say, nearly that time will elapse before the different vegetables are added,—care must be taken to keep the jar which contains the pickle well covered, either with a closely-fitting lid, or a piece of bladder securely tied over, so as perfectly to exclude the air.

Pickled Walnuts* (Very Good)

INGREDIENTS.—100 walnuts, salt and water. To each quart of vinegar allow 2 oz. of whole black pepper, 1 oz. of allspice, 1 oz. of bruised ginger.

Mode.—Procure the walnuts while young; be careful they are not woody, and prick them well with a fork; prepare a strong brine of salt and water (4 lbs. of salt to each gallon of water), into which put the walnuts, letting them remain 9 days, and changing the brine every third day; drain them off, put them on a dish, place it in the sun until they become perfectly black, which will be in 2 or 3 days; have ready dry jars, into which place the walnuts, and do not quite fill the jars. Boil sufficient vinegar to cover them, for 10 minutes, with spices in the above proportion, and pour it hot over the walnuts, which must be quite covered with the pickle; tie down with bladder, and keep in a dry place. They will be fit for use in a month, and will keep good 2 or 3 years.

Time.—10 minutes.

Seasonable.—Make this from the beginning to the middle of July, before the walnuts harden.

Note.—When liked, a few shalots may be added to the vinegar, and boiled with it.

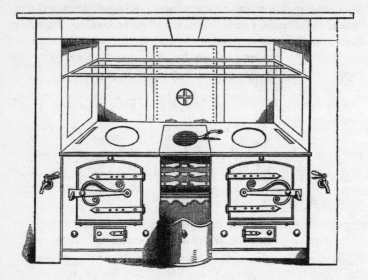

The Leamington Stove, or Kitchener

CHAPTER XI

VARIOUS MODES OF COOKING MEAT:
GENERAL REMARKS

In our 'Introduction to Cookery' (*see* p. 57) we have described the gradual progress of mankind in the art of cookery, the probability being, that the human race, for a long period, lived wholly on fruits. Man's means of attacking animals, even if he had the desire of slaughtering them, were very limited, until he acquired the use of arms. He, however, made weapons for himself, and, impelled by a carnivorous instinct, made prey of the animals that surrounded him. It is natural that man should seek to feed on flesh; he has too small a stomach to be supported alone by fruit, which has not sufficient nourishment to renovate him. It is possible he might subsist on vegetables; but their preparation needs the knowledge of art, only to be obtained after the lapse of many centuries. Man's first weapons were the branches of trees, which were succeeded by bows and arrows; and it is worthy of remark, that these latter weapons have been round with the natives of all climates and latitudes. It is singular how this idea presented itself to individuals so differently placed.

BRILLAT SAVARIN says, that raw flesh has but one inconvenience, —from its viscousness it attaches itself to the teeth. He goes on to say, that it is not, however, disagreeable; but, when seasoned with salt, that it is easily digested. He tells a story of a Croat captain, whom he invited to dinner in 1815, during the occupation of Paris by the allied troops. This officer was amazed at his host's preparations, and said, 'When we are campaigning, and get hungry, we knock over the first animal we find, cut off a steak, powder it with salt, which we always have in the sabretasche, put it under the saddle, gallop over it for half a mile, and then dine like princes.'* Again, of the huntsmen of Dauphiny it is said, that when they are out shooting in September, they take with them both pepper and salt. If they kill a very fat bird, they pluck and season it, and, after carrying it some time in their caps, eat it. This, they declare, is the best way of serving it up.

Subsequently to the Croat Mode, which, doubtless, was in fashion in the earlier ages of the world, fire was discovered. This was an accident; for fire is not, although we are accustomed to call it so, an element, or spontaneous. Many savage nations have been found utterly ignorant of it, and many races had no other way of dressing their food than by exposing it to the rays of the sun.

The inhabitants of the Marian Islands, which were discovered in 1521, had no idea of fire. Never was astonishment greater than theirs when they first saw it, on the descent of Magellan, the navigator, on one of their isles. At first they thought it a kind of animal, that fixed itself to and fed upon wood. Some of them, who approached too near, being burnt, the rest were terrified, and durst only look upon it at a distance. They were afraid, they said, of being bit, or lest that dreadful animal should wound with his violent respiration and dreadful breath; for these were the first notions they formed of the heat and flame. Such, too, probably, were the notions the Greeks originally formed of them.

Fire having been discovered, mankind endeavoured to make use of it for drying, and afterwards for cooking their meat; but they were a considerable time before they hit upon proper and commodious methods of employing it in the preparation of their food.

Meat, then, placed on burning fuel was found better than when raw: it had more firmness, was eaten with less difficulty, and the osmazome being condensed by the carbonization, gave it a pleasing perfume and flavour. Still, however, the meat cooked on the coal would become somewhat befouled, certain portions of the fuel adhering to it. This disadvantage was remedied by passing spits through it, and placing it at a suitable height above the burning fuel. Thus grilling was invented; and it is well known that, simple as is this mode of cookery, yet all meat cooked in this way is richly and pleasantly flavoured. In Homer's time, the art of cookery had not advanced much beyond this; for we read in the 'Iliad,' how the great Achilles and his friend Patroclus regaled the three Grecian leaders on bread, wine, and broiled meat. It is noticeable, too, that Homer does not speak of boiled meat anywhere in his poems. Later, however, the Jews, coming out of their captivity in Egypt, had made much greater progress. They undoubtedly possessed kettles; and in one of these, Esau's mess of pottage, for which he sold his birthright, must have been prepared.

Having thus briefly traced a history of gastronomical progresses, we will now proceed to describe the various methods of cooking meat, and make a few observations on the chemical changes which occur in each of the operations.

In this country, plain boiling, roasting, and baking are the usual methods of cooking animal food. To explain the philosophy of these simple culinary operations, we must advert to the effects that are produced by heat on the principal constituents of flesh. When finely-chopped mutton or beef is steeped for some time in a small quantity of clean water, and then subjected to slight pressure, the juice of the meat is extracted, and there is left a white tasteless residue, consisting chiefly of muscular fibres. When this residue is heated to between 158° and 177° Fahrenheit, the fibres shrink together, and become hard and horny. The influence of an elevated temperature on the soluble extract of flesh is not less remarkable. When the watery infusion, which contains all the savoury constituents of the meat, is gradually heated, it soon becomes turbid; and, when the temperature reaches 133°, flakes of whitish matter separate. These flakes are *albumen*, a substance precisely similar, in all its properties, to the white of egg (*see* p. 73). When the temperature of the watery extract is raised to 158°, the colouring matter of the blood coagulates, and the liquid, which was originally tinged red by this substance, is left perfectly clear, and almost colourless. When evaporated, even at a gentle heat, this residual liquid gradually becomes brown, and acquires the flavour of roast meat.

These interesting facts, discovered in the laboratory, throw a flood of light upon the mysteries of the kitchen. The fibres of meat are surrounded by a liquid which contains albumen in its soluble state, just as it exists in the unboiled egg. During the operation of boiling or roasting, this substance coagulates, and thereby prevents the contraction and hardening of the fibres. The tenderness of well-cooked meat is consequently proportioned to the amount of albumen deposited in its substance. Meat is underdone when it has been heated throughout only to the temperature of coagulating albumen: it is thoroughly done when it has been heated through its whole mass to the temperature at which the colouring matter of the blood coagulates: it is overdone when the heat has been continued long enough to harden the fibres.

The juice of flesh is water, holding in solution many substances besides albumen, which are of the highest possible value as articles of food. In preparing meat for the table, great care should be taken to prevent the escape of this precious juice, as the succulence and sapidity of the meat depend on its retention. The meat to be cooked should be exposed at first to a quick heat, which immediately coagulates the albumen on and near the surface. A kind of shell is thus formed, which effectually retains the whole of the juice within the meat.

During the operations of boiling, roasting, and baking, fresh beef and mutton, when moderately fat, lose, according to Johnston, on an average about—

	In boiling	In baking	In roasting
4 lbs. of beef lose	1 lb.	1 lb. 3 oz.	1 lb. 5 oz.
4 lbs. of mutton lose	14 oz.	1 lb. 4 oz.	1 lb. 6 oz.

BAKING

The difference between roasting meat and baking it, may be generally described as consisting in the fact, that, in baking it, the fumes

Baking-Dish

caused by the operation are not carried off in the same way as occurs in roasting. Much, however, of this disadvantage is obviated by the improved construction of modern ovens, and of especially those in connection with the Leamington kitchener, of which we give an engraving here, and a full description of which can be seen on pp. 41–2, with the prices at which they can be purchased of Messrs R. and J. Slack, of the Strand. With meat baked in the generality of ovens, however, which do not possess ventilators on the principle of this kitchener, there is undoubtedly a peculiar taste, which does not at all equal the flavour developed by roasting meat. The chemistry of baking may be said to be the same as that described in roasting.*

BOILING

Boiling, or the preparation of meat by hot water, though one of the easiest processes in cookery, requires skilful management. Boiled meat should be tender, savoury, and full of its own juice, or natural gravy; but, through the carelessness and ignorance of cooks, it is too often sent to table hard, tasteless, and innutritious. To insure a successful result in boiling flesh, the heat of the fire must be judiciously regulated, the proper quantity of water must be kept up in the pot, and the scum which rises to the surface must be carefully removed.*

Many writers on cookery assert that the meat to be boiled should be put into *cold water*, and that the pot should be heated gradually; but Liebig, the highest authority on all matters connected with the chemistry of food, has shown that meat so treated loses some of its most nutritious constituents. 'If the flesh,' says the great chemist, 'be introduced into the boiler when the water is in a state of brisk ebullition, and if the boiling be kept up for a few minutes, and the pot then placed in a warm place, so that the temperature of the water is kept at 158° to 165°, we have the united conditions for giving to the flesh the qualities which best fit it for being eaten.' When a piece of meat is plunged into boiling water, the albumen which is near the surface immediately coagulates, forming an envelope, which prevents the escape of the internal juice, and most effectually excludes the water, which, by mixing with this juice, would render the meat insipid. Meat treated thus is juicy and well-flavoured, when cooked, as it retains most of its savoury constituents. On the other hand, if the piece of meat be set on the fire with cold water, and this slowly heated to boiling, the flesh undergoes a loss of soluble and nutritious substances, while, as a matter of course, the soup becomes richer in these matters. The albumen is gradually dissolved from the surface to the centre; the fibre loses, more or less, its quality of shortness or tenderness, and becomes hard and tough: the thinner the piece of meat is, the greater is its loss of savoury constituents. In order to obtain well-flavoured and eatable meat, we must relinquish the idea of making good soup from it, as that mode of boiling which yields the best soup gives the driest, toughest, and most vapid meat. Slow boiling whitens the meat; and, we suspect, that it is on this account that it is in such flavour with the cooks. The wholesomeness of food is, however, a matter of much greater moment than the appearance it presents on the table. It should be borne in mind, that the whiteness of meat that has been boiled slowly, is produced by the loss of some important alimentary properties.

The objections we have raised to the practice of putting meat on the fire in cold water, apply with equal force to the practice of soaking meat before cooking it, which is so strongly recommended by some cooks. Fresh meat ought never to be soaked, as all its most nutritive constituents are soluble in water. Soaking, however, is an operation that cannot be entirely dispensed with in the preparation of animal food. Salted and dried meats require to be soaked for some time in water before they are cooked.

A few observations on the nutritive value of salted meat may be properly introduced in this place. Every housewife knows that dry salt in contact with fresh meat gradually becomes fluid brine. The application of salt causes the fibres of the meat to contract, and the juice to flow out from its pores: as much as one-third of the juice of the meat is often forced out in this manner. Now, as this juice is pure extract of meat, containing albumen, osmazome, and other valuable principles, it follows that meat which has been preserved by the action of salt can never have the nutritive properties of fresh meat.

The vessels used for boiling should be made of cast-iron, well tinned within, and provided with closely-fitting lids. They must be kept scrupulously clean, otherwise they will render the meat cooked in them unsightly and unwholesome. Copper pans, if used at all, should be reserved for operations that are performed with rapidity; as, by long contact with copper, food may become dangerously contaminated. The kettle in which a joint is dressed should be large enough to allow room for a good supply of water; if the meat be cramped and be surrounded with but little water, it will be stewed, not boiled.

Boiling-Pot　　　　　　　　　　　　　　　　*Stewpan*

Two useful culinary vessels are represented above. One is a boiling-pot, in which large joints may be boiled; the other is a stewpan, with a closely-fitting lid, to which is attached a long handle; so the cover can be removed without scalding the fingers.

In stewing, it is not requisite to have so great a heat as in boiling. A gentle simmering in a small quantity of water, so that the meat is stewed almost in its own juices, is all that is necessary. It is a method much used on the continent, and is wholesome and economical.

BROILING*

Generally speaking, small dishes only are prepared by this mode of cooking; amongst these, the beef-steak and mutton chop of the solitary English diner may be mentioned as celebrated all the world over. Our beef-steak, indeed, has long crossed the Channel; and, with a view of pleasing the Britons, there is in every *carte* at every French restaurant, by the side of *à la Marengo*, and *à la Mayonnaise,—biftek d'Angleterre*. In order to succeed in a broil, the cook must have a bright, clear fire; so that the surface of the meat may be quickly heated. The result of this is the same as that obtained in roasting; namely, that a crust, so to speak, is formed outside, and thus the juices of the meat are retained. The appetite of an invalid, so difficult to minister to, is often pleased with a broiled dish, as the flavour and sapidity of the meat are so well preserved.

The utensils used for broiling need but little description. The common gridiron, for which see engraving on p. 44, is the same as it has been for ages past, although some little variety has been introduced into its manufacture, by the addition of grooves to the bars, by means of which the liquid fat is carried into a small trough. One point it is well to bear in mind, viz., that the gridiron should be kept in a direction slanting towards the cook, so that as little fat as possible

Revolving Gridiron

may fall into the fire. It has been observed, that broiling is the most difficult manual office the general cook has to perform, and one that requires the most unremitting attention; for she may turn her back upon the stewpan or the spit, but the gridiron can never be left with impunity. The revolving gridiron, shown in the engraving, possesses some advantages of convenience, which will be at once apparent.

FRYING

This very favourite mode of cooking may be accurately described as boiling in fat or oil. Substances dressed in this way are generally well received, for they introduce an agreeable variety, possessing, as they do, a peculiar flavour. By means of frying, cooks can soon satisfy many requisitions made on

Sauté Pan

them, it being a very expeditious mode of preparing dishes for the table, and one which can be employed when the fire is not sufficiently large for the purposes of roasting and boiling. The great point to be borne in mind in frying, is that the liquid must be hot enough to act instantaneously, as all the merit of this culinary operation lies in the invasion of the boiling liquid, which carbonizes or burns, at the very instant of the immersion of the body placed in it. It may be ascertained if the fat is heated to the proper degree, by cutting a piece of bread and dipping it in the frying-pan for five or six seconds; and if it be firm and of a dark brown when taken out, put in immediately what you wish to prepare; if it be not, let the fat be heated until of the right temperature. This having been effected, moderate the fire, so that the action may not be too hurried, and that by a continuous heat the juices of the substance may be preserved, and its flavour enhanced.

The philosophy of frying consists in this, that liquids subjected to the action of fire do not all receive the same quantity of heat. Being differently constituted in their nature, they possess different 'capacities for caloric.' Thus, you may, with impunity, dip your finger in boiling spirits of wine; you would take it very quickly from boiling brandy, yet more rapidly from water; whilst the effects of the most rapid immersion in boiling oil need not be told. As a consequence of this, heated fluids act differently on the sapid bodies presented to them. Those put in water, dissolve, and are reduced to a soft mass; the result being *bouillon*, stock, &c. Those substances, on the contrary, treated with oil, harden, assume a more or less deep colour, and are finally carbonized. The reason of these different results is, that, in the first instance, water dissolves and extracts the interior juices of the alimentary substances placed in it; whilst, in the second, the juices are preserved; for they are insoluble in oil.

It is to be especially remembered, in connection with frying, that all dishes fried in fat should be placed before the fire on a piece of blotting-paper, or sieve reversed, and there left for a few minutes, so that any superfluous greasy moisture may be removed.

COOKING BY GAS

Gas-cooking can scarcely now be considered a novelty,—many establishments, both small and large, have been fitted with apparatus for cooking by this mode, which undoubtedly exhibits some advantages. Thus the heat may be more regularly supplied to the substance cooking, and the operation is essentially a clean one, because there can be no cinders or other dirt to be provided for. Some labour and attention necessary, too, with a coal fire or close stove, may be saved; and, besides this, it may, perhaps, be said that culinary operations are reduced, by this means, to something like a certainty.

There are, however, we think, many objections to this mode of cooking, more especially when applied to small domestic establishments. For instance, the ingenious machinery necessary for carrying it out, requires cooks perfectly conversant with its use; and if the gas, when the cooking operations are finished, be not turned off, there will be a large increase in the cost of cooking, instead of the economy which it has been supposed to bring. For large establishments, such as some of the immense London warehouses, where a large number of young men have to be catered for daily, it may be well adapted, as it is just possible that a slight increase in the supply of gas necessary for a couple of joints, may serve equally to cook a dozen dishes.

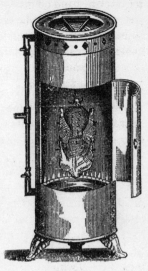

Gas-Stove

ROASTING*

Of the various methods of preparing meat, roasting is that which most effectually preserves its nutritive qualities. Meat is roasted by being exposed to the direct influence of the fire. This is done by placing the meat before an open grate, and keeping it in motion to prevent the scorching on any particular part. When meat is properly roasted, the outer layer of its albumen is coagulated, and thus presents a barrier to the exit of the juice. In roasting meat, the heat must be strongest at first, and it should then be much reduced. To have a good juicy roast, therefore, the fire must be red and vigorous at the very commencement of the operation. In the most careful roasting, some of the juice is squeezed out of the meat: this evaporates on the surface of the meat, and gives it a dark brown colour, a rich lustre, and a strong aromatic taste. Besides these effects on the albumen and the expelled juice, roasting converts the cellular tissue of the meat into gelatine, and melts the fat out of the fat-cells.

If a spit is used to support the meat before the fire, it should be kept quite bright. Sand and water ought to be used to scour it with, for brickdust and oil may give a disagreeable taste to the meat. When well scoured, it must be wiped quite dry with a clean cloth; and, in spitting the meat, the prime parts should be left untouched, so as to avoid any great escape of its juices.

Kitchens in large establishments are usually fitted with what are termed 'smoke-jacks.' By means of these, several spits, if required, may be turned at the same time. This not being, of course, necessary in smaller establishments, a roasting apparatus, more economical in its consumption of coal, is more frequently in use.

The bottle-jack, of which we here give an illustration, with the wheel and hook, and showing the precise manner of using it, is now commonly used in many kitchens. This consists of a spring inclosed in a brass cylinder, and requires winding up before it is used, and sometimes, also, during the operation of roasting. The joint is fixed to an iron hook, which is suspended by a chain connected with a wheel, and which, in its turn, is connected with the bottle-jack. Beneath it stands the dripping-pan, which we have also engraved, together with the basting-ladle, the use of which latter should not be spared; as there can be no good roast without good basting. 'Spare the rod, and spoil the child,' might easily be paraphrased into 'Spare the basting, and spoil the meat.' If the joint is small and light, and so turns unsteadily, this may be remedied by fixing to the wheel one of the kitchen weights. Sometimes this jack is fixed inside a screen; but there is this objection to this apparatus,—that the meat cooked in it resembles the flavour of baked meat. This is derived from its being so completely sur-

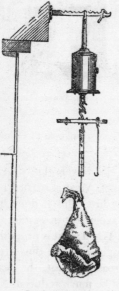

Bottle-Jack, with Wheel and Hook

Dripping-Pan and Basting-Ladle

rounded with the tin, that
no sufficient current of air
gets to it. It will be found
preferable to make use of a
common meat-screen, such
as is shown in the woodcut.
This contains shelves for
warming plates and dishes;
and with this, the reflection
not being so powerful, and

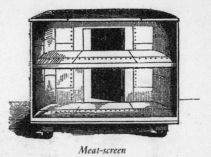

Meat-screen

more air being admitted to the joint, the roast may be very
excellently cooked.

In stirring the fire, or putting fresh coals on it, the dripping-pan
should always be drawn back, so that there may be no danger of the
coal, cinders, or ashes falling down into it.

Under each particular recipe there is stated the time required for
roasting each joint; but, as a general rule, it may be here given, that
for every pound of meat, in ordinary-sized joints, a quarter of an
hour may be allotted.

White meats, and the meat of young animals, require to be very
well roasted, both to be pleasant to the palate and easy of digestion.
Thus veal, pork, and lamb, should be thoroughly done to the centre.

Mutton and beef, on the other hand, do not, generally speaking,
require to be so thoroughly done, and they should be dressed to the
point, that, in carving them, the gravy should just run, but not too
freely.* Of course in this, as in most other dishes, the tastes of individuals vary; and there are many who cannot partake, with satisfaction,
of any joint unless it is what others would call overdressed.

QUADRUPEDS

CHAPTER XII

GENERAL OBSERVATIONS ON QUADRUPEDS*

By the general assent of mankind, the empire of nature has been divided into three kingdoms; the first consisting of minerals, the second of vegetables, and the third of animals. The Mineral Kingdom comprises all substances which are without those organs necessary to locomotion, and the due performance of the functions of life. They are composed of the accidental aggregation of particles, which, under certain circumstances, take a constant and regular figure, but which are more frequently found without any definite conformation. They also occupy the interior parts of the earth, as well as compose those huge masses by which we see the land in some parts guarded against the encroachments of the sea. The Vegetable Kingdom covers and beautifies the earth with an endless variety of form and colour. It consists of organized bodies, but destitute of the power of locomotion. They are nourished by means of roots; they breathe by means of leaves; and propagate by means of seed, dispersed within certain limits. The Animal Kingdom consists of sentient beings, that enliven the external parts of the earth. They possess the powers of voluntary motion, respire air, and are forced into action by the cravings of hunger or the parching of thirst, by the instincts of animal passion, or by pain. Like the vegetable kingdom, they are limited within the boundaries of certain countries by the conditions of climate and soil; and some of the species prey upon each other. Linnaeus* has divided them into six classes;—Mammalia, Birds, Fishes, Amphibious Animals, Insects, and Worms. The three latter do not come within the limits of our domain; of fishes we have already treated, of birds we shall treat, and of mammalia we will now treat.

In the general economy of nature, this class of animals seems destined to preserve a constant equilibrium in the number of animated beings that hold their existence on the surface of the earth. To man they are immediately useful in various ways. Some of their bodies afford him food, their skin shoes, and their fleece clothes. Some of them unite with him in participating the dangers of combat with an enemy, and others assist him in the chase, in exterminating wilder sorts, or banishing them from the haunts of civilization. Many, indeed, are injurious to him; but most of them, in some shape or other, he turns to his service. Of these there is none he has made more subservient to his purposes than the common ox, of which there is scarcely a part that he has not been able to convert into some useful purpose. Of the horns he makes drinking-vessels, knife-handles, combs, and boxes; and when they are softened by means of boiling water, he fashions them into transparent plates for lanterns. This invention is ascribed to King Alfred, who is said to have been the first to use them to preserve his candle time-measures from the wind. Glue is made of the cartilages, gristles, and the finer pieces of the parings and cuttings of the hides. Their bone is a cheap substitute for ivory. The thinnest of the calf-skins are manufactured into vellum. Their blood is made the basis of Prussian blue, and saddlers use a fine sort of thread prepared from their sinews. The hair is used in various valuable manufactures; the suet, fat, and tallow, are moulded into candles; and the milk and cream of the cow yield butter and cheese. Thus is every part of this animal valuable to man, who has spared no pains to bring it to the highest state of perfection.

THE ALDERNEY.*—Among the dairy breeds of England, the Alderney takes a prominent place, not on account of the quantity of milk which it yields, but on account of the excellent quality of the cream and butter which are produced from it. Its docility is marvellous, and in appearance it greatly resembles the Ayrshire breed of Scotland, the excellence of which is supposed to be, in some degree, derived from a mixture of the Alderney blood with that breed. The distinction between them, however, lies both in the quantity and quality of the milk which they severally produce; that of the Alderney being rich in quality, and that of the Ayrshire abundant in quantity. The merit of the former, however, ends with its milk, for as a grazer it is worthless.

Alderney Cow   *Alderney Bull*

The general mode of slaughtering oxen in this country is by striking them a smart blow with a hammer or poleaxe on the head, a little above the eyes. By this means, when the blow is skilfully given, the beast is brought down at one blow, and, to prevent recovery, a cane is generally inserted, by which the spinal cord is perforated, which instantly deprives the ox of all sensation of pain. In Spain, and some other countries on the continent, it is also usual to deprive oxen of life by the operation of pithing or dividing the spinal cord in the neck, close to the back part of the head. This is, in effect, the same mode as is practised in the celebrated Spanish bull-fights by the matador, and it is instantaneous in depriving the animal of sensation, if the operator be skilful. We hope and believe that those men whose disagreeable duty it is to slaughter the 'beasts of the field' to provide meat for mankind, inflict as little punishment and cause as little suffering as possible.*

The manner in which a side of beef is cut up in London, is shown in the engraving on this page. In the metropolis, on account of the large number of its population possessing the means to indulge in the 'best of everything,' the demand for the most delicate joints of meat is great, the price, at the same time, being much higher for these than for the other parts. The consequence is, that in London the carcass is there divided so as to obtain the greatest quantity of meat on the most esteemed joints. In many places, however, where, from a greater equality in the social condition and habits of the inhabitants, the demand and prices for

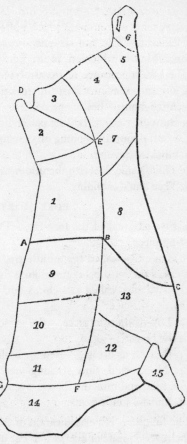

Side of Beef, Showing the Several Joints

the different parts of the carcasses are more equalized, there is not the same reason for the butcher to cut the best joints so large.*

The meat on those parts of the animal in which the muscles are least called into action, is most tender and succulent; as, for instance, along the back, from the rump to the hinder part of the shoulder; whilst the limbs, shoulder, and neck, are the toughest, driest, and least-esteemed.

The names of the several joints in the hind and fore quarters of a side of beef, and the purposes for which they are used, are as follows:—

HIND QUARTER

1. Sirloin.—The two sirloins, cut together in one joint, form a baron; this, when roasted, is the famous national dish of Englishmen, at entertainments, on occasion of rejoicing.
2. Rump,—the finest part for steaks.
3. Aitch-bone,—boiling piece.
4. Buttock,—prime boiling piece.
5. Mouse-round,—boiling or stewing.
6. Hock,—stewing.
7. Thick flank, cut with the udder-fat,—primest boiling piece.
8. Thin flank,—boiling.

FORE QUARTER

9. Five ribs, called the fore-rib.—This is considered the primest roasting piece.
10. Four ribs, called the middle-rib,—greatly esteemed by housekeepers as the most economical joint for roasting.
11. Two ribs, called the chuck-rib,—used for second quality of steaks.
12. Leg-of-mutton piece,—the muscles of the shoulder dissected from the breast.
13. Brisket, or breast,—used for boiling, after being salted.
14. Neck, clod, and sticking-piece,—used for soups, gravies, stocks, pies, and mincing for sausages.
15. Shin,—stewing.

The following is a classification of the qualities of meat, according to the several joints of beef; when cut up in the London manner.

First class—includes the sirloin, with the kidney suet (1), the rump-steak piece (2), the fore-rib (9).

Second class.—The buttock (4), the thick flank (7), the middle-rib (10).

Third class.—The aitch-bone (3), the mouse-round (5), the thin flank (8), the chuck (11), the leg-of-mutton piece (12), the brisket (13).

Fourth class.—The neck, clod, and sticking-piece (14).

Fifth class.—The hock (6), the shin (15).

CHAPTER XIII

RECIPES*

Beef à la Mode*

INGREDIENTS.—6 or 7 lbs. of the thick flank of beef, a few slices of fat bacon, 1 teacupful of vinegar, black pepper, allspice, 2 cloves well mixed and finely pounded, making altogether 1 heaped teaspoonful; salt to taste, 1 bunch of savoury herbs, including parsley, all finely minced and well mixed; 3 onions, 2 large carrots, 1 turnip, 1 head of celery, 1½ pint of water, 1 glass of port wine.

Mode.—Slice and fry the onions of a pale brown, and cut up the other vegetables in small pieces, and prepare the beef for stewing in the following manner:—Choose a fine piece of beef, cut the bacon into long slices, about an inch in thickness, dip them into vinegar, and then into a little of the above seasoning of spice, &c., mixed with the same quantity of minced herbs. With a sharp knife make holes deep enough to let in the bacon; then rub the beef over with the remainder of the seasoning and herbs, and bind it up in a nice shape with tape. Have ready a well-tinned stewpan (it should not be much larger than the piece of meat you are cooking), into which put the beef, with the vegetables, vinegar, and water. Let it simmer *very gently* for 5 hours, or rather longer, should the meat not be extremely tender, and turn it once or twice. When ready to serve, take out the beef, remove the tape, and put it on a hot dish. Skim off every particle of fat from the gravy, add the port wine, just let it boil, pour it over the beef, and it is ready to serve. Great care must be taken that this does not boil fast, or the meat will be tough and tasteless; it should only just bubble. When convenient, all kinds of stews, &c., should be cooked on a hot-plate, as the process is so much more gradual than an open fire.

Time.—5 hours, or rather more.   *Average cost,* 7*d*. per lb.

Sufficient for 7 or 8 persons.

Seasonable all the year, but more suitable for a winter dish.

GOOD MEAT.—The lyer of meat when freshly killed, and the animal, when slaughtered, being in a state of perfect health, adheres firmly to the bones. Beef of the best quality is of a deep-red colour; and when the animal has approached maturity, and been well fed, the lean is intermixed with fat, giving it the mottled appearance which is so much esteemed. It is also full of juice, which resembles in colour claret wine. The fat of the best beef is of a firm and waxy consistency, of a colour resembling that of the finest grass butter; bright in appearance, neither greasy nor friable to the touch, but moderately unctuous, in a medium degree between the last-mentioned properties.

Beef-Steak and Kidney Pudding*

INGREDIENTS.—2 lbs. of rump-steak, 2 kidneys, seasoning to taste of salt and black pepper, suet crust made with milk (see PASTRY), in the proportion of 6 oz. of suet to each 1 lb. of flour.

Mode.—Procure some tender rump steak (that which has been hung a little time), and divide it into pieces about an inch square, and cut each kidney into 8 pieces. Line the dish (of which we have given an engraving) with crust made with suet and flour in the above

Sussex Pudding-Dish

proportion, leaving a small piece of crust to overlap the edge. Then cover the bottom with a portion of the steak and a few pieces of kidney; season with salt and pepper (some add a little flour to thicken the gravy, but it is not necessary), and then add another layer of steak, kidney, and seasoning. Proceed in this manner till the dish is full, when pour in sufficient water to come within 2 inches of the top of the basin. Moisten the edges of the crust, cover the pudding over, press the two crusts together, that the gravy may not escape, and turn up the overhanging paste. Wring out a cloth in hot water, flour it, and tie up the pudding; put it into boiling water, and let it boil for at least 4 hours. If the water diminishes, always replenish with some, hot in a jug, as the pudding should be kept covered all the time, and not allowed to stop boiling. When the cloth is removed, cut out a round piece in the top of the crust, to prevent the pudding bursting, and send it to table in the basin, either in an ornamental dish, or with a napkin pinned round it. Serve quickly.

Time.—For a pudding with 2 lbs. of steak and 2 kidneys allow 4 hours.

Average cost, 2s. 8d.

Sufficient for 6 persons.

Seasonable all the year, but more suitable in winter.

Note.—Beef-steak pudding may be very much enriched by adding a few oysters or mushrooms. The above recipe was contributed to this work by a Sussex lady, in which county the inhabitants are noted for their savoury puddings. It differs from the general way of making them, as the meat is cut up into very small pieces and the basin is differently shaped: on trial, this pudding will be found far nicer, and more full of gravy, than when laid in large pieces in the dish.

BAD MEAT.—In the flesh of animals slaughtered whilst suffering acute inflammation or fever, the hollow fibres, or capillaries, as they are called, which form the substance of the lyer, are filled with congested and unassimilated animal fluid, which, from its impurity, gives the lyer a dark colour, and produces a tendency to rapid putrefaction. In a more advanced stage of such disease, serous, and sometimes purulent matter, is formed in the cellular tissues between the muscles of the flesh; and when such is the case, nothing can be more poisonous than such abominable carrion. In the flesh of animals killed whilst under the influence of any disease of an emaciating effect, the lyer adheres but slightly to the bones, with its fibres contracted and dry; and the little fat that there may be is friable, and shrunk within its integuments. The flesh of animals slaughtered whilst under considerable depression of vital energy (as from previous bleeding) has a diminished tendency to stiffen after death, the feebleness of this tendency being in proportion to the degree of depression. It presents, also, an unnatural blue or pallid appearance, has a faint and slightly sour smell, and soon becomes putrid. When an animal has died otherwise than by slaughtering, its flesh is flaccid and clammy, emits a peculiar faint and disagreeable smell, and, it need scarcely be added, spontaneous decomposition proceeds very rapidly.

To Dress a Bullock's Heart

INGREDIENTS.—1 heart, stuffing of veal forcemeat, p. 128.

Mode.—Put the heart into warm water to soak for 2 hours; then wipe it well with a cloth, and, after cutting off the lobes, stuff the inside with a highly-seasoned forcemeat. Fasten it in, by means of a needle and coarse thread; tie the heart up in paper, and set it before a good fire, being very particular to keep it well basted, or it will eat dry, there being very little of its own fat. Two or three minutes before serving, remove the paper, baste well, and serve with good gravy and red-currant jelly or melted butter. If the heart is very large, it will require 2 hours, and, covered with a caul, may be baked as well as roasted.

Time.—Large heart, 2 hours.

Average cost, 2*s*. 6*d*.

Sufficient for 6 or 8 persons.

Seasonable all the year.

Note.—This is an excellent family dish, is very savoury, and, though not seen at many good tables, may be recommended for its cheapness and economy.

Bubble-and-Squeak* (Cold Meat Cookery)

INGREDIENTS.—A few thin slices of cold boiled beef; butter, cabbage, 1 sliced onion, pepper and salt to taste.

Mode.—Fry the slices of beef gently in a little butter, taking care not to dry them up. Lay them on a flat dish, and cover with fried greens. The greens may be prepared from cabbage sprouts or green savoys. They should be boiled till tender, well drained, minced, and placed, till quite hot, in a frying-pan, with butter, a sliced onion, and seasoning of pepper and salt. When the onion is done, it is ready to serve.

Time.—Altogether, ½ hour.

Average cost, exclusive of the cold beef, 3*d*.

Seasonable at any time.

Roast Fillet of Beef (Larded)

INGREDIENTS.—About 4 lbs. of the inside fillet of the sirloin, 1 onion, a small bunch of parsley, salt and pepper to taste, sufficient vinegar to cover the meat, glaze, Spanish sauce, pp. 127–8.

Mode.—Lard the beef with bacon, and put it into a pan with sufficient vinegar to cover it, with an onion sliced, parsley, and seasoning, and let it remain in this pickle for 12 hours. Roast it before a nice clear fire for about 1¼ hour, and, when done, glaze it. Pour some Spanish sauce round the beef, and the remainder serve in a tureen. It may be garnished with Spanish onions boiled and glazed.

Time.—1¼ hour.   *Average cost*, exclusive of the sauce, 4*s*.

Sufficient for 6 or 8 persons.

Seasonable at any time.

Fried Rump-Steak

INGREDIENTS.—Steaks, butter or clarified dripping.

Mode.—Although broiling is a far superior method of cooking steaks to frying them, yet, when the cook is not very expert, the latter mode may be adopted; and, when properly done, the dish may really look very inviting, and the flavour be good. The steaks should be cut rather thinner than for broiling, and with a small quantity of fat to each. Put some butter or clarified dripping into a frying-pan; let it get quite hot, then lay in the steaks. Turn them frequently until done, which will be in about 8 minutes, or rather more, should the steaks be very thick. Serve on a very hot dish, in which put a small piece of butter and a tablespoonful of ketchup, and season with pepper and salt. They should be sent to table quickly, as, when cold, the steaks are entirely spoiled.

Time.—8 minutes for a medium-sized steak, rather longer for a very thick one.

Average cost, 1s. per lb.

Seasonable all the year, but not good in summer, as the meat cannot hang to get tender.

Note.—Where much gravy is liked, make it in the following manner:—As soon as the steaks are done, dish them, pour a little boiling water into the frying-pan, add a seasoning of pepper and salt, a small piece of butter, and a tablespoonful of Harvey's sauce or mushroom ketchup. Hold the pan over the fire for a minute or two, just let the gravy simmer, then pour on the steak, and serve.

A FRENCHMAN'S OPINION OF BEEF.—The following is translated from a celebrated modern French work, the production of one who in Paris enjoys a great reputation as cook and chemist:*—The flesh of the ox, to be in the best condition, should be taken from an animal of from four to six years old, and neither too fat nor too lean. This meat, which possesses in the highest degree the most nutritive qualities, is generally easily digested; stock is made from it, and it is eaten boiled, broiled, roasted, stewed, braised, and in a hundred other different ways. Beef is the foundation of stock, gravies, braises, &c.; its nutritious and succulent gravy gives body and flavour to numberless ragoûts. It is an exhaustless mine in the hands of a skilful artist, and is truly the king of the kitchen. Without it, no soup, no gravy; and its absence would produce almost a famine in the civilized world!

To Dress Beef Kidney

INGREDIENTS.—1 kidney, clarified butter, pepper and salt to taste, a small quantity of highly-seasoned gravy, 1 tablespoonful of lemon-juice, ¼ teaspoonful of powdered sugar.

Mode.—Cut the kidneys into neat slices, put them into warm water to soak for 2 hours, and change the water 2 or 3 times; then put them on a clean cloth to dry the water from them, and lay them in a frying-pan with some clarified butter, and fry them of a nice brown; season each side with pepper and salt, put them round the dish, and the gravy in the middle. Before pouring the gravy in the dish, add the lemon-juice and sugar.

Time.—From 5 to 10 minutes.   *Average cost,* 9*d.* each.

Seasonable at any time.

Boiled Marrow-Bones*

INGREDIENTS.—Bones, a small piece of common paste, a floured cloth.

Mode.—Have the bones neatly sawed into convenient sizes, and cover the ends with a small piece of common crust, made with flour and water. Over this tie a floured cloth, and place them upright in a saucepan of boiling water, taking care there is sufficient to cover the bones. Boil them for 2 hours, remove the cloth and paste, and serve them upright on a napkin with dry toast. Many persons clear the marrow from the bones after they are cooked, spread it over a slice of toast and add a seasoning of pepper; when served in this manner, it must be very expeditiously sent to table, as it so soon gets cold.

Time.—2 hours.

Seasonable at any time.

Note.—Marrow-bones may be baked after preparing them as in the preceding recipe; they should be laid in a deep dish, and baked for 2 hours.

Marrow-Bones

MARROW-BONES.—Bones are formed of a dense cellular tissue of membranous matter, made stiff and rigid by insoluble earthy salts; of which, phosphate of lime is the most abundant. In a large bone, the insoluble matter is generally deposited in such a manner as to leave a cavity, into which a fatty substance, distinguished by the name of marrow, is thrown. Hollow cylindrical bones possess the qualities of strength and lightness in a remarkable degree. If bones were entirely solid, they would be unnecessarily heavy; and if their materials were brought into smaller compass, they would be weaker, because the strength of a bone is in proportion to the distance at which its fibres are from the centre. Some animals, it must, however, be observed, have no cavities in the centre of their bones; such as the whale tribe, skate, and turtles.

Fried Ox-Feet, or Cow-Heel*

INGREDIENTS.—Ox-feet, the yolk of 1 egg, bread crumbs, parsley, salt and cayenne to taste, boiling butter.

Mode.—Wash, scald, and thoroughly clean the feet, and cut them into pieces about 2 inches long; have ready some fine bread crumbs mixed with a little minced parsley, cayenne, and salt, dip the pieces of heel into the yolk of egg, sprinkle them with the bread crumbs, and fry them until of a nice brown in boiling butter.

Time.—¼ hour.   *Average cost*, 6d. each.

Seasonable at any time.

Note.—Ox-feet may be dressed in various ways, stewed in gravy or plainly boiled and served with melted butter. When plainly boiled, the liquor will answer for making sweet or relishing jellies, and also to give richness to soups or gravies.

Stewed Ox-Tails

INGREDIENTS.—2 ox-tails, 1 onion, 3 cloves, 1 blade of mace, ¼ teaspoonful of whole black pepper, ¼ teaspoonful of allspice, ½ a teaspoonful of salt, a small bunch of savoury herbs, thickening of butter and flour, 1 tablespoonful of lemon-juice, 1 tablespoonful of mushroom ketchup.

Mode.—Divide the tails at the joints, wash, and put them into a stewpan with sufficient water to cover them, and set them on the fire; when the water boils, remove the scum, and add the onion cut into rings, the spice, seasoning, and herbs. Cover the stewpan closely, and let the tails simmer very gently until tender, which will be in about 2½ hours. Take them out, make a thickening of butter and flour, add it to the gravy, and let it boil for ¼ hour. Strain it through a sieve into a saucepan, put back the tails, add the lemon-juice and ketchup; let the whole just boil up, and serve. Garnish with croûtons or sippets of toasted bread.

Time.—2½ hours to stew the tails.

Average cost, 9*d.* to 1*s.* 6*d.*, according to the season.

Sufficient for 8 persons.

Seasonable all the year.

Miniature Round of Beef
(*An Excellent Dish for a Small Family*)*

INGREDIENTS.—From 5 to 10 lbs. of rib of beef, sufficient brine to cover the meat.

Mode.—Choose a fine rib, have the bone removed, rub some salt over the inside, and skewer the meat up into a nice round form, and bind it with tape. Put it into sufficient brine to cover it, and let it remain for 6 days, turning the meat every day. When required to be dressed, drain from the pickle, and put the meat into very hot water; let it boil rapidly for a few minutes, when draw the pot to the side of the fire, and let it simmer very gently until done. Remove the skewer, and replace it by a plated or silver one. Carrots and turnips should be served with this dish, and may be boiled with the meat.

Time.—A small round of 8 lbs., about 2 hours after the water boils; one of 12 lbs., about 3 hours.

Average cost, 9*d.* per lb. *Sufficient* for 6 persons.

Seasonable at any time.

Note.—Should the joint be very small, 4 or 5 days will be sufficient time to salt it.

Roast Sirloin of Beef*

INGREDIENTS.—Beef, a little salt.

Mode.—As a joint cannot be well roasted without a good fire, see that it is well made up about ¾ hour before it is required, so that when the joint is put down, it is clear and bright. Choose a nice sirloin, the weight of which should not exceed 16 lbs., as the outside would be too much done, whilst the inside would not be done enough. Spit it or hook it on to the jack firmly, dredge it slightly with flour, and place it near the fire at first, as directed in the preceding recipe. Then draw it to a distance, and keep continually basting until the meat is done. Sprinkle a small quantity of salt over it, empty the dripping-pan of all the dripping, pour in some boiling water slightly salted, stir it about, and *strain* over the meat. Garnish with tufts of horseradish, and send horseradish sauce and Yorkshire pudding to table with it. For carving, *see* pp. 171–2.

Time.—A sirloin of 10 lbs., 2½ hours; 14 to 16 lbs., about 4 or 4½ hours.

Average cost, 8½d. per lb.

Sufficient.—A joint of 10 lbs. for 8 or 9 persons.

Seasonable at any time.

The rump, round, and other pieces of beef are roasted in the same manner, allowing for solid joints ¼ hour to every lb.

Note.—The above is the usual method of roasting meat; but to have it in perfection and the juices kept in, the meat should at first be laid *close* to the fire, and when the outside is set and firm, drawn away to a good distance, and then left to roast very slowly; where economy is studied, this plan would not answer, as the meat requires to be at the fire double the time of the ordinary way of cooking; consequently, double the quantity of fuel would be consumed.

ORIGIN OF THE WORD 'SIRLOIN'.—The loin of beef is said to have been knighted by King Charles II, at Friday Hall, Chingford. The 'Merry Monarch' returned to this hospitable mansion from Epping Forest literally 'as hungry as a hunter,' and beheld, with delight, a huge loin of beef steaming upon the table. 'A noble joint!' exclaimed the king. 'By St George, it shall have a title,!' Then drawing his sword, he raised it above the meat, and cried, with mock dignity, 'Loin, we dub thee knight; henceforward be Sir Loin!' This anecdote is doubtless apocryphal,

Sirloin of Beef

although the oak table upon which the joint was supposed to have received its knighthood, might have been seen by any one who visited Friday-Hill House, a few years ago. It is, perhaps, a pity to spoil so noble a story; but the interests of truth demand that we declare that *sirloin* is probably a corruption of *surloin*, which signifies the upper part of a loin, the prefix *sur* being equivalent to *over* or *above*. In French we find this joint called *surlonge*, which so closely resembles our *sirloin*, that we may safely refer the two words to a common origin.

Toad-in-the-Hole* (a Homely but Savoury Dish)

INGREDIENTS.—1½ lb. of rump-steak, 1 sheep's kidney, pepper and salt to taste. For the batter, 3 eggs, 1 pint of milk, 4 tablespoonfuls of flour, ½ saltspoonful of salt.

Mode.—Cut up the steak and kidney into convenient-sized pieces, and put them into a pie-dish, with a good seasoning of salt and pepper; mix the flour with a small quantity of milk at first, to prevent its being lumpy; add the remainder, and the 3 eggs, which should be well beaten; put in the salt, stir the batter for about 5 minutes, and pour it over the steak. Place it in a tolerably brisk oven immediately, and bake for 1½ hour.

Time.—1½ hour. *Average cost*, 1s. 9d.

Sufficient for 4 or 5 persons.

Seasonable at any time.

Note.—The remains of cold beef, rather underdone, may be substituted for the steak, and, when liked, the smallest possible quantity of minced onion or shalot may be added.

Boiled Tongue

INGREDIENTS.—1 tongue, a bunch of savoury herbs, water.

Mode.—In choosing a tongue, ascertain how long it has been dried or pickled, and select one with a smooth skin, which denotes its being young and tender. If a dried one, and rather hard, soak it at least for 12 hours previous to cooking it; if, however, it is fresh from the pickle, 2 or 3 hours will be sufficient for it to remain in soak. Put the tongue into a stewpan with plenty of cold water and a bunch of savoury herbs; let it gradually come to a boil, skim well, and simmer very gently until tender. Peel off the skin, garnish with tufts of cauliflowers or Brussels sprouts, and serve. Boiled tongue is frequently sent to table with boiled poultry, instead of ham, and is, by many persons, preferred. If to serve cold, peel it, fasten it down to a piece of board by sticking a fork through the root, and another through the top, to straighten it. When cold, glaze it, and put a paper ruche round the root, and garnish with tufts of parsley.

Time.—A large smoked tongue, 4 to 4½ hours; a small one, 2½ to 3 hours. A large unsmoked tongue, 3 to 3½ hours; a small one, 2 to 2½ hours.

Average cost, for a moderate-sized tongue, 3*s*. 6*d*.

Seasonable at any time.

THE TONGUES OF ANIMALS.—The tongue, whether in the ox or in man, is the seat of the sense of taste. This sense warns the animal against swallowing deleterious substances. Dr Carpenter says, that, among the lower animals, the instinctive perceptions connected with this sense, are much more remarkable than our own; thus, an omnivorous monkey will seldom touch fruits of a poison-

Beef Tongue

ous character, although their taste may be agreeable. However this may be, man's instinct has decided that ox-tongue is better than horse-tongue; nevertheless, the latter is frequently substituted by dishonest dealers for the former. The horse's tongue may be readily distinguished by a spoon-like expansion at its end.

To Dress Tripe*

INGREDIENTS.—Tripe, onion sauce, milk and water.

Mode.—Ascertain that the tripe is quite fresh, and have it cleaned and dressed. Cut away the coarsest fat, and boil it in equal proportions of milk and water for ¾ hour. Should the tripe be entirely undressed, more than double that time should be allowed for it. Have ready some onion sauce, dish the tripe, smother it with the sauce, and the remainder send to table in a tureen.

Time.—¾ hour; for undressed tripe, from 2½ to 3 hours.

Average cost, 7*d*. per lb.

Seasonable at any time.

Note.—Tripe may be dressed in a variety of ways; it may be cut in pieces and fried in batter, stewed in gravy with mushrooms, or cut into collops, sprinkled with minced onion and savoury herbs, and fried a nice brown in clarified butter.

BEEF CARVING

Sirloin of Beef

This dish is served differently at various tables, some preferring it to come to table with the fillet, or, as it is usually called, the undercut, uppermost. The reverse way, as shown in the cut, is that most usually adopted. Still the undercut is best eaten when hot; consequently, the carver himself may raise the joint, and cut some slices from the under side, in the direction of from 1 to 2, as the fillet is very much

preferred by some eaters. The upper part of the sirloin should be cut in the direction of the line from 5 to 6, and care should be taken to carve it evenly and in thin slices. It will be found a great assistance, in carving this joint well, if the knife be first inserted just above the bone at the bottom, and run sharply along between the bone and meat, and also to divide the meat from the bone in the same way at the side of the joint. The slices will then come away more readily. Some carvers cut the upper side of the sirloin across, as shown by the line from 3 to 4; but this is a wasteful plan, and one not to be recommended. With the sirloin, very finely-scraped horseradish is usually served, and a little given, when liked, to each guest. Horseradish sauce is preferable, however, for serving on the plate, although the scraped horseradish may still be used as a garnish.

CHAPTER XIV

GENERAL OBSERVATIONS ON
THE SHEEP AND LAMB

Of all wild or domesticated animals, the sheep is, without exception,
the most useful to man as a food, and the most necessary to his health
and comfort; for it not only supplies him with the lightest and most
nutritious of meats, but, in the absence of the cow, its udder yields
him milk, cream, and a sound though inferior cheese; while from
its fat he obtains light, and from its fleece broadcloth, kerseymere,
blankets, gloves, and hose. Its bones when burnt make an animal
charcoal—ivory black—to polish his boots, and when powdered, a
manure for the cultivation of his wheat; the skin, either split or
whole, is made into a mat for his carriage, a housing for his horse, or
a lining for his hat, and many other useful purposes besides, being
extensively employed in the manufacture of parchment; and finally,
when oppressed by care and sorrow, the harmonious strains that
carry such soothing contentment to the heart, are elicited from the

musical strings, prepared almost exclusively from the intestines of the sheep.*

Different names have been given to sheep by their breeders, according to their age and sex. The male is called a ram, or tup; after weaning, he is said to be a hog, or hogget, or a lamb-hog, tup-hog, or teg; later he is a wether, or wether-hog; after the first shearing, a shearing, or dinmont; and after each succeeding shearing, a two, three, or four-shear ram, tup, or wether, according to circumstances. The female is called a ewe, or gimmer-lamb, till weaned, when she becomes, according to the shepherd's nomenclature, a gimmer-ewe, hog, or teg; after shearing, a gimmer or shearing-ewe, or theave; and in future a two, three, or four-shear ewe, or theave.

The mode of slaughtering sheep is perhaps as humane and expeditious a process as could be adopted to attain the objects sought: the animal being laid on its side in a sort of concave stool, the butcher, while pressing the body with his knee, transfixes the throat near the angle of the jaw, passing his knife between the windpipe and bones of the neck; thus dividing the jugulars, carotids, and large vessels, the death being very rapid from such a hemorrhage.

Almost every large city has a particular manner of cutting up, or, as it is called, dressing the carcase. In London this process is very simple, and as our butchers have found that much skewering back, doubling one part over another, or scoring the inner cuticle or fell, tends to spoil the meat and shorten the time it would otherwise keep, they avoid all such treatment entirely. The carcase when flayed (which operation is performed while yet warm), the sheep when hung up and the head removed, presents the profile shown in our cut; the

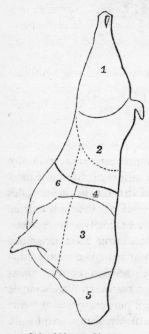

Side of Mutton, Showing the Several Joints

small numerals indicating the parts or joints into which one half of the animal is cut. After separating the hind from the fore quarters, with eleven ribs to the latter, the quarters are usually subdivided in the manner shown in the sketch, in which the several joints are defined by the intervening lines and figures. *Hind quarter*: No. 1, the leg; 2, the loin—the two, when cut in one piece, being called the saddle. *Fore quarter*: No. 3, the shoulder; 4 and 5 the neck; No. 5 being called, for distinction, the scrag, which is generally afterwards separated from 4, the lower and better joint; No. 6, the breast. The haunch of mutton, so often served at public dinners and special entertainments, comprises all the leg and so much of the loin, short of the ribs or lap, as is indicated on the upper part of the carcase by a dotted line.

The gentle and timid disposition of the sheep,* and its defenceless condition, must very early have attached it to man for motives less selfish than either its fleece or its flesh; for it has been proved beyond a doubt that, obtuse as we generally regard it, it is susceptible of a high degree of domesticity, obedience, and affection. In many parts of Europe, where the flocks are guided by the shepherd's voice alone, it is no unusual thing for a sheep to quit the herd when called by its name, and follow the keeper like a dog. In the mountains of Scotland, when a flock is invaded by a savage dog, the rams have been known to form the herd into a circle, and placing themselves on the outside line, keep the enemy at bay, or charging on him in a troop, have despatched him with their horns.

The value of the sheep seems to have been early understood by Adam in his fallen state,* his skin not only affording him protection for his body, but a covering for his tent; and accordingly, we find Abel intrusted with this portion of his father's stock; for the Bible tells us that 'Abel was a keeper of sheep.' What other animals were domesticated at that time we can only conjecture, or at what exact period the flesh of the sheep was first eaten for food by man, is equally, if not uncertain, open to controversy. For though some authorities maintain the contrary, it is but natural to suppose that when Abel brought firstlings of his flock, 'and the fat thereof,' as a sacrifice, the less dainty portions, not being oblations, were hardly likely to have been flung away as refuse. Indeed, without supposing Adam and his descendants to have eaten animal food, we cannot reconcile the fact of Jubal Cain, Cain's son, and his family, living in tents, as they are reported to have done, knowing that both their own garments and the coverings of the tents, were made from the hides and skins of the animals they bred; for the number of sheep and oxen slain for oblations only, would not have supplied sufficient material for two such necessary purposes. The opposite opinion is, that animal food was not eaten till after the Flood, when the Lord renewed his covenant with Noah. From Scriptural authority we learn many interesting facts as regards the sheep: the first, that mutton fat was considered the most delicious portion of any meat, and the tail and adjacent part the most exquisite morsel in the whole body; consequently, such were regarded as especially fit for the offer of sacrifice. From this fact we may reasonably infer that the animal still so often met with in Palestine and Syria, and known as the Fat-tailed sheep, was in use in the days of the patriarchs, though probably not then of the size and weight it now attains to; a supposition that gains greater strength, when it is remembered that the ram Abraham found in the bush, when he went to offer up Isaac, was a horned animal, being entangled in the brake by his curved horns; so far proving that it belonged to the tribe of the Capridae, the fat-tailed sheep appertaining to the same family.

LAMBS

From the large proportion of moisture or fluids contained in the tissues of all young animals, the flesh of lamb and veal is much more prone, in close, damp weather, to become tainted and spoil than the flesh of the more mature, drier, and closer-textured beef and mutton. Among epicures, the most delicious sorts of lamb are those of the South-Down breed, known by their black feet; and of these, those which have been exclusively suckled on the milk of the parent ewe, are considered the finest. Next to these in estimation are those fed on the milk of several dams, and last of all, though the fattest, the grass-fed lamb; this, however, implies an age much greater than either of the others.

In the purchasing of lamb for the table, there are certain signs by which the experienced judgment is able to form an accurate opinion whether the animal has been lately slaughtered, and whether the joints possess that condition of fibre indicative of good and wholesome meat. The first of these doubts may be solved satisfactorily by the bright and dilated appearance of the eye; the quality of the fore quarter can always be guaranteed by the blue or healthy ruddiness of the jugular, or vein of the neck; while the rigidity of the knuckle, and the firm, compact feel of the kidney, will answer in an equally positive manner for the integrity of the hind quarter.

CHAPTER XV

RECIPES*

Braised Leg of Mutton

INGREDIENTS.—1 small leg of mutton, 4 carrots, 3 onions, 1 faggot of savoury herbs, a bunch of parsley, seasoning to taste of pepper and salt, a few slices of bacon, a few veal trimmings, ½ pint of gravy or water.

Mode.—Line the bottom of a braising-pan with a few slices of bacon, put in the carrots, onions, herbs, parsley, and seasoning, and over these place the mutton. Cover the whole with a few more slices of bacon and the veal trimmings, pour in the gravy or water, and stew very *gently* for 4 hours. Strain the gravy, reduce it to a glaze over a sharp fire, glaze the mutton with it, and send it to table, placed on a dish of white haricot beans boiled tender, or garnished with glazed onions.

Time.—4 hours.

Average cost, 5s.

Sufficient for 6 or 7 persons.

Seosonable at any time.

THE ORDER OF THE GOLDEN FLEECE.—This order of knighthood was founded by Philip the Good, duke of Burgundy, in 1429, on the day of his marriage with the Princess Isabella of Portugal. The number of the members was originally fixed at thirty-one, including the sovereign, as the head and chief of the institution. In 1516, Pope Leo X consented to increase the number to fifty-two, including the head. In 1700 the German emperor Charles VI and King Philip of Spain both laid claim to the order. The former, however, on leaving Spain, which he could not maintain by force of arms, took with him, to Vienna, the archives of the order, the inauguration of which he solemnized there in 1713, with great magnificence; but Philip V of Spain declared himself Grand Master, and formally protested, at the congress of Cambrai (1721), against the pretensions of the emperor. The dispute, though subsequently settled by the intercession of France, England, and Holland, was frequently renewed, until the order was tacitly introduced into both countries, and it now passes by the respective names of the Spanish or Austrian 'Order of the Golden Fleece,' according to the country where it is issued.

China Chilo*

INGREDIENTS.—1½ lb. of leg, loin, or neck of mutton, 2 onions, 2 lettuces, 1 pint of green peas, 1 teaspoonful of salt, 1 teaspoonful of pepper, ¼ pint of water, ¼ lb. of clarified butter; when liked, a little cayenne.

Mode.—Mince the above quantity of undressed leg, loin, or neck of mutton, adding a little of the fat, also minced; put it into a stew-pan with the remaining ingredients, previously shredding the lettuce and onion rather fine; closely cover the stewpan, after the ingredients have been well stirred, and simmer gently for rather more than 2 hours. Serve in a dish, with a border of rice round, the same as for curry.

Time.—Rather more than 2 hours.   *Average cost,* 1s. 6d.

Sufficient for 3 or 4 persons.

Seasonable from June to August.

Irish Stew*

INGREDIENTS.—3 lbs. of the loin or neck of mutton, 5 lbs. of potatoes, 5 large onions, pepper and salt to taste, rather more than 1 pint of water.

Mode.—Trim off some of the fat of the above quantity of loin or neck of mutton, and cut it into chops of a moderate thickness. Pare and halve the potatoes, and cut the onions into thick slices. Put a layer of potatoes at the bottom of a stewpan, then a layer of mutton and onions, and season with pepper and salt; proceed in this manner until the stewpan is full, taking care to have plenty of vegetables at the top. Pour in the water, and let it stew very gently for 2½ hours, keeping the lid of the stewpan closely shut the *whole* time, and occasionally shaking it to prevent its burning.

Time.—2½ hours.   *Average cost,* for this quantity, 2s. 8d.

Sufficient for 5 or 6 persons.

Seasonable.—More suitable for a winter dish.

Italian Mutton Cutlets

INGREDIENTS.—About 3 lbs. of the neck of mutton, clarified butter, the yolk of 1 egg, 4 tablespoonfuls of bread crumbs, 1 tablespoonful of minced savoury herbs, 1 tablespoonful of minced parsley,

1 teaspoonful of minced shalot, 1 saltspoonful of finely-chopped lemon-peel; pepper, salt, and pounded mace to taste; flour, ½ pint of hot broth or water, 2 teaspoonfuls of Harvey's sauce, 1 teaspoonful of soy, 2 teaspoonfuls of tarragon vinegar, 1 tablespoonful of port wine.

Mode.—Cut the mutton into nicely-shaped cutlets, flatten them, and trim off some of the fat, dip them in clarified butter, and then into the beaten yolk of an egg. Mix well together bread crumbs, herbs, parsley, shalot, lemon-peel, and seasoning in the above proportion, and cover the cutlets with these ingredients. Melt some butter in a frying-pan, lay in the cutlets, and fry them a nice brown; take them out, and keep them hot before the fire. Dredge some flour into the pan, and if there is not sufficient butter, add a little more; stir till it looks brown, then pour in the hot broth or water, and the remaining ingredients; give one boil, and pour round the cutlets. If the gravy should not be thick enough, add a little more flour. Mushrooms, when obtainable, are a great improvement to this dish, and when not in season, mushroom-powder may be substituted for them.

Time.—10 minutes;—rather longer, should the cutlets be very thick.

Average cost, 2s. 9d.

Sufficient for 5 or 6 persons.

Seasonable at any time.

Roast Leg of Mutton*

INGREDIENTS.—Leg of mutton, a little salt.

Mode.—As mutton, when freshly killed, is never tender, hang it almost as long as it will keep; flour it, and put it in a cool airy place

Leg of Mutton

for a few days, if the weather will permit. Wash off the flour, wipe it very dry, and cut off the shank-bone; put it down to a brisk clear fire, dredge with flour, and keep continually basting the whole time it is cooking. About 20 minutes before serving, draw it near the fire to get nicely brown; sprinkle over it a little salt, dish the meat, pour off the dripping, add some boiling water slightly salted, strain it over the joint, and serve.

Time.—A leg of mutton weighing 10 lbs., about 2¼ or 2½ hours; one of 7 lbs., about 2 hours, or rather less.

Average cost, 8½*d.* per lb.

Sufficient.—A moderate-sized leg of mutton sufficient for 6 or 8 persons.

Seasonable at any time, but not so good in June, July, and August.

Rolled Loin of Mutton (Very Excellent)

INGREDIENTS.—About 6 lbs. of a loin of mutton, ½ teaspoonful of pepper, ¼ teaspoonful of pounded allspice, ¼ teaspoonful of mace, ¼ teaspoonful of nutmeg, 6 cloves, forcemeat (p. 128), 1 glass of port wine, 2 tablespoonfuls of mushroom ketchup.

Mode.—Hang the mutton till tender, bone it, and sprinkle over it pepper, mace, cloves, allspice, and nutmeg in the above proportion, all of which must be pounded very fine. Let it remain for a day, then make a forcemeat, cover the meat with it, and roll and bind it up firmly. Half bake it in a slow oven, let it grow cold, take off the fat, and put the gravy into a stewpan; flour the meat, put it in the gravy, and stew it till perfectly tender. Now take out the meat, unbind it, add to the gravy wine and ketchup as above, give one boil, and pour over the meat. Serve with red-currant jelly; and, if obtainable, a few mushrooms stewed for a few minutes in the gravy, will be found a great improvement.

Time.—1½ hour to bake the meat, 1½ hour to stew gently.

Average cost, 4*s.* 9*d.* *Sufficient* for 5 or 6 persons.

Seasonable at any time.

Note.—This joint will be found very nice if rolled and stuffed, as here directed, and plainly roasted. It should be well basted, and served with a good gravy and currant jelly.

Roast Saddle of Mutton*

INGREDIENTS.—Saddle of mutton; a little salt.

Mode.—To insure this joint being tender, let it hang for ten days or a fortnight, if the weather permits. Cut off the tail and flaps, and trim away every part that has not indisputable pretensions to be eaten, and have the skin taken off and skewered on again. Put it down to a bright, clear fire, and, when the joint has been cooking for

Saddle of Mutton

an hour, remove the skin and dredge it with flour. It should not be placed too near the fire, as the fat should not be in the slightest degree burnt. Keep constantly basting, both before and after the skin is removed; sprinkle some salt over the joint. Make a little gravy in the dripping-pan; pour it over the meat, which send to table with a tureen of made gravy and red-currant jelly.

Time.—A saddle of mutton weighing 10 lbs., 2½ hours; 14 lbs., 3¼ hours. When liked underdone, allow rather less time.

Average cost, 10*d*. per lb.

Sufficient.—A moderate-sized saddle of 10 lbs. for 7 or 8 persons.

Seasonable all the year; not so good when lamb is in full season.

To Dress a Sheep's Head*

INGREDIENTS.—1 sheep's head, sufficient water to cover it, 3 carrots, 3 turnips, 2 or 3 parsnips, 3 onions, a small bunch of parsley, 1 teaspoonful of pepper, 3 teaspoonfuls of salt, ¼ lb. of Scotch oatmeal.

Mode.—Clean the head well, and let it soak in warm water for 2 hours, to get rid of the blood; put it into a saucepan, with sufficient cold water to cover it, and when it boils, add the vegetables, peeled and sliced, and the remaining ingredients; before adding the oatmeal, mix it to a smooth batter with a little of the liquor. Keep stirring till it boils up; then shut the saucepan closely, and let it stew gently for 1½ or 2 hours. It may be thickened with rice or barley, but oatmeal is preferable.

Time.—1½ or 2 hours. *Average cost*, 8*d*. each.

Sufficient for 3 persons.

Seasonable at any time.

SINGED SHEEP'S HEAD.—The village of Dudingston, which stands 'within a mile of Edinburgh town,' was formerly celebrated for this ancient and homely Scottish dish. In the summer months, many opulent citizens used to resort to this place to solace themselves over singed sheep's heads, boiled or baked. The sheep fed upon the neighbouring hills were slaughtered at this village, and the carcases were sent to town; but the heads were left to be consumed in the place. We are not aware whether the custom of eating sheep's heads at Dudingston is still kept up by the good folks of Edinburgh.

Lamb Chops*

INGREDIENTS.—Loin of lamb, pepper and salt to taste.

Mode.—Trim off the flap from a fine loin of lamb, and cut it into chops about ¾ inch in thickness. Have ready a bright clear fire; lay the chops on a gridiron, and broil them of a nice pale brown, turning them when required. Season them with pepper and salt; serve very hot and quickly, and garnish with crisped parsley, or place them on mashed potatoes. Asparagus, spinach, or peas are the favourite accompaniments to lamb chops.

Time.—About 8 or 10 minutes. *Average cost*, 1s. per lb.

Sufficient.—Allow 2 chops to each person.

Seasonable from Easter to Michaelmas.

Roast Shoulder of Lamb

INGREDIENTS.—Lamb; a little salt.

Mode.—Have ready a clear brisk fire, and put down the joint at a sufficient distance from it, that the fat may not burn. Keep constantly basting until done, and serve with a little gravy made in the dripping-pan, and send mint sauce to table with it. Peas, spinach, or cauliflowers are the usual vegetables served with lamb, and also a fresh salad.

Time.—A shoulder of lamb rather more than 1 hour.

Average cost, 10d. to 1s. per lb.

Sufficient for 4 or 5 persons.

Seasonable from Easter to Michaelmas.

Lamb's Sweetbreads, Larded, and
Asparagus (an Entrée)

INGREDIENTS.—2 or 3 sweetbreads, ½ pint of veal stock, white pepper and salt to taste, a small bunch of green onions, 1 blade of pounded mace, thickening of butter and flour, 2 eggs, nearly ½ pint of cream, 1 teaspoonful of minced parsley, a very little grated nutmeg.

Mode.—Soak the sweetbreads in lukewarm water, and put them into a saucepan with sufficient boiling water to cover them, and let them simmer for 10 minutes; then take them out and put them into cold water. Now lard them, lay them in a stewpan, add the stock, seasoning, onions, mace, and a thickening of butter and flour, and stew gently for ¼ hour or 20 minutes. Beat up the egg with the cream, to which add the minced parsley and a very little grated nutmeg. Put this to the other ingredients; stir it well till quite hot, but do not let it boil after the cream is added, or it will curdle. Have ready some asparagus-tops, boiled; add these to the sweetbreads, and serve.

Time.—Altogether ½ hour.   *Average cost*, 2s. 6d. to 3s. 6d. each.

Sufficient.—3 sweetbreads for 1 entrée.

Seasonable from Easter to Michaelmas.

MUTTON AND LAMB CARVING

Leg of Mutton

This homely, but capital English joint, is almost invariably served at table as shown in the engraving. The carving of it is not very difficult: the knife should be carried sharply down in the direction of

Leg of Mutton

the line from 1 to 2, and slices taken from either side, as the guests may desire, some liking the knuckle-end, as well done, and others preferring the more underdone part. The fat should be sought near the line 3 to 4. Some connoisseurs are fond of having this joint dished with the under-side uppermost, so as to get at the finely-grained meat lying under that part of the meat, known as the Pope's eye; but this is an extravagant fashion, and one that will hardly find favour in the eyes of many economical British housewives and housekeepers.*

Saddle of Mutton

Although we have heard, at various intervals, growlings expressed at the inevitable 'saddle of mutton' at the dinner-parties of our middle classes, yet we doubt whether any other joint is better liked, when it has been well hung and artistically cooked.* There is a diversity of opinion respecting the mode of sending this joint to table; but it has only reference to whether or no there shall be any portion of the tail, or, if so, how many joints of the tail. Some trim the tail with a paper frill. The carving is not difficult: it is usually cut in the direction of the line from 2 to 1, quite down to the

Saddle of Mutton

bones, in evenly-sliced pieces. A fashion, however, patronized by some, is to carve it obliquely, in the direction of the line from 4 to 3; in which case the joint would be turned round the other way, having the tail end on the right of the carver.

CHAPTER XVI

GENERAL OBSERVATIONS ON
THE COMMON HOG

The hog belongs to the order *Mammalia*, the genus *Sus scrofa*, and the species *Pachydermata*, or thick-skinned; and its generic characters are, a small head, with long flexible snout truncated; 42 teeth, divided into 4 upper incisors, converging, 6 lower incisors, projecting, 2 upper and 2 lower canine, or tusks,—the former short, the latter projecting, formidable, and sharp, and 14 molars in each jaw; cloven feet furnished with 4 toes, and tail, small, short, and twisted; while, in some varieties, this appendage is altogether wanting.

Whatever difference in its physical nature climate and soil may produce in this animal, his functional characteristics are the same in whatever part of the world he may be found; and whether in the trackless forests of South America, the coral isles of Polynesia, the jungles of India, or the spicy brakes of Sumatra, he is everywhere known for his gluttony, laziness, and indifference to the character and quality of his food. And though he occasionally shows an epicure's relish for a succulent plant or a luscious carrot, which he will discuss with all his salivary organs keenly excited, he will, the next moment, turn with equal gusto to some carrion offal that might excite the forbearance of the unscrupulous cormorant. It is this coarse and repulsive mode of feeding that has, in every country and language, obtained for him the opprobrium of being 'an unclean animal.'

In the Mosaical Law, the pig is condemned as an unclean beast, and consequently interdicted to the Israelites, as unfit for human food. 'And the swine, though he divideth the hoof and be cloven footed, yet he cheweth not the cud. He is unclean to you.'—Lev. xi. 7. Strict, however, as the law was respecting the cud-chewing and hoof-divided animals, the Jews, with their usual perversity and violation of the divine commands, seem afterwards to have ignored the prohibition; for, unless they ate pork, it is difficult to conceive for what purpose they kept droves of swine, as from the circumstance recorded in Matthew xviii. 32, when Jesus was in Galilee, and the devils, cast out of the two men, were permitted to enter the herd of swine that were feeding on the hills in the neighbourhood of the Sea of Tiberias, it is very evident they did. There is only one interpretation by which we can account for a prohibition that debarred the Jews from so many foods which we regard as nutritious luxuries, that, being fat and the texture more hard of digestion than other meats, they were likely, in a hot dry climate, where vigorous exercise could seldom be taken, to produce disease, and especially cutaneous affections; indeed, in this light, as a code of sanitary ethics, the book of Leviticus is the most admirable system of moral government ever conceived for man's benefit.

From the grossness of his feeding, the large amount of aliment he consumes, his gluttonous way of eating it, from his slothful habits, laziness, and indulgence in sleep, the pig is particularly liable to disease, and especially indigestion, heartburn, and affections of the skin.

To counteract the consequence of a violation of the physical laws, a powerful monitor in the brain of the pig teaches him to seek for relief and medicine. To open the pores of his skin, blocked up with mud, and excite perspiration, he resorts to a tree, a stump, or his trough—anything rough and angular, and using it as a curry-comb to his body, obtains the luxury of a scratch and the benefit of cuticular evaporation; he next proceeds with his long supple snout to grub up antiscorbutic roots, cooling salads of mallow and dandelion, and, greatest treat of all, he stumbles on a piece of chalk or a mouthful of delicious cinder, which, he knows by instinct, is the most sovereign remedy in the world for that hot, unpleasant sensation he has had all the morning at his stomach.

It is a remarkable fact that, though every one who keeps a pig knows how prone he is to disease, how that disease injures the quality of the meat, and how eagerly he pounces on a bit of coal or cinder, or any coarse dry substance that will adulterate the rich food on which he lives, and by affording soda to his system, correct the vitiated fluids of his body,—yet very few have the judgment to act on what they see, and by supplying the pig with a few shovelfuls of cinders in his sty, save the necessity of his rooting for what is so needful to his health. Instead of this, however, and without supplying the animal with what its instinct craves for, his nostril is bored with a red-hot iron, and a ring clinched in his nose to prevent rooting for what he feels to be absolutely necessary for his health; and ignoring the fact that, in a domestic state at least, the pig lives on the richest of all food,—scraps of cooked animal substances, boiled vegetables, bread, and other items, given in that concentrated essence of aliment for a quadruped called wash, and that he eats to repletion, takes no exercise, and finally sleeps all the twenty-four hours he is not eating, and then, when the animal at last seeks for those medicinal aids which would obviate the evil of such a forcing diet, his keeper, instead of meeting his animal instinct by human reason, and giving him what he seeks, has the inhumanity to torture him by a ring, that, keeping up a perpetual 'raw' in the pig's snout, prevents his digging for those corrective drugs which would remove the evils of his artificial existence.*

We have already said that no other animal yields man so *many* kinds and varieties of luxurious food as is supplied to him by the flesh of the hog differently prepared; for almost every part of the animal, either fresh, salted, or dried, is used for food; and even those viscera not so employed are of the utmost utility in a domestic point of view.

Though destitute of the hide, horns, and hoofs, constituting the offal of most domestic animals, the pig is not behind the other mammalia in its usefulness to man. Its skin, especially that of the boar, from its extreme closeness of texture, when tanned, is employed for the seats of saddles, to cover powder, shot, and drinking-flasks; and the hair, according to its colour, flexibility, and stubbornness, is manufactured into tooth, nail, and hair-brushes,— others into hat, clothes, and shoe-brushes; while the longer and finer qualities are made into long and short brooms and painters' brushes; and a still more rigid description, under the name of 'bristles,' are used by the shoemaker as needles for the passage of his wax-end. Besides so many benefits and useful services conferred on man by this valuable animal, his fat, in a commercial sense, is quite as important as his flesh, and brings a price equal to the best joints in the carcase. This fat is rendered, or melted out of the caul, or membrane in which it is contained, by boiling water, and, while liquid, run into prepared bladders, when, under the name of *lard*, it becomes an article of extensive trade and value.

The best and most humane mode of killing all large hogs is to strike them down like a bullock, with the pointed end of a poleaxe, on the forehead, which has the effect of killing the animal at once; all the butcher has then to do, is to open the aorta and great arteries, and laying the animal's neck over a trough, let out the blood as quickly as possible. The carcase is then to be scalded, either on a board or by immersion in a tub of very hot water, and all the hair and dirt rapidly scraped off, till the skin is made perfectly white, when it is hung up, opened, and dressed, as it is called, in the usual way. It is then allowed to cool, a sheet being thrown around the carcase, to prevent the air from discolouring the newly-cleaned skin. When meant for bacon, the hair is singed instead of being scalded off.

Pork, to be preserved, is cured in several ways,—either by covering it with salt, or immersing it in ready-made brine, where it is kept till required; or it is only partially salted, and then hung up to dry, when the meat is called white bacon; or, after salting, it is hung in wood smoke till the flesh is impregnated with the aroma from the wood. The Wiltshire bacon, which is regarded as the finest in the kingdom, is prepared by laying the sides of a hog in large wooden troughs, and then rubbing into the flesh quantities of powdered bay-salt, made hot in a frying-pan. This process is repeated for four days; they are then left for three weeks, merely turning the flitches every other day. After that time they are hung up to dry. The hogs usually killed for purposes of bacon in England average from 18 to 20 stone; on the other hand, the hogs killed in the country for farm-house purposes, seldom weigh less than 26 stone. The legs of boars, hogs, and, in Germany, those of bears, are prepared differently, and called hams.

CHAPTER XVII

RECIPES*

Roast Leg of Pork

INGREDIENTS.—Leg of pork, a little oil for stuffing. (*See* Recipe, pp. 138–9.)

Mode.—Choose a small leg of pork, and score the skin across in narrow strips, about ¼ inch apart. Cut a slit in the knuckle, loosen the skin, and fill it with a sage-and-onion stuffing. Brush the joint over with a little salad-oil (this makes the crackling crisper, and a better colour), and put it down to a

Roast Leg of Pork

bright, clear fire, not too near, as that would cause the skin to blister. Baste it well, and serve with a little gravy made in the dripping-pan, and do not omit to send to table with it a tureen of well-made apple-sauce. (*See* Recipe, p. 121.)

Time.—A leg of pork weighing 8 lbs., about 3 hours.

Average cost, 9*d*. per lb.

Sufficient for 6 or 7 persons.

Seasonable from September to March.

To Cure Bacon in the Wiltshire Way*

INGREDIENTS.—1½ lb. of coarse sugar, 1½ lb. of bay-salt, 6 oz. of saltpetre,* 1 lb. of common salt.

Mode.—Sprinkle each flitch with salt, and let the blood drain off for 24 hours; then pound and mix the above ingredients well together and rub it well into the meat, which should be turned every day for a month; then hang it to dry, and afterwards smoke it for 10 days.

Time.—To remain in the pickle 1 month, to be smoked 10 days.

Sufficient.—The above quantity of salt for 1 pig.

HOW PIGS WERE FORMERLY PASTURED AND FED.—Though unquestionably far greater numbers of swine are now kept in England than formerly, every peasant having one or more of that useful animal, in feudal times immense droves of pigs were kept by the franklings and barons; in those days the swine-herds being a regular part of the domestic service of every feudal household, their duty consisted in daily driving the herd of swine from the castle-yard, or outlying farm, to the nearest woods, chase, or forest, where the frankling or vavasour had, either by right or grant, what was called *free warren*, or the liberty to feed his hogs off the acorns, beech, and chestnuts that lay in such abundance on the earth, and far exceeded the power of the royal or privileged game to consume. Indeed, it was the license granted the nobles of free warren, especially for their swine, that kept up the iniquitous forest laws to so late a date, and covered so large a portion of the land with such immense tracts of wood and brake, to the injury of agriculture and the misery of the people. Some idea of the extent to which swine were grazed in the feudal times, may be formed by observing the number of pigs still fed in Epping Forest, the Forest of Dean, and the New Forest, in Hampshire, where, for several months of the year, the beech-nuts and acorns yield them so plentiful a diet. In Germany, where the chestnut is so largely cultivated, the amount of food shed every autumn is enormous; and consequently the pig, both wild and domestic, has, for a considerable portion of the year, an unfailing supply of admirable nourishment. Impressed with the value of this fruit for the food of pigs, the Prince Consort has, with great judgment, of late encouraged the collection of chestnuts in Windsor Park, and by giving a small reward to old people and children for every bushel collected, has not only found an occupation for many of the unemployed poor, but, by providing a gratuitous food for their pig, encouraged a feeling of providence and economy.

HOG NOT BACON. ANECDOTE OF LORD BACON:*—As Lord Bacon, on one occasion, was about to pass sentence of death upon a man of the name of Hogg, who had just been tried for a long career of crime, the prisoner suddenly claimed to be heard in arrest of judgment, saying, with an expression of arch confidence as he addressed the bench, 'I claim indulgence, my lord, on the plea of relationship; for I am convinced your lordship will never be unnatural enough to hang one of your own family.'

'Indeed,' replied the judge, with some amazement, 'I was not aware that I had the honour of your alliance; perhaps you will be good enough to name the degree of our mutual affinity.'

'I am sorry, my lord,' returned the impudent thief, 'I cannot trace the links of consanguinity; but the moral evidence is sufficiently pertinent. My name, my lord, is Hogg, your lordship's is Bacon; and all the world will allow that bacon and hog are *very* closely allied.'

'I am sorry,' replied his lordship, 'I cannot admit the truth of your instance: hog cannot be bacon till it is *hanged*; and so, before I can admit your plea, or acknowledge the family compact, Hogg must be hanged to-morrow morning.'

To Bake a Ham

INGREDIENTS.—Ham; a common crust.*

Mode.—As a ham for baking should be well soaked, let it remain in water for at least 12 hours. Wipe it dry, trim away any rusty places underneath, and cover it with a common crust, taking care that this is of sufficient thickness all over to keep the gravy in. Place it in a moderately-heated oven, and bake for nearly 4 hours. Take off the crust, and skin, and cover with raspings, the same as for boiled ham, and garnish the knuckle with a paper frill. This method of cooking a ham is, by many persons, considered far superior to boiling it, as it cuts fuller of gravy and has a finer flavour, besides keeping a much longer time good.

Time. A medium-sized ham, 4 hours.

Average cost, from 8*d*. to 10*d*. per lb. by the whole ham.

Seasonable all the year.

To Salt Two Hams, about 12 or 15 lbs. each

INGREDIENTS.—2 lbs. of treacle, ½ lb. of saltpetre, 1 lb. of bay-salt, 2 pounds of common salt.

Mode.—Two days before they are put into pickle, rub the hams well with salt, to draw away all slime and blood. Throw what comes from them away, and then rub them with treacle, saltpetre, and salt. Lay them in a deep pan, and let them remain one day; boil the above proportion of treacle, saltpetre, bay-salt, and common salt for ¼ hour, and pour this pickle boiling hot over the hams: there should be sufficient of it to cover them. For a day or two rub them well with it; afterwards they will only require turning. They ought to remain in this pickle for 3 weeks or a month, and then be sent to be smoked, which will take nearly or quite a month to do. An ox-tongue pickled in this way is most excellent, to be eaten either green or smoked.

Time.—To remain in the pickle 3 weeks or a month; to be smoked about a month.

Seasonable from October to March.

To Smoke Hams and Fish at Home

Take an old hogshead, stop up all the crevices, and fix a place to put a cross-stick near the bottom, to hang the articles to be smoked on. Next, in the side, cut a hole near the top, to introduce an iron pan filled with sawdust and small pieces of green wood. Having turned the tub upside down, hang the articles upon the cross-stick, introduce the iron pan in the opening, and place a piece of red-hot iron in the pan, cover it with sawdust, and all will be complete. Let a large ham remain 40 hours, and keep up a good smoke.

Collared Pig's Face (a Breakfast or Luncheon Dish)

INGREDIENTS.—1 pig's face; salt. For brine, 1 gallon of spring water, 1 lb. of common salt, ½ handful of chopped juniper-berries, 6 bruised cloves, 2 bay-leaves, a few sprigs of thyme, basil, sage, ¼ oz. of saltpetre. For forcemeat, ½ lb. of ham, ½ lb. bacon, 1 teaspoonful of mixed spices, pepper to taste, ¼ lb. of lard, 1 tablespoonful of minced parsley, 6 young onions.

Mode.—Singe the head carefully, bone it without breaking the skin, and rub it well with salt. Make the brine by boiling the above

Pig's Face

ingredients for ¼ hour, and letting it stand to cool. When cold, pour it over the head, and let it steep in this for 10 days, turning and rubbing it often. Then wipe, drain, and dry it. For the forcemeat, pound the ham and bacon very finely, and mix with these the remaining ingredients, taking care that the whole is thoroughly incorporated. Spread this equally over the head, roll it tightly in a cloth, and bind it securely with broad tape. Put it into a saucepan with a few meat trimmings, and cover it with stock; let it simmer gently for 4 hours, and be particular that it does not stop boiling the whole time. When quite tender, take it up, put it between 2 dishes with a heavy weight on the top, and when cold, remove the cloth and tape. It should be sent to table on a napkin, or garnished with a piece of deep white paper with a ruche at the top.

Time.—4 hours. *Average cost,* from 2s. to 2s. 6d.

Seasonable from October to March.

Pig's Pettitoes*

INGREDIENTS.—A thin slice of bacon, 1 onion, 1 blade of mace, 6 peppercorns, 3 or 4 sprigs of thyme, 1 pint of gravy, pepper and salt to taste, thickening of butter and flour.

Mode.—Put the liver, heart, and pettitoes into a stewpan with the bacon, mace, peppercorns, thyme, onion, and gravy, and simmer these gently for ¼ hour; then take out the heart and liver, and mince them very fine. Keep stewing the feet until quite tender, which will be in from 20 minutes to ½ hour, reckoning from the time that they boiled up first; then put back the minced liver, thicken the gravy with a little butter and flour, season with pepper and salt, and simmer over a gentle fire for 5 minutes, occasionally stirring the contents. Dish the mince, split the feet, and arrange them round alternately with sippets of toasted bread, and pour the gravy in the middle.

Time.—Altogether 40 minutes.

Sufficient for 3 or 4 persons.

Seasonable from September to March.

Pork Pies* (Warwickshire Recipe)

INGREDIENTS.—For the crust, 5 lbs. of lard to 14 lbs. of flour, milk, and water. For filling the pies, to every 3 lbs. of meat allow 1 oz. of salt, 2¼ oz. of pepper, a small quantity of cayenne, 1 pint of water.

Mode.—Rub into the flour a portion of the lard; the remainder put with sufficient milk and water to mix the crust, and boil this gently for ¼ hour. Pour it boiling on the flour, and knead and beat it till perfectly smooth. Now raise the crust in either a round or oval form, cut up the pork into pieces the size of a nut, season it in the above proportion, and press it compactly into the pie, in alternate layers of fat and lean, and pour in a small quantity of water; lay on the lid, cut the edges smoothly round, and pinch them together. Bake in a brick oven, which should be slow, as the meat is very solid. Very frequently, the inexperienced cook finds much difficulty in raising the crust. She should bear in mind that it must not be allowed to get cold, or it will fall immediately: to prevent this, the operation should be performed as near the fire as possible. As considerable dexterity and expertness are necessary to raise the crust with the hand only, a glass bottle or small jar may be placed in the middle of the paste, and the crust moulded on this; but be particular that it is kept warm the whole time.

Sufficient.—The proportions for 1 pie are 1 lb. of flour and 3 lbs. of meat.

Seasonable from September to March.

To Make Sausages
(*Author's Oxford Recipe*)

INGREDIENTS.—1 lb. of pork, fat and lean, without skin or gristle; 1 lb. of lean veal, 1 lb. of beef suet, ½ lb. of bread crumbs, the rind of ½ lemon, 1 small nutmeg, 6 sage-leaves, 1 teaspoonful of pepper, 2 teaspoonfuls of salt, ½ teaspoonful of savory, ½ teaspoonful of marjoram.

Mode.—Chop the pork, veal, and suet finely together, add the bread crumbs, lemon-peel (which should be well minced), and a small nutmeg grated. Wash and chop the sage-leaves very finely; add these with the remaining ingredients to the sausage-meat, and when thoroughly mixed, either put the meat into skins, or, when wanted for table, form it into little cakes, which should be floured and fried.

Average cost, for this quantity, 2*s*. 6*d*.

Sufficient for about 30 moderate-sized sausages.

Seasonable from October to March.

To Scald a Sucking-Pig

Put the pig into cold water directly it is killed; let it remain for a few minutes, then immerse it in a large pan of boiling water for 2 minutes. Take it out, lay it on a table, and pull off the hair as quickly as possible. When the skin looks clean, make a slit down the belly, take out the entrails, well clean the nostrils and ears, wash the pig in cold water, and wipe it thoroughly dry. Take off the feet at the first joint, and loosen and leave sufficient skin to turn neatly over. If not to be dressed immediately, fold it in a wet cloth to keep it from the air.

THE LEARNED PIG.—That the pig is capable of education, is a fact long known to the world; and though, like the ass, naturally stubborn and obstinate, that he is equally amenable with other animals to caresses and kindness, has been shown from very remote time; the best modern evidence of his docility, however, is the instance of the learned pig, first exhibited about a century since, but which has been continued down to our own time by repeated instances of an animal who will put together all the letters or figures that compose the day, month, hour and date of the exhibition, besides many other unquestioned evidences of memory. The instance already given of breaking a sow into a pointer, till she became more stanch even than the dog itself, though surprising, is far less wonderful than that evidence of education where so generally obtuse an animal may be taught not only to spell, but couple figures and give dates correctly.*

Roast Sucking-Pig

INGREDIENTS.—Pig, 6 oz. of bread crumbs, 16 sage-leaves, pepper and salt to taste, a piece of butter the size of an egg, salad oil or butter to baste with, about ½ pint of gravy, 1 tablespoonful of lemon-juice.

Mode.—A sucking-pig, to be eaten in perfection, should not be more than three weeks old, and should be dressed the same day that it is killed. After preparing the pig for cooking, as in the preceding recipe, stuff it with finely-grated bread crumbs, minced sage, pepper, salt, and a piece of butter the size of an egg, all of which should be well mixed together, and put into the body of the pig. Sew up the slit neatly, and truss the legs back, to allow the inside to be roasted, and the under part to be crisp. Put the pig down to a bright clear fire, not too near, and let it lay till thoroughly dry; then have ready some butter tied up in a piece of thin

Roast Sucking-Pig

cloth, and rub the pig with this in every part. Keep it well rubbed with the butter the whole of the time it is roasting, and do not allow the crackling to become blistered or burnt. When half-done, hang a pig-iron before the middle part (if this is not obtainable, use a flat iron), to prevent its being scorched and dried up before the ends are done. Before it is taken from the fire, cut off the head, and part that and the body down the middle. Chop the brains and mix them with the stuffing; add ½ pint of good gravy, a tablespoonful of lemon-juice, and the gravy that flowed from the pig; put a little of this on the dish with the pig, and the remainder send to table in a tureen. Place the pig back to back in the dish, with one half of the head on each side, and one of the ears at each end, and send it to table as hot as possible. Instead of butter, many cooks take salad oil for basting, which makes the crackling *crisp*; and as this is one of the principal things to be considered, perhaps it is desirable to use it; but be particular that it is very pure, or it will impart an unpleasant flavour to the meat. The brains and stuffing may be stirred into a tureen of melted butter instead of gravy, when the latter is not liked. Apple sauce and the old-fashioned currant sauce are not yet quite obsolete as an accompaniment to roast pig.

Time.—1½ to 2 hours for a small pig.　　*Average cost*, 5s. to 6s.

Sufficient for 9 or 10 persons.

Seasonable from September to February.

HOW ROAST PIG WAS DISCOVERED.—Charles Lamb, who, in the early part of this century, delighted the reading public by his quaint prose sketches, written under the title of 'Essays of Elia,' has, in his own quiet humorous way, devoted one paper to the subject of *Roast Pig*, and more especially to that luxurious and toothsome dainty known as 'CRACKLING ;' and shows, in a manner peculiarly his own, *how crackling first came into the world*.

According to this erudite authority, man in the golden age, or at all events the primitive age, eat his pork and bacon raw, as, indeed, he did his beef and mutton; unless, as Hudibras tells us, he was an epicure, when he used to make a saddle of his saddle of mutton, and after spreading it on his horse's back, and riding on it for a few hours till thoroughly warmed, he sat down to the luxury of a dish cooked to a turn. At the epoch of the story, however, a citizen of some Scythian community had the misfortune to have his hut, or that portion of it containing his live stock of pigs, burnt down. In going over the *débris* on the following day, and picking out all the available salvage, the proprietor touched something unusually or unexpectedly hot, which caused him to shake his hand with great energy, and clap the tips of his suffering fingers to his mouth. The act was simple and natural, but the result was wonderful. He rolled his eyes in ecstatic pleasure, his frame distended, and, conscious of a celestial odour, his nostrils widened, and, while drawing in deep inspirations of the ravishing perfume, he sucked his fingers with a gusto he had never, in his most hungry moments, conceived. Clearing away the rubbish from beneath him, he at last brought to view the carcase of one of his pigs, *roasted to death*. Stooping down to examine this curious object, and touching its body, a fragment of the burnt skin was detached, which, with a sort of superstitious dread, he at length, and in a spirit of philosophical inquiry put into his mouth. Ye gods! the felicity he then enjoyed, no pen can chronicle! Then it was that he—the world—first tasted *crackling*. Like a miser with his gold, the Scythian hid his treasure from the prying eyes of the world, and feasted, in secret, more sumptuously than the gods. When he had eaten up all his pig, the poor man fell into a melancholy; he refused the most tempting steak, though cooked on the horse's back, and turned every half-hour after his own favourite recipe; he fell, in fact, from his appetite, and was reduced to a shadow, till, unable longer to endure the torments of memory he hourly suffered, he rose one night and secretly set fire to his hut and once more was restored to flesh and manhood. Finding it impossible to live in future without roast-pig, he set fire to his house every time his larder became empty; till at last his neighbours, scandalized by the frequency of these incendiary acts, brought his conduct before the supreme council of the nation. To avert the penalty that awaited him, he brought his judges to the smouldering ruins, and discovering the secret, invited them to eat; which having done, with tears of gratitude, the august synod embraced him, and, with an overflowing feeling of ecstasy, dedicated a statue to the memory of the man who first *instituted roast pork*.

CHAPTER XVIII

GENERAL OBSERVATIONS ON THE CALF*

The cow goes with young for nine months, and the affection and solicitude she evinces for her offspring is more human in its tenderness and intensity than is displayed by any other animal; and her distress when she hears its bleating, and is not allowed to reach it with her distended udders, is often painful to witness, and when the calf has died, or been accidentally killed, her grief frequently makes her refuse to give down her milk. At such times, the breeder has adopted the expedient of flaying the dead carcase, and, distending the skin with hay, lays the effigy before her, and then taking advantage of her solicitude, milks her while she is caressing the skin with her tongue.

In some countries, to please the epicurean taste of vitiated appetites, it is the custom to kill the calf for food almost immediately after birth, and any accident that forestalls that event, is considered to enhance its value. We are happy to say, however, that in this country, as far as England and Scotland are concerned, the taste for very young veal has entirely gone out and 'Staggering Bob,' as the poor little animal was called in the language of the shambles, is no longer to be met with in such a place.

There was no species of slaughtering practised in this country so inhuman and disgraceful as that, till very lately, employed in killing this poor animal; when, under the plea of making the flesh *white*, the calf was bled day by day, till, when the final hour came, the animal was unable to stand. This inhumanity is, we believe, now everywhere abolished, and the calf is at once killed, and with the least amount of pain; a sharp-pointed knife is run through the neck, severing all the large veins and arteries up to the vertebrae. The skin is then taken off to the knee, which is disjointed, and to the head, which is removed; it is then reflected backwards, and the carcase having been opened and dressed, is kept apart by stretchers, and the thin membrane, the caul, extended over the organs left in the carcase, as the kidneys and sweetbread; some melted fat is then scattered suddenly over the whole interior, giving that white and frosted appearance to the meat, that is thought to add to its beauty; the whole is then hung up to cool and harden.

CHAPTER XIX

RECIPES*

Stewed Breast of Veal and Peas

INGREDIENTS.—Breast of veal, 2 oz. of butter, a bunch of savoury herbs, including parsley; 2 blades of pounded mace, 2 cloves, 5 or 6 young onions, 1 strip of lemon-peel, 6 allspice, ¼ teaspoonful of pepper, 1 teaspoonful of salt, thickening of butter and flour, 2 table-spoonfuls of sherry, 2 tablespoonfuls of tomato sauce, 1 tablespoon-ful of lemon-juice, 2 tablespoonfuls of mushroom ketchup, green peas.

Mode.—Cut the breast in half, after removing the bone under-neath, and divide the meat into convenient-sized pieces. Put the butter into a frying-pan, lay in the pieces of veal, and fry until of a nice brown colour. Now place these in a stewpan with the herbs, mace, cloves, onions, lemon-peel, allspice, and seasoning; pour over them just sufficient boiling water to cover the meat; well close the lid, and let the whole simmer very gently for about 2 hours. Strain off as much gravy as is required, thicken it with butter and flour, add the remaining ingredients, skim well, let it simmer for about 10 minutes, then pour it over the meat. Have ready some green peas, boiled separately; sprinkle these over the veal, and serve. It may be garnished with forcemeat balls, or rashers of bacon curled and fried. Instead of cutting up the meat, many persons prefer it dressed whole;—in that case it should be half-roasted before the water, &c. are put to it.

Time.—2¼ hours. *Average cost,* 8½d. per lb.

Sufficient for 5 or 6 persons.

Seasonable from March to October.

Veal Cake (a Convenient Dish for a Picnic)

INGREDIENTS.—A few slices of cold roast veal, a few slices of cold ham, 2 hard-boiled eggs, 2 tablespoonfuls of minced parsley, a little pepper, good gravy.

Mode.—Cut off all the brown outside from the veal, and cut the eggs into slices. Procure a pretty mould; lay veal, ham, eggs, and parsley in layers, with a little pepper between each, and when the mould is full, get some *strong* stock, and fill up the shape. Bake for ½ hour, and when cold, turn it out.

Time.—½ hour.

Seasonable at any time.

Boiled Calf's Feet and Parsley and Butter

INGREDIENTS.—2 calf's feet, 2 slices of bacon, 2 oz. of butter, 2 tablespoonfuls of lemon-juice, salt and whole pepper to taste, 1 onion, a bunch of savoury herbs, 4 cloves, 1 blade of mace, water, parsley and butter.

Mode.—Procure 2 white calf's feet; bone them as far as the first joint, and put them into warm water to soak for 2 hours. Then put the bacon, butter, lemon-juice, onion, herbs, spices, and seasoning into a stewpan; lay in the feet, and pour in just sufficient water to cover the whole. Stew gently for about 3 hours; take out the feet, dish them, and cover with parsley and butter. The liquor they were boiled in should be strained and put by in a clean basin for use: it will be found very good as an addition to gravies, &c. &c.

Time.—Rather more than 3 hours.

Average cost, in full season, 9*d.* each.   *Sufficient* for 4 persons.

Seasonable from March to October.

WHEN A CALF SHOULD BE KILLED.—The age at which a calf ought to be killed should not be under four weeks: before that time the flesh is certainly not wholesome, wanting firmness, due development of muscular fibre, and those animal juices on which the flavour and nutritive properties of the flesh depend, whatever the unhealthy palate of epicures may deem to the contrary. In France, a law exists to prevent the slaughtering of calves under *six weeks* of age.* The calf is considered in prime condition at ten weeks, when he will weigh from sixteen to eighteen stone, and sometimes even twenty.

Veal Cutlets (an Entrée)

INGREDIENTS.—About 3 lbs. of the prime part of the leg of veal, egg and bread crumbs, 3 tablespoonfuls of minced savoury herbs, salt and pepper to taste, a small piece of butter.

Mode.—Have the veal cut into slices about ¾ of an inch in thickness, and, if not cut perfectly even, level the meat with a cutlet-bat or rolling-pin. Shape and trim the cutlets, and brush them over with egg. Sprinkle with bread crumbs, with which have been mixed minced herbs and a seasoning of pepper and salt, and press the crumbs down. Fry them of a delicate brown in fresh lard or butter, and be careful not to burn them. They should be very thoroughly done, but not dry. If the cutlets be thick, keep the pan covered for a few minutes at a good distance from the fire, after they have acquired a good colour: by this means, the meat will be done through. Lay the cutlets in a dish, keep them hot, and make a gravy in the pan as follows: Dredge in a little flour, add a piece of butter the size of a walnut, brown it, then pour as much boiling water as is required over it, season with pepper and salt, add a little lemon-juice, give one boil, and pour it over the cutlets. They should be garnished with slices of broiled bacon, and a few forcemeat balls will be found a very excellent addition to this dish.

Time.—For cutlets of a moderate thickness, about 12 minutes; if very thick, allow more time.

Average cost, 10*d.* per lb.   *Sufficient* for 6 persons.

Seasonable from March to October.

Note.—Veal cutlets may be merely floured and fried of a nice brown; the gravy and garnishing should be the same as in the preceding recipe. They may also be cut from the loin or neck.

Veal à la Bourgeoise*
(*Excellent*)

INGREDIENTS.—2 to 3 lbs. of the loin or neck of veal, 10 or 12 young carrots, a bunch of green onions, 2 slices of lean bacon, 2 blades of pounded mace, 1 bunch of savoury herbs, pepper and salt to taste, a few new potatoes, 1 pint of green peas.

Mode.—Cut the veal into cutlets, trim them, and put the trimmings into a stewpan with a little butter; lay in the cutlets and fry them a nice brown colour on both sides. Add the bacon, carrots, onions, spice, herbs, and seasoning; pour in about a pint of boiling water, and stew gently for 2 hours on a very slow fire. When done, skim off the fat, take out the herbs, and flavour the gravy with a little tomato sauce and ketchup. Have ready the peas and potatoes, boiled *separately*; put them with the veal, and serve.

Time.—2 hours.   *Average cost*, 2*s.* 9*d.*

Sufficient for 5 or 6 persons.

Seasonable from June to August with peas;—rather earlier when these are omitted.

Scotch Collops, White (Cold Meat Cookery)

INGREDIENTS.—The remains of cold roast veal, ½ teaspoonful of grated nutmeg, 2 blades of pounded mace, cayenne and salt to taste, a little butter, 1 dessertspoonful of flour, ¼ pint of water, 1 teaspoonful of anchovy sauce, 1 tablespoonful of lemon-juice, ¼ teaspoonful of lemon-peel, 1 tablespoonful of mushroom ketchup, 3 tablespoonfuls of cream, 1 tablespoonful of sherry.

Mode.—Cut the veal into thin slices about 3 inches in width; hack them with a knife, and grate on them the nutmeg, mace, cayenne, and salt, and fry them in a little butter. Dish them, and make a gravy in the pan by putting in the remaining ingredients. Give one boil, and pour it over the collops; garnish with lemon and slices of toasted bacon, rolled. Forcemeat balls may be added to this dish. If cream is not at hand, substitute the yolk of an egg beaten up well with a little milk.

Time.—About 5 or 7 minutes.

Seasonable from May to October.

COOKING COLLOPS.—Dean Ramsay, who tells us, in his 'Reminiscences of Scottish Life and Character,' a number of famous stories of the strong-headed, warm-hearted, and plain-spoken old dames of the north, gives, amongst them, the following:—A strong-minded lady of this class was inquiring the character of a cook she was about to hire. The lady who was giving the character entered a little upon the cook's moral qualifications, and described her as a very decent woman; to which the astounding reply—this was 60 years ago, and a Dean tells the story—'Oh, d——n her decency; can she make good collops?'

Boiled Calf's Head (with the Skin on)

INGREDIENTS.—Calf's head, boiling water, bread crumbs, 1 large bunch of parsley, butter, white pepper and salt to taste, 4 tablespoonfuls of melted butter, 1 tablespoonful of lemon-juice, 2 or 3 grains of cayenne.

Mode.—Put the head into boiling water, and let it remain by the side of the fire for 3 or 4 minutes; take it out, hold it by the ear, and with the back of a knife, scrape off the hair (should it not come off easily, dip the head again into boiling water). When perfectly clean, take the eyes out, cut off the ears, and remove the brain, which soak for an hour in warm water. Put the head into hot water to soak for a few minutes, to make it look white, and then have ready a stewpan, into which lay the head; cover it with cold water, and bring it gradually to boil. Remove the scum, and add a little salt, which assists to throw it up. Simmer it very gently from 2½ to 3 hours, and when nearly done, boil the brains for ¼ hour; skin and chop them, not too finely, and add a tablespoonful of minced parsley which has been previously scalded. Season with pepper and salt, and stir the brains, parsley, &c., into about 4 tablespoonfuls of melted butter; add the lemon-juice and cayenne, and keep these hot by the side of the fire. Take up the head, cut out the tongue, skin it, put it on a small dish with the brains round it; sprinkle over the head a few bread crumbs mixed with a little minced parsley; brown these before the fire, and serve with a tureen of parsley and butter, and either boiled bacon, ham, or pickled pork as an accompaniment.

Time.—2½ to 3 hours.

Average cost, according to the season, from 3*s.* to 7*s.* 6*d.*

Sufficient for 8 or 9 persons.

Seasonable from March to October.

THE CALF'S-HEAD CLUB.—When the restoration of Charles II took the strait waistcoat off the minds and morose religion of the Commonwealth period, and gave a loose rein to the long-compressed spirits of the people, there still remained a large section of society wedded to the former state of things.* The elders of this party retired from public sight, where, unoffended by the reigning saturnalia, they might dream in seclusion over their departed Utopia. The young bloods of this school, however, who were compelled to mingle in the world, yet detesting the politics which had become the fashion, adopted a novel expedient to keep alive their republican sentiments, and mark their contempt of the reigning family. They accordingly met, in considerable numbers, at some convenient inn, on the 30th of January in each year,—the anniversary of Charles's death, and dined together off a feast prepared from *calves' heads*, dressed in every possible variety of way, and with an abundance of wine drank toasts of defiance and hatred to the house of Stuart, and glory to the memory of old Holl Cromwell; and having lighted a large bonfire in the yard, the club of fast young Puritans, with their white handkerchiefs stained *red* in wine, and one of the party in a mask, bearing an axe, followed by the chairman, carrying a *calf's head* pinned up in a napkin, marched in mock procession to the bonfire, into which, with great shouts and uproar, they flung the enveloped head. This odd custom was continued for some time, and even down to the early part of this century it was customary for men of republican politics always to dine off calf's head on the 30th of January.

Calf's Liver and Bacon

INGREDIENTS.—2 or 3 lbs. of liver, bacon, pepper and salt to taste, a small piece of butter, flour, 2 tablespoonfuls of lemon-juice, ¼ pint of water.

Mode.—Cut the liver in thin slices, and cut as many slices of bacon as there are of liver; fry the bacon first, and put that on a hot dish before the fire. Fry the liver in the fat which comes from the bacon, after seasoning it with pepper and salt and dredging over it a very little flour. Turn the liver occasionally to prevent its burning, and when done, lay it round the dish with a piece of bacon between each. Pour away the bacon fat, put in a small piece of butter, dredge in a little flour, add the lemon-juice and water, give one boil, and pour it in the *middle* of the dish. It may be garnished with slices of cut lemon, or forcemeat balls.

Time.—According to the thickness of the slices, from 5 to 10 minutes.

Average cost, 10*d.* per lb.   *Sufficient* for 6 or 7 persons.

Seasonable from March to October.

Minced Veal and Macaroni*
(*A pretty side or corner dish*)

INGREDIENTS.—¾ lb. of minced cold roast veal, 3 oz. of ham, 1 tablespoonful of gravy, pepper and salt to taste, ¼ teaspoonful of grated nutmeg, ¼ lb. of bread crumbs, ¼ lb. of macaroni, 1 or 2 eggs to bind, a small piece of butter.

Mode.—Cut some nice slices from a cold fillet of veal, trim off the brown outside, and mince the meat finely with the above proportion of ham: should the meat be very dry, add a spoonful of good gravy. Season highly with pepper and salt, add the grated nutmeg and bread crumbs, and mix these ingredients with 1 or 2 eggs well beaten, which should bind the mixture and make it like forcemeat. In the mean time, boil the macaroni in salt and water, and drain it;

butter a mould, put some of the macaroni at the bottom and sides of it, in whatever form is liked; mix the remainder with the forcemeat, fill the mould up to the top, put a plate or small dish on it, and steam for ½ hour. Turn it out carefully, and serve with good gravy poured round, but not over, the meat.

Time.—½ hour.   *Average cost*, exclusive of the cold meat, 10*d*.

Seasonable from March to October.

Note.—To make a variety, boil some carrots and turnips separately in a little salt and water; when done, cut them into pieces about ⅛ inch in thickness; butter an oval mould, and place these in it, in white and red stripes alternately, at the bottom and sides. Proceed as in the foregoing recipe, and be very careful in turning it out of the mould.

Veal and Ham Pie*

INGREDIENTS.—2 lbs. of veal cutlets, ½ lb. of boiled ham, 2 table-spoonfuls of minced savoury herbs, ¼ teaspoonful of grated nutmeg, 2 blades of pounded mace, pepper and salt to taste, a strip of lemon-peel finely minced, the yolks of 2 hard-boiled eggs, ½ pint of water, nearly ½ pint of good strong gravy, puff-crust.

Mode.—Cut the veal into nice square pieces, and put a layer of them at the bottom of a pie-dish; sprinkle over these a portion of the herbs, spices, seasoning, lemon-peel, and the yolks of the eggs cut in slices; cut the ham very thin, and put a layer of this in. Proceed in this manner until the dish is full, so arranging it that the ham comes at the top. Lay a puff-paste on the edge of the dish, and pour in about ½ pint of water; cover with crust, ornament it with leaves, brush it over with the yolk of an egg, and bake in a well-heated oven for 1 to 1½ hour, or longer, should the pie be very large. When it is taken out of the oven, pour in at the top, through a funnel, nearly ½ pint of strong gravy: this should be made sufficiently good that, when cold, it may cut in a firm jelly. This pie may be very much enriched by adding a few mushrooms, oysters, or sweetbreads; but it will be found very good without any of the last-named additions.

Time.—1½ hour, or longer, should the pie be very large.

Average cost, 3*s*.

Sufficient for 5 or 6 persons.

Seasonable from March to October.

Baked Sweetbreads (an Entrée)

INGREDIENTS.—3 sweetbreads, egg and bread crumbs, oiled butter, 3 slices of toast, brown gravy.

Mode.—Choose large white sweetbreads; put them into warm water to draw out the blood, and to improve their colour; let them remain for rather more than 1 hour; then put them into boiling water, and allow them to simmer for about 10 minutes, which renders them firm. Take them up, drain them, brush over with egg, sprinkle with bread crumbs; dip them in egg again, and then into more bread crumbs. Drop on them a little oiled butter, and put the sweetbreads into a moderately-heated oven, and let them bake for nearly ¾ hour. Make 3 pieces of toast; place the sweetbreads on the toast, and pour round, but not over them, a good brown gravy.

Time.—To soak 1 hour, to be boiled 10 minutes, baked 40 minutes.

Average cost, 1s. to 5s.   *Sufficient* for an entrée.

Seasonable.—In full season from May to August.

VEAL CARVING

Calf's Head

This is not altogether the most easy-looking dish to cut when it is put before a carver for the first time; there is not much real difficulty in the operation, however, when the head has been attentively examined, and, after the manner of a phrenologist,* you get to know its bumps, good and bad. In the first place, inserting the knife quite down to the bone, cut slices in the direction of the line

Calf's Head

1 to 2; with each of these should be helped a piece of what is called the throat sweetbread, cut in the direction of from 3 to 4. The eye, and the flesh round, are favourite morsels with many, and should be given to those at the table who are known to be the greatest connoisseurs. The jawbone being removed, there will then be found some nice lean; and the palate, which is reckoned by some a tit-bit, lies under the head. On a separate dish there is always served the tongue and brains, and each guest should be asked to take some of these.

CHAPTER XX

GENERAL OBSERVATIONS ON BIRDS

'Birds, the free tenants of land, air, and ocean,
Their forms all symmetry, their motions grace;
In plumage delicate and beautiful;
Thick without burthen, close as fishes' scales,
Or loose as full-blown poppies to the breeze.'

The Pelican Islands

The divisions of birds are founded principally on their habits of life, and the natural resemblance which their external parts, especially their bills, bear to each other. According to Mr Vigors, there are five orders, each of which occupies its peculiar place on the surface of the globe; so that the air, the forest, the land, the marsh, and the water, has each its appropriate kind of inhabitants. These are respectively designated as BIRDS OF PREY, PERCHERS, WALKERS, WADERS, and SWIMMERS; and, in contemplating their variety, lightness, beauty, and wonderful adaptation to the regions they severally inhabit, and the functions they are destined to perform in the grand scheme of creation, our hearts are lifted with admiration at the exhaustless ingenuity, power, and wisdom of HIM who has, in producing them, so strikingly 'manifested His handiwork.'* Not only these, however, but all classes of animals, have their peculiar ends to fulfil; and, in order that this may be effectually performed, they are constructed in such a manner as will enable them to carry out their conditions. Thus the quadrupeds, that are formed to tread the earth in common with man, are muscular and vigorous; and, whether they have passed into the servitude of man, or are permitted to range the forest or the field, they still retain, in a high degree, the energies with which they were originally endowed. Birds, on the contrary, are generally feeble, and, therefore, timid. Accordingly, wings have been given them to enable them to fly through the air, and thus elude the force which, by nature, they are unable to resist. Notwithstanding the natural tendency of all bodies towards the centre of the earth, birds, when raised in the atmosphere, glide through it with the greatest ease, rapidity, and vigour. There, they are in their natural element, and can vary their course with the greatest promptitude— can mount or descend with the utmost facility, and can light on any spot with the most perfect exactness, and without the slightest injury to themselves.

Birds, however, do not lay eggs before they have some place to put them; accordingly, they construct nests for themselves with astonishing art. As builders, they exhibit a degree of architectural skill, niceness, and propriety, that would seem even to mock the imitative talents of man, however greatly these are marked by his own high intelligence and ingenuity.

> 'Each circumstance
> Most artfully contrived to favour warmth.
> Here read the reason of the vaulted roof;
> How Providence compensates, ever kind,
> The enormous disproportion that subsists
> Between the mother and the numerous brood
> Which her small bulk must quicken into life.'*

In building their nests, the male and female generally assist each other, and they contrive to make the outside of their tenement bear as great a resemblance as possible to the surrounding foliage or branches; so that it cannot very easily be discovered even by those who are in search of it. This art of nidification is one of the most wonderful contrivances which the wide field of Nature can show, and which, of itself, ought to be sufficient to compel mankind to the belief, that they and every other part of the creation, are constantly under the protecting power of a superintending Being, whose benign dispensations seem as exhaustless as they are unlimited.*

CHAPTER XXI

RECIPES*

Chicken or Fowl Patties*

INGREDIENTS.—The remains of cold roast chicken or fowl; to every ¼ lb. of meat allow 2 oz. of ham, 3 tablespoonfuls of cream, 2 tablespoonfuls of veal gravy, ½ teaspoonful of minced lemon-peel; cayenne, salt, and pepper to taste; 1 tablespoonful of lemon-juice, 1 oz. of butter rolled in flour; puff paste.

Mode.—Mince very small the white meat from a cold roast fowl, after removing all the skin; weigh it, and to every ¼ lb. of meat allow the above proportion of minced ham. Put these into a stewpan with the remaining ingredients, stir over the fire for 10 minutes or ¼ hour, taking care that the mixture does not burn. Roll out some puff paste about ¼ inch in thickness; line the patty-pans with this, put upon each a small piece of bread, and cover with another layer of paste; brush over with the yolk of an egg, and bake in a brisk oven for about ¼ hr. When done, cut a round piece out of the top, and, with a small spoon, take out the bread (be particular in not breaking the outside border of the crust), and fill the patties with the mixture.

Time.—¼ hour to prepare the meat; not quite ¼ hour to bake the crust.

Seasonable at any time.

Potted Chicken or Fowl (a Luncheon or Breakfast Dish)

INGREDIENTS.—The remains of cold roast chicken; to every lb. of meat allow ¼ lb. of fresh butter, salt and cayenne to taste, 1 teaspoonful of pounded mace, ½ small nutmeg.

Mode.—Strip the meat from the bones of cold roast fowl; when it is freed from gristle and skin, weigh it, and, to every lb. of meat, allow the above proportion of butter, seasoning, and spices. Cut the meat into small pieces, pound it well with the fresh butter, sprinkle in the spices gradually, and keep pounding until reduced to a perfectly smooth paste. Put it into potting-pots for use, and cover it with clarified butter, about ¼ inch in thickness, and, if to be kept for some time, tie over a bladder: 2 or 3 slices of ham, minced and pounded with the above ingredients, will be found an improvement. It should be kept in a dry place.

Seasonable at any time.

Roast Ducks

INGREDIENTS.—A couple of ducks; sage-and-onion stuffing (Recipe, p. 138); a little flour.

Choosing and Trussing—Choose ducks with plump bellies, and with thick and yellowish feet. They should be trussed with the feet on, which should be scalded, and the skin peeled off, and then turned up close to the legs. Run a skewer through the middle of each leg, after having drawn them as close as possible to the body, to plump up the breast, passing the same quite through the body. Cut off the heads and necks, and the pinions at the first joint; bring these close to the sides, twist the feet round, and truss them at the back of the bird. After the duck is stuffed, both ends should be secured with string, so as to keep in the seasoning.

Mode.—To insure ducks being tender, never dress them the same day they are killed; and if the weather permits, they should hang a day or two. Make a stuffing of sage and onion sufficient for one duck, and leave the other unseasoned, as the flavour is not liked by everybody. Put them down to a brisk

Roast Duck

clear fire, and keep them well basted the whole of the time they are cooking. A few minutes before serving, dredge them lightly with flour, to make them froth and look plump; and when the steam draws towards the fire, send them to table hot and quickly, with a good brown gravy poured *round*, but not *over* the ducks, and a little of the same in a tureen. When in season, green peas should invariably accompany this dish.

Time.—Full-grown ducks from ¾ to 1 hour; ducklings from 25 to 35 minutes.

Average cost, from 2s. 3d. to 2s. 6d. each.

Sufficient.—A couple of ducks for 6 or 7 persons.

Seasonable.—Ducklings from April to August; ducks from November to February.

Note.—Ducklings are trussed and roasted in the same manner, and served with the same sauces and accompaniments. When in season, serve apple sauce.

Boiled Fowls or Chickens*

INGREDIENTS.—A pair of fowls; water.

Choosing and Trussing.—In choosing fowls for boiling, it should be borne in mind that those that are not black-legged are generally much whiter when dressed. Pick, draw, singe, wash, and truss them in the following manner, without the livers in the wings; and, in drawing, be careful not to break the gall-bladder:—Cut off the neck, leaving sufficient skin to skewer back. Cut the feet off to the first joint, tuck the stumps into a slit made on each side of the belly, twist the wings over the back of the fowl, and secure the top of the leg and the bottom of the wing together by running a skewer through them and the body. The other side must be done in the same manner. Should the fowl be very large and old, draw the sinews of the legs before tucking them in. Make a slit in the apron of the fowl, large enough to admit the parson's nose, and tie a string on the tops of the legs to keep them in their proper place.

Mode.—When they are firmly trussed, put them into a stewpan with plenty of hot water; bring it to boil, and carefully remove all the scum as it rises. *Simmer very gently* until the fowl is tender, and bear in mind that the slower it boils, the plumper and whiter will the fowl be. Many cooks wrap them in a floured cloth to preserve the colour, and to prevent the scum from clinging to them; in this case, a few slices of lemon should be placed on the breasts; over these a sheet of buttered paper, and then the cloth; cooking them in this manner renders the

Boiled Fowl

flesh very white. Boiled ham, bacon, boiled tongue, or pickled pork, are the usual accompaniments to boiled fowls, and they may be served with Béchamel, white sauce, parsley and butter, oyster, lemon, liver, celery, or mushroom sauce. A little should be poured over the fowls, after the skewers are removed, and the remainder sent in a tureen to table.

Time.—Large fowl, 1 hour; moderate-sized one, ¾ hour; chicken, from 20 minutes to ½ hour.

Average cost, in full season, 5s. the pair.

Sufficient for 7 or 8 persons.

Seasonable all the year, but scarce in early spring.

VARIOUS MODES OF FATTENING FOWLS.—It would, I think, be a difficult matter to find among the entire fraternity of fowl-keepers, a dozen whose mode of fattening 'stock' is the same. Some say that the grand secret is to give them abundance of saccharine food; others say nothing beats heavy corn steeped in milk; while another breeder, celebrated in his day, and the recipient of a gold medal from a learned society, says, 'The best method is as follows:—The chickens are to be taken from the hen the night after they are hatched, and fed with eggs hard-boiled, chopped, and mixed with crumbs of bread, as larks and other small birds are fed, for the first fortnight; after which give them oatmeal and treacle mixed so as to crumble, of which the chickens are very fond, and thrive so fast that, at the end of two months, they will be as large as full-grown fowls.' Others there are who insist that nothing beats oleaginous diet, and cram their birds with ground oats and suet. But, whatever the course of diet favoured, on one point they seem agreed; and that is, that, while fattening, the fowls *should be kept in the dark*. Supposing the reader to be a dealer,—a breeder of gross chicken-meat for the market (against which supposition the chances are 10,000 to 1), and beset with as few scruples as generally trouble the huckster, the advice is valuable. 'Laugh and grow fat' is a good maxim enough; but 'Sleep and grow fat' is, as is well known to folks of porcine attributes, a better. The poor birds, immured in their dark dungeons, ignorant that there is life and sunshine abroad, tuck their heads under their wings and make a long night of it; while their digestive organs, having no harder work than to pile up fat, have an easy time enough. But, unless we are mistaken, he who breeds poultry for his own eating, bargains for a more substantial reward than the questionable pleasure of burying his carving-knife in chicken grease. Tender, delicate, and nutritious *flesh* is the great aim; and these qualities, I can affirm without fear of contradiction, were never attained by a dungeon-fatted chicken: perpetual gloom and darkness is as incompatible with chicken life as it is with human. If you wish to be convinced of the absurdity of endeavouring to thwart nature's laws, plant a tuft of grass, or a cabbage-plant, in the darkest corner of your coal-cellar. The plant or the tuft may increase in length and breadth, but its colour will be as wan and pale, almost, as would be your own face under the circumstances.*

Poulet à la Marengo

INGREDIENTS.—1 large fowl, 4 tablespoonfuls of salad oil, 1 table-spoonful of flour, 1 pint of [medium] stock, or water, about 20 mushroom-buttons, salt and pepper to taste, 1 teaspoonful of powdered sugar, a very small piece of garlic.

Mode.—Cut the fowl into 8 or 10 pieces; put them with the oil into a stewpan, and brown them over a moderate fire; dredge in the above proportion of flour; when that is browned, pour in the stock or water; let it simmer very slowly for rather more than ½ hour, and skim off the fat as it rises to the top; add the mushrooms; season with salt, pepper, garlic, and sugar; take out the fowl, which arrange pyramidically on the dish, with the inferior joints at the bottom. Reduce the sauce by boiling it quickly over the fire, keeping it stirred until sufficiently thick to adhere to the back of a spoon; pour over the fowl, and serve.

Time.—Altogether 50 minutes.   *Average cost*, 3s. 6d.

Sufficient for 3 or 4 persons.

Seasonable at any time.

A FOWL A LA MARENGO.—The following is the origin of the well-known dish Poulet à la Marengo:—On the evening of the battle the first consul was very hungry after the agitation of the day, and a fowl was ordered with all expedition. The fowl was procured, but there was no butter at hand, and unluckily none could be found in the neighbourhood. There was oil in abundance, however; and the cook having poured a certain quantity into his skillet, put in the fowl, with a clove of garlic and other seasoning, with a little white wine, the best the country afforded; he then garnished it with mushrooms, and served it up hot. This dish proved the second conquest of the day, as the first consul found it most agreeable to his palate, and expressed his satisfaction. Ever since, a fowl à la Marengo is a favourite with all lovers of good cheer.

An Indian Dish of Fowl (an Entrée)

INGREDIENTS.—The remains of cold roast fowl, 3 or 4 sliced onions, 1 tablespoonful of curry-powder, salt to taste.

Mode.—Divide the fowl into joints; slice and fry the onions in a little butter, taking care not to burn them; sprinkle over the fowl a little curry-powder and salt; fry these nicely, pile them high in the centre of the dish, cover with the onion, and serve with a cut lemon on a plate. Care must be taken that the onions are not greasy: they should be quite dry, but not burnt.

Time.—5 minutes to fry the onions, 10 minutes to fry the fowl.

Average cost, exclusive of the fowl, 4*d*.

Seasonable during the winter months.

Giblet Pie

INGREDIENTS.—A set of duck or goose giblets, 1 lb. of rump-steak, 1 onion, ½ teaspoonful of whole black pepper, a bunch of savoury herbs, plain crust.

Mode.—Clean, and put the giblets into a stewpan with an onion, whole pepper, and a bunch of savoury herbs; add rather more than a pint of water, and simmer gently for about 1½ hour. Take them out, let them cool, and cut them into pieces; line the bottom of a pie-dish with a few pieces of rump-steak; add a layer of giblets and a few more pieces of steak; season with pepper and salt, and pour in the gravy (which should be strained), that the giblets were stewed in; cover with a plain crust, and bake for rather more than 1½ hour in a brisk oven. Cover a piece of paper over the pie, to prevent the crust taking too much colour.

Time.—1½ hour to stew the giblets, about 1 hour to bake the pie.

Average cost, exclusive of the giblets, 1*s*. 4*d*.

Sufficient for 5 or 6 persons.

Roast Goose*

INGREDIENTS.—Goose, 4 large onions, 10 sage-leaves, ¼ lb. of bread crumbs, 1½ oz. of butter, salt and pepper to taste, 1 egg.

Choosing and Trussing.—Select a goose with a clean white skin, plump breast, and yellow feet: if these latter are red, the bird is old. Should the weather permit, let it hang for a few days: by so doing, the flavour will be very much improved. Pluck, singe, draw, and carefully wash and wipe the goose; cut off the neck close to the back, leaving the skin long enough to turn over; cut off the feet at the first joint, and separate the pinions at the first joint. Beat the breast-bone flat with a rolling-pin, put a skewer through the under part of each wing, and having drawn up the legs closely, put a skewer into the middle of each, and pass the same quite through the body. Insert another skewer into the small of the leg, bring it close down to the side bone, run it through, and do the same to the other side. Now cut off the end of the vent, and make a hole in the skin sufficiently large for the passage of the rump, in order to keep in the seasoning.

Mode.—Make a sage-and-onion stuffing of the above ingredients; put it into the body of the goose, and secure it firmly at both ends, by passing the rump through the hole made in the skin, and the other end by tying the skin of the neck to the back; by this means the seasoning will not escape. Put it down to a brisk fire, keep it well basted, and roast from 1½ to 2 hours, according to the size. Remove the skewers, and serve with a tureen of good gravy, and

Roast Goose

one of well-made apple-sauce. Should a very highly-flavoured seasoning be preferred, the onions should not be parboiled, but minced raw: of the two methods, the mild seasoning is far superior. A ragoût, or pie, should be made of the giblets, or they may be stewed down to make gravy. Be careful to serve the goose before the breast falls, or its appearance will be spoiled by coming flattened to table. As this is rather a troublesome joint to carve, a *large* quantity of gravy should not be poured round the goose, but sent in a tureen.

Time.—A large goose, 1¾ hour; a moderate-sized one, 1¼ to 1½ hour.

Seasonable from September to March; but in perfection from Michaelmas to Christmas.

Average cost, 5s. 6d. each.   *Sufficient* for 8 or 9 persons.

Note.—A teaspoonful of made mustard, a saltspoonful of salt, a few grains of cayenne, mixed with a glass of port wine, are sometimes poured into the goose by a slit made in the apron. This sauce is, by many persons, considered an improvement.

THE GOOSE.—This bird is pretty generally distributed over the face of the globe, being met with in North America, Lapland, Iceland, Arabia, and Persia. Its varieties are numerous; but in England there is only one species, which is supposed to be a native breed. The best geese are found on the borders of Suffolk, and in Norfolk and Berkshire; but the largest flocks are reared in the fens of Lincolnshire and Cambridge. They thrive best where they have an easy access to water, and large herds of them are sent every year to London, to be fattened by the metropolitan poulterers.

Emden Goose

'A Michaelmas goose,' says Dr Kitchener, 'is as famous in the mouths of the million as the minced-pie at Christmas; yet for those who eat with delicacy, it is, at that time, too full-grown. The true period when the goose is in the highest perfection is when it has just acquired its full growth, and not begun to harden; if the March goose is insipid, the Michaelmas goose is rank. The fine time is between both; from the second week in June to the first in September.' It is said that the Michaelmas goose is indebted to Queen Elizabeth for its origin on the table at that season. Her majesty happened to dine on one at the table of an English baronet, when she received the news of the discomfiture of the Spanish Armada. In commemoration of this event, she commanded the goose to make its appearance at table on every Michaelmas. We here give an engraving of the Emden goose.

Roast Larks*

INGREDIENTS.—Larks, egg and bread crumbs, fresh butter.

Mode.—These birds are by many persons esteemed a great delicacy, and may be either roasted or broiled. Pick, gut, and clean them; when they are trussed, brush them over with the yolk of an egg; sprinkle with bread crumbs, and roast them before a quick fire; baste them continually with fresh butter, and keep sprinkling with the bread crumbs until the birds are well covered. Dish them on bread crumbs fried in clarified butter, and garnish the dish with slices of lemon. Broiled larks are also very excellent: they should be cooked over a clear fire, and would take about 10 minutes or ¼ hour.

Time.—¼ hour to roast; 10 minutes to broil.

Seasonable.—In full season in November.

Note.—Larks may also be plainly roasted, without covering them with egg and bread crumbs; they should be dished on fried crumbs.

Pigeon Pie (Epsom Grand-Stand Recipe)*

INGREDIENTS.—1½ lb. of rump-steak, 2 or 3 pigeons, 3 slices of ham, pepper and salt to taste, 2 oz. of butter, 4 eggs, puff crust.

Mode.—Cut the steak into pieces about 3 inches square, and with it line the bottom of a pie-dish, seasoning it well with pepper and salt. Clean the pigeons, rub them with pepper and salt inside and out, and put into the body of each rather more than ½ oz. of butter; lay them on the steak, and a piece of ham on each pigeon. Add the yolks of 4 eggs, and half fill the dish with stock; place a border of puff paste round the edge of the dish, put on the cover, and ornament it in any way that may be preferred. Clean three of the feet, and place them in a hole made in the crust at the top: this shows what kind of pie it is. Glaze the crust,—that is to say, brush it over with the yolk of an egg,—and bake it in a well-heated oven for about 1¼ hour. When liked, a seasoning of pounded mace may be added.

Time.—1¼ hour, or rather less. *Average cost*, 5s. 3d.

Sufficient for 5 or 6 persons. *Seasonable* at any time.

Roast or Baked Rabbit

INGREDIENTS.—1 rabbit, forcemeat (Recipe, p. 128) buttered paper, sausage-meat.

Mode.—Empty, skin, and thoroughly wash the rabbit; wipe it dry, line the inside with sausage-meat and forcemeat, to which has been added the minced liver. Sew the stuffing inside, skewer back the head between the shoulders, cut off the fore-joints of the shoulders and legs, bring them close to the body, and secure them by means of a skewer. Wrap the rabbit in buttered paper, and

Roast Rabbit

put it down to a bright clear fire; keep it well basted, and a few minutes before it is done remove the paper, flour and froth it, and let it acquire a nice brown colour. Take out the skewers, and serve with brown gravy and red-currant jelly. To bake the rabbit, proceed in the same manner as above: in a good oven, it will take about the same time as roasting.

Time.—A young rabbit, 35 minutes; a large one, about ¾ hour.

Average cost, from 1s. to 1s. 6d. each. *Sufficient* for 4 persons.

Seasonable from September to February.

THE RABBIT-HOUSE.—Rabbit-keeping is generally practised by a few individuals in almost every town, and by a few in almost every part of the country. Forty years ago, there were in the metropolis one or two considerable feeders, who, according to report, kept from 1,500 to 2,000 breeding does. These large establishments, however, have ceased to exist, and London receives the supply of tame as well as wild rabbits chiefly from the country. Where they are kept, however, the rabbit-house should be placed upon a dry foundation, and be well ventilated. Exposure to rain, whether externally or internally, is fatal to rabbits, which, like sheep, are liable to the rot, springing from the same causes. Thorough ventilation and good air are indispensable where many rabbits are kept, or they will neither prosper nor remain healthy for any length of time. A thorough draught or passage for the air is, therefore, absolutely necessary, and should be so contrived as to be checked in cold or wet weather by the closing or shutting of opposite doors or windows.

THE HUTCH.—Hutches are generally placed one above another to the height required by the number of rabbits and the extent of the room. Where a large stock is kept, to make the most of room, the hutches may be placed in rows, with a sufficient interval between for feeding and cleaning, instead of being, in the usual way, joined to the wall. It is preferable to rest the hutches upon stands, about a foot above the ground, for the convenience of cleaning under them. Each of the hutches intended for breeding should have two rooms,—a feeding and a bed-room. Those are single for the use of the weaned rabbits, or for the bucks, which are always kept separate. The floors should be planed smooth, that wet may run off, and a common hoe, with a short handle, and a short broom, are most convenient implements for cleaning these houses.

To Bone a Turkey or Fowl without Opening it
(*Miss Acton's Recipe*)

After the fowl has been drawn and singed, wipe it inside and out with a clean cloth, but do not wash it. Take off the head, cut through the skin all round the first joint of the legs, and pull them from the fowl, to draw out the large tendons. Raise the flesh first from the lower part of the backbone, and a little also from the end of the breastbone, if necessary; work the knife gradually to the socket of the thigh; with the point of the knife detach the joint from it, take the end of the bone firmly in the fingers, and cut the flesh clean from it down to the next joint, round which pass the point of the knife carefully, and when the skin is loosened from it in every part, cut round the next bone, keeping the edge of the knife close to it, until the whole of the leg is done. Remove the bones of the other leg in the same manner; then detach the flesh from the back- and breast-bone sufficiently to enable you to reach the upper joints of the wings; proceed with these as with the legs, but be especially careful not to pierce the skin of the second joint: it is usual to leave the pinions unboned, in order to give more easily its natural form to the fowl when it is dressed. The merrythought* and neck-bones may now easily be cut away, the back- and side-bones taken out without being divided, and the breastbone separated carefully from the flesh (which, as the work progresses, must be turned back from the bones upon the fowl, until it is completely inside out). After the one remaining bone is removed, draw the wings and legs back to their proper form, and turn the fowl right side outwards.

A turkey is boned exactly in the same manner; but as it requires a very large proportion of forcemeat to fill it entirely, the legs and wings are sometimes drawn into the body, to diminish the expense of this. If very securely trussed, and sewn, the bird may be either boiled, or stewed in rich gravy, as well as roasted, after being boned and forced; but it must be most gently cooled, or it may burst.

Another Mode of Boning a Turkey or Fowl
(*Miss Acton's Recipe*)

Cut through the skin down the centre of the back, and raise the flesh carefully on either side with the point of a sharp knife, until the sockets of the wings and thighs are reached. Till a little practice has been gained, it will perhaps be better to bone these joints before proceeding further; but after they are once detached from it, the whole of the body may easily be separated from the flesh and taken out entire: only the neck-bones and merrythought will then remain to be removed. The bird thus prepared may either be restored to its original form, by filling the legs and wings with forcemeat, and the body with the livers of two or three fowls, mixed with alternate layers of parboiled tongue freed from the rind, fine sausage-meat, or veal forcemeat, or thin slices of the nicest bacon, or aught else of good flavour, which will give a marbled appearance to the fowl when it is carved; and then be sewn up and trussed as usual; or the legs and wings may be drawn inside the body, and the bird being first flattened on a table, may be covered with sausage-meat, and the various other ingredients we have named, so placed that it shall be of equal thickness in every part; then tightly rolled, bound firmly together with a fillet of broad tape, wrapped in a thin pudding-cloth, closely tied at both ends, and dressed as follows:—Put it into a braising-pan, stewpan, or thick iron saucepan, bright in the inside, and fitted as nearly as may be to its size; add all the chicken-bones, a bunch of sweet herbs, two carrots, two bay-leaves, a large blade of mace, twenty-four white peppercorns, and any trimmings or bones of undressed veal which may be at hand; cover the whole with good veal broth, add salt, if needed, and stew it very softly, from an hour and a quarter to an hour and a half; let it cool in the liquor in which it was stewed; and after it is lifted out, boil down the gravy to a jelly and strain it; let it become cold, clear off the fat, and serve it cut into large dice or roughed, and laid round the fowl, which is to be served cold. If restored to its form, instead of being rolled, it must be stewed gently for an hour, and may then be sent to table hot, covered with mushroom, or any other good sauce that may be preferred; or it may be left until the following day, and served garnished with the jelly, which should be firm, and very clear and well-flavoured: the liquor in which a calf's foot has been boiled down, added to the broth, will give it the necessary degree of consistence.

THE GUINEA-PIG.*—The common hutch companion of the rabbit, although originally a native of Brazil, propagates freely in England and other European countries. Were it not that they suffer cruelly from cats, and numerous other enemies, and that it is the habit of the males to devour

their own offspring, their numbers would soon become overwhelming. Rats, however, it is said, carefully avoid them; and for this reason they are frequently bred by rabbit-fanciers, by way of protection for their young stock against those troublesome vermin. The lower tier of a rabbit-hutch is esteemed excellent quarters by the guinea-

The Guinea-Pig

pig: here, as he runs loose, he will devour the waste food of his more admired companion. Some naturalists assert that the guinea-pig will breed at two months old, the litter varying from four to twelve at a time. It is varied in colour,—white, fawn, and black, and a mixture of the three colours, forming a tortoiseshell, which is the more generally admired hue. Occasionally, the white ones have red eyes, like those of the ferret and the white rabbit. Their flesh, although eatable, is decidedly unfit for food; they have been tasted, however, we presume by some enthusiast eager to advance the cause of science, or by some eccentric epicure in search of a new pleasure for his palate. Unless it has been that they deter rats from intruding within the rabbit-hutch, they are as useless as they are harmless. The usual ornament of an animal's hind quarters is denied them; and were it not for this fact, and also for their difference in colour, the Shaksperean locution, 'a rat without a tail,' would designate them very properly.

THE CYGNET.—The Cygnet, or the young Swan, was formerly much esteemed; but it has 'fallen from its high estate,' and is now rarely seen upon the table. We are not sure that it is not still fattened in Norwich for the corporation of that place. Persons who have property on the river there, take the young birds, and send them to some one who is employed by the corporation, to be fed; and for this trouble he is paid, or was wont to be paid, about half a guinea a bird. It is as the

The Cygnet

future bird of elegance and grace that the young swan is mostly admired; when it has become old enough to grace the waters, then it is that all admire her, when she with

> 'Arched neck,
> Between her white wings mantling, proudly rows
> Her state with oary feet.'

POULTRY CARVING

Roast Turkey

A noble dish is a turkey, roast or boiled. A Christmas dinner, with the middle classes of this empire, would scarcely be a Christmas dinner without its turkey; and we can hardly imagine an object of greater envy than is presented by a respected portly paterfamilias carving, at the season devoted to good cheer and genial charity, his own fat turkey, and carving it well.* The only art consists, as in the carving of a goose, in getting from the breast as many fine slices as possible;

Roast Turkey

and all must have remarked the very great difference in the large number of people whom a good carver will find slices for, and the comparatively few that a bad carver will succeed in serving. As we have stated in both the carving of a duck and goose, the carver should commence cutting slices close to the wing from, 2 to 3, and then proceed upwards towards the ridge of the breastbone: this is not the usual plan, but, in practice, will be found the best. The breast is the only part which is looked on as fine in a turkey, the leg being very seldom cut off and eaten at table: they are usually removed to the kitchen, where they are taken off, as here marked, to appear only in a form which seems to have a special attraction at a bachelor's supper-table,—we mean devilled: served in this way, they are especially liked and relished.

A boiled turkey is carved in the same manner as when roasted.

CHAPTER XXII

GENERAL OBSERVATIONS ON GAME*

The common law of England has a maxim, that goods, in which no person can claim any property, belong, by his or her prerogative, to the king or queen. Accordingly, those animals, those *ferae naturae*, which come under the denomination of game, are, in our laws, styled his or her majesty's, and may therefore, as a matter of course, be granted by the sovereign to another; in consequence of which another may prescribe to possess the same within a certain precinct or lordship. From this circumstance arose the right of lords of manors or others to the game within their respective liberties; and to protect these species of animals, the game laws were originated, and still remain in force. There are innumerable acts of parliament inflicting penalties on persons who may illegally kill game, and some of them are very severe; but they cannot be said to answer their end, nor can it be expected that they ever will, whilst there are so many persons of great wealth who have not otherwise the mean of procuring game, except by purchase, and who will have it. These must necessarily encourage poaching, which, to a very large extent, must continue to render all game laws nugatory as to their intended effects upon the rustic population.

The object of these laws, however, is not wholly confined to the restraining of the illegal sportsman. Even qualified or privileged persons must not kill game at all seasons. During the day, the hours allowed for sporting are from one hour before sunrise till one hour after sunset; whilst the time of killing certain species is also restricted to certain seasons. For example, the season for bustard-shooting is from December 1 to March 1; for grouse, or red grouse, from August 12 to December 10; heath-fowl, or black-game, from August 20 to December 20; partridges from September 1 to February 12; pheasants from October 1 to February 1; widgeons, wild ducks, wild geese, wild fowls, at any time but in June, July, August, and September. Hares may be killed at any time of the year, under certain restrictions defined by an act of parliament of the 10th of George III.

The exercise or diversion of pursuing four-footed beasts of game is called hunting, which, to this day, is followed in the field and the forest, with gun and greyhound. Birds, on the contrary, are not hunted, but shot in the air, or taken with nets and other devices, which is called fowling; or they are pursued and taken by birds of prey, which is called hawking, a species of sport now fallen almost entirely into desuetude in England, although, in some parts, showing signs of being revived.

In pursuing four-footed beasts, such as deer, boars, and hares, properly termed hunting, mankind were, from the earliest ages, engaged. It was the rudest and the most obvious manner of acquiring human support before the agricultural arts had in any degree advanced. It is an employment, however, requiring both art and contrivance, as well as a certain fearlessness of character, combined with the power of considerable physical endurance. Without these, success could not be very great; but, at best, the occupation is usually accompanied with rude and turbulent habits; and, when combined with these, it constitutes what is termed the savage state of man. As culture advances, and as the soil proportionably becomes devoted to the plough or to the sustenance of the tamer or more domesticated animals, the range of the huntsman is proportionably limited; so that when a country has attained to a high state of cultivation, hunting becomes little else than an amusement of the opulent. In the case of fur-bearing animals, however, it is somewhat different; for these continue to supply the wants of civilization with one of its most valuable materials of commerce.

The themes which form the minstrelsy of the earliest ages either relate to the spoils of the chase or the dangers of the battle-field. Even the sacred writings introduce us to Nimrod, the first mighty hunter before the Lord, and tell us that Ishmael, in the solitudes of Arabia, became a skilful bowman; and that David, when yet young, was not afraid to join in combat with the lion or the bear. The Greek mythology teems with hunting exploits. Hercules overthrows the Nemaean lion, the Erymanthean boar, and the hydra of Lerna; Diana descends to the earth, and pursues the stag; whilst Aesculapius, Nestor, Theseus, Ulysses, and Achilles are all followers of the chase. Aristotle, sage as he was, advises young men to apply themselves early to it; and Plato finds in it something divine. Horace exalts it as a preparative exercise for the path of glory, and several of the heroes of Homer are its ardent votaries. The Romans followed the hunting customs of the Greeks, and the ancient Britons were hunters before Julius Caesar invaded their shores.

That hunting has in many instances been carried to an excess is well known, and the match given by the Prince Esterhazy, regent of Hungary, on the signing of the treaty of peace with France, is not the least extraordinary upon record. On that occasion, there were killed 160 deer, 100 wild boars, 300 hares, and 80 foxes: this was the achievement of one day. Enormous, however, as this slaughter may appear, it is greatly inferior to that made by the contemporary king of Naples on a hunting expedition. That sovereign had a larger extent of ground at his command, and a longer period for the exercise of his talents; consequently, his sport, if it can so be called, was proportionably greater. It was pursued during his journey to Vienna, in Austria, Bohemia, and Moravia; when he killed 5 bears, 1,820 boars, 1,950 deer, 1,145 does, 1,625 roebucks, 11,121 rabbits, 13 wolves, 17 badgers, 16,354 hares, and 354 foxes. In birds, during the same expedition, he killed 15,350 pheasants and 12,335 partridges. Such an amount of destruction can hardly be called sport; it resembles more the indiscriminate slaughter of a battle-field, where the scientific engines of civilized warfare are brought to bear upon defenceless savages.

Deer and hares may be esteemed as the only four-footed animals now hunted in Britain for the table; and even these are not followed with the same ardour as they were wont to be. Still, there is no country in the world where the sport of hunting on horseback is carried to such an extent as in Great Britain, and where the pleasures of the chase are so well understood, and conducted on such purely scientific principles. The Fox, of all 'the beasts of the field,' is now considered to afford the best sport. For this, it is infinitely superior to the stag; for the real sportsman can only enjoy that chase when the deer is sought for and found like other game which are pursued with hounds. In the case of finding an outlying fallow-deer, which is unharboured, in this manner, great sport is frequently obtained; but this is now rarely to be met with in Britain. In reference to hare-hunting, it is much followed in many parts of this and the sister island; but, by the true foxhunter, it is considered as a sport only fit to be pursued by women and old men. Although it is less dangerous and exciting than the fox-chase, however, it has great charms for those who do not care for the hard riding which the other requires.

The art of taking or killing birds is called 'fowling,' and is either practised as an amusement by persons of rank or property, or for a livelihood by persons who use nets and other apparatus. When practised as an amusement, it principally consists of killing them with a light firearm called a 'fowling-piece,' and the sport is secured to those who pursue it by the game laws. The other means by which birds are taken, consist in imitating their voices, or leading them, by other artifices, into situations where they become entrapped by nets, birdlime, or otherwise. For taking large numbers of birds, the pipe or call is the most common means employed; and this is done during the months of September and October. We will here briefly give a description of the *modus operandi* pursued in this sport. A thin wood is usually the spot chosen, and, under a tree at a little distance from the others, a cabin is erected, and there are only such branches left on the tree as are necessary for the placing of the birdlime, and which are covered with it. Around the cabin are placed avenues with twisted perches, also covered with birdlime. Having thus prepared all that is necessary, the birdcatcher places himself in the cabin, and, at sunrise and sunset, imitates the cry of a small bird calling the others to its assistance. Supposing that the cry of the owl is imitated, immediately different kinds of birds will flock together at the cry of their common enemy, when, at every instant, they will be seen falling to the ground, their wings being of no use to them, from their having come in contact with the birdlime. The cries of those which are thus situated now attract others, and thus are large numbers taken in a short space of time. If owls were themselves desired to be taken, it is only during the night that this can be done, by counterfeiting the squeak of the mouse. Larks, other birds, and water-fowl, are sometimes taken by nets; but to describe fully the manner in which this is done, would here occupy too much space.

As the inevitable result of social progress is, at least to limit, if not entirely to suppress, such sports as we have here been treating of, much of the romance of country life has passed away. This is more especially the case with falconry, which had its origin about the middle of the fourth century, although, lately, some attempts have been rather successfully made to institute a revival of the 'gentle art' of hawking. Julius Firmicus, who lived about that time, is, so far as we can find, the first Latin author who speaks of falconers, and the art of teaching one species of birds to fly after and catch others. The occupation of these functionaries has now, however, all but ceased. New and nobler efforts characterize the aims of mankind in the development of their civilization, and the sports of the field have, to a large extent, been superseded by other exercises, it may be less healthful and invigorating, but certainly more elegant, intellectual, and humanizing.

CHAPTER XXIII

RECIPES*

Roast Wild Duck

INGREDIENTS.—Wild duck, flour, butter.

Mode.—Carefully pluck and draw them; cut off the heads close to the necks, leaving sufficient skin to turn over, and do not cut off the feet; some twist each leg at the knuckle, and rest the claws on each side of the breast; others truss them as shown in our illustration.

Roast Wild Duck

Roast the birds before a quick fire, and, when they are first put down, let them remain for 5 minutes without basting (this will keep the gravy in); afterwards baste plentifully with butter, and a few minutes before serving dredge them lightly with flour; baste well, and send them to table nicely frothed, and full of gravy. If overdone, the birds will lose their flavour. Serve with a good gravy in the dish, or orange gravy; and send to table with them a cut lemon. To take off the fishy taste which wild fowl sometimes have, baste them for a few minutes with hot water to which have been added an onion and a little salt; then take away the pan, and baste with butter.

Time.—When liked underdressed, 20 to 25 minutes; well done, 25 to 35 minutes.

Average cost, 4s. to 5s. the couple.

Sufficient,—2 for a dish.

Seasonable from November to February.

The Wild Duck

THE WILD DUCK.—The male of the wild duck is called a mallard; and the young ones are called flappers. The time to try to find a brood of these is about the month of July, among the rushes of the deepest and most retired parts of some brook or stream, where, if the old bird is sprung, it may be taken as a certainty that its brood is not far off. When once found, flappers are easily killed, as they attain their full growth before their wings are fledged. Consequently, the sport is more like hunting water-rats than shooting birds. When the flappers take wing, they assume the name of wild ducks, and about the month of August repair to the corn-fields, where they remain until they are disturbed by the harvest-people. They then frequent the rivers pretty early in the evening, and give excellent sport to those who have patience to wait for them. In order to know a wild duck, it is necessary only to look at the claws, which should be black.

Grouse Pie

INGREDIENTS.—Grouse; cayenne, salt, and pepper to taste; 1 lb. of rump-steak, ½ pint of well-seasoned broth, puff paste.

Mode.—Line the bottom of a pie-dish with the rump-steak cut into neat pieces, and, should the grouse be large, cut them into joints; but, if small, they may be laid in the pie whole; season highly with salt, cayenne, and black pepper; pour in the broth, and cover with a puff paste; brush the crust over with the yolk of an egg, and bake from ¾ to 1 hour. If the grouse is cut into joints, the backbones and trimmings will make the gravy, by stewing them with an onion, a little sherry, a bunch of herbs, and a blade of mace: this should be poured in after the pie is baked.

Time.—¾ to 1 hour.

Average cost, exclusive of the grouse, which are seldom bought, 1s. 9d.

Seasonable from the 12th of August to the beginning of December.

Jugged Hare
(*Very Good*)

INGREDIENTS.—1 hare, 1½ lb. of gravy beef, ½ lb. of butter, 1 onion, 1 lemon, 6 cloves; pepper, cayenne, and salt to taste; ½ pint of port wine.

Mode.—Skin; paunch, and wash the hare, cut it into pieces, dredge them with flour, and fry in boiling butter. Have ready 1½ pint of gravy, made from the above proportion of beef, and thickened with a little flour. Put this into a jar; add the pieces of fried hare, an onion stuck with six cloves, a lemon peeled and cut in half, and a good seasoning of pepper, cayenne, and salt; cover the jar down tightly, put it up to the neck into a stewpan of boiling water, and let it stew until the hare is quite tender, taking care to keep the water boiling. When nearly done, pour in the wine, and add a few forcemeat balls: these must be fried or baked in the oven for a few minutes before they are put to the gravy. Serve with red-currant jelly.

Time.—3½ to 4 hours. If the hare is very old, allow 4½ hours.

Average cost, 7s.

Sufficient for 7 or 8 persons.

Seasonable from September to the end of February.

Salmi de Perdrix, or Hashed Partridges*

INGREDIENTS.—3 young partridges, 3 shalots, a slice of lean ham, 1 carrot, 3 or 4 mushrooms, a bunch of savoury herbs, 2 cloves, 6 whole peppers, ¾ pint of stock, 1 glass of sherry or Madeira, a small lump of sugar.

Mode.—After the partridges are plucked and drawn, roast them rather underdone, and cover them with paper, as they should not be browned; cut them into joints, take off the skin from the wings, legs, and breasts; put these into a stewpan, cover them up, and set by until the gravy is ready. Cut a slice of ham into small pieces, and put them, with the carrots sliced, the shalots, mushrooms, herbs, cloves, and pepper, into a stewpan; fry them lightly in a little butter, pour in the stock, add the bones and trimming from the partridges, and simmer for ¼ hour. Strain the gravy, let it cool, and skim off every particle of fat; put it to the legs, wings, and breasts, add a glass of sherry or Madeira and a small lump of sugar, let all gradually warm through by the side of the fire, and when on the point of boiling, serve, and garnish the dish with croûtons. The remains of roast partridge answer very well dressed in this way, although not so good as when the birds are in the first instance only half-roasted. This recipe is equally suitable for pheasants, moor-game, &c.; but care must be taken always to skin the joints.

Time.—Altogether 1 hour.

Sufficient.—2 or 3 partridges for an entrée.

Seasonable from the 1st of September to the beginning of February.

To Dress Plovers

INGREDIENTS.—3 plovers, butter, flour, toasted bread.

Choosing and Trussing.—Choose those that feel hard at the vent, as that shows their fatness. There are three sorts,—the grey, green, and bastard plover, or lapwing. They will keep good for some time, but if very stale, the feet will be very dry. Plovers are scarcely fit for anything but roasting; they are, however, sometimes stewed, or made into a ragoût, but this mode of cooking is not to be recommended.

Mode.—Pluck off the feathers, wipe the outside of the birds with a damp cloth, and do not draw them; truss with the head under the wing, put them down to a clear fire, and lay slices of moistened toast in the dripping-pan, to catch the trail.* Keep them *well basted*, dredge them lightly with flour a few minutes before they are done, and let them be nicely frothed. Dish them on the toasts, over which the *trail* should be equally spread. Pour round the toast a little good gravy, and send some to table in a tureen.

Time.—10 minutes to ¼ hour.

Average cost, 1s. 6d. the brace, if plentiful.

Sufficient for 2 persons.

Seasonable.—In perfection from the beginning of September to the end of January.

THE PLOVER.—There are two species of this bird, the grey and the green, the former being larger than the other, and somewhat less than the woodcock. It has generally been classed with those birds which chiefly live in the water; but it would seem only to seek its food there, for many of the species breed upon the loftiest mountains. Immense flights of these birds are to be seen in the Hebrides, and other parts of Scotland; and, in the winter, large numbers are sent

The Plover

to the London market, which is sometimes so much glutted with them that they are sold very cheap. Previous to dressing, they are kept till they have a game flavour; and although their flesh is a favourite with many, it is not universally relished. The green is preferred to the grey, but both are inferior to the woodcock. Their eggs are esteemed as a great delicacy. Birds of this kind are migratory. They arrive in England in April, live with us all the spring and summer, and at the beginning of autumn prepare to take leave by getting together in flocks. It is supposed that they then retire to Spain, and frequent the sheep-walks with which that country abounds.

Roast Haunch of Venison

INGREDIENTS.—Venison, coarse flour-and-water paste, a little flour.

Mode.—Choose a haunch with clear, bright, and thick fat, and the cleft of the hoof smooth and close; the greater quantity of fat there is, the better quality will the meat be. As many people object to venison when it has too much *haut goût*, ascertain how long it has been kept, by running a sharp skewer into the meat close to the bone: when this is withdrawn, its sweetness can be judged of. With care and attention, it

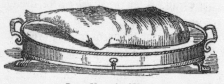

Roast Haunch of Venison

will keep good a fortnight, unless the weather is very mild. Keep it perfectly dry by wiping it with clean cloths till not the least damp remains, and sprinkle over powdered ginger or pepper, as a preventative against the fly. When required for use, wash it in warm water, and *dry* it *well* with a cloth; butter a sheet of white paper, put it over the fat, lay a coarse paste, about ½ inch in thickness, over this, and then a sheet or two of strong paper. Tie the whole firmly on to the haunch with twine, and put the joint down to a strong close fire; baste the venison immediately, to prevent the paper and string from burning, and continue this operation, without intermission, the whole of the time it is cooking. About 20 minutes before it is done, carefully remove the paste and paper, dredge the joint with flour, and baste well with *butter* until it is nicely frothed, and of a nice pale-brown colour; garnish the knuckle-bone with a frill of white paper, and serve with a good, strong, but unflavoured gravy, in a tureen, and currant jelly; or melt the jelly with a little port wine, and serve that also in a tureen. As the principal object in roasting venison is to preserve the fat, the above is the best mode of doing so where expense is not objected to; but, in ordinary cases, the paste may be dispensed with, and a double paper placed over the roast instead: it will not require so long cooking without the paste. Do not omit to send very hot plates to table, as the venison fat so soon freezes: to be thoroughly enjoyed by epicures, it should be eaten on hot-water plates. The neck and shoulder may be roasted in the same manner.

Time.—A large haunch of buck venison, with the paste, 4 to 5 hours; haunch of doe venison, 3¼ to 3¾ hours. Allow less time without the paste.

Average cost, 1s. 4d. to 1s. 6d. per lb.   *Sufficient* for 18 persons.

Seasonable—Buck venison in greatest perfection from June to Michaelmas; doe venison from November to the end of January.

Roast Woodcock

INGREDIENTS.—Woodcocks; butter, flour, toast.

Mode.—Woodcocks should not be drawn, as the trails are, by epicures, considered a great delicacy. Pluck, and wipe them well outside; truss them with the legs close to the body, and the feet pressing upon the thighs; skin the neck and head, and bring the beak round under the wing.* Place some slices of toast in the dripping-pan to catch the trails, allowing a piece of toast for each bird. Roast before a clear fire from 15 to 25 minutes; keep them well basted, and flour and froth them nicely. When done, dish the pieces of toast with the birds upon

Roast Woodcock

them, and pour round a very little gravy; send some more to table in a tureen. These are most delicious birds when well cooked, but they should not be kept too long: when the feathers drop, or easily come out, they are fit for table.

Time.—When liked underdone, 15 to 20 minutes; if liked well done, allow an extra 5 minutes.

Average cost.—Seldom bought.   *Sufficient,*—2 for a dish.

Seasonable from November to February.

GAME CARVING

Roast Hare

The 'Grand Carver' of olden times, a functionary of no ordinary dignity, was pleased when he had a hare to manipulate, for his skill and grace had an opportunity of display. *Diners à la Russe*

may possibly, erewhile, save modern gentlemen the necessity of learning the art which was in auld lang syne one of the necessary accomplishments of the youthful squire; but, until side-tables become universal,

Roast Hare

or till we see the office of 'grand carver' once more instituted, it will be well for all to learn how to assist at the carving of this dish, which, if not the most elegant in appearance, is a very general favourite.* The hare, having its head to the left, as shown in the woodcut, should be first served by cutting slices from each side of the backbone, in the direction of the lines from 3 to 4. After these prime parts are disposed of, the leg should next be disengaged by cutting round the line indicated by the figures 5 to 6. The shoulders will then be taken off by passing the knife round from 7 to 8. The back of the hare should now be divided by cutting quite through its spine, as shown by the line 1 to 2, taking care to feel with the point of the knife for a joint where the back may be readily penetrated. It is the usual plan not to serve any bone in helping hare; and thus the flesh should be sliced from the legs and placed alone on the plate. In large establishments, and where men-cooks are kept,* it is often the case that the backbone of the hare, especially in old animals, is taken out, and then the process of carving is, of course, considerably facilitated. A great point to be remembered in connection with carving hare is, that plenty of gravy should accompany each helping; otherwise this dish, which is naturally dry, will lose half its flavour, and so become a failure. Stuffing is also served with it; and the ears, which should be nicely crisp, and the brains of the hare, are esteemed as delicacies by many connoisseurs.

CHAPTER XXIV

GENERAL OBSERVATIONS ON VEGETABLES

'Strange there should be found
Who, self-imprison'd in their proud saloons,
Renounce the odours of the open field
For the unscented fictions of the loom;
Who, satisfied with only pencilled scenes,
Prefer to the performance of a God,
Th' inferior wonders of an artist's hand!
Lovely, indeed, the mimic works of art,
But Nature's works far lovelier.'

Cowper*

'The animal and vegetable kingdoms,' says Hogg,* in his Natural History of the Vegetable Kingdom, 'may be aptly compared to the primary colours of the prismatic spectrum, which are so gradually and intimately blended, that we fail to discover where the one terminates and where the other begins. If we had to deal with yellow and blue only, the eye would easily distinguish the one from the other; but when the two are blended, and form green, we cannot tell where the blue ends and the yellow begins. And so it is in the animal and vegetable kingdoms. If our powers of observation were limited to the highest orders of animals and plants, if there were only mammals, birds, reptiles, fishes, and insects in the one, and trees, shrubs, and herbs in the other, we should then be able with facility to define the bounds of the two kingdoms; but as we descend the scale of each, and arrive at the lowest forms of animals and plants, we there meet with bodies of the simplest structure, sometimes a mere cell, whose organization, modes of development and reproduction, are so anomalous, and partake so much of the character of both, that we cannot distinguish whether they are plants or whether they are animals.'*

Whilst it is thus difficult to determine where the animal begins and the vegetable ends, it is as difficult to account for many of the singularities by which numbers of plants are characterized. This, however, can hardly be regarded as a matter of surprise, when we recollect that, so far as it is at present known, the vegetable kingdom is composed of upwards of 92,000 species of plants. Of this amazing number the lichens and the mosses are of the simplest and hardiest kinds. These, indeed, may be considered as the very creators of the soil: they thrive in the coldest and most sterile regions, many of them commencing the operations of nature in the growth of vegetables on the barest rocks, and receiving no other nourishment than such as may be supplied to them by the simple elements of air and rain. When they have exhausted their period in such situations as have been assigned them, they pass into a state of decay, and become changed into a very fine mould, which, in the active spontaneity of nature, immediately begins to produce other species, which in their turn become food for various mosses, and also rot. This process of growth and decay, being, from time to time, continued, by-and-by forms a soil sufficient for the maintenance of larger plants, which also die and decay, and so increase the soil, until it becomes deep enough to sustain an oak, or even the weight of a tropical forest. To create soil amongst rocks, however, must not be considered as the only end of the lichen; different kinds of it minister to the elegant arts, in the form of beautiful dyes; thus the *lichen rocella* is used to communicate to silk and wool, various shades of purple and crimson, which greatly enhance the value of these materials. This species is chiefly imported from the Canary Islands, and, when scarce, as an article of commerce has brought as much as £1,000 per ton.*

When Nature has found a soil, her next care is to perfect the growth of her seeds, and then to disperse them. Whilst the seed remains confined in its capsule, it cannot answer its purpose; hence, when it is sufficiently ripe, the pericardium opens, and lets it out. What must strike every observer with surprise is, how nuts and shells, which we can hardly crack with our teeth, or even with a hammer, will divide of themselves, and make way for the little tender sprout which proceeds from the kernel. There are instances, it is said, such as in the Touch-me-not (*impatiens*), and the Cuckoo-flower (*cardamine*), in which the seed-vessels, by an elastic jerk at the moment of their explosion, cast the seeds to a distance. We are all aware, however, that many seeds—those of the most composite flowers, as of the thistle and dandelion—are endowed with, what have not been inappropriately called, wings. These consist of a beautiful silk-looking down, by which they are enabled to float in the air, and to be transported, sometimes, to considerable distances from the parent plant that produced them. The swelling of this downy tuft within the seed-vessel is the means by which the seed is enabled to overcome the resistance of its coats, and to force for itself a passage by which it escapes from its little prison-house.

Birds, as well as quadrupeds, are likewise the means of dispersing the seeds of plants, and placing them in situations where they ultimately grow. Amongst the latter is the squirrel, which is an extensive planter of oaks; nay, it may be regarded as having, in some measure, been one of the creators of the British navy. We have read of a gentleman who was walking one day in some woods belonging to the Duke of Beaufort, near Troy House, in Monmouthshire, when his attention was arrested by a squirrel, sitting very composedly upon the ground. He stopped to observe its motions, when, in a short time, the little animal suddenly quitted its position, and darted to the top of the tree beneath which it had been sitting. In an instant it returned with an acorn in its mouth, and with its paws began to burrow in the earth. After digging a small hole, it therein deposited an acorn, which it hastily covered, and then darted up the tree again. In a moment it was down with another, which it buried in the same manner; and so continued its labour, gathering and burying, as long as the gentleman had patience to watch it. This industry in the squirrel is an instinct which directs it to lay up a store of provision for the winter; and as it is probable that its memory is not sufficiently retentive to enable it to recollect all the spots in which it deposits its acorns, it no doubt makes some slips in the course of the season, and loses some of them. These few spring up, and are, in time, destined to supply the place of the parent tree. Thus may the sons of Britain, in some degree, consider themselves to be indebted to the industry and defective memory of this little animal for the production of some of those 'wooden walls' which have, for centuries, been the national pride, and which have so long 'braved the battle and the breeze' on the broad bosom of the great deep, in every quarter of the civilized globe.

Some of the acorns planted by the squirrel of Monmouthshire may be now in a fair way to become, at the end of some centuries, venerable trees; for not the least remarkable quality of oaks is the strong principle of life with which they are endued. In Major Rooke's 'Sketch of the Forest of Sherwood' we find it stated that, on some timber cut down in Berkland and Bilhaugh, letters were found stamped in the bodies of the trees, denoting the king's reign in which they were marked. The bark appears to have been cut off, and then the letters to have been cut in, and the next year's wood to have grown over them without adhering to where the bark had been cut out. The ciphers were found to be of James I, William and Mary, and one of King John. One of the ciphers of James was about one foot within the tree, and one foot from the centre. It was cut down in 1786. The tree must have been two feet in diameter, or two yards in circumference, when the mark was cut. A tree of this size is generally estimated at 120 years' growth; which number being subtracted from the middle year of the reign of James, would carry the year back to 1492, which would be about the period of its being planted. The tree with the cipher of William and Mary displayed its mark about nine inches within the tree, and three feet three inches from the centre. This tree was felled in 1786. The cipher of John was eighteen inches within the tree, and rather more than a foot from the centre. The middle year of the reign of that monarch was 1207. By subtracting from this 120, the number of years requisite for a tree's growth to arrive at the diameter of two feet, the date of its being planted would seem to have been 1085, or about twenty years after the Conquest.*

In the vascular system of a plant, we at once see the great analogy which it bears to the veins and arteries in the human system; but neither it, nor the cellular tissue combined, is all that is required to perfect the production of a vegetable. There is, besides, a tracheal system, which is composed of very minute elastic spiral tubes, designed for the purpose of conveying air both to and from the plant. There are also fibres, which consist of collections of these cells and vessels closely united together. These form the root and the stem. If we attempt to cut them transversely, we meet with difficulty, because we have to force our way across the tubes, and break them; but if we slit the wood lengthwise, the vessels are separated without breaking. The layers of wood, which appear in the stem or branch of a tree cut transversely, consist of different zones of fibres, each the produce of one year's growth, and separated by a coat of cellular tissue, without which they could not be well distinguished. Besides all these, there is the cuticle, which extends over every part of the plant, and covers the bark with three distinct coats. The *liber*, or inner bark, is said to be formed of hollow tubes, which convey the sap downwards to increase the solid diameter of the tree.*

In accordance with the plan of this work, special notices of culinary vegetables will accompany the various recipes in which they are spoken of; but here we cannot resist the opportunity of declaring it as our conviction, that he or she who introduces a useful or an ornamental plant into our island, ought justly to be considered, to a large extent, a benefactor to the country. No one can calculate the benefits which may spring from this very vegetable, after its qualities have become thoroughly known. If viewed in no other light, it is pleasing to consider it as bestowing upon us a share of the blessings of other climates, and enabling us to participate in the luxury which a more genial sun has produced.

CHAPTER XXV

RECIPES*

Boiled Artichokes*

INGREDIENTS—To each ½ gallon of water, allow 1 heaped table-spoonful of salt, a piece of soda the size of a shilling; artichokes.

Mode.—Wash the artichokes well in several waters; see that no insects remain about them, and trim away the leaves at the bottom. Cut off the stems and put them into *boiling* water, to which have

Artichokes

been added salt and soda in the above proportion. Keep the saucepan uncovered, and let them boil quickly until tender; ascertain when they are done by thrusting a fork in them, or by trying if the leaves can be easily removed. Take them out, let them drain for a minute or two, and serve in a napkin, or with a little white sauce poured over. A tureen of melted butter should accompany them. This vegetable, unlike any other, is considered better for being gathered two or three days; but they must be well soaked and washed previous to dressing.

Time.—20 to 25 minutes, after the water boils.

Sufficient,—a dish of 5 or 6 for 4 persons.

Seasonable from July to the beginning of September.

Asparagus Peas* (Entremets, or to be served as a Side-dish with the Second Course)

INGREDIENTS.—100 heads of asparagus, 2 oz. of butter, a small bunch of parsley, 2 or 3 green onions, flour, 1 lump of sugar, the yolks of 2 eggs, 4 tablespoonfuls of cream, salt.

Mode.—Carefully scrape the asparagus, cut it into pieces of an equal size, avoiding that which is in the least hard or tough, and throw them into cold water. Then boil the asparagus in salt and water until three-parts done; take it out, drain, and place it on a cloth to dry the moisture away from it. Put it into a stewpan with the butter, parsley, and onions, and shake over a brisk fire for 10 minutes. Dredge in a little flour, add the sugar, and moisten with boiling water. When boiled a short time and reduced, take out the parsley and onions, thicken with the yolks of 2 eggs beaten with the cream; add a seasoning of salt, and, when the whole is on the point of simmering, serve. Make the sauce sufficiently thick to adhere to the vegetable.

Time.—Altogether, ½ hour.   *Average cost*, 1s. 6d. a pint.

Seasonable in May, June, and July.

MEDICINAL USES OF ASPARAGUS.—This plant not only acts as a wholesome and nutritious vegetable, but also as a diuretic, aperient, and deobstruent. The chemical analysis of its juice discovers its composition to be a peculiar crystallizable principle, called asparagin, albumen, mannite, malic acid, and some salts. Thours says, the cellular tissue contains a substance similar to sago. The berries are capable of undergoing vinous fermentation, and affording alcohol by distillation. In their unripe state they possess the same properties as the roots, and probably in a much higher degree.

French Mode of Cooking French Beans

INGREDIENTS.—A quart of French beans, 3 oz. of fresh butter, pepper and salt to taste, the juice of ½ lemon.

Mode.—Cut and boil the beans, and when tender, put them into a stewpan, and shake over the fire, to dry away the moisture from the beans. When quite dry and hot, add the butter, pepper, salt, and lemon-juice; keep moving the stewpan, without using a spoon, as that would break the beans; and when the butter is melted, and all is thoroughly hot, serve. If the butter should not mix well, add a tablespoonful of gravy, and serve very quickly.

Time.—About ¼ hour to boil the beans;* 10 minutes to shake them over the fire.

Average cost, in full season, about 1s. 4d a peck.

Sufficient for 4 or 5 persons.

Seasonable from the middle of July to the end of September.

Boiled Broad or Windsor Beans

INGREDIENTS.—To each ½ gallon of water, allow 1 heaped tablespoonful of salt; beans.

Mode.—This is a favourite vegetable with many persons, but to be nice, should be young and freshly gathered.* After shelling the beans, put them into *boiling* water, salted in the above proportion, and let them boil rapidly until tender. Drain them well in a colander; dish, and serve with them separately a tureen of parsley and butter. Boiled bacon should always accompany this vegetable, but the beans should be cooked separately. It is usually served with the beans laid round, and the parsley and butter in a tureen. Beans also make an excellent garnish to a ham, and when used for this purpose, if very old, should have their skins removed.

Time.—Very young beans, 15 minutes; when of a moderate size, 20 to 25 minutes, or longer.

Average cost, unshelled, 6*d*. per peck.

Sufficient.—Allow one peck for 6 or 7 persons.

Seasonable in July and August.

NUTRITIVE PROPERTIES OF THE BEAN.—The produce of beans in meal is, like that of peas, more in proportion to the grain than in any of the cereal grasses. A bushel of beans is supposed to yield fourteen pounds more of flour than a bushel of oats; and a bushel of peas eighteen pounds more, or, according to some, twenty pounds. A thousand parts of bean flour were found by Sir H. Davy to yield 570 parts of nutritive matter, of which 426 were mucilage or starch, 103 gluten, and 41 extract, or matter rendered insoluble during the process.

Boiled Cabbage*

INGREDIENTS.—To each ½ gallon of water allow 1 heaped table-spoonful of salt; a *very small* piece of soda.

Mode.—Pick off all the dead outside leaves, cut off as much of the stalk as possible, and cut the cabbages across twice, at the stalk end; if they should be very large, quarter them. Wash them well in cold water, place them in a colander, and drain; then put them into *plenty* of *fast-boiling* water, to which have been added salt and soda in the above proportions. Stir them down once or twice in the water, keep the pan uncovered, and let them boil quickly until tender. The instant they are done, take them up into a colander, place a plate over them, let them thoroughly drain, dish, and serve.

Time.—Large cabbages, or savoys, ½ to ¾ hour, young summer cabbage, 10 to 12 minutes, after the water boils.

Average cost, 2*d*. each in full season.

Sufficient,—2 large ones for 4 or 5 persons.

Seasonable.—Cabbages and sprouts of various kinds at any time.

To Dress Carrots in the German Way

INGREDIENTS.—8 large carrots, 3 oz. of butter, salt to taste, a very little grated nutmeg, 1 tablespoonful of finely-minced parsley, 1 dessertspoonful of minced onion, rather more than 1 pint of weak stock or broth, 1 tablespoonful of flour.

Mode.—Wash and scrape the carrots, and cut them into rings of about ¼ inch in thickness. Put the butter into a stewpan; when it is melted, lay in the carrots, with salt, nutmeg, parsley, and onion in the above proportions. Toss the stewpan over the fire for a few minutes, and when the carrots are well saturated with the butter, pour in the stock, and simmer gently until they are nearly tender. Then put into another stewpan a small piece of butter; dredge in about a table-spoonful of flour; stir this over the fire, and when of a nice brown colour, add the liquor that the carrots have been boiling in; let this just boil up, pour it over the carrots in the other stewpan, and let them finish simmering until quite tender. Serve very hot. This vege-table, dressed as above, is a favourite accompaniment of roast pork, sausages, &c &c.

Time.—About ¾ hour.   *Average cost*, 6*d*. to 8*d*. per bunch of 18.

Sufficient for 6 or 7 persons.

Seasonable.—Young carrots from April to June, old ones at any time.

Cauliflowers with Parmesan Cheese* (Entremets, or Side-dish, to be served with the Second Course)

INGREDIENTS.—2 or 3 cauliflowers, rather more than ½ pint of white sauce, 2 tablespoonfuls of grated Parmesan cheese, 2 oz. of fresh butter, 3 tablespoonfuls of bread crumbs.

Mode.—Cleanse and boil the cauliflowers, and drain them and dish them with the flowers standing upright. Have ready the above pro-portion of white sauce; pour sufficient of it over the cauliflowers just to cover the top; sprinkle over this some rasped Parmesan cheese and bread crumbs, and drop on these the butter, which should be melted, but not oiled. Brown with a salamander, or before the fire, and pour round, but not over, the flowers the remainder of the sauce, with which should be mixed a small quantity of grated Parmesan cheese.

Time.—Altogether, ½ hour.   *Average cost*, for large cauliflowers, 6*d*. each.

Sufficient,—3 small cauliflowers for 1 dish.

Seasonable from the beginning of June to the end of September.

To Dress Cucumbers*

INGREDIENTS.—3 tablespoonfuls of salad-oil, 4 tablespoonfuls of vinegar, salt and pepper to taste; cucumber.

Mode.—Pare the cucumber, cut it equally into *very thin* slices, and *commence* cutting from the *thick end*; if commenced at the stalk, the cucumber will most likely have an exceedingly bitter taste, far from agreeable. Put the slices into a dish, sprinkle over salt and pepper, and pour over oil and vinegar in the above proportion; turn the cucumber about, and it is ready to serve. This is a favourite accompaniment to boiled salmon, is a nice addition to all descriptions of salads, and makes a pretty garnish to lobster salad.

Average cost, when scarce, 1s. to 2s. 6d.; when cheapest, may be had for 4d. each.

Cucumber

Seasonable.—Forced from the beginning of March to the end of June; in full season in July, August, and September.

GEOGRAPHICAL DISTRIBUTION OF CUCUMBERS.—This family is not known in the frigid zone, is somewhat rare in the temperate, but in the tropical and warmer regions throughout the world they are abundant. They are most plentiful in the continent of Hindostan; but in America are not near so plentiful. Many of the kinds supply useful articles of consumption for food, and others are actively medicinal in their virtues. Generally speaking, delicate stomachs should avoid this plant, for it is cold and indigestible.

Endive

This vegetable, so beautiful in appearance, makes an excellent addition to winter salad, when lettuces and other salad herbs are not obtainable. It is usually placed in the centre of the dish, and looks remarkably pretty with slices of beetroot, hard-boiled eggs, and curled celery placed round it, so that the colours contrast nicely. In preparing it, carefully wash and cleanse it free from insects, which are generally found near the heart; remove any decayed or dead leaves, and dry it thoroughly by shaking in a cloth. This vegetable may also be served hot, stewed in cream, brown gravy, or butter; but when dressed thus, the sauce it is stewed in should not be very highly seasoned, as that would destroy and overpower the flavour of the vegetable.

Average cost, 1*d.* per head.

Sufficient,—1 head for a salad for 4 persons.

Endive

Seasonable from November to March.

ENDIVE.—This is the *C. endivium* of science, and is much used as a salad. It belongs to the family of the *Compositae,* with Chicory, common Goats-beard, and others of the same genus. Withering states, that before the stems of the common Goats-beard shoot up, the roots, boiled like asparagus, have the same flavour, and are nearly as nutritious. We are also informed by Villars that the children in Dauphiné universally eat the stems and leaves of the young plant before the flowers appear, with great avidity. The fresh juice of these tender herbs is said to be the best solvent of bile.

Baked Mushrooms (A Breakfast, Luncheon, or Supper Dish)

INGREDIENTS.—16 to 20 mushroom-flaps, butter, pepper to taste.

Mode.—For this mode of cooking, the mushroom-flaps are better than the buttons, and should not be too large. Cut off a portion of the stalk, peel the top, and wipe the mushrooms carefully with a piece of flannel and a little fine salt. Put them into a tin baking-dish, with a very small piece of butter placed on each mushroom; sprinkle over a little pepper, and let them bake for about 20 minutes, or longer should the mushrooms be very large. Have ready a *very hot* dish, pile the mushrooms high in the centre, pour the gravy round, and send them to table quickly, with very *hot* plates.

Time.—20 minutes; large mushrooms, ½ hour.

Average cost, 1*d.* each for large mushroom-flaps.

Sufficient for 5 or 6 persons.

Seasonable.—Meadow mushrooms in September and October; cultivated mushrooms may be had at any time.

FUNGI.—These are common parasitical plants, originating in the production of copious filamentous threads, called the mycelium, or spawn. Rounded tubers appear on the mycelium; some of these enlarge rapidly, burst an outer covering, which is left at the base, and protrude a thick stalk, bearing at its summit a rounded body, which in a short time expands into the pileus or cap. The gills, which occupy its lower surface, consist of parallel plates, bearing naked sporules over their whole surface. Some of the cells, which are visible by the microscope, produce four small cells at their free summit, apparently by germination and constriction. These are the sporules, and this is the development of the Agarics.

Boiled Green Peas*

INGREDIENTS.—Green peas; to each ½ gallon of water allow 1 *small* teaspoonful of moist sugar, 1 heaped tablespoonful of salt.

Mode.—This delicious vegetable, to be eaten in perfection, should be young, and not *gathered* or *shelled* long before it is dressed. Shell the peas, wash them well in cold water, and drain them; then put them into a saucepan with plenty of *fast-boiling* water, to which salt and *moist sugar* have been added in the above proportion; let them boil quickly over a brisk fire, with the lid of the saucepan uncovered, and be careful that the smoke does not draw in. When tender, pour them into a colander; put them into a hot vegetable-dish, and quite in the centre of the peas place a piece of butter, the size of a walnut. Many cooks boil a small bunch of mint *with* the *peas*, or garnish them with it, by boiling a few sprigs in a saucepan by themselves. Should the peas be very old, and difficult to boil a good colour, a very tiny piece of soda may be thrown in the water previous to putting them in; but this must be very sparingly used, as it causes the peas, when boiled, to have a smashed and broken appearance. With young peas, there is not the slightest occasion to use it.

Time.—Young peas, 10 to 15 minutes; the large sorts, such as marrowfats, &c., 18 to 24 minutes; old peas, ½ hour.

Average cost, when cheapest, 6*d.* per peck; when first in season, 1*s.* to 1*s.* 6*d.* per peck.

Sufficient.—Allow 1 peck of unshelled peas for 4 or 5 persons.

Seasonable from June to the end of August.

To Boil Potatoes in their Jackets

INGREDIENTS.— 10 or 12 potatoes; to each ½ gallon of water, allow 1 heaped tablespoonful of salt.

Mode.—To obtain this wholesome and delicious vegetable cooked in perfection, it should be boiled and sent to table with the skin on. In Ireland, where, perhaps, the cooking of potatoes is better understood than in any country, they are always served so.* Wash the potatoes well, and if necessary, use a clean scrubbing-brush to remove the dirt from them; and if possible, choose the potatoes so that they may all be as nearly the same size as possible. When thoroughly cleansed, fill the saucepan half full with them, and just cover the potatoes with cold water, salted in the above proportion: they are more quickly boiled with a small quantity of water, and, besides, are more savoury than when drowned in it. Bring them to boil, then draw the pan to the side of the fire, and let them simmer gently until tender. Ascertain when they are done by probing them with a fork; then pour off the water, uncover the saucepan, and let the potatoes dry by the side of the fire, taking care not to let them burn. Peel them quickly, put them in a very hot vegetable-dish, either with or without a napkin, and serve very quickly. After potatoes are cooked, they should never be entirely covered up, as the steam, instead of escaping, falls down on them, and makes them watery and insipid. In Ireland they are usually served up with the skins on, and a small plate is placed by the side of each guest.

Time.—Moderate-sized potatoes, with their skins on, 20 to 25 minutes after the water boils; large potatoes, 25 minutes to ¾ hour, or longer; 5 minutes to dry them.

Average cost, 4s. per bushel. *Sufficient* for 6 persons.

Seasonable all the year, but not good just before and whilst new potatoes are in season.

Boiled Sea-Kale

INGREDIENTS.—To each ½ gallon of water allow 1 heaped tablespoonful of salt.

Mode.—Well wash the kale, cut away any wormeaten pieces, and tie it into small bunches; put it into *boiling* water, salted in the above proportion, and let it boil quickly until tender. Take it out, drain, untie the bunches, and serve with plain melted butter or white sauce, a little of which may be poured over the kale. Sea-kale may also be parboiled and stewed in good brown gravy: it will then take about ½ hour altogether.

Time. — 15 minutes; when liked very thoroughly done, allow an extra 5 minutes.

Average cost, in full season, 9*d*. per basket.

Sufficient. — Allow 12 heads for 4 or 5 persons.

Seasonable from February to June.

SEA-KALE. — This plant belongs to the Asparagus tribe, and grows on seashores, especially in the West of England, and in the neighbourhood of Dublin. Although it is now in very general use, it did not come into repute till 1794. It is easily cultivated, and is esteemed as one of the most valuable esculents indigenous to Britain. As a vegetable, it is stimulating to the appetite, easily digestible, and nutritious. It is so light that the most delicate organizations may readily eat it. The flowers form a favourite resort for bees, as their petals contain a great amount of saccharine matter.

Sea-Kale

Summer Salad

INGREDIENTS. — 3 lettuces, 2 handfuls of mustard-and-cress, 10 young radishes, a few slices of cucumber.

Mode. — Let the herbs be as fresh as possible for a salad, and, if at all stale or dead-looking, let them lie in water for an hour or two, which will very much refresh them. Wash and carefully pick them over, remove any decayed or wormeaten leaves, and drain them thoroughly by swinging them gently in a clean cloth. With a silver knife,* cut the lettuces into small pieces, and the radishes and cucumbers into thin slices; arrange all these ingredients lightly on a dish, with the mustard-and-cress, and pour [your choice of dressing] under, but not over the salad, and do not stir it up until it is to be eaten. It may be garnished with hard-boiled eggs, cut in slices, sliced cucumbers, nasturtiums, cut vegetable-flowers, and many other things that taste will always suggest to make a pretty and elegant dish. In making a good salad, care must be taken to have the herbs freshly gathered, and *thoroughly drained* before the sauce is added to them, or it will be watery and thin. Young spring onions, cut small, are by many persons considered an improvement to salads; but, before these are added, the cook should always consult the taste of her employer. Slices of cold meat or poultry added to a salad make a convenient and quickly-made summer luncheon-dish; or cold fish, flaked, will also be found exceedingly nice, mixed with it.

Average cost, 9*d*. for a salad for 5 or 6 persons; but more expensive when the herbs are forced.

Sufficient for 5 or 6 persons.

Seasonable from May to September.

Baked Tomatoes
(*Excellent*)

INGREDIENTS.—8 or 10 tomatoes, pepper and salt to taste, 2 oz. of butter, bread crumbs.

Mode.—Take off the stalks from the tomatoes; cut them into thick slices, and put them into a deep baking-dish; add a plentiful seasoning of pepper and salt, and butter in the above proportion; cover the whole with bread crumbs; drop over these a little clarified butter; bake in a moderate oven from 20 minutes to ½ hour, and serve very hot. This vegetable, dressed as above, is an exceedingly nice accompaniment to all kinds of roast meat. The tomatoes, instead of being cut in slices, may be baked whole; but they will take rather longer time to cook.

Time.—20 minutes to ½ hour.

Average cost, in full season, 9*d*. per basket.

Sufficient for 5 or 6 persons.

Seasonable in August, September, and October; but may be had, forced, much earlier.

The Tomato

TOMATOES.—The Tomato is a native of tropical countries, but is now cultivated considerably both in France and England. Its skin is of a brilliant red, and its flavour, which is somewhat sour, has become of immense importance in the culinary art.* It is used both fresh and preserved. When eaten fresh, it is served as an *entremets*; but its principal use is in sauce and gravy; its flavour stimulates the appetite, and is almost universally approved. The Tomato is a wholesome fruit, and digests easily. From July to September, they gather the tomatoes green in France, not breaking them away from the stalk; they are then hung, head downwards, in a dry and not too cold place; and there they ripen.

To Dress Truffles with Champagne*

INGREDIENTS.—12 fine black truffles, a few slices of fat bacon, 1 carrot, 1 turnip, 2 onions, a bunch of savoury herbs, including parsley, 1 bay-leaf, 2 cloves, 1 blade of pounded mace, 2 glasses of champagne, ½ pint of stock.

Mode.—Carefully select the truffles, reject those that have a musty smell, and wash them well with a brush, in cold water only, until perfectly clean. Put the bacon into a stewpan, with the truffles and the remaining ingredients; simmer these gently for an hour, and let the whole cool in the stewpan. When to be served, rewarm them, and drain them on a clean cloth; then arrange them on a delicately-white napkin, that it may contrast as strongly as possible with the truffles, and serve. The trimmings of truffles are used to flavour gravies, stock, sauces, &c.; and are an excellent addition to ragoûts, made dishes of fowl, &c.

Time.—1 hour. *Average cost.*—Not often bought in this country. *Seasonable* from November to March.

THE TRUFFLE.—The Truffle belongs to the family of the Mushroom. It is certain that the truffle must possess, equally with other plants, organs of reproduction; yet, notwithstanding all the efforts of art and science, it has been impossible to subject it to a regular culture. Truffles grow at a considerable depth under the earth, never appearing on the surface. They are found in many parts of France; those of Périgord and Magny are the most esteemed for their odour. There are three varieties of the species,— the black, the red, and the white: the latter are of little value. The red are very rare, and their use is restricted. The black has the highest repute, and its consumption is enormous. When the peasantry go to gather truffles, they take a pig with them to scent out the spot where they grow. When that is found, the pig turns up the surface with his snout, and the men then dig until they find the truffles. Good truffles are easily distinguished by their agreeable perfume; they should be light in proportion to their size, and elastic when pressed by the finger. To have them in perfection, they should be quite fresh, as their aroma is considerably diminished by any conserving process. Truffles are stimulating and heating. Weak stomachs digest them with difficulty. Some of the culinary uses to which they are subjected render them more digestible; but they should always be eaten sparingly. Their chief use is in seasoning and garnitures. In short, a professor has said, 'Meats with truffles are the most distinguished dishes that opulence can offer to the epicure.' The Truffle grows in clusters, some inches below the surface of the soil, and is of an irregular globular form. Those which grow wild in England are about the size of a hen's egg, and have no roots. As there is nothing to indicate the places where they are, dogs have been trained to discriminate their scent, by which they are discovered. Hogs are very fond of them, and frequently lead to their being found, from their rutting up the ground in search of them.

Fried Vegetable Marrow

INGREDIENTS.—3 medium-sized vegetable marrows, egg and bread crumbs, hot lard.

Mode.—Peel, and boil the marrows until tender in salt and water; then drain them and cut them in quarters, and take out the seeds. When thoroughly-drained, brush the marrows over with egg, and sprinkle with bread crumbs; have ready some hot lard, fry the marrow in this, and, when of a nice brown, dish; sprinkle over a little salt and pepper, and serve.

Time.—About ½ hour to boil the marrow, 7 minutes to fry it.

Average cost, in full season, 1s. per dozen.

Sufficient for 4 persons.

Seasonable in July, August, and September.

Boiled Indian Wheat or Maize

INGREDIENTS—The ears of young and green Indian wheat; to every ½ gallon of water allow 1 heaped tablespoonful of salt.

Mode.—This vegetable, which makes one of the most delicious dishes brought to table, is unfortunately very rarely seen in Britain; and we wonder that, in the gardens of the wealthy, it is not invariably cultivated. Our sun, it is true, possesses hardly power sufficient to ripen maize; but, with well-prepared ground, and in a favourable position, it might be sufficiently advanced by the beginning of autumn to serve as a vegetable. The outside sheath being taken off and the waving fibres removed, let the ears be placed in boiling water, where they should remain for about 25 minutes (a longer time may be necessary for larger ears than ordinary); and, when sufficiently boiled and well drained, they may be sent to table whole, and with a piece of toast underneath them. Melted butter should be served with them.

Time.—25 to 35 minutes. *Average cost.*—Seldom bought.

Sufficient,—1 ear for each person. *Seasonable* in autumn.

Note.—William Cobbett, the English radical writer and politician, was a great cultivator and admirer of maize, and constantly ate it as a vegetable, boiled. We believe he printed a special recipe for it, but we have been unable to lay our hands on it.* Mr Buchanan, the present president of the United States, was in the habit, when ambassador here, of receiving a supply of Indian corn from America in hermetically-sealed cases; and the publisher of this work remembers, with considerable satisfaction, his introduction to a dish of this vegetable, when in America. He found it to combine the excellences of the young green pea and the finest asparagus; but he felt at first slightly awkward in holding the large ear with one hand, whilst the other had to be employed in cutting off with a knife the delicate green grains.

CHAPTER XXVI

GENERAL OBSERVATIONS ON PUDDINGS AND PASTRY

Puddings and pastry, familiar as they may be, and unimportant as they may be held in the estimation of some, are yet intimately connected with the development of agricultural resources in reference to the cereal grasses. When they began to be made is uncertain; but we may safely presume, that a simple form of pudding was amongst the first dishes made after discovering a mode of grinding wheat into flour. Traditional history enables us to trace man back to the time of the Deluge. After that event he seems to have recovered himself in the central parts of Asia, and to have first risen to eminence in the arts of civilization on the banks of the Nile. From this region, Greece, Carthage, and some other parts along the shores of the Mediterranean Sea, were colonized. In process of time, Greece gave to the Romans the arts which she had thus received from Egypt, and these subsequently diffused them over Europe. How these were carried to or developed in India and China, is not so well ascertained; and in America their ancient existence rests only on very indistinct traditions. As to who was the real discoverer of the use of corn, we have no authentic knowledge. The traditions of different countries ascribe it to various fabulous personages, whose names it is here unnecessary to introduce. In Egypt, however, corn must have grown abundantly; for Abraham, and after him Jacob, had recourse to that country for supplies during times of famine.

The habits of a people, to a great extent, are formed by the climate in which they live, and by the native or cultivated productions in which their country abounds. Thus we find that the agricultural produce of the ancient Egyptians is pretty much the same as that of the present day, and the habits of the people are not materially altered. In Greece, the products cultivated in antiquity were the same kinds of grains and legumes as are cultivated at present, with the vine, the fig, the olive, the apple, and other fruits. So with the Romans, and so with other nations. As to the different modes of artificially preparing these to please the taste, it is only necessary to say that they arise from the universal desire of novelty, characteristic of man in the development of his social conditions. Thus has arisen the whole science of cookery, and thus arose the art of making puddings. The porridge of the Scotch is nothing more than a species of hasty-pudding,* composed of oatmeal, salt, and water; and the 'red pottage' for which Esau sold his birthright, must have been something similar. The barley-gruel of the Lacedaemonians, of the Athenian gladiators and common people, was the same, with the exception of the slight seasoning it had beyond the simplicity of Scottish fare. Here is the ancient recipe for the Athenian national dish:—'Dry near the fire, in the oven, twenty pounds of barley-flour; then parch it; add three pounds of linseed-meal, half a pound of coriander-seed, two ounces of salt, and the quantity of water necessary.' To this sometimes a little millet was added, in order to give the paste greater cohesion and delicacy.

However great may have been the qualifications of the ancients, however, in the art of pudding-making, we apprehend that such preparations as gave gratification to their palates, would have generally found little favour amongst the insulated inhabitants of Great Britain. Here, from the simple suet dumpling up to the most complicated Christmas production, the grand feature of substantiality is primarily attended to. Variety in the ingredients, we think, is held only of secondary consideration with the great body of the people, provided that the whole is agreeable and of sufficient abundance.*

Although from puddings to pastry is but a step, it requires a higher degree of art to make the one than to make the other. Indeed, pastry is one of the most important branches of the culinary science. It unceasingly occupies itself with ministering pleasure to the sight as well as to the taste; with erecting graceful monuments, miniature fortresses, and all kinds of architectural imitations, composed of the sweetest and most agreeable products of all climates and countries. At a very early period, the Orientals were acquainted with the art of manipulating in pastry, but they by no means attained to the taste, variety, and splendour of design, by which it is characterized amongst the moderns. At first it generally consisted of certain mixtures of flour, oil, and honey, to which it was confined for centuries, even among the southern nations of the European continent. At the commencement of the middle ages, a change began to take place in the art of mixing it. Eggs, butter, and salt came into repute in the making of paste, which was forthwith used as an inclosure for meat, seasoned with spices. This advance attained, the next step was to inclose cream, fruit, and marmalades; and the next, to build pyramids and castles; when the summit of the art of the pastry-cook may be supposed to have been achieved.

DIRECTIONS IN CONNECTION WITH THE MAKING OF PUDDINGS AND PASTRY

A few general remarks respecting the various ingredients of which puddings and pastry are composed, may be acceptable as preliminary to the recipes in this department of Household Management.

Flour should be of the best quality, and perfectly dry, and sifted before being used; if in the least damp, the paste made from it will certainly be heavy.

Butter, unless fresh is used, should be washed from the salt, and well squeezed and wrung in a cloth, to get out all the water and buttermilk, which, if left in, assists to make the paste heavy.

Suet should be finely chopped, perfectly free from skin, and quite sweet; during the process of chopping, it should be lightly dredged with flour, which prevents the pieces from sticking together. Beef suet is considered the best; but veal suet, or the outside fat of a loin or neck of mutton, makes good crusts; as also the skimmings in which a joint of mutton has been boiled, but *without* vegetables.

Clarified Beef Dripping answers very well for kitchen pies, puddings, cakes, or for family use. A very good short crust may be made by mixing with it a small quantity of moist sugar; but care must be taken to use the dripping sparingly, or a very disagreeable flavour will be imparted to the paste.

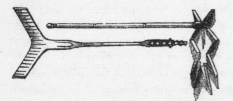

Paste-Cutter and Corner-Cutter

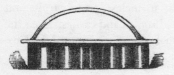

Ornamental Paste-Cutter

Puff-paste requires a brisk oven, but not too hot, or it would blacken the crust; on the other hand, if the oven be too slack, the paste will be soddened, and will not rise, nor will it have any colour. Tart-tins, cake-moulds, dishes for baked puddings, patty-pans, &c., should all be buttered before the article intended to be baked is put in them: things to be baked on sheets should be placed on buttered paper. Raised-pie paste should have a soaking heat, and paste glazed must have rather a slack oven, that the icing be not scorched. It is better to ice tarts, &c. when they are three-parts baked.

Raised-Pie Mould

Raised-Pie Mould, Open

Scrupulous attention should be paid to the cleanliness of pudding-cloths, as, from neglect in this particular, the outsides of boiled puddings frequently taste very disagreeably. As soon as possible after

it is taken off the pudding, it should
be soaked in water, and then well
washed, without soap, unless it be
very greasy. It should be dried out of
doors, then folded up and kept in a
dry place. When wanted for use, dip
it in boiling water, and dredge it
slightly with flour.

Pudding-Basin

CHAPTER XXVII

RECIPES*

Very Good Puff-Paste*

INGREDIENTS.—To every lb. of flour allow 1 lb. of butter, and not quite ½ pint of water.

Mode.—Carefully weigh the flour and butter, and have the exact proportion; squeeze the butter well, to extract the water from it, and afterwards wring it in a clean cloth, that no moisture may remain. Sift the flour; see that it is perfectly dry, and proceed in the following manner to make the paste, using a very *clean* paste-board and rolling-pin:—Supposing the quantity to be 1 lb. of flour, work the whole into a smooth paste, with not quite ½ pint of water, using a knife to mix it with: the proportion of this latter ingredient must be regulated by the discretion of the cook; if too much be added, the paste, when baked, will be tough. Roll it out until it is of an equal thickness of about an inch; break 4 oz. of the butter into small pieces; place these on the paste, sift over it a little flour, fold it over, roll out again, and put another 4 oz. of butter. Repeat the rolling and buttering until the paste has been rolled out 4 times, or equal quantities of flour and butter have been used. Do not omit, every time the paste is rolled out, to dredge a little flour over that and the rolling-pin, to prevent both from sticking. Handle the paste as lightly as possible, and do not press heavily upon it with the rolling-pin. The next thing to be considered is the oven, as the baking of pastry requires particular attention. Do not put it into the oven until it is sufficiently hot to raise the paste; for the best-prepared paste, if not properly baked, will be good for nothing. Brushing the paste as often as rolled out, and the pieces of butter placed thereon, with the white of an egg, assists it to rise in *leaves* or *flakes*. As this is the great beauty of puff-paste, it is as well to try this method.

Average cost, 1s. 4d. per lb.

Suet Crust, for Pies or Puddings

INGREDIENTS.—To every lb. of flour allow 5 or 6 oz. of beef suet, ½ pint of water.

Mode.—Free the suet from skin and shreds; chop it extremely fine, and rub it well into the flour ; work the whole to a smooth paste with the above proportion of water; roll it out, and it is ready for use. This crust is quite rich enough for ordinary purposes, but when a better one is desired, use from ½ to ¾ lb. of suet to every lb. of flour. Some cooks, for rich crusts, pound the suet in a mortar, with a small quantity of butter. It should then be laid on the paste in small pieces, the same as for puff-crust, and will be found exceedingly nice for hot tarts. 5 oz. of suet to every lb. of flour will make a very good crust; and even ¼ lb. will answer very well for children, or where the crust is wanted very plain.

Average cost, 5*d*. per lb.

Common Crust for Raised Pies*

INGREDIENTS.—To every lb. of flour allow ½ pint of water, 1½ oz. of butter, 1½ oz. of lard, ½ saltspoonful of salt.

Mode.—Put into a saucepan the water; when it boils, add the butter and lard; and when these are melted, make a hole in the middle of the flour; pour in the water gradually; beat it well with a wooden spoon, and be particular in not making the paste too soft. When it is well mixed, knead it with the hands until quite stiff, dredging a little flour over the paste and board, to prevent them from sticking. When it is well kneaded, place it before the fire, with a cloth covered over it, for a few minutes; it will then be more easily worked into shape. This paste does not taste so nicely as the preceding one, but is worked with greater facility, and answers just as well for raised pies, for the crust is seldom eaten.

Average cost, 5*d*. per lb.

Almond Cheesecakes*

INGREDIENTS.—¼ lb. of sweet almonds, 4 bitter ones, 3 eggs, 2 oz. of butter, the rind of ¼ lemon, 1 tablespoonful of lemon-juice, 3 oz. of sugar.

Mode.—Blanch and pound the almonds smoothly in a mortar, with a little rose- or spring-water; stir in the eggs, which should be well beaten, and the butter, which should be warmed; add the grated lemon-peel and -juice, sweeten, and stir well until the whole is thoroughly mixed. Line some pattypans with puff-paste, put in the mixture, and bake for 20 minutes, or rather less in a quick oven.

Time.—20 minutes, or rather less.

Average cost, 10*d.*

Sufficient for about 12 cheesecakes.

Seasonable at any time.

BITTER ALMONDS.—The Bitter Almond is a variety of the common almond, and is injurious to animal life, on account of the great quantity of hydrocyanic acid it contains, and is consequently seldom used in domestic economy, unless it be to give flavour to confectionery; and even then it should be used with great caution. A single drop of the essential oil of bitter almonds is sufficient to destroy a bird, and four drops have caused the death of a middle-sized dog.

Boiled Apple Dumplings*

INGREDIENTS.—6 apples, ¾ lb. of suet-crust (Recipe, pp. 262–3), sugar to taste.

Mode.—Pare and take out the cores of the apples without dividing them; sweeten, and roll each apple in a piece of crust; be particular that the paste is nicely joined; put the dumplings into floured cloths, tie them securely, and put them into boiling water. Keep them boiling from ½ to ¾ hour; remove the cloths, and send them hot and quickly to table. Dumplings boiled in knitted cloths have a very pretty appearance when they come to table. The cloths should be made square, just large enough to hold one dumpling, and should be knitted in plain knitting, with *very coarse* cotton.

Time.—¾ to 1 hour, or longer should the dumplings be very large.

Average cost, 1½*d.* each.   *Sufficient* for 4 persons.

Seasonable from August to March, but flavourless after the end of January.

Creamed Apple Tart*

INGREDIENTS.—Puff-crust, apples; to every lb. of pared and cored apples, allow 2 oz. of moist sugar, ½ teaspoonful of minced lemon-peel, 1 tablespoonful of lemon juice, ½ pint of boiled custard.

Mode.—Make an apple tart by the preceding recipe, with the exception of omitting the icing. When the tart is baked, cut out the middle of the lid or crust, leaving a border all round the dish. Fill up with a nicely-made boiled custard, grate a little nutmeg over the top, and the pie is ready for table. This tart is usually eaten cold; is rather an old-fashioned dish, but, at the same time, extremely nice.

Time.—½ to ¾ hour.   *Average cost,* 1s. 3d.

Sufficient for 5 or 6 persons.   *Seasonable* from August to March.

Baked or Boiled Arrowroot Pudding

INGREDIENTS.—2 tablespoonfuls of arrowroot, 1½ pint of milk, 1 oz. of butter, the rind of ½ lemon, 2 heaped tablespoonfuls of moist sugar, a little grated nutmeg.

Mode.—Mix the arrowroot with as much cold milk as will make it into a smooth batter, moderately thick; put the remainder of the milk into a stewpan with the lemon-peel, and let it infuse for about ½ hour; when it boils, strain it gently to the batter, stirring it all the time to keep it smooth; then add the butter; beat this well in until thoroughly mixed, and sweeten with moist sugar. Put the mixture into a pie-dish, round which has been placed a border of paste, grate a little nutmeg over the top, and bake the pudding from 1 to 1¼ hour, in a moderate oven, or boil it the same length of time in a well-buttered basin. To enrich this pudding, stir to the other ingredients, just before it is put in the oven, 3 well-whisked eggs, and add a tablespoonful of brandy. For a nursery pudding, the addition of the latter ingredients will be found quite superfluous, as also the paste round the edge of the dish.

Time.—1 to 1¼ hour, baked or boiled.   *Average cost,* 7d.

Sufficient for 5 or 6 persons.   *Seasonable* at any time.

ARROWROOT.—In India, and in the colonies, by the process of rasping, they extract from a vegetable (*Maranta arundinacea*) a sediment nearly resembling tapioca. The grated pulp is sifted into a quantity of water, from which it is afterwards strained and dried, and the sediment thus produced is called arrowroot. Its qualities closely resemble those of tapioca.

Bakewell Pudding*
(*Very Rich*)

INGREDIENTS.—¼ lb. of puff-paste, 5 eggs, 6 oz. of sugar, ¼ lb. of butter, 1 oz. of almonds, jam.

Mode.—Cover a dish with thin paste, and put over this a layer of any kind of jam, ½ inch thick; put the yolks of 5 eggs into a basin with the white of 1, and beat these well; add the sifted sugar, the butter, which should be melted, and the almonds, which should be well pounded; beat all together until well mixed, then pour it into the dish over the jam, and bake for an hour in a moderate oven.

Time.—1 hour. *Average cost*, 1s. 6d.

Sufficient for 4 or 5 persons. *Seasonable* at any time.

Baroness Pudding
(*Author's Recipe*)

INGREDIENTS.—¾ lb. of suet, ¾ lb. of raisins weighed after being stoned, ¾ lb. of flour, ½ pint of milk, ¼ saltspoonful of salt.

Mode.—Prepare the suet, by carefully freeing it from skin, and chop it finely; stone the raisins, and cut them in halves, and mix both these ingredients with the salt and flour; moisten the whole with the above proportion of milk, stir the mixture well, and tie the pudding in a floured cloth, which has been previously wrung out in boiling water. Put the pudding into a saucepan of boiling water, and let it boil, without ceasing, 4½ hours. Serve merely with plain sifted sugar, a little of which may be sprinkled over the pudding.

Time.—4½ hours. *Average cost*, 1s. 4d.

Sufficient for 7 or 8 persons.

Seasonable in winter, when fresh fruit is not obtainable.

Note.—This pudding the editress cannot too highly recommend. The recipe was kindly given to her family by a lady who bore the title here prefixed to it; and with all who have partaken of it, it is an especial favourite.* Nothing is of greater consequence, in the above directions, than attention to the time of boiling, which should never be *less* than that mentioned.

Baked Batter Pudding

INGREDIENTS.—1½ pint of milk; 4 tablespoonfuls of flour, 2 oz. of butter, 4 eggs, a little salt.

Mode.—Mix the flour with a small quantity of cold milk; make the remainder hot, and pour it on to the flour, keeping the mixture well stirred; add the butter, eggs, and salt; beat the whole well, and put the pudding into a buttered pie-dish; bake for ¾ hour, and serve with sweet sauce, wine sauce, or stewed fruit. Baked in small cups, this makes very pretty little puddings, and should be eaten with the same accompaniments as above.

Time.—¾ hour.   *Average cost*, 9*d*.

Sufficient for 5 or 6 persons.   *Seasonable* at any time.

Boiled Bread Pudding*

INGREDIENTS.— 1½ pint of milk; ¾ pint of bread crumbs, sugar to taste, 4 eggs, 1 oz. of butter, 3 oz. of currants, ¼ teaspoonful of grated nutmeg.

Mode.—Make the milk boiling, and pour it on the bread crumbs; let these remain till cold; then add the other ingredients, taking care that the eggs are well beaten and the currants well washed, picked, and dried. Beat the pudding well, and put it into a buttered basin; tie it down tightly with a cloth, plunge it into boiling water, and boil for 1¼ hour; turn it out of the basin, and serve with sifted sugar. Any odd pieces or scraps of bread answer for this pudding; but they should be soaked overnight, and, when wanted for use, should have the water well squeezed from them.

Time.— 1¼ hour.   *Average cost*, 1*s*.

Sufficient for 6 or 7 persons.   *Seasonable* at any time.

Baked Bread-and-Butter Pudding

INGREDIENTS.—9 thin slices of bread and butter, 1½ pint of milk, 4 eggs, sugar to taste, ¼ lb. of currants, flavouring of vanilla, grated lemon-peel or nutmeg.

Mode.—Cut 9 slices of bread and butter not very thick, and put them into a pie-dish, with currants between each layer and on the top. Sweeten and flavour the milk, either by infusing a little lemon-peel in it, or by adding a few drops of essence of vanilla; well whisk the eggs, and stir these to the milk. *Strain* this over the bread and butter, and bake in a moderate oven for 1 hour, or rather longer. This pudding may be very much enriched by adding cream, candied peel, or more eggs than stated above. It should not be turned out, but sent to table in the pie-dish, and is better for being made about 2 hours before it is baked.

Time.—1 hour, or rather longer. *Average cost*, 9*d*.
Sufficient for 6 or 7 persons.
Seasonable at any time.

Canary Pudding*

INGREDIENTS.—The weight of 3 eggs in sugar and butter, the
weight of 2 eggs in flour, the rind of 1 small lemon, 3 eggs.

Mode.—Melt the butter to a liquid state, but do not allow it to oil;
stir to this the sugar and finely-minced lemon-peel, and gradually
dredge in the flour, keeping the mixture well stirred; whisk the eggs;
add these to the pudding; beat all the ingredients until thoroughly
blended, and put them into a buttered mould or basin; boil for
2 hours, and serve with sweet sauce.

Time.—2 hours. *Average cost* 9*d*.
Sufficient for 4 or 5 persons. *Seasonable* at any time.

College Puddings*

INGREDIENTS.—1 pint of bread crumbs, 6 oz. of finely-chopped
suet, ¼ lb. of currants, a few thin slices of candied peel, 3 oz. of
sugar, ¼ nutmeg, 3 eggs, 4 tablespoonfuls of brandy.

Mode.—Put the bread crumbs into a basin; add the suet, currants,
candied peel, sugar, and nutmeg, grated, and stir these ingredients
until they are thoroughly mixed. Beat up the eggs, moisten the pudding with these, and put in the brandy; beat well for a few minutes,
then form the mixture into round balls or egg-shaped pieces; fry
these in hot butter or lard, letting them stew in it until thoroughly
done, and turn them two or three times, till of a fine light brown;
drain them on a piece of blotting-paper before the fire; dish, and
serve with wine sauce.

Time.—15 to 20 minutes. *Average cost*, 1*s*.
Sufficient for 7 or 8 puddings. *Seasonable* at any time.

Baked Custard Pudding*

INGREDIENTS.—1½ pint of milk, the rind of ¼ lemon, ¼ lb. of
moist sugar, 4 eggs.

Mode.—Put the milk into a saucepan with the sugar and lemon-
rind, and let this infuse for about ½ hour, or until the milk is well

flavoured; whisk the eggs, yolks and whites; pour the milk to them, stirring all the while; then have ready a pie-dish, lined at the edge with paste ready baked; strain the custard into the dish, grate a little nutmeg over the top, and bake in a *very slow* oven for about ½ hour, or rather longer. The flavour of this pudding may be varied by substituting bitter almonds for the lemon-rind; and it may be very much enriched by using half cream and half milk, and doubling the quantity of eggs.

Time.—½ to ¾ hour.   *Average cost,* 9*d.*

Sufficient for 5 or 6 persons.   *Seasonable* at any time.

Note.—This pudding is usually served cold with fruit tarts.

Empress Pudding

INGREDIENTS.—½ lb. of rice; 2 oz. of butter, 3 eggs, jam, sufficient milk to soften the rice.

Mode.—Boil the rice in the milk until very soft; then add the butter; boil it for a few minutes after the latter ingredient is put in, and set it by to cool. Well beat the eggs, stir these in, and line a dish with puff-paste; put over this a layer of rice, then a thin layer of any kind of jam, then another layer of rice, and proceed in this manner until the dish is full; and bake in a moderate oven for ¾ hour. This pudding may be eaten hot or cold; if the latter, it will be much improved by having a boiled custard poured over it.

Time.—¾ hour.   *Average cost,* 1*s.*

Sufficient for 6 or 7 persons.   *Seasonable* at any time.

Exeter Pudding
(*Very rich*)

INGREDIENTS.—10 oz. of bread crumbs, 4 oz. of sago, 7 oz. of finely-chopped suet, 6 oz. of moist sugar, the rind of ½ lemon, ¼ pint of rum, 7 eggs, 4 tablespoonfuls of cream, 4 small sponge cakes, 2 oz. of ratafias, ½ lb. of jam.

Mode.—Put the bread crumbs into a basin with the sago, suet, sugar, minced lemon-peel, rum, and 4 eggs; stir these ingredients well together, then add 3 more eggs and the cream, and let the mixture be well beaten. Then butter a mould, strew in a few bread crumbs, and cover the bottom with a layer of ratafias; then put in a layer of the mixture, then a layer of sliced sponge cake spread thickly with any kind of jam; then add some ratafias, then some of the mixture and sponge cake, and so on until the mould is full, taking care that a layer of the mixture is on the top of the pudding. Bake in a good oven from ¾ to 1 hour, and serve with the following sauce:— Put 3 tablespoonfuls of black-currant jelly into a stewpan, add 2 glasses of sherry, and, when warm, turn the pudding out of the mould, pour the sauce over it, and serve hot.

Time.—From 1 to 1¼ hour.

Average cost, 2s. 6d.

Sufficient for 7 or 8 persons.

Seasonable at any time.

Dampfnudeln, or German Puddings*

INGREDIENTS.—1 lb. of flour, ¼ lb. of butter, 5 eggs, 2 small tablespoonfuls of yeast, 2 tablespoonfuls of finely-pounded sugar, milk, a very little salt.

Mode.—Put the flour into a basin, make a hole in the centre, into which put the yeast, and rather more than ¼ pint of warm milk; make this into a batter with the middle of the flour, and let the sponge rise in a warm temperature. When sufficiently risen, mix the eggs, butter, sugar, and salt with a little more warm milk, and knead the whole well together with the hands, beating the dough until it is perfectly smooth, and it drops from the fingers. Then cover the basin with a cloth, put it in a warm place, and when the dough has nicely risen, knead it into small balls; butter the bottom of a deep sauté-pan, strew over some pounded sugar, and let the dampfnudeln be laid in, but do not let them touch one another; then pour over sufficient milk to cover them, put on the lid, and let them rise to twice their original size by the side of the fire. Now place them in the oven for a few minutes, to acquire a nice brown colour, and serve them on a napkin, with custard sauce flavoured with vanilla, or a *compôte* of any fruit that may be preferred.

Time.—½ to ¾ hour for the sponge to rise; 10 to 15 minutes for the puddings to rise; 10 minutes to bake them in a brisk oven.

Sufficient for 10 or 12 dampfnudeln.

Seasonable at any time.

Half-Pay Pudding*

INGREDIENTS.—¼ lb. of suet, ¼ lb. of currants, ¼ lb. of raisins, ¼ lb. of flour, ¼ lb. of bread crumbs, 2 tablespoonfuls of treacle, ½ pint of milk.

Mode.—Chop the suet finely; mix with it the currants, which should be nicely washed and dried, the raisins, which should be stoned, the flour, bread crumbs, and treacle; moisten with the milk, beat up the ingredients until all are thoroughly mixed, put them into a buttered basin, and boil the pudding for 3½ hours.

Time.—3½ hours.　*Average cost*, 8*d*.

Sufficient for 5 or 6 persons.　*Seasonable* at any time.

Herodotus Pudding*

INGREDIENTS.—½ lb. of bread crumbs, ½ lb. of good figs, 6 oz. of suet, 6 oz. of moist sugar, ½ saltspoonful of salt, 3 eggs, nutmeg to taste.

Mode.—Mince the suet and figs very finely; add the remaining ingredients, taking care that the eggs are well whisked; beat the mixture for a few minutes, put it into a buttered mould, tie it down with a floured cloth, and boil the pudding for 5 hours. Serve with wine sauce.

Time.—5 hours.　*Average cost*, 10*d*.

Sufficient for 5 or 6 persons.　*Seasonable* at any time.

Baked Lemon Pudding
(*Very rich*)

INGREDIENTS.—The rind and juice of 2 large lemons, ½ lb. of loaf sugar, ¼ pint of cream, the yolks of 8 eggs, 2 oz. of almonds, ½ lb. of butter, melted.

Mode.—Mix the pounded sugar with the cream, and add the yolks of eggs and the butter, which should be previously warmed. Blanch and pound the almonds, and put these, with the grated rind and strained juice of the lemons, to the other ingredients. Stir all well together; line a dish with puff-paste, put in the mixture, and bake for 1 hour.

Time.—1 hour.　*Average cost*, 2*s*.

Sufficient for 6 or 7 persons.　*Seasonable* at any time.

Sweet Macaroni Pudding

INGREDIENTS.—2½ oz. of macaroni, 2 pints of milk, the rind of ½ lemon, 3 eggs, sugar and grated nutmeg to taste, 2 tablespoonfuls of brandy.

Mode.—Put the macaroni, with a pint of the milk, into a saucepan with the lemon-peel, and let it simmer gently until the macaroni is tender; then put it into a pie-dish without the peel; mix the other pint of milk with the eggs; stir these well together, adding the sugar and brandy, and pour the mixture over the macaroni. Grate a little nutmeg over the top, and bake in a moderate oven for ½ hour. To make this pudding look nice, a paste should be laid round the edges of the dish, and, for variety, a layer of preserve or marmalade may be placed on the macaroni: in this case omit the brandy.

Time.—¾ hour to simmer the macaroni; ½ hour to bake the pudding.

Macaroni

Average cost, 11*d.*

Sufficient for 5 or 6 persons.

Seasonable at any time.

MACARONI is composed of wheaten flour, flavoured with other articles, and worked up with water into a paste, to which, by a peculiar process, a tubular or pipe form is given, in order that it may cook more readily in hot water. That of smaller diameter than macaroni (which is about the thickness of a goose-quill) is called *vermicelli*; and when smaller still, *fidelini*. The finest is made from the flour of the hard-grained Black-Sea wheat. Macaroni is the principal article of food in many parts of Italy, particularly Naples, where the best is manufactured, and from whence, also, it is exported in considerable quantities. In this country, macaroni and vermicelli are frequently used in soups.*

Excellent Mincemeat*

INGREDIENTS.—3 large lemons, 3 large apples, 1 lb. of stoned raisins, 1 lb. of currants, 1 lb. of suet, 2 lbs. of moist sugar, 1 oz. of sliced candied citron, 1 oz. of sliced candied orange-peel, and the same quantity of lemon-peel, 1 teacupful of brandy, 2 tablespoonfuls of orange marmalade.

Mode.—Grate the rinds of the lemons; squeeze out the juice, strain it, and boil the remainder of the lemons until tender enough to pulp or chop very finely. Then add to this pulp the apples, which should be baked, and their skins and cores removed; put in the remaining ingredients one by one, and, as they are added, mix everything very thoroughly together. Put the mincemeat into a stone jar with a closely-fitting lid, and in a fortnight it will be ready for use.

Seasonable.—This should be made the first or second week in December.

Monday's Pudding*

INGREDIENTS.—The remains of cold plum-pudding, brandy, custard made with 5 eggs to every pint of milk.

Mode.—Cut the remains of a *good* cold plum-pudding into finger-pieces, soak them in a little brandy, and lay them cross-barred in a mould until full. Make a custard with the above proportion of milk and eggs, flavouring it with nutmeg or lemon-rind; fill up the mould with it; tie it down with a cloth, and boil or steam it for an hour. Serve with a little of the custard poured over, to which has been added a tablespoonful of brandy.

Time.—1 hour.   *Average cost*, exclusive of the pudding, 6*d*.

Sufficient for 5 or 6 persons.   *Seasonable* at any time.

SMALL DISHES OF PASTRY FOR ENTREMETS, SUPPER-DISHES, &C.

Fanchonnettes, or Custard Tartlets

INGREDIENTS.—For the custard, 4 eggs, ¾ pint of milk, 2 oz. of butter, 2 oz. of pounded sugar, 3 dessert-spoonfuls of flour, flavouring to taste; the whites of 2 eggs, 2 oz. of pounded sugar.

Mode.—Well beat the eggs; stir to them the milk, the butter, which should be beaten to a cream, the sugar, and flour; mix these ingredients well together, put them into a very clean saucepan, and bring them to the simmering point, but do not allow them to boil. Flavour with essence of vanilla, bitter almonds, lemon, grated chocolate, or any flavouring ingredient that may be preferred. Line some round tartlet-pans with good puff-paste; fill them with the custard, and bake in a moderate oven for about 20 minutes; then take them out of the pans; let them cool, and in the mean time whisk the whites of the eggs to a stiff froth; stir into this the pounded sugar, and spread smoothly over the tartlets a little of this mixture. Put them in the oven again to set the icing, but be particular that they do not scorch: when the icing looks crisp, they are done. Arrange them, piled high in the centre, on a white napkin, and garnish the dish, and in between the tartlets, with strips of bright jelly, or very firmly-made preserve.

Time.—20 minutes to bake the tartlets; 5 minutes after being iced.

Average cost, exclusive of the paste, 1s.

Sufficient to fill 10 or 12 tartlets.   *Seasonable* at any time.

Note.—The icing may be omitted on the top of the tartlets, and a spoonful of any kind of preserve put at the bottom of the custard instead: this varies both the flavour and appearance of this dish.

Pease Pudding*

INGREDIENTS.—1½ pint of split peas, 2 oz. of butter, 2 eggs, pepper and salt to taste.

Mode.—Put the peas to soak over-night, in rain-water, and float off any that are wormeaten or discoloured. Tie them loosely in a clean cloth, leaving a little room for them to swell, and put them on to boil in cold rain-water, allowing 2½ hours after the water has simmered up. When the peas are tender, take them up and drain; rub them through a colander with a wooden spoon; add the butter, eggs, pepper, and salt; beat all well together for a few minutes, until the ingredients are well incorporated; then tie them tightly in a floured cloth; boil the pudding for another hour, turn it on to the dish, and serve very hot. This pudding should always be sent to table with boiled leg of pork, and is an exceedingly nice accompaniment to boiled beef.

Time.—2½ hours to boil the peas, tied loosely in the cloth; 1 hour for the pudding.

Average cost, 6d.

Sufficient for 7 or 8 persons.

Seasonable from September to March.

An Unrivalled Plum-Pudding*

INGREDIENTS.—1½ lb. of muscatel raisins, 1¾ lb. of currants, 1 lb. of sultana raisins, 2 lbs. of the finest moist sugar, 2 lbs. of bread crumbs, 16 eggs, 2 lbs. of finely-chopped suet, 6 oz. of mixed candied peel, the rind of 2 lemons, 1 oz. of ground nutmeg, 1 oz. of ground cinnamon, ½ oz. of pounded bitter almonds, ¼ pint of brandy.

Mode.—Stone and cut up the raisins, but do not chop them; wash and dry the currants, and cut the candied peel into thin slices. Mix all the dry ingredients well together, and moisten with the eggs, which should be well beaten and strained, to the pudding; stir in the brandy, and, when all is thoroughly mixed, well butter and flour a stout new pudding-cloth; put in the pudding, tie it down very tightly and closely, boil from 6 to 8 hours, and serve with brandy-sauce. A few sweet almonds, blanched and cut in strips, and stuck on the pudding, ornament it prettily. This quantity may be divided and boiled in buttered moulds. For small families this is the most desirable way; as the above will be found to make a pudding of rather large dimensions.

Time.—6 to 8 hours.   *Average cost*, 7s. 6d.

Seasonable in winter.   *Sufficient* for 12 or 14 persons.

Note.—The muscatel raisins can be purchased at a cheap rate loose (not in bunches): they are then scarcely higher in price than the ordinary raisins, and impart a much richer flavour to the pudding.

Plum Tart*

INGREDIENTS.—½ lb. of good short crust, 1½ pint of plums, ¼ lb. of moist sugar.

Mode.—Line the edges of a deep tart-dish with crust; fill the dish with plums, and place a small cup or jar, upside down, in the midst of them. Put in the sugar, cover the pie with crust, ornament the edges, and bake in a good oven from ½ to ¾ hour. When

Plum Tart

puff-crust is preferred to short crust, glaze the top by brushing it over with the white of an egg beaten to a stiff froth with a knife; sprinkle over a little sifted sugar, and put the pie in the oven to set the glaze.

Time.—½ to ¾ hour.   *Average cost*, 1s.

Sufficient for 5 or 6 persons.

Seasonable, with various kinds of plums, from the beginning of August to the beginning of October.

Potato Pasty*

INGREDIENTS.—1½ lb. of rump-steak or mutton cutlets, pepper and salt to taste, ⅓ pint of weak broth or gravy, 1 oz. of butter, mashed potatoes.

Mode.—Place the meat, cut in small pieces, at the bottom of the pan; season it with pepper and salt, and add the gravy and butter

Potato-Pasty Pan

broken into small pieces. Put on the perforated plate, with its valve-pipe screwed on, and fill up the whole space to the top of the tube with nicely-mashed potatoes mixed with a little milk, and finish the surface of them in any ornamental manner. If carefully baked, the potatoes will be covered with a delicate brown crust, retaining all the savoury steam rising from the meat. Send it to table as it comes from the oven, with a napkin folded round it.

Time.—40 to 60 minutes. *Average cost,* 2s.

Sufficient for 4 or 5 persons. *Seasonable* at any time.

Raised Pie of Veal and Ham*

INGREDIENTS.—3 or 4 lbs. of veal cutlets, a few slices of bacon or ham, seasoning of pepper, salt, nutmeg, and allspice, forcemeat, 2 lbs. of hot-water paste (p. 263), ½ pint of good strong gravy.

Mode.—To raise the crust for a pie with the hands is a very difficult task, and can only be accomplished by skilled and experienced cooks. The process should be seen to be satisfactorily learnt,

Raised Pie

and plenty of practice given to the making of raised pies, as by that means only will success be insured. Make a hot-water paste by recipe on p. 263, and from the mass raise the pie with the hands; if this cannot be accomplished, cut out pieces for the top and bottom, and a long piece for the sides, fasten the bottom and side-piece together by means of egg, and pinch the edges well together; then line the pie with forcemeat, put in a layer of veal, and a plentiful seasoning of salt, pepper, nutmeg, and allspice, as, let it be remembered, these pies taste very insipid unless highly seasoned. Over the seasoning place a layer of sliced bacon or cooked ham, and then a layer of forcemeat, veal seasoning, and bacon, and so on until the meat rises to about an inch above the paste; taking care to finish with a layer of forcemeat, to fill all the cavities of the pie, and to lay in the meat firmly and compactly. Brush the top edge of the pie with beaten egg, put on the cover, press the edges, and pinch them round with paste-pincers. Make a hole in the middle of the lid, and ornament the pie with leaves, which should be stuck on with the white of an egg; then brush it all over with the beaten yolk of an egg, and bake the pie in an oven with a soaking heat from 3 to 4 hours. To ascertain when it is done, run a sharp-pointed knife or skewer through the hole at the top into the middle of the pie, and if the meat feels tender, it is sufficiently baked. Have ready about ½ pint of very strong gravy, pour it through a funnel into the hole at the top, stop up the hole with a small leaf of baked paste, and put the pie away until wanted for use. Should it acquire too much colour in the baking, cover it with white paper, as the crust should not in the least degree be burnt. Mushrooms, truffles, and many other ingredients, may be added to enrich the flavour of these pies, and the very fleshy parts of the meat may be larded. These pies are more frequently served cold than hot, and form excellent dishes for cold suppers or breakfasts. The cover of the pie is sometimes carefully removed, leaving the perfect edges, and the top decorated with square pieces of very bright aspic jelly: this has an exceedingly pretty effect.

Time.—About 4 hours.   *Average cost*, 6s. 6d.

Sufficient for a very large pie.   *Seasonable* from March to October.

Baked Rice Pudding

INGREDIENTS.—1 small teacupful of rice, 4 eggs, 1 pint of milk, 2 oz. of fresh butter, 2 oz. of beef marrow,* ¼ lb. of currants, 2 tablespoonfuls of brandy, nutmeg, ¼ lb. of sugar, the rind of ½ lemon.

Mode.—Put the lemon-rind and milk into a stewpan, and let it infuse till the milk is well flavoured with the lemon; in the mean time, boil the rice until tender in water, with a very small quantity of salt, and, when done, let it be thoroughly drained. Beat the eggs, stir to them the milk, which should be strained, the butter, marrow, currants, and remaining ingredients; add the rice, and mix all well together. Line the edges of the dish with puff-paste, put in the pudding, and bake for about ¾ hour in a slow oven. Slices of candied-peel may be added at pleasure, or Sultana raisins may be substituted for the currants.

Time.—¾ hour. *Average cost*, 1s. 3d.

Sufficient for 5 or 6 persons.

Seasonable.—Suitable for a winter pudding, when fresh fruits are not obtainable.

Boiled Rice for Curries, &c.*

INGREDIENTS.—¾ lb. of rice, water, salt.

Mode.—Pick, wash, and soak the rice in plenty of cold water; then have ready a saucepan of boiling water, drop the rice into it, and keep it boiling quickly, with the lid uncovered, until it is tender, but not soft. Take it up, drain it, and put it on a dish before the fire to dry: do not handle it much with a spoon, but shake it about a little with two forks, that it may all be equally dried, and strew over a little salt. It is now ready to serve, and may be heaped lightly on a dish by itself, or be laid round the dish as a border, with a curry or fricassee in the centre. Some cooks smooth the rice with the back of a spoon, and then brush it over with the yolk of an egg, and set it in the oven to colour; but the rice well boiled, white, dry, and with every grain distinct, is by far the more preferable mode of dressing it. During the process of boiling, the rice should be attentively watched, that it be not overdone, as, if this is the case, it will have a mashed and soft appearance.

Time.—15 to 25 minutes, according to the quality of the rice.

Average cost, 3d.

Sufficient for a large dish of curry. *Seasonable* at any time.

Lemon Sauce for Sweet Puddings*

INGREDIENTS.—The rind and juice of 1 lemon, 1 tablespoonful of flour, 1 oz. of butter, 1 large wineglassful of sherry, 1 wineglassful of water, sugar to taste, the yolks of 4 eggs.

Mode.—Rub the rind of the lemon on to some lumps of sugar; squeeze out the juice, and strain it; put the butter and flour into a saucepan, stir them over the fire, and when of a pale brown, add the wine, water, and strained lemon-juice. Crush the lumps of sugar that were rubbed on the lemon; stir these into the sauce, which should be very sweet. When these ingredients are well mixed, and the sugar is melted, put in the beaten yolks of 4 eggs; keep stirring the sauce until it thickens, when serve. Do not, on any account, allow it to boil, or it will curdle, and be entirely spoiled.

Time.—Altogether, 15 minutes.   *Average cost*, 1s. 2d.

Sufficient for 7 or 8 persons.

An Excellent Wine Sauce for Puddings

INGREDIENTS.—The yolks of 4 eggs, 1 teaspoonful of flour, 2 oz. of pounded sugar, 2 oz. of fresh butter, ¼ saltspoonful of salt, ½ pint of sherry or Madeira.

Mode.—Put the butter and flour into a saucepan, and stir them over the fire until the former thickens; then add the sugar, salt, and wine, and mix these ingredients well together. Separate the yolks from the whites of 4 eggs; beat up the former, and stir them briskly to the sauce; let it remain over the fire until it is on the point of simmering; but do not allow it to boil, or it will instantly curdle. This sauce is delicious with plum, marrow, or bread puddings; but should be served separately, and not poured over the pudding.

Time.—From 5 to 7 minutes to thicken the butter; about 5 minutes to stir the sauce over the fire.

Average cost, 1s. 10d.   *Sufficient* for 7 or 8 persons.

Rolled Treacle Pudding

INGREDIENTS.— 1 lb. of suet crust, ¼ lb. of treacle, ½ teaspoonful of grated ginger.

Mode.—Make, with 1 lb. of flour, a suet crust by recipe on pp. 262–3; roll it out to the thickness of ½ inch, and spread the treacle equally over it, leaving a small margin where the paste joins; close the ends securely, tie the pudding in a floured cloth, plunge it into boiling water, and boil for 2 hours. We have inserted this pudding, being economical, and a favourite one with children; it is, of course, only suitable for a nursery, or very plain family dinner.* Made with a lard instead of a suet crust, it would be very nice baked, and would be sufficiently done in from 1½ to 2 hours.

Time.—Boiled pudding, 2 hours; baked pudding, 1½ to 2 hours.

Average cost, 7d.

Sufficient for 5 or 6 persons.   *Seasonable* at any time.

Yorkshire Pudding, to serve with hot Roast Beef

INGREDIENTS.—1½ pint of milk, 6 *large* tablespoonfuls of flour, 3 eggs, 1 saltspoonful of salt.

Mode.—Put the flour into a basin with the salt, and stir gradually to this enough milk to make it into a stiff batter. When this is perfectly smooth, and all the lumps are well rubbed down, add the remainder of the milk and the eggs, which should be well beaten. Beat the mixture for a few minutes, and pour it into a shallow tin, which has been previously well rubbed with beef dripping. Put the pudding into the oven, and bake it for an hour; then, for another ½ hour, place it under the meat, to catch a little of the gravy that flows from it. Cut the pudding into small square pieces, put them on a hot dish, and serve. If the meat is baked, the pudding may at once be placed under it, resting the former on a small three-cornered stand.

Time.—1½ hour.   *Average cost*, 7d.

Sufficient for 5 or 6 persons.   *Seasonable* at any time.

CHAPTER XXVIII

GENERAL OBSERVATIONS ON CREAMS, JELLIES, SOUFFLÉS, OMELETS, AND SWEET DISHES

CREAMS.—The yellowish-white, opaque fluid, smooth and unctuous to the touch, which separates itself from new milk, and forms a layer on its surface, when removed by skimming, is employed in a variety of culinary preparations. The analyses of the contents of cream have been decided to be, in 100 parts—butter, 3.5; curd, or matter of cheese, 3.5; whey, 92.0. That cream contains an oil, is evinced by its staining clothes in the manner of oil; and when boiled for some time, a little oil floats upon the surface. The thick animal oil which it contains, the well-known *butter*, is separated only by agitation, as in the common process of *churning*, and the cheesy matter remains blended with the whey in the state of *buttermilk*. Of the several kinds of cream, the principal are the Devonshire and Dutch clotted creams, the Costorphin cream, and the Scotch sour cream. The Devonshire cream is produced by nearly boiling the milk in shallow tin vessels over a charcoal fire, and kept in that state until the whole of the cream is thrown up. It is used for eating with fruits and tarts. The cream from Costorphin, a village of that name near Edinburgh, is accelerated in its separation from three or four days' old milk, by a certain degree of heat; and the Dutch clotted cream—a coagulated mass in which a spoon will stand upright—is manufactured from fresh-drawn milk, which is put into a pan, and stirred with a spoon two or three times a day, to prevent the cream from separating from the milk. The Scotch 'sour cream' is a misnomer; for it is a material produced without cream. A small tub filled with skimmed milk is put into a larger one, containing hot water, and after remaining there all night, the thin milk (called *wigg*) is drawn off, and the remainder of the contents of the smaller vessel is 'sour cream.'

JELLIES are not the nourishing food they were at one time considered to be, and many eminent physicians are of opinion that they are less digestible than the flesh, or muscular part of animals; still, when acidulated with lemon-juice and flavoured with wine, they are very suitable for some convalescents. Vegetable jelly is a distinct principle, existing in fruits, which possesses the property of gelatinizing when boiled and cooled; but it is a principle entirely different from the gelatine of animal bodies, although the name of jelly, common to both, sometimes leads to an erroneous idea on that subject. Animal jelly, or gelatine, is glue, whereas vegetable jelly is rather analogous to gum. Liebig* places gelatine very low indeed in the scale of usefulness. He says, 'Gelatine, which by itself is tasteless, and when eaten, excites nausea, possesses no nutritive value; that, even when accompanied by the savoury constituents of flesh, it is not capable of supporting the vital process, and when added to the usual diet as a substitute for plastic matter, does not increase, but, on the contrary, diminishes the nutritive value of the food, which it renders insufficient in quantity and inferior in quality.' It is this substance which is most frequently employed in the manufacture of the jellies supplied by the confectioner; but those prepared at home from calves' feet do possess some nutrition, and are the only sort that should be given to invalids. Isinglass is the purest variety of gelatine, and is prepared from the sounds or swimming-bladders of certain fish, chiefly the sturgeon. From its whiteness it is mostly used for making blanc-mange and similar dishes.

The WHITE OF EGGS is perhaps the best substance that can be employed in clarifying jelly, as well as some other fluids, for the reason that when albumen (and the white of eggs is nearly pure albumen) is put into a liquid that is muddy, from substances suspended in it, on boiling the liquid, the albumen coagulates in a flocculent manner, and, entangling with it the impurities, rises with them to the surface as a scum, or sinks to the bottom, according to their weight.

SOUFFLÉS, OMELETS, and SWEET DISHES, in which eggs form the principal ingredient, demand, for their successful manufacture, an experienced cook. They are the prettiest, but most difficult of all entremets. The most essential thing to insure success is to secure the best ingredients from an honest tradesman. The entremets coming within the above classification, are healthy, nourishing, and pleasant to the taste, and may be eaten with safety by persons of the most delicate stomachs.

CHAPTER XXIX

RECIPES*

Flanc of Apples, or Apples in a Raised Crust*
(*Sweet Entremets*)

INGREDIENTS.—¾ lb. of short crust, 9 moderate-sized apples, the rind and juice of ½ lemon, ½ lb. of white sugar, ¾ pint of water, a few strips of candied citron.

Mode.—Make a short crust; roll it out to the thickness of ½ inch, and butter an oval mould; line it with the crust, and press it carefully all round the sides, to obtain the form of the mould, but be particular not to break the paste. Pinch the part that just rises above the mould with the paste-pincers, and fill the case with flour; bake it for about ¾ hour; then take it out of the oven, remove the flour, put the case back in the oven for another ¼ hour, and do not allow it to get scorched. It is now ready for the apples, which should be prepared in the following manner: peel, and take out the cores with a small knife, or a cutter for the purpose, without dividing the apples; put them into a small lined saucepan, just capable of holding them, with sugar, water, lemon juice and rind, in the above proportion. Let them simmer very gently until tender; then take out the apples, let them cool, arrange them in the flanc or case, and boil down the syrup until reduced to a thick jelly; pour it over the apples, and garnish them with a few slices of candied citron.

A MORE SIMPLE FLANC may be made by rolling out the paste, cutting the bottom of a round or oval shape, and then a narrow strip for the sides: these should be stuck on with the white of an egg, to the bottom piece, and the flanc then filled with raw fruit, with sufficient sugar to sweeten it nicely. It will not require so long baking as in a mould; but the crust must be made everywhere of an equal thickness, and so perfectly joined, that the juice does not escape. This dish may also be served hot, and should be garnished in the same manner, or a little melted apricot jam may be poured over the apples, which very much improves their flavour.

Time.—Altogether, 1 hour to bake the flanc, from 30 to 40 minutes to stew the apples very gently.

Average cost, 1s. 6d.

Sufficient for 1 entremets or side-dish.

Seasonable from July to March.

Apple Fritters*

INGREDIENTS.—For the batter, ½ lb. of flour, ½ oz. of butter, ½ saltspoonful of salt, 2 eggs, milk, apples, hot lard or clarified beef-dripping.

Mode.—Break the eggs; separate the whites from the yolks, and beat them separately. Put the flour into a basin, stir in the butter, which should be melted to a cream; add the salt, and moisten with sufficient warm milk to make it of a proper consistency, that is to say, a batter that will drop from the spoon. Stir this well, rub down any lumps that may be seen, and add the whites of the eggs, which have been previously well whisked; beat up the batter for a few minutes, and it is ready for use. Now peel and cut the apples into rather thick whole slices, without dividing them, and stamp out the middle of each slice, where the core is, with a cutter. Throw the slices into the batter; have ready a pan of boiling lard or clarified dripping; take out the pieces of apple one by one, put them into the hot lard, and fry a nice brown, turning them when required. When done, lay them on a piece of blotting-paper before the fire, to absorb the greasy moisture; then dish on a white d'oyley, piled one above the other; strew over them some pounded sugar, and serve very hot. The flavour of the fritters would be very much improved by soaking the pieces of apple in a little wine, mixed with sugar and lemon-juice, for 3 or 4 hours before wanted for table; the batter, also, is better for being mixed some hours before the fritters are made

Time.—About 10 minutes to fry them; 5 minutes to drain them.

Average cost, 9d.

Sufficient for 4 or 5 persons.

Seasonable from July to March.

A Pretty Dish of Apples and Rice

INGREDIENTS.—6 oz. of rice, 1 quart of milk, the rind of ½ lemon, sugar to taste, ½ saltspoonful of salt, 8 apples, ¼ lb. of sugar, ¼ pint of water, ½ pint of boiled custard.

Mode.—Flavour the milk with lemon-rind, by boiling them together for a few minutes; then take out the peel, and put in the rice, with sufficient sugar to sweeten it nicely, and boil gently until the rice is quite soft; then let it cool. In the mean time pare, quarter, and core the apples, and boil them until tender in a syrup made with sugar and water in the above proportion; and, when soft, lift them out on a sieve to drain. Now put a middling-sized gallipot* in the centre of a dish; lay the rice all round till the top of the gallipot is reached; smooth the rice with the back of a spoon, and stick the apples into it in rows, one row sloping to the right and the next to the left. Set it in the oven to colour the apples; then, when required for table, remove the gallipot, garnish the rice with preserved fruits, and pour in the middle sufficient custard to be level with the top of the rice, and serve hot.

Time.—From 20 to 30 minutes to stew the apples; ¾ hour to simmer the rice; ¼ hour to bake.   *Average cost, 1s. 6d.*

Sufficient for 5 or 6 persons.   *Seasonable* from July to March.

Blanc-mange*
(*A Supper Dish*)

INGREDIENTS.—1 pint of new milk, 1¼ oz. of isinglass, the rind of ½ lemon, ¼ lb. of loaf sugar, 10 bitter almonds, ½ oz. of sweet almonds, 1 pint of cream.

Mode.—Put the milk into a saucepan, with the isinglass, lemon-rind, and sugar, and let these ingredients stand by the side of the

Blanc-Mange Mould

fire until the milk is well flavoured; add the almonds, which should be blanched and pounded in a mortar to a paste, and let the milk just boil up; strain it through a fine sieve or muslin into a jug, add the cream, and stir the mixture occasionally until nearly cold. Let it stand for a few minutes, then pour it into the mould, which should be previously oiled with the purest salad-oil, or dipped in cold water. There will be a sediment at the bottom of the jug, which must not be poured into the mould, as, when turned out, it would very much disfigure the appearance of the blanc-mange. This blanc-mange may be made very much richer by using 1½ pint of cream, and melting the isinglass in ½ pint of boiling water. The flavour may also be very much varied by adding bay-leaves, laurel-leaves, or essence of vanilla, instead of the lemon-rind and almonds. Noyeau, Maraschino, Curaçoa, or any favourite liqueur, added in small proportions, very much enhances the flavour of this always favourite dish. In turning it out, just loosen the edges of the blanc-mange from the mould, place a dish on it, and turn it quickly over: it should come out easily, and the blanc-mange have a smooth glossy appearance when the mould is oiled, which it frequently has not when it is only dipped in water. It may be garnished as fancy dictates.

Time.—About 1½ hour to steep the lemon-rind and almonds in the milk.

Average cost, with cream at 1s. per pint, 1s. 8d.*

Sufficient to fill a quart mould.   *Seasonable* at any time.

Bread-and-Butter* Fritters

INGREDIENTS.—Batter, 8 slices of bread and butter, 3 or 4 tablespoonfuls of jam.

Mode.—Make a batter, the same as for apple fritters (p. 285); cut some slices of bread and butter, not very thick; spread half of them with any jam that may be preferred, and cover with the other slices; slightly press them together, and cut them out in square, long, or round pieces. Dip them in the batter, and fry in boiling lard for about 10 minutes; drain them before the fire on a piece of blotting-paper or cloth. Dish them, sprinkle over sifted sugar, and serve.

Time.—About 10 minutes.

Average cost, 1s.

Sufficient for 4 or 5 persons.   *Seasonable* at any time.

To Make the Stock for Jelly, and to Clarify it

INGREDIENTS.—2 calf's feet, 6 pints of water.

Mode.—The stock for jellies should always be made the day before it is required for use, as the liquor has time to cool, and the fat can be so much more easily and effectually removed when thoroughly set. Procure from the butcher's 2 nice calf's feet; scald them, to take off the hair; slit them in two, remove the fat from between the claws, and wash the feet well in warm water; put them into a stewpan, with the above proportion of cold water, bring it gradually to boil, and remove every particle of scum as it rises. When it is

well skimmed, boil it very gently for 6 or 7 hours, or until the liquor is reduced rather more than half; then strain it through a sieve into a basin, and put it in a cool place to set. As the liquor is strained, measure it, to ascertain the proportion for the jelly, allowing something for the sediment and fat at the top. To

Jelly-Mould

clarify it, carefully remove all the fat from the top, pour over a little warm water, to wash away any that may remain, and wipe the jelly with a clean cloth; remove the jelly from the sediment, put it into a saucepan, and, supposing the quantity to be a quart, add to it 6 oz. of

loaf sugar, the shells and well-whisked whites of 5 eggs, and stir these ingredients together cold; set the saucepan on the fire, but *do not stir the jelly after it begins to warm*. Let it boil about 10 minutes after it rises to a head, then throw in a teacupful of cold water; let it boil 5 minutes longer, then take the saucepan off, cover it closely, and let it remain ½ hour near the fire. Dip the jelly-bag into hot water, wring it out quite dry, and fasten it on to a stand or the back of a chair, which must be

Jelly-Bag

placed near the fire, to prevent the jelly from setting before it has run through the bag. Place a basin underneath to receive the jelly; then pour it into the bag, and should it not be clear the first time, run it through the bag again. This stock is the foundation of all *really good* jellies, which may be varied in innumerable ways, by colouring and flavouring with liqueurs, and by moulding it with fresh and preserved fruits. To insure the jelly being firm when turned out, ½ oz. of isinglass clarified might be added to the above proportion of stock. Substitutes for calf's feet are now frequently used in making jellies, which lessen the expense and trouble in preparing this favourite dish; isinglass and gelatine being two of the principal materials employed; but, although they may *look* as nicely as jellies made from good stock, they are never so delicate, having very often an unpleasant flavour, somewhat resembling glue, particularly when made with gelatine.

Time.—About 6 hours to boil the feet for the stock; to clarify it,—¼ hour to boil, ½ hour to stand in the saucepan covered.

Average cost.—Calf's feet may be purchased for 6*d.* each when veal is in full season, but more expensive when it is scarce.

Sufficient.—2 calf's feet should make 1 quart of stock.

Seasonable from March to October, but may be had all the year.

How to make a Jelly-bag.—The very stout flannel called double-mill, used for ironing-blankets, is the best material for a jelly-bag: those of home manufacture are the only ones to be relied on for thoroughly clearing the jelly. Care should be taken that the seam of the bag be stitched twice, to secure it against unequal filtration. The most convenient mode of using the bag is to tie it upon a hoop the exact size of the outside of its mouth; and, to do this, strings should be sewn round it at equal distances. The jelly-bag may, of course, be made any size; but one of twelve or fourteen inches deep, and seven or eight across the mouth, will be sufficient for ordinary use. The form of a jelly-bag is the fool's cap.

Calf's-Feet Jelly

INGREDIENTS.— 1 quart of calf's-feet stock, ½ lb. of sugar, ½ pint of sherry, 1 glass of brandy, the shells and whites of 5 eggs, the rind and juice of 2 lemons, ½ oz. of isinglass.

Mode.—Prepare the stock as directed in [previous] recipe, taking care to leave the sediment, and to remove all the fat from the surface. Put it into a saucepan, cold, without clarifying it; add the remaining ingredients, and stir them well together before the saucepan is placed on the fire. Then simmer the mixture gently for ¼ hour, *but do not stir it after it begins to warm.* Throw in a teacupful of cold water, boil for another 5 minutes, and keep the saucepan covered by the side of the fire for about ½ hour, but do not let it boil again. In simmering, the head or scum may be carefully removed as it rises; but particular attention must be given to the jelly, that

Jelly-Mould

it be not stirred in the slightest degree after it is heated. The isinglass should be added when the jelly begins to boil: this assists to clear it, and makes it firmer for turning out. Wring out a jelly-bag in hot water; fasten it on to a stand, or the back of a chair; place it near the fire with a basin underneath it, and run the jelly through it. Should it not be perfectly clear the first time, repeat the process until the desired brilliancy is obtained. Soak the moulds in water, drain them for half a second, pour in the jelly, and put it in a cool place to set. If ice is at hand, surround the moulds with it, and the jelly will set sooner, and be firmer when turned out. In summer it is necessary to have ice in which to put the moulds, or the cook will be, very likely, disappointed, by her jellies being in too liquid a state to turn out properly, unless a great deal of isinglass is used. When wanted for table, dip the moulds in hot water for a minute, wipe the outside with a cloth, lay a dish on the top of the mould, turn it quickly over, and the jelly should slip out easily. It is sometimes served broken into square lumps, and piled high in glasses. Earthenware moulds are preferable to those of pewter or tin, for red jellies, the colour and transparency of the composition being often spoiled by using the latter.

To make this jelly more economically, raisin wine may be substituted for the sherry and brandy, and the stock made from cow-heels, instead of calf's feet.

Time.—20 minutes to simmer the jelly, ½ hour to stand covered.

Average cost, reckoning the feet at 6*d.* each, 3*s.* 6*d.*

Sufficient to fill two 1½-pint moulds.   *Seasonable* at any time.

Note.—As lemon-juice, unless carefully strained, is liable to make the jelly muddy, see that it is clear before it is added to the other ingredients. Omit the brandy when the flavour is objected to.

Charlotte Russe
(*An Elegant Sweet Entremets*)

INGREDIENTS.—About 18 Savoy biscuits, ¾ pint of cream, flavouring of vanilla, liqueurs, or wine, 1 tablespoonful of pounded sugar, ½ oz. of isinglass.

Mode.—Procure about 18 Savoy biscuits, or ladies'-fingers, as they are sometimes called; brush the edges of them with the white of an egg, and line the bottom of a plain round mould, placing them like a star or rosette. Stand them upright all round the edge; carefully put them so closely together that the white of the egg connects them firmly, and place this case in the oven for about 5 minutes, just to dry the egg. Whisk the cream to a stiff froth, with the sugar, flavouring, and melted isinglass; fill the charlotte with it, cover with a slice of sponge-cake cut in the shape of the mould; place it in ice, where let it remain till ready for table; then turn it on a dish, remove the mould, and serve. 1 tablespoonful of liqueur of any kind, or 4 tablespoonfuls of wine, would nicely flavour the above proportion of cream. For arranging the biscuits in the mould, cut them to the shape required, so that they fit in nicely, and level them with the mould at the top, that, when turned out, there may be something firm to rest upon. Great care and attention is required in the turning out of this dish, that the cream does not burst the case; and the edges of the biscuits must have the smallest quantity of egg brushed over them, or it would stick to the mould, and so prevent the charlotte from coming away properly.

Time.— 5 minutes in the oven.

Average cost, with cream at 1s. per pint, 1s. 6d.

Sufficient for 1 charlotte.   *Seasonable* any time.

Chocolate Cream

INGREDIENTS.— 3 oz. of grated chocolate, ¼ lb. of sugar, 1½ pint of cream, 1½ oz. of clarified isinglass, the yolks of 6 eggs.

Mode.—Beat the yolks of the eggs well; put them into a basin with the grated chocolate, the sugar, and 1 pint of the cream; stir these ingredients well together, pour them into a jug, and set this jug in a saucepan of boiling water; stir it one way until the mixture thickens, but *do not allow it to boil*, or it will curdle. Strain the cream through a sieve into a basin; stir in the isinglass and the other ½ pint of cream, which should be well

Cream-Mould

whipped; mix all well together, and pour it into a mould which has been previously oiled with the purest salad-oil, and, if at hand, set it in ice until wanted for table.

Time.—About 10 minutes to stir the mixture over the fire.

Average cost, 3*s*., with cream at 1*s*. per pint..

Sufficient to fill a quart mould.   *Seasonable* at any time.

Ginger Cream

INGREDIENTS.—The yolks of 4 eggs, 1 pint of cream, 3 oz. of preserved ginger, 2 dessert-spoonfuls of syrup, sifted sugar to taste, 1 oz. of isinglass.

Mode.—Slice the ginger finely; put it into a basin with the syrup, the well-beaten yolks of eggs, and the cream; mix these ingredients well together, and stir them over the fire for about 10 minutes, or until the mixture thickens; then take it off the fire, whisk till nearly cold, sweeten to taste, add the isinglass, which should be melted and strained, and serve the cream in a glass dish. It may be garnished with slices of preserved ginger or candied citron.

Time.—About 10 minutes to stir the cream over the fire.

Average cost, with cream at 1*s*. per pint, 2*s*. 3*d*.

Sufficient for a good-sized dish.   *Seasonable* at any time.

PRESERVED GINGER comes to us from the West Indies. It is made by scalding the roots when they are green and full of sap, then peeling them in cold water, and putting them into jars, with a rich syrup; in which state we receive them. It should be chosen of a bright yellow colour, with a little transparency: what is dark-coloured, fibrous, and stringy, is not good. Ginger roots, fit for preserving, and in size equal to West Indian, have been produced in the Royal Agricultural Garden in Edinburgh.

To Make Gooseberry Fool

INGREDIENTS.—Green gooseberries; to every pint of pulp add 1 pint of milk, or ½ pint of cream and ½ pint of milk; sugar to taste.

Mode.—Cut the tops and tails off the gooseberries; put them into a jar, with 2 tablespoonfuls of water and a little good moist sugar; set this jar in a saucepan of boiling water, and let it boil until the fruit is soft enough to mash. When done enough, beat it to a pulp, work this pulp through a colander, and stir to every pint the above proportion of milk, or equal quantities of milk and cream. Ascertain if the mixture is sweet enough, and put in plenty of sugar, or it will not be eatable; and in mixing the milk and gooseberries, add the former very gradually to these: serve in a glass dish, or in small glasses.

This, although a very old-fashioned and homely dish, is, when well made, very delicious, and, if properly sweetened, a very suitable preparation for children.

Time.—From ¾ to 1 hour.   *Average cost*, 6d. per pint, with milk.

Sufficient.—A pint of milk and a pint of gooseberry pulp for 5 or 6 children.

Seasonable in May and June.

Italian Cream*

INGREDIENTS.—½ pint of milk, ½ pint of cream, sugar to taste, 1 oz. of isinglass, 1 lemon, the yolks of 4 eggs.

Mode.—Put the cream and milk into a saucepan, with sugar to sweeten, and the lemon-rind. Boil until the milk is well flavoured; then strain it into a basin, and add the beaten yolks of eggs. Put this mixture into a jug; place the jug in a saucepan of boiling water over the fire, and stir the contents until they thicken, but do not allow them to boil. Take the cream off the fire, stir in the lemon-juice and isinglass, which should be melted, and whip well; fill a mould, place it in ice if at hand, and, when set, turn it out on a dish, and garnish as taste may dictate. The mixture may be whipped and drained, and then put into small glasses, when this mode of serving is preferred.

Time.—From 5 to 8 minutes to stir the mixture in the jug.

Average cost, with the best isinglass, 2s. 6d.

Sufficient to fill 1½-pint mould.   *Seasonable* at any time.

Jelly of Two Colours*

INGREDIENTS.—1½ pint of calf's-feet jelly, a few drops of prepared cochineal.

Mode.—Make 1½ pint of jelly by recipe on pp. 289–90, or, if wished more economical, of clarified syrup and gelatine, flavouring it in any way that may be preferred. Colour one-half of the jelly with a few drops of prepared cochineal, and the other half leave as pale as possible. Have ready a mould well wetted in every part; pour in a small quantity of the red jelly, and let this set; when quite firm, pour

Jelly of Two Colours

on it the same quantity of the pale jelly, and let this set; then proceed in this manner until the mould is full, always taking care to let one jelly set before the other is poured in, or the colours would run one into the other. When turned out, the jelly should have a striped appearance. For variety, half the mould may be filled at once with one of the jellies, and, when firm, filled up with the other: this, also, has a very pretty effect, and is more expeditiously prepared than when the jelly is poured in small quantities into the mould. Blanc-mange and red jelly, or blancmange and raspberry cream, moulded in the above manner, look very well. The layers of blancmange and jelly should be about an inch in depth, and each layer should be perfectly hardened before another is added. Half a mould of blancmange and half a mould of jelly are frequently served in the same manner. A few pretty dishes may be made, in this way, of jellies or blancmanges left from the preceding day, by melting them separately in a jug placed in a saucepan of boiling water, and then moulding them by the foregoing directions.

Time.— ¾ hour to make the jelly.

Average cost, with calf's-feet jelly, 2s.; with gelatine and syrup, more economical.

Sufficient to fill 1½-pint mould.　*Seasonable* at any time.

Note.—In making the jelly, use for flavouring a very pale sherry, or the colour will be too dark to contrast nicely with the red jelly.

To Make a Plain Omelet*

INGREDIENTS.—6 eggs, 1 saltspoonful of salt, ½ saltspoonful of pepper, ¼ lb. of butter.

Mode.—Break the eggs into a basin, omitting the whites of 3, and beat them up with the salt and pepper until extremely light; then add 2 oz. of the butter broken into small pieces, and stir this into the mixture. Put the other 2 oz. of butter into a frying-pan, make it quite hot, and, as soon as it begins to bubble, whisk the eggs, &c. very briskly for a minute or two, and pour them into the pan; stir the omelet with a spoon one way until the mixture thickens and becomes firm, and when the whole is set, fold the edges over, so that the omelet assumes an oval form; and when it is nicely brown on one side, and quite firm, it is done. To take off the rawness on the upper side, hold the pan before the fire for a minute or two, and brown it with a salamander or hot shovel. Serve very expeditiously on a very hot dish, and never cook it until it is just wanted. The flavour of this omelet may be very much enhanced by adding minced parsley, minced onion or eschalot, or grated cheese, allowing 1 tablespoonful of the former, and half the quantity of the latter, to the above proportion of eggs. Shrimps or oysters may also be added: the latter should be scalded in their liquor, and then bearded and cut into small pieces. In making an omelet, be particularly careful that it is not too thin, and, to avoid this, do not make it in too large a frying-pan, as the mixture would then spread too much, and taste of the outside. It should also not be greasy, burnt, or too much done, and should be cooked over a gentle fire, that the whole of the substance may be heated without drying up the outside. Omelets are sometimes served with gravy; but *this should never be poured over them*, but served in a tureen, as the liquid causes the omelet to become heavy and flat, instead of eating light and soft. In making the gravy, the flavour should not overpower that of the omelet, and should be thickened with arrowroot or rice flour.

Time.—With 6 eggs, in a frying-pan 18 or 20 inches round, 4 to 6 minutes. *Average cost*, 9*d*.

Sufficient for 4 persons. *Seasonable* at any time.

A Pretty Dish of Oranges

INGREDIENTS.—6 large oranges, ½ lb. of loaf sugar, ¼ pint of water, ½ pint of cream, 2 tablespoonfuls of any kind of liqueur, sugar to taste.

Mode.—Put the sugar and water into a saucepan, and boil them until the sugar becomes brittle, which may be ascertained by taking up a small quantity in a spoon, and dipping it in cold water; if the sugar is sufficiently boiled, it will easily snap. Peel the oranges, remove as much of the white pith as possible, and divide them into nice-sized slices, without breaking the thin white skin which surrounds the juicy pulp. Place the pieces of orange on small skewers, dip them into the hot sugar, and arrange them in layers round a plain mould, which should be well oiled with the purest salad oil. The sides of the mould only should be lined with the oranges, and the centre left open for the cream. Let the sugar become firm by cooling; turn the oranges carefully out on a dish, and fill the centre with whipped cream, flavoured with any kind of liqueur, and sweetened with pounded sugar. This is an exceedingly ornamental and nice dish for the supper-table.

Time.— 10 minutes to boil the sugar. *Average cost*, 1s. 8d.

Sufficient for 1 mould. *Seasonable* from November to May.

Pears à l'Allemande*

INGREDIENTS.—6 to 8 pears, water, sugar, 2 oz. of butter, the yolk of an egg, ½ oz. of gelatine.

Mode.—Peel and cut the pears into any form that may be preferred, and steep them in cold water to prevent them turning black; put them into a saucepan with sufficient cold water to cover them, and boil them with the butter and enough sugar to sweeten them nicely, until tender; then brush the pears over with the yolk of an egg, sprinkle them with sifted sugar, and arrange them on a dish. Add the gelatine to the syrup, boil it up quickly for about 5 minutes, strain it over the pears, and let it remain until set. The syrup may be coloured with a little prepared cochineal, which would very much improve the appearance of the dish.

Time.—From 20 minutes to ½ hour to stew the pears; 5 minutes to boil the syrup.

Average cost, 1s. 3d.

Sufficient for a large dish.

Seasonable from August to February.

Rice Soufflé

INGREDIENTS.—3 tablespoonfuls of ground rice, 1 pint of milk, 5 eggs, pounded sugar to taste, flavouring of lemon-rind, vanilla, coffee, chocolate, or anything that may be preferred, a piece of butter the size of a walnut.

Mode.—Mix the ground rice with 6 tablespoonfuls of the milk quite smoothly, and put it into a saucepan with the remainder of the milk and butter, and keep stirring it over the fire for about ¼ hour, or until the mixture thickens. Separate the yolks from the whites of the eggs, beat the former in a basin, and stir to them the rice and sufficient pounded sugar to sweeten the soufflé; but add this latter ingredient as sparingly as possible, as, the less sugar there is used, the lighter will be the soufflé. Now whisk the whites of the eggs to a stiff froth or snow; mix them with the other preparation, and pour the whole into a soufflé-dish, and put it instantly into the oven; bake it about ½ hour in a moderate oven; take it out, hold a salamander or hot shovel over the top, sprinkle sifted sugar over it, and send the soufflé to table in the dish it was baked in, either with a napkin pinned round, or inclosed in a more ornamental dish. The excellence of this fashionable dish entirely depends on the proper whisking of the whites of the eggs, the manner of baking, and the expedition with which it is sent to table. Soufflés should be served *instantly* from the oven, or they will sink, and be nothing more than an ordinary pudding.

Time.—About ½ hour.   *Average cost*, 1s.

Sufficient for 3 or 4 persons.   *Seasonable* at any time.

Snow Eggs, or Œufs à la Neige*
(*A very pretty Supper Dish*)

INGREDIENTS.—4 eggs, ¾ pint of milk, pounded sugar to taste, flavouring of vanilla, lemon-rind, or orange-flower water.

Mode.—Put the milk into a saucepan with sufficient sugar to sweeten it nicely, and the rind of ½ lemon. Let this steep by the side of the fire for ½ hour, when take out the peel; separate the whites from the yolks of the eggs, and whisk the former to a perfectly stiff froth, or until there is no liquid remaining; bring the milk to the boiling-point, and drop in the snow a tablespoonful at a time, and keep turning the eggs until sufficiently cooked. Then place them on a glass dish, beat up the yolks of the eggs, stir to them the milk, add a little more sugar, and strain this mixture into a jug; place the jug in a saucepan of boiling water, and stir it one way until the mixture thickens, but do not allow it to boil, or it will curdle. Pour this custard over the eggs, when they should rise to the surface. They make an exceedingly pretty addition to a supper, and should be put in a cold place after being made. When they are flavoured with vanilla or orange-flower water, it is not necessary to steep the milk. A few drops of the essence of either may be poured in the milk just before the whites are poached. In making the custard, a little more flavouring and sugar should always be added.

Time.—About 2 minutes to poach the whites; 8 minutes to stir the custard.

Average cost, 8*d*.

Sufficient for 4 or 5 persons.   *Seasonable* at any time.

To Make Syllabub

INGREDIENTS.—1 pint of sherry or white wine, ½ grated nutmeg, sugar to taste, 1½ pint of milk.

Mode.—Put the wine into a bowl, with the grated nutmeg and plenty of pounded sugar, and milk into it* the above proportion of milk frothed up. Clouted cream may be laid on the top, with pounded cinnamon or nutmeg and sugar; and a little brandy may be added to the wine before the milk is put in. In some counties, cider is substituted for the wine: when this is used, brandy must always be added. Warm milk may be poured on from a spouted jug or teapot; but it must be held very high.

Average cost, 2*s*.

Sufficient for 5 or 6 persons.   *Seasonable* at any time.

To Make a Trifle

INGREDIENTS.—For the whip, 1 pint of cream, 3 oz. of pounded sugar, the whites of 2 eggs, a small glass of sherry or raisin wine. For the trifle, 1 pint of custard, made with 8 eggs to a pint of milk; 6 small sponge-cakes, or 6 slices of sponge-cake; 12 macaroons, 2 dozen ratafias, 2 oz. of sweet almonds, the grated rind of 1 lemon, a layer of raspberry or strawberry jam, ½ pint of sherry or sweet wine, 6 tablespoonfuls of brandy.

Trifle

Mode.—The whip to lay over the top of the trifle should be made the day before it is required for table, as the flavour is better, and it is much more solid than when prepared the same day. Put into a large bowl the pounded sugar, the whites of the eggs, which should be beaten to a stiff froth, a glass of sherry or sweet wine, and the cream. Whisk these ingredients well in a cool place, and take off the froth with a skimmer as fast as it rises, and put it on a sieve to drain; continue the whisking till there is sufficient of the whip, which must be put away in a cool place to drain. The next day, place the sponge-cakes, macaroons, and ratafias at the bottom of a trifle-dish; pour over them ½ pint of sherry or sweet wine, mixed with 6 tablespoonfuls of brandy, and, should this proportion of wine not be found quite sufficient, add a little more, as the cakes should be well soaked. Over the cakes put the grated lemon-rind, the sweet almonds, blanched and cut into strips, and a layer of raspberry or strawberry jam. Make a good custard using 8 eggs to the pint of milk, and let this cool a little; then pour it over the cakes, &c. The whip being made the day previously, and the trifle prepared, there remains nothing to do now but heap the whip lightly over the top: this should stand as high as possible, and it may be garnished with strips of bright currant jelly, crystallized sweetmeats, or flowers ; the small coloured comfits are sometimes used for the purpose of garnishing a trifle, but they are now considered rather old-fashioned.

Average cost, with cream at 1s. per pint, 5s. 6d.

Sufficient for 1 trifle.   *Seasonable* at any time.

CHAPTER XXX

GENERAL OBSERVATIONS ON PRESERVES, CONFECTIONARY, ICES, AND DESSERT DISHES

PRESERVES*

From the nature of vegetable substances, and chiefly from their not passing so rapidly into the putrescent state as animal bodies, the mode of preserving them is somewhat different, although the general principles are the same. All the means of preservation are put in practice occasionally for fruits and the various parts of vegetables, according to the nature of the species, the climate, the uses to which they are applied, &c. Some are dried, as nuts, raisins, sweet herbs, &c.; others are preserved by means of sugar, such as many fruits whose delicate juices would be lost by drying; some are preserved by means of vinegar, and chiefly used as condiments or pickles; a few also by salting, as French beans; while others are preserved in spirits. We have, however, in this place to treat of the best methods of preserving fruits. Fruit is a most important item in the economy of health; the epicurean can scarcely be said to have any luxuries without it; therefore, as it is so invaluable, when we cannot have it fresh, we must have it preserved. It has long been a desideratum to preserve fruits by some cheap method, yet by such as would keep them fit for the various culinary purposes, as making tarts and other similar dishes. The expense of preserving them with sugar is a serious objection; for, except the sugar is used in considerable quantities, the success is very uncertain. Sugar also overpowers and destroys the sub-acid taste so desirable in many fruits: those which are preserved in this manner are chiefly intended for the dessert. Fruits intended for preservation should be gathered in the morning, in dry weather, with the morning sun upon them, if possible; they will then have their fullest flavour, and keep in good condition longer than when gathered at any other time. Until fruit can be used, it should be placed in the dairy, an ice-house, or a refrigerator. In an ice-house it will remain fresh and plump for several days. Fruit gathered in wet or foggy weather will soon be mildewed, and be of no service for preserves.

The fruits that are the most fit for preservation in syrup are, apricots, peaches, nectarines, apples, greengages, plums of all kinds, and pears. As an example, take some apricots not too ripe, make a small slit at the stem end, and push out the stone; simmer them in water till they are softened and about half done, and afterwards throw them into cold water. When they have cooled, take them out and drain them. Put the apricots into the preserving-pan with sufficient syrup to cover them; let them boil up three or four times, and then skim them; remove them from the fire, pour them into an earthen pan, and let them cool till next day. Boil them up three days successively, skimming each time, and they will then be finished and in a state fit to be put into pots for use. After each boiling, it is proper to examine into the state of the syrup when cold; if too thin, it will bear additional boiling; if too thick, it may be lowered with more syrup of the usual standard. The reason why the fruit is emptied out of the preserving-pan into an earthen pan is, that the acid of the fruit acts upon the copper, of which the preserving-pans are usually made. From this example the process of preserving fruits by syrup will be easily comprehended. The first object is to soften the fruit by blanching or boiling it in water, in order that the syrup by which it is preserved may penetrate through its substance.

Any of the fruits that have been preserved in syrup may be converted into dry preserves, by first draining them from the syrup, and then drying them in a stove or very moderate oven, adding to them a quantity of powdered loaf sugar, which will gradually penetrate the fruit, while the fluid parts of the syrup gently evaporate. They should be dried in the stove or oven on a sieve, and turned every six or eight hours, fresh powdered sugar being sifted over them every time they are turned. Afterwards, they are to be kept in a dry situation, in drawers or boxes. Currants and cherries preserved whole in this manner, in bunches, are extremely elegant, and have a fine flavour. In this way it is, also, that orange and lemon chips are preserved.

Marmalades, jams, and fruit pastes are of the same nature, and are now in very general request. They are prepared without difficulty, by attending to a very few directions; they are somewhat expensive, but may be kept without spoiling for a considerable time. Marmalades and jams differ little from each other: they are preserves of a half-liquid consistency, made by boiling the pulp of fruits, and sometimes part of the rinds, with sugar. The appellation of marmalade is applied to those confitures which are composed of the firmer fruits, as pineapples or the rinds of oranges; whereas jams are made of the more juicy berries, such as strawberries, raspberries, currants, mulberries, &c. Fruit pastes are a kind of marmalades, consisting of the pulp of fruits, first evaporated to a proper consistency, and afterwards boiled with sugar. The mixture is then poured into a mould, or spread on sheets of tin, and subsequently dried in the oven or stove till it has acquired the state of a paste. From a sheet of this paste, strips may be cut and formed into any shape that may be desired, as knots, rings, &c. Jams require the same care and attention in the boiling as marmalade; the slightest degree of burning communicates a disagreeable empyreumatic taste, and if they are not boiled sufficiently, they will not keep. That they may keep, it is necessary not to be sparing of sugar.

DESSERT DISHES*

With moderns the dessert is not profuse, nor does it hold the same relationship to the dinner that it held with the ancients,—the Romans more especially. On ivory tables they would spread hundreds of different kinds of raw, cooked, and preserved fruits, tarts and cakes, as substitutes for the more substantial comestibles with which the guests were satiated. However, as late as the reigns of our two last Georges, fabulous sums were often expended upon fanciful desserts. The dessert certainly repays, in its general effect, the expenditure upon it of much pains; and it may be said, that if there be any poetry at all in meals, or the process of feeding, there is poetry in the dessert, the materials for which should be selected with taste, and, of course, must depend, in a great measure, upon the season. Pines, melons, grapes, peaches, nectarines, plums, strawberries, apples, pears, oranges, almonds, raisins, figs, walnuts, filberts, medlars, cherries, &c. &c., all kinds of dried fruits, and choice and delicately-flavoured cakes and biscuits, make up the dessert, together with the most costly and *recherché* wines. The shape of the dishes varies at different periods, the prevailing fashion at present being oval and circular dishes on stems. The patterns and colours are also subject to changes of fashion; some persons selecting china, chaste in pattern and colour; others, elegantly-shaped glass dishes on stems, with gilt edges. The beauty of the dessert services at the tables of the wealthy tends to enhance the splendour of the plate. The general mode of putting a dessert on table, now the elegant tazzas are fashionable, is, to place them down the middle of the table, a tall and short dish alternately; the fresh fruits being arranged on the tall dishes, and dried fruits, bon-bons, &c., on small round or oval glass plates. The garnishing needs especial attention, as the contrast of the brilliant-coloured fruits with nicely-arranged foliage is very charming. The garnish *par excellence* for dessert is the ice-plant; its crystallized dewdrops producing a marvellous effect in the height of summer, giving a most inviting sense of coolness to the fruit it encircles. The double-edged mallow, strawberry, and vine leaves have a pleasing effect; and for winter desserts, the bay, cuba, and laurel are sometimes used. In town, the expense and difficulty of obtaining natural foliage is great, but paper and composite leaves are to be purchased at an almost nominal price. Mixed fruits of the larger sort are now frequently served on one dish. This mode admits of the display of much taste in the arrangement of the fruit: for instance, a pine in the centre of the dish, surrounded with large plums of various sorts and colours, mixed with pears, rosy-cheeked apples, all arranged with a due regard to colour, have a very good effect. Again, apples and pears look well mingled with plums and grapes, hanging from the border of the dish in a *négligé* sort of manner, with a large bunch of the same fruit lying on the top of the apples. A dessert would not now be considered complete without candied and preserved fruits and confections. The candied fruits may be purchased at a less cost than they can be manufactured at home. They are preserved abroad in most ornamental and elegant forms. And since, from the facilities of travel, we have become so familiar with the tables of the French, chocolate in different forms is indispensable to our desserts.

ICES

Ices are composed, it is scarcely necessary to say, of congealed cream or water, combined sometimes with liqueurs or other flavouring ingredients, or more generally with the juices of fruits. At desserts, or at some evening parties, ices are scarcely to be dispensed with. The principal utensils required for making ice-creams are ice-tubs, freezing-pots, spaddles, and a cellaret. The tub must be large enough to contain about a bushel of ice, pounded small, when brought out of the ice-house,* and mixed very carefully with either *salt*, *nitre*, or *soda*. The freezing-pot is best made of pewter. If it be of tin, as is sometimes the case, the congelation goes on too rapidly in it for the thorough intermingling of its contents, on which the excellence of the ice greatly depends. The spaddle is generally made of copper, kept bright and clean. The cellaret is a tin vessel, in which ices are kept for a short time from dissolving. The method to be pursued in the freezing process must be attended to. When the ice-tub is prepared with fresh-pounded ice and salt, the freezing-pot is put into it up to its cover. The articles to be congealed are then poured into it and covered over; but to prevent the ingredients from separating and the heaviest of them from falling to the bottom of the mould, it is requisite to turn the freezing-pot round and round by the handle, so as to keep its contents moving until the congelation commences. As soon as this is perceived (the cover of the pot being occasionally taken off for the purpose of noticing when freezing takes place), the cover is immediately closed over it, ice is put upon it, and it is left in this state till it is served. The use of the spaddle is to stir up and remove from the sides of the freezing-pot the cream, which in the shaking may have washed against it, and by stirring it in with the rest, to prevent waste of it occurring. Any negligence in stirring the contents of the freezing-pot before congelation takes place, will destroy the whole: either the sugar sinks to the bottom and leaves the ice insufficiently sweetened, or lumps are formed, which disfigure and discolour it.

The aged, the delicate, and children should abstain from ices or iced beverages; even the strong and healthy should partake of them in moderation. They should be taken immediately after the repast, or some hours after, because the taking these substances *during* the process of digestion is apt to provoke indisposition. It is necessary, then, that this function should have scarcely commenced, or that it should be completely finished, before partaking of ices. It is also necessary to abstain from them when persons are very warm, or immediately after taking violent exercise, as in some cases they have produced illnesses which have ended fatally.

Do ladies know to whom they are indebted for the introduction of ices, which all the fair sex are passionately fond of?—To Catherine de' Medici. Will not this fact cover a multitude of sins committed by the instigator of St Bartholomew?*

CHAPTER XXXI

RECIPES*

To Make Syrup for Compotes,* &c.

INGREDIENTS.—To every lb. of sugar allow 1½ pint of water.

Mode.—Boil the sugar and water together for ¼ hour, carefully removing the scum as it rises: the syrup is then ready for the fruit. The articles boiled in this syrup will not keep for any length of time, it being suitable only for dishes intended to be eaten immediately. A larger proportion of sugar must be added for a syrup intended to keep.

Time.—¼ hour.

To Preserve Apples in Quarters, in imitation of Ginger

INGREDIENTS.—To every lb. of apples allow ¾ lb. of sugar, 1½ oz. of the best white ginger; 1 oz. of ginger to every ½ pint of water.

Mode.—Peel, core, and quarter the apples, and put the fruit, sugar, and ginger in layers into a wide-mouthed jar, and let them remain for 2 days; then infuse 1 oz. of ginger in ½ pint of boiling water, and cover it closely, and let it remain for 1 day: this quantity of ginger and water is for 3 lbs. of apples, with the other ingredients in proportion. Put the apples, &c., into a preserving-pan with the water strained from the ginger, and boil till the apples look clear and the syrup is rich, which will be in about an hour. The rind of a lemon may be added just before the apples have finished boiling; and great care must be taken not to break the pieces of apple in putting them into the jars. Serve on glass dishes for dessert.

Time.—2 days for the apples to remain in the jar with sugar, &c.; 1 day to infuse the ginger; about 1 hour to boil the apples.

Average cost, for 3 lbs. of apples, with the other ingredients in proportion, 2s. 3d.

Sufficient.—3 lbs. should fill 3 moderate-sized jars.

Seasonable.—This should be made in September, October, or November.

Compote of Apricots
(*An elegant Dish*)

INGREDIENTS.—½ pint of syrup, 12 green apricots.

Mode.—Make the syrup by recipe on p. 306, and, when it is ready, put in the apricots whilst the syrup is boiling. Simmer them very gently until tender, taking care not to let them break; take them out carefully, arrange them on a glass dish, let the syrup cool a little, pour it over the apricots, and, when cold, serve.

Time.—From 15 to 20 minutes to simmer the apricots.

Average cost, 9*d*.

Sufficient for 4 or 5 persons.

Seasonable in June and July, with green apricots.

Carrot Jam to Imitate Apricot Preserve*

INGREDIENTS.—Carrots; to every lb. of carrot pulp allow 1 lb. of pounded sugar, the grated rind of 1 lemon, the strained juice of 2, 6 chopped bitter almonds, 2 tablespoonfuls of brandy.

Mode.—Select young carrots; wash and scrape them clean, cut them into round pieces, put them into a saucepan with sufficient water to cover them, and let them simmer until perfectly soft; then beat them through a sieve. Weigh the pulp, and to every lb. allow the above ingredients. Put the pulp into a preserving-pan with the sugar, and let this boil for 5 minutes, stirring and skimming all the time. When cold, add the lemon-rind and juice, almonds and brandy; mix these well with the jam; then put it into pots, which must be well covered and kept in a dry place. The brandy may be omitted, but the preserve will then not keep: with the brandy it will remain good for months.

Time.—About ¾ hour to boil the carrots; 5 minutes to simmer the pulp.

Average cost, 1*s*. 2*d*. for 1 lb. of pulp, with the other ingredients in proportion.

Sufficient to fill 3 pots. *Seasonable* from July to December.

Dried Cherries

Cherries may be put in a slow oven and thoroughly dried before they begin to change colour. They should then be taken out of the oven, tied in bunches, and stored away in a dry place. In the winter, they may be cooked with sugar for dessert, the same as Normandy pippins. Particular care must be taken that the oven be not too hot. Another method of drying cherries is to stone them, and to put them into a preserving-pan, with plenty of loaf sugar strewed amongst them. They should be simmered till the fruit shrivels, when they should be strained from the juice. The cherries should then be placed in an oven, cool enough to dry without baking them. About 5 oz. of sugar would be required for 1 lb. of cherries, and the same syrup may be used again to do another quantity of fruit.

Damson Cheese*

INGREDIENTS.—Damsons; to every lb. of fruit pulp allow ½ lb. of loaf sugar.

Mode.—Pick the stalks from the damsons, and put them into a preserving-pan; simmer them over the fire until they are soft, occasionally stirring them; then beat them through a coarse sieve, and put the pulp and juice into the preserving-pan, with sugar in the above proportion, having previously carefully weighed them. Stir the sugar well in, and simmer the damsons slowly for 2 hours. Skim well; then boil the preserve quickly for ½ hour, or until it looks firm and hard in the spoon; put it quickly into shallow pots, or very tiny earthenware moulds, and, when cold, cover it with oiled papers, and the jars with tissue-paper brushed over on both sides with the white of an egg. A few of the stones may be cracked, and the kernels boiled with the damsons, which very much improves the flavour of the cheese.

Time.—1 hour to boil the damsons without the sugar; 2 hours to simmer them slowly, ½ hour quickly.

Average cost, from 8*d.* to 10*d.* per ¼-lb. pot.

Sufficient.—1 pint of damsons to make a *very small* pot of cheese.

Seasonable.—Make this in September or October.

Compote of Green Figs

INGREDIENTS.—1 pint of syrup, 1½ pint of green figs, the rind of ½ lemon.

Mode.—Make a syrup by recipe on p. 306, boiling with it the lemon-rind, and carefully remove all the scum as it rises. Put in the figs, and simmer them very slowly until tender; dish them on a glass dish; reduce the syrup by boiling it quickly for 5 minutes; take out the lemon-peel, pour the syrup over the figs, and the compôte, when cold, will be ready for table. A little port wine, or lemon-juice, added just before the figs are done, will be found an improvement.

Time.—2 to 3 hours to stew the figs.

Average cost, figs, 2*s.* to 3*s.* per dozen.

Seasonable in August and September.

Gooseberry Jam

INGREDIENTS.—To every lb. of fruit allow ¾ lb. of loaf sugar; currant-juice.

Mode.—Select red hairy gooseberries; have them gathered in dry weather, when quite ripe, without being too soft. Weigh them; with a pair of scissors, cut off the tops and tails, and to every 6 lbs. of fruit have ready ½ pint of red-currant juice, drawn as for jelly. Put the gooseberries and currant-juice into a preserving pan; let them boil tolerably quickly, keeping them well stirred; when they begin to break, add to them the sugar, and keep simmering until the jam becomes firm, carefully skimming and stirring it, that it does not burn at the bottom. It should be boiled rather a long time, or it will not keep. Put it into pots (not too large); let it get perfectly cold; then cover the pots down with oiled and egged papers.

Time.—About 1 hour to boil the gooseberries in the currant-juice; from ½ to ¾ hour with the sugar.

Average cost, per lb. pot, from 6*d.* to 8*d.*

Sufficient.—Allow 1½ pint of fruit for a lb. pot.

Seasonable.—Make this in June or July.

To Preserve and Dry Greengages

INGREDIENTS.—To every lb. of sugar allow 1 lb. of fruit, ¼ pint of water.

Mode.—For this purpose, the fruit must be used before it is quite ripe, and part of the stalk must be left on. Weigh the fruit, rejecting all that is in the least degree blemished, and put it into a lined saucepan with the sugar and water, which should have been previously boiled together to a rich syrup. Boil the fruit in this for 10 minutes, remove it from the fire, and drain the greengages. The next day, boil up the syrup and put in the fruit again, and let it simmer for 3 minutes, and drain the syrup away. Continue this process for 5 or 6 days, and the last time place the greengages, when drained, on a hair sieve, and put them in an oven or warm spot to dry; keep them in a box, with paper between each layer, in a place free from damp.

Time.—10 minutes the first time of boiling.

Seasonable.—Make this in August or September.

To Make Fruit Ice-Creams

INGREDIENTS.—To every pint of fruit-juice allow 1 pint of cream; sugar to taste.

Mode.—Let the fruit be well ripened; pick it off the stalks, and put it into a large earthen pan. Stir it about with a wooden spoon, breaking it until it is well mashed; then, with the back of the

Dish of Ices

spoon, rub it through a hair sieve. Sweeten it nicely with pounded sugar; whip the cream for a few minutes, add it to the fruit, and whisk the whole again for another

5 minutes. Put the mixture into the freezing-pot, and freeze, taking care to stir the cream, &c., two or three times, and to remove it from the sides of the vessel, that the mixture may be equally frozen and smooth. Ices are usually served in glasses, but if moulded, as they sometimes are for dessert, must have a small quantity of melted isinglass added to them, to enable them to keep their shape. Raspberry, strawberry, currant, and all fruit ice-creams, are made in the same manner. A little pounded sugar sprinkled over the fruit before it is mashed assists to extract the juice. In winter, when fresh fruit is not obtainable, a little jam may be substituted for it: it should be melted and worked through a sieve before being added to the whipped cream; and if the colour should not be good, a little prepared cochineal or beetroot may be put in to improve its appearance.

Time.—½ hour to freeze the mixture.

Average cost, with cream at 1s. per pint, 4d. each ice.

Seasonable, with fresh fruit, in June, July, and August.

Orange Marmalade*

INGREDIENTS.—Equal weight of fine loaf sugar and Seville oranges; to 12 oranges allow 1 pint of water.

Mode.—Let there be an equal weight of loaf sugar and Seville oranges, and allow the above proportion of water to every dozen oranges. Peel them carefully, remove a little of the white pith, and boil the rinds in water 2 hours, changing the water three times to take off a little of the bitter taste. Break the pulp into small pieces, take out all the pips, and cut the boiled rind into chips. Make a syrup with the sugar and water; boil this well, skim it, and, when clear, put in the pulp and chips. Boil all together from 20 minutes to ½ hour; pour it into pots, and, when cold, cover down with bladders or tissue-paper brushed over on both sides with the white of an egg. The juice and grated rind of 2 lemons to every dozen of oranges, added with the pulp and chips to the syrup, are a very great improvement to this marmalade.

Time.—2 hours to boil the orange-rinds; 10 minutes to boil the syrup; 20 minutes to ½ hour to boil the marmalade.

Average cost, from 6d. to 8d. per lb. pot.

Seasonable.—This should be made in March or April, as Seville oranges are then in perfection.

Peaches Preserved in Brandy

INGREDIENTS.—To every lb. of fruit weighed before being stoned, allow ¼ lb. of finely-pounded loaf sugar; brandy.

Mode.—Let the fruit be gathered in dry weather; wipe and weigh it, and remove the stones as carefully as possible, without injuring the peaches much. Put them into a jar, sprinkle amongst them pounded loaf sugar in the above proportion, and pour brandy over the fruit. Cover the jar down closely, place it in a saucepan of boiling water over the fire, and bring the brandy to the simmering-point, but do not allow it to boil. Take the fruit out carefully, without breaking it; put it into small jars, pour over it the brandy, and, when cold, exclude the air by covering the jars with bladders, or tissue-paper brushed over on both sides with the white of an egg. Apricots may be done in the same manner, and, if properly prepared, will be found delicious.

Time.—From 10 to 20 minutes to bring the brandy to the simmering-point.

Seasonable in August and September.

Preserved Pineapple, for Present Use

INGREDIENTS.—Pineapple, sugar, water.

Mode.—Cut the pine into slices ¼ inch in thickness; peel them, and remove the hard part from the middle. Put the parings and hard pieces into a stewpan with sufficient water to cover them, and boil for ¼ hour. Strain the liquor, and put in the slices of pine. Stew them for 10 minutes, add sufficient sugar to sweeten the whole nicely, and boil again for another ¼ hour; skim well, and the preserve will be ready for use. It must be eaten soon, as it will keep but a very short time.

Time.—¼ hour to boil the parings in water; 10 minutes to boil the pine without sugar, ¼ hour with sugar.

Average cost.—Foreign pines, 1s. to 3s. each; English,* from 2s. to 12s. per lb.

Seasonable.—Foreign, in July and August; English, all the year.

Quince Jelly

INGREDIENTS.—To every pint of juice allow 1 lb. of loaf sugar.

Mode.—Pare and slice the quinces, and put them into a preserving-pan with sufficient water to float them. Boil them until tender, and the fruit is reduced to a pulp; strain off the clear juice, and to each pint allow the above proportion of loaf sugar. Boil the juice and sugar together for about ¾ hour; remove all the scum as it rises, and, when the jelly appears firm when a little is poured on a plate, it is done. The residue left on the sieve will answer to make a common marmalade, for immediate use, by boiling it with ½ lb. of common sugar to every lb. of pulp.

Time.—3 hours to boil the quinces in water; ¾ hour to boil the jelly.

Average cost, from 8d. to 10d. per lb. pot.

Seasonable from August to October.

Rhubarb Jam

INGREDIENTS.—To every lb. of rhubarb allow 1 lb. of loaf sugar, the rind of ½ lemon.

Mode.—Wipe the rhubarb perfectly dry, take off the string or peel, and weigh it; put it into a preserving-pan, with sugar in the above proportion; mince the lemon-rind very finely, add it to the other ingredients, and place the preserving-pan by the side of the fire; keep stirring to prevent the rhubarb from burning, and when the sugar is well dissolved, put the pan more over the fire, and let the jam boil until it is done, taking care to keep it well skimmed and stirred with a wooden or silver spoon. Pour it into pots, and cover down with oiled and egged papers.

Time.—If the rhubarb is young and tender, ¾ hour, reckoning from the time it simmers equally; old rhubarb, 1¼ to 1½ hour.

Average cost, 5*d*. to 7*d*. per lb. pot.

Sufficient.—About 1 pint of sliced rhubarb to fill a lb. pot.

Seasonable from February to April.

To Make Everton Toffee

INGREDIENTS.— 1 lb. of powdered loaf sugar, 1 teacupful of water, ¼ lb. of butter, 6 drops of essence of lemon.

Mode.—Put the water and sugar into a brass pan, and beat the butter to a cream. When the sugar is dissolved, add the butter, and keep stirring the mixture over the fire until it sets, when a little is poured on to a buttered dish; and just before the toffee is done, add the essence of lemon. Butter a dish or tin, pour on it the mixture, and when cool, it will easily separate from the dish. Butter-Scotch, an excellent thing for coughs, is made with brown, instead of white sugar, omitting the water, and flavoured with ½ oz. of powdered ginger. It is made in the same manner as toffee.

Time.— 18 to 35 minutes.   *Average cost*, 10*d*.

Sufficiently to make a lb. of toffee.

DESSERT DISHES

The tazza, or dish with stem, the same as that shown in our illustrations [overleaf], is now the favourite shape for dessert-dishes. The fruit can be arranged and shown to better advantage on these tall high

Dish of Nuts

Box of French Plums

Dish of Mixed Fruit

Box of Chocolate

dishes than on the short flat ones. All the dishes are now usually placed down the centre of the table, dried and fresh fruit alternately, the former being arranged on small round or oval glass plates, and the latter on the dishes with stems. The fruit should always be gathered on the same day that it is required for table, and should be tastefully arranged on the dishes, with leaves between and round it. By purchasing fruits that *are in season*, a dessert can be supplied at a very moderate cost. These, with a few fancy biscuits, crystallized fruit, bon-bons, &c., are sufficient for an ordinary dessert. When fresh fruit cannot be obtained, dried and foreign fruits, compôtes, baked pears, stewed Normandy pippins, &c. &c., must supply its place, with the addition of preserves, bon-bons, cakes, biscuits, &c. At fashionable tables, forced fruit is served growing in pots, these pots being hidden in more ornamental ones, and arranged with the other dishes. A few vases of fresh flowers, tastefully arranged, add very much to the appearance of the dessert; and, when these are not obtainable, a few paper ones, mixed with green leaves, answer very well as a substitute. In decorating a table, whether for luncheon, dessert, or supper, a vase or two of flowers should never be forgotten, as they add so much to the elegance of the *tout ensemble*. In summer and autumn, ladies residing in the country can always manage to have a few freshly-gathered flowers on their tables, and should never be without this inexpensive luxury. On the continent, vases or epergnes filled with flowers are invariably placed down the centre of the dinner-table at regular distances. Ices for dessert are usually moulded: when this is not the case, they are handed round in glasses with wafers to accompany them. Preserved ginger is frequently handed round after ices, to prepare the palate for the delicious dessert wines. A basin or glass of finely-pounded lump sugar must never be omitted at a dessert, as also a glass jug of fresh cold water (iced, if possible), and two goblets by its side. Grape-scissors, a melon-knife and fork, and nutcrackers, should always be put on table, if there are dishes of fruit requiring them. Zests are sometimes served at the close of the dessert; such as anchovy toasts or biscuits.* The French often serve plain or grated cheese with a dessert of fresh or dried fruits. At some tables, finger-glasses are placed at the right of each person, nearly half filled with cold spring water, and in winter with tepid water. These precede the dessert. At other tables, a glass or vase is simply handed round, filled with perfumed water, into which each guest dips the corner of his napkin, and, when needful, refreshes his lips and the tips of his fingers. After the dishes are placed, and every one is provided with plates, glasses, spoons, &c., the

Dish of Apples

Dish of Mixed Summer Fruit

Almonds and Raisins

Dish of Strawberries

wine should be put at each end of the table, cooled or otherwise, according to the season. If the party be small, the wine may be placed only at the top of the table, near the host.

Box of French Plums*

If the box which contains them is exceedingly ornamental, it may be placed on the table; if small, on a glass dish; if large, without one. French plums may also be arranged on a glass plate, and garnished with bright-coloured sweetmeats, which make a very good effect. All fancy boxes of preserved and crystallized fruit may be put on the table or not, at pleasure. These little matters of detail must, of course, be left to individual taste.

Seasonable.—May be purchased all the year; but are in greater perfection in the winter, and are more suitable for that season, as fresh fruit cannot be obtained.

Dish of Mixed Fruit

For a centre dish, a mixture of various fresh fruits has a remarkably good effect, particularly if a pine be added to the list. A high raised appearance should be given to the fruit, which is done in the following manner. Place a tumbler in the centre of the dish, and, in this tumbler, the pine, crown uppermost; round the tumbler put a thick layer of moss, and, over this, apples, pears, plums, peaches, and such fruit as is simultaneously in season. By putting a layer of moss underneath, so much fruit is not required, besides giving a better shape to the dish. Grapes should be placed on the top of the fruit, a portion of some of the bunches hanging over the sides of the dish in a *négligé* kind of manner, which takes off the formal look of the dish. In arranging the plums, apples, &c., let the colours contrast well.

Seasonable.—Suitable for a dessert in September or October.

GRAPES.—France produces about a thousand varieties of the grape, which is cultivated more extensively in that country than in any other. Hygienists agree in pronouncing grapes as among the best of fruits. The grape possesses several rare qualities: it is nourishing and fattening, and its prolonged use has often overcome the most obstinate cases of constipation. The skins and pips of grapes should not be eaten.

Dish of Strawberries

Fine strawberries, arranged in the manner shown in the engraving, look exceedingly well. The inferior ones should be placed at the bottom of the dish, and the others put in rows pyramidically, with the stalks downwards; so that when the whole is completed, nothing but the red part of the fruit is visible. The fruit should be gathered with rather long stalks, as there is then something to support it, and it can be placed more upright in each layer. A few of the finest should be reserved to crown the top.

To Have Walnuts Fresh throughout the Season

INGREDIENTS.—To every pint of water allow 1 teaspoonful of salt.

Mode.—Place the walnuts in the salt and water for 24 hours at least; then take them out, and rub them dry. Old nuts may be freshened in this manner; or walnuts, when first picked, may be put into an earthen pan with salt sprinkled amongst them, and with damped hay placed on the top of them, and then covered down with a lid. They must be well wiped before they are put on table.

Seasonable.—Should be stored away in September or October.

CHAPTER XXXII

GENERAL OBSERVATIONS ON MILK, BUTTER, CHEESE, AND EGGS*

MILK

Milk is obtained only from the class of animals called Mammalia, and is intended by Nature for the nourishment of their young. The milk of each animal is distinguished by some peculiarities; but as that of the cow is by far the most useful to us in this part of the world, our observations will be confined to that variety.

Milk, considered as an aliment, is of such importance in domestic economy as to render all the improvements in its production extremely valuable. To enlarge upon the antiquity of its use is unnecessary; it has always been a favourite food in Britain. 'Lacte et carne vivunt,' says Caesar, in his Commentaries; the English of which is, 'the inhabitants subsist upon flesh and milk.' The breed of the cow has received great improvement in modern times, as regards the quantity and quality of the milk which she affords; the form of milch-cows, their mode of nourishment, and progress, are also manifest in the management of the dairy.

Milk of the *human subject* is much thinner than cow's milk; *Ass's milk* comes the nearest to human milk of any other; *Goat's milk* is something thicker and richer than cow's milk; *Ewe's milk* has the appearance of cow's milk, and affords a larger quantity of cream; *Mare's milk* contains more sugar than that of the ewe; *Camel's milk* is used only in Africa; *Buffalo's milk* is employed in India.

From no other substance, solid or fluid, can so great a number of distinct kinds of aliment be prepared as from milk; some forming food, others drink; some of them delicious, and deserving the name of luxuries; all of them wholesome, and some medicinal: indeed, the variety of aliments that seems capable of being produced from milk, appears to be quite endless. In every age this must have been a subject for experiment, and every nation has added to the number by the invention of some peculiarity of its own.

BUTTER

Beckman, in his 'History of Inventions,' states that butter was not used either by the Greeks or Romans in cooking, nor was it brought upon their tables at certain meals, as is the custom at present. In England it has been made from time immemorial, though the art of making cheese is said not to have been known to the ancient Britons, and to have been learned from their conquerors.

The taste of butter is peculiar, and very unlike any other fatty substance. It is extremely agreeable when of the best quality; but its flavour depends much upon the food given to the cows: to be good, it should not adhere to the knife.

Butter, with regard to its dietetic properties, may be regarded nearly in the light of vegetable oils and animal fats; but it becomes sooner rancid than most other fat oils. When fresh, it cannot but be considered as very wholesome; but it should be quite free from rancidity. If slightly salted when it is fresh, its wholesomeness is probably not at all impaired; but should it begin to turn rancid, salting will not correct its unwholesomeness. When salt butter is put into casks, the upper part next the air is very apt to become rancid, and this rancidity is also liable to affect the whole cask.

CHEESE

Cheese is the curd formed from milk by artificial coagulation, pressed and dried for use. Curd, called also casein and caseous matter, or the basis of cheese, exists in the milk, and not in the cream, and requires only to be separated by coagulation. The coagulation, however, supposes some alteration of the curd. By means of the substance employed to coagulate it, it is rendered insoluble in water. When the curd is freed from the whey, kneaded and pressed to expel it entirely, it becomes cheese. This assumes a degree of transparency, and possesses many of the properties of coagulated albumen. If it be well dried, it does not change by exposure to the air; but if it contain moisture, it soon putrefies. It therefore requires some salt to preserve it, and this acts likewise as a kind of seasoning. All our cheese is coloured more or less, except that made from skim milk. The colouring substances employed are arnatto, turmeric, or marigold, all perfectly harmless unless they are adulterated; and it is said that arnatto sometimes contains red lead.*

Cheese varies in quality and richness according to the materials of which it is composed. It is made—1. Of entire milk, as in Cheshire; 2. of milk and cream, as at Stilton; 3. of new milk mixed with skimmed milk, as in Gloucestershire; 4. of skimmed milk only, as in Suffolk, Holland, and Italy.

The principal varieties of cheese used in England are the following:—*Cheshire cheese*, famed all over Europe for its rich quality and fine piquant flavour. It is made of entire new milk, the cream not being taken off. *Gloucester cheese* is much milder in its taste than the Cheshire. There are two kinds of Gloucester cheese,—single and double. *Single Gloucester* is made of skimmed milk, or of the milk deprived of half the cream; *Double Gloucester* is a cheese that pleases almost every palate: it is made of the whole milk and cream. *Stilton cheese* is made by adding the cream of one day to the entire milk of the next: it was first made at Stilton, in Leicestershire. *Sage cheese* is so called from the practice of colouring some curd with bruised sage, marigold-leaves, and parsley, and mixing this with some uncoloured curd. With the Romans, and during the middle ages, this practice was extensively adopted. *Cheddar cheese* much resembles Parmesan. It has a very agreeable taste and flavour, and has a spongy appearance. *Brickbat cheese* has nothing remarkable except its form. It is made by turning with rennet a mixture of cream and new milk. The curd is put into a wooden vessel the shape of a brick, and is then pressed and dried in the usual way. *Dunlop cheese* has a peculiarly mild and rich taste: the best is made entirely from new milk. *New cheese* (as it is called in London) is made chiefly in Lincolnshire, and is either made of all cream, or, like Stilton, by adding the cream of one day's milking to the milk that comes immediately from the cow: they are extremely thin, and are compressed gently two or three times, turned for a few days, and then eaten new with radishes, salad, &c. *Skimmed Milk cheese* is made for sea voyages principally. *Parmesan cheese* is made in Parma and Piacenza. It is the most celebrated of all cheese: it is made entirely of skimmed cow's milk. The high flavour which it has, is supposed to be owing to the rich herbage of the meadows of the Po, where the cows are pastured. The best Parmesan is kept for three or four years, and none is carried to market till it is at least six months old. *Dutch cheese* derives its peculiar pungent taste from the practice adopted in Holland of coagulating the milk with muriatic acid instead of rennet. *Swiss cheeses* in their several varieties are all remarkable for their fine flavour. That from *Gruyère*, a baili-wick in the canton of Fribourg, is best known in England. It is flavoured by the dried herb of *Melilotos officinalis* in powder. Cheese from milk and potatoes is manufactured in Thuringia and Saxony. *Cream cheese*, although so called, is not properly cheese, but is nothing more than cream dried sufficiently to be cut with a knife.

EGGS

There is only one opinion as to the nutritive properties of eggs, although the qualities of those belonging to different birds vary somewhat. Those of the common hen are most esteemed as delicate food, particularly when 'new-laid.' The quality of eggs depends much upon the food given to the hen. Eggs in general are considered most easily digestible when little subjected to the art of cookery. The lightest way of dressing them is by poaching, which is effected by putting them for a minute or two into brisk boiling water: this coagulates the external white, without doing the inner part too much. Eggs are much better when new-laid than a day or two afterwards. The usual time allotted for boiling eggs in the shell is 3 to 3¾ minutes:

less time than that in boiling water will not be sufficient to solidify the white, and more will make the yolk hard and less digestible: it is very difficult to *guess* accurately as to the time. Great care should be employed in putting them into the water, to prevent cracking the shell, which inevitably causes a portion of the white to exude, and lets water into the egg. Eggs are often beaten up raw in nutritive beverages.

Eggs are employed in a very great many articles of cookery, entrées, and entremets, and they form an essential ingredient in pastry, creams, flip, &c. It is particularly necessary that they should be quite fresh, as nothing is worse than stale eggs. Cobbett justly says, stale, or even preserved eggs, are things to be run from, not after.

The Metropolis is supplied with eggs from all parts of the kingdom, and they are likewise largely imported from various places on the continent; as France, Holland, Belgium, Guernsey, and Jersey. It appears from official statements mentioned in McCulloch's 'Commercial Dictionary,' that the number imported from France alone amounts to about 60,000,000 a year; and supposing them on an average to cost fourpence a dozen, it follows that we pay our continental neighbours above £83,000 a year for eggs.

CHAPTER XXXIII

RECIPES

Separation of Milk and Cream

If it be desired that the milk should be freed entirely from cream, it should be poured into a very shallow broad pan or dish, not more than 1½ inch deep, as cream cannot rise through a great depth of milk. In cold and wet weather, milk is not so rich as it is in summer and warm weather, and the morning's milk is always richer than the evening's. The last-drawn milk of each milking, at all times and seasons, is richer than the first-drawn, and on that account should be set apart for cream. Milk should be shaken as little as possible when carried from the cow to the dairy, and should be poured into the pans very gently. Persons not keeping cows, may always have a little cream, provided the milk they purchase be pure and unadulterated. As soon as it comes in, it should be poured into very shallow open pie-dishes, and set by in a very cool place, and in 7 or 8 hours a nice cream should have risen to the surface.

To Keep Milk and Cream in Hot Weather

When the weather is very warm, and it is very difficult to prevent milk from turning sour and spoiling the cream, it should be scalded, and it will then remain good for a few hours. It must on no account be allowed to boil, or there will be a skin instead of a cream upon the milk; and the slower the process, the safer will it be. A very good plan to scald milk, is to put the pan that contains it into a saucepan or wide kettle of boiling water. When the surface looks thick, the milk is sufficiently scalded, and it should then be put away in a cool place in the same vessel that it was scalded in. Cream may be kept for 24 hours, if scalded without sugar; and by the addition of the latter ingredient, it will remain good double the time, if kept in a cool place. All pans, jugs, and vessels intended for milk, should be kept beautifully clean, and well scalded before the milk is put in, as any negligence in this respect may cause large quantities of it to be spoiled; and milk should never be kept in vessels of zinc or copper. Milk may be preserved good in hot weather, for a few hours, by placing the jug which contains it in ice, or very cold water; or a pinch of bicarbonate of soda may be introduced into the liquid.

MILK, when of good quality, is of an opaque white colour: the cream always comes to the top; the well-known milky odour is strong; it will boil without altering its appearance in these respects; the little bladders which arise on the surface will renew themselves if broken by the spoon. To boil milk is, in fact, the simplest way of testing its quality. The commonest adulterations of milk are not of a hurtful character. It is a good deal thinned with water, and sometimes thickened with a little starch, or coloured with yolk of egg, or even saffron; but these processes have nothing murderous in them.

Curds and Whey*

INGREDIENTS.—A very small piece of rennet, ½ gallon of milk.

Mode.—Procure from the butcher's a small piece of rennet, which is the stomach of the calf, taken as soon as it is killed, scoured, and well rubbed with salt, and stretched on sticks to dry. Pour some boiling water on the rennet, and let it remain for 6 hours; then use the liquor to turn the milk. The milk should be warm and fresh from the cow: if allowed to cool, it must be heated till it is of a degree quite equal to new milk; but do not let it be too hot. About a tablespoonful, or rather more, would be sufficient to turn the above proportion of milk into curds and whey; and whilst the milk is turning, let it be kept in rather a warm place.

Time.—From 2 to 3 hours to turn the milk.

Seasonable at any time.

To Preserve and to Choose Salt Butter*

In large families, where salt butter is purchased a tub at a time, the first thing to be done is to turn the whole of the butter out, and, with a clean knife, to scrape the outside; the tub should then be wiped with a clean cloth, and sprinkled all round with salt, the butter replaced, and the lid kept on to exclude the air. It is necessary to take these precautions, as sometimes a want of proper cleanliness in the dairymaid causes the outside of the butter to become rancid, and if the scraping be neglected, the whole mass would soon become spoiled. To choose salt butter, plunge a knife into it, and if, when drawn out, the blade smells rancid or unpleasant, the butter is bad.

The layers in tubs will vary greatly, the butter being made at different times; so, to try if the whole tub be good, the cask should be unhooped, and the butter tried between the staves.

It is not necessary to state that butter is extracted from cream, or from unskimmed milk, by the churn. Of course it partakes of the qualities of the milk, and winter butter is said not to be so good as spring butter.

A word of caution is necessary about *rancid* butter. Nobody eats it on bread, but it is sometimes used in cooking, in forms in which the acidity can be more or less disguised. So much the worse; it is almost poisonous, disguise it as you may. Never, under any exigency whatever, be tempted into allowing butter with even a *soupçon* of 'turning' to enter into the composition of any dish that appears on your table. And, in general, the more you can do without the employment of butter that has been subjected to the influence of heat, the better. The woman of modern times is not a 'leech;' but she might often keep the 'leech' from the door, if she would give herself the trouble to invent *innocent* sauces.*

Cheese

In families where much cheese is consumed, and it is bought in large quantities, a piece from the whole cheese should be cut, the larger quantity spread with a thickly-buttered sheet of white paper, and the outside occasionally wiped. To keep cheeses moist that are in daily use, when they come from table a damp cloth should be wrapped round them, and the cheese put into a pan with a cover to it, in a cool but not very dry place. To ripen cheeses, and bring them forward, put them into a damp cellar; and, to check too large a production of mites, spirits may be poured into the parts affected. Pieces of cheese which are too near the rind, or too dry to put on table, may be made into Welsh rare-bits, or grated down and mixed with macaroni. Cheeses may be preserved in a perfect state for years, by covering them with parchment made pliable by soaking in water, or by rubbing them over with a coating of melted fat. The cheeses selected should be free from cracks or bruises of any kind.

CHEESE.—It is well known that some persons like cheese in a state of decay, and even 'alive.' There is no accounting for tastes, and it may be hard to show why mould, which is vegetation, should not be eaten as well as salad, or maggots as well as eels. But, generally speaking, decomposing bodies are not wholesome eating, and the line must be drawn somewhere.

Stilton Cheese

Stilton cheese, or British Parmesan, as it is sometimes called, is generally preferred to all other cheeses by those whose authority few will dispute. Those made in May or June are usually served at Christmas; or, to be in prime order, should be kept from 10 to 12 months, or even longer. An artificial ripeness in Stilton cheese is sometimes produced by inserting a small piece of decayed Cheshire into an aperture at the top. From 3 weeks to

Stilton Cheese

a month is sufficient time to ripen the cheese. An additional flavour may also be obtained by scooping out a piece from the top, and pouring therein port, sherry, Madeira, or old ale, and letting the cheese absorb these for 2 or 3 weeks. But that cheese is the finest which is ripened without any artificial aid, is the opinion of those who are judges in these matters. In serving a Stilton cheese, the top of it should be cut off to form a lid, and a napkin or piece of white paper, with a frill at the top, pinned round. When the cheese goes from table, the lid should be replaced.

Mode of Serving Cheese*

The usual mode of serving cheese at good tables is to cut a small quantity of it into neat square pieces, and to put them into a glass

Cheese-Glass

cheese-dish, this dish being handed round. Should the cheese crumble much, of course this method is rather wasteful, and it may then be put on the table in the piece, and the host may cut from it. When served thus, the

cheese must always be carefully scraped,* and laid on a white d'oyley or napkin, neatly folded. Cream cheese is often served in a cheese course, and, sometimes, grated Parmesan: the latter should be put into a covered glass dish. Rusks, cheese-biscuits, pats or slices of butter, and salad, cucumber, or water-cresses, should always form part of a cheese course.

SMOKING CHEESES.—The Romans smoked their cheeses, to give them a sharp taste. They possessed public places expressly for this use, and subject to police regulations which no one could evade.

A celebrated gourmand* remarked that a dinner without cheese is like a woman with one eye.

Cheese Sandwiches*

INGREDIENTS.—Slices of brown bread-and-butter, thin slices of cheese.

Mode.—Cut from a nice fat Cheshire, or any good rich cheese, some slices about ½ inch thick, and place them between some slices of brown bread-and-butter, like sandwiches. Place them on a plate in the oven, and, when the bread is toasted, serve on a napkin very hot and very quickly.

Time.—10 minutes in a brisk oven.

Average cost, 1½d. each sandwich.

Sufficient.—Allow a sandwich for each person.

Seasonable at any time.

CHEESE.—One of the most important products of coagulated milk is cheese. Unfermented, or cream-cheese, when quite fresh, is good for sub-jects with whom milk does not disagree; but cheese, in its commonest shape, is only fit for sedentary people, as an after-dinner stimulant; and in very small quantity. Bread and cheese, as a meal, is only fit for soldiers on march or labourers in the open air, who like it because it 'holds the stomach a long time.'*

Macaroni, as usually served with the Cheese Course

INGREDIENTS.—½ lb. of pipe macaroni, ¼ lb. of butter, 6 oz. of Parmesan or Cheshire cheese, pepper and salt to taste, 1 pint of milk, 2 pints of water, bread crumbs.

Mode.—Put the milk and water into a saucepan with sufficient salt to flavour it; place it on the fire, and, when it boils quickly, drop in the macaroni. Keep the water boiling until it is quite tender; drain the macaroni, and put it into a deep dish. Have ready the grated cheese, either Parmesan or Cheshire; sprinkle it amongst the maca-roni and some of the butter cut into small pieces, reserving some of the cheese for the top layer. Season with a little pepper, and cover the top layer of cheese with some very fine bread crumbs. Warm, without oiling, the remainder of the butter, and pour it gently over the bread crumbs. Place the dish before a bright fire to brown the crumbs; turn it once or twice, that it may be equally coloured, and serve very hot. The top of the macaroni may be browned with a salamander,* which is even better than placing it before the fire, as the process is more expeditious; but it should never be browned in the oven, as the butter would oil, and so impart a very disagreeable flavour to the dish. In boiling the macaroni, let it be perfectly tender but firm, no part beginning to melt, and the form entirely preserved. It may be boiled in plain water, with a little salt instead of using milk, but should then have a small piece of butter mixed with it.

Time.—1½ to 1¾ hour to boil the macaroni, 5 minutes to brown it before the fire.

Average cost, 1s. 6d.

Sufficient for 6 or 7 persons.   *Seasonable* at any time.

Note.—Riband macaroni may be dressed in the same manner, but does not require boiling so long a time.

Toasted Cheese, or Scotch Rare-bit*

INGREDIENTS.—A few slices of rich cheese, toast, mustard, and pepper.

Mode.—Cut some nice rich sound cheese into rather thin slices; melt it in a cheese-toaster on a hot plate, or over steam, and, when melted, add a small quantity of mixed mustard and a seasoning of

Hot-Water Cheese-Dish

pepper; stir the cheese until it is completely dissolved, then brown it before the fire, or with a salamander. Fill the bottom of the cheese-toaster with hot water, and serve with dry or buttered toasts, whichever may be preferred. Our engraving illustrates a cheese-toaster with hot-water reservoir: the cheese is melted in the upper tin, which is placed in another vessel of boiling water, so keeping the preparation beautifully hot. A small quantity of porter, or port wine, is sometimes mixed with the cheese; and, if it be not very rich, a few pieces of butter may be mixed with it to great advantage. Sometimes the melted cheese is spread on the toasts, and then laid in the cheese-dish at the top of the hot water. Whichever way it is served, it is highly necessary that the mixture be very hot, and very quickly sent to table, or it will be worthless.

Time.—About 5 minutes to melt the cheese.

Average cost, 1½d. per slice.

Sufficient.—Allow a slice to each person.   *Seasonable* at any time.

Scotch Woodcock*

INGREDIENTS.—A few slices of hot buttered toast; allow 1 anchovy to each slice. For the sauce,—¼ pint of cream, the yolks of 3 eggs.

Mode.—Separate the yolks from the whites of the eggs; beat the former, stir to them the cream, and bring the sauce to the boiling-point, but do not allow it to boil, or it will curdle. Have ready some hot buttered toast, spread with anchovies pounded to a paste; pour a little of the hot sauce on the top, and serve very hot and very quickly.

Time.—5 minutes to make the sauce hot.

Sufficient.—Allow ½ slice to each person.   *Seasonable* at any time.

To Keep Eggs Fresh for Several Weeks

Have ready a large saucepan, capable of holding 3 or 4 quarts, full of boiling water. Put the eggs into a cabbage-net, say 20 at a time, and hold them in the water (which must be kept boiling) *for 20 seconds.* Proceed in this manner till you have done as many eggs as you wish to preserve; then pack them away in sawdust. We have tried this method of preserving eggs, and can vouch for its excellence: they will be found, at the end of 2 or 3 months, quite good enough for culinary purposes; and although the white may be a little tougher than that of a new-laid egg, the yolk will be nearly the same. Many persons keep eggs for a long time by smearing the shells with butter or sweet oil: they should then be packed in plenty of bran or saw-dust, and the eggs not allowed to touch each other. Eggs for storing should be collected in fine weather, and should not be more than 24 hours old when they are packed away, or their flavour, when used, cannot be relied on. Another simple way of preserving eggs is to immerse them in lime-water soon after they have been laid, and then to put the vessel containing the lime-water in a cellar or cool outhouse.

Seasonable.—The best time for preserving eggs is from July to September.

EGGS.—The quality of eggs is said to be very much affected by the food of the fowls who lay them. Herbs and grain together make a better food than grain only. When the hens eat too many insects, the eggs have a disagreeable flavour.

CHAPTER XXXIV

GENERAL OBSERVATIONS ON BREAD, BISCUITS, AND CAKES

BREAD AND BREAD-MAKING

Among the numerous vegetable products yielding articles of food for man, the Cereals hold the first place. By means of skilful cultivation, mankind have transformed the original forms of these growths, poor and ill-flavoured as they perhaps were, into various fruitful and agreeable species, which yield an abundant and pleasant supply. Classified according to their respective richness in alimentary elements, the Cereals stand thus:—Wheat, and its varieties, Rye, Barley, Oats, Rice, Indian Corn. Everybody knows it is wheat flour which yields the best bread. Rye-bread is viscous, hard, less easily soluble by the gastric juice, and not so rich in nutritive power. Flour produced from barley, Indian corn, or rice, is not so readily made into bread; and the article, when made, is heavy and indigestible.

On examining a grain of corn from any of the numerous cereals[1]

[1] *Cereal*, a corn-producing plant; from Ceres, the goddess of agriculture.

used in the preparation of flour, such as wheat, maize, rye, barley, &c., it will be found to consist of two parts,—the husk, or exterior covering, which is generally of a dark colour, and the inner, or albuminous part, which is more or less white. In grinding, these two portions are separated, and the husk being blown away in the process of winnowing, the flour remains in the form of a light brown powder, consisting principally of starch and gluten. In order to render it white, it undergoes a process called 'bolting.' It is passed through a series of fine sieves, which separate the coarser parts, leaving behind fine white flour,—the 'fine firsts' of the corn-dealer. The process of bolting, as just described, tends to deprive flour of its gluten, the coarser and darker portion containing much of that substance; while the lighter part is peculiarly rich in starch. Bran contains a large proportion of gluten; hence it will be seen why brown bread is so much more nutritious than white; in fact, we may lay it down as a general rule, that the whiter the bread the less nourishment it contains. Majendie proved this by feeding a dog for forty days with white wheaten bread, at the end of which time he died; while another dog, fed on brown bread made with flour mixed with bran, lived without any disturbance of his health. The 'bolting' process, then, is rather injurious than beneficial in its result; and is one of the numerous instances where fashion has chosen a wrong standard to go by. In ancient times, down to the Emperors, no bolted flour was known. In many parts of Germany the entire meal is used; and in no part of the world are the digestive organs of the people in a better condition. In years of famine, when corn is scarce, the use of bolted flour is most culpable, for from 18 to 20 per cent is lost in bran. Brown bread has, of late years, become very popular; and many physicians have recommended it to invalids with weak digestions with great success.* This rage for white bread has introduced adulterations of a very serious character, affecting the health of the whole community. Potatoes are added for this purpose; but this is a comparatively harmless cheat, only reducing the nutritive property of the bread; but bone-dust and alum are also put in, which are far from harmless.

BREAD-MAKING

One word as to the unwholesomeness of new bread and hot rolls. When bread is taken out of the oven, it is full of moisture; the starch is held together in masses, and the bread, instead of being crusted so as to expose each grain of starch to the saliva, actually prevents their digestion by being formed by the teeth into leathery poreless masses, which lie on the stomach like so many bullets. Bread should always be at least a day old before it is eaten; and, if properly made, and kept in a *cool dry* place, ought to be perfectly soft and palatable at the end of three or four days. Hot rolls, swimming in melted butter, and new bread, ought to be carefully shunned by everybody who has the slightest respect for that much-injured individual—the Stomach.

AËRATED BREAD.—It is not unknown to some of our readers that Dr Dauglish, of Malvern, has recently patented a process for making bread 'light' without the use of leaven. The ordinary process of bread-making by fermentation is tedious, and much labour of human hands is requisite in the kneading, in order that the dough may be thoroughly interpenetrated with the leaven. The new process impregnates the bread, by the application of machinery, with carbonic acid gas, or fixed air. Different opinions are expressed about the bread; but it is curious to note, that, as corn is now reaped by machinery, and dough is baked by machinery, the whole process of bread-making is probably in course of undergoing changes which will emancipate both the housewife and the professional baker from a large amount of labour.*

A FEW HINTS RESPECTING THE MAKING AND BAKING OF CAKES

Loaf Sugar should be well pounded, and then sifted through a fine sieve.

Currants should be nicely washed, picked, dried in a cloth, and then carefully examined, that no pieces of grit or stone may be left amongst them. They should then be laid on a dish before the fire, to become thoroughly dry; as, if added damp to the other ingredients, cakes will be liable to be heavy.

Good Butter should always be used in the manufacture of cakes; and if beaten to a cream, it saves much time and labour to warm, but not melt, it before beating.

BISCUITS

Since the establishment of the large modern biscuit manufactories, biscuits have been produced both cheap and wholesome, in, comparatively speaking, endless variety. Their actual component parts are, perhaps, known only to the various makers; but there are several kinds of biscuits which have long been in use, that may here be advantageously described.*

Biscuits belong to the class of unfermented bread, and are, perhaps, the most wholesome of that class. In cases where fermented bread does not agree with the human stomach, they may be recommended: in many instances they are considered lighter, and less liable to create acidity and flatulence. The name is derived from the French *bis cuit* 'twice-baked,' because, originally, that was the mode of entirely depriving them of all moisture, to insure their keeping; but, although that process is no longer employed, the name is retained. The use of this kind of bread on land is pretty general, and some varieties are luxuries; but, at sea, biscuits are articles of the first necessity.

SEA, or SHIP BISCUITS, are made of wheat-flour from which only the coarsest bran has been separated. The dough is made up as stiff as it can be worked, and is then formed into shapes, and baked in an oven; after which, the biscuits are exposed in lofts over the oven until perfectly dry, to prevent them from becoming mouldy when stored.

CAPTAINS' BISCUITS are made in a similar manner, only of fine flour.

CHAPTER XXXV

RECIPES*

To Make Good Home-made Bread
(*Miss Acton's Recipe*)

INGREDIENTS.—1 quartern of flour, 1 large tablespoonful of solid brewer's yeast, or nearly 1 oz. of fresh German yeast,* 1¼ to 1½ pint of warm milk-and-water.

Mode.—Put the flour into a large earthenware bowl or deep pan; then, with a strong metal or wooden spoon, hollow out the middle; but do not clear it entirely away from the bottom of the pan, as, in that case, the sponge (or leaven, as it was formerly termed) would stick to it, which it ought not to do. Next take either a large table-spoonful of brewer's yeast which has been rendered solid by mixing it with plenty of cold water, and letting it afterwards stand to settle for a day and night; or nearly an ounce of German yeast; put it into a large basin, and proceed to mix it, so that it shall be as smooth as

Cottage Loaf

Tin Bread

cream, with ¾ pint of warm milk-and-water, or with water only; though even a very little milk will much improve the bread. Pour the yeast into the hole made in the flour, and stir into it as much of that which lies round it as will make a thick batter, in which there must be no lumps. Strew plenty of flour on the top; throw a thick clean cloth over, and set it where the air is warm; but do not place it upon the kitchen fender, for it will become too much heated there. Look at it from time to time: when it has been laid for nearly an hour, and when the yeast has risen and broken through the flour, so that bubbles appear in it, you will know that it is ready to be made up into dough. Then place the pan on a strong chair, or dresser, or table, of convenient height; pour into the sponge the remainder of the warm milk-and-water; stir into it as much of the flour as you can with the spoon; then wipe it out clean with your fingers, and lay it aside. Next take plenty of the remaining flour, throw it on the top of the leaven, and begin, with the knuckles of both hands, to knead it well. When the flour is nearly all kneaded in, begin to draw the edges of the dough towards the middle, in order to mix the whole thoroughly; and when it is free from flour and lumps and crumbs, and does not stick to the hands when touched, it will be done, and may again be covered with the cloth, and left to rise a second time. In ¾ hour look at it, and should it have swollen very much, and begin to crack, it will be light enough to bake. Turn it then on to a paste-board or very clean dresser, and with a large sharp knife divide it in two; make it up quickly into loaves, and dispatch it to the oven: make one or two incisions across the tops of the loaves, as they will rise more easily if this be done. If baked in tins or pans, rub them with a tiny piece of butter laid on a piece of clean paper, to prevent the dough from sticking to them. All bread should be turned upside down, or on its side, as soon as it is drawn from the oven: if this be neglected, the under part of the loaves will become wet and blistered from the steam, which cannot then escape from them. *To make the dough without setting a sponge*, merely mix the yeast with the greater part of the warm milk-and-water, and wet up the whole of the flour at once after a little salt has been stirred in, proceeding exactly, in every other respect, as in the directions just given. As the dough will *soften* in the rising, it should be made quite firm at first, or it will be too lithe by the time it is ready for the oven.

Time.—To be left to rise an hour the first time, ¾ hour the second time; to be baked from 1 to 1¼ hour, or baked in one loaf from 1½ to 2 hours.

To Make Hot Buttered Toast

A loaf of household bread about two days old answers for making toast better than cottage bread, the latter not being a good shape, and too crusty for the purpose. Cut as many nice even slices as may be required, rather more than ¼ inch in thickness, and toast them before a very bright fire, without allowing the bread to blacken, which spoils the appearance and flavour of all toast. When of a nice colour on both sides, put it on a hot plate; divide some good butter into small pieces, place them on the toast, set this before the fire, and when the butter is just beginning to melt, spread it lightly over the toast. Trim off the crust and ragged edges, divide each round into 4 pieces, and send the toast quickly to table. Some persons cut the slices of toast across from corner to corner, so making the pieces of a three-cornered shape. Soyer recommends that each slice should be cut into pieces as soon as it is buttered, and when all are ready, that they should be piled lightly on the dish they are intended to be served on. He says that by cutting through 4 or 5 slices at a time, all the butter is squeezed out of the upper ones, while the bottom one is swimming in fat liquid. It is highly essential to use good butter for making this dish.*

Muffins*

INGREDIENTS.—To every quart of milk allow 1½ oz. of German yeast, a little salt; flour.

Mode.—Warm the milk, add to it the yeast, and mix these well together; put them into a pan, and stir in sufficient flour to make the whole into a dough of rather a soft consistence; cover it over with a cloth, and place it in a warm place to rise, and, when light and nicely risen, divide the dough into pieces, and round them to the proper shape with the hands; place them,

Muffins

in a layer of flour about two inches thick, on wooden trays, and let them rise again; when this is effected, they each will exhibit a semi-globular shape. Then place them carefully on a hot-plate or stove, and bake them until they are slightly browned, turning them when they are done on one side. Muffins are not easily made, and are more generally purchased than manufactured at home. *To toast them*, divide the edge of the muffin all round, by pulling it open, to the depth of about an inch, with the fingers. Put it on a toasting-fork, and hold it before a very clear fire until one side is nicely browned, but not burnt; turn, and toast it on the other. Do not toast them too quickly, as, if this is done, the middle of the muffin will not be warmed through. When done, divide them by pulling them open; butter them slightly on both sides, put them together again, and cut them into halves: when sufficient are toasted and buttered, pile them on a very hot dish, and send them very quickly to table.

Time.—From 20 minutes to ½ hour to bake them.

Sufficient.—Allow 1 muffin to each person.

Macaroons

INGREDIENTS.—½ lb. of sweet almonds, ½ lb. of sifted loaf sugar, the whites of 3 eggs, wafer-paper.

Mode.—Blanch, skin, and dry the almonds, and pound them well with a little orange-flower water or plain water; then add to them the sifted sugar and the whites of the eggs, which should be beaten to a stiff froth, and mix all the ingredients well together. When the paste looks soft, drop it at equal distances from a biscuit-syringe on to sheets of wafer-paper; put a strip of almond on the top of each; strew some sugar over, and bake the macaroons in rather a slow oven, of a light brown colour. When hard and set, they are done, and must not be allowed to get very brown, as that would spoil their appearance. If the cakes, when baked, appear heavy, add a little more white of egg, but let this always be well whisked before it is added to the other ingredients.* We have given a recipe for making these cakes, but we think it almost or quite as economical to purchase such articles as these at a good confectioner's.

Time.—From 15 to 20 minutes, in a slow oven.

Average cost, 1s. 8d. per lb.

Rock Biscuits*

INGREDIENTS.—6 eggs, 1 lb. of sifted sugar, ½ lb. of flour, a few currants.

Mode.—Break the eggs into a basin, beat them well until very light, add the pounded sugar, and when this is well mixed with the eggs, dredge in the flour gradually, and add the currants. Mix all well together, and put the dough, with a fork, on the tins, making it look as rough as possible. Bake the cakes in a moderate oven from 20 minutes to ½ hour; when they are done, allow them to get cool, and store them away in a tin canister, in a dry place.

Time.—20 minutes to ½ hour.   *Average cost*, 1s. 2d.

Seasonable at any time.

Savoy Biscuits or Cakes*

INGREDIENTS.—4 eggs, 6 oz. of pounded sugar, the rind of 1 lemon, 6 oz. of flour.

Mode.—Break the eggs into a basin, separating the whites from the yolks; beat the yolks well, mix with them the pounded sugar and grated lemon-rind, and beat these ingredients together for ¼ hour. Then dredge in the flour gradually, and when the whites of the eggs have been whisked to a solid froth, stir them to the flour, &c.; beat the mixture well for another 5 minutes, then draw it along in strips upon thick cartridge paper to the proper size of the biscuit, and bake them in rather a hot oven; but let them be carefully watched, as they are soon done, and a few seconds over the proper time will scorch and spoil them. These biscuits, or ladies'-fingers, as they are called, are used for making Charlotte russes, and for a variety of fancy sweet dishes.

Time.—5 to 8 minutes, in a quick oven.

Average cost, 1s. 8d. per lb., or ½d. each.

Rich Bride* or Christening Cake

INGREDIENTS.—5 lbs. of the finest flour, 3 lbs. of fresh butter, 5 lbs. of currants, 2 lbs. of sifted loaf sugar, 2 nutmegs, ¼ oz. of mace, half ¼ oz. of cloves, 16 eggs, 1 lb. of sweet almonds, ½ lb. of candied citron, ½ lb. each of candied orange and lemon peel, 1 gill of wine, 1 gill of brandy.

Mode.—Let the flour be as fine as possible, and well dried and sifted; the currants washed, picked, and dried before the fire; the sugar well pounded and sifted; the nutmegs grated, the spices pounded; the eggs thoroughly whisked, whites and yolks separately; the almonds pounded with a little orange-flower water, and the candied peel cut in neat slices. When all these ingredients are prepared, mix them in the following manner. Begin working the butter with the hand till it becomes of a cream-like consistency; stir in the sugar, and when the whites of the eggs are whisked to a solid froth, mix them with the butter and sugar; next, well beat up the yolks for 10 minutes, and, adding them to the flour, nutmegs, mace, and cloves, continue beating the whole together for ½ hour or longer, till wanted for the oven. Then mix in lightly the currants, almonds, and candied peel with the wine and brandy; and having lined a hoop with buttered paper, fill it with the mixture, and bake the cake in a tolerably quick oven, taking care, however, not to burn it: to prevent this, the top of it may be covered with a sheet of paper. To ascertain whether the cake is done, plunge a clean knife into the middle of it, withdraw it directly, and if the blade is not sticky, and looks bright, the cake is sufficiently baked. These cakes are usually spread with a thick layer of almond icing, and over that another layer of sugar icing, and afterwards ornamented. In baking a large cake like this, great attention must be paid to the heat of the oven; it should not be too fierce, but have a good soaking heat.

Time.—5 to 6 hours. *Average cost*, 2s. per lb.

Common Cake, suitable for sending to
Children at School

INGREDIENTS.—2 lbs. of flour, 4 oz. of butter or clarified dripping, ½ oz. of caraway seeds, ¼ oz. of allspice, ½ lb. of pounded sugar, 1 lb. of currants, 1 pint of milk, 3 tablespoonfuls of fresh yeast.

Mode.—Rub the butter lightly into the flour; add all the dry ingredients, and mix these well together. Make the milk warm, but not hot; stir in the yeast, and with this liquid make the whole into a light dough; knead it well, and line the cake-tins with strips of buttered paper; this paper should be about 6 inches higher than the top of the tin. Put in the dough; stand it in a warm place to rise for more than an hour; then bake the cakes in a well-heated oven. If this quantity be divided in two, they will take from 1½ to 2 hours' baking.

Time.—1¾ to 2¼ hours. *Average cost*, 1s. 9d.

Sufficient to make 2 moderate-sized cakes.

A Nice Useful Cake

INGREDIENTS.—¼ lb. of butter, 6 oz. of currants, ¼ lb. of sugar, 1 lb. of dried flour, 2 teaspoonfuls of baking-powder, 3 eggs, 1 teacupful of milk, 2 oz. of sweet almonds, 1 oz. of candied peel.

Mode.—Beat the butter to a cream; wash, pick, and dry the currants; whisk the eggs; blanch and chop the almonds, and cut the peel into neat slices. When all these are ready, mix the dry ingredients together; then add the butter, milk, and eggs, and beat the mixture well for a few minutes. Put the cake into a buttered mould or tin, and bake it for rather more than 1½ hour. The currants and candied peel may be omitted, and a little lemon or almond flavouring substituted for them: made in this manner, the cake will be found very good.

Time.—Rather more than 1½ hour. *Average cost*, 1s. 9d.

Sunderland Gingerbread Nuts*
(An Excellent Recipe)

INGREDIENTS.—1¾ lb. treacle, 1 lb. of moist sugar, 1 lb. of butter, 2¾ lbs. of flour, 1½ oz. of ground ginger, 1½ oz. of allspice, 1½ oz. of coriander seeds.

Mode.—Let the allspice, coriander seeds, and ginger be freshly ground; put them into a basin, with the flour and sugar, and mix these ingredients well together; warm the treacle and butter together; then with a spoon work it into the flour, &c., until the whole forms a nice smooth paste. Drop the mixture from the spoon on to a piece of buttered paper, and bake in rather a slow oven from 20 minutes to ½ hour. A little candied lemon-peel mixed with the above is an improvement, and a great authority in culinary matters suggests the addition of a little cayenne pepper in gingerbread. Whether it be advisable to use this latter ingredient or not, we leave our readers to decide.

Time.—20 minutes to ½ hour.   *Average cost*, 1s. to 1s. 4d. per lb.

Seasonable at any time.

Pound Cake*

INGREDIENTS.—1 lb. of butter, 1¼ lb. of flour, 1 lb. of pounded loaf sugar, 1 lb. of currants, 9 eggs, 2 oz. of candied peel, ½ oz. of citron, ½ oz. of sweet almonds; when liked, a little pounded mace.

Mode.—Work the butter to a cream; dredge in the flour; add the sugar, currants, candied peel, which should be cut into neat slices, and the almonds, which should be blanched and chopped, and mix all these well together; whisk the eggs, and let them be thoroughly blended with the dry ingredients. Beat the cake well for 20 minutes, and put it into a round tin, lined at the bottom and sides with a strip of white

Pound Cake

buttered paper. Bake it from 1½ to 2 hours, and let the oven be well heated when the cake is first put in, as, if this is not the case, the currants will all sink to the bottom of it. To make this preparation light, the yolks and whites of the eggs should be beaten separately, and added separately to the other ingredients. A glass of wine is sometimes added to the mixture; but this is scarcely necessary, as the cake will be found quite rich enough without it.*

Time.—1½ to 2 hours. *Average cost*, 3s. 6d.

Sufficient.—The above quantity divided in two will make two nice-sized cakes.

Seasonable at any time.

A Very Good Seed-Cake*

INGREDIENTS.—1 lb. of butter, 6 eggs, ¾ lb. of sifted sugar, pounded mace and grated nutmeg to taste, 1 lb. of flour, ¾ oz. of caraway seeds, 1 wineglassful of brandy.

Mode.—Beat the butter to a cream; dredge in the flour; add the sugar, mace, nutmeg, and caraway seeds, and mix these ingredients well together. Whisk the eggs, stir to them the brandy, and beat the cake again for 10 minutes. Put it into a tin lined with buttered paper, and bake it from 1½ to 2 hours. This cake would be equally nice made with currants, and omitting the caraway seeds.

Time.—1½ to 2 hours. *Average cost*, 2s. 6d.

Seasonable at any time.

Scrap-Cakes

INGREDIENTS.—2 lbs. of leaf, or the inside fat of a pig; 1½ lb. of flour, ¼ lb. of moist sugar, ½ lb. of currants, 1 oz. of candied lemon-peel, ground allspice to taste.

Mode.—Cut the leaf, or flead, as it is sometimes called, into small pieces; put it into a large dish, which place in a quick oven; be careful that it does not burn, and in a short time it will be reduced to oil, with the small pieces of leaf floating on the surface; and it is of these that the cakes should be made. Gather all the scraps together, put them into a basin with the flour, and rub them well together. Add the currants, sugar, candied peel, cut into thin slices, and the ground allspice. When all these ingredients are well mixed, moisten with sufficient cold water to make the whole into a nice paste; roll it out thin, cut it into shapes, and bake the cakes in a quick oven from 15 to 20 minutes. These are very economical and wholesome cakes for children, and the lard, melted at home, produced from the flead, is generally better than that you purchase. To prevent the lard from burning, and to insure its being a good colour, it is better to melt it in a jar placed in a saucepan of boiling water; by doing it in this manner, there will be no chance of its discolouring.

Time.—15 to 20 minutes.

Sufficient to make 3 or 4 dozen cakes.

Seasonable from September to March.

Scotch Shortbread

INGREDIENTS.—2 lbs. of flour, 1 lb. of butter, ¼ lb. of pounded loaf sugar, ½ oz. of caraway seeds, 1 oz. of sweet almonds, a few strips of candied orange-peel.

Mode.—Beat the butter to a cream, gradually dredge in the flour, and add the sugar, caraway seeds, and sweet almonds, which should be blanched and cut into small pieces.

Work the paste until it is quite smooth, and divide it into six pieces. Put each cake on a separate piece of

Shortbread

paper, roll the paste out square to the thickness of about an inch, and pinch it upon all sides. Prick it well, and ornament with one or two strips of candied orange-peel. Put the cakes into a good oven, and bake them from 25 to 30 minutes.

Time.—25 to 30 minutes.   *Average cost,* for this quantity, 2s.

Sufficient to make 6 cakes.   *Seasonable* at any time.

Note.—Where the flavour of the caraway seeds is disliked, omit them, and add rather a larger proportion of candied peel.

Tea-Cakes

INGREDIENTS.—2 lbs. of flour, ½ teaspoonful of salt, ¼ lb. of butter or lard, 1 egg, a piece of German yeast the size of a walnut, warm milk.

Mode.—Put the flour (which should be perfectly dry) into a basin; mix with it the salt, and rub in the butter or lard; then beat the egg well, stir to it the yeast, and add these to the flour with as much warm milk as will make the whole into a smooth paste, and knead it well. Let it rise near the fire, and, when well risen, form it into cakes; place them on tins, let them rise again for a few minutes before putting them into the oven, and bake from ¼ to ½ hour in a moderate oven. These are very nice with a few currants and a little sugar added to the other ingredients: they should be put in after the butter is rubbed in. These cakes should be buttered, and eaten hot as soon as baked; but, when stale, they are very nice split and toasted; or, if dipped in milk, or even water, and covered with a basin in the oven till hot, they will be almost equal to new.

Time.—¼ to ½ hour.　　*Average cost*, 10*d*.

Sufficient to make 8 tea-cakes.　　*Seasonable* at any time.

To Toast Tea-Cakes*

Cut each tea-cake into three or four slices, according to its thickness; toast them on both sides before a nice clear fire, and as each slice is done, spread it with butter on both sides. When a cake is toasted, pile the slices one on the top of the other, cut them into quarters, put them on a very hot plate, and send the cakes immediately to table. As they are wanted, send them in hot, one or two at a time, as, if allowed to stand, they spoil, unless kept in a muffin-plate over a basin of boiling water.

CHAPTER XXXVI

GENERAL OBSERVATIONS ON BEVERAGES

Beverages are innumerable in their variety; but the ordinary beverages drunk in the British isles, may be divided into three classes:—
1. Beverages of the simplest kind not fermented. 2. Beverages, consisting of water, containing a considerable quantity of carbonic acid. 3. Beverages composed partly of fermented liquors. Of the first class may be mentioned,—water, toast-and-water, barley-water, eau sucré, lait sucré, cheese and milk whey, milk-and-water, lemonade, orangeade, sherbet, apple and pear juice, capillaire, vinegar-and-water, raspberry vinegar and water.

Of the common class of beverages, consisting of water impregnated with carbonic acid gas, we may name soda-water, single and double, ordinary effervescing draughts, and ginger-beer.

The beverages composed partly of fermented liquors, are hot spiced wines, bishop, egg-flip, egg-hot, ale posset, sack posset, punch, and spirits-and-water.

We will, however, forthwith treat on the most popular of our beverages, beginning with the one which makes 'the cup that cheers but not inebriates.'

The beverage called tea has now become almost a necessary of life. Previous to the middle of the 17th century it was not used in England, and it was wholly unknown to the Greeks and Romans. Pepys says, in his Diary,—'September 25th, 1661.—I sent for a cup of tea (a China drink), of which I had never drunk before.' Two years later it was so rare a commodity in England, that the English East-India Company bought 2 lbs. 2 oz. of it, as a present for his majesty. In 1666 it was sold in London for sixty shillings a pound. From that date the consumption has gone on increasing from 5,000 lbs. to 50,000,000 lbs.

The various names by which teas are sold in the British market are corruptions of Chinese words. There are about a dozen different kinds; but the principal are Bohea, Congou, and Souchong, and signify, respectively, inferior, middling, and superior. Teas are often perfumed and flavoured with the leaves of different kinds of plants grown on purpose. Different tea-farms in China produce teas of various qualities, raised by skilful cultivation on various soils.

Chinese tea has frequently been adulterated in this country, by the admixture of the dried leaves of certain plants. The leaves of the sloe, white thorn, ash, elder, and some others, have been employed for this purpose; such as the leaves of the speedwell, wild germander, black currants, syringa, purple-spiked willow-herb, sweet-brier, and cherry-tree. Some of these are harmless, others are to a certain degree poisonous; as, for example, are the leaves of all the varieties of the plum and cherry tribe, to which the sloe belongs. Adulteration by means of these leaves is by no means a new species of fraud; and several acts of parliament, from the time of George II, have been passed, specifying severe penalties against those guilty of the offence, which, notwithstanding numerous convictions, continues to the present time.

In the purchase of tea, that should be chosen which possesses an agreeable odour and is as whole as possible, in order that the leaf may be easily examined. The greatest care should be taken that it has not been exposed to the air, which destroys its flavour.

It would be impossible, in the space at our command, to enumerate the various modes adopted in different countries for 'making coffee;' that is, the phrase commonly understood to mean the complete preparation of this delicious beverage for drinking. For performing this operation, such recipes or methods as we have found most practical will be inserted in their proper place; but the following facts connected with coffee will be found highly interesting.

It appears that coffee was first introduced into England by Daniel Edwards, a Turkey merchant, whose servant, Pasqua, a Greek, understood the manner of roasting it. This servant, under the patronage of Edwards, established the first coffee-house in London, in George Yard, Lombard Street. Coffee was then sold at four or five guineas a pound, and a duty was soon afterwards laid upon it of fourpence a gallon, when made into a beverage. In the course of two centuries, however, this berry, unknown originally as an article of food, except to some savage tribes on the confines of Abyssinia, has made its way through the whole of the civilized world. Mahommedans of all ranks drink coffee twice a day; it is in universal request in France; and the demand for it throughout the British isles is daily increasing, the more especially since so much attention has been given to mechanical contrivances for roasting and grinding the berry and preparing the beverage.

To have coffee in perfection, it should be roasted and ground just before it is used, and more should not be ground at a time than is wanted for immediate use, or, if it be necessary to grind more, it should be kept closed from the air. Coffee readily imbibes exhalations from other substances, and thus often acquires a bad flavour: brown sugar placed near it will communicate a disagreeable flavour. It is stated that the coffee in the West Indies has often been injured by being laid in rooms near the sugar-works, or where rum is distilled; and the same effect has been produced by bringing over coffee in the same ships with rum and sugar. Dr Moseley mentions that a few bags of pepper, on board a ship from India, spoiled a whole cargo of coffee.

With respect to the quantity of coffee used in making the decoction, much depends upon the taste of the consumer. The greatest and most common fault in English coffee is the too small quantity of the ingredient. Count Rumford says that to make good coffee for drinking after dinner, a pound of good Mocha coffee, which, when roasted and ground, weighs only thirteen ounces, serves to make fifty-six full cups, or a little less than a quarter of an ounce to a coffee-cup of moderate size.

CHAPTER XXXVII

RECIPES*

To Make Chocolate

INGREDIENTS.—Allow ½ oz. of chocolate to each person; to every oz. allow ½ pint of water, ½ pint of milk.

Mode.—Make the milk-and-water hot; scrape the chocolate into it, and stir the mixture constantly and quickly until the chocolate is dissolved; bring it to the boiling-point, stir it well, and serve directly with white sugar. Chocolate prepared within a mill, as shown in the engraving, is made by putting in the scraped chocolate, pouring over it the boiling milk-and-water, and milling it over the fire until hot and frothy.

Sufficient.—Allow ½ oz. of cake chocolate to each person.

Mill

CHOCOLATE AND COCOA.—Both these preparations are made from the seeds or beans of the cacao-tree, which grows in the West Indies and South America. The Spanish, and the proper name, is cacao, not cocoa, as it is generally spelt. From this mistake, the tree from which the beverage is procured has been often confounded with the palm that produces the edible cocoa-nuts, which are the produce of the cocoa-tree (*Cocos nucifera*), whereas the tree from which chocolate is procured is very different (the *Theobroma cacao*). The cocoa-tree was cultivated by the aboriginal inhabitants of South America, particularly in Mexico, where, according to Humboldt, it was reared by Montezuma. It was transplanted thence into other dependencies of the Spanish monarchy in 1520; and it was so highly esteemed by Linnaeus as to receive from him the name now conferred upon it, of Theobroma, a term derived from the Greek, and signifying '*food for gods.*' Chocolate has always been a favourite beverage among the Spaniards and Creoles, and was considered here as a great luxury when first introduced, after the discovery of America; but the high duties laid upon it, confined it long almost entirely to the wealthier classes. Before it was subjected to duty, Mr Bryan Edwards stated that cocoa plantations were numerous in Jamaica, but that the duty caused their almost entire ruin. The removal of this duty has increased their cultivation.

To Make Coffee

INGREDIENTS.—Allow ½ oz., or 1 tablespoonful, of ground coffee to each person; to every oz. of coffee allow ⅓ pint of water.

Mode.—To make coffee good, *it should never be boiled*, but the boiling water merely poured on it, the same as for tea. The coffee should always be purchased in the berry,—if possible, freshly roasted; and it should never be ground long before it is wanted for use. There are very many new kinds of coffee-pots, but the method of making the coffee is nearly always the same; namely, pouring the boiling water on the powder, and allowing it to filter through. Our illustration shows one of Loysel's Hydrostatic Urns, which are admirably adapted for making good and clear coffee, which should be made in the following manner:—

Loysel's Hydrostatic Urn

Warm the urn with boiling water, remove the lid and movable filter, and place the ground coffee at the bottom of the urn. Put the movable filter over this, and screw the lid, inverted, tightly on the end of the centre pipe. Pour into the inverted lid the above proportion of boiling water, and when all the water so poured has disappeared from the funnel, and made its way down the centre pipe and up again through the ground coffee by *hydrostatic pressure*, unscrew the lid and cover the urn. Pour back direct into the urn, *not through the funnel*, one, two, or three cups, according to the size of the percolater, in order to make the infusion of uniform strength; the contents will then be ready for use, and should run from the tap strong, hot, and clear. The coffee made in these urns generally turns out very good, and there is but one objection to them,—the coffee runs rather slowly from the tap. This is of no consequence where there is a small party, but tedious where there are many persons to provide for. A remedy for this objection may be suggested; namely, to make the coffee very strong, so that not more than ⅓ of a cup would be required, as the rest would be filled up with milk. Making coffee in filters or percolaters does away with the necessity of using isinglass, white of egg, and various other preparations to clear it. Coffee should always be served very hot, and, if possible, in the same vessel in which it is made, as pouring it from one pot to another cools, and consequently spoils it. Many persons may think that the proportion of water we have given for each oz. of coffee is rather small; it is so, and the coffee produced from it will be very strong; ⅓ of a cup will be found quite sufficient, which should be filled with nice hot milk, or milk and cream mixed. This is the *café au lait* for which our neighbours over the Channel are so justly celebrated. Should the ordinary method of making coffee be preferred, use double the quantity of water, and, in pouring it into the cups, put in more coffee and less milk.

Sufficient.—For very good coffee, allow ½ oz., or 1 tablespoonful, to each person.

To Make Tea*

There is very little art in making good tea; if the water is boiling, and there is no sparing of the fragrant leaf, the beverage will almost invariably be good. The old-fashioned plan of allowing a teaspoonful to each person, and one over, is still practised. Warm the teapot with boiling water; let it remain for two or three minutes for the vessel to become thoroughly hot, then pour it away. Put in the tea, pour in from ½ to ¾ pint of *boiling* water, close the lid, and let it stand for the tea to draw from 5 to 10 minutes; then fill up the pot with water. The tea will be quite spoiled unless made with water that is actually *boiling*, as the leaves will not open, and the flavour not be extracted from them; the beverage will consequently be colourless and tasteless,—in fact, nothing but tepid water. Where there is a very large party to make tea for, it is a good plan to have two teapots instead of putting a large quantity of tea into one pot; the tea, besides, will go farther. When the infusion has been once completed, the addition of fresh tea adds very little to the strength; so, when more is required, have the pot emptied of the old leaves, scalded, and fresh tea made in the usual manner. Economists say that a few grains of carbonate of soda, added before the boiling water is poured on the tea, assist to draw out the goodness: if the water is very hard, perhaps it is a good plan, as the soda softens it; but care must be taken to use this ingredient sparingly, as it is liable to give the tea a soapy taste if added in too large a quantity. For mixed tea, the usual proportion is four spoonfuls of black to one of green; more of the latter when the flavour is very much liked; but strong green tea is highly pernicious, and should never be partaken of too freely.

Time.—2 minutes to warm the teapot, 5 to 10 minutes to draw the strength from the tea.

Sufficient.—Allow 1 teaspoonful to each person, and one over.

Cowslip Wine*

INGREDIENTS.—To every gallon of water allow 3 lbs. of lump sugar, the rind of 2 lemons, the juice of 1, the rind and juice of 1 Seville orange, 1 gallon of cowslip pips. To every 4½ gallons of wine allow 1 bottle of brandy.

Mode.—Boil the sugar and water together for ½ hour, carefully removing all the scum as it rises. Pour this boiling liquor on the orange and lemon-rinds, and the juice, which should be strained; when milk-warm, add the cowslip pips or flowers, picked from the stalks and seeds; and to 9 gallons of wine 3 tablespoonfuls of good fresh brewers' yeast. Let it ferment 3 or 4 days; then put all together in a cask with the brandy, and let it remain for 2 months, when bottle it off for use.

Time.—To be boiled ½ hour; to ferment 3 or 4 days; to remain in the cask 2 months.

Average cost, exclusive of the cowslips, which may be picked in the fields, 2s. 9d. per gallon.

Seasonable.—Make this in April or May.

Raspberry Vinegar*

INGREDIENTS.—To every 3 pints of the best vinegar allow 4½ pints of freshly-gathered raspberries; to each pint of liquor allow 1 lb. of pounded loaf sugar, 1 wineglassful of brandy.

Mode.—Let the raspberries be freshly gathered; pick them from the stalks, and put 1½ pint of them into a stone jar; pour 3 pints of the best vinegar over them, and let them remain for 24 hours; then strain the liquor over another 1½ pint of fresh raspberries. Let them remain another 24 hours, and the following day repeat the process for the third time; then drain off the liquor without pressing, and pass it through a jelly-bag (previously wetted with plain vinegar), into a stone jar. Add to every pint of the liquor 1 lb. of pounded loaf sugar; stir them together, and, when the sugar is dissolved, cover the jar; set it upon the fire in a saucepan of boiling water, and let it boil for an hour, removing the scum as fast as it rises; add to each pint a glass of brandy, bottle it, and seal the corks. This is an excellent drink in cases of fevers and colds: it should be diluted with cold water, according to the taste or requirement of the patient.

Time.—To be boiled 1 hour. *Average cost,* 1s. per pint.

Sufficient to make 2 quarts.

Seasonable.—Make this in July or August, when raspberries are most plentiful.

Claret-Cup*

INGREDIENTS.—1 bottle of claret, 1 bottle of soda-water, about ½ lb. of pounded ice, 4 tablespoonfuls of powdered sugar, ¼ teaspoonful of grated nutmeg, 1 liqueur-glass of Maraschino, a sprig of green borage.

Mode.—Put all the ingredients into a silver cup, regulating the proportion of ice by the state of the weather: if very warm, a larger quantity would be necessary. Hand the cup round with a clean napkin passed through one of the handles, that the edge of the cup may be wiped after each guest has partaken of the contents thereof.

Claret-Cup

Seasonable in summer.

Ginger Beer

INGREDIENTS.—2½ lbs. of loaf sugar, 1½ oz. of bruised ginger, 1 oz. of cream of tartar, the rind and juice of 2 lemons, 3 gallons of boiling water, 2 large tablespoonfuls of thick and fresh brewer's yeast.

Mode.—Peel the lemons, squeeze the juice, strain it, and put the peel and juice into a large earthen pan, with the bruised ginger, cream of tartar, and loaf sugar. Pour over these ingredients 3 gallons of *boiling* water; let it stand until just warm, when add the yeast, which should be thick and perfectly fresh. Stir the contents of the pan well, and let them remain near the fire all night, covering the pan over with a cloth. The next day skim off the yeast, and pour the liquor carefully into another vessel, leaving the sediment; then bottle immediately, and tie the corks down, and in 3 days the ginger beer will be fit for use. For some tastes, the above proportion of sugar may be found rather too large, when it may be diminished; but the beer will not keep so long good.

Average cost for this quantity, 2s.; or ½d. per bottle.

Sufficient to fill 4 dozen ginger-beer bottles.

Seasonable.—This should be made during the summer months.

To Make Hot Punch*

INGREDIENTS.—½ pint of rum, ½ pint of brandy, ¼ lb. of sugar, 1 large lemon, ½ teaspoonful of nutmeg, 1 pint of boiling water.

Mode.—Rub the sugar over the lemon until it has absorbed all the yellow part of the skin, then put the sugar into a punchbowl; add the

lemon-juice (free from pips), and mix these two ingredients well together. Pour over them the boiling water, stir well together, add the rum, brandy, and nutmeg; mix thoroughly, and the punch

Punch-Bowl and Ladle

will be ready to serve. It is very important in making good punch that all the ingredients are thoroughly incorporated; and, to insure success, the processes of mixing must be diligently attended to.

Sufficient.—Allow a quart for 4 persons; but this information must be taken *cum grano salis*; for the capacities of persons for this kind of beverage are generally supposed to vary considerably.

PUNCH is a beverage made of various spirituous liquors or wine, hot water, the acid juice of fruits, and sugar. It is considered to be very intoxicating; but this is probably because the spirit, being partly sheathed by the mucilaginous juice and the sugar, its strength does not appear to the taste so great as it really is. Punch, which was almost universally drunk among the middle classes about fifty or sixty years ago, has almost disappeared from our domestic tables, being superseded by wine. There are many different varieties of punch. It is sometimes kept cold in bottles, and makes a most agreeable summer drink. In Scotland, instead of the Madeira or sherry generally used in its manufacture, whiskey is substituted, and then its insidious properties are more than usually felt. Where fresh lemons cannot be had for punch or similar beverages, crystallized citric acid and a few drops of the essence of lemon will be very nearly the same thing. In the composition of 'Regent's punch,' champagne, brandy, and *veritable Martinique* are required; 'Norfolk punch' requires Seville oranges; 'Milk punch' may be extemporized by adding a little hot milk to lemonade, and then straining it through a jelly-bag. Then there are 'Wine punch,' 'Tea punch,' and 'French punch,' made with lemons, spirits, and wine, in fantastic proportions. But of all the compounds of these materials, perhaps, for a *summer* drink, the North-American 'mint julep' is the most inviting. Captain Marryat gives the following recipe for its preparation:—'Put into a tumbler about a dozen sprigs of the tender shoots of mint; upon them put a spoonful of white sugar, and equal proportions of peach and common brandy, so as to fill up one third, or, perhaps, a little less; then take rasped or pounded ice, and fill up the tumbler. Epicures rub the lips of the tumbler with a piece of fresh pine-apple; and the tumbler itself is very often encrusted outside with stalactites of ice. As the ice melts, you drink.' The Virginians, says Captain Marryat, claim the merit of having invented this superb compound; but, from a passage in the 'Comus' of Milton, he claims it for his own country.

CHAPTER XXXVIII

INVALID COOKERY

A FEW RULES TO BE OBSERVED IN COOKING FOR INVALIDS

Let all the kitchen utensils used in the preparation of invalids' cookery be delicately and *scrupulously clean*, if this is not the case, a disagreeable flavour may be imparted to the preparation, which flavour may disgust, and prevent the patient from partaking of the refreshment when brought to him or her.

For invalids, never make a large quantity *of one thing*, as they seldom require much at a time; and it is desirable that variety be provided for them.

Always have something in readiness; a little beef tea, nicely made and nicely skimmed, a few spoonfuls of jelly, &c. &c., that it may be administered as soon almost as the invalid wishes for it. If obliged to wait a long time, the patient loses the desire to eat, and often turns against the food when brought to him or her.

In sending dishes or preparations up to invalids, let everything look as tempting as possible. Have a clean tray-cloth laid smoothly over the tray; let the spoons, tumblers, cups and saucers, &c., be very clean and bright. Gruel served in a tumbler is more appetizing than when served in a basin or cup and saucer.

As milk is an important article of food for the sick, in warm weather let it be kept on ice, to prevent its turning sour. Many other delicacies may also be preserved good in the same manner for some little time.

If the patient be allowed to eat vegetables, never send them up undercooked, or half raw; and let a small quantity only be temptingly arranged on a dish. This rule will apply to every preparation, as an invalid is much more likely to enjoy his food if small delicate pieces are served to him.

Never leave food about a sick room; if the patient cannot eat it when brought to him, take it away, and bring it to him in an hour or two's time. Miss Nightingale says, 'To leave the patient's untasted food by his side, from meal to meal, in hopes that he will eat it in the interval, is simply to prevent him from taking any food at all.' She says, 'I have known patients literally incapacitated from taking one article of food after another by this piece of ignorance. Let the food come at the right time, and be taken away, eaten or uneaten, at the right time, but never let a patient have "something always standing" by him, if you don't wish to disgust him of everything.'

Never serve beef tea or broth with the *smallest particle* of fat or grease on the surface. It is better, after making either of these, to allow them to get perfectly cold, when *all the fat* may be easily removed; then warm up as much as may be required. Two or three pieces of clean whity-brown paper laid on the broth will absorb any greasy particles that may be floating at the top, as the grease will cling to the paper.

Roast mutton, chickens, rabbits, calves' feet or head, game, fish (simply dressed), and simple-puddings, are all light food, and easily digested. Of course, these things are only partaken of, supposing the patient is recovering.

A mutton chop, nicely cut, trimmed, and broiled to a turn, is a dish to be recommended for invalids; but it must not be served *with all the fat* at the end, nor must it be too thickly cut. Let it be cooked over a fire free from smoke, and sent up with the gravy in it, between two very hot plates. Nothing is more disagreeable to an invalid than *smoked* food.

In making toast-and-water, never blacken the bread, but toast it only a nice brown. Never leave toast-and-water to make until the moment it is required, as it cannot then be properly prepared,—at least, the patient will be obliged to drink it warm, which is anything but agreeable.

In boiling eggs for invalids, let the white be just set; if boiled hard, they will be likely to disagree with the patient.

In Miss Nightingale's admirable 'Notes on Nursing,' a book that no mother or nurse should be without, she says,—'You cannot be too careful as to quality in sick diet. A nurse should never put before a patient milk that is sour, meat or soup that is turned, an egg that is bad, or vegetables underdone.' Yet often, she says, she has seen these things brought in to the sick, in a state perfectly perceptible to every nose or eye except the nurse's. It is here that the clever nurse appears,—she will not bring in the peccant article; but, not to disappoint the patient, she will whip up something else in a few minutes. Remember, that sick cookery should half do the work of your poor patient's weak digestion.

She goes on to caution nurses, by saying,—'Take care not to spill into your patient's saucer; in other words, take care that the outside bottom rim of his cup shall be quite dry and clean. If, every time he lifts his cup to his lips, he has to carry the saucer with it, or else to drop the liquid upon and to soil his sheet, or bedgown, or pillow, or, if he is sitting up, his dress, you have no idea what a difference this minute want of care on your part makes to his comfort, and even to his willingness for food.'

CHAPTER XXXIX

RECIPES*

To Make Barley-Water

INGREDIENTS.—2 oz. of pearl barley, 2 quarts of boiling water, 1 pint of cold water.

Mode.—Wash the barley in cold water; put it into a saucepan with the above proportion of cold water, and when it has boiled for about ¼ hour, strain off the water, and add the 2 quarts of fresh boiling water. Boil it until the liquid is reduced one half; strain it, and it will be ready for use. It may be flavoured with lemon-peel, after being sweetened, or a small piece may be simmered with the barley. When the invalid may take it, a little lemon-juice gives this pleasant drink in illness a very nice flavour.

Time.—To boil until the liquid is reduced one half.

Sufficient to make 1 quart of barley-water.

To Make Beef Tea

INGREDIENTS.—1 lb. of lean gravy-beef, 1 quart of water, 1 salt-spoonful of salt.

Mode.—Have the meat cut without fat and bone, and choose a nice fleshy piece. Cut it into small pieces about the size of dice, and put it into a clean saucepan. Add the water *cold* to it; put it on the fire, and bring it to the boiling-point; then skim well. Put in the salt when the water boils, and *simmer* the beef tea *gently* from ½ to ¾ hour, removing any more scum should it appear on the surface. Strain the tea through a hair sieve, and set it by in a cool place. When wanted for use, remove every particle of fat from the top; warm up as much as may be required, adding, if necessary, a little more salt. This preparation is simple beef tea, and is to be administered to those invalids to whom flavourings and seasonings are not allowed. When the patient is very low, use double the quantity of meat to the same proportion of water. Beef tea is always better when made the day before it is wanted, and then warmed up. It is a good plan to put the tea into a small cup or basin, and to place this basin in a saucepan of boiling water. When the tea is warm, it is ready to serve.

Time.—½ to ¾ hour.   *Average cost,* 6*d.* per pint.

Sufficient.—Allow 1 lb. of meat for a pint of good beef tea.

Miss Nightingale says, one of the most common errors among nurses, with respect to sick diet, is the belief that beef tea is the most nutritive of all articles. She says, 'Just try and boil down a lb. of beef into beef tea; evaporate your beef tea, and see what is left of your beef; you will find that there is barely a teaspoonful of solid nourishment to ½ pint of water in beef tea. Nevertheless, there is a certain reparative quality in it,—we do not know what,—as there is in tea; but it may be safely given in almost any inflammatory disease, and is as little to be depended upon with the healthy or convalescent, where much nourishment is required.'

Dr Christison says that 'every one will be struck with the readiness with which certain classes of patient will often take diluted meat juice, or beef tea repeatedly, when they refuse all other kinds of food.' This is particularly remarkable in cases of gastric fever, in which, he says, little or nothing else besides beef tea, or diluted meat juice, has been taken for weeks, or even months; and yet a pint of beef tea contains scarcely ¼ oz. of anything but water. The result is so striking, that he asks, 'What is its mode of action? Not simple nutriment; ¼ oz. of the most nutritive material cannot nearly replace the daily wear and tear of the tissue in any circumstances.' Possibly, he says, it belongs to a new denomination of remedies.

To Make Gruel*

Ingredients.—1 tablespoonful of Robinson's patent groats, 2 tablespoonfuls of cold water, 1 pint of boiling water.

Mode.—Mix the prepared groats smoothly with the cold water in a basin; pour over them the boiling water, stirring it all the time. Put it into a very clean saucepan; boil the gruel for 10 minutes, keeping it well stirred; sweeten to taste, and serve. It may be flavoured with a small piece of lemon-peel, by boiling it in the gruel, or a little grated nutmeg may be put in; but in these matters the taste of the patient should be consulted. Pour the gruel in a tumbler and serve. When wine is allowed to the invalid, 2 tablespoonfuls of sherry or port make this preparation very nice. In cases of colds, the same quantity of spirits is sometimes added instead of wine.

Time.—10 minutes.

Sufficient to make a pint of gruel.

To Make Mutton Broth

INGREDIENTS.—1 lb. of the scrag end of the neck of mutton, 1 onion, a bunch of sweet herbs, ½ turnip, 3 pints of water, pepper and salt to taste.

Mode.—Put the mutton into a stewpan; pour over the water cold, and add the other ingredients. When it boils, skim it very carefully, cover the pan closely, and let it simmer very gently for an hour; strain it, let it cool, take off all the fat from the surface, and warm up as much as may be required, adding, if the patient be allowed to take it, a teaspoonful of minced parsley which has been previously scalded. Pearl barley or rice are very nice additions to mutton broth, and should be boiled as long as the other ingredients. When either of these is added, the broth must not be strained, but merely thoroughly skimmed. Plain mutton broth without seasoning is made by merely boiling the mutton, water, and salt together, straining it, letting the broth cool, skimming all the fat off, and warming up as much as is required. This preparation would be very tasteless and insipid, but likely to agree with very delicate stomachs, whereas the least addition of other ingredients would have the contrary effect.

Time.—1 hour. *Average cost,* 7*d.*

Sufficient to make from 1½ to 2 pints of broth.

Seasonable at any time.

Note.—Veal broth may be made in the same manner; the knuckle of a leg or shoulder is the part usually used for this purpose. It is very good with the addition of the inferior joints of a fowl, or a few shank-bones.

To Make Toast-and-Water*

INGREDIENTS.—A slice of bread, 1 quart of boiling water.

Mode.—Cut a slice from a stale loaf (a piece of hard crust is better than anything else for the purpose), toast it of a nice brown on every side, but *do not allow it to burn or blacken*. Put it into a jug, pour the boiling water over it, cover it closely, and let it remain until cold. When strained, it will be ready for use. Toast-and-water should always be made a short time before it is required, to enable it to get cold: if drunk in a tepid or lukewarm state, it is an exceedingly disagreeable beverage. If, as is sometimes the case, this drink is wanted in a hurry, put the toasted bread into a jug, and only just cover it with the boiling water; when this is cool, cold water may be added in the proportion required,—the toast-and-water strained; it will then be ready for use, and is more expeditiously prepared than by the above method.

Toast Sandwiches*

INGREDIENTS.—Thin cold toast, thin slices of bread-and-butter, pepper and salt to taste.

Mode.—Place a very thin piece of cold toast between 2 slices of thin bread-and-butter in the form of a sandwich, adding a seasoning of pepper and salt. This sandwich may be varied by adding a little pulled meat, or very fine slices of cold meat, to the toast, and in any of these forms will be found very tempting to the appetite of an invalid.

Besides the recipes contained in this chapter, there are, in the previous chapters on cookery, many others suitable for invalids, which it would be useless to repeat here. Recipes, fish simply dressed, light soups, plain roast meat, well-dressed vegetables, poultry, simple puddings, jelly, stewed fruits, &c. &c., all of which dishes may be partaken of by invalids and convalescents, will be found in preceding chapters.

CHAPTER XL

DINNERS AND DINING

Man, it has been said, is a dining animal. Creatures of the inferior races eat and drink; man only dines. It has also been said that he is a cooking animal; but some races eat food without cooking it. A Croat captain said to M. Brillat Savarin,* 'When, in campaign, we feel hungry, we knock over the first animal we find, cut off a steak, powder it with salt, put it under the saddle, gallop over it for half a mile, and then eat it.' Huntsmen in Dauphiny, when out shooting, have been known to kill a bird, pluck it, salt and pepper it, and cook it by carrying it some time in their caps. It is equally true that some races of men do not dine any more than the tiger or the vulture. It is not a *dinner* at which sits the aboriginal Australian, who gnaws his bone half bare and then flings it behind to his squaw. And the native of Terra-del-Fuego does not dine when he gets his morsel of red clay. Dining is the privilege of civilization. The rank which a people occupy in the grand scale may be measured by their way of taking their meals, as well as by their way of treating their women. The nation which knows how to dine has learnt the leading lesson of progress. It implies both the will and the skill to reduce to order, and surround with idealisms and graces, the more material conditions of human existence; and wherever that will and that skill exist, life cannot be wholly ignoble.

Dinner, being the grand solid meal of the day, is a matter of considerable importance; and a well-served table is a striking index of human ingenuity and resource. 'Their table', says Lord Byron, in describing a dinner-party given by Lord and Lady Amundeville at Norman Abbey,—

> 'Their table was a board to tempt even ghosts
> To pass the Styx for more substantial feasts.
> I will not dwell upon ragoûts or roasts,
> Albeit all human history attests
> That happiness for man—the hungry sinner!—
> Since Eve ate apples, much depends on dinner.'*

And then he goes on to observe upon the curious complexity of the results produced by human cleverness and application catering for

the modifications which occur in civilized life, one of the simplest of
the primal instincts:—

> 'The mind is lost in mighty contemplation
>   Of intellect expended on two courses;
> And indigestion's grand multiplication
>   Requires arithmetic beyond my forces.
> Who would suppose, from Adam's simple ration,
>   That cookery could have call'd forth such resources,
> As form a science and a nomenclature
> From out the commonest demands of nature?'*

And we may well say, Who, indeed, would suppose it? The gulf
between the Croat, with a steak under his saddle, and Alexis Soyer
getting up a great dinner at the Reform Club, or even Thackeray's
Mrs Raymond Gray giving 'a little dinner' to Mr Snob (with one of
those famous 'roly-poly puddings' of hers),*—what a gulf it is!

That Adam's 'ration,' however, was 'simple,' is a matter on which
we have contrary judgments given by the poets. When Raphael paid
that memorable visit to Paradise,—which we are expressly told by
Milton he did exactly at dinner-time,—Eve seems to have prepared
'a little dinner' not wholly destitute of complexity, and to have added
ice-creams and perfumes. Nothing can be clearer than the testimony
of the poet on these points:—

> 'And Eve within, due at her home prepared
> For dinner savoury fruits, of taste to please
> True appetite, and not disrelish thirst
> Of nectarous draughts between . . .
> . . . With dispatchful looks in haste
> She turns, on hospitable thoughts intent,
> What choice to choose for delicacy best,
> What order so contrived as not to mix
> Tastes not well join'd, inelegant, but bring
> Taste after taste, upheld with kindliest change—
>
> .   .   .   .   .   .
>
> She *tempers dulcet creams* . . .
>   . . . *then strews the ground*
> *With rose and odours*.'*

It may be observed, in passing, that the poets, though they have more
to say about wine than solid food, because the former more directly
stimulates the intellect and the feelings, do not flinch from the subject of eating and drinking. There is infinite zest in the above passage

from Milton, and even more in the famous description of a dainty supper, given by Keats in his 'Eve of Saint Agnes.' Could Queen Mab herself desire to sit down to anything nicer, both as to its appointments and serving, and as to its quality, than the collation served by Porphyro in the lady's bedroom while she slept?—

> 'There by the bedside, where the faded moon
> Made a dim silver twilight, soft he set
> A table, and, half-anguish'd, threw thereon
> A cloth of woven crimson, gold, and jet.
>
> .   .   .   .   .
>
> While he, from forth the closet, brought a heap
> Of candied apple, quince, and plum, and gourd;
> With jellies smoother than the creamy curd,
> And lucent syrups tinct with cinnamon;
> Manna and dates, in argosy transferr'd
> From Fez; and spicèd dainties, every one,
> From silken Samarcand to cedar'd Lebanon.'*

But Tennyson has ventured beyond dates, and quinces, and syrups, which may be thought easy to be brought in by a poet. In his idyl of 'Audley Court' he gives a most appetizing description of a pasty at a pic-nic:—

> 'There, on a slope of orchard, Francis laid
> A damask napkin wrought with horse and hound;
> Brought out a dusky loaf that smelt of home,
> And, half cut down, a pasty costly made,
> Where quail and pigeon, lark and leveret, lay
> Like fossils of the rock, with golden yolks
> Imbedded and injellied.'*

We gladly quote passages like these, to show how eating and drinking may be surrounded with poetical associations, and how man, using his privilege to turn any and every repast into a 'feast of reason,' with a warm and plentiful 'flow of soul,'* may really count it as not the least of his legitimate prides, that he is 'a dining animal.'

It has been said, indeed, that great men, in general, are great diners. This, however, can scarcely be true of any great men but men of action; and, in that case, it would simply imply that persons of vigorous constitution, who work hard, eat heartily; for, of course, a life of action *requires* a vigorous constitution; even though there may be much illness, as in such cases as William III and our brave General Napier.* Of men of thought, it can scarcely be true that they eat so much, in a general way, though even they eat more than they are apt to suppose they do; for, as Mr Lewes observes, 'nerve-tissue is very expensive.' Leaving great men of all kinds, however, to get their own dinners, let us, who are not great, look after ours. Dine we must, and we may as well dine elegantly as well as wholesomely.

There are plenty of elegant dinners in modern days, and they were not wanting in ancient times. It is well known that the dinner-party, or symposium, was a not unimportant, and not unpoetical, feature in the life of the sociable, talkative, tasteful Greek. Douglas Jerrold* said that such is the British humour for dining and giving of dinners, that if London were to be destroyed by an earthquake, the Londoners would meet at a public dinner to consider the subject. The Greeks, too, were great diners: their social and religious polity gave them many chances of being merry and making others merry on good eating and drinking. Any public or even domestic sacrifice to one of the gods, was sure to be followed by a dinner-party, the remains of the slaughtered 'offering' being served up on the occasion as a pious *pièce de résistance*; and as the different gods, goddesses, and demigods, worshipped by the community in general, or by individuals, were very numerous indeed, and some very religious people never let a day pass without offering up something or other, the dinner-parties were countless. A birthday, too, was an excuse for a dinner; a birthday, that is, of any person long dead and buried, as well as of a living person, being a member of the family, or otherwise esteemed. Dinners were, of course, eaten on all occasions of public rejoicing. Then, among the young people, subscription dinners, very much after the manner of modern times, were always being got up; only that they would be eaten not at an hotel, but probably at the house of one of the *heterae**. A Greek dinner-party was a handsome, well-regulated affair. The guests came in elegantly dressed and crowned with flowers. A slave, approaching each person as he entered, took off his sandals and washed his feet. During the repast, the guests reclined on couches with pillows, among and along which were set small tables. After the solid meal came the 'symposium' proper, a scene of music, merriment, and dancing, the two latter being supplied chiefly by young girls. There was a chairman, or symposiarch, appointed by the company to regulate the drinking; and it was his duty to mix the wine in the 'mighty bowl.' From this bowl the attendants ladled the liquor into goblets, and, with the goblets, went round and round the tables, filling the cups of the guests.

The elegance with which a dinner is served is a matter which depends, of course, partly upon the means, but still more upon the taste of the master and mistress of the house. It may be observed, in general, that there should always be flowers on the table, and as they form no item of expense, there is no reason why they should not be employed every day.

The variety in the dishes which furnish forth a modern dinner-table, does not necessarily imply anything unwholesome, or anything capricious. Food that is not well relished cannot be well digested; and the appetite of the over-worked man of business, or statesman, or of any dweller in towns, whose occupations are exciting and exhausting, is jaded, and requires stimulation. Men and women who are in rude health, and who have plenty of air and exercise, eat the simplest food with relish, and consequently digest it well; but those conditions are out of the reach of many men. They must suit their mode of dining to their mode of living, if they cannot choose the latter. It is in serving up food that is at once appetizing and wholesome that the skill of the modern housewife is severely tasked; and she has scarcely a more important duty to fulfil. It is, in fact, her particular vocation, in virtue of which she may be said to hold the health of the family, and of the friends of the family, in her hands from day to day. It has been said that 'the destiny of nations depends on the manner in which they are fed;' and a great gastronomist exclaims, 'Tell me what kind of food you eat, and I will tell you what kind of man you are.' The same writer has some sentences of the same kind, which are rather hyperbolical, but worth quoting:—'The pleasures of the table belong to all ages, to all conditions, to all countries, and to all eras; they mingle with all other pleasures, and remain, at last, to console us for their departure. The discovery of a new dish confers more happiness upon humanity than the discovery of a new star.'

The gastronomist from whom we have already quoted, has some aphorisms and short directions in relation to dinner-parties, which are well deserving of notice:—'Let the number of your guests never exceed twelve, so that the conversation may be general.[1] Let the

---

[1] We have seen this varied by saying that the number should never exceed that of the Muses or fall below that of the Graces.

temperature of the dining-room be about 68°. Let the dishes be few in number in the first course, but proportionally good. The order of food is from the most substantial to the lightest. The order of drinking wine is from the mildest to the most foamy and most perfumed. To invite a person to your house is to take charge of his happiness so long as he is beneath your roof. The mistress of the house should always be certain that the coffee be excellent; whilst the master should be answerable for the quality of his wines and liqueurs.'*

BILLS OF FARE*

JANUARY

Dinner for 18 Persons

First Course

Mock Turtle Soup,
removed by
Cod's Head and Shoulders

Stewed Eels

Vase of
Flowers

Red Mullet

Clear Oxtail Soup,
removed by
Fried Filleted Soles

Entrées

Riz de Veau aux
Tomates

Ragoût of
Lobster

Vase of
Flowers

Cotelettes de Porc
à la Robert

Poulet à la Marengo

Second Course

Roast Turkey

Pigeon Pie

Boiled Turkey and
Celery Sauce

Vase of
Flowers

Boiled Ham

Tongue, garnished

Saddle of Mutton

Third Course

Pheasants,
removed by
Plum-pudding

Charlotte
à la Parisienne

Jelly

Apricot-Jam
Tartlets

Cream

Vase of
Flowers

Cream

Jelly

Mince
Pies

Maids
of Honour

Snipes,
removed by
Pommes à la Condé

We have given above the plan of placing the various dishes of the 1st Course, Entrées, 2nd Course, and 3rd Course. Following this will be found bills of fare for smaller parties; and it will be readily seen, by studying the above arrangement of dishes, how to place a less number for the more limited company. Several *menus* for dinners *à la Russe*, are also included in the present chapter.*

Dinner for 6 Persons (January)

First Course

Julienne Soup

Soles à la Normandie

Entrées

Sweetbreads, with Sauce Piquante

Mutton Cutlets, with Mashed Potatoes

Second Course

Haunch of Venison

Boiled-Fowls and Bacon, garnished with Brussels Sprouts

Third Course

Plum-pudding   Custards in Glasses   Apple Tart

Fondue à la Brillat Savarin

Dessert

Plain Family Dinners for January*

Sunday.—1. Boiled turbot and oyster sauce, potatoes. 2. Roast leg or griskin of pork, apple sauce, brocoli, potatoes. 3. Cabinet pudding, and damson tart made with preserved damsons.

Monday.—1. The remains of turbot warmed in oyster sauce, potatoes. 2. Cold pork, stewed steak. 3. Open jam tart, which should have been made with the pieces of paste left from the damson tart; baked arrowroot pudding.

Tuesday.—1. Boiled neck of mutton, carrots, mashed turnips, suet dumplings, and caper sauce: the broth should be served first, and a little rice or pearl barley should be boiled with it along with the meat. 2. Rolled jam pudding.

Wednesday.—1. Roast rolled ribs of beef, greens, potatoes, and horseradish sauce. 2. Bread-and-butter pudding, cheesecakes.

Thursday.—1. Vegetable soup (the bones from the ribs of beef should be boiled down with this soup), cold beef, mashed potatoes. 2. Pheasants, gravy, bread sauce. 3. Macaroni.

Friday.—1. Fried whitings or soles. 2. Boiled rabbit and onion sauce, minced beef, potatoes. 3. Currant dumplings.

Saturday.—1. Rump-steak pudding or pie, greens, and potatoes. 2. Baked custard pudding and stewed apples.

FEBRUARY

Dinner for 12 Persons

First Course

Soup à la Reine   Clear Gravy Soup
Brill and Lobster Sauce   Fried Smelts

Entrées

Lobster Rissoles   Beef Palates   Pork Cutlets à la Soubise
Grilled Mushrooms

Second Course

Braised Turkey   Haunch of Mutton   Boiled Capon and Oysters
Tongue, garnished with tufts of Brocoli   Vegetables and Salads

Third Course

Wild Ducks   Plovers
Orange Jelly   Clear Jelly   Charlotte Russe   Nesselrode Pudding
Gâteau de Riz   Sea-kale   Maids of Honour

Dessert and Ices

Dinner for 6 Persons (February)

First Course

Spring Soup
Boiled Turbot and Lobster Sauce

Entrees

Fricasseed Rabbit   Oyster Patties

Second Course

Boiled Round of Beef and Marrow-bones
Roast Fowls, garnished with Water-cresses and rolled Bacon
Vegetables

Third Course

Marrow Pudding   Cheesecakes   Tartlets of Greengage Jam
Lemon Cream   Rhubarb Tart

Dessert

MARCH

Dinner for 10 Persons

First Course

Macaroni Soup
Boiled Turbot and Lobster Sauce   Salmon Cutlets

Entrées

Compôte of Pigeons   Mutton Cutlets and Tomato Sauce

Second Course

Roast Lamb   Boiled Half Calf's Head, Tongue, and Brains
Boiled Bacon-cheek, garnished with spoonfuls of Spinach
Vegetables

Third Course

Ducklings
Plum-pudding   Ginger Cream   Trifle   Rhubarb Tart
Cheesecakes   Fondues, in cases

Dessert and Ices

Dinner for 6 Persons (March)

First Course

Ox-tail Soup
Boiled Mackerel

Entrées

Stewed Mutton Kidneys   Minced Veal and Oysters

Second Course

Stewed Shoulder of Veal
Roast Ribs of Beef and Horseradish Sauce
Vegetables

Third Course

Ducklings

Tartlets of Strawberry Jam   Cheesecakes   Gâteau de Riz
Carrot Pudding   Sea-kale

Dessert

Plain Family Dinners for March

Sunday.—1. Boiled ½ calf's head, pickled pork, the tongue on a small dish with the brains round it; mutton cutlets and mashed potatoes. 2. Plum tart made with bottled fruit, baked custard pudding, Baroness pudding.

Monday.—1. Roast shoulder of mutton and onion sauce, brocoli, baked potatoes. 2. Slices of Baroness pudding warmed, and served with sugar sprinkled over. Cheesecakes.

Tuesday.—1. Mock turtle soup, made with liquor that calf's head was boiled in, and the pieces of head. 2. Hashed mutton, rump-steaks and oyster sauce. 3. Boiled plum-pudding.

Wednesday.—1. Fried whitings, melted butter, potatoes. 2. Boiled beef, suet dumplings, carrots, potatoes, marrow-bones. 3. Arrowroot blancmange, and stewed rhubarb.

Thursday.—1. Pea-soup made from liquor that beef was boiled in. 2. Stewed rump-steak, cold beef, mashed potatoes. 3. Rolled jam pudding.

Friday.—1. Fried soles, melted butter, potatoes. 2. Roast loin of mutton, brocoli, potatoes, bubble-and-squeak. 3. Rice pudding.

Saturday.—1. Rump-steak pie, haricot mutton made with remains of cold loin. 2. Pancakes, ratafia pudding.

APRIL

Dinner for 12 Persons

First Course

Soup à la Reine   Julienne Soup
Turbot and Lobster Sauce   Slices of Salmon à la Genévése

Entrées

Croquettes of Leveret   Fricandeau de Veau
Vol-au-Vent   Stewed Mushrooms

Second Course

Fore-quarter of Lamb   Saddle of Mutton
Boiled Chickens and Asparagus Peas
Boiled Tongue garnished with Tufts of Brocoli   Vegetables

Third Course

Ducklings   Larded Guinea-Fowls   Charlotte à la Parisienne
Orange Jelly   Meringues
Ratafia Ice Pudding   Lobster Salad   Sea-kale

Dessert and Ices

Dinner for 6 Persons (April)

First Course

Ox-tail Soup
Crimped Salmon

Entrées

Croquettes of Chicken   Mutton Cutlets and Soubise Sauce

Second Course

Roast Fillet of Veal   Boiled Bacon-cheek garnished with Sprouts
Boiled Capon   Vegetables

Third Course

Sea-kale   Lobster Salad   Cabinet Pudding   Ginger Cream
Raspberry Jam Tartlets   Rhubarb Tart   Macaroni

Dessert

MAY

Dinner for 10 Persons

First Course

Spring Soup
Salmon à la Genévése   Red Mullet

Entrées

Chicken Vol-au-Vent   Calf's Liver and Bacon aux Fines Herbes

Second Course

Saddle of Mutton   Half Calf's Head, Tongue, and Brains
Braised Ham   Asparagus

Third Course

Roast Pigeons   Ducklings
Sponge-cake Pudding   Charlotte à la Vanille   Gooseberry Tart
Cream   Cheesecakes   Apricot-jam Tart

Dessert and Ices

Dinner for 6 Persons (May)

First Course

Macaroni Soup
Boiled Mackerel à la Maître d'Hôtel   Fried Smelts

Entrées

Scollops of Fowl   Lobster Pudding

Second Course

Boiled Leg of Lamb and Spinach
Roast Sirloin of Beef and Horseradish Sauce
Vegetables

Third Course

Roast Leveret   Salad   Soufflé of Rice
Ramakins   Strawberry-jam Tartlets
Orange Jelly

Dessert

Plain Family Dinners for May

Sunday.—1. Boiled salmon and lobster or caper sauce. 2. Roast lamb, mint sauce, asparagus, potatoes. 3. Plum-pudding, gooseberry tart.

Monday.—1. Salmon warmed in remains of lobster sauce and garnished with croûtons. 2. Stewed knuckle of veal and rice, cold lamb and dressed cucumber. 3. Slices of pudding warmed, and served with sugar sprinkled over. Baked rice pudding.

Tuesday.—1. Roast ribs of beef, horseradish sauce, Yorkshire pudding, spinach and potatoes. 2. Boiled lemon pudding.

Wednesday.—1. Fried soles, melted butter. 2. Cold beef and dressed cucumber or salad, veal cutlets and bacon. 3. Baked plumpudding.

Thursday.—1. Spring soup. 2. Calf's liver and bacon, broiled beef-bones, spinach and potatoes. 3. Gooseberry tart.

Friday.—1. Roast shoulder of mutton, baked potatoes, onion sauce, spinach. 2. Currant dumplings.

Saturday.—1. Broiled mackerel, fennel sauce or plain melted butter. 2. Rump-steak pie, hashed mutton, vegetables. 2. Baked arrowroot pudding.

JUNE

Dinner for 18 Persons

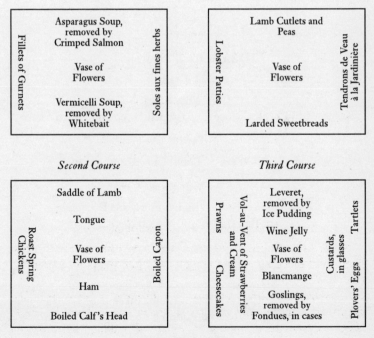

First Course

| Fillets of Gurnets | Asparagus Soup, removed by Crimped Salmon

Vase of Flowers

Vermicelli Soup, removed by Whitebait | Soles aux fines herbs |

Entrées

| Lobster Patties | Lamb Cutlets and Peas

Vase of Flowers

Larded Sweetbreads | Tendrons de Veau à la Jardinière |

Second Course

| Roast Spring Chickens | Saddle of Lamb

Tongue

Vase of Flowers

Ham

Boiled Calf's Head | Boiled Capon |

Third Course

Prawns	Vol-au-Vent of Strawberries and Cream	Leveret, removed by Ice Pudding Wine Jelly Vase of Flowers Blancmange Goslings, removed by Fondues, in cases	Custards, in glasses	Plovers' Eggs	Tartlets
	Cheesecakes				

Desserts and Ices

Dinner for 6 Persons (June)

First Course

Spring Soup
Boiled Salmon and Lobster Sauce

Entrées

Veal Cutlets and Endive   Ragoût of Duck and Green Peas

Second Course

Roast Loin of Veal   Boiled Leg of Lamb and White Sauce
Tongue, garnished   Vegetables

Third Course

Strawberry Cream   Gooseberry Tartlets
Almond Pudding   Lobster Salad

Dessert

JULY

Dinner for 8 Persons

First Course

Green-Pea Soup
Salmon and Lobster Sauce   Crimped Perch and Dutch Sauce

Entrées

Stewed Veal and Peas   Lamb Cutlets and Cucumbers

Second Course

Haunch of Venison   Boiled Fowls à la Béchamel
Braised Ham   Vegetables

Third Course

Peas à la Française   Lobster Salad
Strawberry Cream   Blancmange
Cherry Tart   Cheesecakes
Iced Pudding

Dessert and Ices

Dinner for 6 Persons (July)

First Course

Soup à la Jardinière

Salmon Trout and Parsley-and-Butter

Fillets of Mackerel à la Maître d'Hôtel

Entrées

Lobster Cutlets   Beef Palates à la Italienne

Second Course

Roast Lamb   Boiled Capon and White Sauce

Boiled Tongue, garnished with small Vegetable Marrows

Bacon and Beans

Third Course

Goslings

Whipped Strawberry Cream   Raspberry-and-Currant Tart

Meringues   Cherry Tartlets   Iced Pudding

Dessert and Ices

Plain Family Dinners for July

Sunday.—1. Julienne Soup. 2. Roast lamb, half calf's head, tongue and brains, boiled ham, peas and potatoes. 3. Cherry tart, custards.

Monday.—1. Hashed calf's head, cold lamb and salad. 2. Vegetable marrow and white sauce, instead of pudding.

Tuesday.—1. Stewed veal, with peas, young carrots, and potatoes. Small meat pie. 2. Raspberry-and-currant pudding.

Wednesday.—1. Roast ducks stuffed, gravy, peas, and potatoes; the remains of stewed veal rechauffé. 2. Macaroni served as a sweet pudding.

Thursday.—1. Slices of salmon and caper sauce. 2. Boiled knuckle of veal, parsley-and-butter, vegetable marrow and potatoes. 3. Black-currant pudding.

Friday.—1. Roast shoulder of mutton, onion sauce, peas and potatoes. 2. Cherry tart, baked custard pudding.

Saturday.—1. Minced mutton, rumpsteak-and-kidney pudding. 2. Baked lemon pudding.

AUGUST

Dinner for 12 Persons

First Course

Vermicelli Soup   Soup à la Reine
Boiled Salmon   Fried Flounders   Trout en Matelot

Entrées

Stewed Pigeons   Sweetbreads   Ragoût of Ducks
Fillets of Chickens and Mushrooms

Second Course

Quarter of Lamb   Cotelette de Bœuf à la Jardinière
Roast Fowls and Boiled Tongue   Bacon and Beans

Third Course

Grouse   Wheatears
Greengage Tart   Whipped Cream   Vol-au-Vent of Plums
Fruit Jelly   Iced Pudding   Cabinet Pudding

Dessert and Ices

Dinner for 6 Persons (August)

First Course

Vegetable-Marrow Soup
Stewed Mullet   Fillets of Salmon and Ravigotte Sauce

Entrées

Curried Lobster   Fricandeau de Veau à la Jardinière

Second Course

Roast Saddle of Mutton   Stewed Shoulder of Veal, garnished with
Forcemeat Balls   Vegetables

Third Course

Roast Grouse and Bread Sauce
Vol-au-Vent of Greengages   Fruit Jelly   Raspberry Cream
Custards   Fig Pudding

Dessert

SEPTEMBER

Dinner for 18 Persons

First Course

Red Mullet & Italian Sauce

Julienne Soup,
removed by
Brill and Shrimp Sauce

Vase of
Flowers

Giblet Soup,
removed by
Salmon and Lobster Sauce

Fried Eels

Entrées

Fillets of Chicken
and Truffles

Lamb Cutlets and
French Beans

Vase of
Flowers

Sweetbreads and
Tomata Sauce

Oysters au gratin

Second Course

Chickens à la Béchamel

Saddle of Mutton

Veal-and-Ham Pie

Vase of
Flowers

Broiled Ham, garnished
with Cauliflowers

Fillet of Veal

Braised Goose

Third Course

Custards

Noyeau Jelly

Plum Tart

Partridges,
removed by
Plum-pudding

Compôte of Greengages

Vase of
Flowers

Pastry Sandwiches

Grouse & Bread Sauce,
removed by
Nesselrode Pudding

Lemon Cream

Custards

Apple Tart

Dessert and Ices

Dinner for 6 Persons (September)

First Course

Thick Gravy Soup

Fillets of Turbot à la Crême   Stewed Eels

Entrées

Vol-au-Vent of Lobster   Salmi of Grouse

Second Course

Haunch of Venison   Rump of Beef à la Jardinière

Hare, boned and larded, with Mushrooms

Third Course

Roast Grouse

Apricot Blancmange   Compôte of Peaches   Plum Tart
Custards   Plum-pudding

Dessert

Plain Family Dinners for September

Sunday.—1. Fried filleted soles and anchovy sauce. 2. Roast leg of mutton, brown onion sauce, French beans, and potatoes; half calf's head, tongue, and brains. 3. Plum tart, custards, in glasses.

Monday.—1. Vegetable-marrow soup. 2. Calf's head à la maître d'hôtel, from remains of cold head; boiled brisket of beef and vegetables. 3. Stewed fruit and baked rice pudding.

Tuesday.—1. Roast fowls and water-cresses; boiled bacon, garnished with tufts of cauliflower; hashed mutton, from remains of mutton of Sunday. 2. Baked plum-pudding.

Wednesday.—1. Boiled knuckle of veal and rice, turnips, potatoes; small ham, garnished with French beans. 2. Baked apple pudding.

Thursday.—1. Brill and shrimp sauce. 2. Roast hare, gravy, and red-currant jelly; mutton cutlets and mashed potatoes. 3. Scalloped oysters, instead of pudding.

Friday.—1. Small roast loin of mutton; the remains of hare, jugged; vegetable marrow, and potatoes. 2. Damson pudding.

Saturday.—1. Rump-steaks, broiled, and oyster sauce, mashed potatoes; veal-and-ham pie,—the ham may be cut from that boiled on Wednesday, if not all eaten cold for breakfast. 2. Lemon pudding.

OCTOBER

Dinner for 8 Persons

First Course

Calf's-Head Soup

Crimped Cod and Oyster Sauce   Stewed Eels

Entrées

Stewed Mutton Kidneys   Curried Sweetbreads

Second Course

Boiled Leg of Mutton, garnished with Carrots and Turnips
Roast Goose

Third Course

Partridges

Fruit Jelly   Italian Cream   Vol-au-Vent of Pears   Apple Tart
Cabinet Pudding

Dessert and Ices

Dinner for 6 Persons (October)

First Course

Hare Soup
Broiled Cod à la Maître d'Hôtel   Haddocks and Egg Sauce

Entrées

Veal Cutlets, garnished with French Beans   Haricot Mutton

Second Course

Roast Haunch of Mutton   Boiled Capon and Rice   Vegetables

Third Course

Pheasants

Punch Jelly   Blancmange   Apples à la Portugaise
Charlotte à la Vanille   Marrow Pudding

Dessert

NOVEMBER

Dinner for 8 Persons

First Course

Mulligatawny Soup
Fried slices of Codfish and Oyster Sauce   Eels en Matelote

Entrées

Broiled Pork Cutlets and Tomata Sauce
Tendrons de Veau à la Jardinière

Second Course

Boiled Leg of Mutton and Vegetables   Roast Goose
Cold Game Pie

Third Course

Snipes   Teal

Apple Soufflé   Iced Charlotte   Tartlets   Champagne Jelly

Coffee Cream   Mince Pies

Dessert and Ices

Dinner for 6 Persons (November)

First Course

Oyster Soup

Crimped Cod and Oyster Sauce   Fried Perch and Dutch Sauce

Entrées

Pigs' Feet à la Béchamel   Curried Rabbit

Second Course

Roast Sucking-Pig   Boiled Fowls and Oyster Sauce   Vegetables

Third Course

Jugged Hare

Meringues à la Crême   Apple Custard   Vol-au-Vent of Pears

Whipped Cream   Cabinet Pudding

Dessert

Plain Family Dinners for November

Sunday.—1. Crimped cod and oyster sauce. 2. Roast fowls, small boiled ham, vegetables; rump-steak pie. 3. Baked apple pudding, open jam tart.

Monday.—1. The remainder of cod warmed in maître d'hôtel sauce. 2. Boiled aitchbone of beef, carrots, parsnips, suet dumplings. 3. Baked bread-and-butter pudding.

Tuesday.—1. Pea-soup, made from liquor in which beef was boiled. 2. Cold beef, mashed potatoes; mutton cutlets and tomata sauce. 3. Carrot pudding.

Wednesday.—1. Fried soles and melted butter. 2. Roast leg of pork, apple sauce, vegetables. 3. Macaroni with Parmesan cheese.

Thursday.—1. Bubble-and-squeak from remains of cold beef; curried pork. 2. Baked Semolina pudding.

Friday.—1. Roast leg of mutton, stewed Spanish onions, potatoes. 2. Apple tart.

Saturday.—1. Hashed mutton; boiled rabbit and onion sauce; vegetables. 2. Damson pudding made with bottled fruit.

DECEMBER

Dinner for 10 Persons

First Course

Mulligatawny Soup

Fried Slices of Codfish   Soles à la Crême

Entrées

Croquettes of Fowl   Pork Cutlets and Tomata Sauce

Second Course

Roast Ribs of Beef   Boiled Turkey and Celery Sauce

Tongue, garnished   Lark Pudding   Vegetables

Third Course

Roast Hare   Grouse

Plum-pudding   Mince Pies   Charlotte à la Parisienne

Cheesecakes   Apple Tart   Nesselrode Pudding

Dessert and Ices

Dinner for 6 Persons (December)

First Course

Rabbit Soup

Brill and Shrimp Sauce

Entrées

Curried Fowl   Oyster Patties

Second Course

Roast Turkey and Sausages   Boiled Leg of Pork   Vegetables

Third Course

Hunters' Pudding   Lemon Cheesecakes   Apple Tart

Custards, in glasses   Raspberry Cream

Dessert

Bill of Fare for a Game Dinner for
30 Persons (November)

First Course

Purée of Grouse

Hare Soup

Vase of Flowers

Soup à la Reine

Pheasant Soup

Entrées

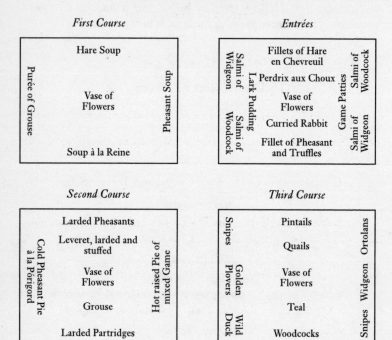

Salmi of Widgeon

Lark Pudding

Salmi of Woodcock

Fillets of Hare en Chevreuil

Perdrix aux Choux

Vase of Flowers

Curried Rabbit

Fillet of Pheasant and Truffles

Salmi of Woodcock

Salmi of Widgeon

Game Patties

Second Course

Cold Pheasant Pie à la Périgord

Larded Pheasants

Leveret, larded and stuffed

Vase of Flowers

Grouse

Larded Partridges

Hot raised Pie of mixed Game

Third Course

Snipes

Golden Plovers

Wild Duck

Pintails

Quails

Vase of Flowers

Teal

Woodcocks

Ortolans

Widgeon

Snipes

Entremets and Removes

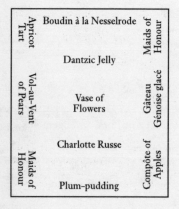

Apricot Tart

Vol-au-Vent of Pears

Maids of Honour

Boudin à la Nesselrode

Dantzic Jelly

Vase of Flowers

Charlotte Russe

Plum-pudding

Maids of Honour

Compôte of Apples

Gâteau Génoise glacé

Dessert

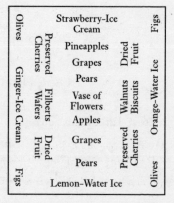

Olives

Preserved Cherries

Ginger-Ice Cream

Wafers

Filberts

Dried Fruit

Figs

Strawberry-Ice Cream

Pineapples

Grapes

Pears

Vase of Flowers

Apples

Grapes

Pears

Lemon-Water Ice

Dried Fruit

Preserved Cherries

Walnuts

Biscuits

Orange-Water Ice

Figs

Olives

MENU

Service à la Russe (July)

———

Julienne Soup   Vermicelli Soup

———

Boiled Salmon   Turbot and Lobster Sauce

Soles-Water Souchy   Perch-Water Souchy

Matelote d'Anguilles à la Toulouse   Filets de Soles à la Normandie

Red Mullet   Trout

Lobster Rissoles   Whitebait

———

Riz de Veau à la Banquière   Filets de Poulets aux Coucombres

Canards à la Rouennaise   Mutton Cutlets à la Jardinière

Braised Beef à la Flamande   Spring Chickens

Roast Quarter of Lamb   Roast Saddle of Mutton

Tongue   Ham and Peas

———

Quails, larded   Roast Ducks   Turkey Poult, larded

Mayonnaise of Chicken   Tomatas   Green Peas à la Française

Suédoise of Strawberries   Charlotte Russe   Compôte of Cherries

Neapolitan Cakes   Pastry   Madeira Wine Jelly

Iced Pudding à la Nesselrode

———

Dessert and Ices

———

Note.—Dinners à la Russe differ from ordinary dinners in the mode of serving the various dishes. In a dinner à la Russe, the dishes are cut up on a sideboard, and handed round to the guests, and each dish may be considered a course. The table for a dinner à la Russe should be laid with flowers and plants in fancy flowerpots down the middle, together with some of the dessert dishes. A *menu* or bill of fare should be laid by the side of each guest.

MENU

Service à la Russe (November)

———

Ox-tail Soup   Soup à la Jardinière

———

Turbot and Lobster Sauce   Crimped Cod and Oyster Sauce

Stewed Eels   Soles à la Normandie

Pike and Cream Sauce   Fried Filleted Soles

———

Filets de Bœuf à la Jardinière

Croquettes of Game aux Champignons

Chicken Cutlets   Mutton Cutlets and Tomata Sauce

Lobster Rissoles   Oyster Patties

Partridges aux fines herbes   Larded Sweetbreads

Roast Beef   Poulets aux Cressons

Haunch of Mutton   Roast Turkey

Boiled Turkey and Celery Sauce   Ham

———

Grouse   Pheasants   Hare

Salad   Artichokes   Stewed Celery

Italian Cream   Charlotte aux Pommes   Compôte of Pears

Croûtes madrées aux Fruits   Pastry   Punch Jelly

Iced Pudding

———

Dessert and Ices

Note.—Dinners à la Russe are scarcely suitable for small establishments; a large number of servants being required to carve, and to help the guests; besides there being a necessity for more plates, dishes, knives, forks, and spoons, than are usually to be found in any other than a very large establishment. Where, however, a service à la Russe is practicable, there is, perhaps, no mode of serving a dinner so enjoyable as this.

SUPPERS

Much may be done in the arrangement of a supper-table, at a very small expense, provided *taste* and *ingenuity* are exercised. The colours and flavours of the various dishes should contrast nicely; there should be plenty of fruit and flowers on the table, and the room should be well lighted. We have endeavoured to show how the various dishes may be placed; but of course these little matters entirely depend on the length and width of the table used, on individual taste, whether the tables are arranged round the room, whether down the centre, with a cross one at the top, or whether the supper is laid in two separate rooms, &c. &c. The garnishing of the dishes has also much to do with the appearance of a supper-table. Hams and tongues should be ornamented with cut vegetable flowers, raised pies with aspic jelly cut in dice, and all the dishes garnished sufficiently to be in good taste without looking absurd. The eye, in fact, should be as much gratified as the palate. Hot soup is now often served at suppers, but is not placed on the table. The servants fill the plates from a tureen on the buffet, and then hand them to the guests: when these plates are removed, the business of supper commences.

Where small rooms and large parties necessitate having a standing supper, many things enumerated in the following bill of fare may be placed on the buffet. Dishes for these suppers should be selected which may be eaten standing without any trouble. The following list may, perhaps, assist our readers in the arrangement of a buffet for a standing supper.

Beef, ham, and tongue sandwiches, lobster and oyster patties, sausage rolls, meat rolls, lobster salad, dishes of fowls, the latter *all cut up*; dishes of sliced ham, sliced tongue, sliced beef, and galantine of veal; various jellies, blancmanges and creams; custards in glasses, compôtes of fruit, tartlets of jam, and several dishes of small fancy pastry; dishes of fresh fruit, bonbons, sweetmeats, two or three sponge cakes, a few plates of biscuits, and the buffet ornamented with vases of fresh or artificial flowers. The above dishes are quite sufficient for a standing supper; where more are desired, a supper must then be laid and arranged in the usual manner.

BILL OF FARE FOR A BALL SUPPER FOR 60 PERSONS (for Winter)

	Left	Centre	Right	
Lobster Salad		**BOAR'S HEAD,** garnished with Aspic Jelly		**Lobster Salad**
	Fruited Jelly	Mayonnaise of Fowl	Charlotte Russe	
	Small Pastry	Small Ham, garnished	Biscuits	
		Iced Savoy Cake		
Two Roast Fowls, cut up	Vanilla Cream	Epergne, with Fruit	Fruited Jelly	**Two Roast Fowls, cut up**
	Prawns	Two Boiled Fowls, with Béchamel Sauce	Prawns	
	Biscuits		Small Pastry	
		Tongue, ornamented		
	Custards, in glasses	Trifle, ornamented	Custards, in glasses	
		Raised Chicken Pie		
Lobster Salad	Fruited Jelly	Tipsy Cake	Swiss Cream	**Lobster Salad**
		Roast Pheasant		
	Meringues	Epergne, with Fruit	Meringues	
	Raspberry Cream	Galantine of Veal	Fruited Jelly	
		Tipsy Cake		
Two Roast Fowls, cut up	Small Pastry	Raised Game Pie	Biscuits	**Two Roast Fowls, cut up**
	Custards, in glasses	Trifle, ornamented	Custards, in glasses	
		Tongue, ornamented		
	Prawns	Two Boiled Fowls, with Béchamel Sauce	Prawns	
	Biscuits		Small Pastry	
		EPERGNE, WITH FRUIT		
Lobster Salad	Fruited Jelly	Iced Savoy Cake	Blancmange	**Lobster Salad**
		Small Ham, garnished		
	Charlotte Russe	Mayonnaise of Fowl	Fruited Jelly	
		Larded Capon		

Note.—When soup is served from the buffet, Mock Turtle and Julienne may be selected. Besides the articles enumerated above, Ices, Wafers, Biscuits, Tea, Coffee, Wines, and Liqueurs will be required. Punch à la Romaine may also be added to the list of beverages.

BILL OF FARE FOR A BALL SUPPER, or a Cold Collation for a Summer Entertainment, or Wedding or Christening Breakfast for 70 or 80 Persons (July)

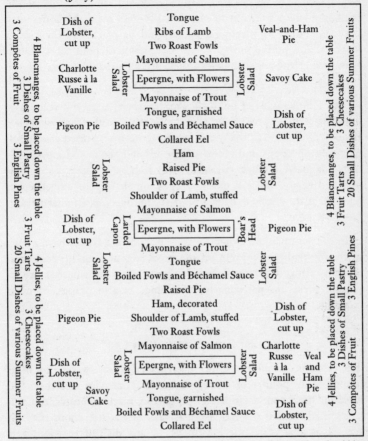

Note.—The length of the page will not admit of our giving the dishes as they should be placed on the table; they should be arranged with the large and high dishes down the centre, and the spaces filled up with the smaller dishes, fruit, and flowers, taking care that the flavours and colours contrast nicely, and that no two dishes of a sort come together. This bill of fare may be made to answer three or four purposes, placing a wedding cake or christening cake in the centre on a high stand, if required for either of these occasions. A few dishes of fowls, lobster salads, &c. &c., should be kept in reserve to replenish those that are most likely to be eaten first. A joint of cold roast and boiled beef should be placed on the buffet, as being something substantial for the gentlemen of the party to partake of. Besides the articles enumerated in the bill of fare, biscuits and wafers will be required, cream-and-water ices, tea, coffee, wines, liqueurs, soda-water, ginger-beer, and lemonade.

BREAKFASTS*

It will not be necessary to give here a long bill of fare of cold joints, &c., which may be placed on the side-board, and do duty at the breakfast-table. Suffice it to say, that any cold meat the larder may furnish, should be nicely garnished, and be placed on the buffet. Collared and potted meats or fish, cold game or poultry, veal-and-ham pies, game-and-rumpsteak pies, are all suitable dishes for the breakfast table; as also cold ham, tongue, &c. &c.

The following list of hot dishes may perhaps assist our readers in knowing what to provide for the comfortable meal called breakfast. Broiled fish, such as mackerel, whiting, herrings, dried haddocks, &c.; mutton chops and rump-steaks, broiled sheep's kidneys, kidneys à la mâtre d'hôtel, sausages, plain rashers of bacon, bacon and poached eggs, ham and poached eggs, omelets, plain boiled eggs, œufs-au-plat, poached eggs on toast, muffins, toast, marmalade, butter, &c. &c.

In the summer, and when they are obtainable, always have a vase of freshly-gathered flowers on the breakfast-table, and, when convenient, a nicely-arranged dish of fruit: when strawberries are in season, these are particularly refreshing; as also grapes, or even currants.

LUNCHEONS AND SUPPERS*

The remains of cold joints, nicely garnished, a few sweets, or a little hashed meat, poultry or game, are the usual articles placed on the table for luncheon, with bread and cheese, biscuits, butter, &c. If a substantial meal is desired, rump-steaks or mutton chops may be served, as also veal cutlets, kidneys, or any dish of that kind. In families where there is a nursery, the mistress of the house often partakes of the meal with the children, and makes it her luncheon. In the summer, a few dishes of fresh fruit should be added to the luncheon, or, instead of this, a compôte of fruit or fruit tart, or pudding.

Of suppers we have little to say, as we have already given two bills of fare for a large party, which will answer very well for a smaller number, by reducing the quantity of dishes and by omitting a few.

Hot suppers are now very little in request, as people now generally dine at an hour which precludes the possibility of requiring supper; at all events, not one of a substantial kind. Should, however, a bill of fare be required, one of those under the head of DINNERS, with slight alterations, will be found to answer for a hot supper.

BILL OF FARE FOR A PICNIC FOR 40 PERSONS

A joint of cold roast beef, a joint of cold boiled beef, 2 ribs of lamb, 2 shoulders of lamb, 4 roast fowls, 2 roast ducks, 1 ham, 1 tongue, 2 veal-and-ham pies, 2 pigeon pies, 6 medium-sized lobsters, 1 piece of collared calf's head, 18 lettuces, 6 baskets of salad, 6 cucumbers.

Stewed fruit well sweetened, and put into glass bottles well corked; 3 or 4 dozen plain pastry biscuits to eat with the stewed fruit, 2 dozen fruit turnovers, 4 dozen cheesecakes, 2 cold cabinet puddings in moulds, 2 blancmanges in moulds, a few jam puffs, 1 large cold plum-pudding (this must be good), a few baskets of fresh fruit, 3 dozen plain biscuits, a piece of cheese, 6 lbs. of butter (this, of course, includes the butter for tea), 4 quartern loaves of household bread, 3 dozen rolls, 6 loaves of tin bread (for tea), 2 plain plum cakes, 2 pound cakes, 2 sponge cakes, a tin of mixed biscuits, ½ lb. of tea. Coffee is not suitable for a picnic, being difficult to make.

Things not to be Forgotten at a Picnic

A stick of horseradish, a bottle of mint-sauce well corked, a bottle of salad dressing, a bottle of vinegar, made mustard, pepper, salt, good oil, and pounded sugar. If it can be managed, take a little ice. It is scarcely necessary to say that plates, tumblers, wine-glasses, knives, forks, and spoons, must not be forgotten; as also teacups and saucers, 3 or 4 teapots, some lump sugar, and milk, if this last-named article cannot be obtained in the neighbourhood. Take 3 corkscrews.

Beverages.—3 dozen quart bottles of ale, packed in hampers; ginger-beer, soda-water, and lemonade, of each 2 dozen bottles; 6 bottles of sherry, 6 bottles of claret, champagne à discrétion, and any other light wine that may be preferred, and 2 bottles of brandy. Water can usually be obtained; so it is useless to take it.

CHAPTER XLI

DOMESTIC SERVANTS*

It is the custom of 'Society' to abuse its servants,—a *façon de parler*,* such as leads their lords and masters to talk of the weather, and, when rurally inclined, of the crops,—leads matronly ladies, and ladies just entering on their probation in that honoured and honourable state, to talk of servants, and, as we are told wax eloquent over the greatest plague in life while taking a quiet cup of tea. Young men at their clubs, also, we are told, like to abuse their 'fellows,' perhaps not without a certain pride and pleasure at the opportunity of intimating that they enjoy such appendages to their state. It is another conviction of 'Society' that the race of good servants has died out, at least in England, although they do order these things better in France; that there is neither honesty, conscientiousness, nor the careful and industrious habits which distinguished the servants of our grandmothers and great-grandmothers; that domestics no longer know their place; that the introduction of cheap silks and cottons, and, still more recently, these ambiguous 'materials' and tweeds, have removed the landmarks between the mistress and her maid, between the master and his man.

When the distinction really depends on things so insignificant, this is very probably the case when the lady of fashion chooses her footman without any other consideration than his height, shape, and *tournure* of his calf, it is not surprising that she should find a domestic who has no attachment for the family, who considers the figure he cuts behind her carriage, and the late hours he is compelled to keep, a full compensation for the wages he exacts, for the food he wastes, and for the perquisites he can lay his hands on. Nor should the fast young man, who chooses his groom for his knowingness in the ways of the turf and in the tricks of low horse-dealers, be surprised if he is sometimes the victim of these learned ways. But these are the exceptional cases, which prove the existence of a better state of things. The great masses of society among us are not thus deserted; there are few families of respectability, from the shopkeeper in the next street to the nobleman whose mansion dignifies the next square, which do not contain among their dependents attached and useful servants; and where these are absent altogether, there are good reasons for it. The sensible master and the kind mistress know, that if servants depend on them for their means of living, in their turn they are dependent on their servants for very many of the comforts of life; and that, with a proper amount of care in choosing servants, and treating them like reasonable beings, and making slight excuses for the shortcomings of human nature, they will, save in some exceptional case, be tolerably well served, and, in most instances, surround themselves with attached domestics.

This remark, which is applicable to all domestics, is especially so to men-servants. Families accustomed to such attendants have always about them humble dependents, whose children have no other prospect than domestic service to look forward to; to them it presents no degradation, but the reverse, to be so employed; they are initiated step by step into the mysteries of the household, with the prospect of rising in the service, if it is a house admitting of promotion,—to the respectable position of butler or house-steward. In families of humbler pretensions, where they must look for promotion elsewhere, they know that can only be attained by acquiring the good-will of their employers. Can there be any stronger security for their good conduct,—any doubt that, in the mass of domestic servants, good conduct is the rule, the reverse the exception?*

The number of the male domestics in a family varies according to the wealth and position of the master, from the owner of the ducal mansion, with a retinue of attendants, at the head of which is the chamberlain and house-steward, to the occupier of the humbler house, where a single footman, or even the odd man-of-all-work, is the only male retainer. The majority of gentlemen's establishments probably comprise a servant out of livery, or butler, a footman, and coachman, or coachman and groom, where the horses exceed two or three.

DUTIES OF THE BUTLER

The domestic duties of the butler are to bring in the eatables at breakfast, and wait upon the family at that meal, assisted by the footman, and see to the cleanliness of everything at table. On taking away, he removes the tray with the china and plate, for which he is responsible. At luncheon, he arranges the meal, and waits unassisted, the footman being now engaged in other duties. At dinner, he places the silver and plated articles on the table, sees that everything is in its place, and rectifies what is wrong. He carries in the first dish, and announces in the drawing-room that dinner is on the table, and respectfully stands by the door until the company are seated, when he takes his place behind his master's chair on the left, to remove the covers, handing them to the other attendants to carry out. After the first course of plates is supplied, his place is at the sideboard to serve the wines, but only when called on.

The first course ended, he rings the cook's bell, and hands the dishes from the table to the other servants to carry away, receiving from them the second course, which he places on the table, removing the covers as before, and again taking his place at the sideboard.

At dessert, the slips* being removed, the butler receives the dessert from the other servants, and arranges it on the table, with plates and glasses, and then takes his place behind his master's chair to hand the wines and ices, while the footman stands behind his mistress for the same purpose, the other attendants leaving the room. Where the old-fashioned practice of having the dessert on the polished table, without any cloth, is still adhered to, the butler should rub off any marks made by the hot dishes before arranging the dessert.

Before dinner, he has satisfied himself that the lamps, candles, or gas-burners are in perfect order, if not lighted, which will usually be the case. Having served every one with their share of the dessert, put the fires in order (when these are used), and seen the lights are all right, at a signal from his master, he and the footman leave the room.

He now proceeds to the drawing-room, arranges the fireplace, and sees to the lights; he then returns to his pantry, prepared to answer the bell, and attend to the company, while the footman is clearing away and cleaning the plate and glasses.

At tea he again attends. At bedtime he appears with the candles; he locks up the plate, secures doors and windows, and sees that all the fires are safe.

In addition to these duties, the butler, where only one footman is kept, will be required to perform some of the duties of the valet, to pay bills, and superintend the other servants. But the real duties of the butler are in the wine-cellar; there he should be competent to advise his master as to the price and quality of the wine to be laid in; 'fine,' bottle, cork, and seal it, and place it in the binns. Brewing, racking, and bottling malt liquors, belong to his office, as well as their distribution. These and other drinkables are brought from the cellar every day by his own hands, except where an under-butler is kept; and a careful entry of every bottle used, entered in the cellar-book; so that the book should always show the contents of the cellar.

The office of butler is thus one of very great trust in a household. Here, as elsewhere, honesty is the best policy: the butler should make it his business to understand the proper treatment of the different wines under his charge, which he can easily do from the wine-merchant, and faithfully attend to it; his own reputation will soon compensate for the absence of bribes from unprincipled wine-merchants, if he serves a generous and hospitable master. Nothing spreads more rapidly in society than the reputation of a good wine-cellar, and all that is required is wines well chosen and well cared for; and this a little knowledge, carefully applied, will soon supply.

The butler, we have said, has charge of the contents of the cellars, and it is his duty to keep them in a proper condition, to fine down wine in wood,* bottle it off, and store it away in places suited to the sorts. Where wine comes into the cellar ready bottled, it is usual to return the same number of empty bottles; the butler has not, in this case, the same inducements to keep the bottles of the different sorts separated; but where the wine is bottled in the house, he will find his account, not only in keeping them separate, but in rinsing them well, and even washing them with clean water as soon as they are empty.

There are various modes of fining wine: isinglass, gelatine, and gum Arabic are all used for the purpose. Whichever of these articles is used, the process is always the same. Supposing eggs (the cheapest) to be used,—Draw a gallon or so of the wine, and mix one quart of it with the whites of four eggs, by stirring it with a whisk; afterwards, when thoroughly mixed, pour it back into the cask through the bunghole, and stir up the whole cask, in a rotatory direction, with a clean split stick inserted through the bunghole. Having stirred it sufficiently, pour in the remainder of the wine drawn off, until the cask is full; then stir again, skimming off the bubbles that rise to the surface. When thoroughly mixed by stirring, close the bunghole, and leave it to stand for three or four days. This quantity of clarified wine will fine thirteen dozen of port or sherry. The other clearing ingredients are applied in the same manner, the material being cut into small pieces, and dissolved in the quart of wine, and the cask stirred in the same manner.

To Bottle Wine.—Having thoroughly washed and dried the bottles, supposing they have been before used for the same kind of wine, provide corks, which will be improved by being slightly boiled, or at least steeped in hot water,—a wooden hammer or mallet, a bottling-boot, and a squeezer for the corks. Bore a hole in the lower part of the cask with a gimlet, receiving the liquid stream which follows in the bottle and filterer, which is placed in a tub or basin. This operation is best performed by two persons, one to draw the wine, the other to cork the bottles. The drawer is to see that the bottles are up to the mark, but not too full, the bottle being placed in a clean tub to prevent waste. The corking-boot is buckled by a strap to the knee, the bottle placed in it, and the cork, after being squeezed in the press, driven in by a flat wooden mallet.

As the wine draws near to the bottom of the cask, a thick piece of muslin is placed in the strainer, to prevent the viscous grounds from passing into the bottle.

Having carefully counted the bottles, they are stored away in their respective binns, a layer of sand or sawdust being placed under the first tier, and another over it; a second tier is laid over this, protected by a lath, the head of the second being laid to the bottom of the first; over this another bed of sawdust is laid, not too thick, another lath; and so on till the binn is filled.

Wine so laid in will be ready for use according to its quality and age. Port wine, old in the wood, will be ready to drink in five or six months; but if it is a fruity wine, it will improve every year. Sherry, if of good quality, will be fit to drink as soon as the 'sickness' (as its first condition after bottling is called) ceases, and will also improve; but the cellar must be kept at a perfectly steady temperature, neither too hot nor too cold, but about 55° or 60°, and absolutely free from draughts of cold air.

DUTIES OF THE FOOTMAN

Where a single footman, or odd man, is the only male servant, then, whatever his ostensible position, he is required to make himself generally useful. He has to clean the knives and shoes, the furniture, the plate; answer the visitors who call, the drawing-room and parlour bells; and do all the errands. His life is no sinecure; and a methodical arrangement of his time will be necessary, in order to perform his many duties with any satisfaction to himself or his master.

The footman only finds himself* in stockings, shoes, and washing. Where silk stockings, or other extra articles of linen are worn, they are found by the family, as well as his livery, a working dress, consisting of a pair of overalls, a waistcoat, a fustian jacket, with a white or jean* one for times when he is liable to be called to answer the door or wait at breakfast; and, on quitting his service, he is expected to leave behind him any livery had within six months.

The footman is expected to rise early, in order to get through all his dirty work before the family are stirring. Boots and shoes, and knives and forks, should be cleaned, lamps in use trimmed, his master's clothes brushed, the furniture rubbed over; so that he may put aside his working dress, tidy himself, and appear in a clean jean jacket to lay the cloth and prepare breakfast for the family.

We need hardly dwell on the boot-cleaning process: three good brushes and good blacking must be provided; one of the brushes hard, to brush off the mud; the other soft, to lay on the blacking; the third of a medium hardness, for polishing; and each should be kept for its particular use. The blacking should be kept corked up, except when in use, and applied to the brush with a sponge tied to a stick, which, when put away, rests in a notch cut in the cork. When boots come in very muddy, it is a good practice to wash off the mud, and wipe them dry with a sponge; then leave them to dry very gradually on their sides, taking care they are not placed near the fire, or scorched. Much delicacy of treatment is required in cleaning ladies' boots, so as to make the leather look well-polished, and the upper part retain a fresh appearance, with the lining free from hand-marks, which are very offensive to a lady of refined tastes.

Patent leather boots require to be wiped with a wet sponge, and afterwards with a soft dry cloth, and occasionally with a soft cloth and sweet oil, blacking and polishing the edge of the soles in the usual way, but so as not to cover the patent polish with blacking. A little milk may also be used with very good effect for patent leather boots.

Top boots* are still occasionally worn by gentlemen. While cleaning the lower part in the usual manner, protect the tops, by inserting a cloth or brown paper under the edges and bringing it over them. In cleaning the tops, let the covering fall down over the boot; wash the tops clean with soap and flannel, and rub out any spots with pumice-stone. If the tops are to be whiter, dissolve an ounce of oxalic acid and half an ounce of pumice-stone in a pint of soft water; if a brown colour is intended, mix an ounce of muriatic acid, half an ounce of alum, half an ounce of gum Arabic, and half an ounce of spirit of lavender, in a pint and a half of skimmed milk 'turned.' These mixtures apply by means of a sponge, and polish, when dry, with a rubber made of soft flannel.

Knives are now generally cleaned by means of Kent's or Masters's machine, which gives very little trouble, and is very effective; before, however, putting the knives into the machine, it is highly necessary that they be first washed in a little warm (not hot) water, and then thoroughly wiped: if put into the machine with any grease on them, it adheres to the brushes, and consequently renders them unfit to use for the next knives that may be put in. When this precaution is not taken the machine must come to pieces, so causing an immense amount of trouble, which may all be avoided by having the knives thoroughly free from grease before using the machine. Brushes are also used for cleaning forks, which facilitate the operation. When knives are so cleaned, see that they are carefully polished, wiped, and with a good edge, the ferules and prongs free from dirt, and place them in the basket with the handles all one way.

Lamp-trimming requires a thorough acquaintance with the mechanism; after that, constant attention to cleanliness, and an occasional entire clearing out with hot water: when this is done, all the parts should be carefully dried before filling again with oil. When lacquered, wipe the lacquered parts with a soft brush and cloth, and wash occasionally with weak soapsuds, wiping carefully afterwards. Brass lamps may be cleaned with oil and rottenstone* every day when trimmed. With bronze, and other ornamental lamps, more care will be required, and soft flannel and oil only used, to prevent the removal of the bronze or enamel. Brass-work, or any metalwork not lacquered, is cleaned by a little oil and rottenstone made into a paste, or with fine emery-powder and oil mixed in the same manner. A small portion of sal ammoniac,* beat into a fine powder and moistened with soft water, rubbed over brass ornaments, and heated over a charcoal fire, and rubbed dry with bran or whitening, will give to brass-work the brilliancy of gold. In trimming moderator lamps, let the wick be cut evenly all round; as, if left higher in one place than it is in another, it will cause it to smoke and burn badly. The lamp should then be filled with oil from a feeder, and afterwards well wiped with a cloth or rag kept for the purpose. If it can be avoided, never wash the chimneys of a lamp, as it causes them to crack when they become hot. Small sticks, covered with wash-leather pads, are the best things to use for cleaning the glasses inside, and a clean duster for polishing the outside. The globe of a moderator lamp should be occasionally washed in warm soap-and-water, then well rinsed in cold water, and either wiped dry or left to drain. Where candle-lamps are used, take out the springs occasionally, and free them well from the grease that adheres to them.

French polish, so universally applied to furniture, is easily kept in condition by dusting and rubbing with a soft cloth, or a rubber of old silk; but dining-tables can only be kept in order by hard rubbing, or rather by quick rubbing, which warms the wood and removes all spots.

Brushing clothes is a very simple but very necessary operation. Fine cloths require to be brushed lightly, and with rather a soft brush, except where mud is to be removed, when a hard one is necessary, being previously beaten lightly to dislodge the dirt. Lay the garment on a table, and brush it in the direction of the nap. Having brushed it properly, turn the sleeves back to the collar, so that the folds may come at the elbow-joints; next turn the lappels or sides back over the folded sleeves; then lay the skirts over level with the collar, so that the crease may fall about the centre, and double one half over the other, so as the fold comes in the centre of the back.

Having got through his dirty work, the single footman has now to clean himself and prepare the breakfast. He lays the cloth on the table; over it the breakfast-cloth, and sets the breakfast things in order, and then proceeds to wait upon his master, if he has any of the duties of a valet to perform.

Where a valet is not kept, a portion of his duties falls to the footman's share,—brushing the clothes among others. When the hat is silk, it requires brushing every day with a soft brush; after rain, it requires wiping the way of the nap before drying, and, when nearly dry, brushing with the soft brush and with the hat-stick in it. If the footman is required to perform any part of a valet's duties, he will have to see that the housemaid lights a fire in the dressing-room in due time; that the room is dusted and cleaned; that the washhand-ewer is filled with soft water; and that the bath, whether hot or cold, is ready when required; that towels are at hand; that hair-brushes and combs are properly cleansed, and in their places; that hot water is ready at the hour ordered; the dressing-gown and slippers in their place, the clean linen aired, and the clothes to be worn for the day in their proper places. After the master has dressed, it will be the footman's duty to restore everything to its place properly cleansed and dry, and the whole restored to order.

At breakfast, when there is no butler, the footman carries up the tea-urn, and, assisted by the housemaid, he waits during breakfast. Breakfast over, he removes the tray and other things off the table, folds up the breakfast-cloth, and sets the room in order, by sweeping up all crumbs, shaking the cloth, and laying it on the table again, making up the fire, and sweeping up the hearth.

At luncheon-time nearly the same routine is observed, except where the footman is either out with the carriage or away on other business, when, in the absence of any butler, the housemaid must assist.

For dinner, the footman lays the cloth, taking care that the table is not too near the fire, if there is one, and that passage-room is left. A table-cloth should be laid without a wrinkle; and this requires two persons: over this the slips are laid, which are usually removed preparatory to placing dessert on the table. He prepares knives, forks, and glasses, with five or six plates for each person. This done, he places chairs enough for the party, distributing them equally on each side of the table, and opposite to each a napkin neatly folded, within it a piece of bread or small roll, and a knife on the right side of each plate, a fork on the left, and a carving-knife and fork at the top and bottom of the table, outside the others, with the rests opposite to them, and a gravy-spoon beside the knife. The fish-slice should be at the top, where the lady of the house, with the assistance of the gentleman next to her, divides the fish, and the soup-ladle at the bottom: it is sometimes usual to add a dessert-knife and fork; at the same time, on the right side also of each plate, put a wine-glass for as many kinds of wine as it is intended to hand round, and a finger-glass or glass-cooler about four inches from the edge. The latter are frequently put on the table with the dessert.

About half an hour before dinner, he rings the dinner-bell, where that is the practice, and occupies himself with carrying up everything he is likely to require. At the expiration of the time, having communicated with the cook, he rings the real dinner-bell, and proceeds to take it up with such assistance as he can obtain. Having ascertained that all is in order, that his own dress is clean and presentable, and his white cotton gloves are without a stain, he announces in the drawing-room that dinner is served, and stands respectfully by the door until the company are seated: he places himself on the left, behind his master, who is to distribute the soup; where soup and fish are served together, his place will be at his mistress's left hand; but he must be on the alert to see that whoever is assisting him, whether male or female, are at their posts. If any of the guests has brought his own servant with him, his place is behind his master's chair, rendering such assistance to others as he can, while attending to his master's wants throughout the dinner, so that every guest has what he requires. This necessitates both activity and intelligence, and should be done without bustle, without asking any questions, except where it is the custom of the house to hand round dishes or wine, when it will be necessary to mention, in a quiet and unobtrusive manner, the dish or wine you present.

Salt-cellars should be placed on the table in number sufficient for the guests, so that each may help themselves, or at least, their immediate neighbours.

Dinners à la Russe

In some houses the table is laid out with plate and glass, and ornamented with flowers, the dessert only being placed on the table, the dinner itself being placed on the sideboard, and handed round in succession, in courses of soup, fish, entrées, meat, game, and sweets. This is not only elegant but economical, as fewer dishes are required, the symmetry of the table being made up with the ornaments and dessert. The various dishes are also handed round when hot; but it involves additional and superior attendance, as the wines are also handed round; and unless the servants are very active and intelligent, many blunders are likely to be made. (*See* p. 385.)

General Observations

While attentive to all, the footman should be obtrusive to none; he should give nothing but on a waiter, and always hand it with the left hand and on the left side of the person he serves, and hold it so that the guest may take it with ease. In lifting dishes from the table, he should use both hands, and remove them with care, so that nothing is spilt on the table-cloth or on the dresses of the guests.

Masters as well as servants sometimes make mistakes; but it is not expected that a servant will correct any omissions, even if he should have time to notice them, although with the best intentions: thus it would not be correct, for instance, if he observed that his master took wine with the ladies all round, as some gentlemen still continue to do, but stopped at some one:—to nudge him on the shoulder and say, as was done by the servant of a Scottish gentleman, 'What ails you at her in the green gown?' It will be better to leave the lady unnoticed than for the servant thus to turn his master into ridicule.

During dinner each person's knife, fork, plate, and spoon should be changed as soon as he has done with it; the vegetables and sauces belonging to the different dishes presented without remark to the guests; and the footman should tread lightly in moving round, and, if possible, should bear in mind, if there is a wit or humorist of the party, whose good things keep the table in a roar, that they are not expected to reach his ears.

In opening wine, let it be done quietly, and without shaking the bottle; if crusted, let it be inclined to the crusted side, and decanted while in that position. In opening champagne, it is not necessary to discharge it with a pop; properly cooled, the cork is easily extracted without an explosion; when the cork is out, the mouth of the bottle should be wiped with the napkin over the footman's arm.

At the end of the first course, notice is conveyed to the cook, who is waiting to send up the second, which is introduced in the same way as before; the attendants who remove the fragments, carrying the dishes from the kitchen, and handing them to the footman or butler, whose duty it is to arrange them on the table. After dinner, the dessert-glasses and wines are placed on the table by the footman, who places himself behind his master's chair, to supply wine and hand round the ices and other refreshments, all other servants leaving the room.

As soon as the drawing-room bell rings for tea, the footman enters with the tray, which has been previously prepared; hands the tray round to the company, with cream and sugar, the tea and coffee being generally poured out, while another attendant hands cakes, toast, or biscuits. If it is an ordinary family party, where this social meal is prepared by the mistress, he carries the urn or kettle, as the case may be; hands round the toast, or such other eatable as may be required, removing the whole in the same manner when tea is over.

After each meal, the footman's place is in his pantry: here perfect order should prevail—a place for everything and everything in its place. A sink,

with hot and cold water laid on, is very desirable,—cold absolutely necessary. Wooden bowls or tubs of sufficient capacity are required, one for hot
and another for cold water. Have the bowl three parts full of clean hot
water; in this wash all plate and plated articles which are greasy, wiping
them before cleaning with the brush.

The footman in small families, where only one man is kept, has many of
the duties of the upper servants to perform as well as his own, and more
constant occupation; he will also have the arrangement of his time more
immediately under his own control, and he will do well to reduce it to a
methodical division. All his rough work should be done before breakfast is
ready, when he must appear clean, and in a presentable state. After breakfast, when everything belonging to his pantry is cleaned and put in its
place, the furniture in the dining- and drawing-rooms requires rubbing.
Towards noon, the parlour luncheon is to be prepared; and he must be at
his mistress's disposal to go out with the carriage, or follow her if she
walks out.*

Glass is a beautiful and most fragile article: hence it requires great care in
washing. A perfectly clean wooden bowl is best for this operation, one for
moderately hot and another for cold water. Wash the glasses well in the
first and rinse them in the second, and turn them down on a linen cloth
folded two or three times, to drain for a few minutes. When sufficiently
drained, wipe them with a cloth and polish with a finer one, doing so
tenderly and carefully. Accidents will happen; but nothing discredits a
servant in the drawing-room more than continual reports of breakages,
which, of course, must reach that region.

Decanters and water-jugs require still more tender treatment in cleaning, inasmuch as they are more costly to replace. Fill them about two-
thirds with hot but not boiling water, and put in a few pieces of
well-soaped brown paper; leave them thus for two or three hours; then
shake the water up and down in the decanters; empty this out, rinse them
well with clean cold water, and put them in a rack to drain. When dry,
polish them outside and inside, as far as possible, with a fine cloth. To
remove the crust of port or other wines, add a little muriatic acid to the
water, and let it remain for some time.

When required to go out with the carriage, it is the footman's duty
to see that it has come to the door perfectly clean, and that the
glasses, and sashes and linings, are free from dust. In receiving messages at the carriage door, he should turn his ear to the speaker, so as
to comprehend what is said, in order that he may give his directions
to the coachman clearly. When the house he is to call at is reached, he

should knock, and return to the carriage for orders. In closing the door upon the family, he should see that the handle is securely turned, and that no part of the ladies' dress is shut in.

It is the footman's duty to carry messages or letters for his master or mistress to their friends, to the post, or to the tradespeople; and nothing is more important than dispatch and exactness in doing so, although writing even the simplest message is now the ordinary and very proper practice. Dean Swift, among his other quaint directions, all of which are to be read by contraries, recommends a perusal of all such epistles, in order that you may be the more able to fulfil your duty to your master. An old lady of Forfarshire had one of those odd old Caleb Balderston* sort of servants, who construed the Dean of St Patrick more literally. On one occasion, when dispatch was of some importance, knowing his inquiring nature, she called her Scotch Paul Pry to her, opened the note, and read it to him herself, saying, 'Now, Andrew, you ken a'aboot it, and needna' stop to open and read it, but just take it at once.' Probably most of the notes you are expected to carry might, with equal harmlessness, be communicated to you; but it will be better not to take so lively an interest in your mistress's affairs.

Politeness and civility to visitors is one of the things masters and mistresses have a right to expect, and should exact rigorously. When visitors present themselves, the servant charged with the duty of opening the door will open it promptly, and answer, without hesitation, if the family are 'not at home,' or 'engaged;' which generally means the same thing, and might be oftener used with advantage to morals. On the contrary, if he has no such orders, he will answer affirmatively, open the door wide to admit them, and precede them to open the door of the drawing-room. If the family are not there, he will place chairs for them, open the blinds (if the room is too dark), and intimate civilly that he goes to inform his mistress. If the lady is in her drawing-room, he announces the name of the visitors, having previously acquainted himself with it. In this part of his duty it is necessary to be very careful to repeat the names correctly; mispronouncing names is very apt to give offence, and leads sometimes to other disagreeables. The writer was once initiated into some of the secrets on the 'other side' of a legal affair in which he took an interest, before he could correct a mistake made by the servant in announcing him.* When the visitor is departing, the servant should be at hand, ready, when rung for, to open the door; he should open it with a respectful manner, and close it gently when the visitors are fairly beyond the threshold. When several visitors arrive together, he should take care not to mix up the different names together, where they belong to the same family, as Mr, Mrs, and Miss; if they are strangers, he should announce each as distinctly as possible.

Receptions and Evening Parties.—The drawing-rooms being prepared, the card-tables laid out with cards and counters, and such other arrangements as are necessary made for the reception of the company, the rooms should be lighted up as the hour appointed approaches. Attendants in the drawing-room, even more than in the dining-room, should move about actively but noiselessly; no creaking of shoes, which is an abomination; watching the lights from time to time, so as to keep up their brilliancy. But even if the attendant likes a game of cribbage or whist himself, he must not interfere in his master or mistress's game, nor even seem to take an interest in it. We once knew a lady who had a footman, and both were fond of a game of cribbage,—John in the kitchen, the lady in her drawing-room. The lady was a giver of evening parties, where she frequently enjoyed her favourite amusement. While handing about the tea and toast, John could not always suppress his disgust at her mistakes. 'There is more in that hand, ma'am,' he has been known to say; or, 'Ma'am, you forgot to count his nob;' in fact, he identified himself with his mistress's game, and would have lost twenty places rather than witness a miscount. It is not necessary to adopt his example on this point, although John had many qualities a good servant might copy with advantage.

THE COACHHOUSE AND STABLES

THE HORSE is the noblest of quadrupeds, whether we view him in his strength, his sagacity, or his beauty. He is also the most useful to man of all the animal creation; but his delicacy is equal to his power and usefulness. No other animal, probably, is so dependent on man in the state of domestication to which he has been reduced, or deteriorates so rapidly under exposure, bad feeding, or bad grooming. It is, therefore, a point of humanity, not to speak of its obvious impolicy, for the owner of horses to overlook any neglect in their feeding or grooming. His interest dictates that so valuable an animal should be well housed, well fed, and well groomed; and he will do well to acquire so much of stable lore as will enable him to judge of these points himself. In a general way, where a horse's coat is habitually rough and untidy, there is a sad want of elbow-grease in the stable. When a horse of tolerable breeding is dull and spiritless, he is getting ill or badly fed; and where he is observed to perspire much in the stables, is overfed, and probably eats his litter in addition to his regular supply of food.

Stables.—The architectural form of the stables will be subject to other influences than ours; we confine ourselves, therefore, to their internal arrangements. They should be roomy in proportion to the number of stalls; warm, with good ventilation, and perfectly free from cold draughts; the stalls roomy, without excess, with good and well-trapped drainage, so as to exclude bad smells; a sound ceiling to prevent the entrance of dust from the hayloft, which is usually above them; and there should be plenty of light, coming, however, either from above or behind, so as not to glare in the horse's eye.

Heat.—The first of these objects is attained, if the stables are kept within a degree or two of 50° in winter, and 60° in summer; although some grooms insist on a much higher temperature, in the interests of their own labour.

Ventilation is usually attained by the insertion of one or more tubes or boxes of wood or iron through the ceiling and the roof, with a sloping covering over the opening, to keep out rain, and valves or ventilators below to regulate the atmosphere, with openings in the walls for the admission of fresh air: this is still a difficulty, however; for the effluvium of the stable is difficult to dispel, and draughts must be avoided. This is sometimes accomplished by means of hollow walls with gratings at the bottom outside, for the exit of bad air, which is carried down through the hollow walls and discharged at the bottom, while, for the admission of fresh air, the reverse takes place: the fresh by this means gets diffused and heated before it is discharged into the stable.

The Stalls should be divided by partitions of wood-work eight or nine feet high at the head and six at the heels, and nine feet deep, so as to separate each horse from its neighbour. A hay-rack placed within easy reach of the horse, of wood or iron, occupies either a corner or the whole breadth of the stall, which should be about six feet for an ordinary-sized horse. A manger, formerly of wood, but of late years more generally of iron lined with enamel, occupies a corner of the stall. The pavement of the stall should be nearly level, with a slight incline towards the gutter, to keep the bed dry, paved with hard Dutch brick laid on edge, or asphalte, or smithy clinkers, or rubble-stones, laid in strong cement. In the centre, about five feet from the wall, a grating should be firmly fixed in the pavement, and in communication with a well-trapped drain to carry off the water; the gutter outside the stall should also communicate with the drains by trapped openings. The passage between the stall and the hall should be from five to six feet broad at least; on the wall, opposite to each stall, pegs should be placed for receiving the harness and other things in daily use.

A Harness-room is indispensable to every stable. It should be dry and airy, and furnished with a fireplace and boiler, both for the protection of the harness and to prepare mashes for the horses when required. The partition-wall should be boarded where the harness goes, with pegs to hang the various pieces of harness on, with saddle-trees to rest the saddles on, a cupboard for the brushes, sponges, and leathers, and a lock-up corn-bin.

The furniture of a stable with coachhouse, consists of coach-mops, jacks for raising the wheels, horse-brushes, spoke-brushes, water-brushes, crest and bit-brushes, dandy-brushes, currycombs, birch and heath brooms, trimming-combs, scissors and pickers, oil-cans and brushes, harness-brushes of three sorts, leathers, sponges for horse and carriage, stable-forks, dung-baskets or wheelbarrow, corn-sieves and measures, horse-cloths and stable pails, horn or glass lanterns. Over the stables there should be accommodation for the coachman or groom to sleep. Accidents sometimes occur, and he should be at hand to interfere.

DUTIES OF THE COACHMAN, GROOM, AND STABLE-BOY

The Establishment we have in view will consist of coachman, groom, and stable-boy, who are capable of keeping in perfect order four horses, and perhaps the pony. Of this establishment the coachman is chief. Besides skill in driving, he should possess a good general knowledge of horses; he has usually to purchase provender, to see that the horses are regularly fed and properly groomed, watch over their condition, apply simple remedies to trifling ailments in the animals under his charge, and report where he observes symptoms of more serious ones which he does not understand. He has either to clean the carriage himself; or see that the stable-boy does it properly.

The Groom's first duties are to keep his horses in condition; but he is sometimes expected to perform the duties of a valet, to ride out with his master, on occasions, to wait at table, and otherwise assist in the house: in these cases, he should have the means of dressing himself, and keeping his clothes entirely away from the stables. In the morning, about six o'clock, or rather before, the stables should be opened and cleaned out, and the horses fed, first by cleaning the rack and throwing in fresh hay, putting it lightly in the rack, that the horses may get it out easily; a short time afterwards their usual morning feed of oats should be put into the manger. While this is going on, the stable-boy has been removing the stable-dung, and sweeping and washing out the stables, both of which should be done every day, and every corner carefully swept, in order to keep the stable sweet and clean. The real duties of the groom follow: where the horses are not taken out for early exercise, the work of grooming immediately commences. 'Having tied up the head,' to use the excellent description of the process given by old Barrett, 'take a currycomb and curry him all over the body, to raise the dust, beginning first at the neck, holding the left cheek of the headstall in the left hand, and curry him from the setting-on of his head all over the body to the buttocks, down to the point of the hock; then change your hands, and curry him before, on his breast, and, laying your right arm over his back, join your right side to his left, and curry him all under the belly near the fore-bowels, and so all over from the knees and back upwards; after that, go to the far side and do that likewise. Then take a dead horse's tail, or, failing that, a cotton dusting-cloth, and strike that away which the currycomb hath raised. Then take a round brush made of bristles, with a leathern handle, and dress him all over, both head, body, and legs, to the very fetlocks, always cleansing the brush from the dust by rubbing it with the currycomb. In the curry-combing process, as well as brushing, it must be applied with mildness, especially with fine-skinned horses; otherwise the tickling irritates them much. The brushing is succeeded by a hair-cloth, with which rub him all over again very hard, both to take away loose hairs and lay his coat; then wash your hands in fair water, and rub him all over while they are wet, as well over the head as the body. Lastly, take a clean cloth, and rub him all over again till he be dry; then take another hair-cloth, and rub all his legs exceeding well from the knees and hocks downwards to his hoofs, picking and dressing them very carefully about the fetlocks, so as to remove all gravel and dust which will sometimes lie in the bending of the joints.' In addition to the practice of this old writer, modern grooms add wisping, which usually follows brushing. The best wisp is made from a hayband, untwisted, and again doubled up after being moistened with water: this is applied to every part of the body, as the brushing had been, by changing the hands, taking care in all these operations to carry the hand in the direction of the coat. Stains on the hair are removed by sponging, or, when the coat is very dirty, by the water-brush; the whole being finished off by a linen or flannel cloth. The horsecloth should now be put on by taking the cloth in both hands, with the outside next you, and, with your right hand to the off side, throw it over his back, placing it no farther back than will leave it straight and level, which will be about a foot from the tail. Put the roller round, and the pad-piece under it, about six or eight inches from the fore legs. The horse's head is now loosened; he is turned about in his stall to have his head and ears rubbed and brushed over every part, including throat, with the dusting-cloth, finishing by 'pulling his ears,' which all horses seem to enjoy very much. This done, the mane and foretop should be combed out, passing a wet sponge over them, sponging the mane on both sides, by throwing it back to the midriff, to make it lie smooth. The horse is now returned to his headstall, his tail combed out, cleaning it of stains with a wet brush or sponge, trimming both tail and mane, and forelock when necessary, smoothing them down with a brush on which a little oil has been dropped.

Watering usually follows dressing; but some horses refuse their food until they have drunk: the groom should not, therefore, lay down exclusive rules on this subject, but study the temper and habits of his horse.

Exercise.—All horses not in work require at least two hours' exercise daily; and in exercising them a good groom will put them through the paces to which they have been trained. In the case of saddle-horses he will walk, trot, canter, and gallop them, in order to keep them up to their work. With draught horses they ought to be kept up to a smart walk and trot.

Feeding must depend on their work, but they require feeding three times a day, with more or less corn each time, according to their work. In the fast coaching days it was a saying among proprietors that, 'his belly was the measure of his food;' but the horse's appetite itself is not to be taken as a criterion of the quantity of food under any circumstances. Horses have been known to consume 40 lbs. of hay in twenty-four hours, whereas 16 lbs. to 18 lbs. is the utmost which should have been given. Mr Croall, an extensive coach proprietor in Scotland, limited his horses to 4½ lbs. cut straw, 8 lbs. bruised oats, and 24 lbs. bruised beans, in the morning and noon, giving them at night 25 lbs. of the following; viz., 560 lbs. steamed potatoes, 36 lbs. barley-dust, 40 lbs. cut straw, and 6 lbs. salt, mixed up together: under this the horses did their work well. The ordinary measure given to a horse is a peck of oats, about 40 lbs. to the bushel, twice a day, a third feed and a rack-ful of hay, which may be about 15 lbs. or 18 lbs., when he is in full work.

You cannot take up a paper without having the question put, 'Do you bruise your oats?' Well, that depends on circumstances: a fresh young horse can bruise its own oats when it can get them; but aged horses, after a time, lose the power of masticating and bruising them, and bolt them whole; thus much impeding the work of digestion. For an old horse, then, bruise the oats; for a young one it does no harm and little good. Oats should be bright and dry and not too new. Where they are new, sprinkle them with salt and water; otherwise, they overload the horse's stomach. Chopped straw mixed with oats, in the proportion of a third of straw or hay, is a good food for horses in full work; and carrots, of which horses are remarkably fond, have a perceptible effect in a short time on the gloss of the coat.

The water given to a horse merits some attention; it should not be too cold; hard water is not to be recommended; stagnant or muddy water is positively injurious; river water is the best for all purposes; and anything is preferable to spring water, which should be exposed to the sun in summer for an hour or two, and stirred up before using it: a handful of oatmeal thrown into the pail will much improve its quality.

Shoeing.—A horse should not be sent on a journey or any other hard work immediately after new shoeing;—the stiffness incidental to new shoes is not unlikely to bring him down. A day's rest, with reasonable exercise, will not be thrown away after this operation. On reaching home very hot, the groom should walk him about for a few minutes; this done, he should take off the moisture with the scraper, and afterwards wisp him over with a handful of straw and a flannel cloth: if the cloth is dipped in some spirit, all the better. He should wash, pick, and wipe dry the legs and feet, take off the bridle and crupper, and fasten it to the rack, then the girths, and put a wisp of straw under the saddle. When sufficiently cool, the horse should have some hay given him, and then a feed of oats: if he refuse the latter, offer him a little wet bran, or a handful of oatmeal in tepid water. When he has been fed, he should be thoroughly cleaned, and his body-clothes put on, and, if very much harassed with fatigue, a little good ale or wine will be well bestowed on a valuable horse, adding plenty of fresh litter under the belly.

Bridles.—Every time a horse is unbridled, the bit should be carefully washed and dried, and the leather wiped, to keep them sweet, as well as the girths and saddle, the latter being carefully dried and beaten with a switch before it is again put on. In washing a horse's feet after a day's work, the master should insist upon the legs and feet being washed thoroughly with a sponge until the water flows over them, and then rubbed with a brush till quite dry.

Harness, if not carefully preserved, very soon gets a shabby tarnished appearance. Where the coachman has a proper harness-room and sufficient assistance, this is inexcusable and easily prevented. The harness-room should have a wooden lining all round, and be perfectly dry and well ventilated. Around the walls, hooks and pegs should be placed, for the several pieces of harness, at such a height as to prevent their touching the ground; and every part of the harness should have its peg or hook,—one for the halters, another for the reins, and others for snaffles and other bits and metal-work; and either a wooden horse or saddle-trees for the saddles and pads. All these parts should be dry, clean, and shining. This is only to be done by careful cleaning and polishing, and the use of several requisite pastes. The metallic parts, when white, should be cleaned by a soft brush and plate-powder; the copper and brass parts burnished with rottenstone-powder and oil,—steel with emery-powder; both made into a paste with a little oil.

An excellent paste for polishing harness and the leather-work of carriages, is made by melting 8 lbs. of yellow wax, stirring it till completely dissolved. Into this pour 1 lb. of litharge of the shops, which has been pounded up with water, and dried and sifted through a sieve, leaving the two, when mixed, to simmer on the fire, stirring them continually till all is melted. When it is a little cool, mix this with 1½ lb. of good ivory-black;

place this again on the fire, and stir till it boils anew, and suffer it to cool. When cooled a little, add distilled turpentine till it has the consistence of a thickish paste, scenting it with any essence at hand, thinning it when necessary from time to time, by adding distilled turpentine.

When the leather is old and greasy, it should be cleaned before applying this polish, with a brush wetted in a weak solution of potass and water, washing afterwards with soft river water, and drying thoroughly. If the leather is not black, one or two coats of black ink may be given before applying the polish. When quite dry, the varnish should be laid on with a soft shoe-brush, using also a soft brush to polish the leather.

When the leather is very old, it may be softened with fish-oil, and, after putting on the ink, a sponge charged with distilled turpentine passed over, to scour the surface of the leather, which should be polished as above.

For fawn or yellow-coloured leather, take a quart of skimmed milk, pour into it 1 oz. of sulphuric acid, and, when cold, add to it 4 oz. of hydrochloric acid, shaking the bottle gently until it ceases to emit white vapours; separate the coagulated from the liquid part, by straining through a sieve, and store it away till required. In applying it, clean the leather by a weak solution of oxalic acid, washing it off immediately, and apply the composition when dry with a sponge.

Wheel-grease is usually purchased at the shops; but a good paste is made as follows:—Melt 80 parts of grease, and stir into it, mixing it thoroughly and smoothly, 20 parts of fine black-lead in powder, and store away in a tin box for use. This grease is used in the mint at Paris, and is highly approved.

*Carriages** in endless variety of shapes and names are continually making their appearance; but the hackney cab or clarence seems most in request for light carriages; the family carriage of the day being a modified form of the clarence adapted for family use. The carriage is a valuable piece of furniture,* requiring all the care of the most delicate upholstery, with the additional disadvantage of continual exposure to the weather and to the muddy streets.

It requires, therefore, to be carefully cleaned before putting away, and a coach house perfectly dry and well ventilated, for the woodwork swells with moisture; it shrinks also with heat, unless the timber has undergone a long course of seasoning: it should also have a dry floor, a boarded one being recommended. It must be removed from the ammoniacal influence of the stables, from open drains and cesspools, and other gaseous influences likely to affect the paint and varnish. When the carriage returns home, it should be carefully washed and dried, and that, if possible, before the mud has time to dry on it. This is done by first well slushing it with clean water, so as to wash away all particles of sand, having first closed the sashes to avoid wetting the linings. The body is then gone carefully over with a soft mop, using plenty of clean water, and penetrating into every corner of the carved work, so that not an atom of dirt remains; the body of the carriage is then raised by placing the jack under the axletree and raising it so that the wheel turns freely; this is now thoroughly washed with the mop until the dirt is removed, using a water-brush for corners where the mop does not penetrate. Every particle of mud and sand removed by the mop, and afterwards with a wet sponge, the carriage is wiped dry, and, as soon after as possible, the varnish is carefully polished with soft leather, using a little sweet oil for the leather parts, and even for the panels, so as to check any tendency of the varnish to crack. Stains are removed by rubbing them with the leather and sweet oil; if that fails, a little Tripoli powder mixed with the oil will be more successful.

In preparing the carriage for use, the whole body should be rubbed over with a clean leather and carefully polished, the iron-work and joints oiled, the plated and brass-work occasionally cleaned,—the one with plate-powder, or with well-washed whiting mixed with sweet oil, and leather kept for the purpose,—the other with rottenstone mixed with a little oil, and applied without too much rubbing, until the paste is removed; but, if rubbed every day with the leather, little more will be required to keep it untarnished. The linings require careful brushing every day, the cushions being taken out and beaten, and the glass sashes should always be bright and clean. The wheel-tires and axletree are carefully seen to, and greased when required, the bolts and nuts tightened, and all the parts likely to get out of order overhauled.

These duties, however, are only incidental to the coachman's office, which is to drive; and much of the enjoyment of those in the carriage depends on his proficiency in his art,—much also of the wear of the carriage and horses. He should have sufficient knowledge of the construction of the carriage to know when it is out of order,—to know, also, the pace at which he can go over the road he has under him, without risking the springs, and without shaking those he is driving too much.

Having, with or without the help of the groom or stable-boy, put his horses to the carriage, and satisfied himself, by walking round them, that everything is properly arranged, the coachman proceeds to the off-side of the carriage, takes the reins from the back of the horses, where they were thrown, buckles them together, and, placing his foot on the step, ascends to his box, having his horses now entirely under control. In ordinary circumstances, he is not expected to descend, for where no footman accompanies the carriage, the doors are usually so arranged that even a lady may let herself out, if she wishes it, from the inside. The coachman's duties are to avoid everything approaching an accident, and all his attention is required to guide his horses.

The pace at which he drives will depend upon his orders,—in all prob-ability a moderate pace of seven or eight miles an hour; less speed is injurious to the horses, getting them into lazy and sluggish habits; for it is wonderful how soon these are acquired by some horses. The writer* was once employed to purchase a horse for a country friend, and he picked a very handsome gelding out of Collins's stables, which seemed to answer to his friend's wants. It was duly committed to the coachman who was to drive it, after some very successful trials in harness and out of it, and seemed likely to give great satisfaction. After a time, the friend got tired of his carriage, and gave it up; as the easiest mode of getting rid of the horse, it was sent up to the writer's stables,—a present. Only twelve months had elapsed; the horse was as handsome as ever, with plenty of flesh, and a sleek glossy coat, and he was thankfully enough received; but, on trial, it was found that a stupid coachman, who was imbued with one of their old maxims, that 'it's the pace that kills,' had driven the horse, capable of doing his nine miles an hour with ease, at a jog-trot of four miles, or four and a half; and now, no persuasion of the whip could get more out of him. After many unsuccessful efforts to bring him back to his pace; in one of which a break-down occurred, under the hands of a professional trainer, he was sent to the hammer, and sold for a sum that did not pay for the attempt to break him in. This maxim, therefore, 'that it's the pace that kills,' is altogether fallacious in the moderate sense in which we are view-ing it. In the old coaching days, indeed, when the Shrewsbury 'Wonder' drove into the inn yard while the clock was striking, week after week and month after month, with unerring regularity, twenty-seven hours to a hundred and sixty-two miles; when the 'Quicksilver' mail was timed to eleven miles an hour between London and Plymouth, with a fine of £5 to the driver if behind time; when the Brighton 'Age,' 'tool'd' and horsed by the late Mr Stevenson, used to dash round the square as the fifth hour was striking, having stopped at the half-way house while his servant handed a sandwich and a glass of sherry to his passengers,—then the pace was indeed 'killing.' But the truth is, horses that are driven at a jog-trot pace lose that *élan* with which a good driver can inspire them, and they are left to do their work by mere weight and muscle; therefore, unless he has contrary orders, a good driver will choose a smart pace, but not enough to make his horses perspire: on level roads this should never be seen.

In choosing his horses, every master will see that they are properly paired,—that their paces are about equal. When their habits differ, it is the coachman's duty to discover how he can, with least annoyance to the horses, get that pace out of them. Some horses have been accustomed to be driven on the check, and the curb irritates them; others, with harder mouths, cannot be controlled with the slight leverage this affords; he must, therefore, accommodate the horses as he best can. The reins should always be held so that the horses are 'in hand;' but he is a very bad driver who always drives with a tight rein; the pain to the horse is intolerable, and causes him to rear and plunge, and finally break away, if he can. He is also a bad driver when the reins are always slack; the horse then feels abandoned to himself; he is neither directed nor supported, and if no accident occurs, it is great good luck.

The true coachman's hands are so delicate and gentle, that the mere weight of the reins is felt on the bit, and the directions are indicated by a turn of the wrist rather than by a pull; the horses are guided and encouraged, and only pulled up when they exceed their intended pace, or in the event of a stumble; for there is a strong though gentle hand on the reins.

The Whip, in the hands of a good driver, and with well-bred cattle, is there, more as a precaution than a 'tool' for frequent use; if he uses it, it is to encourage, by stroking the flanks; except, indeed, he has to punish some waywardness of temper, and then he does it effectually, taking care, however, that it is done on the flank, where there is no very tender part, never on the crupper. In driving, the coachman should never give way to temper. How often do we see horses stumble from being conducted, or at least 'allowed,' to go over bad ground by some careless driver, who immediately wreaks that vengeance on the poor horse which might, with much more justice, be applied to his own brutal shoulders. The whip is of course useful, and even necessary, but should be rarely used, except to encourage and excite the horses.

DUTIES OF THE VALET

Attendants on the Person.—'No man is a hero to his valet,' saith the proverb;* and the corollary may run, 'No lady is a heroine to her maid.' The infirmities of humanity are, perhaps, too numerous and too equally distributed to stand the severe microscopic tests which attendants on the person have opportunities of applying. The valet and waiting-maid are placed near the persons of the master and mistress, receiving orders only from them, dressing them, accompanying them in all their journeys, the confidants and agents of their most unguarded moments, of their most secret habits, and of course subject to their commands,—even to their caprices; they themselves being subject to erring judgment, aggravated by an imperfect education. All that can be expected from such servants is polite manners, modest demeanour, and a respectful reserve, which are indispensable. To these, good sense, good temper, some self-denial, and consideration for the feelings of others, whether above or below them in the social scale, will be useful qualifications. Their duty leads them to wait on those who are, from sheer wealth, station, and education, more polished, and consequently more susceptible of annoyance; and any vulgar familiarity of manner is opposed to all their notions of self-respect. Quiet unobtrusive manners, therefore, and a delicate reserve in speaking of their employers, either in praise or blame, is as essential in their absence, as good manners and respectful conduct in their presence.

Some of the duties of the valet we have just hinted at in treating of the duties of the footman in a small family. His day commences by seeing that his master's dressing room is in order; that the housemaid has swept and dusted it properly; that the fire is lighted and burns cheerfully; and some time before his master is expected, he will do well to throw up the sash to admit fresh air, closing it, however, in time to recover the temperature which he knows his master prefers. It is now his duty to place the body-linen on the horse before the fire, to be aired properly; to lay the trousers intended to be worn, carefully brushed and cleaned, on the back of his master's chair; while the coat and waistcoat, carefully brushed and folded, and the collar cleaned, are laid in their place ready to put on when required. All the articles of the toilet should be in their places, the razors properly set and stropped, and hot water ready for use.

Gentlemen generally prefer performing the operation of shaving themselves, but a valet should be prepared to do it if required; and he should, besides, be a good hairdresser. Shaving over, he has to brush the hair, beard, and moustache, where that appendage is encouraged, arranging the whole simply and gracefully, according to the age and style of countenance. Every fortnight, or three weeks at the utmost, the hair should be cut, and the points of the whiskers trimmed as often as required. A good valet will now present the various articles of the toilet as they are wanted; afterwards, the body-linen, neck-tie, which he will put on, if required, and, afterwards, waistcoat, coat, and boots, in suitable order, and carefully brushed and polished.

Having thus seen his master dressed, if he is about to go out, the valet will hand him his cane, gloves, and hat, the latter well brushed on the outside with a soft brush, and wiped inside with a clean handkerchief; respectfully attend him to the door, and open it for him, and receive his last orders for the day.

He now proceeds to put everything in order in the dressing-room, cleans the combs and brushes, and brushes and folds up any clothes that may be left about the room, and puts them away in the drawers.

Gentlemen are sometimes indifferent as to their clothes and appearance; it is the valet's duty, in this case, where his master permits it, to select from the wardrobe such things as are suitable for the occasion, so that he may appear with scrupulous neatness and cleanliness; that his linen and neck-tie, where that is white or coloured, are unsoiled; and where he is not accustomed to change them every day, that the cravat is turned, and even ironed, to remove the crease of the previous fold. The coat collar,—which where the hair is oily and worn long, is apt to get greasy—should also be examined; a careful valet will correct this by removing the spots day by day as they appear, first by moistening the grease-spots with a little rectified spirits of wine or spirits of hartshorn, which has a renovating effect, and the smell of which soon disappears. The grease is dissolved and removed by gentle scraping. The grease removed, add a little more of the spirit, and rub with a piece of clean cloth; finish by adding a few drops more; rub it with the palm of the hand, in the direction of the grain of the cloth, and it will be clean and glossy as the rest of the garment.

Polish for the boots is an important matter to the valet, and not always to be obtained good by purchase; never so good, perhaps, as he can make for himself after the following recipes:—Take of ivory-black and treacle each 4 oz., sulphuric acid 1 oz., best olive-oil 2 spoonfuls, best white-wine vinegar 3 half-pints: mix the ivory-black and treacle well in an earthen jar; then add the sulphuric acid, continuing to stir the mixture; next pour in the oil; and, lastly, add the vinegar, stirring it in by degrees, until thoroughly incorporated.

Another polish is made by mixing 1 oz. each of pounded galls and logwood-chips, and 3 lbs. of red French wine (ordinaire). Boil together till the liquid is reduced to half the quantity, and pour it off through a strainer. Now take ½ lb. each of pounded gum-arabic and lump-sugar, 1 oz. of green copperas, and 3 lbs. of brandy. Dissolve the gum-arabic in the preceding decoction, and add the sugar and copperas: when all is dissolved and mixed together, stir in the brandy, mixing it smoothly. This mixture will yield 5 or 6 lbs. of a very superior polishing paste for boots and shoes.

It is, perhaps, unnecessary to add, that having discharged all the commissions intrusted to him by his master, such as conveying notes or messages to friends, or the tradesmen, all of which he should punctually and promptly attend to, it is his duty to be in waiting when his master returns home to dress for dinner, or for any other occasion, and to have all things prepared for this second dressing. Previous to this, he brings under his notice the cards of visitors who may have called, delivers the messages he may have received for him, and otherwise acquits himself of the morning's commissions, and receives his orders for the remainder of the day. The routine of his evening duty is to have the dressing-room and study, where there is a separate one, arranged comfortably for his master, the fires lighted, candles prepared, dressing-gown and slippers in their place, and aired, and everything in order that is required for his master's comforts.

FEMALE DOMESTICS

DUTIES OF THE LADY'S-MAID

The duties of a lady's-maid are more numerous, and perhaps more onerous, than those of the valet; for while the latter is aided by the tailor, the hatter, the linen-draper, and the perfumer, the lady's-maid has to originate many parts of the mistress's dress herself: she should, indeed, be a tolerably expert milliner and dressmaker, a good hairdresser, and possess some chemical knowledge of the cosmetics with which the toilet-table is supplied, in order to use them with safety and effect. Her first duty in the morning, after having performed her own toilet, is to examine the clothes put off by her mistress the evening before, either to put them away, or to see that they are all in order to put on again. During the winter, and in wet weather, the dresses should be carefully examined, and the mud removed. Dresses of tweed, and other woollen materials, may be laid out on a table and brushed all over; but in general, even in woollen fabrics, the lightness of the tissues renders brushing unsuitable to dresses, and it is better to remove the dust from the folds by beating them lightly with a handkerchief or thin cloth. Silk dresses should never be brushed, but rubbed with a piece of merino, or other soft material, of a similar colour, kept for the purpose. Summer dresses of barège, muslin, mohair, and other light materials, simply require shaking; but if the muslin be tumbled, it must be ironed afterwards. If the dresses require slight repair, it should be done at once: 'a stitch in time saves nine.'

The bonnet should be dusted with a light feather plume, in order to remove every particle of dust; but this has probably been done, as it ought to have been, the night before. Velvet bonnets, and other velvet articles of dress, should be cleaned with a soft brush. If the flowers with which the bonnet is decorated have been crushed or displaced, or the leaves tumbled, they should be raised and readjusted by means of flower-pliers. If feathers have suffered from damp, they should be held near the fire for a few minutes, and restored to their natural state by the hand or a soft brush.

The Chausserie, or foot-gear of a lady, is one of the few things left to mark her station,* and requires special care. Satin boots or shoes should be dusted with a soft brush, or wiped with a cloth. Kid or varnished leather should have the mud wiped off with a sponge charged with milk, which preserves its softness and polish. The following is also an excellent polish for applying to ladies' boots, instead of blacking them:—Mix equal proportions of sweet-oil, vinegar, and treacle, with 1 oz. of lamp-black. When all the ingredients are thoroughly incorporated, rub the mixture on the boots with the palm of the hand, and put them in a cool place to dry. Ladies' blacking, which may be purchased in 6*d*. and 1*s*. bottles, is also very much used for patent leather and kid boots, particularly when they are a little worn. This blacking is merely applied with a piece of sponge, and the boots should not be put on until the blacking is dry and hardened.

These various preliminary offices performed, the lady's-maid should prepare for dressing her mistress, arranging her dressing-room, toilet-table, and linen, according to her mistress's wishes and habits. The details of dressing we need not touch upon,—every lady has her own mode of doing so; but the maid should move about quietly, perform any offices about her mistress's person, as lacing stays, gently, and adjust her linen smoothly.

Having prepared the dressing-room by lighting the fire, sweeping the hearth, and made everything ready for dressing her mistress, placed her linen before the fire to air, and laid out the various articles of dress she is to wear, which will probably have been arranged the previous evening, the lady's-maid is prepared for the morning's duties.

Hairdressing is the most important part of the lady's-maid's office. If ringlets are worn, remove the curl-papers, and, after thoroughly brushing the back hair both above and below, dress it according to the prevailing fashion. If bandeaux are worn, the hair is thoroughly brushed and frizzed outside and inside, folding the hair back round the head, brushing it perfectly smooth, giving it a glossy appearance by the use of pomades, or oil, applied by the palm of the hand, smoothing it down with a small brush dipped in bandoline. Double bandeaux are formed by bringing most of the hair forward, and rolling it over frizettes made of hair the same colour as that of the wearer: it is finished behind by plaiting the hair, and arranging it in such a manner as to look well with the head-dress.

Lessons in hairdressing may be obtained, and at not an unreasonable charge. If a lady's-maid can afford it, we would advise her to initiate herself in the mysteries of hairdressing before entering on her duties. If a mistress finds her maid handy, and willing to learn, she will not mind the expense of a few lessons, which are almost necessary, as the fashion and mode of dressing the hair is so continually changing. Brushes and combs should be kept scrupulously clean, by washing them about twice a week: to do this oftener spoils the brushes, as very frequent washing makes them so very soft.

To Wash Brushes

Dissolve a piece of soda in some hot water, allowing a piece the size of a walnut to a quart of water. Put the water into a basin, and, after combing out the hair from the brushes, dip them, bristles downwards, into the water and out again, keeping the backs and handles as free from the water as possible. Repeat this until the bristles look clean; then rinse the brushes in a little cold water; shake them well, and wipe the handles and backs with a towel, *but not the bristles*, and set the brushes to dry in the sun, or near the fire; but take care not to put them too close to it. Wiping the bristles of a brush makes them soft, as does also the use of soap.

To Clean Combs

If it can be avoided, never wash combs, as the water often makes the teeth split, and the tortoiseshell or horn of which they are made, rough. Small brushes, manufactured purposely for cleaning combs, may be purchased at a trifling cost: with this the comb should be well brushed, and afterwards wiped with a cloth or towel.

A Good Wash for the Hair

INGREDIENTS.— 1 pennyworth of borax, ½ pint of olive-oil, 1 pint of boiling water.

Mode.—Pour the boiling water over the borax and oil; let it cool; then put the mixture into a bottle. Shake it before using, and apply it with a flannel. Camphor and borax, dissolved in boiling water and left to cool, make a very good wash for the hair; as also does rosemary-water mixed with a little borax. After using any of these washes, when the hair becomes thoroughly dry, a little pomatum or oil should be rubbed in, to make it smooth and glossy.

To Make Pomade for the Hair

INGREDIENTS.— ¼ lb. of lard, 2 pennyworth of castor-oil; scent.

Mode.—Let the lard be unsalted; beat it up well; then add the castor-oil, and mix thoroughly together with a knife, adding a few drops of any scent that may be preferred. Put the pomatum into pots, which keep well covered to prevent it turning rancid.

Another Recipe for Pomatum

INGREDIENTS.—8 oz. of olive-oil, 1 oz. of spermaceti,* 3 penny-worth of essential oil of almonds, 3 pennyworth of essence of lemon.

Mode.—Mix these ingredients together, and store away in jars for use.

To Make Bandoline

INGREDIENTS.—1 oz. of gum-tragacanth, ¼ pint of cold water, 3 pennyworth of essence of almonds, 2 teaspoonfuls of old rum.

Mode.—Put the gum-tragacanth into a wide-mouthed bottle with the cold water; let it stand till dissolved, then stir into it the essence of almonds; let it remain for an hour or two, when pour the rum on the top. This should make the stock bottle, and when any is required for use, it is merely necessary to dilute it with a little cold water until the desired consistency is obtained, and to keep it in a small bottle, well corked, for use. This bandoline, instead of injuring the hair, as many other kinds often do, improves it, by increasing its growth, and making it always smooth and glossy.

An Excellent Pomatum

INGREDIENTS.—1½ lb. of lard, ½ pint of olive-oil, ½ pint of caster-oil, 4 oz. of spermaceti, bergamot, or any other scent; elder-flower water.

Mode.—Wash the lard well in the elder-flower water; drain, and beat it to a cream. Mix the two oils together, and heat them sufficiently to dissolve the spermaceti, which should be beaten fine in a mortar. Mix all these ingredients together with the brandy and whatever kind of scent may be preferred; and whilst warm pour into glass bottles for use, keeping them well corked. The best way to liquefy the pomatum is to set the bottle in a saucepan of warm water. It will remain good for many months.

To Promote the Growth of Hair

INGREDIENTS.—Equal quantities of olive-oil and spirit of rosemary; a few drops of oil of nutmeg.

Mode.—Mix the ingredients together, rub the roots of the hair every night with a little of this liniment, and the growth of it will very soon sensibly increase.

Our further remarks on dressing must be confined to some general advice. In putting on a band, see that it is laid quite flat, and is drawn tightly round the waist before it is pinned in front; that the pin is a strong one, and that it is secured to the stays, so as not to slip up or down, or crease in the folds. Arrange the folds of the dress over the crinoline petticoats; if the dress fastens behind, put a small pin in the slit to prevent it from opening. See that the sleeves fall well over the arms. If it is finished with a jacket, or other upper dress, see that it fits smoothly under the arms; pull out the flounces, and spread out the petticoat at the bottom with the hands, so that it falls in graceful folds. In arranging the petticoat itself, a careful lady's-maid will see that this is firmly fastened round the waist.

Where sashes are worn, pin the bows securely on the inside with a pin, so as not to be visible; then raise the bow with the fingers. The collar is arranged and carefully adjusted with brooch or bow in the centre.

Having dressed her mistress for breakfast, and breakfasted herself, the further duties of the lady's-maid will depend altogether upon the habits of the family, in which hardly two will probably agree. Where the duties are entirely confined to attendance on her mistress, it is probable that the bedroom and dressing-room will be committed to her care; that, the housemaid will rarely enter, except for the weekly or other periodical cleaning; she will, therefore, have to make her mistress's bed, and keep it in order; and as her duties are light and easy, there can be no allowance made for the slightest approach to uncleanliness or want of order. Every morning, immediately after her mistress has left it, and while breakfast is on, she should throw the bed open, by taking off the clothes; open the windows (except in rainy weather), and leave the room to air for half an hour. After breakfast, except when her attendance on her mistress prevents it, if the rooms are carpeted, she should sweep them carefully, having previously strewed the room with moist tea-leaves, dusting every table and chair, taking care to penetrate to every corner, and moving every article of furniture that is portable. This done satisfactorily, and having cleaned the dressing-glass, polished up the furniture and the ornaments, and made the glass jug and basin clean and bright, emptied all slops, emptied the water-jugs and filled them with fresh water, and arranged the rooms, the dressing-room is ready for the mistress when she thinks proper to appear.

The dressing-room thoroughly in order, the same thing is to be done in the bedroom, in which she will probably be assisted by the housemaid to make the bed and empty the slops. In making the bed, she will study her lady's wishes, whether it is to be hard or soft, sloping or straight,* and see that it is done accordingly.

Having swept the bedroom with equal care, dusted the tables and chairs, chimney-ornaments, and put away all articles of dress left from yesterday, and cleaned and put away any articles of jewellery, her next care is to see, before her mistress goes out, what requires replacing in her department, and furnish her with a list of them, that she may use her discretion about ordering them. All this done, she may settle herself down to any work on which she is engaged. This will consist chiefly in mending; which is first to be seen to; everything, except stockings, being mended before washing. Plain work will probably be one of the lady's-maid's chief employments.

A waiting-maid, who wishes to make herself useful, will study the fashion-books with attention, so as to be able to aid her mistress's judgment in dressing, according to the prevailing fashion, with such modifications as her style of countenance requires. She will also, if she has her mistress's interest at heart, employ her spare time in repairing and making up dresses which have served one purpose, to serve another also; or turning many things, unfitted for her mistress to use, for the younger branches of the family. The lady's-maid may thus render herself invaluable to her mistress, and increase her own happiness in so doing. The exigencies of fashion and luxury are such, that all ladies, except those of the very highest rank, will consider themselves fortunate in having about them a thoughtful person, capable of diverting their finery to a useful purpose.

Among other duties, the lady's-maid should understand the various processes for washing, and cleaning, and repairing laces; edging of collars; removing stains and grease-spots from dresses, and similar processes, for which the following recipes will be found very useful. In washing—

Blonde, fine toilet-soap is used; the blonde is soaped over very slightly, and washed in water in which a little fig-blue is dissolved, rubbing it very gently; when clean, dry it. Dip it afterwards in very thin gum-water, dry it again in linen, spread it out as flat as it will lie, and iron it. Where the blonde is of better quality, and wider, it may be stretched on a hoop to dry after washing in the blue-water, applying the gum with a sponge; or it may be washed finally in water in which a lump of sugar has been dissolved, which gives it more the appearance of new blonde.

Lace collars soil very quickly when in contact with the neck; they are cleaned by beating the edge of the collar between the folds of a fine linen cloth, then washing the edges as directed above, and spreading it out on an ironing-board, pinning it at each corner with fine pins; then going carefully over it with a sponge charged with water in which some gum-dragon and fig-blue have been dissolved, to give it a proper consistence. To give the collar the same tint throughout, the whole collar should be sponged with the same water, taking care not to touch the flowers.

A multiplicity of accidents occur to soil and spot dresses, which should be removed at once. To remove—

Grease-spots from cotton or woollen materials of fast colours, absorbent pastes, purified bullock's-blood, and even common soap, are used, applied to the spot when dry. When the colours are not fast, use fuller's-earth or pulverized potter's-clay, laid in a layer over the spot, and press it with a very hot iron.

For Silks, Moires, and plain or brocaded Satins, begin by pouring over the spot two drops of rectified spirits of wine; cover it over with a linen cloth, and press it with a hot iron, changing the linen instantly. The spot will look tarnished, for a portion of the grease still remains: this will be removed entirely by a little sulphuric ether dropped on the spot, and a very little rubbing. If neatly done, no perceptible mark or circle will remain; nor will the lustre of the richest silk be changed, the union of the two liquids operating with no injurious effects from rubbing.

Fruit-spots are removed from white and fast-coloured cottons by the use of chloride of soda. Commence by cold-soaping the article, then touch the spot with a hair-pencil or feather dipped in the chloride, dipping it immediately into cold water, to prevent the texture of the article being injured.

Ink-spots are removed, when fresh applied to the spot, by a few drops of hot water being poured on immediately afterwards. By the same process, iron-mould in linen or calico may be removed, dipping immediately in cold water to prevent injury to the fabric.

Wax dropped on a shawl, table-cover, or cloth dress, is easily discharged by applying spirits of wine.

Syrups or Preserved Fruits, by washing in lukewarm water with a dry cloth, and pressing the spot between two folds of clean linen.

Essence of Lemon will remove grease, but will make a spot itself in a few days.

To Clean Silk or Ribbons

INGREDIENTS.—½ pint of gin, ½ lb. of honey, ½ lb. of soft soap, ½ pint of water.

Mode.—Mix the above ingredients together; then lay each breadth of silk upon a clean kitchen table or dresser, and scrub it well on the soiled side with the mixture. Have ready three vessels of cold water; take each piece of silk at two corners, and dip it up and down in each vessel, but do not wring it; and take care that each breadth has one vessel of quite clean water for the last dip. Hang it up dripping for a minute or two, then dab it in a cloth, and iron it quickly with a very hot iron.

To Remove Paint-Spots from Silk Cloth

If the fabric will bear it, sharp rubbing will frequently entirely discharge a newly-made paint-stain; but, if this is not successful, apply spirit of turpentine with a quill till the stains disappear.

To Make Old Crape* Look Nearly Equal to New

Place a little water in a teakettle, and let it boil until there is plenty of steam from the spout; then, holding the crape in both hands, pass it to and fro several times through the steam, and it will be clean and look nearly equal to new.

Linen.—Before sending linen to wash, the lady's-maid should see that everything under her charge is properly mended; for her own sake she should take care that it is sent out in an orderly manner, each class of garments by themselves, with a proper list, of which she retains a copy. On its return, it is still more necessary to examine every piece separately, so that all missing buttons be supplied, and only the articles properly washed and in perfect repair passed into the wardrobe.

Ladies who keep a waiting-maid for their own persons are in the habit of paying visits to their friends, in which it is not unusual for the maid to accompany them; at all events, it is her duty to pack the trunks; and this requires not only knowledge but some practice, although the improved trunks and portmanteaus now made, in which there is a place for nearly everything, render this more simple than formerly. Before packing, let the trunks be thoroughly well cleaned, and, if necessary, lined with paper, and everything intended for packing laid out on the bed or chairs, so that it may be seen what is to be stowed away; the nicer articles of dress neatly folded in clean calico wrappers. Having satisfied herself that everything wanted is laid out, and that it is in perfect order, the packing is commenced by disposing of the most bulky articles, the dressing-case and work-box, skirts, and other articles requiring room, leaving the smaller articles to fill up; finally, having satisfied herself that all is included, she should lock and cover up the trunk in its canvas case, and then pack her own box, if she is to accompany her mistress.

On reaching the house, the lady's-maid will be shown her lady's apartment; and her duties here are what they were at home; she will arrange her mistress's things, and learn which is her bell, in order to go to her when she rings. Her meals will be taken in the housekeeper's room; and here she must be discreet and guarded in her talk to any one of her mistress or her concerns. Her only occupation here will be attending in her lady's room, keeping her things in order, and making her rooms comfortable for her.

The evening duties of a lady's-maid are pretty nearly a repetition of those of the morning. She is in attendance when her mistress retires; she assists her to undress if required, brushes her hair, and renders such other assistance as is demanded; removes all slops; takes care that the fire, if any, is safe, before she retires to rest herself.

Ironing is a part of the duties of a lady's-maid, and she should be able to do it in the most perfect manner when it becomes necessary. Ironing is often badly done from inattention to a few very simple requirements. Cleanliness is the first essential: the ironing-board, the fire, the iron, and the ironing-blanket should all be perfectly clean. It will not be necessary here to enter into details on ironing, as full directions are given in the 'Duties of the Laundry-maid.' A lady's-maid will have a great deal of 'ironing-out' to do; such as light evening dresses, muslin dresses, &c., which are not dirty enough to be washed, but merely require smoothing out to remove the creases. In summer, particularly, an iron will be constantly required, as also a skirt-board, which should be covered with a nice clean piece of flannel. To keep muslin dresses in order, they almost require smoothing out every time they are worn, particularly if made with many flounces. The lady's-maid may often have to perform little services for her mistress which require care; such as restoring the colour to scorched linen, &c. &c. The following recipe is, we believe, a very good one.

To Restore Whiteness to Scorched Linen

INGREDIENTS.—½ pint of vinegar, 2 oz. of fuller's-earth, 1 oz. of dried fowls' dung, ½ oz. of soap, the juice of 2 large onions.

Mode.—Boil all these ingredients together to the consistency of paste; spread the composition thickly over the damaged part, and if the threads be not actually consumed, after it has been allowed to dry on, and the place has subsequently been washed once or twice, every trace of scorching will disappear.

Furs, Feathers, and Woollens require the constant care of the waiting-maid. Furs and feathers not in constant use should be wrapped up in linen washed in lye. From May to September they are subject to being made the depositary of the moth-eggs. They should be looked to, and shaken and beaten, from time to time, in case some of the eggs should have been lodged in them, in spite of every precaution; laying them up again, or rather folding them up as before, wrapping them in brown paper, which is itself a preservative. Shawls and cloaks, which would be damaged by such close folds, must be looked to, and aired and beaten, putting them away dry before the evening.

Preservatives against the Ravages of Moths

Place pieces of camphor, cedar-wood, Russia leather, tobacco-leaves, bog-myrtle, or anything else strongly aromatic, in the drawers or boxes where furs or other things to be preserved from moths are kept, and they will never take harm.

Jewels are generally wrapped up in cotton, and kept in their cases; but they are subject to tarnish from exposure to the air, and require cleaning. This is done by preparing clean soap-suds, using fine toilet-soap. Dip any article of gold, silver, gilt, or precious stones into this lye, and dry them by brushing with a brush of soft badgers' hair, or a fine sponge; afterwards with a piece of fine cloth, and, lastly, with a soft leather.

Epaulettes of gold or silver, and, in general, all articles of jewellery, may be dressed by dipping them in spirits of wine warmed in a *bain marie*, or shallow kettle, placed over a slow fire or hot-plate.

The valet and lady's-maid, from their supposed influence with their master and mistress, are exposed to some temptations to which other servants are less subjected. They are probably in communication with the tradespeople who supply articles for the toilet; such as hatters, tailors, dressmakers, and perfumers. The conduct of waiting-maid and valet to these people should be civil but independent, making reasonable allowance for want of exact punctuality, if any such can be made; they should represent any inconvenience respectfully, and if an excuse seems unreasonable, put the matter fairly to master or mistress, leaving it to them to notice it further, if they think it necessary. No expectations of a personal character should influence them one way or the other. It would be acting unreasonably to any domestic to make them refuse such presents as tradespeople choose to give them; the utmost that can be expected is that they should not influence their judgment in the articles supplied—that they should represent them truly to master or mistress, without fear and without favour. Civility to all, servility to none, is a good maxim for every one. Deference to a master and mistress, and to their friends and visitors, is one of the implied terms of their engagement; and this deference must apply even to what may be considered their whims. A servant is not to be seated, or wear a hat in the house, in his master's or mistress's presence; nor offer any opinion, unless asked for it; nor even to say 'good night,' or 'good morning,' except in reply to that salutation.

To Preserve Cut Flowers

A bouquet of freshly-cut flowers may be preserved alive for a long time by placing them in a glass or vase with fresh water, in which a little charcoal has been steeped, or a small piece of camphor dissolved. The vase should be set upon a plate or dish, and covered with a bell-glass, around the edges of which, when it comes in contact with the plate, a little water should be poured to exclude the air.

To Revive Cut Flowers after Packing

Plunge the stems into boiling water, and by the time the water is
cold, the flowers will have revived. Then cut afresh the ends of the
stems, and keep them in fresh cold water.

UPPER AND UNDER HOUSEMAIDS

Housemaids, in large establishments, have usually one or more
assistants; in this case they are upper and under housemaids. Dividing the work between them, the upper housemaid will probably
reserve for herself the task of dusting the ornaments and cleaning
the furniture of the principal apartments, but it is her duty to see
that every department is properly attended to. The number of assistants depends on the number in the family, as well as on the style in
which the establishment is kept up. In wealthy families it is not
unusual for every grown-up daughter to have her waiting-maid,
whose duty it is to keep her mistress's apartments in order, thus
abridging the housemaid's duties. In others, perhaps, one waiting-
maid attends on two or three, when the housemaid's assistance will
be more requisite. In fact, every establishment has some customs
peculiar to itself, on which we need not dwell; the general duties are
the *same in all*, perfect cleanliness and order being the object.

DUTIES OF THE HOUSEMAID

'Cleanliness is next to godliness,' saith the proverb, and 'order' is in
the next degree; the housemaid, then, may be said to be the hand-
maiden to two of the most prominent virtues. Her duties are very
numerous, and many of the comforts of the family depend on their
performance; but they are simple and easy to a person naturally
clean and orderly, and desirous of giving satisfaction. In all families,
whatever the habits of the master and mistress, servants will find it
advantageous to rise early; their daily work will thus come easy to
them. If they rise late, there is a struggle to overtake it, which throws
an air of haste and hurry over the whole establishment. Where the
master's time is regulated by early business or professional engagements, this will, of course, regulate the hours of the servants; but
even where that is not the case, servants will find great personal
convenience in rising early and getting through their work in an

orderly and methodical manner. The housemaid who studies her own ease will certainly be at her work by six o'clock in the summer, and, probably, half-past six or seven in the winter months, having spent a reasonable time in her own chamber in dressing. Earlier than this would, probably, be an unnecessary waste of coals and candle in winter.

The first duty of the housemaid in winter is to open the shutters of all the lower rooms in the house, and take up the hearth-rugs of those rooms which she is going to 'do' before breakfast. In some families, where there is only a cook and housemaid kept, and where the drawing-rooms are large, the cook has the care of the dining-room, and the housemaid that of the breakfast-room, library, and drawing-rooms. After the shutters are all opened, she sweeps the breakfast-room, sweeping the dust towards the fire-place, of course previously removing the

Carpet-Brooms

fender. She should then lay a cloth (generally made of coarse wrappering) over the carpet in front of the stove, and on this should place her housemaid's box, containing black-lead brushes, leathers, emery-paper, cloth, black lead, and all utensils necessary for cleaning a grate, with the cinder-pail on the other side.

She now sweeps up the ashes, and deposits them in her cinder-pail, which is a japanned tin pail, with a wire-sifter inside, and a closely-fitting top. In this pail the cinders are sifted, and reserved for use in the kitchen or under the copper, the ashes only being thrown away. The cinders disposed of, she proceeds to black-lead the grate, producing the black lead, the soft brush for laying it on, her blacking and polishing brushes, from the box which contains her tools. This housemaid's box should be kept

Stove-Brushes

well stocked. Having blackened, brushed, and polished every part, and made all clean and bright, she now proceeds to lay the fire.

Sometimes it is very difficult to get a proper polish to black grates, particularly if they have been neglected, and allowed to rust at all. Brunswick black, which is an excellent varnish for grates, may be prepared in the following manner:—

Housemaid's Box

INGREDIENTS.—1 lb. of common asphaltum, ½ pint of linseed oil, 1 quart of oil of turpentine.

Mode.—Melt the asphaltum, and add gradually to it the other two ingredients. Apply this with a small painter's brush, and leave it to become perfectly dry. The grate will need no other cleaning, but will merely require dusting every day, and occasionally brushing with a dry black-lead brush. This is, of course, when no fires are used. When they are required, the bars, cheeks, and back of the grate will need black-leading in the usual manner.

Fire-lighting, however simple, is an operation requiring some skill; a fire is readily made by laying a few cinders at the bottom in open order; over this a few pieces of paper, and over that again eight or ten pieces of dry wood; over the wood, a course of moderate-sized pieces of coal, taking care to leave hollow spaces between for air at the centre; and taking care to lay the whole well back in the grate, so that the smoke may go up the chimney, and not into the room. This done, fire the paper with a match from below, and, if properly laid, it will soon burn up; the stream of flame from the wood and paper soon communicating to the coals and cinders, provided there is plenty of air at the centre.

A new method of lighting a fire is sometimes practised with advantage, the fire lighting from the top and burning down, in place of being lighted and burning up from below. This is arranged by laying the coals at the bottom, mixed with a few good-sized cinders, and the wood at the top with another layer of coals and some paper over it; the paper is lighted in the usual way, and soon burns down to a good fire, with some economy of fuel, as is said.

Bright grates require unceasing attention to keep them in perfect order. A day should never pass without the housemaid rubbing with a dry leather the polished parts of a grate, as also the fender and fire-irons. A careful and attentive housemaid should have no occasion ever to use emery-paper for any part but the bars, which, of course, become blackened by the fire. (Some mistresses, to save labour, have a double set of bars, one set bright for the summer, and another black set to use when fires are in requisition.) When bright grates are once neglected, small rust-spots begin to show themselves, which a plain leather will not remove; the following method of cleaning them must then be resorted to:—First, thoroughly clean with emery-paper; then take a large smooth pebble from the road, sufficiently large to hold comfortably in the hand, with which rub the steel backwards and forwards one way, until the desired polish is obtained. It may appear at first to scratch, but continue rubbing, and the result will be success. The following is also an excellent polish for bright stoves and steel articles:—

INGREDIENTS.—1 tablespoonful of turpentine, 1 ditto of sweet oil, emery powder.

Mode.—Mix the turpentine and sweet oil together, stirring in sufficient emery powder to make the mixture of the thickness of cream. Put it on the article with a piece of soft flannel, rub off quickly with another piece, then polish with a little dry emery powder and clean leather.

The several fires lighted, the housemaid proceeds with her dusting, and polishing the several pieces of furniture in the breakfast-parlour, leaving no corner unvisited. Before sweeping the carpet, it is a good practice to sprinkle it all over with tea-leaves, which not only lay all dust, but give a slightly fragrant smell to the room. It is now in order for the reception of the family; and where there is neither footman nor parlour-maid, she now proceeds to the dressing-room, and lights her mistress's fire, if she is in the habit of having one to dress by. Her mistress is called, hot water placed in the dressing-room for her use, her clothes—as far as they are under the housemaid's charge—put before the fire to air, hanging a fire-guard on the bars where there is one, while she proceeds to prepare the breakfast.

In summer the housemaid's work is considerably abridged: she throws open the windows of the several rooms not occupied as bed-rooms, that they may receive the fresh morning air before they are occupied; she prepares the breakfast-room by sweeping the carpet, rubbing tables and chairs, dusting mantel-shelf and picture-frames with a light brush, dusting the furniture, and beating and sweeping the rug; she cleans the grate when necessary, and replaces the white paper or arranges the shavings with which it is filled, leaving every-thing clean and tidy for breakfast. It is not enough, however, in cleaning furniture, just to pass lightly over the surface; the rims and legs of tables, and the backs and legs of chairs and sofas, should be rubbed vigorously daily; if there is a book-case, every corner of every pane and ledge requires to be carefully wiped, so that not a speck of dust can be found in the room.

After the breakfast-room is finished, the housemaid should pro-ceed to sweep down the stairs, commencing at the top, while the cook has the charge of the hall, door-step, and passages. After this she should go into the drawing-room, cover up every article of furniture that is likely to spoil, with large dusting-sheets, and put the chairs together, by turning them seat to seat, and, in fact, make as much room as possible, by placing all the loose fur-niture in the middle of the room, whilst she sweeps the corners and sides. When this is accomplished, the furniture can then be put back in its place, and the middle of the room swept, sweeping the dirt, as before said, towards the fireplace. The same rules should be observed in cleaning the drawing-room grates as we have just stated, putting down the cloth, before commencing, to prevent the carpet from getting soiled. In the country, a room would not require sweeping thoroughly like this more than twice a week; but the housemaid should go over it every morning with a dust-pan and broom, taking up every crumb and piece she may see. After the sweeping she should leave the room, shut the door, and proceed to lay the break-fast. Where there is neither footman nor parlour-maid kept, the duty of laying the breakfast-cloth rests on the housemaid.

Banister-Broom

Staircase-Broom

Before laying the cloth for breakfast, the heater of the tea-urn is to be placed in the hottest part of the kitchen fire; or, where the kettle is used, boiled on the kitchen fire, and then removed to the parlour, where it is kept hot. Having washed herself free from the dust arising from the morning's work, the housemaid collects the breakfast-things on her tray, takes the breakfast-cloth from the napkin press, and carries them all on the tray into the parlour; arranges them on the table, placing a sufficiency of knives, forks, and salt-cellars for the family, and takes the tray back to the pantry; gets a supply of milk, cream, and bread; fills the butter-dish, taking care that the salt is plentiful, and soft and dry, and that hot plates and egg-cups are ready where warm meat or eggs are served, and that butter-knife and bread-knife are in their places. And now she should give the signal for breakfast, holding herself ready to fill the urn with hot water, or hand the kettle, and take in the rolls, toast, and other eatables, with which the cook supplies her, when the breakfast-room bell rings; bearing in mind that she is never to enter the parlour with dirty hands or with a dirty apron, and that everything is to be handed on a tray; that she is to hand everything she may be required to supply, on the left hand of the person she is serving, and that all is done quietly and without bustle or hurry. In some families, where there is a large number to attend on, the cook waits at breakfast whilst the housemaid is busy upstairs in the bedrooms, or sweeping, dusting, and putting the drawing-room in order.

Breakfast served, the housemaid proceeds to the bed-chambers, throws up the sashes, if not already done, pulls up the blinds, throwing back curtains at the same time, and opens the beds, by removing the clothes, placing them over a horse, or, failing that, over the backs of chairs. She now proceeds to empty the slops. In doing this, everything is emptied into the slop-pail, leaving a little scalding-hot water for a minute in such vessels as require it; adding a drop of turpentine to the water, when that is not sufficient to cleanse them. The basin is emptied, well rinsed with clean water, and carefully wiped; the ewers emptied and washed; finally, the water-jugs themselves emptied out and rinsed, and wiped dry. As soon as this is done, she should remove and empty the pails, taking care that they also are well washed, scalded, and wiped as soon as they are empty.

Next follows bedmaking, at which the cook or kitchen-maid, where one is kept, usually assists; but, before beginning, velvet chairs, or other things injured by dust, should be removed to another room. In bedmaking, the fancy of its occupant should be consulted; some like beds sloping from the top towards the feet, swelling slightly in the middle; others, perfectly flat: a good housemaid will accommodate each bed to the taste of the sleeper, taking care to shake, beat, and turn it well in the process. Some persons prefer sleeping on the mattress; in which case a feather bed is usually beneath, resting on a second mattress, and a straw paillasse at the bottom. In this case, the mattresses should change places daily; the feather bed placed on the mattress shaken, beaten, taken up and opened several times, so as thoroughly to separate the feathers: if too large to be thus handled, the maid should shake and beat one end first, and then the other, smoothing it afterwards equally all over into the required shape, and place the mattress gently over it. Any feathers which escape in this process a tidy servant will put back through the seam of the tick; she will also be careful to sew up any stitch that gives way the moment it is discovered. The bedclothes are laid on, beginning with an under blanket and sheet, which are tucked under the mattress at the bottom. The bolster is then beaten and shaken, and put on, the top of the sheet rolled round it, and the sheet tucked in all round. The pillows and other bedclothes follow, and the counterpane over all, which should fall in graceful folds, and at equal distance from the ground all round. The curtains are drawn to the head and folded neatly across the bed, and the whole finished in a smooth and graceful manner. Where spring-mattresses are used, care should be taken that the top one is turned every day. The housemaid should now take up in a dustpan any pieces that may be on the carpet; she should dust the room, shut the door, and proceed to another room. When all the bedrooms are finished, she should dust the stairs, and polish the handrail of the banisters, and see that all ledges, window-sills, &c., are quite free from dust. It will be necessary for the housemaid to divide her work, so that she may not have too much to do on certain days, and not sufficient to fill up her time on other days. In the country, bedrooms should be swept and thoroughly cleaned once a week; and to be methodical and regular in her work, the housemaid should have certain days for doing certain rooms thoroughly. For instance, the drawing-room on Monday, two bedrooms on Tuesday, two on Wednesday, and so on, reserving a day for thoroughly cleaning the plate, bedroom candlesticks, &c. &c., which she will have to do where there is no parlour-maid or footman kept. By this means the work will be divided, and there will be no unnecessary bustling and hurrying, as is the case where the work is done any time, without rule or regulation.

Once a week, when a bedroom is to be thoroughly cleaned, the housemaid should commence by brushing the mattresses of the bed before it is made; she should then make it, shake the curtains, lay them smoothly on the bed, and pin or tuck up the bottom valance, so that she may be able to sweep under the bed. She should then unloop the window-curtains, shake them, and pin them high up out of the way. After clearing the dressing-table, and the room altogether of little articles of china, &c. &c., she should shake the toilet-covers, fold them up, and lay them on the bed, over which a large dusting-sheet should be thrown. She should then sweep the room; first of all sprinkling the carpet with well-squeezed tea-leaves, or a little freshly-pulled grass, when this is obtain-

Scrubbing-Brush

Long Hair-Broom

able. After the carpet is swept, and the grate cleaned, she should wash with soap and water, with a little soda in it, the washing-table appar-atus, removing all marks or fur round the jugs, caused by the water. The water-bottles and tumblers must also have her attention, as well as the top of the washing-stand, which should be cleaned with soap and flannel if it be marble: if of polished mahogany, no soap must be used. When these are all clean and arranged in their places, the housemaid should scrub the floor where it is not covered with carpet, under the beds, and round the wainscot. She should use as little soap and soda as possible, as too free a use of these articles is liable to give the boards a black appearance. In the country, cold soft water, a clean scrubbing-brush, and a willing arm, are all that are required to make bedroom floors look white. In winter it is not advisable to scrub rooms too often, as it is difficult to dry them thoroughly at that season of the year, and nothing is more dangerous than to allow persons to sleep in a damp room. The housemaid should now dust the furniture, blinds, ornaments, &c.; polish the looking-glass; arrange the toilet-cover and muslin; remove the cover from the bed, and straighten and arrange the curtains and counterpane. A bedroom should be cleaned like this every week. There are times, however, when it is necessary to have the carpet up; this should be done once a year in the country, and twice a year in large cities. The best time for these arrangements is spring and autumn, when the bed-furniture requires changing to suit the seasons of the year. After arranging the furniture, it should all be well rubbed and polished; and for this purpose the housemaid should provide herself with an old silk pocket-handkerchief, to finish the polishing.

As modern furniture is now nearly always French-polished, it should often be rubbed with an old silk rubber, or a fine cloth or duster, to keep it free from smears. Three or four times a year any of the following polishes may be applied with very great success, as any of them make French-polished furniture look very well. One precaution must be taken,—not to put too much of the polish on at one time, and *to rub, not smear* it over the articles.

Furniture Polish

INGREDIENTS.—¼ pint of linseed-oil, ¼ pint of vinegar, 1 oz. of spirits of salts, ½ oz. of muriatic antimony.
Mode.—Mix all well together, and shake before using.

Furniture Polish

INGREDIENTS.—Equal proportions of linseed-oil, turpentine, vinegar, and spirits of wine.
Mode.—When used, shake the mixture well, and rub on the furniture with a piece of linen rag, and polish with a clean duster. Vinegar and oil, rubbed in with flannel, and the furniture rubbed with a clean duster, produce a very good polish.

Furniture Paste

INGREDIENTS.—3 oz. of common beeswax, 1 oz. of white wax, 1 oz. of curd soap, 1 pint of turpentine, 1 pint of boiled water.
Mode.—Mix the ingredients together, adding the water when cold; shake the mixture frequently in the bottle, and do not use it for 48 hours after it is made. It

Furniture-Brush should be applied with a piece of flannel, the furniture polished with a duster, and then with an old silk rubber.

The chambers are finished, the chamber candlesticks brought down and cleaned, the parlour lamps trimmed;—and here the housemaid's utmost care is required. In cleaning candlesticks, as in every other cleaning, she should have cloths and brushes kept for that purpose alone; the knife used to scrape them should be applied to no other purpose; the tallow-grease should be thrown into a box kept for the purpose; the same with everything connected with the lamp-trimming; the best mode of doing which she will do well to learn from the tradesman who supplies the oil; always bearing in mind, however, that without perfect cleanliness, which involves occasional scalding, no lamp can be kept in order.

The drawing- and dining-room, inasmuch as everything there is more costly and valuable, require even more care. When the carpets are of the kind known as velvet-pile, they require to be swept firmly by a hard whisk brush, made of cocoanut fibre.

The furniture must be carefully gone over in every corner with a soft cloth, that it may be left perfectly free from dust; or where that is beyond reach, with a brush made of long feathers, or a goose's wing. The sofas are swept in the same manner, slightly beaten, the cushions shaken and smoothed, the picture-frames swept, and everything arranged in its proper place. This, of course, applies to dining- as well as drawing-room and morning-room. And now the housemaid may dress herself for the day, and prepare for the family dinner, at which she must attend.

We need not repeat the long instructions already given for laying the dinner-table. At the family dinner, even where no footman waits, the routine will be the same. In most families the cloth is laid with the slips on each side, with napkins, knives, forks, spoons, and wine and finger glasses on all occasions.

She should ascertain that her plate is in order, glasses free from smears, water-bottles and decanters the same, and everything ready on her tray, that she may be able to lay her cloth properly. Few things add more to the neat and comfortable appearance of a dinner-table than

Butler's Tray and Stand

well-polished plate; indeed, the state of the plate is a certain indication of a well-managed or ill-managed household. Nothing is easier than to keep plate in good order, and yet many servants, from stupidity and ignorance, make it the greatest trouble of all things under their care. It should be remembered, that it is utterly impossible to make greasy silver take a polish; and that as spoons and forks in daily use are continually in contact with grease, they must require good washing in soap-and-water to remove it. Silver should be washed with a soapy flannel in one water, rinsed in another, and then wiped dry with a dry cloth. The plate so washed may be polished with the plate-rags, as in the following directions:—Once a week all the plate should receive a thorough cleaning with the hartshorn powder, as directed in the first recipe for cleaning plate; and where the housemaid can find time, rubbed every day with the plate-rags.

Hartshorn, we may observe, is one of the best possible ingredients for plate-powder in daily use. It leaves on the silver a deep, dark polish, and at the same time does less injury than anything else. It has also the advantage of being very cheap; almost all the ordinary powders sold in boxes containing more or less of quicksilver, in some form or another; and this in process of time is sure to make the plate brittle. If any one wishes to be convinced of the effect of quicksilver on plate, he has only to rub a little of it on one place for some time,—on the handle of a silver teaspoon for instance, and he will find it break in that spot with very little pressure.

To Clean Plate
A very excellent method

Wash the plate well to remove all grease, in a strong lather of common yellow soap and boiling water, and wipe it quite dry; then mix

Plate-Brush

as much hartshorn powder as will be required, into a thick paste, with cold water or spirits of wine; smear this lightly over the plate with a piece of soft rag, and leave it for some little time to dry. When perfectly dry, brush it off quite clean with a soft plate-brush, and polish the plate with a dry leather. If the plate be very dirty, or much tarnished, spirits of wine will be found to answer better than the water for mixing the paste.

Plate-rags for Daily Use

Boil soft rags (nothing is better for the purpose than the tops of old cotton stockings) in a mixture of new milk and hartshorn powder, in the proportion of 1 oz. of powder to a pint of milk; boil them for 5 minutes; wring them as soon as they are taken out, for a moment, in cold water, and dry them before the fire. With these rags rub the plate briskly as soon as it has been well washed and dried after daily use. A most beautiful deep polish will be produced, and the plate will require nothing more than merely to be dusted with a leather or a dry soft cloth, before it is again put on the table.

For waiting at table, the housemaid should be neatly and cleanly dressed, and, if possible, her dress made with closed sleeves, the large open ones dipping and falling into everything on the table, and being very much in the way. She should not wear creaking boots, and should move about the room as noiselessly as possible, anticipating people's wants by handing them things without being asked for them, and altogether be as quiet as possible. It will be needless here to repeat what we have already said respecting waiting at table, in the duties of the butler and footman: rules that are good to be observed by them, are equally good for the parlour-maid or housemaid.

The housemaid having announced that dinner is on the table, will hand the soup, fish, meat, or side-dishes to the different members of the family; but in families who do not spend much of the day together, they will probably prefer being alone at dinner and breakfast; the housemaid will be required, after all are helped, if her master does not wish her to stay in the room, to go on with her work of cleaning up in the pantry, and answer the bell when rung. In this case she will place a pile of plates on the table or a dumb-waiter, within reach of her master and mistress, and leave the room.

Dinner over, the housemaid removes the plates and dishes on the tray, places the dirty knives and forks in the basket prepared for them, folds up the napkins in the ring which indicates by which member of the family it has been used, brushes off the crumbs on the hand-tray kept for the purpose, folds up the table-cloth in the folds

Crumb-Brush

already made, and places it in the linen-press to be smoothed out. After every meal the table should be rubbed, all marks from hot plates removed, and the table-cover thrown over, and the room restored to its usual order. If the family retire to the drawing-room, or any other room, it is a good practice to throw up the sash to admit fresh air and ventilate the room.

The housemaid's evening service consists in washing up the dinner things, the plate, plated articles, and glasses, restoring everything to its place; cleaning up her pantry, and putting away everything for use when next required; lastly, preparing for tea, as the time approaches, by setting the things out on the tray, getting the urn or kettle ready, with cream and other things usually partaken of at that meal.

In summer-time the windows of all the bedrooms, which have been closed during the heat of the day, should be thrown open for an hour or so after sunset, in order to air them. Before dark they should be closed, the bedclothes turned down, and the night-clothes laid in order for use when required. During winter, where fires are required in the dressing-rooms, they should be lighted an hour before the usual time of retiring, placing a fire-guard before each fire. At the same time, the night-things on the horse should be placed before it to be aired, with a tin can of hot water, if the mistress is in the habit of washing before going to bed. We may add, that there is no greater preservative of beauty than washing the face every night in hot water. The housemaid will probably be required to assist her mistress to undress and put her dress in order for the morrow; in which case her duties are very much those of the lady's-maid.

And now the fire is made up for the night, the fireguard replaced, and everything in the room in order for the night, the housemaid taking care to leave the night-candle and matches together in a convenient place, should they be required. It is usual in summer to remove all highly fragrant flowers from sleeping-rooms, the impression being that their scent is injurious in a close chamber.

On leisure days, the housemaid should be able to do some needlework for her mistress,—such as turning and mending sheets and darning the house linen, or assist her in anything she may think fit to give her to do. For this reason it is almost essential that a housemaid, in a small family, should be an expert needlewoman; as, if she be a good manager and an active girl, she will have time on her hands to get through plenty of work.

Periodical Cleanings.—Besides the daily routine which we have described, there are portions of every house which can only be thoroughly cleaned occasionally; at which time the whole house usually undergoes a more thorough cleaning than is permitted in the general way. On these occasions it is usual to begin at the top of the house and clean downwards; moving everything out of the room; washing the wainscoting or paint with soft soap and water; pulling down the beds and thoroughly cleansing all the joints; 'scrubbing' the floor; beating feather beds, mattress, and paillasse, and thoroughly purifying every article of furniture before it is put back in its place.

This general cleaning usually takes place in the spring or early summer, when the warm curtains of winter are replaced by the light and cheerful muslin curtains. Carpets are at the same time taken up and beaten, except where the mistress of the house has been worried into an experiment by the often-reiterated question, 'Why beat your carpets?' In this case she will probably have made up her mind to try the cleaning process, and arranged with the company to send for them on the morning when cleaning commenced.* It is hardly necessary to

House-Pail

repeat, that on this occasion every article is to be gone over, the French-polished furniture well rubbed and polished. The same thorough system of cleaning should be done throughout the house; the walls cleaned where painted, and swept down with a soft broom or feather brush where papered; the window and bed curtains, which have been replaced with muslin ones, carefully brushed, or, if they require it, cleaned; lamps not likely to be required, washed out with hot water, dried, and cleaned. The several grates are now to be furnished with their summer ornaments;

Cornice-Brush

Dusting-Brush

and we know none prettier than the following, which the housemaid may provide at a small expense to her mistress:—Purchase two yards and a half of crinoline muslin, and tear it into small strips, the selvage way of the material, about an inch wide; strip this thread by thread on each side, leaving the four centre threads; this gives about six-and-thirty pieces, fringed on each side, which are tied together at one end, and fastened to the trap of the register, while the threads, unravelled, are spread gracefully about the grate, the lower part of which is filled with paper shavings. This makes a very elegant and very cheap ornament, which is much stronger, besides, than those usually purchased.*

As winter approaches, this house-cleaning will have to be repeated, and the warm bed and window curtains replaced. The process of scouring and cleaning is again necessary, and must be gone through, beginning at the top, and going through the house, down to the kitchens.

Independently of these daily and periodical cleanings, other occupations will present themselves from time to time, which the housemaid will have to perform. When spots show on polished furniture, they can generally be restored by soap-and-water and a sponge, the polish being brought out by using a little polish, and then well rubbing it. Again, drawers which draw out stiffly may be made to move more easily if the spot where they press is rubbed over with a little soap.

Chips broken off any of the furniture should be collected and replaced, by means of a little glue applied to it. Liquid glue, which is sold prepared in bottles, is very useful to have in the house, as it requires no melting; and anything broken can be so quickly repaired.

Breaking glass and china is about the most disagreeable thing that can happen in a family,* and it is, probably, a greater annoyance to a right-minded servant than to the mistress. A neat-handed house-maid may sometimes repair these breakages, where they are not broken in very conspicuous places, by joining the pieces very neatly together with a cement made as follows:—Dissolve an ounce of gum mastic in a quantity of highly-rectified spirits of wine; then soften an ounce of isinglass in warm water, and, finally, dissolve it in rum or brandy, till it forms a thick jelly. Mix the isinglass and gum mastic together, adding a quarter of an ounce of finely-powdered gum ammoniac; put the whole into an earthen pipkin, and in a warm place, till they are thoroughly incorporated together; pour it into a small phial, and cork it down for use.

In using it, dissolve a small piece of the cement in a silver teaspoon over a lighted candle. The broken pieces of glass or china being warmed, and touched with the now liquid cement, join the parts neatly together, and hold in their places till the cement has set; then wipe away the cement adhering to the edge of the joint, and leave it for twelve hours without touching it: the joint will be as strong as the china itself, and if neatly done, it will show no joining. It is essential that neither of the pieces be wetted either with hot or cold water.

USEFUL RECIPES FOR HOUSEMAIDS

To Clean Marble

Mix with ¼ pint of soap lees, ½ gill of turpentine, sufficient pipe-clay and bullock's gall to make the whole into rather a thick paste. Apply it to the marble with a soft brush, and after a day or two, when quite dry, rub it off with a soft rag. Apply this a second or third time till the marble is quite clean.

Another Method

Take two parts of soda, one of pumice-stone, and one of finely-powdered chalk. Sift these through a fine sieve, and mix them into a paste with water. Rub this well all over the marble, and the stains will be removed; then wash it with soap-and-water, and a beautiful bright polish will be produced.

To Clean Floorcloth*

After having washed the floorcloth in the usual manner with a damp flannel, wet it all over with milk and rub it well with a dry cloth, when a most beautiful polish will be brought out. Some persons use for rubbing a well-waxed flannel; but this in general produces an unpleasant slipperiness, which is not the case with the milk.

To Clean Decanters

Roll up in small pieces some soft brown or blotting paper; wet them, and soap them well. Put them into the decanters about one quarter full of warm water; shake them well for a few minutes, then rinse with clear cold water; wipe the outsides with a nice dry cloth, put the decanters to drain, and when dry they will be almost as bright as new ones.

To Brighten Gilt Frames

Take sufficient flour of sulphur to give a golden tinge to about 1½ pint of water, and in this boil 4 or 5 bruised onions, or garlic, which will answer the same purpose. Strain off the liquid, and with it, when cold, wash, with a soft brush, any gilding which requires restoring, and when dry it will come out as bright as new work.

To Preserve Bright Grates or Fire-irons from Rust

Make a strong paste of fresh lime and water, and with a fine brush smear it as thickly as possible over all the polished surface requiring preservation. By this simple means, all the grates and fire-irons in an empty house may be kept for months free from harm, without further care or attention.

German Furniture-Gloss

INGREDIENTS.—¼ lb. yellow wax, 1 oz. black rosin, 2 oz. of oil of turpentine.

Mode.—Cut the wax into small pieces, and melt it in a pipkin, with the rosin pounded very fine. Stir in gradually, while these two ingredients are quite warm, the oil of turpentine. Keep this composition well covered for use in a tin or earthen pot. A little of this gloss should be spread on a piece of coarse woollen cloth, and the furniture well rubbed with it; afterwards it should be polished with a fine cloth.

DUTIES OF THE MAID-OF-ALL-WORK

The general servant, or maid-of-all-work, is perhaps the only one of her class deserving of commiseration: her life is a solitary one, and, in some places, her work is never done. She is also subject to rougher treatment than either the house or kitchen-maid, especially in her earlier career: she starts in life, probably a girl of thirteen, with some small tradesman's wife as her mistress, just a step above her in the social scale; and although the class contains among them many excellent, kind-hearted women, it also contains some very rough specimens of the feminine gender, and to some of these it occasionally falls to give our maid-of-all-work her first lessons in her multifarious occupations: the mistress's commands are the measure of the maid-of-all-work's duties. By the time she has become a tolerable servant, she is probably engaged in some respectable tradesman's house, where she has to rise with the lark, for she has to do in her own person all the work which in larger establishments is performed by cook, kitchen-maid, and housemaid, and occasionally the part of a footman's duty, which consists in carrying messages.*

The general servant's duties commence by opening the shutters (and windows, if the weather permits) of all the lower apartments in the house; she should then brush up her kitchen-range, light the fire, clear away the ashes, clean the hearth, and polish with a leather the bright parts of the range, doing all as rapidly and as vigorously as possible, that no more time be wasted than is necessary. After putting on the kettle, she should then proceed to the dining-room or parlour to get it in order for breakfast. She should first roll up the rug, take up the fender, shake and fold up the table-cloth, then sweep the room, carrying the dirt towards the fireplace; a coarse cloth should then be laid down over the carpet, and she should proceed to clean the grate, having all her utensils close to her. When the grate is finished, the ashes cleared away, the hearth cleaned, and the fender put back in its place, she must dust the furniture, not omitting the legs of the tables and chairs; and if there are any ornaments or things on the sideboard, she must not dust round them, but lift them up on to another place, dust well where they have been standing, and then replace the things. Nothing annoys a particular mistress so much as to find, when she comes down stairs, different articles of furniture looking as if they had never been dusted. If the servant is at all methodical, and gets into a habit of *doing* a room in a certain way, she will scarcely ever leave her duties neglected. After the rug is put down, the table-cloth arranged, and everything in order, she should lay the cloth for breakfast, and then shut the dining-room door.

The hall must now be swept, the mats shaken, the door-step cleaned, and any brass knockers or handles polished up with the leather. If the family breakfast very early, the tidying of the hall must then be deferred till after that meal. After cleaning the boots that are absolutely required, the servant should now wash her hands and face, put on a clean white apron, and

Blacking-Brush Box

be ready for her mistress when she comes down stairs. In families where there is much work to do before breakfast, the master of the house frequently has two pairs of boots in wear, so that they may be properly cleaned when the servant has more time to do them, in the daytime. This arrangement is, perhaps, scarcely necessary in the summer-time, when there are no grates to clean every morning; but in the dark days of winter it is only kind and thoughtful to lighten a servant-of-all-work's duties as much as possible.

She will now carry the urn into the dining-room, where her mistress will make the tea or coffee, and sometimes will boil the eggs, to insure them being done to her liking. In the mean time the servant cooks, if required, the bacon, kidneys, fish, &c.;—if cold meat is to be served, she must always send it to table on a clean dish, and nicely garnished with tufts of parsley, if this is obtainable.

After she has had her own breakfast, and whilst the family are finishing theirs, she should go upstairs into the bedrooms, open all the windows, strip the clothes off the beds, and leave them to air whilst she is clearing away the breakfast things. She should then take up the crumbs in a dustpan from under the table, put the chairs in their places, and sweep up the hearth.

The breakfast things washed up, the kitchen should be tidied, so that it may be neat when her mistress comes in to give the orders for the day: after receiving these orders, the servant should go upstairs again, with a jug of boiling water, the slop-pail, and two cloths. After emptying the slops, and scalding the vessels with the boiling water, and wiping them thoroughly dry, she should wipe the top of the wash-table and arrange it all in order. She then proceeds to make the beds, in which occupation she is generally assisted by the mistress, or, if she have any daughters, by one of them. Before commencing to make the bed, the servant should put on a large bed-apron, kept for this purpose only, which should be made very wide, to button round the waist and meet behind, while it should be made as long as the dress. By adopting this plan, the blacks and dirt on servants' dresses (which at all times it is impossible to help) will not rub off on to the bed-clothes, mattresses, and bed furniture. When the beds are made, the rooms should be dusted, the stairs lightly swept down, hall furniture, closets, &c., dusted. The lady of the house, where there is but one servant kept, frequently takes charge of the drawing-room herself, that is to say, dusting it; the servant sweeping, cleaning windows, looking-glasses, grates, and rough work of that sort. If there are many ornaments and knick-knacks about the room, it is certainly better for the mistress to dust these herself, as a maid-of-all-work's hands are not always in a condition to handle delicate ornaments.

Now she has gone the rounds of the house and seen that all is in order, the servant goes to her kitchen to see about the cooking of the dinner, in which very often her mistress will assist her. She should put on a coarse apron with a bib to do her dirty work in, which may be easily replaced by a white one if required.

Half an hour before dinner is ready, she should lay the cloth, that everything may be in readiness when she is dishing up the dinner, and take all into the dining-room that is likely to be required, in the way of knives, forks, spoons, bread, salt, water, &c. &c. By exercising a little forethought, much confusion and trouble may be saved both to mistress and servant, by getting everything ready for the dinner in good time.

After taking in the dinner, when everyone is seated, she removes the covers, hands the plates round, and pours out the beer; and should be careful to hand everything on the left side of the person she is waiting on.

We need scarcely say that a maid-of-all-work cannot stay in the dining-room during the whole of dinner-time, as she must dish up her pudding, or whatever is served after the first course. When she sees every one helped, she should leave the room to make her preparations for the next course; and anything that is required, such as bread, &c., people may assist themselves to in the absence of the servant.

When the dinner things are cleared away, the servant should sweep up the crumbs in the dining-room, sweep the hearth, and lightly dust the furniture, then sit down to her own dinner.

After this, she washes up and puts away the dinner things, sweeps the kitchen, dusts and tidies it, and puts on the kettle for tea. She should now, before dressing herself for the afternoon, clean her knives, boots, and shoes, and do any other dirty work in the scullery that may be necessary. Knife-cleaning machines are rapidly taking the place, in most households, of the old knife-board. The saving of

Knife-Cleaning Machine

labour by the knife-cleaner is very great, and its performance of the work is very satisfactory. Small and large machines are manufactured, some cleaning only four knives, whilst others clean as many as twelve at once. Nothing can be more simple than the process of machine knife-cleaning; and although, in a very limited household, the substitution of the machine for the board may not be necessary, yet we should advise all housekeepers, to whom the outlay is not a difficulty, to avail themselves of the services of a machine. We have already spoken of its management in the 'Duties of the Footman,' p. 398.

When the servant is dressed, she takes in the tea, and after tea turns down the beds, sees that the water-jugs and bottles are full, closes the windows, and draws down the blinds. If the weather is very warm, these are usually left open until the last thing at night, to cool the rooms.

The routine of a general servant's duties depends upon the kind of situation she occupies; but a systematic maid-of-all-work should so contrive to divide her work, that every day in the week may have its proper share. By this means she is able to keep the house clean with less fatigue to herself than if she left all the cleaning to do at the end of the week. Supposing there are five bedrooms in the house, two sitting-rooms, kitchen, scullery, and the usual domestic offices:*—on Monday she should thoroughly clean the drawing-room; on Tuesday, two of the bedrooms; on Wednesday, two more; on Thursday, the other bedroom and stairs; on Friday morning she should sweep the dining-room very thoroughly, clean the hall, and in the afternoon her kitchen tins and bright utensils. By arranging her work in this manner, no undue proportion will fall to Saturday's share, and she will then have this day for cleaning plate, cleaning her kitchen, and arranging everything in nice order. The regular work must, of course, be performed in the usual manner, as we have endeavoured to describe.

Before retiring to bed, she will do well to clean up glasses, plates, &c. which have been used for the evening meal, and prepare for her morning's work by placing her wood near the fire, on the hob, to dry, taking care there is no danger of it igniting, before she leaves the kitchen for the night. Before retiring, she will have to lock and bolt the doors, unless the master undertakes this office himself.

If the washing, or even a portion of it, is done at home, it will be impossible for the maid-of-all-work to do her household duties thoroughly, during the time it is about, unless she have some assistance. Usually, if all the washing is done at home, the mistress hires some one to assist at the wash-tub, and sees to little matters herself, in the way of dusting, clearing away breakfast things, folding, starching, and ironing the fine things. With a little management much can be accomplished, provided the mistress be industrious, energetic, and willing to lend a helping hand. Let washing-week be not the excuse for having everything in a muddle; and although 'things' cannot be cleaned so thoroughly, and so much time spent upon them, as ordinarily, yet the house may be kept tidy and clear from litter without a great deal of exertion either on the part of the mistress or servant. We will conclude our remarks with an extract from an admirably-written book, called 'Home Truths for Home Peace.' The authoress says, with respect to the great wash—'Amongst all the occasions in which it is most difficult and glorious to keep muddle out of a family, "the great wash" stands pre-eminent; and as very little money is now saved by having *everything* done at home, many ladies, with the option of taking another servant or putting out the chief part of the washing, have thankfully adopted the latter course.' She goes on to say—'When a gentleman who dines at home can't bear washing in the house, but gladly pays for its being done elsewhere, the lady should gratefully submit to his wishes, and put out anything in her whole establishment rather than put out a good and generous husband.'

A bustling and active girl will always find time to do a little needlework for herself, if she lives with consistent and reasonable people. In the summer evenings she should manage to sit down for two or three hours, and for a short time in the afternoon in leisure days. A general servant's duties are so multifarious, that unless she be quick and active, she will not be able to accomplish this. To

discharge these various duties properly is a difficult task, and sometimes a thankless office; but it must be remembered that a good
maid-of-all-work will make a good servant in any capacity, and
may be safely taken not only without fear of failure, but with every
probability of giving satisfaction to her employer.

DUTIES OF THE DAIRY-MAID

The duties of the dairy-maid differ considerably in different districts. In Scotland, Wales, and some of the northern counties,
women milk the cows. On some of the large dairy farms in other
parts of England, she takes her share in the milking, but in private
families the milking is generally performed by the cowkeeper, and
the dairy-maid only receives the milkpails from him morning and
night, and empties and cleans them preparatory to the next milking;
her duty being to supply the family with milk, cream, and butter, and
other luxuries depending on the 'milky mothers' of the herd.

The Dairy.—The object with which gentlemen keep cows is to procure
milk unadulterated, and sweet butter, for themselves and families: in order
to obtain this, however, great cleanliness is required, and as visitors, as
well as the mistress of the house, sometimes visit the dairy, some efforts
are usually made to render it ornamental and picturesque. The locality is
usually fixed near to the house; it should neither be exposed to the fierce
heat of the summer's sun nor to the equally unfavourable frosts of
winter—it must be both sheltered and shaded. If it is a building apart
from the house and other offices, the walls should be tolerably thick, and if
hollow, the temperature will be more equable. The walls inside are usually
covered with Dutch glazed tiles; the flooring also of glazed tiles set in
asphalte, to resist water; and the ceiling, lath and plaster, or closely-jointed
woodwork, painted. Its architecture will be a matter of fancy: it should
have a northern aspect, and a thatched roof is considered most suitable,
from the shade and shelter it affords; and it should contain at least two
apartments, besides a cool place for storing away butter. One of the apartments, in which the milk is placed to deposit cream, or to ripen for
churning, is usually surrounded by shelves of marble or slate, on which
the milk-dishes rest; but it will be found a better plan to have a large
square or round table of stone in the centre, with a water-tight ledge all
round it, in which water may remain in hot weather, or, if some attempt at
the picturesque is desired, a small fountain might occupy the centre,
which would keep the apartment cool and fresh. Round this table the
milk-dishes should be ranged; one shelf, or dresser, of slate or marble,

being kept for the various occupations of the dairy-maid: it will be found a better plan than putting them on shelves and corners against the wall. There should be a funnel or ventilator in the ceiling, communicating with the open air, made to open and shut as required. Double windows are recommended, but of the lattice kind, so that they may open, and with wire-gauze blinds fitted into the opening, and calico blinds, which may be wetted when additional coolness is required. The other apartment will be used for churning, washing, and scrubbing—in fact, the scullery of the dairy, with a boiler for hot water, and a sink with cold water laid on, which should be plentiful and good. In some dairies a third apartment, or, at least, a cool airy pantry, is required for storing away butter, with shelves of marble or slate, to hold the cream-jars while it is ripening; and where cheeses are made, a fourth becomes necessary. The dairy utensils are not numerous,—*churns*, *milk-pails* for each cow, *hair-sieves*, *slices of tin*, milk-pans, marble dishes for cream for family use, scales and weights, a portable rack for drying the utensils, *wooden-bowls*, butter-moulds and butter-patters, and *wooden tubs* for washing the utensils, comprising pretty nearly everything.

Pails are made of maple-wood or elm, and hooped, or of tin, more or less ornamented. One is required for each cow.

The Hair-Sieve is made of closely-twisted horse-hair, with a rim, through which the milk is strained to remove any hairs which may have dropped from the cow in milking.

Milk-Dishes are shallow basins of glass, of glazed earthenware, or tin, about 16 inches in diameter at top, and 12 at the bottom, and 5 or 6 inches deep, holding about 8 to 10 quarts each when full.

Churns are of all sorts and sizes, from that which churns 70 or 80 gallons by means of a strap from the engine, to the square box in which a pound of butter is made. The churn used for families is a square box, 18 inches by 12 or 13, and 17 deep, bevelled below to the plane of the *dashers*, with a loose lid or cover. The dasher consists of an axis of wood, to which the four beaters or fanners are attached; these fans are simply four pieces of elm strongly dovetailed together, forming an oblong square, with a space left open, two of the openings being left broader than the others; attached to an axle, they form an axis with four projecting blades; the axle fits into supports at the centre of the box; a handle is fitted to it, and the act of churning is done by turning the handle.

Such is the temple in which the dairy-maid presides: it should be removed both from stable and cowhouse, and larder; no animal smells should come near it, and the drainage should be perfect.

The dairy-maid receives the milk from the cowkeeper, each pail being strained through the hair sieve into one of the milk-basins. This is left in the basins from twenty-four to thirty-six hours in the summer, according to the weather; after which it is skimmed off by means of the slicer, and poured into glazed earthenware jars to 'turn' for churning. Some persons prefer making up a separate churning for the milk of each cow; in which there is some advantage. In this case the basins of each cow, for two days, would either be kept together or labelled. As soon as emptied, the pails should be scalded and every particle of milk washed out, and placed away in a dry place till next required; and all milk spilt on the floor, or on the table or dresser, cleaned up with a cloth and hot water. Where very great attention is paid to the dairy, the milk-coolers are used larger in winter, when it is desirable to retard the cooling down and increase the creamy deposit, and smaller in summer, to hasten it; the temperature required being from 55° to 50°. In summer it is sometimes expedient, in very sultry weather, to keep the dairy fresh and cool by suspending cloths dipped in chloride of lime across the room.

In some dairies it is usual to churn twice, and in others three times a week: the former produces the best butter, the other the greatest quantity. With three cows, the produce should be 27 to 30 quarts a day. The dairy-maid should churn every day when very hot, if they are in full milk, and every second day in more temperate weather; besides supplying the milk and cream required for a large establishment. The churning should always be done in the morning: the dairy-maid will find it advantageous in being at work on churning mornings by five o'clock. The operation occupies from 20 minutes to half an hour in summer, and considerably longer in winter. A steady uniform motion is necessary to produce sweet butter; neither too quick nor too slow. Rapid motion causes the cream to heave and swell, from too much air being forced into it: the result is a tedious churning, and soft, bad-coloured butter.

In spring and summer, when the cow has her natural food, no artificial colour is required; but in winter, under stall-feeding, the colour is white and tallowy, and some persons prefer a higher colour. This is communicated by mixing a little finely-powdered arnotto with the cream before putting it into the churn; a still more natural and delicate colour is communicated by scraping a red carrot into a clean piece of linen cloth, dipping it into water, and squeezing it into the cream.

As soon as the butter comes, the milk is poured off, and the butter put into a shallow wooden tub or bowl, full of pure spring water, in which it is washed and kneaded, pouring off the water, and renewing it until it comes away perfectly free from milk. Imperfect washing is the frequent cause of bad butter, and in nothing is the skill of the dairy-maid tested more than in this process; moreover, it is one in which cleanliness of habits and person are most necessary. In this operation we want the aid of Phyllis's* neat, soft, and perfectly clean hand; for no mechanical operation can so well squeeze out the sour particles of milk or curd.

The operations of churning and butter-making over, the butter-milk is disposed of: usually, in England, it goes to the pigs; but it is a very wholesome beverage when fresh, and some persons like it; the disposal, therefore, will rest with the mistress: the dairy-maid's duty is to get rid of it. She must then scald with boiling water and scrub out every utensil she has used; brush out the churn, clean out the cream-jars, which will probably require the use of a little common soda to purify; wipe all dry, and place them in a position where the sun can reach them for a short time, to sweeten them.

In Devonshire, celebrated for its dairy system, the milk is always scalded. The milk-pans, which are of tin, and contain from 10 to 12 quarts, after standing 10 or 12 hours, are placed on a hot plate of iron, over a stove, until the cream has formed on the surface, which is indicated by the air-bubbles rising through the milk, and producing blisters on the surface-coating of cream. This indicates its approach to the boiling point: and the vessel is now removed to cool. When sufficiently, that is, quite cool, the cream is skimmed off with the slice: it is now the clouted cream for which Devonshire is so famous. It is now placed in the churn, and churned until the butter comes, which it generally does in a much shorter time than by the other process. The butter so made contains more *caseine* than butter made in the usual way, but does not keep so long.

It is a question frequently discussed, how far it is economical for families to keep cows and make their own butter. It is calculated that a good cow costs from May 1 to October 1, when well but economically kept, £5. 16s. 6d.; and from October 1 to April 30, £10. 2s. 6d. During that time she should produce 227 lbs. of butter, besides the skimmed milk. Of course, if new milk and cream are required, that will diminish the quantity of butter.

Besides churning and keeping her dairy in order, the dairy-maid has charge of the whole produce, handing it over to the cook, butler, or housemaid as required; and she will do well to keep an exact account both of what she receives and how and when she disposes of it.

DUTIES OF THE LAUNDRY-MAID

The laundry-maid is charged with the duty of washing and getting-up the family linen,—a situation of great importance where the washing is all done at home; but in large towns, where there is little convenience for bleaching and drying, it is chiefly done by professional laundresses and companies, who apply mechanical and chemical processes to the purpose. These processes, however, are supposed to injure the fabric of the linen; and in many families the fine linen, cottons, and muslins, are washed and got-up at home, even where the bulk of the washing is given out. In country and suburban houses, where greater conveniences exist, washing at home is more common,—in country places universal.

The laundry establishment consists of a washing-house, an ironing and drying-room, and sometimes a drying-closet heated by furnaces. The washing-house will probably be attached to the kitchen; but it is better that it should be completely detached from it, and of one story, with a funnel or shaft to carry off the steam. It will be of a size proportioned to the extent of the washing to be done. A range of tubs, either round or oblong, opposite to, and sloping towards, the light, narrower at the bottom than the top, for convenience in stooping over, and fixed at a height suited to the convenience of the women using them; each tub having a tap for hot and cold water, and another in the bottom, communicating with the drains, for drawing off foul water. A boiler and furnace, proportioned in size to the wants of the family, should also be fixed. The flooring should be York stone, laid on brick piers, with good drainage, or asphalte, sloping gently towards a gutter connected with the drain.

Adjoining the bleaching-house, a second room, about the same size, is required for ironing, drying, and mangling. The contents of this room should comprise an ironing-board, opposite to the light; a strong white deal table, about twelve or fourteen feet long, and about three and a half feet broad, with drawers for ironing-blankets; a mangle in one corner, and clothes-horses for drying and airing; cupboards for holding the various irons, starch, and other articles used in ironing; a hot-plate built in the chimney, with furnace beneath it for heating the irons; sometimes arranged with a flue for carrying the hot air round the room for drying. Where this is the case, however, there should be a funnel in the ceiling for ventilation and carrying off steam; but a better arrangement is to have a hot-air closet adjoining, heated by hot-air pipes, and lined with iron, with proper arrangements for carrying off steam, and clothes-horses on castors running in grooves, to run into it for drying purposes. This leaves the laundry free from unwholesome vapour.

The laundry-maid should commence her labours on Monday morning by a careful examination of the articles committed to her care, and enter them in the washing-book; separating the white linen and collars, sheets and body-linen, into one heap, fine muslins into another, coloured cotton and linen fabrics into a third, woollens into a fourth, and the coarser kitchen and other greasy cloths into a fifth. Every article should be examined for ink- or grease-spots, or for fruit- or wine-stains. Ink-spots are removed by dipping the part into hot water, and then spreading it smoothly on the hand or on the back of a spoon, pouring a few drops of oxalic acid or salts of sorel over the ink-spot, rubbing and rinsing it in cold water till removed; grease-spots, by rubbing over with yellow soap, and rinsing in hot water; fruit- and wine-spots, by dipping in a solution of sal ammonia or spirits of wine, and rinsing.

Every article having been examined and assorted, the sheets and fine linen should be placed in one of the tubs and just covered with lukewarm water, in which a little soda has been dissolved and mixed, and left there to soak till the morning. The greasy cloths and dirtier things should be laid to soak in another tub, in a liquor composed of ½ lb. of unslaked lime to every 6 quarts of water which has been boiled for two hours, then left to settle, and strained off when clear. Each article should be rinsed in this liquor to wet it thoroughly, and left to soak till the morning, just covered by it when the things are pressed together. Coppers and boilers should now be filled, and the fires laid ready to light.

Early on the following morning the fires should be lighted, and as soon as hot water can be procured, washing commenced; the sheets and body-linen being wanted to whiten in the morning, should be taken first; each article being removed in succession from the lye in which it has been soaking, rinsed, rubbed, and wrung, and laid aside until the tub is empty, when the foul water is drawn off. The tub should be again filled with lukewarm water, about 80°, in which the articles should again be plunged, and each gone over carefully with soap, and rubbed. Novices in the art sometimes rub the linen against the skin; more experienced washerwomen rub one linen surface against the other, which saves their hands, and enables them to continue their labour much longer, besides economizing time, two parts being thus cleaned at once.

After this first washing, the linen should be put into a second water as hot as the hand can bear, and again rubbed over in every part, examining every part for spots not yet moved, which require to be again soaped over and rubbed till thoroughly clean; then rinsed and wrung, the larger and stronger articles by two of the women; the smaller and more delicate articles requiring gentler treatment.

In order to remove every particle of soap, and produce a good colour, they should now be placed, and boiled for about an hour and a half in the copper, in which soda, in the proportion of a teaspoonful to every two gallons of water, has been dissolved. Some very careful laundresses put the linen into a canvas bag to protect it from the scum and the sides of the copper. When taken out, it should again be rinsed, first in clean hot water, and then in abundance of cold water slightly tinged with fig-blue, and again wrung dry. It should now be removed from the washing-house and hung up to dry or spread out to bleach, if there are conveniences for it; and the earlier in the day this is done, the clearer and whiter will be the linen.

Coloured muslins, cottons, and linens, require a milder treatment; any application of soda will discharge the colour, and soaking all night, even in pure water, deteriorates the more delicate tints. When ready for washing, if not too dirty, they should be put into cold water and washed very speedily, using the common yellow soap, which should be rinsed off immediately. One article should be washed at a time, and rinsed out immediately before any others are wetted. When washed thoroughly, they should be rinsed in succession in soft water, in which common salt has been dissolved, in the proportion of a handful to three or four gallons, and afterwards wrung gently, as soon as rinsed, with as little twisting as possible, and then hung out to dry. Delicate-coloured articles should not be exposed to the sun, but dried in the shade, using clean lines and wooden pegs.

Woollen articles are liable to shrink, unless the flannel has been well shrunk before making up. This liability is increased where very hot water is used: cold water would thus be the best to wash woollens in; but, as this would not remove the dirt, lukewarm water, about 85°, and yellow soap, are recommended. When thoroughly washed in this, they require a good deal of rinsing in cold water, to remove the soap.

Greasy cloths, which have soaked all night in the liquid described, should be now washed out with soap-and-water as hot as the hands can bear, first in one water, and rinsed out in a second; and afterwards boiled for two hours in water in which a little soda is dissolved. When taken out, they should be rinsed in cold water, and laid out or hung up to dry.

Silk handkerchiefs require to be washed alone. When they contain snuff, they should be soaked by themselves in lukewarm water two or three hours; they should be rinsed out and put to soak with the others in cold water for an hour or two; then washed in lukewarm water, being soaped as they are washed. If this does not remove all stains, they should be washed a second time in similar water, and, when finished, rinsed in soft water in which a handful of common salt has been dissolved. In washing stuff or woollen dresses, the band at the waist and the lining at the bottom should be removed, and wherever it is gathered into folds; and, in furniture, the hems and gatherings. A black silk dress, if very dirty, must be washed; but, if only soiled, soaking for four-and-twenty hours will do; if old and rusty, a pint of common spirits should be mixed with each gallon of water, which is an improvement under any circumstances. Whether soaked or washed, it should be hung up to drain, and dried without wringing.

Satin and silk ribbons, both white and coloured, may be cleaned in the same manner.

Silks, when washed, should be dried in the shade, on a linen-horse, taking care that they are kept smooth and unwrinkled. If black or blue, they will be improved if laid again on the table, when dry, and sponged with gin, or whiskey, or other white spirit.

The operations should be concluded by rinsing the tubs, cleaning the coppers, scrubbing the floors of the washing-house, and restoring everything to order and cleanliness.

Thursday and Friday, in a laundry in full employ, are usually devoted to mangling, starching, and ironing.

Linen, cotton, and other fabrics, after being washed and dried, are made smooth and glossy by mangling and by ironing. The mangling process, which is simply passing them between rollers subjected to a very considerable pressure, produced by weight, is confined to sheets, towels, table-linen, and similar articles, which are without folds or plaits. Ironing is necessary to smooth body-linen, and made-up articles of delicate texture or gathered into folds. The mangle is too well known to need description.

Ironing.—The irons consist of the common flat-iron, which is of different sizes, varying from 4 to 10 inches in length, triangular in form, and from 2½ to 4½ inches in width at the broad end; the oval iron, which is used for more delicate articles; and the box-iron, which is hollow, and heated by a red-hot iron inserted into the box. The Italian iron is a hollow tube, smooth on the outside, and raised on a slender pedestal with a footstalk. Into the hollow cylinder a red-hot iron is pushed, which heats it; and the smooth outside of the latter is used, on which articles such as frills, and plaited articles, are drawn. Crimping- and gauffering-machines are used for a kind of plaiting where much regularity is required, the articles being passed through two iron rollers fluted so as to represent the kind of plait or fold required.

Starching is a process by which stiffness is communicated to certain parts of linen, as the collar and front of shirts, by dipping them in a paste made of starch boiled in water, mixed with a little gum Arabic, where extra stiffness is required.

To Make Starch

INGREDIENTS.—Allow ½ pint of cold water and 1 quart of boiling water to every 2 tablespoonfuls of starch.

Mode.—Put the starch into a tolerably large basin; pour over it the cold water, and stir the mixture well with a wooden spoon until it is perfectly free from lumps, and quite smooth. Then take the basin to the fire, and whilst the water is *actually boiling* in the kettle or boiler, pour it over the starch, stirring it the whole time. If made properly in this manner, the starch will require no further boiling; but should the water not be boiling when added to the starch, it will not thicken, and must be put into a clean saucepan, and stirred over the fire until it boils. Take it off the fire, strain it into a clean basin, cover it up to prevent a skin forming on the top, and, when sufficiently cool that the hand may be borne in it, starch the things. Many persons, to give a shiny and smooth appearance to the linen when ironed, stir round two or three times in the starch a piece of wax candle, which also prevents the iron from sticking.

When the 'things to be starched' are washed, dried, and taken off the lines, they should be dipped into the hot starch made as directed, squeezed out of it, and then just dipped into cold water, and immediately squeezed dry. If fine things be wrung, or roughly used, they are very liable to tear; so too much care cannot be exercised in this respect. If the article is lace, clap it between the hands a few times, which will assist to clear it; then have ready laid out on the table a large clean towel or cloth; shake out the starched things, lay them on the cloth, and roll it up tightly, and let it remain for three or four hours, when the things will be ready to iron.

To be able to iron properly requires much practice and experience. Strict cleanliness with all the ironing utensils must be observed, as, if this is not the case, not the most expert ironer will be able to make her things look clear and free from smears, &c. After wiping down her ironing-table, the laundry-maid should place a coarse cloth on it, and over that the ironing-blanket, with her stand and iron-rubber; and having ascertained that her irons are quite clean and of the right heat, she proceeds with her work.

It is a good plan to try the heat of the iron on a coarse cloth or apron before ironing anything fine: there is then no danger of scorching. For ironing fine things, such as collars, cuffs, muslins, and laces, there is nothing so clean and nice to use as the box-iron; the bottom being bright, and never placed near the fire, it is always perfectly clean; it should, however, be kept in a dry place, for fear of its rusting. Gauffering-tongs or irons must be placed in a clear fire for a minute, then withdrawn, wiped with a coarse rubber, and the heat of them tried on a piece of paper, as, unless great care is taken, these will very soon scorch.

The skirts of muslin dresses should be ironed on a skirt-board covered with flannel, and the fronts of shirts on a smaller board, also covered with flannel; this board being placed between the back and front.

After things are mangled, they should also be ironed in the folds and gathers; dinner-napkins smoothed over, as also table-cloths, pillow-cases, and sometimes sheets. The bands of flannel petticoats, and shoulder-straps to flannel waistcoats, must also undergo the same process.

UPPER AND UNDER NURSEMAIDS

The nursery is of great importance in every family, and in families of distinction, where there are several young children, it is an establishment kept apart from the rest of the family, under the charge of an upper nurse, assisted by under nursery-maids proportioned to the work to be done. The responsible duties of upper nursemaid commence with the weaning of the child: it must now be separated from the mother or wet-nurse, at least for a time, and the cares of the nursemaid, which have hitherto been only occasionally put in requisition, are now to be entirely devoted to the infant. She washes, dresses, and feeds it; walks out with it, and regulates all its little wants; and, even at this early age, many good qualities are required to do so in a satisfactory manner. Patience and good temper are indispensable qualities; truthfulness, purity of manners, minute cleanliness, and docility and obedience, almost equally so. She ought also to be acquainted with the art of ironing and trimming little caps, and be handy with her needle.

There is a considerable art in carrying an infant comfortably for itself and for the nursemaid. If she carry it always seated upright on her arm, and presses it too closely against her chest, the stomach of the child is apt to get compressed, and the back fatigued. For her own comfort, a good nurse will frequently vary this position, by changing from one arm to the other, and sometimes by laying it across both, raising the head a little. When teaching it to walk, and guiding it by the hand, she should change the hand from time to time, so as to avoid raising one shoulder higher than the other. This is the only way in which a child should be taught to walk; leading-strings and other foolish inventions, which force an infant to make efforts, with its shoulders and head forward, before it knows how to use its limbs, will only render it feeble, and retard its progress.

Most children have some bad habit, of which they must be broken; but this is never accomplished by harshness without developing worse evils: kindness, perseverance, and patience in the nurse, are here of the utmost importance. When finger-sucking is one of these habits, the fingers are sometimes rubbed with bitter aloes, or some equally disagreeable substance. Others have dirty habits, which are only to be changed by patience, perseverance, and, above all, by regularity in the nurse. She should never be permitted to inflict punishment on these occasions, or, indeed, on any occasion. But, if punishment is to be avoided, it is still more necessary that all kinds of indulgences and flattery be equally forbidden. Yielding to all the whims of a child,—picking up its toys when thrown away in mere wantonness, would be intolerable. A child should never be led to think others inferior to it, to beat a dog, or even the stone against which it falls, as some children are taught to do by silly nurses. Neither should the nurse affect or show alarm at any of the little accidents which must inevitably happen: if it falls, treat it as a trifle; otherwise she encourages a spirit of cowardice and timidity. But she will take care that such accidents are not of frequent occurrence, or the result of neglect.

The nurse should keep the child as clean as possible, and particularly she should train it to habits of cleanliness, so that it should feel uncomfortable when otherwise; watching especially that it does not soil itself in eating. At the same time, vanity in its personal appearance is not to be encouraged by over-care in this respect, or by too tight lacing or buttoning of dresses, nor a small foot cultivated by the use of tight shoes.

Nursemaids would do well to repeat to the parents faithfully and truly the defects they observe in the dispositions of very young children. If properly checked in time, evil propensities may be eradicated; but this should not extend to anything but serious defects; otherwise, the intuitive perceptions which all children possess will construe the act into 'spying' and 'informing,' which should never be resorted to in the case of children, nor, indeed, in any case.

Such are the cares which devolve upon the nursemaid, and it is her duty to fulfil them personally. In large establishments she will have assistants proportioned to the number of children of which she has the care. The under nursemaid lights the fires, sweeps, scours, and dusts the rooms, and makes the beds; empties slops, and carries up water; brings up and removes the nursery meals; washes and dresses all the children, except the infant, and assists in mending. Where there is a nursery girl to assist, she does the rougher part of the cleaning; and all take their meals in the nursery together, after the children of the family have done.

In smaller families, where there is only one nursemaid kept, she is assisted by the housemaid, or servant-of-all-work, who will do the rougher part of the work, and carry up the nursery meals. In such circumstances she will be more immediately under the eye of her mistress, who will probably relieve her from some of the cares of the infant. In higher families, the upper nurse is usually permitted to sup or dine occasionally at the housekeeper's table by way of relaxation, when the children are all well, and her subordinates trustworthy.

Where the nurse has the entire charge of the nursery, and the mother is too much occupied to do more than pay a daily visit to it, it is desirable that she be a person of observation, and possess some acquaintance with the diseases incident to childhood, as also with such simple remedies as may be useful before a medical attendant can be procured, or where such attendance is not considered necessary. All these little ailments are preceded by symptoms so minute as to be only perceptible to close observation; such as twitching of the brows, restless sleep, grinding the gums, and, in some inflammatory diseases, even to the child abstaining from crying, from fear of the increased pain produced by the movement. Dentition, or cutting the teeth, is attended with many of these symptoms. Measles, thrush, scarlatina, croup, hooping-cough, and other childish complaints, are all preceded by well-known symptoms, which may be alleviated and rendered less virulent by simple remedies instantaneously applied.

Dentition is usually the first serious trouble, bringing many other disorders in its train. The symptoms are most perceptible to the mother: the child sucks feebly, and with gums hot, inflamed, and swollen. In this case, relief is yielded by rubbing them from time to time with a little of Mrs Johnson's soothing syrup, a valuable and perfectly safe medicine. Selfish and thoughtless nurses, and mothers too, sometimes give cordials and sleeping-draughts, whose effects are too well known.*

Convulsion Fits sometimes follow the feverish restlessness produced by these causes; in which case a hot bath should be administered without delay, and the lower parts of the body rubbed, the bath being as hot as it can be without scalding the tender skin; at the same time, the doctor should be sent for immediately, for no nurse should administer medicine in this case, unless the fits have been repeated and the doctor has left directions with her how to act.

Croup is one of the most alarming diseases of childhood; it is accompanied with a hoarse, croaking, ringing cough, and comes on very suddenly, and most so in strong, robust children. A very hot bath should be instantly administered, followed by an emetic, either in the form of tartar-emetic, croup-powder, or a teaspoonful of ipecacuhana, wrapping the body warmly up in flannel after the bath. The slightest delay in administering the bath, or the emetic, may be fatal; hence, the importance of nurses about very young children being acquainted with the symptoms.

Hooping-Cough is generally preceded by the moaning noise during sleep, which even adults threatened with the disorder cannot avoid: it is followed by violent fits of coughing, which little can be done to relieve. A child attacked by this disorder should be kept as much as possible in the fresh, pure air, but out of draughts, and kept warm, and supplied with plenty of nourishing food. Many fatal diseases flow from this scourge of childhood, and a change to purer air, if possible, should follow convalescence.

Worms are the torment of some children: the symptoms are, an unnatural craving for food, even after a full meal: costiveness, suddenly followed by the reverse; fetid breath, a livid circle under the eyes, enlarged abdomen, and picking the nose; for which the remedies must be prescribed by the doctor.

Measles and *Scarlatina* much resemble each other in their early stages: headache, restlessness, and fretfulness are the symptoms of both. Shivering fits, succeeded by a hot skin; pains in the back and limbs, accompanied by sickness, and, in severe cases, sore throat; pain about the jaws, difficulty in swallowing, running at the eyes, which become red and inflamed, while the face is hot and flushed, often distinguish scarlatina and scarlet fever, of which it is only a mild form.

While the case is doubtful, a dessert-spoonful of spirit of nitre diluted in water, given at bedtime, will throw the child into a gentle perspiration, and will bring out the rash in either case. In measles, this appears first on the face; in scarlatina, on the chest; and in both cases a doctor should be called in. In scarlatina, tartar-emetic powder or ipecacuhana may be administered in the mean time.

In all cases, cleanliness, fresh air, clean utensils, and frequent washing of the person, both of nurse and children, are even more necessary in the nursery than in either drawing-room or sick-room, inasmuch as the delicate organs of childhood are more susceptible of injury from smells and vapours than adults.

It may not be out of place if we conclude this brief notice of the duties of a nursemaid, by an extract from Florence Nightingale's admirable 'Notes on Nursing.' Referring to children, she says:—

'They are much more susceptible than grown people to all noxious influences. They are affected by the same things, but much more quickly and seriously; by want of fresh air, of proper warmth; want of cleanliness in house, clothes, bedding, or body; by improper food, want of punctuality, by dulness, by want of light, by too much or too little covering in bed or when up.' And all this in health; and then she quotes a passage from a lecture on sudden deaths in infancy, to show the importance of careful nursing of children:—'In the great majority of instances, when death suddenly befalls the infant or young child, it is an *accident*; it is not a necessary, inevitable result of any disease. That which is known to injure children most seriously is foul air; keeping the rooms where they sleep closely shut up is destruction to them; and, if the child's breathing be disordered by disease, a few hours only of such foul air may endanger its life, even where no inconvenience is felt by grown-up persons in the room.'

Persons moving in the best society will see, after perusing Miss Nightingale's book, that this 'foul air,' 'want of light,' 'too much or too little clothing,' and improper food, is not confined to Crown Street or St

Giles's; that Belgravia and the squares have their north room, where the rays of the sun never reach. 'A wooden bedstead, two or three mattresses piled up to above the height of the table, a vallance attached to the frame,—nothing but a miracle could ever thoroughly dry or air such a bed and bedding,'—is the ordinary bed of a private house, than which nothing can be more unwholesome. 'Don't treat your children like sick,' she sums up; 'don't dose them with tea. Let them eat meat and drink milk, or half a glass of light beer. Give them fresh, light, sunny, and open rooms, cool bedrooms, plenty of outdoor exercise, facing even the cold, and wind, and weather, in sufficiently warm clothes, and with sufficient exercise, plenty of amusements and play; more liberty, and less schooling, and cramming, and training; more attention to food and less to physic.'

DUTIES OF THE SICK-NURSE

All women are likely, at some period of their lives, to be called on to perform the duties of a sick-nurse, and should prepare themselves as much as possible, by observation and reading, for the occasion when they may be required to perform the office. The main requirements are good temper, compassion for suffering, sympathy with sufferers, which most women worthy of the name possess, neat-handedness, quiet manners, love of order, and cleanliness. With these qualifications there will be very little to be wished for; the desire to relieve suffering will inspire a thousand little attentions, and surmount the disgusts which some of the offices attending the sick-room are apt to create. Where serious illness visits a household, and protracted nursing is likely to become necessary, a professional nurse will probably be engaged, who has been trained to its duties; but in some families, and those not a few let us hope, the ladies of the family would oppose such an arrangement as a failure of duty on their part. There is, besides, even when a professional nurse is ultimately called in, a period of doubt and hesitation, while disease has not yet developed itself, when the patient must be attended to; and, in these cases, some of the female servants of the establishment must give their attendance in the sick-room. There are, also, slight attacks of cold, influenza, and accidents in a thousand forms, to which all are subject, where domestic nursing becomes a necessity; where disease, though unattended with danger, is nevertheless accompanied by the nervous irritation incident to illness, and when all the attention of the domestic nurse becomes necessary.

In the first stage of sickness, while doubt and a little perplexity hang over the household as to the nature of the sickness, there are some things about which no doubt can exist: the patient's room must be kept in a perfectly pure state, and arrangements made for proper attendance; for the first canon of nursing, according to Florence Nightingale, its apostle, is to 'keep the air the patient breathes as pure as the external air, without chilling him.' This can be done without any preparation which might alarm the patient; with proper windows, open fireplaces, and a supply of fuel, the room may be as fresh as it is outside, and kept at a temperature suitable for the patient's state.

Windows, however, must be opened from above, and not from below, and draughts avoided; cool air admitted beneath the patient's head chills the lower strata and the floor. The careful nurse will keep the door shut when the window is open; she will also take care that the patient is not placed between the door and the open window, nor between the open fireplace and the window. If confined to bed, she will see that the bed is placed in a thoroughly ventilated part of the room, but out of the current of air which is produced by the momentary opening of doors, as well as out of the line of draught between the window and the open chimney, and that the temperature of the room is kept about 64°. Where it is necessary to admit air by the door, the windows should be closed; but there are few circumstances in which good air can be obtained through the chamber-door; through it, on the contrary, the gases generated in the lower parts of the house are likely to be drawn into the invalid chamber.

These precautions taken, and plain nourishing diet, such as the patient desires, furnished, probably little more can be done, unless more serious symptoms present themselves; in which case medical advice will be sought.

Under no circumstances is ventilation of the sick-room so essential as in cases of febrile diseases, usually considered infectious; such as typhus and puerperal fevers, influenza, hooping-cough, small- and chicken-pox, scarlet fever, measles, and erysipelas: all these are considered communicable through the air; but there is little danger of infection being thus communicated, provided the room is kept thoroughly ventilated. On the contrary, if this essential be neglected, the power of infection is greatly increased and concentrated in the confined and impure air; it settles upon the clothes of the attendants and visitors, especially where they are of wool, and is frequently communicated to other families in this manner.

Under all circumstances, therefore, the sick-room should be kept as fresh and sweet as the open air, while the temperature is kept up by artificial heat, taking care that the fire burns clear, and gives out no smoke into the room; that the room is perfectly clean, wiped over with a damp cloth every day, if boarded; and swept, after sprinkling with damp tea-leaves, or other aromatic leaves, if carpeted; that all utensils are emptied and cleaned as soon as used, and not once in four-and-twenty hours, as is sometimes done. 'A slop-pail,' Miss Nightingale says, 'should never enter a sick-room; everything should be carried direct to the water-closet, emptied there, and brought up clean; in the best hospitals the slop-pail is unknown.' 'I do not approve,' says Miss Nightingale, 'of making housemaids of nurses,—that would be waste of means; but I have seen surgical sisters, women whose hands were worth to them two or three guineas a week, down on their knees, scouring a room or hut, because they thought it was not fit for their patients: these women had the true nurse spirit.'

Bad smells are sometimes met by sprinkling a little liquid chloride of lime on the floor; fumigation by burning pastiles is also a common expedient for the purification of the sick-room. They are useful, but only in the sense hinted at by the medical lecturer, who commenced his lecture thus:—'Fumigations, gentlemen, are of essential impor-tance; they make so abominable a smell, that they compel you to open the windows and admit fresh air.' In this sense they are useful, but ineffectual unless the cause be removed, and fresh air admitted.

The sick-room should be quiet; no talking, no gossiping, and, above all, no whispering,—this is absolute cruelty to the patient; he thinks his complaint the subject, and strains his ear painfully to catch the sound. No rustling of dresses, nor creaking shoes either; where the carpets are taken up, the nurse should wear list shoes, or some other noiseless material, and her dress should be of soft material that does not rustle. Miss Nightingale denounces crinoline, and quotes Lord Melbourne on the subject of women in the sick-room, who said, 'I would rather have men about me, when ill, than women; it requires very strong health to put up with women.' Ungrateful man! but absolute quiet is necessary in the sick-room.

Never let the patient be waked out of his first sleep by noise, never roused by anything like a surprise. Always sit in the apartment, so that the patient has you in view, and that it is not necessary for him to turn in speaking to you. Never keep a patient standing; never speak to one while moving. Never lean on the sick-bed. Above all, be calm and decisive with the patient, and prevent all noises over-head.

A careful nurse, when a patient leaves his bed, will open the sheets wide, and throw the clothes back so as thoroughly to air the bed. She will avoid drying or airing anything damp in the sick-room.

'It is another fallacy,' says Florence Nightingale, 'to suppose that night air is injurious; a great authority told me that, in London, the air is never so good as after ten o'clock, when smoke has diminished; but then it must be air from without, not within, and not air vitiated by gaseous airs.' 'A great fallacy prevails also,' she says, in another section, 'about flowers poisoning the air of the sick-room: no one ever saw them over-crowding the sick-room; but, if they did, they actually absorb carbonic acid and give off oxygen.' Cut flowers also decompose water, and produce oxygen gas. Lilies, and some other very odorous plants, may perhaps give out smells unsuited to a close room, while the atmosphere of the sick-room should always be fresh and natural.

'Patients,' says Miss Nightingale, 'are sometimes starved in the midst of plenty, from want of attention to the ways which alone make it possible for them to take food. A spoonful of beef-tea, or arrowroot and wine, or some other light nourishing diet, should be given every hour, for the patient's stomach will reject large supplies. In very weak patients there is often a nervous difficulty in swallowing, which is much increased if food is not ready and presented at the moment when it is wanted: the nurse should be able to discriminate, and know when this moment is approaching.'

Diet suitable for patients will depend, in some degree, on their natural likes and dislikes, which the nurse will do well to acquaint herself with. Beef-tea is useful and relishing, but possesses little nourishment; when evaporated, it presents a teaspoonful of solid meat to a pint of water. Eggs are not equivalent to the same weight of meat. Arrowroot is less nourishing than flour. Butter is the lightest and most digestible kind of fat. Cream, in some diseases, cannot be replaced. But, to sum up with some of Miss Nightingale's useful maxims:—Observation is the nurse's best guide, and the patient's appetite the rule. Half a pint of milk is equal to a quarter of a pound of meat. Beef-tea is the least nourishing food administered to the sick; and tea and coffee, she thinks; are both too much excluded from the sick-room.

THE MONTHLY NURSE

The choice of a monthly nurse is of the utmost importance; and in the case of a young mother with her first child, it would be well for her to seek advice and counsel from her more experienced relatives in this matter. In the first place, the engaging a monthly nurse in good time is of the utmost importance, as, if she be competent and clever, her services will be sought months beforehand; a good nurse having seldom much of her time disengaged. There are some qualifications which it is evident the nurse should possess: she should be scrupulously clean and tidy in her person; honest, sober, and noiseless in her movements; should possess a natural love for children, and have a strong nerve in case of emergencies. Snuff-taking and spirit-drinking must not be included in her habits; but these are happily much less frequent than they were in former days.

Receiving, as she often will, instructions from the doctor, she should bear these in mind, and carefully carry them out. In those instances where she does not feel herself sufficiently informed, she should ask advice from the medical man, and not take upon herself to administer medicines, &c., without his knowledge.

A monthly nurse should be between 30 and 50 years of age, sufficiently old to have had a little experience, yet not too old or infirm to be able to perform various duties requiring strength and bodily vigour. She should be able to wake the moment she is called,—at any hour of the night, that the mother or child may have their wants immediately attended to. Good temper, united to a kind and gentle disposition, is indispensable; and, although the nurse will frequently have much to endure from the whims and caprices of the invalid, she should make allowances for these, and command her temper, at the same time exerting her authority when it is necessary.

What the nurse has to do in the way of cleaning and dusting her lady's room, depends entirely on the establishment that is kept. Where there are plenty of servants, the nurse, of course, has nothing whatever to do but attend on her patient, and ring the bell for anything she may require. Where the number of domestics is limited, she should not mind keeping her room in order; that is to say, sweeping and dusting it every morning. If fires be necessary, the housemaid should always clean the grate, and do all that is wanted in that way, as this, being rather dirty work, would soil the nurse's dress, and unfit her to approach the bed, or take the infant without soiling its clothes. In small establishments, too, the nurse should herself fetch things she may require, and not ring every time she wants anything; and she must, of course, not leave her invalid unless she sees everything is comfortable; and then only for a few minutes. When down stairs, and in company with the other servants, the nurse should not repeat what she may have heard in her lady's room, as much mischief may be done by a gossiping nurse. As in most houses the monthly nurse is usually sent for a few days before her services may be required, she should see that all is in readiness; that there be no bustle and hurry at the time the confinement takes place. She should keep two pairs of sheets thoroughly aired, as well as night-dresses, flannels, &c. &c. All the things which will be required to dress the baby the first time should be laid in the basket in readiness, in the order in which they are to be put on; as well as scissors, thread, a few pieces of soft linen rag, and two or three flannel squares. If a berceaunette is to be used immediately, the nurse should ascertain that the mattresses, pillow, &c. are all well aired; and if not already done before she arrives, she should assist in covering and trimming it, ready for the little occupant. A monthly nurse should be handy at her needle, as, if she is in the house some time before the baby is born, she will require some work of this sort to occupy her time. She should also understand the making-up of little caps, although we can scarcely say this is one of the nurse's duties. As most children wear no caps, except out of doors, her powers in this way will not be much taxed.

A nurse should endeavour to make her room as cheerful as possible, and always keep it clean and tidy. She should empty the chamber utensils as soon as used, and on no account put things under the bed. Soiled baby's napkins should be rolled up and put into a pan, when they should be washed out every morning, and hung out to dry: they are then in a fit state to send to the laundress; and should, on no account, be left dirty, but done every morning in this way. The bedroom should be kept rather dark, particularly for the first week or ten days; of a regular temperature, and as free as possible from draughts, at the same time well ventilated and free from unpleasant smells.

The infant during the month must not be exposed to strong light, or much air; and in carrying it about the passages, stairs, &c., the nurse should always have its head-flannel on, to protect the eyes and ears from the currents of air. For the management of children, we must refer our readers to the following chapters; and we need only say, in conclusion, that a good nurse should understand the symptoms of various ills incident to this period, as, in all cases, prevention is better than cure. As young mothers with their first baby are very often much troubled at first with their breasts, the nurse should understand the art of emptying them by suction, or some other contrivance. If the breasts are kept well drawn, there will be but little danger of inflammation; and as the infant at first cannot take all that is necessary, something must be done to keep the inflammation down. This is one of the greatest difficulties a nurse has to contend with, and we can only advise her to be very persevering, to rub the breasts well, and to let the infant suck as soon and as often as possible, until they get in proper order.

THE WET-NURSE

We are aware that, according to the opinion of some ladies, there is no domestic theme, during a certain period of their married lives, more fraught with vexation and disquietude than that ever-fruitful source of annoyance, 'the Nurse;' but, as we believe, there are thousands of excellent wives and mothers who pass through life without even a temporary embroglio in the kitchen, or suffering a state of moral hectic the whole time of a nurse's empire in the nursery or bedroom. Our own experience goes to prove, that although many unqualified persons palm themselves off on ladies as fully competent for the duties they so rashly and dishonestly undertake to perform, and thus expose themselves to ill-will and merited censure, there are still very many fully equal to the legitimate exercise of what they undertake; and if they do not in every case give entire satisfaction, some of the fault,—and sometimes a great deal of it,—may be honestly placed to the account of the ladies themselves, who, in many instances, are so impressed with the propriety of their own method of performing everything, as to insist upon the adoption of *their* system in preference to that of the nurse, whose plan is probably based on a comprehensive forethought, and rendered perfect in all its details by an ample experience.

In all our remarks on this subject, we should remember with gentleness the order of society from which our nurses are drawn; and that those who make their duty a study, and are termed professional nurses, have much to endure from the caprice and egotism of their employers; while others are driven to the occupation from the laudable motive of feeding their own children, and who, in fulfilling that object, are too often both selfish and sensual, performing, without further interest than is consistent with their own advantage, the routine of customary duties.

Properly speaking, there are two nurses,—the nurse for the mother and the nurse for the child, or, the monthly and the wet-nurse. Of the former we have already spoken, and will now proceed to describe the duties of the latter, and add some suggestions as to her age, physical health, and moral conduct, subjects of the utmost importance as far as the charge intrusted to her is concerned, and therefore demanding some special remarks.

When from illness, suppression of the milk, accident, or some natural process, the mother is deprived of the pleasure of rearing her infant,* it becomes necessary at once to look around for a fitting substitute, so that the child may not suffer, by any needless delay, a physical loss by the deprivation of its natural food. The first consideration should be as regards age, state of health, and temper.

The age, if possible, should not be less than twenty nor exceed thirty years, with the health sound in every respect, and the body free from all eruptive disease or local blemish. The best evidence of a

sound state of health will be found in the woman's clear open countenance, the ruddy tone of the skin, the full, round, and elastic state
of the breasts, and especially in the erectile, firm condition of the
nipple, which, in all unhealthy states of the body, is pendulous,
flabby, and relaxed; in which case, the milk is sure to be imperfect in
its organization, and, consequently, deficient in its nutrient qualities.
Appetite is another indication of health in the suckling nurse or
mother; for it is impossible a woman can feed her child without
having a corresponding appetite; and though inordinate craving for
food is neither desirable nor necessary, a natural vigour should be
experienced at meal-times, and the food taken should be anticipated
and enjoyed.

Besides her health, the moral state of the nurse is to be taken into
account, or that mental discipline or principle of conduct which
would deter the nurse from at any time gratifying her own pleasures
and appetites at the cost or suffering of her infant charge.

The conscientiousness and good faith that would prevent a nurse
so acting are, unfortunately, very rare; and many nurses, rather than
forego the enjoyment of a favourite dish, though morally certain of
the effect it will have on the child, will, on the first opportunity, feed
with avidity on fried meats, cabbage, cucumbers, pickles, or other
crude and injurious aliments, in defiance of all orders given, or confidence reposed in their word, good sense, and humanity. And when
the infant is afterwards racked with pain, and a night of disquiet
alarms the mother, the doctor is sent for, and the nurse, covering her
dereliction by a falsehood, the consequence of her gluttony is treated
as a disease, and the poor infant is dosed for some days with medicines, that can do it but little if any good, and, in all probability,
materially retard its physical development. The selfish nurse, in her
ignorance, believes, too, that as long as she experiences no admoni-
tory symptoms herself, the child cannot suffer; and satisfied that,
whatever is the cause of its screams and plunges, neither she, nor
what she had eaten, had anything to do with it, with this flattering
assurance at her heart, she watches her opportunity, and has another
luxurious feast off the prescribed dainties, till the increasing disturbance in the child's health, or treachery from the kitchen, opens the
eyes of mother and doctor to the nurse's unprincipled conduct. In all
such cases the infant should be spared the infliction of medicine,

and, as a wholesome corrective to herself, and relief to her charge, a good sound dose administered to the nurse.*

Respecting the diet of the wet-nurse, the first point of importance is to fix early and definite hours for every meal; and the mother should see that no cause is ever allowed to interfere with their punctuality. The food itself should be light, easy of digestion, and simple. Boiled or roast meat, with bread and potatoes, with occasionally a piece of sago, rice, or tapioca pudding, should constitute the dinner, the only meal that requires special comment; broths, green vegetables, and all acid or salt foods, must be avoided. Fresh fish, once or twice a week, may be taken; but it is hardly sufficiently nutritious to be often used as a meal. If the dinner is taken early,—at one o'clock,—there will be no occasion for luncheon, which too often, to the injury of the child, is made the cover for a first dinner. Half a pint of stout, with a Reading biscuit, at eleven o'clock, will be abundantly sufficient between breakfast at eight and a good dinner, with a pint of porter at one o'clock. About eight o'clock in the evening, half a pint of stout, with another biscuit may be taken; and for supper, at ten or half-past, a pint of porter, with a slice of toast or a small amount of bread and cheese, may conclude the feeding for the day.

Animal food once in twenty-four hours is quite sufficient. All spirits, unless in extreme cases, should be avoided; and wine is still more seldom needed. With a due quantity of plain digestible food, and the proportion of stout and porter ordered, with early hours and regularity, the nurse will not only be strong and healthy herself, but fully capable of rearing a child in health and strength. There are two points all mothers, who are obliged to employ wet-nurses, should remember, and be on their guard against. The first is, never to allow a nurse to give medicine to the infant on her own authority: many have such an infatuated idea of the *healing excellence* of castor-oil, that they would administer a dose of this disgusting grease twice a week, and think they had done a meritorious service to the child. The next point is, to watch carefully, lest, to insure a night's sleep for herself, she does not dose the infant with Godfrey's cordial, syrup of poppies, or some narcotic potion, to insure tranquillity to the one and give the opportunity of sleep to the other. The fact that scores of nurses keep secret bottles of these deadly syrups, for the purpose of stilling their charges, is notorious; and that many use them to a fearful extent, is sufficiently patent to all.

It therefore behoves the mother, while obliged to trust to a nurse, to use her best discretion to guard her child from the unprincipled treatment of the person she must, to a certain extent, depend upon and trust; and to remember, in all cases, rather than resort to castor-oil or sedatives, to consult a medical man for her infant in preference to following the counsel of her nurse.

CHAPTER XLII

THE REARING, MANAGEMENT, AND DISEASES OF INFANCY AND CHILDHOOD*

PHYSIOLOGY OF LIFE, AS ILLUSTRATED BY RESPIRATION, CIRCULATION, AND DIGESTION

The infantine management of children, like the mother's love for her offspring, seems to be born with the child, and to be a direct intelligence of Nature. It may thus, at first sight, appear as inconsistent and presumptuous to tell a woman how to rear her infant as to instruct her in the manner of loving it. Yet, though Nature is unquestionably the best nurse, Art makes so admirable a foster-mother, that no sensible woman, in her novitiate of parent, would refuse the admonitions of art, or the teachings of experience, to consummate her duties of nurse. It is true that, in a civilized state of society, few young wives reach the epoch that makes them mothers without some insight, traditional or practical, into the management of infants: consequently, the cases wherein a woman is left to her own unaided intelligence, or what, in such a case, may be called instinct, and obliged to trust to the promptings of nature alone for the well-being of her child, are very rare indeed. Again, every woman is not gifted with the same physical ability for the harassing duties of a mother; and though Nature, as a general rule, has endowed all female creation with the attributes necessary to that most beautiful and, at the same time, holiest function,—the healthy rearing of their offspring,—the cases are sufficiently numerous to establish the exception, where the mother is either physically or socially incapacitated from undertaking those most pleasing duties herself, and where, consequently, she is compelled to trust to adventitious aid for those natural benefits which are at once the mother's pride and delight to render to her child.

In these cases, when obliged to call in the services of hired assistance, she must trust the dearest obligation of her life to one who, from her social sphere, has probably notions of rearing children diametrically opposed to the preconceived ideas of the mother, and at enmity with all her sentiments of right and prejudices of position.

It has justly been said—we think by Hood—that the children of the poor are not brought up, but *dragged up*. However facetious this remark may seem, there is much truth in it; and that children, reared in the reeking dens of squalor and poverty, live at all, is an apparent anomaly in the course of things, that, at first sight, would seem to set the laws of sanitary provision at defiance, and make it appear a perfect waste of time to insist on pure air and exercise as indispensable necessaries of life, and especially so as regards infantine existence.

We see elaborate care bestowed on a family of children, everything studied that can tend to their personal comfort,—pure air, pure water, regular ablution, a dietary prescribed by art, and every precaution adopted that medical judgment and maternal love can dictate, for the well-being of the parents' hope; and find, in despite of all this care and vigilance, disease and death invading the guarded treasure. We turn to the foetor and darkness that, in some obscure court, attend the robust brood who, coated in dirt, and with mud and refuse for playthings, live and thrive, and grow into manhood, and, in contrast to the pale face and flabby flesh of the aristocratic child, exhibit strength, vigour, and well-developed frames, and our belief in the potency of the life-giving elements of air, light, and cleanliness receives a shock that, at first sight, would appear fatal to the implied benefits of these, in reality, all-sufficient attributes of health and life.*

But as we must enter more largely on this subject hereafter, we shall leave its consideration for the present, and return to what we were about to say respecting trusting to others' aid in the rearing of children. Here it is that the young and probably inexperienced mother may find our remarks not only an assistance but a comfort to her, in as far as, knowing the simplest and best system to adopt, she may be able to instruct another, and see that her directions are fully carried out.

The human body, materially considered, is a beautiful piece of mechanism, consisting of many parts, each one being the centre of a system, and performing its own vital function irrespectively of the others, and yet dependent for its vitality upon the harmony and health of the whole. It is, in fact, to a certain extent, like a watch, which, when once wound up and set in motion, will continue its function of recording true time only so long as every wheel, spring, and lever performs its allotted duty, and at its allotted time; or till the limit that man's ingenuity has placed to its existence as a moving automaton has been reached, or, in other words, till it has run down.

What the key is to the mechanical watch, air is to the physical man. Once admit air into the mouth and nostrils, and the lungs expand, the heart beats, the blood rushes to the remotest part of the body, the mouth secretes saliva, to soften and macerate the food; the liver forms its bile, to separate the nutriment from the digested aliment; the kidneys perform their office; the eye elaborates its tears, to facilitate motion and impart that glistening to the orb on which depends so much of its beauty; and a dewy moisture exudes from the skin, protecting the body from the extremes of heat and cold, and sharpening the perception of touch and feeling. At the same instant, and in every part, the arteries, like innumerable bees, are everywhere laying down layers of muscle, bones, teeth, and, in fact, like the coral zoophyte, building up a continent of life and matter; while the veins, equally busy, are carrying away the *débris* and refuse collected from where the zoophyte arteries are building,—this refuse, in its turn, being conveyed to the liver, there to be converted into bile.

All these—and they are but a few of the vital actions constantly taking place—are the instant result of one gasp of life-giving air. No subject can be fraught with greater interest than watching the first spark of life, as it courses with electric speed 'through all the gates and alleys' of the soft, insensate body of the infant. The effect of air on the new-born child is as remarkable in its results as it is wonderful in its consequence; but to understand this more intelligibly, it must first be remembered that life consists of the performance of *three* vital functions—RESPIRATION, CIRCULATION, and DIGESTION. The lungs digest the air, taking from it its most nutritious element, the *oxygen*, to give to the impoverished blood that circulates through them. The stomach digests the food, and separates the nutriment— *chyle*—from the aliment, which it gives to the blood for the development of the frame; and the blood, which is understood by the term circulation, digests in its passage through the lungs the nutriment— *chyle*—to give it quantity and quality, and the *oxygen* from the air to give it vitality. Hence it will be seen, that, speaking generally, the three vital functions resolve themselves into one,—DIGESTION; and that the lungs are the primary and the most important of the vital organs; and respiration, the first in fact, as we all know it is the last in deed, of all the functions performed by the living body.

The Lungs—Respiration

The first effect of air on the infant is a slight tremor about the lips and angles of the mouth, increasing to twitchings, and finally to a convulsive contraction of the lips and cheeks, the consequence of sudden cold to the nerves of the face. This spasmodic action pro- duces a gasp, causing the air to rush through the mouth and nostrils, and enter the windpipe and upper portion of the flat and contracted lungs, which, like a sponge partly immersed in water, immediately expand. This is succeeded by a few faint sobs or pants, by which larger volumes of air are drawn into the chest, till, after a few sec- onds, and when a greater bulk of the lungs has become inflated, the breast-bone and ribs rise, the chest expands, and, with a sudden start, the infant gives utterance to a succession of loud, sharp cries, which have the effect of filling every cell of the entire organ with air and life. To the anxious mother, the first voice of her child is, doubtless, the sweetest music she ever heard; and the more loudly it peals, the greater should be her joy, as it is an indication of health and strength, and not only shows the perfect expansion of the lungs, but that the process of life has set in with vigour. Having welcomed in its own existence, like the morning bird, with a shrill note of gladness, the infant ceases its cry, and, after a few short sobs, usually subsides into sleep or quietude.

At the same instant that the air rushes into the lungs, the valve, or door between the two sides of the heart—and through which the blood had previously passed—is closed and hermetically sealed, and the blood taking a new course, bounds into the lungs, now expanded with air, and which we have likened to a wetted sponge, to which they bear a not unapt affinity, air being substituted for water. It here receives the *oxygen* from the atmosphere, and the *chyle*, or white blood, from the digested food, and becomes, in an instant, arterial blood, a vital principle, from which every solid and fluid of the body is constructed. Besides the lungs, Nature has provided another respiratory organ, a sort of supplemental lung, that, as well as being a covering to the body, *in*spires air and *ex*pires moisture;—this is the cuticle, or skin; and so intimate is the connection between the skin and lungs, that whatever injures the first, is certain to affect the latter.

Hence the difficulty of breathing experienced after scalds or burns on the cuticle, the cough that follows the absorption of cold or damp by the skin, the oppressed and laborious breathing experienced by children in all eruptive diseases, while the rash is coming to the surface, and the hot, dry skin that always attends congestion of the lungs, and fever.

The great practical advantage derivable from this fact is, the knowledge that whatever relieves the one benefits the other. Hence, too, the great utility of hot baths in all affections of the lungs or diseases of the skin; and the reason why exposure to cold or wet is, in nearly all cases, followed by tightness of the chest, sore throat, difficulty of breathing, and cough. These symptoms are the consequence of a larger quantity of blood than is natural remaining in the lungs, and the cough is a mere effort of Nature to throw off the obstruction caused by the presence of too much blood in the organ of respiration. The hot bath, by causing a larger amount of blood to rush suddenly to the skin, has the effect of relieving the lungs of their excess of blood, and by equalizing the circulation, and promoting perspiration from the cuticle, affords immediate and direct benefit, both to the lungs and the system at large.

The Stomach—Digestion

The organs that either directly or indirectly contribute to the process of digestion are, the mouth, teeth, tongue, and gullet, the stomach, small intestines, the pancreas, the salivary glands, and the liver. Next to respiration, digestion is the chief function in the economy of life, as, without the nutritious fluid digested from the aliment, there would be nothing to supply the immense and constantly recurring waste of the system, caused by the activity with which the arteries at all periods, but especially during infancy and youth, are building up the frame and developing the body. In infancy (the period of which our present subject treats), the series of parts engaged in the process of digestion may be reduced simply to the stomach and liver, or rather its secretion,—the bile. The stomach is a thick muscular bag, connected above with the gullet, and, at its lower extremity, with the commencement of the small intestines. The duty or function of the stomach is to secrete from the arteries spread over its inner surface, a sharp acid liquid called the *gastric juice*; this, with a due mixture of saliva, softens, dissolves, and gradually digests the food or contents of the stomach, reducing the whole into a soft pulpy mass, which then passes into the first part of the small intestines, where it comes in contact with the bile from the gall-bladder, which immediately separates the digested food into two parts; one is a white creamy fluid called *chyle*, and the absolute concentration of all nourishment, which is taken up by proper vessels, and, as we have before said, carried directly to the heart, to be made blood of, and vitalized in the lungs, and thus provide for the wear and tear of the system. It must be here observed that the stomach can only digest *solids*, for fluids, being incapable of that process, can only be *absorbed*; and without the result of digestion, animal, at least human life, could not exist. Now, as Nature has ordained that infantine life shall be supported on liquid aliment, and as, without a digestion the body would perish, some provision was necessary to meet this difficulty, and that provision was found in the nature of the liquid itself, or in other words, THE MILK. The process of making cheese, or fresh curds and whey, is familiar to most persons; but as it is necessary to the elucidation of our subject, we will briefly repeat it. The internal membrane, or the lining coat of a calf's stomach, having been removed from the organ, is hung up, like a bladder, to dry; when required, a piece is cut off, put in a jug, a little warm water poured upon it, and after a few hours it is fit for use; the liquid so made being called *rennet*. A little of this rennet, poured into a basin of warm milk, at once coagulates the greater part, and separates from it a quantity of thin liquor, called *whey*. This is precisely the action that takes place in the infant's stomach after every supply from the breast. The cause is the same in both cases, the acid of the gastric juice in the infant's stomach immediately converting the milk into a soft cheese. It is gastric juice, adhering to the calf's stomach, and drawn out by the water, forming rennet, that makes the curds in the basin. The cheesy substance being a solid, at once undergoes the process of digestion, is separated into *chyle* by the bile, and, in a few hours, finds its way to the infant's heart, to become blood, and commence the architecture of its little frame. This is the simple process of a baby's digestion:—milk converted into cheese, cheese into *chyle*, chyle into blood, and blood into flesh, bone, and tegument—how simple is the cause, but how sublime and wonderful are the effects!

We have described the most important of the three functions that take place in the infant's body—respiration and digestion; the third, namely, circulation, we hardly think it necessary to enter on, not being called for by the requirements of the nurse and mother; so we shall omit its notice, and proceed from theoretical to more practical considerations. Children of weakly constitutions are just as likely to be born of robust parents, and those who earn their bread by toil, as the offspring of luxury and affluence; and, indeed, it is against the ordinary providence of Nature to suppose the children of the hard-working and necessitous to be hardier and more vigorous than those of parents blessed with ease and competence.

All children come into the world in the same imploring helplessness, with the same general organization and wants, and demanding either from the newly-awakened mother's love, or from the memory of motherly feeling in the nurse, or the common appeals of humanity in those who undertake the earliest duties of an infant, the same assistance and protection, and the same fostering care.

THE INFANT

We have already described the phenomena produced on the new-born child by the contact of air, which, after a succession of muscular twitchings, becomes endowed with voice, and heralds its advent by a loud but brief succession of cries. But though this is the general rule, it sometimes happens (from causes it is unnecessary here to explain) that the infant does not cry, or give utterance to any audible sounds, or if it does, they are so faint as scarcely to be distinguished as human accents, plainly indicating that life, as yet, to the new visitor, is neither a boon nor a blessing; the infant being, in fact, in a state of suspended or imperfect vitality,—a state of *quasi* existence, closely approximating the condition of a *still-birth*.

As soon as this state of things is discovered, the child should be turned on its right side, and the whole length of the spine, from the head downwards, rubbed with all the fingers of the right hand, sharply and quickly, without intermission, till the quick action has not only evoked heat, but electricity in the part, and till the loud and sharp cries of the child have thoroughly expanded the lungs, and satisfactorily established its life. The operation will seldom require above a minute to effect, and less frequently demands a repetition. If there is brandy at hand, the fingers before rubbing may be dipped into that, or any other spirit.

There is another condition of what we may call 'mute births,' where the child only makes short ineffectual gasps, and those at intervals of a minute or two apart, when the lips, eyelids, and fingers become of a deep purple or slate colour, sometimes half the body remaining white, while the other half, which was at first swarthy, deepens to a livid hue. This condition of the infant is owing to the valve between the two sides of the heart remaining open, and allowing the unvitalized venous blood to enter the arteries and get into the circulation.

The object in this case, as in the previous one, is to dilate the lungs as quickly as possible, so that, by the sudden effect of a vigorous inspiration, the valve may be firmly closed, and the impure blood, losing this means of egress, be sent directly to the lungs. The same treatment is therefore necessary as in the previous case, with the addition, if the friction along the spine has failed, of a warm bath at a temperature of about 80°, in which the child is to be plunged up to the neck, first cleansing the mouth and nostrils of the mucus that might interfere with the free passage of air.

While in the bath, the friction along the spine is to be continued, and if the lungs still remain unexpanded, while one person retains the child in an inclined position in the water, another should insert the pipe of a small pair of bellows into one nostril, and while the mouth is closed and the other nostril compressed on the pipe with the hand of the assistant, the lungs are to be slowly inflated by steady puffs of air from the bellows, the hand being removed from the mouth and nose after each inflation, and placed on the pit of the stomach, and by a steady pressure expelling it out again by the mouth. This process is to be continued, steadily inflating and expelling the air from the lungs till, with a sort of tremulous leap, Nature takes up the process, and the infant begins to gasp, and finally to cry, at first low and faint, but with every engulp of air increasing in length and strength of volume, when it is to be removed from the water, and instantly wrapped (all but the face and mouth) in a flannel. Sometimes, however, all these means will fail in effecting an utterance from the child, which will lie, with livid lips and a flaccid body, every few minutes opening its mouth with a short gasping pant, and then subsiding into a state of pulseless inaction, lingering probably some hours, till the spasmodic pantings growing further apart, it ceases to exist.

The time that this state of negative vitality will linger in the frame of an infant is remarkable; and even when all the previous operations, though long-continued, have proved ineffectual, the child will often rally from the simplest of means—the application of dry heat. When removed from the bath, place three or four hot bricks or tiles on the hearth, and lay the child, loosely folded in a flannel, on its back along them, taking care that there is but one fold of flannel between the spine and heated bricks or tiles. When neither of these articles can be procured, put a few clear pieces of red cinder in a warming-pan, and extend the child in the same manner along the closed lid. As the heat gradually diffuses itself over the spinal marrow, the child that was dying, or seemingly dead, will frequently give a sudden and energetic cry, succeeded in another minute by a long and vigorous peal, making up, in volume and force, for the previous delay, and instantly confirming its existence by every effort in its nature.

With these two exceptions,—restored by the means we have pointed out to the functions of life,—we will proceed to the consideration of the child HEALTHILY BORN. Here the first thing that meets us on the threshold of inquiry, and what is often between mother and nurse not only a vexed question, but one of vexatious import, is the *crying* of the child; the mother, in her natural anxiety, maintaining that her infant *must be ill* to cause it to cry so much or so often, and the nurse insisting that *all* children cry, and that nothing is the matter with it, and that crying does good, and is, indeed, an especial benefit to infancy. The anxious and unfamiliar mother, though not convinced by these abstract sayings of the truth or wisdom of the explanation, takes both for granted; and, giving the nurse credit for more knowledge and experience on this head than she can have, contentedly resigns herself to the infliction, as a thing necessary to be endured for the good of the baby, but thinking it, at the same time, an extraordinary instance of the imperfectibility of Nature as regards the human infant; for her mind wanders to what she has observed in her childhood with puppies and kittens, who, except when rudely torn from their nurse, seldom give utterance to any complaining.

We, undoubtedly, believe that crying, to a certain extent, is not only conducive to health, but positively necessary to the full development and physical economy of the infant's being. But though holding this opinion, we are far from believing that a child does not very often cry from pain, thirst, want of food, and attention to its personal comfort; but there is as much difference in the tone and expression of a child's cry as in the notes of an adult's voice; and the mother's ear will not be long in discriminating between the sharp peevish whine of irritation and fever, and the louder intermitting cry that characterizes the want of warmth and sleep. All these shades of expression in the child's inarticulate voice every nurse *should* understand, and every mother will soon teach herself to interpret them with an accuracy equal to language.

There is no part of a woman's duty to her child that a young mother should so soon make it her business to study, as the voice of her infant, and the language conveyed in its cry. The study is neither hard nor difficult; a close attention to its tone, and the expression of the baby's features, are the two most important points demanding attention. The key to both the mother will find in her own heart, and the knowledge of her success in the comfort and smile of her infant. We have two reasons—both strong ones—for urging on mothers the imperative necessity of early making themselves acquainted with the nature and wants of their child: the first, that when left to the entire responsibility of the baby, after the departure of the nurse, she may be able to undertake her new duties with more confidence than if left to her own resources and mother's instinct, without a clue to guide her through the mysteries of those calls that vibrate through every nerve of her nature; and, secondly, that she may be able to guard her child from the nefarious practices of unprincipled nurses, who, while calming the mother's mind with false statements as to the character of the baby's cries, rather than lose their rest, or devote that time which would remove the cause of suffering, administer, behind the curtains, those deadly narcotics which, while stupefying Nature into sleep, insure for herself a night of many unbroken hours. Such nurses as have not the hardihood to dose their infant charges, are often full of other schemes to still that constant and reproachful cry. The most frequent means employed for this purpose is giving it something to suck,—something easily hid from the mother,—or, when that is impossible, under the plea of keeping it warm, the nurse covers it in her lap with a shawl, and, under this blind, surreptitiously inserts a finger between the parched lips, which possibly moan for drink; and, under this inhuman cheat and delusion, the infant is pacified, till Nature, balked of its desires, drops into a troubled sleep. These are two of our reasons for impressing upon mothers the *early*, the *immediate* necessity of putting themselves sympathetically in communication with their child, by at once learning its hidden language as a delightful task.

We must strenuously warn all mothers on *no* account to allow the nurse to sleep with the baby, never herself to lay down with it by her side for a night's rest, never to let it sleep in the parents' bed, and on no account keep it, longer than absolutely necessary, confined in an atmosphere loaded with the breath of many adults.*

The amount of *oxygen* required by an infant is so large, and the quantity consumed by mid-life and age, and the proportion of carbonic acid thrown off from both, so considerable, that an infant breathing the same air cannot possibly carry on its healthy existence while deriving its vitality from so corrupted a medium. This objection, always in force, is still more objectionable at night-time, when doors and windows are closed, and amounts to a condition of poison, when placed between two adults in sleep, and shut in by bed-curtains; and when, in addition to the impurities expired from the lungs, we remember, in quiescence and sleep, how large a portion of mephitic gas is given off from the skin.

Mothers, in the fulness of their affection, believe there is no harbour, sleeping or awake, where their infants can be so secure from all possible or probable danger as in their own arms; yet we should astound our readers if we told them the statistical number of infants who, in despite of their motherly solicitude and love, are annually killed, unwittingly, by such parents themselves, and this from the persistency in the practice we are so strenuously condemning. The mother frequently, on awaking, discovers the baby's face closely impacted between her bosom and her arm, and its body rigid and lifeless; or else so enveloped in the 'head-blanket' and superincumbent bedclothes, as to render breathing a matter of physical impossibility. In such cases the jury in general returns a verdict of '*Accidentally overlaid*;' but one of 'Careless suffocation' would be more in accordance with truth and justice. The only possible excuse that can be urged, either by nurse or mother, for this culpable practice, is the plea of imparting warmth to the infant. But this can always be effected by an extra blanket in the child's crib, or, if the weather is particularly cold, by a bottle of hot water enveloped in flannel and placed at the child's feet; while all the objections already urged—as derivable from animal heat imparted by actual contact—are entirely obviated. There is another evil attending the sleeping together of the mother and infant, which, as far as regards the latter, we consider quite as formidable, though not so immediate as the others, and is always followed by more or less of mischief to the mother. The evil we now allude to is that most injurious practice of letting the child *suck* after the mother has *fallen asleep*, a custom that naturally results from the former, and which, as we have already said, is injurious to both mother and child. It is injurious to the infant by allowing it, without control, to imbibe to distension a fluid sluggishly secreted and deficient in those vital principles which the want of mental energy, and of the sympathetic appeals of the child on the mother, so powerfully produce on the secreted nutriment, while the mother wakes in a state of clammy exhaustion, with giddiness, dimness of sight, nausea, loss of appetite, and a dull aching pain through the back and between the shoulders. In fact, she wakes languid and unrefreshed from her sleep, with febrile symptoms and hectic flushes, caused by her baby vampire, who, while dragging from her, her health and strength, has excited in itself a set of symptoms directly opposite, but fraught with the same injurious consequences—'functional derangement.'

THE MILK

As Nature has placed in the bosom of the mother the natural food of her offspring, it must be self-evident to every reflecting woman, that it becomes her duty to study, as far as lies in her power, to keep that reservoir of nourishment in as pure and invigorating a condition as possible; for she must remember that the *quantity* is no proof of the *quality* of this aliment.

The mother, while suckling, as a general rule, should avoid all sedentary occupations, take regular exercise, keep her mind as lively and pleasingly occupied as possible, especially by music and singing. Her diet should be light and nutritious, with a proper sufficiency of animal food, and of that kind which yields the largest amount of nourishment; and, unless the digestion is naturally strong, vegetables and fruit should form a very small proportion of the general dietary, and such preparations as broths, gruels, arrowroot, &c., still less. Tapioca, or ground-rice pudding, made with several eggs, may be taken freely; but all slops and thin potations, such as that delusion called chicken-broth, should be avoided, as yielding a very small amount of nutriment, and a large proportion of flatulence. All purely stimulants should be avoided as much as possible, especially spirits, unless taken for some special object, and that medicinally; but as a part of the dietary they should be carefully shunned. Lactation is always an exhausting process, and as the child increases in size and strength, the drain upon the mother becomes great and depressing. Then something more even than an abundant diet is required to keep the mind and body up to a standard sufficiently healthy to admit of a constant and nutritious secretion being performed without detriment to the physical integrity of the mother, or injury to the child who imbibes it; and as stimulants are inadmissible, if not positively injurious, the substitute required is to be found in *malt liquor*. To the lady accustomed to her Madeira and sherry, this may appear a very vulgar potation for a delicate young mother to take instead of the more subtle and condensed elegance of wine; but as we are writing from experience, and with the avowed object of imparting useful facts and beneficial remedies to our readers, we allow no social distinctions to interfere with our legitimate object.

We have already said that the suckling mother should avoid stimulants, especially spirituous ones; and though something of this sort is absolutely necessary to support her strength during the exhausting process, it should be rather of a *tonic* than of a stimulating character; and as all wines contain a large percentage of brandy, they are on that account less beneficial than the pure juice of the fermented grape might be. But there is another consideration to be taken into account on this subject; the mother has not only to think of herself, but also of her infant. Now wines, especially port wine, very often—indeed, most frequently—affect the baby's bowels, and what might have been grateful to the mother becomes thus a source of pain and irritation to the child afterwards. Sherry is less open to this objection than other wines, yet still *it* very frequently does influence the second participator, or the child whose mother has taken it.

The nine or twelve months a woman usually suckles must be, to some extent, to most mothers, a period of privation and penance, and unless she is deaf to the cries of her baby, and insensible to its kicks and plunges, and will not see in such muscular evidences the griping pains that rack her child, she will avoid every article that can remotely affect the little being who draws its sustenance from her. She will see that the babe is acutely affected by all that in any way influences her, and willingly curtail her own enjoyments, rather than see her infant rendered feverish, irritable, and uncomfortable. As the best tonic, then, and the most efficacious indirect stimulant that a mother can take at such times, there is no potation equal to *porter* and *stout*, or, what is better still, an equal part of porter and stout. Ale, except for a few constitutions, is too subtle and too sweet, generally causing acidity or heartburn, and stout alone is too potent to admit of a full draught, from its proneness to affect the head; and quantity, as well as moderate strength, is required to make the draught effectual; the equal mixture, therefore, of stout and porter yields all the properties desired or desirable as a medicinal agent for this purpose.

Independently of its invigorating influence on the constitution, *porter exerts a marked and specific effect on the secretion of milk, more powerful in exciting an abundant supply of that fluid than any other article within the range of the physician's art*; and, in cases of deficient quantity, is the most certain, speedy, and the healthiest means that can be employed to insure a quick and abundant flow. In cases where malt liquor produces flatulency, a few grains of the 'carbonate of soda' may advantageously be added to each glass immediately before drinking, which will have the effect of neutralizing any acidity that may be in the porter at the time, and will also prevent its after-disagreement with the stomach. The quantity to be taken must depend upon the natural strength of the mother, the age and demand made by the infant on the parent, and other causes; but the amount should vary from *one* to *two* pints a day, never taking less than half a pint at a time, which should be repeated three or four times a day.

We have said that the period of suckling is a season of penance to the mother, but this is not invariably the case; and, as so much must depend upon the natural strength of the stomach, and its power of assimilating all kinds of food into healthy *chyle*, it is impossible to define exceptions. Where a woman feels she can eat any kind of food, without inconvenience or detriment, she should live during her suckling as she did before; but, as a general rule, we are bound to advise all mothers to abstain from such articles as pickles, fruits, cucumbers, and all acid and slowly digestible foods, unless they wish for restless nights and crying infants.

As regards exercise and amusement, we would certainly neither prohibit a mother's dancing, going to a theatre, nor even from attending an assembly. The first, however, is the best indoor recreation she can take, and a young mother will do well to often amuse herself in the nursery with this most excellent means of healthful circulation. The only precaution necessary is to avoid letting the child suck the milk that has lain long in the breast, or is heated by excessive action.

Every mother who can, should be provided with a breast-pump, or glass tube, to draw off the superabundance that has been accumulating in her absence from the child, or the first gush excited by undue exertion: the subsequent supply of milk will be secreted under the invigorating influence of a previous healthy stimulus.

As the first milk that is secreted contains a large amount of the saline elements, and is thin and innutritious, it is most admirably adapted for the purpose Nature designed it to fulfil,—that of an aperient;* but which, unfortunately, it is seldom permitted, in our artificial mode of living, to perform.

So opposed are we to the objectionable plan of physicking newborn children, that, unless for positive illness, we would much rather advise that medicine should be administered *through* the mother for the first eight or ten weeks of its existence. This practice, which few mothers will object to, is easily effected by the parent, when such a course is necessary for the child, taking either a dose of castor-oil, half an ounce of tasteless salts (the phosphate of soda), one or two teaspoonfuls of magnesia, a dose of lenitive electuary, manna, or any mild and simple aperient, which, almost before it can have taken effect on herself, will exhibit its action on her child.

One of the most common errors that mothers fall into while suckling their children, is that of fancying they are always hungry, and consequently overfeeding them; and with this, the great mistake of applying the child to the breast on every occasion of its crying, without investigating the cause of its complaint, and, under the belief that it wants food, putting the nipple into its crying mouth, until the infant turns in revulsion and petulance from what it should accept with eagerness and joy. At such times, a few teaspoonfuls of water, slightly chilled, will often instantly pacify a crying and restless child, who has turned in loathing from the offered breast; or, after imbibing a few drops, and finding it not what nature craved, throws back its head in disgust, and cries more petulantly than before. In such a case as this, the young mother, grieved at her baby's rejection of the tempting present, and distressed at its cries, and in terror of some injury, over and over ransacks its clothes, believing some insecure pin can alone be the cause of such sharp complaining, an accident that, from her own care in dressing, however, is seldom or ever the case.

These abrupt cries of the child, if they do not proceed from thirst, which a little water will relieve, not unfrequently occur from some unequal pressure, a fold or twist in the '*roller*,' or some constriction round the tender body. If this is suspected, the mother must not be content with merely slackening the strings; the child should be undressed, and the creases and folds of the hot skin, especially those about the thighs and groins, examined, to see that no powder has caked, and, becoming hard, irritated the parts. The violet powder should be dusted freely over all, to cool the skin, and everything put on fresh and smooth. If such precautions have not afforded relief, and, in addition to the crying, the child plunges or draws up its legs, the mother may be assured some cause of irritation exists in the stomach or bowels,—either acidity in the latter or distension from overfeeding in the former; but, from whichever cause, the child should be 'opened' before the fire, and a heated napkin applied all over the abdomen, the infant being occasionally elevated to a sitting position, and while gently jolted on the knee, the back should be lightly patted with the hand.

Should the mother have any reason to apprehend that the *cause* of inconvenience proceeds from the bladder—a not unfrequent source of pain,—the napkin is to be dipped in hot water, squeezed out, and immediately applied over the part, and repeated every eight or ten minutes, for several times in succession, either till the natural relief is afforded, or a cessation of pain allows of its discontinuance. The pain that young infants often suffer, and the crying that results from it, is, as we have already said, frequently caused by the mother inconsiderately overfeeding her child, and is produced by the pain of distension, and the mechanical pressure of a larger quantity of fluid in the stomach than the gastric juice can convert into cheese and digest.

Some children are stronger in the enduring power of the stomach than others, and get rid of the excess by vomiting, concluding every process of suckling by an emission of milk and curd. Such children are called by nurses 'thriving children;' and generally they are so, simply because their digestion is good, and they have the power of expelling with impunity that superabundance of aliment which in others is a source of distension, flatulence, and pain.

The length of time an infant should be suckled must depend much on the health and strength of the child, and the health of the mother, and the quantity and quality of her milk; though, when all circumstances are favourable, it should never be less than *nine*, nor exceed *fifteen* months; but perhaps the true time will be found in the medium between both. But of this we may be sure, that Nature never ordained a child to live on suction after having endowed it with teeth to bite and to grind; and nothing is more out of place and unseemly than to hear a child, with a set of twenty teeth, ask for the 'breast.'

The practice of protracted wet-nursing is hurtful to the mother, by keeping up an uncalled-for, and, after the proper time, an unhealthy drain on her system, while the child either derives no benefit from what it no longer requires, or it produces a positive injury on its constitution. After the period when Nature has ordained the child shall live by other means, the secretion of milk becomes thin and deteriorated, showing in the flabby flesh and puny features of the child both its loss of nutritious properties and the want of more stimulating aliment.

Though we have said that twelve months is about the medium time a baby should be suckled, we by no means wish to imply that a child should be fed exclusively on milk for its first year; quite the reverse; the infant can hardly be too soon made independent of the mother. Thus, should illness assail her, her milk fail, or any domestic cause abruptly cut off the natural supply, the child having been annealed to an artificial diet, its life might be safely carried on without seeking for a wet-nurse, and without the slightest danger to its system.

The advantage to the mother of early accustoming the child to artificial food is as considerable to herself as beneficial to her infant; the demand on her physical strength in the first instance will be less severe and exhausting, the child will sleep longer on a less rapidly digestible aliment, and yield to both more quiet nights, and the mother will be more at liberty to go out for business or pleasure, another means of sustenance being at hand till her return. Besides these advantages, by a judicious blending of the two systems of feeding, the infant will acquire greater constitutional strength, so that, if attacked by sickness or disease, it will have a much greater chance of resisting its virulence than if dependent alone on the mother, whose milk, affected by fatigue and the natural anxiety of the parent for her offspring, is at such a time neither good in its properties nor likely to be beneficial to the patient.

All that we have further to say on suckling is an advice to mothers, that if they wish to keep a sound and unchapped nipple, and possibly avoid what is called a 'broken breast,' never to put it up with a wet nipple, but always to have a soft handkerchief in readiness, and the moment that delicate part is drawn from the child's mouth, to dry it carefully of the milk and saliva that moisten it; and, further, to make a practice of suckling from each breast alternately.

DRESS AND DRESSING, WASHING, &C

As respects the dress and dressing of a new-born infant, or of a child in arms, during any stage of its nursing, there are few women who will require us to give them guidance or directions for their instruction; and though a few hints on the subject may not be out of place here, yet most women intuitively 'take to a baby,' and, with a small amount of experience, are able to perform all the little offices necessary to its comfort and cleanliness with ease and completeness. We shall, therefore, on this delicate subject hold our peace; and only, from afar, *hint* 'at what we would,' leaving our suggestions to be approved or rejected, according as they chime with the judgment and the apprehension of our motherly readers.*

In these days of intelligence, there are few ladies who have not, in all probability, seen the manner in which the Indian squaw, the aborigines of Polynesia, and even the Lapp and Esquimaux, strap down their baby on a board, and by means of a loop suspend it to the bough of a tree, hang it up to the rafters of the hut, or on travel, dangle it on their backs, outside the domestic implements, which, as the slave of her master, man, the wronged but uncomplaining woman carries, in order that her lord may march in unhampered freedom. Cruel and confining as this system of 'backboard' dressing may seem to our modern notions of freedom and exercise, it is positively less irksome, less confining, and infinitely less prejudicial to health, than the mummying of children by our grandmothers a hundred, ay, fifty years ago: for what with chin-stays, back-stays, body-stays, forehead-cloths, rollers, bandages, &c., an infant had as many girths and strings, to keep head, limbs, and body in one exact position, as a ship has halyards.*

Much of this—indeed we may say all—has been abolished; but still the child is far from being dressed loosely enough; and we shall never be satisfied till the abominable use of the *pin* is avoided *in toto* in an infant's dressing, and a texture made for all the under garments of a child of a cool and elastic material.

The manner in which an infant is encircled in a bandage called the 'roller,' as if it had fractured ribs, compressing those organs—that, living on suction, must be, for the health of the child, to a certain degree distended, to obtain sufficient aliment from the fluid imbibed—is perfectly preposterous. Our humanity, as well as our duty, calls upon us at once to abrogate and discountenance by every means in our power. Instead of the process of washing and dressing being made, as with the adult, a refreshment and comfort, it is, by the dawdling manner in which it is performed, the multiplicity of things used, and the perpetual change of position of the infant to adjust its complicated clothing, rendered an operation of positive irritation and annoyance. We, therefore, entreat all mothers to regard this subject in its true light, and study to the utmost, simplicity in dress, and dispatch in the process.

Children do not so much cry from the washing as from the irritation caused by the frequent change of position in which they are placed, the number of times they are turned on their face, on their back, and on their side, by the manipulations demanded by the multiplicity of articles to be fitted, tacked, and carefully adjusted on their bodies. What mother ever found her girl of six or seven stand quiet while she was curling her hair? How many times nightly has she not to reprove her for not standing still during the process! It is the same with the unconscious infant, who cannot bear to be moved about, and who has no sooner grown reconciled to one position than it is forced reluctantly into another. It is true, in one instance the child has intelligence to guide it, and in the other not; but the *motitory nerves*, in both instances, resent coercion, and a child cannot be too little handled.

On this account alone, and, for the moment, setting health and comfort out of the question, we beg mothers to simplify their baby's dress as much as possible; and not only to put on as little as is absolutely necessary, but to make that as simple in its contrivance and adjustment as it will admit of; to avoid belly-bands, rollers, girths, and everything that can impede or confine the natural expansion of the digestive organs, on the due performance of whose functions the child lives, thrives, and develops its physical being.

REARING BY HAND

Articles necessary, and how to use them—Preparation of Foods—Baths*—Advantages of Rearing by Hand

As we do not for a moment wish to be thought an advocate for an artificial, in preference to the natural course of rearing children, we beg our readers to understand us perfectly on this head; all we desire to prove is the fact that a child *can* be brought up as well on a spoon dietary as the best example to be found of those reared on the breast; having more strength, indeed, from the more nutritious food on which it lives. It will be thus less liable to infectious diseases, and more capable of resisting the virulence of any danger that may attack it; and without in any way depreciating the nutriment of its natural food, we wish to impress on the mother's mind that there are many cases of infantine debility which might eventuate in rickets, curvature of the spine, or mesenteric disease, where the addition to, or total substitution of, an artificial and more stimulating aliment, would not only give tone and strength to the constitution, but at the same time render the employment of mechanical means totally unnecessary. And, finally, though we would never—where the mother had the strength to suckle her child—supersede the breast, we would insist on making it a rule to accustom the child as early as possible to the use of an artificial diet, not only that it may acquire more vigour to help it over the ills of childhood, but that, in the absence of the mother, it might not miss the maternal sustenance; and also for the parent's sake, that, should the milk, from any cause, become vitiated, or suddenly cease, the child can be made over to the bottle and the spoon without the slightest apprehension of hurtful consequences.

To those persons unacquainted with the system, or who may have been erroneously informed on the matter, the rearing of a child by hand may seem surrounded by innumerable difficulties, and a large amount of personal trouble and anxiety to the nurse or mother who undertakes the duty. This, however, is a fallacy in every respect, except as regards the fact of preparing the food; but even this extra amount of work, by adopting the course we shall lay down, may be reduced to a very small sum of inconvenience; and as respects anxiety, the only thing calling for care is the display of judgment in the preparation of the food. The articles required for the purpose of feeding an infant are a night-lamp, with its pan and lid, to keep the food warm; a nursing-bottle, with a prepared teat; and a small pap saucepan, for use by day. Of the lamp we need hardly speak, most mothers being acquainted with its operation: but to those to whom it is unknown we may observe, that the flame from the floating rush-light heats the water in the reservoir above, in which the covered pan that contains the food floats, keeping it at such a heat that, when thinned by milk, it will be of a temperature suitable for immediate use. Though many kinds of nursing-bottles have been lately invented, and some mounted with India-rubber nipples, the common glass bottle, with the calf's teat, is equal in cleanliness and utility to any; besides, the nipple put into the child's mouth is so white and natural in appearance, that no child taken from the breast will refuse it. The black artificial one of caoutchouc or gutta-percha are unnatural. The prepared teats can be obtained at any chemist's, and as they are kept in spirits, they will require a little soaking in warm water, and gentle washing, before being tied securely, by means of fine twine, round the neck of the bottle, just sufficient being left projecting for the child to grasp freely in its lips; for if left the full length, or over long, it will be drawn too far into the mouth, and possibly make the infant heave. When once properly adjusted, the nipple need never be removed till replaced by a new one, which will hardly be necessary oftener than once a fortnight, though with care one will last for several weeks. The nursing-bottle should be thoroughly washed and cleaned every day, and always rinsed out before and after using it, the warm water being squeezed through the nipple, to wash out any particles of food that might lodge in the aperture, and become sour. The teat can always be kept white and soft by turning the end of the bottle, when not in use, into a narrow jug containing water, taking care to dry it first, and then to warm it by drawing the food through before putting it into the child's mouth.

Food, and its Preparation

The articles generally employed as food for infants consist of arrowroot, bread, flour, baked flour, prepared groats, farinaceous food, biscuit-powder, biscuits, tops-and-bottoms, and semolina, or manna croup, as it is otherwise called, which, like tapioca, is the prepared pith of certain vegetable substances. Of this list the least efficacious, though, perhaps, the most believed in, is arrowroot, which only as a mere agent, for change, and then only for a very short time, should ever be employed as a means of diet to infancy or childhood. It is a thin, flatulent, and innutritious food, and incapable of supporting infantine life with energy. Bread, though the universal *régime* with the labouring poor, where the infant's stomach and digestive powers are a reflex, in miniature, of the father's, should never be given to an infant under three months, and, even then, however finely beaten up and smoothly made, is a very questionable diet. Flour, when well boiled, though infinitely better than arrowroot, is still only a kind of fermentative paste, that counteracts its own good by after-acidity and flatulence.

Baked flour, when cooked into a pale brown mass, and finely powdered, makes a far superior food to the others, and may be considered as a very useful diet, especially for a change. Prepared groats may be classed with arrowroot and raw flour, as being innutritious. The articles that now follow in our list are all good, and such as we could, with conscience and safety, trust to for the health and development of any child whatever.

We may observe in this place, that an occasional change in the character of the food is highly desirable, both as regards the health and benefit of the child; and though the interruption should only last for a day, the change will be advantageous.

The packets sold as farinaceous food are unquestionably the best aliment that can be given from the first to a baby, and may be continued, with the exception of an occasional change, without alteration of the material, till the child is able to take its regular meals of animal and vegetable food. Some infants are so constituted as to require a frequent and total change in their system of living, seeming to thrive for a certain time on any food given to them, but if persevered in too long, declining in bulk and appearance as rapidly as they had previously progressed. In such cases the food should be immediately changed, and when that which appeared to agree best with the child is resumed, it should be altered in its quality, and perhaps in its consistency.

For the farinaceous food there are directions with each packet, containing instructions for the making; but, whatever the food employed is, enough should be made at once to last the day and night; at first, about a pint basinful, but, as the child advances, a quart will hardly be too much. In all cases, let the food boil a sufficient time, constantly stirring, and taking every precaution that it does not get burnt, in which case it is on no account to be used.

The food should always be made with water, the whole sweetened at once, and of such a consistency that, when poured out, and it has

had time to cool, it will cut with the firmness of a pudding or custard. One or two spoonfuls are to be put into the pap saucepan and
stood on the hob till the heat has softened it, when enough milk is
to be added, and carefully mixed with the food, till the whole has
the consistency of ordinary cream; it is then to be poured into the
nursing-bottle, and the food having been drawn through to warm the
nipple, it is to be placed in the child's mouth. For the first month or
more, half a bottleful will be quite enough to give the infant at one
time; but, as the child grows, it will be necessary not only to increase
the quantity given at each time, but also gradually to make its food
more consistent, and, after the third month, to add an egg to every
pint basin of food made. At night the mother puts the food into the
covered pan of her lamp, instead of the saucepan—that is, enough
for one supply, and, having lighted the rush, she will find, on the
waking of her child, the food sufficiently hot to bear the cooling
addition of the milk. But, whether night or day, the same food should
never be heated twice, and what the child leaves should be thrown
away.

Many persons entertain a belief that cow's milk is hurtful to
infants, and, consequently, refrain from giving it; but this is a very
great mistake, for both sugar and milk should form a large portion of
every meal an infant takes.

TEETHING AND CONVULSIONS

Fits, &c., the consequence of Dentition, and how to be treated—The number and order of the Teeth, and manner in which they are cut—First and Second Set

About three months after birth, the infant's troubles may be said to
begin; teeth commence forming in the gums, causing pain and irritation in the mouth, and which, but for the saliva it causes to flow so
abundantly, would be attended with very serious consequences. At
the same time the mother frequently relaxes in the punctuality of the
regimen imposed on her, and, taking some unusual or different food,
excites diarrhoea or irritation in her child's stomach, which not
unfrequently results in a rash on the skin, or slight febrile symptoms;
which, if not subdued in their outset, superinduce some more serious form of infantine disease. But, as a general rule, the teeth are the

primary cause of much of the child's sufferings, in consequence of the state of nervous and functional irritation into which the system is thrown by their formation and progress out of the jaw and through the gums. We propose beginning this branch of our subject with that most fertile source of an infant's suffering—

Teething

That this subject may be better understood by the nurse and mother, and the reason of the constitutional disturbance that, to a greater or less degree, is experienced by all infants, may be made intelligible to those who have the care of children, we shall commence by giving a brief account of the formation of the teeth, the age at which they appear in the mouth, and the order in which they pierce the gums. The organs of mastication in the adult consist of 32 distinct teeth, 16 in either jaw; being, in fact, a double set. The teeth are divided into 4 incisors, 2 canine, 4 first and second grinders, and 6 molars; but in childhood the complement or first set consists of only twenty, and these only make their appearance as the development of the frame indicates the requirement of a different kind of food for the support of the system. At birth some of the first-cut teeth are found in the cavities of the jaw, in a very small and rudimentary form; but this is by no means universal. About the third month, the jaws, which are hollow and divided into separate cells, begin to expand, making room for the slowly developing teeth, which, arranged for beauty and economy of space lengthwise, gradually turn their tops upwards, piercing the gum by their edges, which, being sharp, assist in cutting a passage through the soft parts. There is no particular period at which children cut their teeth, some being remarkably early, and others equally late. The earliest age that we have ever ourselves known as a reliable fact was, *six weeks*. Such peculiarities are generally hereditary, and, as in this case, common to a whole family. The two extremes are probably represented by six and sixteen months. Pain and drivelling are the usual, but by no means the general, indications of teething.

About the sixth month the gums become tense and swollen, presenting a red, shiny appearance, while the salivary glands pour out an unusual quantity of saliva. After a time, a white line or round spot is observed on the top of one part of the gums, and the sharp edge of the tooth may be felt beneath if the finger is gently pressed on the part. Through these white spots the teeth burst their way in the following order:—

Two incisors in the lower jaw are first cut, though, in general, some weeks elapse between the appearance of the first and the advent of the second. The next teeth cut are the four incisors of the upper jaw. The next in order are the remaining two incisors of the bottom, one on each side, then two top and two bottom on each side, but not joining the incisors; and lastly, about the eighteenth or twentieth month, the four eye teeth, filling up the space left between the side teeth and the incisors; thus completing the infant's set of sixteen. Sometimes at the same period, but more frequently some months later, four more double teeth slowly make their appearance, one on each side of each jaw, completing the entire series of the child's first set of twenty teeth. It is asserted that a child, while cutting its teeth, should either dribble excessively, vomit after every meal, or be greatly relaxed. Though one or other, or all of those at once, may attend a case of teething, it by no means follows that any one of them should accompany this process of nature, though there can be no doubt that where the pain consequent on the unyielding state of the gums, and the firmness of the skin that covers the tooth, is severe, a copious discharge of saliva acts beneficially in saving the head, and also in guarding the child from those dangerous attacks of fits to which many children in their teething are liable.

The *Symptoms* that generally indicate the cutting of teeth, in addition to the inflamed and swollen state of the gums, and increased flow of saliva, are the restless and peevish state of the child, the hands being thrust into the mouth, and the evident pleasure imparted by rubbing the finger or nail gently along the gum; the lips are often excoriated, and the functions of the stomach or bowels are out of order. In severe cases, occurring in unhealthy or scrofulous children, there are, from the first, considerable fever, disturbed sleep, fretfulness, diarrhoea, rolling of the eyes, convulsive startings, laborious breathing, coma, or unnatural sleep, ending, unless the head is quickly relieved, in death.

The *Treatment* in all cases of painful teething is remarkably simple, and consists in keeping the body cool by mild aperient medicines, allaying the irritation in the gums by friction with a rough ivory ring or a stale crust of bread, and when the head, lungs, or any organ is overloaded or unduly excited, to use the hot bath, and by throwing the body into a perspiration, equalize the circulation, and relieve the system from the danger of a fatal termination.

Besides these, there is another means, but that must be employed by a medical man; namely, scarifying the gums—an operation always safe, and which, when judiciously performed, and at a critical opportunity, will often snatch the child from the grasp of death.

There are few subjects on which mothers have often formed such strong and mistaken opinions as on that of lancing an infant's gums, some rather seeing their child go into fits—and by the unrelieved irritation endangering inflammation of the brain, water on the head, rickets, and other lingering affections—than permit the surgeon to afford instant relief by cutting through the hard skin, which, like a bladder over the stopper of a bottle, effectually confines the tooth to the socket, and prevents it piercing the soft, spongy substance of the gum. This prejudice is a great error, as we shall presently show; for, so far from hurting the child, there is nothing that will so soon convert an infant's tears into smiles as scarifying the gums in painful teething; that is, if effectually done, and the skin of the tooth be divided.

Though teething is a natural function, and to an infant in perfect health should be unproductive of pain, yet in general it is not only a fertile cause of suffering, but often a source of alarm and danger; the former, from irritation in the stomach and bowels, deranging the whole economy of the system, and the latter, from coma and fits, that may excite alarm in severe cases; and the danger, that eventuates in some instances, from organic disease of the head or spinal marrow.

We shall say nothing in this place of 'rickets,' or 'water on the head,' which are frequent results of dental irritation, but proceed to finish our remarks on the treatment of teething. Though strongly advocating the lancing of the gums in teething, and when there are any severe head-symptoms, yet it should never be needlessly done, or before being satisfied that the tooth is fully formed, and is out of the socket, and under the gum. When assured on these points, the gum should be cut lengthwise, and from the top of the gum downwards to the tooth, in an horizontal direction, thus —— and for about half an inch in length. The operation is then to be repeated in a transverse direction, cutting across the gum, in the centre of the first incision, and forming a cross, thus + . The object of this double incision is to insure a retraction of the cut parts, and leave an open way for the tooth to start from—an advantage not to be obtained when only one incision is made; for unless the tooth immediately follows the lancing, the opening reunites, and the operation has to be repeated. That this operation is very little or not at all painful, is evidenced by the suddenness with which the infant falls asleep after the lancing, and awakes in apparently perfect health, though immediately before the use of the gum-lancet, the child may have been shrieking or in convulsions.

Convulsions, or Infantine Fits

From their birth till after teething, infants are more or less subject or liable to sudden fits, which often, without any assignable cause, will attack the child in a moment, and while in the mother's arms; and which, according to their frequency, and the age and strength of the infant, are either slight or dangerous.

Whatever may have been the remote cause, the immediate one is some irritation of the nervous system, causing convulsions, or an effusion to the head, inducing coma. In the first instance, the infant cries out with a quick, short scream, rolls up its eyes, arches its body backwards, its arms become bent and fixed, and the fingers parted; the lips and eyelids assume a dusky leaden colour, while the face remains pale, and the eyes open, glassy, or staring. This condition may or may not be attended with muscular twitchings of the mouth, and convulsive plunges of the arms. The fit generally lasts from one to three minutes, when the child recovers with a sigh, and the relaxation of the body. In the other case, the infant is attacked at once with total insensibility and relaxation of the limbs, coldness of the body and suppressed breathing; the eyes, when open, being dilated, and presenting a dim glistening appearance; the infant appearing, for the moment, to be dead.

Treatment.—The first step in either case is, to immerse the child in a hot bath up to the chin; or if sufficient hot water cannot be procured to cover the body, make a hip-bath of what can be obtained;

and, while the left hand supports the child in a sitting or recumbent position with the right scoop up the water, and run it over the chest of the patient. When sufficient water can be obtained, the spine should be briskly rubbed while in the bath; when this cannot be done, lay the child on the knees, and with the fingers dipped in brandy, rub the whole length of the spine vigorously for two or three minutes, and when restored to consciousness, give occasionally a teaspoonful of weak brandy and water or wine and water.

An hour after the bath, it may be necessary to give an aperient powder, possibly also to repeat the dose for once or twice every three hours; in which case the following prescription is to be employed. Take of

Powdered scammony*	6 grains
Grey powder	6 grains
Antimonial powder	4 grains
Lump sugar	20 grains

Mix thoroughly, and divide into three powders, which are to be taken as advised for an infant one year old; for younger or weakly infants, divide into four powders, and give as the other. For thirst and febrile symptoms, give drinks of barley-water, or cold water, and every three hours put ten to fifteen drops of spirits of sweet nitre in a dessert-spoonful of either beverage.

THRUSH, AND ITS TREATMENT

This is a disease to which infants are peculiarly subject, and in whom alone it may be said to be a disease; for when thrush shows itself in adult or advanced life, it is not as a disease proper, but only as a symptom, or accessory, of some other ailment, generally of a chronic character, and should no more be classed as a separate affection than the petechae, or dark-coloured spots that appear in malignant measles, may be considered a distinct affection.

Thrush is a disease of the follicles of the mucous membrane of the alimentary canal, whereby there are formed small vesicles, or bladders, filled with a thick mucous secretion, which, bursting, discharge their contents, and form minute ulcers in the centre of each vessel. To make this formal but unavoidable description intelligible, we must beg the reader's patience while we briefly explain terms that may appear to many so unmeaning, and make the pathology of thrush fully familiar.

The whole digestive canal, of which the stomach and bowels are only a part, is covered, from the lips, eyes, and ears downwards, with a thin glairy tissue, like the skin that lines the inside of an egg, called the mucous membrane; this membrane is dotted all over, in a state of health, by imperceptible points, called follicles, through which the saliva, or mucus secreted by the membrane, is poured out.

These follicles, or little glands, then, becoming enlarged, and filled with a congealed fluid, constitute thrush in its first stage; and when the child's lips and mouth appear a mass of small pearls, then, as these break and discharge, the second stage, or that of ulceration, sets in.

Symptoms.—Thrush is generally preceded by considerable irritation, by the child crying and fretting, showing more than ordinary redness of the lips and nostrils, hot fetid breath, with relaxed bowels, and dark feculent evacuations; the water is scanty and high-coloured; whilst considerable difficulty in swallowing, and much thirst, are the other symptoms, which a careful observation of the little patient makes manifest.

The situation and character of thrush show at once that the cause is some irritation of the mucous membrane, and can proceed only from the nature and quality of the food. Before weaning, this must be looked for in the mother, and the condition of the milk; after that time, in the crude and indigestible nature of the food given. In either case, this exciting cause of the disease must be at once stopped. When it proceeds from the mother, it is always best to begin by physicking the infant through the parent; that is to say, let the parent first take the medicine, which will sufficiently affect the child through the milk: this plan has the double object of benefiting the patient and, at the same time correcting the state of the mother, and improving the condition of her milk. In the other case, when the child is being fed by hand, then proceed by totally altering the style of aliment given, and substituting farinaceous food, custards, blancmange, and ground-rice puddings.

As an aperient medicine for the mother, the best thing she can take is a dessert-spoonful of carbonate of magnesia once or twice a day, in a cup of cold water; and every second day, for two or three times, an aperient pill.

As the thrush extends all over the mouth, throat, stomach, and bowels, the irritation to the child from such an extent of diseased surface is proportionately great, and before attempting to act on such a tender surface by opening medicine, the better plan is to soothe by an emollient mixture; and, for that purpose, let the following be prepared. Take of

Castor oil	2 drachms
Sugar	1 drachm
Mucilage, or powdered gum Arabic	half a drachm

Triturate till the oil is incorporated, then add slowly—

Mint-water	One ounce and a half
Laudanum	Ten drops

Half a teaspoonful three times a day, to an infant from one to two years old; a teaspoonful from two to three years old; and a dessert-spoonful at any age over that time. After two days' use of the mixture, one of the following powders should be given twice a day, accompanied with one dose daily of the mixture:—

Grey powder	20 grains
Powdered rhubarb	15 grains
Scammony	10 grains

Mix. Divide into twelve powders, for one year; eight powders, from one to two; and six powders, from two to six years old. After that age, double the strength, by giving the quantity of two powders at once.

It is sometimes customary to apply borax and honey to the mouth for thrush; but it is always better to treat the disease constitutionally rather than locally. The first steps, therefore, to be adopted are, to remove or correct the exciting cause—the mother's milk or food; allay irritation by a warm bath and the castor-oil mixture, followed by and conjoined with the powders.

To those, however, who wish to try the honey process, the best preparation to use is the following:—Rub down one ounce of honey with two drachms of tincture of myrrh, and apply it to the lips and mouth every four or six hours.

It is a popular belief, and one most devoutly cherished by many nurses and elderly persons, that everybody must, at some time of their life, between birth and death, have an attack of thrush, and if not in infancy, or prime of life, it will surely attack them on their death-bed, in a form more malignant than if the patient had been affected with the malady earlier; the black thrush with which they are then reported to be affected being, in all probability, the petechae, or purple spots that characterize the worst form, and often the last stage, of typhoid fever.

The class of diseases we are now approaching are the most important, both in their pathological features and in their consequences on the constitution, of any group or individual disease that assails the human body; and though more frequently attacking the undeveloped frame of childhood, are yet by no means confined to that period. These are called Eruptive Fevers, and embrace chicken-pox, cow-pox, small-pox, scarlet fever, measles, milary fever, and erysipelas or St Anthony's fire.

The general character of all these is, that they are contagious, and, as a general rule, attack a person only once in his lifetime; that their chain of diseased actions always begins with fever, and that, after an interval of from one to four days, the fever is followed by an eruption of the skin.

CHICKEN-POX, OR GLASS-POX; AND COW-POX, OR VACCINATION

CHICKEN-POX, or GLASS-POX, may, in strict propriety, be classed as a mild variety of small-pox, presenting all the mitigated symptoms of that formidable disease. Among many physicians it is, indeed, classed as small-pox, and not a separate disease; but as this is not the place to discuss such questions, and as we profess to give only facts, the result of our own practical experience, we shall treat this affection of glass-pox or chicken-pox, as we ourselves have found it, as a distinct and separate disease.

Chicken-pox is marked by all the febrile symptoms presented by small-pox, with this difference, that, in the case of chicken-pox, each symptom is particularly slight. The heat of body is much less acute, and the principal symptoms are difficulty of breathing, headache, coated tongue, and nausea, which sometimes amounts to vomiting. After a term of general irritability, heat, and restlessness, about the fourth day, or between the third and fourth, an eruption makes its appearance over the face, neck, and body, in its first two stages closely resembling small-pox, with this especial difference, that whereas the pustules in small-pox have *flat* and *depressed* centres—an infallible characteristic of small-pox—the pustules in chicken-pox remain *globular*, while the fluid in them changes from a transparent white to a straw-coloured liquid, which begins to exude and disappear about the eighth or ninth day, and, in mild cases, by the twelfth desquamates, or peels off entirely.

There can be no doubt that chicken-pox, like small-pox, is contagious, and under certain states of the atmosphere becomes endemic. Parents should, therefore, avoid exposing young children to the danger of infection by taking them where it is known to exist, as chicken-pox, in weakly constitutions, or in very young children, may superinduce small-pox, the one disease either running concurrently with the other, or discovering itself as the other declines. This, of course, is a condition that renders the case very hazardous, as the child has to struggle against two diseases at once, or before it has recruited strength from the attack of the first.

Treatment.—In all ordinary cases of chicken-pox—and it is very seldom it assumes any complexity—the whole treatment resolves itself into the use of the warm bath, and a course of gentle aperients. The bath should be used when the oppression of the lungs renders the breathing difficult, or the heat and dryness of the skin, with the undeveloped rash beneath the surface, shows the necessity for its use.

As the pustules in chicken-pox very rarely run to the state of suppuration, as in the other disease, there is no fear of *pitting* or disfigurement, except in very severe forms, which, however, happen so seldom as not to merit apprehension. When the eruption subsides, however, the face may be washed with elder-flower water, and the routine followed which is prescribed in the convalescent state of small-pox.

Cow-Pox, properly speaking, is an artificial disease, established in a healthy body as a prophylactic, or preventive agent, against the more serious attack of small-pox, and is merely that chain of slight febrile symptoms and local irritation, consequent on the specific action of the lymph of the vaccination, in its action on the circulating system of the body. This is not the place to speak of the benefits conferred on mankind by the discovery of vaccination, not only as the preserver of the human features from a most loathsome disfigurement, but as a sanitary agent in the prolongation of life.*

Fortunately the State has now made it imperative on all parents to have their children vaccinated before, or by the end of, the twelfth week; thus doing away, as far as possible, with the danger to public health proceeding from the ignorance or prejudice of those parents whose want of information on the subject makes them object to the employment of this specific preventive; for though vaccination has been proved *not* to be *always* an infallible guard against small-pox, the attack is always much lighter, should it occur, and is seldom, if indeed *ever*, fatal after the precaution of vaccination. The best time to vaccinate a child is after the sixth and before the twelfth week, if it is in perfect health, but still earlier if small-pox is prevalent, and any danger exists of the infant taking the disease. It is customary, and always advisable, to give the child a mild aperient powder one or two days before inserting the lymph in the arm; and should measles, scarlet fever, or any other disease arise during the progress of the pustule, the child, when recovered, should be *re-vaccinated*, and the lymph taken from its arm on no account used for vaccinating purposes.

The disease of cow-pox generally takes twenty days to complete its course; in other words, the maturity and declension of the pustule takes that time to fulfil its several changes. The mode of vaccination is either to insert the matter, or lymph, taken from a healthy child, under the cuticle in several places on both arms, or, which is still better, to make three slight scratches, or abrasions, with a lancet on one arm in this manner, ₍"₎ and work into the irritated parts the lymph, allowing the arm to dry thoroughly before putting down the infant's sleeve; by this means absorption is insured and the unnecessary pain of several pustules on both arms avoided. No apparent change is observable by the eye for several days; indeed, not till the fourth, in many cases, is there any evidence of a vesicle; about the fifth day, however, a pink areola, or circle, is observed round one or all of the places, surrounding a small pearly vesicle or bladder. This goes on deepening in hue till the seventh or eighth day, when the vesicle is about an inch in diameter, with a depressed centre; on the ninth the edges are elevated, and the surrounding part hard and inflamed. The disease is now at its height, and the pustule should be opened, if not for the purpose of vaccinating other children, to allow the escape of the lymph, and subdue the inflammatory action. After the twelfth day the centre is covered by a brown scab, and the colour of the swelling becomes darker, gradually declining in hardness and colour till the twentieth, when the scab falls off, leaving a small pit, or cicatrix, to mark the seat of the disease, and for life prove a certificate of successful vaccination.

In some children the inflammation and swelling of the arm is excessive, and extremely painful, and the fever, about the ninth or tenth day, very high; the pustule, therefore, at that time, should sometimes be opened, the arm fomented every two hours with a warm bread poultice, and an aperient powder given to the infant.

MEASLES AND SCARLET FEVER, WITH THE TREATMENT OF BOTH

Measles

This much-dreaded disease, which forms the next subject in our series of infantine diseases, and which entails more evils on the health of childhood than any other description of physical suffering to which that age of life is subject, may be considered more an affection of the venous circulation, tending to general and local congestion, attended with a diseased condition of the blood, than either as a fever or an inflammation; and though generally classed before or after scarlet fever, is, in its pathology and treatment, irrespective of its after-consequences, as distinct and opposite as one disease can well be from another.

As we have already observed, measles are always characterized by the running at the nose and eyes, and great oppression of breathing; so, in the mode of treatment, two objects are to be held especially in view; first, to unload the congested state of the lungs,—the cause of the oppressed breathing; and, secondly, to act vigorously, both during the disease and afterwards, on the bowels. At the same time it cannot be too strongly borne in mind, that though the patient in measles should on no account be kept unduly hot, more care than in most infantine complaints should be taken to guard the body from *cold*, or any abrupt changes of temperature. With these special observations, we shall proceed to give a description of the disease, as recognized by its usual—

Symptoms, which commence with cold chills and flushes, lassitude, heaviness, pain in the head, and drowsiness, cough, hoarseness, and extreme difficulty of breathing, frequent sneezing, defluction or running at the eyes and nose, nausea, sometimes vomiting, thirst, a furred tongue; the pulse throughout is quick, and sometimes full and soft, at others hard and small, with other indications of an inflammatory nature.

On the third day, small red points make their appearance, first on the face and neck, gradually extending over the upper and lower part of the body. On the fifth day, the vivid red of the eruption changes into a brownish hue; and, in two or three days more, the rash entirely disappears, leaving a loose powdery desquamation on the skin, which rubs off like dandriff. At this stage of the disease a diarrhoea frequently comes on, which, being what is called 'critical,' should never be checked, unless seriously severe. Measles sometimes assume a typhoid or malignant character, in which form the symptoms are all greatly exaggerated, and the case from the first becomes both doubtful and dangerous. In this condition the eruption comes out sooner, and only in patches; and often, after showing for a few hours, suddenly recedes, presenting, instead of the usual florid red, a dark purple or blackish hue; a dark brown fur forms on the gums and mouth, the breathing becomes laborious, delirium supervenes, and, if unrelieved, is followed by coma; a fetid diarrhoea takes place, and the patient sinks under the congested state of the lungs and the oppressed functions of the brain.

The unfavourable symptoms in measles are a high degree of fever, the excessive heat and dryness of the skin, hurried and short breathing, and a particularly hard pulse. The sequelae, or after-consequences, of measles are, croup, bronchitis, mesenteric disease, abscesses behind the ear, ophthalmia, and glandular swellings in other parts of the body.

Treatment.—In the first place, the patient should be kept in a cool room, the temperature of which must be regulated to suit the child's feelings of comfort, and the diet adapted to the strictest principles of abstinence. When the inflammatory symptoms are severe, bleeding, in some form, is often necessary, though, when adopted, it must be in the *first stage* of the disease; and, if the lungs are the apprehended seat of the inflammation, two or more leeches,* according to the age and strength of the patient, must be applied to the upper part of the chest, followed by a small blister; or the blister may be substituted for the leeches, the attendant bearing in mind, that the benefit effected by the blister can always be considerably augmented by plunging the feet into very hot water about a couple of hours after applying the blister, and kept in the water for about two minutes. And let it further be remembered, that this immersion of the feet in hot water may be adopted at any time or stage of the disease; and that, whenever the *head* or *lungs* are oppressed, relief will *always* accrue from its sudden and brief employment. When the symptoms commence with much shivering, and the skin early assumes a hot, dry character, the appearance of the rash will be facilitated, and all the other symptoms rendered milder, if the patient is put into a warm bath, and kept in the water for about three minutes. Or, where that is not convenient, the following process, which will answer quite as well, can be substituted:—Stand the child, naked, in a tub, and, having first prepared several jugs of sufficiently warm water, empty them, in quick succession, over the patient's shoulders and body; immediately wrap in a hot blanket, and put the child to bed till it rouses from the sleep that always follows the effusion or bath. This agent, by lowering the temperature of the skin, and opening the pores, producing a natural perspiration, and unloading the congested state of the lungs, in most cases does away entirely with the necessity both for leeches and a blister. Whether any of these external means have been employed or not, the first internal remedies should commence with a series of aperient powders and a saline mixture as prescribed in the following formularies; at the same time, as a beverage to quench the thirst, let a quantity of barley-water be made, slightly acidulated by the juice of an orange, and partially sweetened by some sugar-candy; and of which, when properly made and cold, let the patient drink as often as thirst, or the dryness of the mouth, renders necessary.

Aperient Powders.—Take of scammony and jalap,* each 24 grains; grey powder and powdered antimony, each 18 grains. Mix and divide into 12 powders, if for a child between two and four years of age; into 8 powders, if for a child between four and eight years of age; and into 6 powders for between eight and twelve years. One powder to be given, in a little jelly or sugar-and-water, every three or four hours, according to the severity of the symptoms.

Saline Mixture.—Take of mint-water, 6 ounces; powdered nitre, 20 grains; antimonial wine, 3 drachms; spirits of nitre, 2 drachms; syrup of saffron, 2 drachms. Mix. To children under three years, give a teaspoonful every two hours; from that age to six, a dessert-spoonful at the same times; and a tablespoonful every three or four hours to children between six and twelve.

The object of these aperient powders is to keep up a steady but gentle action on the bowels; but, whenever it seems necessary to administer a stronger dose, and effect a brisk action on the digestive organs,—a course particularly imperative towards the close of the disease,—two of these powders given at once, according to the age, will be found to produce that effect; that is, two of the twelve for a child under four years, and two of the eight, and two of the six, according to the age of the patient.

When the difficulty of breathing becomes oppressive, as it generally does towards night, a hot bran poultice, laid on the chest, will be always found highly beneficial. The diet throughout must be light, and consist of farinaceous food, such as rice and sago puddings, beef-tea and toast; and not till convalescence sets in should hard or animal food be given.

When measles assume the malignant form, the advice just given must be broken through; food of a nutritious and stimulating character should be at once substituted, and administered in conjunction with wine, and even spirits, and the disease regarded and treated as a case of typhus. But, as this form of measles is not frequent, and, if occurring, hardly likely to be treated without assistance, it is unnecessary to enter on the minutiae of its practice here. What we have prescribed, in almost all cases, will be found sufficient to meet every emergency, without resorting to a multiplicity of agents.

The great point to remember in measles is, not to give up the treatment with the apparent subsidence of the disease, as the *after consequences* of measles are too often *more serious*, and to be more dreaded, than the measles themselves. To guard against this danger, and thoroughly purify the system, after the subsidence of all the symptoms of the disease, a corrective course of medicine, and a regimen of exercise, should be adopted for some weeks after the cure of the disease. To effect this, an active aperient powder should be given every three or four days, with a daily dose of the subjoined tonic mixture, with as much exercise, by walking, running after a hoop, or other bodily exertion, as the strength of the child and the state of the atmosphere will admit, the patient being, wherever possible, removed to a purer air as soon as convalescence warrants the change.

Tonic Mixture.—Take of infusion of rose-leaves, 6 ounces; quinine, 8 grains; diluted sulphuric acid, 15 drops. Mix. Dose, from half a teaspoonful up to a dessert-spoonful, once a day, according to the age of the patient.

Scarlatina, or Scarlet Fever

Though professional accuracy has divided this disease into several forms, we shall keep to the one disease most generally met with, the common or simple scarlet fever, which, in all cases, is characterized by an excessive heat on the skin, sore throat, and a peculiar speckled appearance of the tongue.

Symptoms.—Cold chills, shivering, nausea, thirst, hot skin, quick pulse, with difficulty of swallowing; the tongue is coated, presenting through its fur innumerable specks, the elevated papillae of the tongue, which gives it the speckled character, that, if not the invariable sign of scarlet fever, is only met with in cases closely analogous to that disease. Between the *second* and *third* day, but most frequently on the *third*, a bright red efflorescence break out in patches on the face, neck, and back, from which it extends over the trunk and extremities, always showing thicker and deeper in colour wherever there is any pressure, such as the elbows, back, and hips; when the eruption is well out, the skin presents the appearance of a boiled lobster-shell. At first, the skin is smooth, but, as the disease advances, perceptible roughness is apparent, from the elevation of the rash, or, more properly, the pores of the skin. On the *fifth* and *sixth* days the eruption begins to decline, and by the *eighth* has generally entirely disappeared. During the whole of this period, there is, more or less, constant sore throat.

The *Treatment* of scarlet fever is, in general, very simple. Where the heat is great, and the eruption comes out with difficulty, or recedes as soon as it appears, the body should be sponged with cold vinegar-and-water, or tepid water, as in measles, poured over the chest and body, the patient being, as in that disease, wrapped in a blanket and put to bed, and the same powders and mixture ordered in measles administered, with the addition of a constant hot bran poultice round the throat, which should be continued from the first symptom till a day or two after the declension of the rash. The same low diet and cooling drink, with the same general instructions, are to be obeyed in this as in the former disease.

When the fever runs high in the first stage, and there is much nausea, before employing the effusions of water, give the patient an emetic, of equal parts of ipecacuanha and antimonial wine, in doses of from a teaspoonful to a tablespoonful, according to age. By these means, nine out of every ten cases of scarlatina may be safely and expeditiously cured, especially if the temperature of the patient's room is kept at an even standard of about sixty degrees.

HOOPING-COUGH, CROUP, AND DIARRHOEA, WITH THEIR MODE OF TREATMENT

Hooping-Cough

This is purely a spasmodic disease, and is only infectious through the faculty of imitation, a habit that all children are remarkably apt to fall into; and even where adults have contracted hooping-cough, it has been from the same cause, and is as readily accounted for, on the principle of imitation, as that the gaping of one person will excite or predispose a whole party to follow the same spasmodic example. If any one associates for a few days with a person who stammers badly, he will find, when released from his company, that the sequence of his articulation and the fluency of his speech are, for a time, gone; and it will be a matter of constant vigilance, and some difficulty, to overcome the evil of so short an association. The manner in which a number of school-girls will, one after another, fall into a fit on beholding one of their number attacked with epilepsy, must be familiar to many. These several facts lead us to a juster notion of how to treat this spasmodic disease. Every effort should, therefore, be directed, mentally and physically, to break the chain of nervous action, on which the continuance of the cough depends.

Symptoms.—Hooping-cough comes on with a slight oppression of breathing, thirst, quick pulse, hoarseness, and a hard, dry cough. This state may exist without any change from one to two or three weeks before the peculiar feature of the disease—the *hoop*—sets in. As the characteristics of this cough are known to all, it is unnecessary to enter here, physiologically, on the subject. We shall, therefore, merely remark that the frequent vomiting and bleeding at the mouth or nose are favourable signs, and proceed to the. . . .

Treatment, which should consist in keeping up a state of nausea and vomiting. For this purpose, give the child doses of ipecacuanha and antimonial wines, in equal parts, and quantities varying from half to one and a half teaspoonful once a day, or, when the expectoration is hard and difficult of expulsion, giving the following cough mixture every four hours. Take of

Syrup of squills	½ ounce
Antimonial wine	1 ounce
Laudanum	15 drops
Syrup of Toulou	2 drachms
Water	1½ ounce

Mix. The dose is from half a spoonful to a dessert-spoonful. When the cough is urgent, the warm bath is to be used, and either one or two leeches applied over the breastbone, or else a small blister laid on the lower part of the throat.

Such is the medical treatment of hooping-cough; but there is a moral regimen, based on the nature of the disease, which should never be omitted. And, on the principle that a sudden start or diversion of the mind will arrest a person in the act of sneezing or gaping, so the like means should be adopted with the hooping-cough patient; and, in the first stage, before the *hooping* has been added, the parent should endeavour to break the paroxysm of the cough by abruptly attracting the patient's attention, and thus, if possible, preventing the cough from reaching that height when the ingulp of air gives the hoop or crow that marks the disease; but when once that symptom has set in, it becomes still more necessary to endeavour, by even measures of intimidation, to break the spasmodic chain of the cough. Exercise in the open air, when dry, is also requisite, and change of scene and air in all cases is of absolute necessity, and may be adopted at any stage of the disease.

Croup

This is by far the most formidable and fatal of all the diseases to which infancy and childhood are liable, and is purely an inflammatory affection, attacking that portion of the mucous membrane lining the windpipe and bronchial tubes, and from the effect of which a false or loose membrane is formed along the windpipe, resembling in appearance the finger of a glove suspended in the passage, and, consequently, terminating the life of the patient by suffocation; for, as the lower end grows together and becomes closed, no air can enter the lungs, and the child dies choked. All dull, fat, and heavy children are peculiarly predisposed to this disease, and those with short necks and who make a wheezing noise in their natural breathing. Croup is always sudden in its attack, and rapid in its career, usually proving fatal within three days; most frequently commences in the night, and generally attacking children between the ages of three and ten years. Mothers should, therefore, be on their guard who have children predisposed to this disease, and immediately resort to the means hereafter advised.

Symptoms.—Languor and restlessness, hoarseness, wheezing, and short, dry cough, with occasional rattling in the throat during sleep, the child often plucking at its throat with its fingers; difficulty of breathing, which quickly becomes hard and laboured, causing great anxiety of the countenance, and the veins of the neck to swell and become knotted; the voice in speaking acquires a sharp, crowing, or croupy sound, while the inspirations have a harsh, metallic intonation. After a few hours, a quantity of thick, ropy mucus is thrown out, hanging about the mouth, and causing suffocating fits of coughing to expel.

Treatment.—Place the child immediately in a hot bath up to the

throat; and, on removal from the water, give an emetic of the antimonial or ipecacuanha wine, and, when the vomiting has subsided,
lay a long blister down the front of the throat, and administer one of
the following powders every twenty minutes to a child from three to
six years of age.

Take of calomel, 12 grains; tartar emetic, 2 grains; lump sugar,
30 grains. Mix accurately, and divide into 12 powders. For a child
from six to twelve years, divide into 6 powders, and give one every
half-hour.

Should the symptoms remain unabated after a few hours, apply
one or two leeches to the throat, and put mustard poultices to the
feet and thighs, retaining them about eight minutes; and, in extreme
cases, a mustard poultice to the spine between the shoulders, and at
the same time rub mercurial ointment into the armpits and the
angles of the jaws.

Such is a vigorous and reliable system of treatment in severe cases
of croup; but, in the milder and more general form, the following
abridgment will, in all probability, be all that will be required:—
First, the hot bath; second, the emetic; third, a mustard plaster
round the throat for five minutes; fourth, the powders; fifth, another
emetic in six hours, if needed, and the powders continued without
intermission while the urgency of the symptoms continues. When
relief has been obtained, these are to be discontinued, and a dose of
senna tea given to act on the bowels.

Diarrhoea

The diarrhoea with which children are so frequently affected, especially in infancy, should demand the nurse's immediate attention,
and when the secretion, from its clayey colour, indicates an absence
of bile, a powder composed of 3 grains of grey powder and 1 grain of
rhubarb, should be given twice, with an interval of four hours
between each dose, to a child from one to two years, and, a day or two
afterwards, an aperient powder containing the same ingredients and
quantities, with the addition of 2 or 3 grains of scammony. For the
relaxation consequent on an overloaded stomach, or acidity in the
bowels, a little magnesia dissolved in milk should be employed two or
three times a day.

When much griping and pain attend the diarrhoea, half a teaspoonful of Dalby's Carminative (the best of all patent medicines) should be given, either with or without a small quantity of castor oil to carry off the exciting cause.

For any form of diarrhoea that, by excessive action, demands a speedy correction, the most efficacious remedy that can be employed in all ages and conditions of childhood is the tincture of Kino, of which from 10 to 30 drops, mixed with a little sugar and water in a spoon, are to be given every two or three hours till the undue action has been checked. Often the change of diet to rice, milk, eggs, or the substitution of animal for vegetable food, or *vice versa*, will correct an unpleasant and almost chronic state of diarrhoea.

A very excellent carminative powder for flatulent infants may be kept in the house, and employed with advantage, whenever the child is in pain or griped, by dropping 5 grains of oil of aniseed and 2 of peppermint on half an ounce of lump sugar, and rubbing it in a mortar, with a drachm of magnesia, into a fine powder. A small quantity of this may be given in a little water at any time, and always with benefit.

CHAPTER XLIII

THE DOCTOR*

'Time,' according to the old proverb, 'is money;' and it may also, in many cases, and with equal truthfulness, be said to be life; for a few moments, in great emergencies, often turn the balance between recovery and death. This applies more especially to all kinds of poisoning, fits, submersion in water, or exposure to noxious gases; and many accidents. If people knew how to act during the interval that must necessarily elapse from the moment that a medical man is sent for until he arrives, many lives might be saved, which now, unhappily, are lost. Generally speaking, however, nothing is done— all is confusion and fright; and the surgeon, on his arrival, finds that death has already seized its victim, who, had his friends but known a few rough rules for their guidance, might have been rescued. We shall, therefore, in a series of papers, give such information as to the means to be employed in event of accidents, injuries, &c., as, by the aid of a gentleman of large professional experience, we are warranted in recommending.

LIST OF DRUGS, &C., NECESSARY TO CARRY OUT ALL INSTRUCTIONS

We append at once a LIST OF DRUGS, &c., and a few PRESCRIPTIONS necessary to carry out all the instructions given in this series of articles. It will be seen that they are few—they are not expensive; and by laying in a little stock of them, our instructions will be of instant value in all cases of accident, &c.—The drugs are— Antimonial Wine.* Antimonial Powder. Blister Compound. Blue Pill.* Calomel. Carbonate of Potash.* Compound Iron Pills. Compound Extract of Colocynth.* Compound Tincture of Camphor. Epsom Salts. Goulard's Extract.* Jalap in Powder. Linseed Oil. Myrrh and Aloes Pills.* Nitre.* Oil of Turpentine.* Opium, powdered, and Laudanum.* Sal Ammoniac. Senna Leaves. Soap Liniment, Opodeldoc.* Sweet Spirits of Nitre. Turner's Cerate.—To which should be added: Common Adhesive Plaster. Isinglass Plaster. Lint. A pair of small Scales with Weights. An ounce and a drachm

Measure-glass. A Lancet, A Probe. A pair of Forceps, and some curved Needles.

The following PRESCRIPTIONS may be made up for a few shillings; and, by keeping them properly labelled, and by referring to the remarks on the treatment of any particular case, much suffering, and, perhaps, some lives, may be saved.

Draught.—Twenty grains of sulphate of zinc in an ounce and a half of water. This draught is to be repeated in a quarter of an hour if vomiting does not take place.

Clyster.—Two tablespoonfuls of oil of turpentine in a pint of warm gruel.

Liniments.—1. Equal parts of lime-water and linseed-oil well mixed together. [Lime-water is made thus: Pour 6 pints of boiling water upon ¼ lb. of lime; mix well together, and when cool, strain the liquid from off the lime which has fallen to the bottom, taking care to get it as clear as possible.], 2. Compound camphor liniment.

Lotions.—1. Mix a dessert-spoonful of Goulard's extract and 2 tablespoonfuls of vinegar in a pint of water.—2. Mix ½ oz. of sal-ammoniac, 2 tablespoonfuls of vinegar, and the same quantity of gin or whisky, in half a pint of water.

Goulard Lotion.—1 drachm of sugar of lead,* 2 pints of rain-water, 2 teaspoonfuls of spirits of wine. For inflammation of the eyes or elsewhere:—The better way of making Goulard Lotion, if for the eyes, is to add to 6 oz. of distilled water, or water that has been well boiled, 1 drachm of the extract of lead.

Opodeldoc.—This lotion being a valuable application for sprains, lumbago, weakness of joints, &c., and it being difficult to procure either pure or freshly made, we give a recipe for its preparation. Dissolve 1 oz. of camphor in a pint of rectified spirits of wine; then dissolve 4 oz. of hard white Spanish soap, scraped thin, in 4 oz. of oil of rosemary, and mix them together.

The Common Black Draught.—Infusion of senna 10 drachms; Epsom salts 10 drachms; tincture of senna, compound tincture of cardamums, compound spirit of lavender, of each 1 drachm.

Families who make black draught in quantity, and wish to preserve it for some time without spoiling, should add about 2 drachms of spirits of hartshorn to each pint of the strained mixture, the use of this drug being to prevent its becoming mouldy or decomposed. A simpler and equally efficacious form of black draught is made by infusing ½ oz. of Alexandrian senna, 3 oz. of Epsom salts, and 2 drachms of bruised ginger and coriander-seeds, for several hours in a pint of boiling water, straining the liquor, and adding either 2 drachms of sal-volatile or spirits of hartshorn to the whole, and giving 3 tablespoonfuls for a dose to an adult.

Mixtures—1. *Aperient.*—Dissolve an ounce of Epsom salts in half a pint of senna tea: take a quarter of the mixture as a dose, and repeat it in three or four hours if necessary.

2. *Fever Mixture.*—Mix a drachm of powdered nitre, 2 drachms of carbonate of potash, 2 teaspoonfuls of antimonial wine, and a table-spoonful of sweet spirits of nitre, in half a pint of water.

3. *Myrrh and Aloes Pills.*—Ten grains made into two pills are the dose for a full-grown person.

4. *Compound Iron Pills.*—Dose for a full-grown person: 10 grains made into two pills.

Pills.—1. Mix 5 grains of calomel and the same quantity of anti-monial powder with a little bread-crumb, and make into two pills. Dose for a full-grown person: two pills.—2. Mix 5 grains of blue pill and the same quantity of compound extract of colocynth together, and make into two pills, the dose for a full-grown person.

Powders.—Mix a grain of calomel and 4 grains of powdered jalap together.

In all cases, the dose of medicines given is to be regulated by the age of the patient.

An ordinary Blister.—Spread a little blister compound on a piece of common adhesive plaster with the right thumb. It should be put on just thickly enough to conceal the appearance of the plaster beneath. The part from which a blister has been taken should be covered till it heals over with soft linen rags smeared with lard.

BATHS AND FOMENTATIONS

All fluid applications to the body are exhibited either in a hot or cold form; and the object for which they are administered is to produce a stimulating effect over the entire, or a part, of the system; for the effect, though differently obtained, and varying in degree, is the same in principle, whether procured by hot or cold water.

Heat.—There are three forms in which heat is universally applied to the body,—that of the tepid, warm, and vapour bath; but as the first is too inert to be worth notice, and the last dangerous and inapplicable, except in public institutions, we shall confine our remarks to the really efficacious and always attainable one—the . . .

Warm and Hot Bath.—These baths are used whenever there is congestion, or accumulation of blood in the internal organs, causing pain, difficulty of breathing, or stupor, and are employed, by their stimulating property, to cause a rush of blood to the surface, and, by unloading the great organs, produce a temporary inflammation in the skin, and so equalize the circulation. The effect of the hot bath is to increase the fulness of the pulse, accelerate respiration, and excite perspiration. In all inflammations of the stomach and bowels, the hot bath is of the utmost consequence; the temperature of the warm bath varies from 92° to 100°, and may be obtained by those who have no thermometer to test the exact heat, by mixing one measure of boiling with two of cold water.

Fomentations are generally used to effect, in a part, the benefit produced on the whole body by the bath; to which a sedative action is occasionally given by the use of roots, herbs, or other ingredients; the object being to relieve the internal organ, as the throat, or muscles round a joint, by exciting a greater flow of blood to the skin *over* the affected part. As the real agent of relief is heat, the fomentation should always be as hot as it can comfortably be borne, and, to insure effect, should be repeated every half-hour. Warm fluids are applied in order to render the swelling which accompanies inflammation less painful, by the greater readiness with which the skin yields, than when it is harsh and dry. They are of various kinds; but the most simple, and oftentimes the most useful, that can be employed, is 'Warm Water.' Another kind of fomentation is composed of dried poppyheads, 4 oz. Break them to pieces, empty out the seeds, put them into 4 pints of water, boil for a quarter of an hour, then strain through a cloth or sieve, and keep the water for use. Or, chamomile flowers, hemlock, and many other plants, may be boiled, and the part fomented with the hot liquor, by means of flannels wetted with the decoction.

Cold, when applied in excess to the body, drives the blood from the surface to the centre, reduces the pulse, makes the breathing hard and difficult, produces coma, and, if long continued, death. But when medicinally used, it excites a reaction on the surface equivalent to a stimulating effect; as in some cases of fever, when the body has been sponged with cold water, it excites, by reaction, increased circulation on the skin. Cold is sometimes used to keep up a repellent action, as, when local inflammation takes place, a remedy is applied, which, by its benumbing and astringent effect, causes the blood, or the excess of it in the part, to recede, and, by contracting the vessels, prevents the return of any undue quantity, till the affected part recovers its tone. Such remedies are called *Lotions*, and should, when used, be applied with the same persistency as the fomentation; for, as the latter should be renewed as often as the heat passes off, so the former should be applied as often as the heat from the skin deprives the application of its cold.

Poultices are only another form of fomentation, though chiefly used for abscesses. The ingredient best suited for a poultice is that which retains heat the longest; of these ingredients, the best are linseed-meal, bran, and bread. Bran sewed into a bag, as it can be reheated, will be found the cleanest and most useful; especially for sore throats.

HOW TO BLEED

In cases of great emergency, such as the strong kind of apoplexy, and when a surgeon cannot possibly be obtained for some considerable time, the life of the patient depends almost entirely upon the fact of his being bled or not. We therefore give instructions how the operation of bleeding is to be performed, but caution the reader only to attempt it in cases of the greatest emergency. Place a handkerchief or piece of tape rather but not too tightly round the arm, about three or four inches above the elbow. This will cause the veins below to swell and become very evident. If this is not sufficient, the hand should be constantly and quickly opened and shut for the same purpose. There will now be seen, passing up the middle of the fore-arm, a vein which, just below the bend of the elbow, sends a branch inwards and outwards, each branch shortly joining another large vein. It is from the *outer* branch that the person is to be bled. The right arm is the one mostly operated on. The operator should take the lancet in his right hand, between the thumb and first finger, place the thumb of his left hand on the vein below the part where he is going to bleed from, and then gently thrust the tip of the lancet into the vein, and taking care not to push it too deeply, cut in a gently curved direction, thus ⌣ and bring it out, point upwards, at about half an inch from the part of the vein into which he had thrust it. The vein must be cut lengthways, and not across. When sufficient blood has been taken away, remove the bandage from above the elbow, and place the thumb of the left hand firmly over the cut, until all the bleeding ceases. A small pad of lint is then to be put over the cut, with a larger pad over it, and the two kept in their places by means of a hand-kerchief or linen roller bound pretty tightly over them and round the arm.

When a person is bled, he should always be in the standing, or at any rate in the sitting, position; for if, as is often the case, he should happen to faint, he can, in most cases at least, easily be brought to again by the operator placing him flat on his back, and stopping the bleeding. *This is of the greatest importance.* It has been recommended, for what supposed advantages we don't know, to bleed people when they are lying down. Should a person, under these circumstances, faint, what could be done to bring him to again? The great treatment of lowering the body of the patient to the flat position cannot be followed here. It is in that position already, and cannot be placed lower than it at present is—except, as is most likely to be the case, under the ground.*

Spitting of blood, or hemorrhage from the lungs, is generally known from blood from the stomach by its being of a brighter colour, and in less quantities than that, which is always grumous and mixed with the half-digested food. In either case, rest should be immedi-ately enjoined, total abstinence from stimulants, and a low, poor diet, accompanied with the horizontal position, and bottles of boiling water to the feet. At the same time the patient should suck through a quill, every hour, half a wine-glass of water in which 10 or 15 drops of the elixir of vitriol has been mixed, and, till further advice has been procured, keep a towel wrung out of cold water on the chest or stomach, according to the seat of the hemorrhage.

BITES AND STINGS

Bites and stings may be divided into three kinds:—1. Those of Insects. 2. Those of Snakes. 3. Those of Dogs and other Animals.

1. *The Bites or Stings of Insects*, such as gnats, bees, wasps, &c., need cause very little alarm, and are, generally speaking, easily cured. They are very serious, however, when they take place on some delicate part of the body, such as near the eye, or in the throat. *The treatment* is very simple in most cases; and consists in taking out the sting, if it is left behind, with a needle, and applying to the part a liniment made of finely-scraped chalk and olive-oil, mixed together to about the thickness of cream.

Bathing the part bitten with warm turpentine or warm vinegar is also of great use. If the person feels faint, he should lie quietly on his back, and take a little brandy-and-water, or sal-volatile and water. When the inside of the throat is the part stung, there is great danger of violent inflammation taking place. In this case, from eight to twelve leeches should be immediately put to the outside of the throat, and when they drop off, the part to which they had been applied should be well fomented with warm water. The inside of the throat is to be constantly gargled with salt and water. Bits of ice are to be sucked. Rubbing the face and hands well over with plain olive-oil, before going to bed, will often keep gnats and musquitoes from biting during the night. Strong scent, such as eau-de-Cologne, will have the same effect.

2. *Bites of Snakes.*—These are much more dangerous than the preceding, and require more powerful remedies. The bites of the different kinds of snakes do not all act alike, but affect people in different ways.—*Treatment of the part bitten*. The great thing is to prevent the poison getting into the blood; and, if possible, to remove the whole of it at once from the body. A pocket-handkerchief, a piece of

tape or cord, or, in fact, of anything that is at hand, should be tied tightly round the part of the body bitten; if it be the leg or arm, immediately *above* the bite, and between it and the heart. The bite should then be sucked several times by any one who is near. There is no danger in this, provided the person who does it has not got the skin taken off any part of his mouth. What has been sucked into the mouth should be immediately spit out again. But if those who are near have sufficient nerve for the operation, and a suitable instrument, they should cut out the central part bitten, and then bathe the wound for some time with warm water, to make it bleed freely. The wound should afterwards be rubbed with a stick of lunar caustic, or, what is better, a solution of this—60 grains of lunar caustic dissolved in an ounce of water—should be dropped into it. The band should be kept on the part during the whole of the time that these means are being adopted. The wound should afterwards be covered with lint dipped in cold water. The best plan, however, to be adopted, if it can be managed, is the following:—take a common wine-glass, and, holding it upside down, put a lighted candle or a spirit-lamp into it for a minute or two. This will take out the air. Then clap the glass suddenly over the bitten part, and it will become attached, and hold on to the flesh. The glass being nearly empty, the blood containing the poison will, in consequence, flow into it from the wound of its own accord. This process should be repeated three or four times, and the wound sucked, or washed with warm water, before each application of the glass. As a matter of course, when the glass is removed, all the blood should be washed out of it before it is applied again.— *Constitutional Treatment.* There is mostly at first great depression of strength in these cases, and it is therefore requisite to give some stimulant; a glass of hot brandy-and-water, or twenty drops of sal-volatile, is the best that can be given. When the strength has returned, and if the patient has not already been sick, a little mustard in hot water should be given, to make him so. If, on the other hand, as is often the case, the vomiting is excessive, a large mustard poultice should be placed over the stomach, and a grain of solid opium swallowed in the form of a pill, for the purpose of stopping it. Only one of these pills should be given by a non-professional person. In all cases of bites from snakes, send for a surgeon as quickly as possible, and act according to the above directions until he arrives. If he is within any reasonable distance, content yourself by putting on the band, sucking the wound, applying the glass, and, if necessary, giving a little brandy-and-water.

3. *Bites of Dogs.*—For obvious reasons, these kinds of bites are more frequently met with than those of snakes. *The treatment* is the same as that for snake-bites, more especially that of the bitten part. The majority of writers on the subject are in favour of keeping the wound open as long as possible. This may be done by putting a few beans on it, and then by applying a large linseed-meal poultice over them.

BURNS AND SCALDS

BURNS AND SCALDS being essentially the same in all particulars, and differing only in the manner of their production, may be spoken of together. As a general rule, scalds are less severe than burns, because the heat of water, by which scalds are mostly produced, is not, even when it is boiling, so intense as that of flame; oil, however, and other liquids, whose boiling-point is high, produce scalds of a very severe nature. Burns and scalds have been divided into three classes. The first class comprises those where the burn is altogether superficial, and merely reddens the skin; the second, where the injury is greater, and we get little bladders containing a fluid (called serum) dotted over the affected part; in the third class we get, in the case of burns, a charring, and in that of scalds, a softening or pulpiness, perhaps a complete and immediate separation of the part. This may occur at once, or in the course of a little time. The pain from the second kind of burns is much more severe than that in the other two, although the danger, as a general rule, is less than it is in the third class. These injuries are much more dangerous when they take place on the trunk than when they happen on the arms or legs. The danger arises more from the extent of surface that is burnt than from the depth to which the burn goes. This rule, of course, has certain exceptions; because a small burn on the chest or belly penetrating deeply is more dangerous than a more extensive but superficial one on the arm or leg. When a person's clothes are in flames, the best way of extinguishing them is to wind a rug, or some thick material, tightly round the whole of the body.*

CONCUSSION OF BRAIN—STUNNING.—This may be caused by a blow or a fall.—*Symptoms.* Cold skin; weak pulse; almost total insensibility; slow, weak breathing; pupil of eye sometimes bigger, sometimes smaller, than natural; inability to move; unwillingness to answer when spoken to. These symptoms come on directly after the accident.—*Treatment.* Place the patient quietly on a warm bed, send for a surgeon, *and do nothing else for the first four or six hours.* After this time the skin will become hot, the pulse full, and the patient feverish altogether. If the surgeon has not arrived by the time these symptoms have set in, shave the patient's head, and apply the following lotion (No. 2): Mix half an ounce of sal-ammoniac, two tablespoonfuls of vinegar; and the same quantity of gin or whisky, in half a pint of water. Then give this pill (No. 1): Mix five grains of calomel and the same quantity of antimonial powder with a little bread-crumb, and make into two pills. Give a black draught three hours after the pill, and two tablespoonfuls of the above-mentioned fever-mixture every four hours. Keep on low diet. Leeches are sometimes to be applied to the head. These cases are often followed by violent inflammation of the brain. They can, there-fore, only be attended to properly throughout by a surgeon. The great thing for people to do in these cases is—nothing; contenting them-selves with putting the patient to bed, and waiting the arrival of a surgeon.

THE CHOLERA* and AUTUMNAL COMPLAINTS.—To oppose cholera, there seems no surer or better means than cleanliness, sobriety, and judicious ventilation. Where there is dirt, that is the place for cholera; where windows and doors are kept most jealously shut, there cholera will find easiest entrance; and people who indulge in intemperate diet during the hot days of autumn are actually court-ing death. To repeat it, cleanliness, sobriety, and free ventilation almost always defy the pestilence; but, in case of attack, immediate recourse should be had to a physician. The faculty say that a large number of lives have been lost, in many seasons, solely from delay in seeking medical assistance. They even assert that, taken early, the cholera is by no means a fatal disorder. The copious use of salt is recommended on very excellent authority. Other autumnal com-plaints there are, of which diarrhoea is the worst example. They come on with pain, flatulence, sickness, with or without vomiting, followed by loss of appetite, general lassitude, and weakness. If attended to at the first appearance, they may soon be conquered; for which purpose it is necessary to assist nature in throwing off the contents of the bowels, which may be done by means of the following prescription:—Take of calomel 3 grains, rhubarb 8 grains; mix and take it in a little honey or jelly, and repeat the dose three times, at the intervals of four or five hours. The next purpose to be answered is the defence of the lining membrane of the intestines from their acrid contents, which will be best effected by drinking copiously of linseed tea, or of a drink made by pouring boiling water on quince-seeds, which are of a very mucilaginous nature; or, what is still better, full draughts of whey. If the complaint continue after these means have been employed, some astringent or binding medicine will be required, as the subjoined:—Take of prepared chalk 2 drachms, cinnamon-water 7 oz., syrup of poppies 1 oz.; mix, and take 3 table-spoonfuls every four hours. Should this fail to complete the cure, ½ oz. of tincture of catechu, or of kino, may be added to it, and then it will seldom fail; or a teaspoonful of the tincture of kino alone, with a little water, every three hours, till the diarrhoea is checked. While any symptoms of derangement are present, particular attention must be paid to the diet, which should be of a soothing, lubricating, and light nature, as instanced in veal or chicken broth, which should contain but little salt. Rice, batter, and bread puddings will be gener-ally relished, and be eaten with advantage; but the stomach is too much impaired to digest food of a more solid nature. Indeed, we should give that organ, together with the bowels, as little trouble as possible, while they are so incapable of acting in their accustomed manner. Much mischief is frequently produced by the absurd prac-tice of taking tincture of rhubarb, which is almost certain of aggra-vating that species of disorder of which we have now treated; for it is a spirit as strong as brandy, and cannot fail of producing harm upon a surface which is rendered tender by the formation and contact of vitiated bile. But our last advice is, upon the first appearance of such symptoms as are above detailed, have *immediate* recourse to a doctor, where possible.

To Cure a Cold.—Put a large teacupful of linseed, with ¼ lb. of sun raisins and 2 oz. of stick liquorice, into 2 quarts of soft water, and let it simmer over a slow fire till reduced to one quart; add to it ¼ lb. of pounded sugar-candy, a tablespoonful of old rum, and a tablespoonful of the best white-wine vinegar, or lemon-juice. The rum and vinegar should be added as the decoction is taken; for, if they are put in at first, the whole soon becomes flat and less efficacious. The dose is half a pint, made warm, on going to bed; and a little may be taken whenever the cough is troublesome. The worst cold is generally cured by this remedy in two or three days; and, if taken in time, is considered infallible.

COLD ON THE CHEST.—A flannel dipped in boiling water, and sprinkled with turpentine, laid on the chest as quickly as possible, will relieve the most severe cold or hoarseness.

SUBSTANCES IN THE EYE.—To remove fine particles of gravel, lime, &c., the eye should be syringed with lukewarm water till free from them. Be particular not to worry the eye, under the impression that the substance is still there, which the enlargement of some of the minute vessels makes the patient believe is actually the case.

SORE EYES.—Incorporate thoroughly, in a glass mortar or vessel, one part of strong citron ointment with three parts of spermaceti ointment. Use the mixture night and morning, by placing a piece of the size of a pea in the corner of the eye affected, only to be used in cases of chronic or long-standing inflammation of the organ, or its lids.

LIME IN THE EYE.—Bathe the eye with a little weak vinegar-and-water, and carefully remove any little piece of lime which may be seen, with a feather. If any lime has got entangled in the eyelashes, carefully clear it away with a bit of soft linen soaked in vinegar-and-water. Violent inflammation is sure to follow; a smart purge must be therefore administered, and in all probability a blister must be applied on the temple, behind the ear, or nape of the neck.

STYE IN THE EYE.—Styes are little abscesses which form between the roots of the eyelashes, and are rarely larger than a small pea. The best way to manage them is to bathe them frequently with warm water, or in warm poppy-water, if very painful. When they have burst, use an ointment composed of one part of citron ointment and four of spermaceti, well rubbed together, and smear along the edge of the eyelid. Give a grain or two of calomel with 5 or 8 grains of rhubarb, according to the age of the child, twice a week. The old-fashioned and apparently absurd practice of rubbing the stye with a ring, is as good and speedy a cure as that by any process of medicinal application; though the number of times it is rubbed, or the quality of the ring and direction of the strokes, has nothing to do with its success. The pressure and the friction excite the vessels of the part, and cause an absorption of the effused matter under the eyelash. The edge of the nail will answer as well as a ring.

INFLAMMATION OF THE EYELIDS.—The following ointment has been found very beneficial in inflammations of the eyeball and edges of the eyelids:—Take of prepared calomel, 1 scruple; spermaceti ointment, ½ oz. Mix them well together in a glass mortar; apply a small quantity to each corner of the eye every night and morning, and also to the edges of the lids, if they are affected. If this should not eventually remove the inflammation, elder-flower water may be applied three or four times a day, by means of an eye-cup. The bowels should be kept in a laxative state, by taking occasionally a quarter of an ounce of the Cheltenham or Epsom salts.

FASTING.—It is said by many able physicians that fasting is a means of removing incipient disease, and of restoring the body to its customary healthy sensations. Howard, the celebrated philanthropist (says a writer), used to fast one day in every week. Napoleon, when he felt his system unstrung, suspended his wonted repast, and took his exercise on horseback.

FITS

FITS come on so suddenly, often without even the slightest warning, and may prove fatal so quickly, that all people should be acquainted at least with their leading symptoms and treatment, as a few moments, more or less, will often decide the question between life and death. The treatment, in very many cases at least, to be of the slightest use, should be *immediate*, as a person in a fit (of apoplexy for instance) may die while a surgeon is being fetched from only the next street. We shall give, as far as the fact of our editing a work for non-professional readers will permit, the peculiar and distinctive symptoms of all kind of fits, and the immediate treatment to be adopted in each case.

APOPLEXY.*—These fits may be divided into two kinds—the *strong* and the *weak*.

1. *The strong kind.*—These cases mostly occur in stout, strong, short-necked, bloated-faced people, who are in the habit of living well.—*Symptoms.* The patient may or may not have had headache, sparks before his eyes, with confusion of ideas and giddiness, for a day or two before the attack. When it takes place, he falls down insensible; the body becomes paralyzed, generally more so on one side than the other; the face and head are hot, and the blood-vessels about them swollen; the pupils of the eyes are larger than natural, and the eyes themselves are fixed; the mouth is mostly drawn down at one corner; the breathing is like loud snoring; the pulse full and hard.—*Treatment.* Place the patient immediately in bed, with his head well raised; take off everything that he has round his neck, and bleed freely and at once from the arm. If you have not got a lancet, use a pen-knife or anything suitable that may be at hand. Apply warm mustard poultices to the soles of the feet and the insides of the thighs and legs; put two drops of castor oil, mixed up with eight grains of calomel, on the top of the tongue, as far back as possible; a most important part of the treatment being to open the bowels as quickly and freely as possible. The patient cannot swallow; but these medicines, especially the oil, will be absorbed into the stomach altogether independent of any voluntary action. If possible, throw up a warm turpentine clyster (two tablespoonfuls of oil of turpentine in a pint of warm gruel), or, if this cannot be obtained, one composed of about a quart of warm salt-and-water and soap. Cut off the hair, and apply rags dipped in weak vinegar-and-water, or weak gin-and-water, or even simple cold water, to the head. If the blood-vessels about the head and neck are much swollen, put from eight to ten leeches on the temple opposite to the paralyzed side of the body. Always send for a surgeon immediately, and act according to the above rules, doing more or less, according to the means at hand, and the length of time that must necessarily elapse until he arrives. A pint, or even a quart of blood in a very strong person, may be taken away. When the patient is able to swallow, give him the No. 1 pills, and the No. 1 mixture directly. (The No. 1 pills are made as follows:—Mix 5 grains of calomel and the same quantity of anti-monial powder with a little bread-crumb: make into two pills, the dose for a full-grown person. For the No. 1 mixture, dissolve an ounce of Epsom salts in half a pint of senna tea: take a quarter of the mixture as a dose.) Repeat these remedies if the bowels are not well

opened. Keep the patient's head well raised, and cool as above. Give very low diet indeed: gruel, arrowroot, and the like. When a person is recovering, he should have blisters applied to the nape of the neck, his bowels should be kept well open, light diet given, and fatigue, worry, and excess of all kinds avoided.

2. *The weak kind.*—*Symptoms*. These attacks are more frequently preceded by warning symptoms than the first kind. The face is pale, the pulse weak, and the body, especially the hands and legs, cold. After a little while, these symptoms sometimes alter to those of the first class in a mild degree.—*Treatment*. At first, if the pulse is *very feeble indeed*, a little brandy-and-water or sal-volatile must be given. Mustard poultices are to be put, as before, to the soles of the feet and the insides of the thighs and legs. Warm bricks, or bottles filled with warm water, are also to be placed under the armpits. When the strength has returned, the body become warmer, and the pulse fuller and harder, the head should be shaved, and wet rags applied to it, as before described. Leeches should be put, as before, to the temple opposite the side paralyzed; and the bowels should be opened as freely and as quickly as possible. Bleeding from the arm is often necessary in these cases, but a non-professional person should never have recourse to it. Blisters may be applied to the nape of the neck at once. The diet in these cases should not be so low as in the former—indeed, it is often necessary, in a day or so after one of these attacks, to give wine, strong beef-tea, &c., according to the condition of the patient's strength.

Distinctions between Apoplexy and Epilepsy.—1. Apoplexy mostly happens in people *over thirty*, whereas epilepsy generally occurs under that age; at any rate for the first time. A person who has epileptic fits over thirty, has generally suffered from them for some years. 2. Again, *in apoplexy*, the body is *paralyzed*; and, therefore, has not the *convulsions which take place in epilepsy*. 3. The peculiar *snoring* will also distinguish apoplexy from epilepsy.

Distinctions between Apoplexy and Drunkenness.—1. The known habits of the person. 2. The fact of a person who was perfectly sober and sensible a little time before, being found in a state of insensibility. 3. The absence, in apoplexy, of the *smell of drink* on applying the nose to the mouth. 4. A person in a fit of apoplexy cannot be roused at all; in drunkenness he mostly can, to a certain extent.

Distinction between Apoplexy and Hysterics.—Hysterics mostly happen in young, nervous, unmarried women; and are attended with convulsions, sobbing, laughter, throwing about of the body, &c. &c.

Distinction between Apoplexy and Poisoning by Opium.—It is exceedingly difficult to distinguish between these two cases. In poisoning by opium, however, we find the particular smell of the drug in the patient's breath. We should also, in forming our opinion, take into consideration the person's previous conduct—whether he has been low and desponding for some time before, or has ever talked about committing suicide.

EPILEPSY.—*Falling Sickness.*—These fits mostly happen, at any rate for the first time, to young people, and are more common in boys than girls. They are produced by numerous causes.—*Symptoms.* The fit may be preceded by pains in the head, palpitations, &c. &c.; but it mostly happens that the person falls down insensible suddenly, and without any warning whatever. The eyes are distorted, so that only their whites can be seen; there is mostly foaming from the mouth; the fingers are clinched; and the body, especially on one side, is much agitated; the tongue is often thrust out of the mouth. When the fit goes off, the patient feels drowsy and faint, and often sleeps soundly for some time.—*Treatment.* During the fit, keep the patient flat on his back, with his head slightly raised, and prevent him from doing any harm to himself; dash cold water into his face, and apply smelling-salts to his nose; loosen his shirt collar, &c.; hold a piece of wood about as thick as a finger—the handle of a tooth-brush or knife will do as well—between the two rows of teeth, at the back part of the mouth. This will prevent the tongue from being injured. A teaspoonful of common salt thrust into the patient's mouth, during the fit, is of much service. The after-treatment of these fits is various, and depends entirely upon their causes. A good general rule, however, is always to keep the bowels well open, and the patient quiet, and free from fatigue, worry, and excess of all kinds.

*Fainting Fits** are sometimes very dangerous, and at others perfectly harmless; the question of danger depending altogether upon the causes which have produced them, and which are exceedingly various. For instance, fainting produced by disease of the heart is a very serious symptom indeed; whereas, that arising from some slight cause, such as the sight of blood, &c., need cause no alarm whatever. The symptoms of simple fainting are so well known that it would be quite superfluous to enumerate them here. The *treatment* consists in laying the patient at full length upon his back, with his head upon a level with the rest of his body, loosening everything about the neck, dashing cold water into the face, and sprinkling vinegar and water about the mouth; applying smelling-salts to the nose; and, when the patient is able to swallow, in giving a little warm brandy-and-water, or about 20 drops of sal-volatile in water.

Hysterics.*—These fits take place, for the most part, in young, nervous, unmarried women. They happen much less often in married women; and even (in some rare cases indeed) in men. Young women, who are subject to these fits, are apt to think that they are suffering from 'all the ills that flesh is heir to;' and the false symptoms of disease which they show are so like the true ones, that it is often exceedingly difficult to detect the difference. The fits themselves are mostly preceded by great depression of spirits, shedding of tears, sickness, palpitation of the heart, &c. A pain, as if a nail were being driven in, is also often felt at one particular part of the head. In almost all cases, when a fit is coming on, pain is felt on the left side. This pain rises gradually until it reaches the throat, and then gives the patient a sensation as if she had a pellet there, which prevents her from breathing properly, and, in fact, seems to threaten actual suffocation. The patient now generally becomes insensible, and faints; the body is thrown about in all directions, froth issues from the mouth, incoherent expressions are uttered, and fits of laughter, crying, or screaming, take place. When the fit is going off, the patient mostly cries bitterly, sometimes knowing all, and at others nothing, of what has taken place, and feeling general soreness all over the body. *Treatment during the fit*. Place the body in the same position as for simple fainting, and treat, in other respects, as directed in the article on Epilepsy. *Always well loosen the patient's stays*; and, when she is recovering, and able to swallow, give 20 drops of sal volatile in a little water. The *after-treatment* of these cases is very various. If the patient is of a strong constitution, she should live on plain diet, take plenty of exercise, and take occasional doses of castor oil, or an aperient mixture. If, as is mostly the case, the patient is weak and delicate, she will require a different mode of treatment altogether. Good nourishing diet, gentle exercise, cold baths, occasionally a dose of No. 3 myrrh and aloes pills at night, and a dose of compound iron pills twice a day. (As to the myrrh and aloes pills (No. 3), 10 grains made into two pills are a dose for a full-grown person. Of the compound iron pills (No. 4), the dose for a full-grown person is also 10 grains, made into two pills.) In every case, amusing the mind, and avoiding all causes of over-excitement, are of great service in bringing about a permanent cure.

LIVER COMPLAINT AND SPASMS.—A very obliging correspondent recommends the following, from personal experience:—Take 4 oz. of dried dandelion root, 1 oz. of the best ginger, ¼ oz. of Columba root; bruise and boil all together in 3 pints of water till it is reduced to a quart: strain, and take a wine-glassful every four hours. Our correspondent says it is a 'safe and simple medicine for both liver complaint and spasms.'

LUMBAGO.—A 'new and successful mode' of treating lumbago, advocated by Dr Day, is a form of counter-irritation, said to have been introduced into this country by the late Sir Anthony Carlisle, and which consists in the instantaneous application of a flat iron button, gently heated in a spirit-lamp, to the skin. Dr Corrigan published, about three years ago, an account of some cases very successfully treated by nearly similar means. Dr Corrigan's plan was, however, to touch the surface of the part affected, at intervals of half an inch, as lightly and rapidly as possible. Dr Day has found greater advantages to result from drawing the flat surface of the heated button lightly over the affected part, so as to act on a greater extent of surface. The doctor speaks so enthusiastically of the benefit to be derived from this practice, that it is evidently highly deserving attention.

PALPITATION OF THE HEART.—Where palpitation occurs as symptomatic of indigestion, the treatment must be directed to remedy that disorder; when it is consequent on a plethoric state, purgatives will be effectual. In this case the patient should abstain from every kind of diet likely to produce a plethoric condition of body.

Animal food and fermented liquor must be particularly avoided. Too much indulgence in sleep will also prove injurious. When the attacks arise from nervous irritability, the excitement must be allayed by change of air and a tonic diet. Should the palpitation originate from organic derangement, it must be, of course, beyond domestic management. Luxurious living, indolence, and tight-lacing often produce this affection: such cases are to be conquered with a little resolution.

POISONS*

shall be the next subject for remark; and we anticipate more detailed instructions for the treatment of persons poisoned, by giving a simple LIST OF THE principal POISONS, with their ANTIDOTES or REMEDIES.

Oil of Vitriol Aquafortis Spirit of Salt	Magnesia, Chalk, Soap-and-Water
Emetic Tartar	Oily Drinks, Solution of Oak-bark
Salt of Lemons, or Acid of Sugar	Chalk, Whiting, Lime, or Magnesia and Water. Sometimes an Emetic Draught
Prussic Acid	Pump on back, Smelling-salts to nose, Artificial Breathing, Chloride of Lime to nose
Pearlash Soap-Lees Smelling-Salts Nitre Hartshorn Sal-Volatile	Lemon-Juice and Vinegar-and-Water
Arsenic Fly-Powder, or White Arsenic King's Yellow, or Yellow Arsenic	Emetics, Lime-Water, Soap-and-Water, Sugar-and-Water, Oily Drinks
Mercury Corrosive Sublimate Calomel	White of Eggs, Soap-and-Water
Opium Laudanum	Emetic Draught, Vinegar-and-Water, dashing Cold Water on chest and face, walking up and down for two or three hours

Lead White Lead Sugar of Lead Goulard's Extract	Epsom Salts, Castor Oil, Emetics
Copper Blue-stone Verdigris	Whites of Eggs, Sugar-and-Water, Castor Oil, Gruel
Zinc	Lime-Water, Chalk-and-Water, Soap-and-Water
Iron	Magnesia, Warm Water
Henbane Hemlock Nightshade Foxglove	Emetics and Castor Oil; Brandy-and-Water, if necessary
Poisonous Food	Emetics and Castor Oil

The symptoms of poisoning may be known for the most part from those of some diseases, which they are very like, from the fact of their coming on *immediately* after eating or drinking something; whereas those of disease come on, in most cases at least, by degrees, and with warnings. In most cases where poison is known, or suspected, to have been taken, the first thing to be done is to empty the stomach, well and immediately, by means of mustard mixed in warm water, or plain warm salt-and-water, or, better, this draught, which we call No. 1:—Twenty grains of sulphate of zinc in an ounce and a half of water. This draught to be repeated in a quarter of an hour if vomiting does not ensue. The back part of the throat should be well tickled with a feather, or two of the fingers thrust down it, to induce vomiting. The cases where vomiting must not be used are those where the skin has been taken off, and the parts touched irritated and inflamed by the poison taken, and where the action of vomiting would increase the evil. Full instructions are given in the article on each particular poison as to where emetics are or are not to be given. The best and safest way of emptying the stomach is by means of the stomach-pump, as in certain cases the action of vomiting is likely to increase the danger arising from the swollen and congested condition of the blood-vessels of the head, which often takes place. In the hands, however, of any one else than a surgeon, it would be not only useless, but harmful, as a great deal of dexterity, caution, and experience are required to use it properly. After having made these brief introductory remarks, we shall now proceed to particulars.

Sulphuric Acid, or *Oil of Vitriol* (a clear, colourless liquid, of an oily appearance).—*Symptoms in those who have swallowed it*. When much is taken, these come on immediately. There is great burning pain, extending from the mouth to the stomach; vomiting of a liquid of a dark coffee-colour, often mixed with shreds of flesh and streaks of blood; the skin inside the mouth is taken off; and the exposed surface is at first white, and after a time becomes brownish. There are sometimes spots of a brown colour round the lips and on the neck, caused by drops of the acid falling on these parts. There is great difficulty of breathing, owing to the swelling at the back part of the mouth. After a time there is much depression of strength, with a quick, weak pulse, and cold, clammy skin. The face is pale, and has a very anxious look. When the acid swallowed has been greatly diluted in water, the same kind of symptoms occur, only in a milder degree.—*Treatment*. Give a mixture of magnesia in milk-and-water, or, if this cannot be obtained, of finely powdered chalk, or whiting, or even of the plaster torn down from the walls or ceiling, in milk-and-water. The mixture should be nearly as thick as cream, and plenty of it given. As well as this, simple gruel, milk, or thick flour-and-water, are very useful, and should be given in large quantities. Violent inflammation of the parts touched by the acid is most likely to take place in the course of a little time, and can only be properly attended to by a surgeon; but if one cannot be obtained, leeches, the fever-mixtures (the recipe for which appears repeatedly in previous paragraphs), thick drinks, such as barley-water, gruel, arrowroot, &c., must be had recourse to, according to the symptoms of each particular case and the means at hand. The inflamed condition of the back part of the mouth requires particular attention. When the breathing is very laboured and difficult in consequence, from fifteen to twenty leeches are to be immediately applied to the outside of the throat, and when they drop off, warm poppy fomentations constantly kept to the part. When the pain over the stomach is very great, the same local treatment is necessary; but if it is only slight, a good mustard poultice will be sufficient without the leeches. In all these cases, two tablespoonfuls of the fever-mixture should be given every four hours, and only gruel or arrowroot allowed to be eaten for some days.

Nitric Acid, commonly known as *Aqua Fortis*, or *Red Spirit of Nitre* (a straw-coloured fluid, of the consistence of water, and which gives off dense white fumes on exposure to the air).—*Symptoms produced in those who have swallowed it.* Much the same as in the case of sulphuric acid. In this case, however, the surface touched by the acid becomes *yellowish*. The tongue is mostly much swollen.—*Treatment.* The same as for sulphuric acid.

Muriatic Acid, *Spirit of Salt* (a thin yellow fluid, emitting dense white fumes on exposure to the air).—This is not often taken as a poison. The *symptoms* and *treatment* are much the same as those of *nitric acid*.

N.B. *In no case of poisoning by these three acids should emetics ever be given.*

Oxalic Acid, commonly called *Salt of Lemons*.—This poison may be taken by mistake for Epsom salts, which it is a good deal like. It may be distinguished from them by its very acid taste and its shape, which is that of needle-formed crystals, each of which, if put into a drop of ink, will turn it to a *reddish brown*, whereas Epsom salts will not change its colour at all. When a large dose of this poison has been taken, death takes place very quickly indeed.—*Symptoms produced in those who have swallowed it.* A hot, burning, acid taste is felt in the act of swallowing, and vomiting of a *greenish-brown* fluid is produced, sooner or later, according to the quantity and strength of the poison taken. There is great tenderness felt over the stomach, followed by clammy perspirations and convulsions; the legs are often drawn up, and there is generally stupor, from which the patient, however, can easily be roused, and always great prostration of strength. The pulse is small and weak, and the breathing faint.—*Treatment.* Chalk or magnesia, made into a cream with water, should be given in large quantities, and afterwards the emetic draught above prescribed, or some mustard-and-water, if the draught cannot be got. The back part of the throat to be tickled with a feather, to induce vomiting. Arrow-root, gruel, and the like drinks, are to be taken. When the prostration of strength is very great and the body cold, warmth is to be applied to it, and a little brandy-and-water, or sal-volatile and water, given.

Prussic Acid (a thin, transparent, and colourless liquid, with a peculiar smell, which greatly resembles that of bitter almonds).— *Symptoms produced in those who have swallowed it*. These come on *immediately* after the poison has been taken, and may be produced by merely *smelling* it. The patient becomes perfectly insensible, and falls down in convulsions—his eyes are fixed and staring, the pupils being bigger than natural, the skin is cold and clammy, the pulse scarcely perceptible, and the breathing slow and gasping.—*Treatment*. Very little can be done in these cases, as death takes place so quickly after the poison has been swallowed, when it takes place at all. The best treatment—which should always be adopted in all cases, even though the patient appears quite dead—is to dash quantities of cold water on the back, from the top of the neck downwards. Placing the patient under a pump, and pumping on him, is the best way of doing this. Smelling-salts are also to be applied to the nose, and the chest well rubbed with a camphor liniment.

ALKALIS: *Potash, Soda*, and *Ammonia*, or common *Smelling-Salts*, with their principal preparations—*Pearlash, Soap Lees, Liquor Potassae, Nitre, Sal Prunella, Hartshorn*, and *Sal Volatile.*—Alkalis are seldom taken or given with the view of destroying life. They may, however, be swallowed by mistake.*—*Symptoms produced in those who have swallowed them*. There is at first a burning, acrid taste in, and a sensation of tightness round, the throat, like that of strangling; the skin touched is destroyed; retching mostly followed by actual vomiting, then sets in; the vomited matters often containing blood of a dark brown colour, with little shreds of flesh here and there, and always changing vegetable blue colours green. There is now great tenderness over the whole of the belly. After a little while, great weakness, with cold, clammy sweats, a quick weak pulse, and purging of bloody matters, takes place. The brain, too, mostly becomes affected.—*Treatment*. Give two tablespoonfuls of vinegar or lemon-juice in a glassful of water every few minutes until the burning sensation is relieved. Any kind of oil or milk may also be given, and will form soap when mixed with the poison in the stomach. Barley-water, gruel, arrowroot, linseed-tea, &c., are also very useful, and should be taken constantly, and in large quantities. If inflammation should take place, it is to be treated by applying leeches and warm poppy fomentations to the part where the pain is most felt, and giving two tablespoonfuls of the fever mixture every four hours. The diet in all these cases should only consist of arrowroot or gruel for the first few days, and then of weak broth or beef-tea for some time after.

When very strong fumes of smelling-salts have in any way been inhaled, there is great difficulty of breathing, and alarming pain in the mouth and nostrils. In this case let the patient inhale the steam of warm vinegar, and treat the feverish symptoms as before.

Arsenic.—Mostly seen under the form of white arsenic, or fly-powder, and yellow arsenic, or king's yellow.—*Symptoms produced in those who have swallowed it.* These vary very much, according to the form and dose in which the poison has been taken. There is faintness, depression, and sickness, with an intense burning pain in the region of the stomach, which gets worse and worse, and is increased by pressure. There is also vomiting of dark brown matter, sometimes mixed with blood; and mostly great thirst, with a feeling of tightness round, and of burning in, the throat. Purging also takes place, the matters brought away being mixed with blood. The pulse is small and irregular, and the skin sometimes cold and clammy, and at others hot. The breathing is painful. Convulsions and spasms often occur.—*Treatment.* Give a couple of teaspoonfuls of mustard in a glass of water, to bring on or assist vomiting, and also use the other means elsewhere recommended for the purpose. A solution, half of lime-water and half of linseed-oil, well mixed, may be given, as well as plenty of arrowroot, gruel, or linseed-tea. Simple milk is also useful. A little castor-oil should be given, to cleanse the intestines of all the poison, and the after-symptoms treated on general principles.

Corrosive Sublimate.—Mostly seen in the form of little heavy crystalline masses, which melt in water, and have a metallic taste. It is sometimes seen in powder. This is a most powerful poison.—*Symptoms.* These mostly come on *immediately* after the poison has been taken. There is a coppery taste experienced in the act of swallowing, with a burning heat, extending from the top of the throat down to the stomach; and also a feeling of great tightness round the throat. In a few minutes great pain is felt over the region of the stomach, and frequent vomiting of long, stringy white masses, mixed with blood, takes place. There is also mostly great purging. The countenance is generally pale and anxious; the pulse always small and frequent; the skin cold and clammy, and the breathing difficult. Convulsions and insensibility often occur, and are very bad symptoms indeed. The inside of the mouth is more or less swollen.— *Treatment*. Mix the whites of a dozen eggs in two pints of cold water, and give a glassful of the mixture every three or four minutes, until the stomach can contain no more. If vomiting does not now come on naturally, and supposing the mouth is not very sore or much swollen, an emetic draught, No. 1, may be given, and vomiting induced. (The No. 1 draught, we remind our readers, is thus made:—Twenty grains of sulphate of zinc in an ounce and a half of water; the draught to be repeated if vomiting does not take place in a quarter of an hour.) After the stomach has been well cleaned out, milk, flour-and-water, linseed-tea, or barley-water, should be taken in large quantities. If eggs cannot be obtained, milk, or flour-and-water, should be given as a substitute for them at once. When the depression of strength is very great indeed, a little warm brandy-and-water must be given. In the course of an hour or two the patient should take two tablespoonfuls of castor-oil, and if inflammation comes on, it is to be treated as directed in the article on acids and alkalis. The diet should also be the same. If the patient recovers, great soreness of the gums is almost certain to take place. The simplest, and at the same time one of the best modes of treatment, is to wash them well three or four times a day with brandy-and-water.

Calomel.—A heavy white powder, without taste, and insoluble in water. It has been occasionally known to destroy life.—*Symptoms*. Much the same as in the case of corrosive sublimate.—*Treatment*. The same as for corrosive sublimate. If the gums are sore, wash them, as recommended in the case of corrosive sublimate, with brandy-and-water three or four times a day, and keep the patient on *fluids*, such as arrowroot, gruel, broth, or beef-tea, according to the other symptoms. Eating hard substances would make the gums more sore and tender.

Copper.—The preparations of this metal which are most likely to be the ones producing poisonous symptoms, are *blue-stone* and *verdigris*. People are often taken ill after eating food that has been cooked in copper saucepans. When anything has been cooked in one of these vessels, *it should never be allowed to cool in it.*—*Symptoms*. Headache, pain in the stomach, and purging; vomiting of green or blue matters, convulsions, and spasms.—*Treatment*. Give whites of eggs, sugar-and-water, castor-oil, and drinks, such as arrowroot and gruel.

Emetic Tartar.—Seen in the form of a white powder, or crystals, with a slightly metallic taste. It has not often been known to destroy life.—*Symptoms*. A strong metallic taste in the act of swallowing, followed by a burning pain in the region of the stomach, vomiting, and great purging. The pulse is small and rapid, the skin cold and clammy, the breathing difficult and painful, and the limbs often much cramped. There is also great prostration of strength.—*Treatment*. Promote the vomiting by giving plenty of warm water, or warm arrowroot and water. Strong tea, in large quantities, should be drunk; or, if it can be obtained, a decoction of oak bark. The after-treatment is the same as that for acids and alkalis; the principal object in all these cases being to keep down the inflammation of the parts touched by the poison by means of leeches, warm poppy fomentations, fever-mixtures, and very low diet.

Lead, and its preparations, *Sugar of Lead, Goulard's Extract, White Lead.*—Lead is by no means an active poison, although it is popularly considered to be so. It mostly affects people by being taken into the system slowly, as in the case of painters and glaziers.* A newly-painted house, too, often affects those living in it.—*Symptoms produced when taken in a large dose*. There is at first a burning, prick-ing sensation in the throat, to which thirst, giddiness, and vomiting follow. The belly is tight, swollen, and painful; *the pain being relieved by pressure*. The bowels are mostly bound. There is great depression of strength, and a cold skin.—*Treament*. Give an emetic draught (No. 1, see above) at once, and shortly afterwards a solution of Epsom salts in large quantities. A little brandy-and-water must be taken if the depression of strength is very great indeed. Milk, whites of eggs, and arrowroot are also useful. After two or three hours, cleanse the stomach and intestines well out with two tablespoonfuls of castor-oil, and treat the symptoms which follow according to the rules laid down in other parts of these articles.—*Symptoms when it is taken into the body slowly*. Headache, pain about the navel, loss of appetite and flesh, offensive breath, *a blueness of the edges of the gums*; the belly is tight, hard, and knotty, and the pulse slow and languid. There is also sometimes a difficulty in swallowing.—*Treatment*. Give five grains of calomel and half a grain of opium directly, in the form of a pill, and half an ounce of Epsom salts in two hours, and repeat this treatment until the bowels are well opened. Put the patient into a warm bath, and throw up a clyster of warmish water when he is in it. Fomentations of warm oil of turpentine, if they can be obtained, should be put over the whole of the belly. The great object is to open the bowels as freely and as quickly as possible. When this has been done, a grain of pure opium may be given. Arrowroot or gruel should be taken in good large quantities. The after-treatment must depend altogether upon the symptoms of each particular case.

Opium, and its preparations, *Laudanum*, &c.—Solid opium is mostly seen in the form of rich brown flattish cakes, with little pieces of leaves sticking on them here and there, and a bitter and slightly warm taste. The most common form in which it is taken as a poison, is that of laudanum.—*Symptoms*. These consist at first in giddiness and stupor, followed by insensibility, the patient, however, being roused to consciousness by a great noise, so as to be able to answer a question, but becoming insensible again almost immediately. The pulse is now quick and small, the breathing hurried, and the skin warm and covered with perspiration. After a little time, these symptoms change; the person becomes *perfectly insensible*, the breathing slow and *snoring*, as in apoplexy, the skin cold, and the pulse slow and full. The pupil of the eye is mostly smaller than natural. On applying his nose to the patient's mouth, a person may smell the poison very distinctly.—*Treatment*. Give an emetic draught (No. 1, see above) directly, with large quantities of warm mustard-and-water, warm salt-and-water, or simple warm water. Tickle the top of the throat with a feather, or put two fingers down it to bring on vomiting, which rarely takes place of itself. Dash cold water on the head, chest, and spine, and flap these parts well with the ends of wet towels. Give strong coffee or tea. Walk the patient up and down in the open air for two or three hours; the great thing being to keep him from sleeping. Electricity is of much service. When the patient is recovering, mustard poultices should be applied to the soles of the feet and the insides of the thighs and legs. The head should be kept cool and raised.

The following preparations, which are constantly given to children by their nurses and mothers, for the purpose of making them sleep, often prove fatal: *Syrup of Poppies*, and *Godfrey's Cordial*. The author would most earnestly urge all people caring for their children's lives, never to allow any of these preparations to be given, unless ordered by a surgeon.

The treatment in the case of poisoning by *Henbane, Hemlock, Nightshade*, and *Foxglove*, is much the same as that for opium. Vomiting should be brought on in all of them.

Poisonous Food.—It sometimes happens that things which are in daily use, and mostly perfectly harmless, give rise, under certain unknown circumstances, and in certain individuals, to the symptoms of poisoning. The most common articles of food of this description are *Mussels, Salmon*, and certain kinds of *Cheese* and *Bacon*. The general symptoms are thirst, weight about the stomach, difficulty of breathing, vomiting, purging, spasms, prostration of strength, and, in the case of mussels more particularly, an eruption on the body, like that of nettle-rash.—*Treatment*. Empty the stomach well with No. 1 draught and warm water, and give two tablespoonfuls of castor-oil immediately after. Let the patient take plenty of arrowroot, gruel, and the like drinks, and if there is much depression of strength, give a little warm brandy-and-water. Should symptoms of fever or inflammation follow, they must be treated as directed in the articles on other kinds of poisoning.

Mushrooms, and similar kinds of vegetables, often produce poisonous effects. The symptoms are various, sometimes giddiness and stupor, and at others pain in and swelling of the belly, with vomiting and purging, being the leading ones. When the symptoms come on quickly after taking the poison, it is generally the head that is affected.—The treatment consists in bringing on vomiting in the usual manner, as quickly and as freely as possible. The other symptoms are to be treated on general principles; if they are those of depression, by brandy-and-water or sal-volatile; if those of inflammation, by leeches, fomentations, fever-mixtures, &c. &c.

FOR CURE OF RINGWORM.—Take of subcarbonate of soda 1 drachm, which dissolve in ½ pint of vinegar. Wash the head every morning with soft soap, and apply the lotion night and morning. One teaspoonful of sulphur and treacle should also be given occasionally night and morning. The hair should be cut close, and round the spot it should be shaved off, and the part, night and morning, bathed with a lotion made by dissolving a drachm of white vitriol in 6 oz. of water. A small piece of either of the two subjoined ointments rubbed into the part when the lotion has dried in. No. 1.—Take of citron ointment 1 drachm; sulphur and tar ointment, of each ½ oz.: mix thoroughly, and apply twice a day. No. 2.—Take of simple cerate 1 oz.; creosote 1 drachm; calomel 30 grains: mix and use in the same manner as the first. Concurrent with these external remedies, the child should take an alterative powder every morning, or, if they act too much on the bowels, only every second day. The following will be found to answer all the intentions desired.

Alterative Powders for Ringworm.—Take of

Sulphuret of antimony, precipitated	24 grains
Grey powder	12 grains
Calomel	6 grains
Jalap powder	36 grains

Mix carefully, and divide into 12 powders for a child from 1 to 2 years old; into 9 powders for a child from 2 to 4 years; and into 6 powders for a child 4 to 6 years. Where the patient is older, the strength may be increased by enlarging the quantities of the drugs ordered, or by giving one and a half or two powders for one dose. The ointment is to be well washed off every morning with soap-and-water, and the part bathed with the lotion before re-applying the ointment. An imperative fact must be remembered by mother or nurse,—never to use the same comb employed for the child with ringworm, for the healthy children, or let the affected little one sleep with those free from the disease; and, for fear of any contact by hands or otherwise, to keep the child's head enveloped in a nightcap, till the eruption is completely cured.

SCRATCHES.—Trifling as scratches often seem, they ought never to be neglected, but should be covered and protected, and kept clean and dry until they have completely healed. If there is the least appearance of inflammation, no time should be lost in applying a large bread-and-water poultice, or hot flannels repeatedly applied, or even leeches in good numbers may be put on at some distance from each other.

For SHORTNESS OF BREATH, or DIFFICULT BREATHING.—
Vitriolated spirits of ether 1 oz., camphor 12 grains: make a solution,
of which take a teaspoonful during the paroxysm. This is found to
afford instantaneous relief in difficulty of breathing, depending on
internal diseases and other causes, where the patient, from a very
quick and laborious breathing, is obliged to be in an erect posture.

SPRAINS.—A sprain is a stretching of the leaders or ligaments of
a part through some violence, such as slipping, falling on the hands,
pulling a limb, &c. &c. The most common are those of the ankle and
wrist. These accidents are more serious than people generally suppose, and often more difficult to cure than a broken leg or arm. The
first thing to be done is to place the sprained part in the straight
position, and to raise it a little as well. Some recommend the application of cold lotions at first. The editress, however, is quite convinced
that *warm* applications are, in most cases, the best for the first three
or four days. These fomentations are to be applied in the following
manner:—Dip a good-sized piece of flannel into a pail or basin full
of hot water or hot poppy fomentation,—six poppy heads boiled in
one quart of water for about a quarter of an hour; wring it almost
dry, and apply it, as hot as the patient can bear, right round the
sprained part. Then place another piece of flannel, quite dry, over it,
in order that the steam and warmth may not escape. This process
should be repeated as often as the patient feels that the flannel next
to his skin is getting cold—the oftener the better. The bowels should
be opened with a black draught, and the patient kept on low diet. If
he has been a great drinker, he may be allowed to take a little beer;
but it is better not to do so. A little of the cream of tartar drink,
ordered in the case of burns, may be taken occasionally if there is
much thirst. When the swelling and tenderness about the joint are
very great, from eight to twelve leeches may be applied. When the
knee is the joint affected, the greatest pain is felt at the inside, and
therefore the greater quantity of the leeches should be applied to
that part. When the shoulder is sprained, the arm should be kept
close to the body by means of a linen roller,* which is to be taken
four or five times round the whole of the chest. It should also be
brought two or three times underneath the elbow, in order to raise
the shoulder. This is the best treatment for these accidents during
the first three or four days. After that time, supposing that no

unfavourable symptoms have taken place, a cold lotion, composed of a tablespoonful of sal-ammoniac to a quart of water, or vinegar-and-water, should be constantly applied. This lotion will strengthen the part, and also help in taking away any thickening that may have formed about the joint. In the course of two or three weeks, according to circumstances, the joint is to be rubbed twice a day with flannel dipped in opodeldoc, a flannel bandage rolled tightly round the joint, the pressure being greatest at the lowest part, and the patient allowed to walk about with the assistance of a crutch or stick. He should also occasionally, when sitting or lying down, quietly bend the joint backwards and forwards, to cause its natural motion to return, and to prevent stiffness from taking place. When the swelling is very great immediately after the accident has occurred, from the breaking of the blood-vessels, it is best to apply cold applications at first. If it can be procured, oil-silk may be put over the warm-fomentation flannel, instead of the dry piece of flannel. Old flannel is better than new.

CURE FOR STAMMERING.—Where there is no malformation of the organs of articulation, stammering may be remedied by reading aloud with the teeth closed. This should be practised for two hours a day, for three or four months. The advocate of this simple remedy says, 'I can speak with certainty of its utility.'

STAMMERING.—At a recent meeting of the Boston Society of Natural History, Dr Warren stated, 'A simple, easy, and effectual cure of stammering.' It is, simply, at every syllable pronounced, to tap at the same time with the finger; by so doing, 'the most inveterate stammerer will be surprised to find that he can pronounce quite fluently, and, by long and constant practice, he will pronounce perfectly well.'

SUFFOCATION, APPARENT.—Suffocation may arise from many different causes. Anything which prevents the air getting into the lungs will produce it. We shall give the principal causes, and the treatment to be followed in each case.

1. *Carbonic Acid Gas.* Choke-Damp of Mines.*—This poisonous gas is met with in rooms where charcoal is burnt, and where there is not sufficient draught to allow it to escape; in coalpits, near limekilns, in breweries, and in rooms and houses where a great many people

live huddled together in wretchedness and filth, and where the air in consequence becomes poisoned. This gas gives out no smell, so that we cannot know of its presence. A candle will not burn in a room which contains much of it.—*Effects*. At first there is giddiness, and a great wish to sleep; after a little time, or where there is much of it present, a person feels great weight in the head, and stupid; gets by degrees quite unable to move, and snores as if in a deep sleep. The limbs may or may not be stiff. The heat of the body remains much the same at first.—*Treatment*. Remove the person affected into the open air, and, even though it is cold weather, take off his clothes. Then lay him on his back, with his head slightly raised. Having done this, dash vinegar-and-water over the whole of the body, and rub it hard, especially the face and chest, with towels dipped in the same mixture. The hands and feet also should be rubbed with a hard brush. Apply smelling-salts to the nose, which may be tickled with a feather. Dashing cold water down the middle of the back is of great service. If the person can swallow, give him a little lemon-water, or vinegar-and-water to drink. The principal means, however, to be employed in this, as, in fact, in most cases of apparent suffocation, is what is called *artificial breathing*. This operation should be performed by three persons, and in the following manner:—The first person should put the nozzle of a common pair of bellows into one of the patient's nostrils; the second should push down, and then thrust back, that part of the throat called 'Adam's apple;' and the third should first raise and then depress the chest, one hand being placed over each side of the ribs. These three actions should be performed in the following order:—First of all, the throat should be drawn down and thrust back; then the chest should be raised, and the bellows gently blown into the nostril. Directly this is done, the chest should be depressed, so as to imitate common breathing. This process should be repeated about eighteen times a minute. The mouth and the other nostril should be closed while the bellows are being blown. Persevere, if necessary, with this treatment for seven or eight hours—in fact, till absolute signs of death are visible. Many lives are lost by giving it up too quickly. When the patient becomes roused, he is to be put into a warm bed, and a little brandy-and-water, or twenty drops of sal-volatile, given cautiously now and then. This treatment is to be adopted in all cases where people are affected from breathing bad air, smells, &c. &c.

2. *Drowning*. This is one of the most frequent causes of death by suffocation.—*Treatment*. Many methods have been adopted, and as some of them are not only useless, but hurtful, we will mention them here, merely in order that they may be avoided. In the first place, then, never hang a person up by his heels, as it is an error to suppose that water gets into the lungs. Hanging a person up by his heels would be quite as bad as hanging him up by his neck. It is also a mistake to suppose that rubbing the body with salt and water is of service.—*Proper Treatment*. Directly a person has been taken out of the water, he should be wiped dry and wrapped in blankets; but if these cannot be obtained, the clothes of the bystanders must be used for the purpose. His head being slightly raised, and any water, weeds, or froth that may happen to be in his mouth, having been removed, he should be carried as quickly as possible to the nearest house. He should now be put into a warm bath, about as hot as the hand can pleasantly bear, and kept there for about ten minutes, artificial breathing being had recourse to while he is in it. Having been taken out of the bath, he should be placed flat on his back, with his head slightly raised, upon a warm bed in a warm room, wiped perfectly dry, and then rubbed constantly all over the body with warm flannels. At the same time, mustard poultices should be put to the soles of the feet, the palms of the hands, and the inner surface of the thighs and legs. Warm bricks, or bottles filled with warm water, should be placed under the armpits. The nose should be tickled with a feather, and smelling-salts applied to it. This treatment should be adopted while the bath is being got ready, as well as when the body has been taken out of it. The bath is not absolutely necessary; constantly rubbing the body with flannels in a warm room having been found sufficient for resuscitation. Sir B. Brodie says that warm air is quite as good as warm water. When symptoms of returning consciousness begin to show themselves, give a little wine, brandy, or twenty drops of sal-volatile and water. In some cases it is necessary, in about twelve or twenty-four hours after the patient has revived, to bleed him, for peculiar head-symptoms which now and then occur. Bleeding, however, even in the hands of professional men themselves, should be very cautiously used—non-professional ones should never think of it. The best thing to do in these cases is to keep the head well raised, and cool with a lotion such as that recommended above for sprains; to

administer an aperient draught, and to abstain from giving anything that stimulates, such as wine, brandy, sal-volatile, &c. &c. As a general rule, a person dies in three minutes and a half after he has been under water. It is difficult, however, to tell how long he has actually been *under* it, although we may know well exactly how long he has been *in* it, This being the case, always persevere in your attempts at resuscitation until actual signs of death have shown themselves, even for six, eight, or ten hours. Dr Douglas, of Glasgow, resuscitated a person who had been under water for fourteen minutes, by simply rubbing the whole of his body with warm flannels, in a warm room, for eight hours and a half, at the end of which time the person began to show the *first* symptoms of returning animation. Should the accident occur at a great distance from any house, this treatment should be adopted as closely as the circumstances will permit of. Breathing through any tube, such as a piece of card or paper rolled into the form of a pipe, will do as a substitute for the bellows. To recapitulate: Rub the body dry; take matters out of mouth; cover with blankets or clothes; slightly raise the head, and place the body in a warm bath, or on a bed in a warm room; apply smelling-salts to nose; employ artificial breathing; rub well with warm flannels; put mustard poultices to feet, hands, and insides of thighs and legs, with warm bricks or bottles to armpits. *Don't bleed*. Give wine, brandy, or sal-volatile when recovering, and *persevere till actual signs of death are seen*.

Briefly to conclude what we have to say of suffocation, let us treat of *Lightning*. When a person has been struck by lightning, there is a general paleness of the whole body, with the exception of the part struck, which is often blackened, or even scorched.—*Treatment*. Same as for drowning. It is not, however, of much use; for when death takes place at all, it is generally instantaneous.

CURE FOR THE TOOTHACHE.—Take a piece of sheet zinc, about the size of a sixpence, and a piece of silver, say a shilling; place them together, and hold the defective tooth between them or contiguous to them; in a few minutes the pain will be gone, as if by magic. The zinc and silver, acting as a galvanic battery, will produce on the nerves of the tooth sufficient electricity to establish a current, and consequently to relieve the pain. Or smoke a pipe of tobacco and caraway-seeds. Again—

A small piece of the pellitory root will, by the flow of saliva it causes, afford relief. Creosote, or a few drops of tincture of myrrh, or friar's balsam, on cotton, put on the tooth, will often subdue the pain. A small piece of camphor, however, retained in the mouth, is the most reliable and likely means of conquering the paroxysms of this dreaded enemy.

WARTS.—Eisenberg says, in his 'Advice on the Hand,' that the hydrochlorate of lime is the most certain means of destroying warts; the process, however, is very slow, and demands perseverance, for, if discontinued before the proper time, no advantage is gained. The following is a simple cure:—On breaking the stalk of the crowfoot plant in two, a drop of milky juice will be observed to hang on the upper part of the stem; if this be allowed to drop on a wart, so that it be well saturated with the juice, in about three or four dressings the warts will die, and may be taken off with the fingers. They may be removed by the above means from the teats of cows, where they are sometimes very troublesome, and prevent them standing quiet to be milked. The wart touched lightly every second day with lunar caustic, or rubbed every night with blue-stone, for a few weeks, will destroy the largest wart, wherever situated.

TO CURE A WHITLOW.*—As soon as the whitlow has risen distinctly, a pretty large piece should be snipped out, so that the watery matter may readily escape, and continue to flow out as fast as produced. A bread-and-water poultice should be put on for a few days, when the wound should be bound up lightly with some mild ointment, when a cure will be speedily completed. Constant poulticing both before and after the opening of the whitlow, is the only practice needed; but as the matter lies deep, when it is necessary to open the abscess, the incision must be made *deep* to reach the suppuration.

WOUNDS.—There are several kinds of wounds, which are called by different names, according to their appearance, or the manner in which they are produced. As, however, it would be useless, and even hurtful, to bother the reader's head with too many nice professional distinctions, we shall content ourselves with dividing wounds into three classes.

1. *Incised wounds or cuts*—those produced by a knife, or some sharp instrument.

2. *Lacerated, or torn wounds*—those produced by the claws of an animal, the bite of a dog, running quickly against some projecting blunt object, such as a nail, &c.

3. *Punctured or penetrating wounds*—those produced by anything running deeply into the flesh; such as a sword, a sharp nail, a spike, the point of a bayonet, &c.

Class 1. Incised wounds or cuts—The danger arising from these accidents is owing more to their position than to their extent. Thus, a cut of half an inch long, which goes through an artery, is more serious than a cut of two inches long, which is not near one. Again, a small cut on the head is more often followed by dangerous symptoms than a much larger one on the legs.—*Treatment.* If the cut is not a very large one, and no artery or vein is wounded, this is very simple. If there are any foreign substances left in the wound, they must be taken out, and the bleeding must be quite stopped before the wound is strapped up. If the bleeding is not very great, it may easily be stopped by raising the cut part, and applying rags dipped in cold water to it. All clots of blood must be carefully removed; for, if they are left behind, they prevent the wound from healing. When the bleeding has been stopped, and the wound perfectly cleaned, its two edges are to be brought closely together by thin straps of common adhesive plaster, which should remain on, if there is not great pain or heat about the part, for two or three days, without being removed. The cut part should be kept raised and cool. When the strips of plaster are to be taken off, they should first be well bathed with lukewarm water. This will cause them to come away easily, and without opening the lips of the wound; which accident is very likely to take place, if they are pulled off without having been first moistened with the warm water. If the wound is not healed when the strips of plaster are taken off, fresh ones must be applied. Great care is required in treating cuts of the head, as they are often followed by erysipelas* taking place round them. They should be strapped with isinglass-plaster, which is much less irritating than the ordinary adhesive plaster. Only use as many strips as are actually requisite to keep the two edges of the wound together; keep the patient quite quiet, on low diet, for a week or so, according to his symptoms. Purge him well with the No. 2 pills (five grains of blue pill mixed with the same quantity of compound extract of colocynth; make into two pills, the dose for an adult). If the patient is feverish, give him two tablespoonfuls of the fever-mixture three times a day. (The fever-mixture, we remind our readers, is thus made: Mix a drachm of powdered nitre, 2 drachms of carbonate of potash, 2 teaspoonfuls of antimonial wine, and a tablespoonful of sweet spirits of nitre in half a pint of water.) A person should be very careful of himself for a month or two after having had a bad cut on the head. His bowels should be kept constantly open, and all excitement and excess avoided. When a vein or artery is wounded, the danger is, of course, much greater. These accidents, therefore, should always be attended to by a surgeon, if he can possibly be procured. Before he arrives, however, or in case his assistance cannot be obtained at all, the following treatment should be adopted:—Raise the cut part, and press rags dipped in cold water firmly against it. This will often be sufficient to stop the bleeding, if the divided artery or vein is not dangerous. When an artery is divided, the blood is of a bright red colour, and comes away in jets. In this case, and supposing the leg or arm to be the cut part, a handkerchief is to be tied tightly round the limb *above* the cut; and, if possible, the two bleeding ends of the artery should each be tied with a piece of silk. If the bleeding is from a vein, the blood is much darker, and does not come away in jets. In this case, the handkerchief is to be tied *below* the cut, and a pad of lint or linen pressed firmly against the divided ends of the vein. Let every bad cut, especially where there is much bleeding, and even although it may to all appearance have been stopped, be attended to by a surgeon if one can by any means be obtained.

Class 2. *Lacerated or torn wounds.*—There is not so much bleeding in these cases as in clean cuts, because the blood-vessels are torn across in a zigzag manner, and not divided straight across. In other respects, however, they are more serious than ordinary cuts, being often followed by inflammation, mortification, fever, and in some cases by locked-jaw. Foreign substances are also more likely to remain in them.—*Treatment*. Stop the bleeding, if there is any, in the manner directed for cuts; remove all substances that may be in the wound; keep the patient quite quiet, and on low diet—gruel, arrowroot, and the like; purge with the No. 1 pills and the No. 1 mixture. (The No. 1 pill: Mix 5 grains of calomel and the same quantity of antimonial powder, with a little bread crumb, and make into two pills, which is the dose for an adult. The No. 1 mixture: Dissolve an ounce of Epsom salts in half a pint of senna tea. A quarter of the mixture is a dose.) If there are feverish symptoms, give two tablespoonfuls of fever-mixture (see above) every four hours. If possible, bring the two edges of the wound together, *but do not strain the parts to do this*. If they cannot be brought together, on account of a piece of flesh being taken clean out, or the raggedness of their edges, put lint dipped in cold water over the wound, and cover it with oiled silk. It will then fill up from the bottom. If the wound, after being well washed, should still contain any sand, or grit of any kind, or if it should get red and hot from inflammation, a large warm bread poultice will be the best thing to apply until it becomes quite clean, or the inflammation goes down. When the wound is a very large one, the application of warm poppy fomentations is better than that of the lint dipped in cold water. If the redness and pain about the part, and the general feverish symptoms, are great, from eight to twelve leeches are to be applied round the wound, and a warm poppy fomentation or warm bread poultice applied after they drop off.

Class 3. *Punctured or penetrating wounds.*—These, for many reasons, are the most serious of all kinds of wounds.—*Treatment.* The same as that for lacerated wounds. Pus (matter) often forms at the bottom of these wounds, which should, therefore, be kept open at the top, by separating their edges every morning with a bodkin, and applying a warm bread poultice immediately afterwards. They will then, in all probability, heal up from the bottom, and any matter which may form will find its own way out into the poultice. Sometimes, however, in spite of all precautions, collections of matter (abscesses) will form at the bottom or sides of the wound. These are to be opened with a lancet, and the matter thus let out. When matter is forming, the patient has cold shiverings, throbbing pain in the part, and flushes on the face, which come and go. A swelling of the part is also often seen. The matter in the abscesses may be felt to move backwards and forwards, when pressure is made from one side of the swelling to the other with the first and second fingers (the middle and that next the thumb) of each hand.

MEDICAL MEMORANDA

ADVANTAGES OF CLEANLINESS.—Health and strength cannot be long continued unless the skin—*all* the skin—is washed frequently with a sponge or other means. Every morning is best; after which the skin should be rubbed very well with a rough cloth. This is the most certain way of preventing cold, and a little substitute for exercise, as it brings blood to the surface, and causes it to circulate well through the fine capillary vessels. Labour produces this circulation naturally. The insensible perspiration cannot escape well if the skin is not clean, as the pores get choked up. It is said that in health about half the aliment we take passes out through the skin.

THE TOMATO MEDICINAL.—To many persons there is something unpleasant, not to say offensive, in the flavour of this excellent fruit. It has, however, long been used for culinary purposes in various countries of Europe. Dr Bennett, a professor of some celebrity, considers it an invaluable article of diet, and ascribes to it very important medicinal properties. He declares:—1. That the tomato is one of the most powerful deobstruents of the *materia medica*; and that, in all those affections of the liver and other organs where calomel is indicated, it is probably the most effective and least harmful remedial agent known in the profession. 2. That a chemical extract can be obtained from it, which will altogether supersede the use of calomel in the cure of diseases. 3. That he has successfully treated diarrhoea with this article alone. 4. That when used as an article of diet, it is almost a sovereign remedy for dyspepsia and indigestion.

WARM WATER.—Warm water is preferable to cold water, as a drink, to persons who are subject to dyspeptic and bilious complaints, and it may be taken more freely than cold water, and consequently answers better as a diluent for carrying off bile, and removing obstructions in the urinary secretion, in cases of stone and gravel. When water of a temperature equal to that of the human body is used for drink, it proves considerably stimulant, and is particularly suited to dyspeptic, bilious, gouty, and chlorotic subjects.

CAUTIONS IN VISITING SICK-ROOMS.—Never venture into a sick-room if you are in a violent perspiration (if circumstances require your continuance there), for the moment your body becomes cold, it is in a state likely to absorb the infection, and give you the disease. Nor visit a sick person (especially if the complaint be of a contagious nature) with *an empty stomach*; as this disposes the system more readily to receive the contagion. In attending a sick person, place yourself where the air passes from the door or window to the bed of the diseased, not betwixt the diseased person and any fire that is in the room, as the heat of the fire will draw the infectious vapour in that direction, and you would run much danger from breathing it.

NECESSITY OF GOOD VENTILATION in rooms lighted with gas.—In dwelling-houses lighted by gas, the frequent renewal of the air is of great importance. A single gas-burner will consume more oxygen, and produce more carbonic acid to deteriorate the atmosphere of a room, than six or eight candles. If, therefore, when several burners are used, no provision is made for the escape of the corrupted air and for the introduction of pure air from without, the health will necessarily suffer.

CHAPTER XLIV

LEGAL MEMORANDA*

Humorists tell us there is no act of our lives which can be performed without breaking through some one of the many meshes of the law by which our rights are so carefully guarded; and those learned in the law, when they do give advice without the usual fee, and in the confidence of friendship, generally say, 'Pay, pay anything rather than go to law;' while those having experience in the courts of Themis have a wholesome dread of its pitfalls. There are a few exceptions, however, to this fear of the law's uncertainties; and we hear of those to whom a lawsuit is an agreeable relaxation, a gentle excitement. One of this class, when remonstrated with, retorted, that while one friend kept dogs, and another horses, he, as he had a right to do, kept a lawyer; and no one had a right to dispute his taste. We cannot pretend, in these few pages, to lay down even the principles of law, not to speak of its contrary exposition in different courts; but there are a few acts of legal import which all men—and women too*—must perform; and to these acts we may be useful in giving a right direction. There is a house to be leased or purchased, servants to be engaged, a will to be made, or property settled, in all families; and much of the welfare of its members depends on these things being done in proper legal form.

The relations of landlord and tenant are most important to both parties, and each should clearly understand his position. The proprietor of a house, or house and land, agrees to let it either to a tenant-at-will, a yearly tenancy, or under lease. A tenancy-at-will may be created by parol or by agreement; and as the tenant may be turned out when his landlord pleases, so he may leave when he himself thinks proper; but this kind of tenancy is extremely inconvenient to both parties. Where an annual rent is attached to the tenancy, in construction of law, a lease or agreement without limitation to any certain period is a lease from year to year, and both landlord and tenant are entitled to notice before the tenancy can be determined by the other. This notice must be given at least six months before the expiration of the current year of the tenancy, and it can only terminate at the end of any whole year from the time at which it began; so that the tenant entering into possession at Midsummer, the notice must be given to or by him, so as to terminate at the same term. When once he is in possession, he has a right to remain for a whole year; and if no notice be given at the end of the first half-year of his tenancy, he will have to remain two years, and so on for any number of years.

TENANCY BY SUFFERANCE.—This is a tenancy, not very uncommon, arising out of the unwillingness of either party to take the initiative in a more decided course at the expiry of a lease or agreement. The tenant remains in possession, and continues to pay rent as before, and becomes, from sufferance, a tenant from year to year, which can only be terminated by one party or the other giving the necessary six months' notice to quit at the term corresponding with the commencement of the original tenancy. This tenancy at sufferance applies also to an under-tenant, who remains in possession and pays rent to the reversioner or head landlord. A six months' notice will be insufficient for this tenancy. A notice was given (in Right *v.* Darby, ITR 159) to quit a house held by plaintiff as tenant from year to year, on the 17th June, 1840, requiring him 'to quit the premises on the 11th October following, or such other day as his said tenancy might expire.' The tenancy had commenced on the 11th October in a former year, but it was held that this was not a good notice for the year ending October 11, 1841. A tenant from year to year gave his landlord notice to quit, ending the tenancy at a time within the half-year; the landlord acquiesced at first, but afterwards refused to accept the notice. The tenant quitted the premises; the landlord entered, and even made some repairs, but it was afterwards held that the tenancy was not determined. A notice to quit must be such as the tenant may safely act on at the time of receiving it; therefore it can only be given by an agent properly authorized at the time, and cannot be made good by the landlord adopting it afterwards. An unqualified notice, given at the proper time, should conclude with 'On failure whereof, I shall require you to pay me double the former rent for so long as you retain possession.'

LEASES.—A lease is an instrument in writing, by which one person grants to another the occupation and use of lands or tenements for a term of years for a consideration, the lessor granting the lease, and the lessee accepting it with all its conditions.

AGREEMENTS.—It is usual, where the lease is a repairing one, to agree for a lease to be granted on completion of repairs according to specification. This agreement should contain the names and designation of the parties, a description of the property, and the term of the intended lease, and all the covenants which are to be inserted, as no verbal agreement can be made to a written agreement. It should also declare that the instrument is an agreement for a lease, and not the lease itself. The points to be settled in such an agreement are, the rent, term, and especially covenants for insuring and rebuilding in the event of a fire; and if it is intended that the lessor's consent is to be obtained before assigning or underleasing, a covenant to that effect is required in the agreement. In building-leases, usually granted for 99 years, the tenant is to insure the property; and even where the agreement is silent on that point, the law decides it so. It is otherwise with ordinary tenements, when the tenant pays a full, or what the law terms rack-rent; the landlord is then to insure, unless it is otherwise arranged by the agreement.

NOXIOUS TRADES.—A clause is usually introduced prohibiting the carrying on of any trade in some houses, and of noxious or particular trades in others. This clause should be jealously inspected, otherwise great annoyance may be produced. It has been held that a general clause of this description prohibited a tenant from keeping a school, for which he had taken it, although a lunatic asylum and public-house have been found admissible; the keeping an asylum not being deemed a trade, which is defined as 'conducted by buying and selling.' It is better to have the trades, or class of trades objected to, defined in the lease.

FIXTURES.—In houses held under lease, it has been the practice with landlords to lease the bare walls of the tenement only, leaving the lessee to put in the stoves, cupboards, and such other conveniences as he requires, at his own option. These, except under particular circumstances, are the property of the lessee, and may either be sold to an incoming tenant, or removed at the end of his term. The articles which may not be removed are subject to considerable doubt, and are a fruitful source of dispute. Mr Commissioner Fonblanque has defined as tenants' property all goods and chattels; 2ndly, all articles 'slightly connected one with another, and with the freehold, but capable of being separated without materially injuring the freehold;' 3rdly, articles fixed to the freehold by nails and screws, bolts or pegs, are also tenants' goods and chattels; but when sunk in the soil, or built on it, they are integral parts of the freehold, and cannot be removed. Thus, a greenhouse or conservatory attached to the house by the tenant is not removable; but the furnace and hot-water pipes by which it is heated, may be removed or sold to the in-coming tenant. A brick flue does not come under the same category, but remains. Window-blinds, grates, stoves, coffee-mills, and, in a general sense, everything he has placed which can be removed without injury to the freehold, he may remove, if they are separated from the tenement during his term, and the place made good. It is not unusual to leave the fixtures in their place, with an undertaking from the landlord that, when again let, the in-coming tenant shall pay for them, or permit their removal. In a recent case, however, a tenant having held over beyond his term and not removed his fixtures, the landlord let the premises to a new tenant, who entered into possession, and would not allow the fixtures to be removed—it was held by the courts, on trial, that he was justified. A similar case occurred to the writer: he left his fixtures in the house, taking a letter from the landlord, undertaking that the in-coming tenant should pay for them by valuation, or permit their removal. The house was let; the landlord died. His executors, on being applied to, pleaded ignorance, as did the tenant, and on being furnished with a copy of the letter, the executors told applicant that if he was aggrieved, he knew his remedy; namely, an action at law. He thought the first loss the least, and has not altered his opinion.

DILAPIDATIONS.—At the termination of a lease, supposing he has not done so before, a landlord can, and usually does, send a surveyor to report upon the condition of the tenement, and it becomes his duty to ferret out every defect. A litigious landlord may drag the outgoing tenant into an expensive lawsuit, which he has no power to prevent. He may even compel him to pay for repairing improvements which he has effected in the tenement itself, if dilapidations exist. When the lessor covenants to do all repairs, and fails to do so, the lessee may repair, and deduct the cost from the rent.

RECOVERY OF RENT.—The remedies placed in the hands of landlords are very stringent. The day after rent falls due, he may proceed to recover it, by action at law, by distress on the premises, or by action of ejectment, if the rent is half a year in arrear. Distress is the remedy usually applied, the landlord being authorized to enter the premises, seize the goods and chattels of his tenant, and sell them, on the fifth day, to reimburse himself for all arrears of rent and the charges of the distress. There are a few exceptions; but, generally, all goods found on the premises may be seized. The exceptions are—dogs, rabbits, poultry, fish, tools and implements of a man's trade actually in use, the books of a scholar, the axe of a carpenter, wearing apparel on the person, a horse at the plough, or a horse he may be riding, a watch in the pocket, loose money, deeds, writings, the cattle at a smithy forge, corn sent to a mill for grinding, cattle and goods of a guest at an inn; but, curiously enough, carriages and horses standing at livery at the same inn may be taken. Distress can only be levied in the daytime, and if made after the tender of arrears, it is illegal. If tender is made after the distress, but before it is *impounded*, the landlord must abandon the distress and bear the cost himself. Nothing of a perishable nature, which cannot be restored in the same condition—as milk, fruit, and the like, must be taken.

The law does not regard a day as consisting of portions. The popular notion that a notice to quit should be served before noon is an error. Although distraint is one of the remedies, it is seldom advisable in a landlord to resort to distraining for the recovery of rent. If a tenant cannot pay his rent, the sooner he leaves the premises the better. If he be a rogue and won't pay, he will probably know that nine out of ten distresses are illegal, through the carelessness, ignorance, or extortion of the brokers who execute them. Many, if not most, of the respectable brokers will not execute distresses, and the business falls into the hands of persons whom it is by no means desirable to employ.

THE I.O.U.—The law is not particular as to orthography; in fact, it distinctly refuses to recognize the existence of that delightful science. You may bring your action against Mr Jacob Phillips, under the fanciful denomination of Jaycobb Fillipse, if you like, and the law won't care, because the law goes by ear; and, although it insists upon having everything written, things written are only supposed in law to have any meaning when read, which is, after all, a common-sense rule enough. So, instead of 'I owe you,' persons of a cheerful disposition, so frequently found connected with debt, used to write facetiously I.O.U., and the law approved of their so doing. An I.O.U. is nothing more than a written admission of a debt, and may run thus:—

15th October, 1860

To Mr W. BROWN.

I.O.U. ten pounds for coals.

£10   JOHN JONES

If to this you add the time of payment, as 'payable in one month from this date,' your I.O.U. is worthless and illegal; for it thus ceases to be a mere acknowledgment, and becomes a promissory note. Now a promissory note requires a stamp, which an I.O.U. does not, Many persons, nevertheless, stick penny stamps upon them, probably for ornamental effect, or to make them look serious and authoritative. If for the former purpose, the postage-stamp looks better than the receipt stamp upon blue paper. If you are W. Brown, and you didn't see the I.O.U. signed, and can't find anybody who knows Jones's autograph, and Jones's won't pay, the I.O.U. will be of no use to you in the county court, except to make the judge laugh. He will, however, allow you to prove the consideration, and as, of course, you won't be prepared to do anything of the sort, he will, if you ask him politely, adjourn the hearing for a week, when you can produce the coalheavers who delivered the article, and thus gain a glorious victory.

APPRENTICES.—By the statute 5 Eliz. cap. 4, it is enacted that, in cases of ill-usage by masters towards apprentices, or of neglect of duty by apprentices, the complaining party may apply to a justice of the peace, who may make such order as equity may require. If, for want of conformity on the part of the master, this cannot be done, then the master may be bound to appear at the next sessions. Authority is given by the act to the justices in sessions to discharge the apprentice from his indentures. They are also empowered, on proof of misbehaviour of the apprentice, to order him to be corrected or imprisoned with hard labour.

HUSBAND AND WIFE.—Contrary to the vulgar opinion, second cousins, as well as first, may legally marry. When married, a husband is liable for his wife's debts contracted before marriage. A creditor desirous of suing for such a claim should proceed against both. It will, however, be sufficient if the husband be served with process, the names of both appearing therein, thus:—John Jones and Ann his wife. A married woman, if sued alone, may plead her marriage, or, as it is called in law, coverture. The husband is liable for debts of his wife contracted for necessaries while living with him. If she voluntarily leaves his protection, this liability ceases. He is also liable for any debts contracted by her with his authority. If the husband have abjured the realm, or been transported by a sentence of law, the wife is liable during his absence, as if she were a single woman, for debts contracted by her.

In civil cases, a wife may now give evidence on behalf of her husband; in criminal cases she can neither be a witness for or against her husband. The case of assault by him upon her forms an exception to this rule.

The law does not at this day admit the ancient principle of allowing moderate correction by a husband upon the person of his wife. Although this is said to have been anciently limited to the use of 'a stick not bigger than the thumb,' this barbarity is now altogether exploded. He may, notwithstanding, as has been recently shown in the famous Agapemone case, keep her under restraint, to prevent her leaving him, provided this be effected without cruelty.

By the Divorce and Matrimonial Causes Act, 1857,* a wife deserted by her husband may apply to a magistrate, or to the petty sessions, for an order to protect her lawful earnings or property acquired by her after such desertion, from her husband and his creditors. In this case it is indispensable that such order shall, within ten days, be entered at the county court of the district within which she resides. It will be seen that the basis of an application for such an order is *desertion*. Consequently, where the parties have separated by common consent, such an order cannot be obtained, any previous cruelty or misconduct on the husband's part notwithstanding.

When a husband allows his wife* to invest money in her own name in a savings-bank, and he survives her, it is sometimes the rule of such establishments to compel him to take out administration in order to receive such money, although it is questionable whether such rule is legally justifiable. Widows and widowers pay no legacy-duty for property coming to them through their deceased partners.

Receipts for sums above £2 should now be given upon penny stamps. A bill of exchange may nevertheless be discharged by an indorsement stating that it has been paid, and this will not be liable to the stamp. A receipt is not, as commonly supposed, conclusive evidence as to a payment. It is only what the law terms *primâ facie* evidence; that is, good until contradicted or explained. Thus, if A sends wares or merchandise to B, with a receipt, as a hint that the transaction is intended to be for ready money, and B detain the receipt without paying the cash, A will be at liberty to prove the circumstances and to recover his claim. The evidence to rebut the receipt must, however, be clear and indubitable, as, after all, written evidence is of a stronger nature than oral testimony.

BOOKS OF ACCOUNT.—A tradesman's books of account cannot be received as evidence in his own behalf; unless the entries therein be proved to have been brought under the notice of, and admitted to be correct by the other party, as is commonly the case with the 'pass-books' employed backwards and forwards between bakers, butchers, and the like domestic traders, and their customers. The defendant may, however, compel the tradesman to produce his books to show entries adverse to his own claim.

WILLS.—The last proof of affection which we can give to those left behind, is to leave their worldly affairs in such a state as to excite neither jealousy, nor anger, nor heartrendings of any kind, at least for the immediate future. This can only be done by a just, clear, and intelligible disposal of whatever there is to leave. Without being advocates for every man being his own lawyer, it is not to be denied that the most elaborately prepared wills have been the most fruitful sources of litigation, and it has even happened that learned judges left wills behind them which could not be carried out. Except in cases where the property is in land or in leases of complicated tenure, very elaborate details are unnecessary; and we counsel no man to use words in making his will of which he does not perfectly understand the meaning and import.

All men over twenty-one years of age, and of sound mind, and all unmarried women of like age and sanity, may by will bequeath their property to whom they please. Infants, that is, all persons under twenty-one years of age, and married women, except where they have an estate to their 'own separate use,' are incapacitated, without the concurrence of the husband; the law taking the disposal of any property they die possessed of. A person born deaf and dumb cannot make a will, unless there is evidence that he could read and comprehend its contents. A person convicted of felony cannot make a will, unless subsequently pardoned; neither can persons outlawed; but the wife of a felon transported for life may make a will, and act in all respects as if she were unmarried. A suicide may bequeath real estate, but personal property is forfeited to the crown.

Except in the case of soldiers on actual service, and sailors at sea, every will must be made in writing. It must be signed by the testator, or by some other person in his presence, and at his request, and the signature must be made or acknowledged in the presence of two or more witnesses, who are required to be present at the same time, who declare by signing that the will was signed by the testator, or acknowledged in their presence, and that they signed as witnesses in testator's presence.

By the act of 1852 it was enacted that no will shall be valid unless signed at the foot or end thereof by the testator, or by some person in his presence, and by his direction; but a subsequent act proceeds to say that every will shall, as far only as regards the position of the signature of the testator, or of the person signing for him, be deemed valid if the signature shall be so placed at, or after, or following, or under, or beside, or opposite to the end of the will, that it shall be apparent on the face of it that the testator intended to give it effect by such signature. Under this clause, a will of several sheets, all of which were duly signed, except the last one, has been refused probate; while, on the other hand, a similar document has been admitted to probate where the last sheet only, and none of the other sheets, was signed. In order to be perfectly formal, however, each separate sheet should be numbered, signed, and witnessed, and attested on the last sheet. This witnessing is an important act: the witnesses must subscribe it in the presence of the testator and of each other; and by their signature they testify to having witnessed the signature of the testator, he being in sound mind at the time. Wills made under any kind of coercion, or even importunity, may become void, being contrary to the wishes of the testator. Fraud or imposition also renders a will void, and where two wills made by the same person happen to exist, neither of them dated, the maker of the wills is declared to have died intestate.

A will may always be revoked and annulled, but only by burning or entirely destroying the writing, or by adding a codicil, or making a subsequent will duly attested; but as the alteration of a will is only a revocation to the extent of the alteration, if it is intended to revoke the original will entirely, such intention should be declared,—no merely verbal directions can revoke a written will; and the act of running the pen through the signatures, or down the page, is not sufficient to cancel it, without a written declaration to that effect signed and witnessed.

A will made before marriage is revoked thereby.

A codicil is a supplement or addition to a will, either explaining or altering former dispositions; it may be written on the same or separate paper, and is to be witnessed and attested in the same manner as the original document.

WITNESSES.—Any persons are qualified to witness a will who can write their names; but such witness cannot be benefitted by the will. If a legacy is granted to the persons witnessing, it is void. The same rule applies to the husband or wife of a witness; a bequest made to either of these is void.

FORM OF WILLS.—Form is unimportant, provided the testator's intention is clear. It should commence with his designation; that is, his name and surname, place or abode, profession, or occupation. The legatees should also be clearly described. In leaving a legacy to a married woman, if no trustees are appointed over it, and no specific directions given, 'that it is for her sole and separate use, free from the control, debts, and incumbrances of her husband,' the husband will be entitled to the legacy. In the same manner a legacy to an unmarried woman will vest in her husband after marriage, unless a settlement of it is made on her before marriage.

In sudden emergencies a form may be useful, and the following has been considered a good one for a death-bed will, where the assistance of a solicitor could not be obtained; indeed, few solicitors can prepare a will on the spur of the moment: they require time and legal forms, which are by no means necessary, before they can act.

I, A.B., of No. 10, ——, Street, in the city of —— [gentleman, builder, or grocer, as the case may be,] being of sound mind, thus publish and declare my last will and testament. Revoking and annulling all former dispositions of my property, I give and bequeath as follows:—to my son J.B., of ——, I give and bequeath the sum of ——; to my daughter M., the wife of J., of ——, I give and bequeath the sum of —— [if intended for her own use, add, 'to her sole and separate use, free from the control, debts, and incumbrances of her husband'], both in addition to any sum or sums of money or other property they have before had from me. All the remaining property I die possessed of I leave to my dear wife M.B., for her sole and separate use during her natural life, together with my house and furniture, situate at No. 10, —— Street, aforesaid. At her death, I desire that the said house shall be sold, with all the goods and chattels therein [*or*, I give and bequeath the said house, with all the goods and chattels therein, to ——], and the money realized from the sale, together with that in which my said wife had a life-interest, I give and bequeath in equal moieties to my son and daughter before named. I appoint my dear friend T.S., of ——, and T.B., of ——, together with my wife M.B., as executors to this my last will and testament.

Signed by A.B., this 10th day of October, 1861, in our presence, both being present together, and both having signed as witnesses, in the presence of the testator:— } A.B.

T.S., Witness,
F.M., Witness.

It is to be observed that the signature of the testator after this attestation has been signed by the witnesses, is not a compliance with the act; he must sign first.

STAMP-DUTIES.—In the case of persons dying intestate, when their effects are administered to by their family, the stamp-duty is half as much more as it would have been under a will. Freehold and copyhold estates are now subject to a special impost on passing, by the Stamp Act of 1857.

The legacy-duty only commences when it amounts to £20 and upwards; and where it is not directed otherwise, the duty is deducted from the legacy.

You cannot compound for past absence of charity by bequeathing land or tenements, or money to purchase such, to any charitable use, by your last will and testament; but you may devise them to the British Museum, to either of the two universities of Oxford and Cambridge, to Eton, Winchester, and Westminster; and you may, if so inclined, leave it for the augmentation of Queen Anne's bounty. You may, however, order your executors to sell land and hand over the money received to any charitable institution.

In making provision for a wife, state whether it is in lieu of, or in addition to, dower.

If you have advanced money to any child, and taken an acknowledgment for it, or entered it in any book of account, you should declare whether any legacy left by will is in addition to such advance, or whether it is to be deducted from the legacy.

A legacy left by will to any one would be cancelled by your leaving another legacy by a codicil to the same person, unless it is stated to be in addition to the former bequest.

Your entire estate is chargeable with your debts, except where the real estate is settled. Let it be distinctly stated out of which property, the real or personal, they are paid, where it consists of both.

Whatever is *devised*, let the intention be clearly expressed, and without any condition, if you intend it to take effect.

Attestation is not necessary to a will, as the act of witnessing is all the law requires, and the will itself declares the testator to be of sound mind in his own estimation; but, wherever there are erasures or interlineations, one becomes necessary. No particular form is prescribed; but it should state that the testator either signed it himself; or that another signed it by his request, or that he acknowledged the signature to be his in their presence, both being present together, and signed as witnesses in his presence. When there are erasures, the attestation must declare that—The words interlined in the third line of page 4, and the erasure in the fifth line of page 6, having been first made. These are the acts necessary to make a properly-executed will; and, being simple in themselves and easily performed, they should be strictly complied with, and always attested.

A witness may, on being requested, sign for testator; and he may also sign for his fellow-witness, supposing he can only make his mark, declaring that he does so; but a husband cannot sign for his wife, either as testator or witness, nor can a wife for her husband.

EXPLANATORY NOTES

1 *Milton*: *Paradise Lost*, ix. 232–3.

3 *'Englishwoman's Domestic Magazine'*: see Introduction

   A diligent study of the best modern writers on cookery: these include most notably Eliza Acton (*Modern Cookery for Private Families*, 1845) and Alexis Soyer (*The Gastronomic Regenerator*, 1846 and *The Pantropheon, or History of Food and Its Preparation, from the Earliest Ages of the World*, 1853), from both of whom Isabella borrowed shamelessly (see Introduction).

4 *coloured plates*: not included in this edition.

7 *the author of 'The Vicar of Wakefield'*: Oliver Goldsmith (1730?–74); the novel was published in 1766, and gradually attained great popular success. It is a gentle story of vicissitudes borne with fortitude, and of fortunes finally restored.

8 *The great Lord Chatham*: William Pitt 'the elder', 1st Earl of Chatham (1708–78).

   Dr Johnson: the great lexicographer Samuel Johnson (1709–84), many of whose pronouncements were recorded by his biographer James Boswell (1740–95).

   Bishop Hall: Joseph Hall (1574–1656), Bishop of Exeter 1627–41 and of Norwich 1641–7. The author of a number of controversial diatribes on doctrinal subjects, he also wrote poems, meditations, and devotional tracts, and claimed to be the first English satirist.

9 *Thomson*: James Thomson (1700–48), Scottish nature poet, whose development of the range of topographical poetry influenced Wordsworth, and inspired some of Turner's paintings.

   Addison: Joseph Addison (1672–1719), essayist, critic, poet, dramatist, and statesman. Best known for his foundation and editorship of, and contributions to, the daily periodical the *Spectator*.

   Joanna Baillie: Scottish dramatist and poet (1762–1851), whose work was admired by Walter Scott.

10 *Washington Irving*: American essayist, story-writer, and poet (1783–1859).

   Cowper: William Cowper (1731–1800), a poet best known for 'The Castaway' and his long poem *The Task* (1785). Although little read today, Cowper, a pre-Romantic poet, was extremely popular with the Victorians.

11 *'no style . . . them all'*: see note above on Dr Johnson.

   The writer: Isabella Beeton herself.

11 *the quaint Fuller*: Thomas Fuller (1608–61), author of ecclesiastical works distinguished by a fondness for puns, quibbles, and what Leslie Stephen called 'fantastic caprices'.

12 *True Charity . . . the skies*: William Cowper, 'Charity' (1782), ll. 573–8. See note on Cowper above.

13 *Judge Haliburton*: Thomas Chandler Haliburton (1796–1865), a Canadian humorist, prose writer, and politician, who wrote satirical sketches and contributed a series of tales from Canadian folklore to the English Tory journal *Fraser's Magazine*, which were later published as *The Old Judge: or, Life in a Colony* (1849).

15 *The following table*: the table contains a wealth of information about rank, wages, income, and size of establishments. It is noteworthy that the lady's-maid and valet are ranked higher than the nurse and cook and the butler respectively, while receiving equal or lesser wages: their notionally higher status stems from their personal proximity to the master and mistress. In practice, the downstairs hierarchy was considerably more contested than this table would allow, with conflicts between the head nurse and cook often recorded. The various levels of income given denote particular stages within the middle class, with most historians including those with incomes ranging from £100 to £1,000 pa. in this broad grouping. According to E. J. Hobsbawm's assessment (in *Industry and Empire*, 1968), the effective economic point of entry to 'the genuine middle class' was an income of £300 a year. The aspirant lower-middle classes, particularly clerks, usually fell into Beeton's lower wage band. It is notable that this lower rung of the economic middle class was by far the most populous: the average middle-class income in 1867 was £154 pa. (see François Crouzet, *The Victorian Economy*, 1982).

17 *'Recreation . . . sharpening'*: see note on Bishop Hall.

18 MORNING CALLS the word 'morning' was habitually applied to visits, functions, and dress, up to the evening.

21 *nous avons changé tout cela*: we have changed all that.

22 *'How sad it is . . . all our pain'*: not traced.

not less than the number of the Graces, or more than that of the Muses: in Greek mythology there are three Graces (Aglaia, Euphrosyne, and Thalia, daughters of Zeus and Hera) and nine Muses (daughters of Zeus and Mnemosyne—goddess of memory—and inspirers of the creative arts).

23 *en règle*: the rule.

'Before dinner . . . his defects': from James Boswell, *The Life of Samuel Johnson*, first published 1791. The conversation in which Boswell reports Johnson making the statement took place on 12 April 1776.

25 *wine negus*: hot sweetened wine and water, invented by a Colonel F. Negus in the early eighteenth century.

28 *Lord Bacon*: Francis Bacon (1561–1626), jurist and essayist concerned with a broad range of philosophical, scientific, and political matters. The quotation is taken from 'Of Studies', *Essays* (1625). Appointed Lord Chancellor in 1618 by James I, he was judged guilty of corruption in 1621 by the House of Lords for taking bribes and devoted the rest of his life to writing.

29 *'her children . . . praiseth her'*: Proverbs 31: 28–9.

Campbell: Thomas Campbell (1777–1844) a poet very popular in his own time, now chiefly remembered for war songs, such as 'Ye Mariners of England' and ballads, particularly 'Lord Ullin's Daughter'. The quotation is from *Pleasures of Hope* (1799), line 37.

Jeremy Taylor: (1613–67), Bishop of Down and Connor, author of theological works famous for their combination of style and simplicity.

30 *'three removes . . . a fire'*: a proverb, first recorded in B. Franklin's *Poor Richard's Almanack* (1758).

33 *'there should . . . in its place'*: one of Isabella Beeton's earliest biographers, Nancy Spain, claims that Beeton herself coined this well-known phrase.

'Short reckonings . . . friends': this may also be one of Beeton's own coinages, as it is otherwise unattributable.

36 *'Caesar's wife . . . suspicion'*: the phrase probably originates with Plutarch, the Roman biographer (AD 46?–120?), who in his *Roman Apophthegms* has Caesar saying that 'Caesar's wife ought to be free from suspicion' as his justification for divorcing her when a man was found to have broken into the private women's quarter of the palace.

Note: one of a number of plans Beeton gives for the efficient organization of time in running the household, this brief yearly scheme adheres to the traditional principles of seasonal household duties, including spring cleaning, the preservation of foods, and ritual celebrations, and maintains the tone of proverbial wisdom that particularly characterizes the 'House-keeper' chapter.

37 *sheets . . . 'sides to middle'*: an economical practice of cutting sheets in half lengthways and sewing together again with the less worn side portions now in the middle.

40 *Thus we are told*: the source of this mythological material is Alexis Soyer's *Pantropheon, or History of Food and Its Preparation, from the Earliest Ages of the World* (London: Simpkin, Marshall & Co., 1853).

43 *bread-moulds*: earthenware moulds in which the bread was baked. Still in use in Victorian times, although in the process of being replaced by tins. Elizabeth David (in *English Bread and Yeast Cookery*, 1977) notes that the ancient Greek bread moulds were originally used for special white loaves baked in honour of religious festivals.

caldrons . . . cisterns . . . chafing-dishes . . . cheese-rasps: cauldrons; any reservoirs for storing water; dishes with an outer pan of hot water to keep the contents warm; graters.

43 *ovens of the Dutch kind*: a Dutch oven is variously a metal box with an open side turned towards an ordinary fire, and a covered cooking pot for braising.

presses: for the extracting of liquids (ie: from fruits), and for the compressing of meats: tongue, in particular, was pressed in the nineteenth century.

trenchers: wooden platters.

44 *braziers*: pans or stands for holding lighted coals.

gridirons: utensils with metal bars for grilling: see Figs. 15 and 17.

47 *Leamington range*: one of the most popular makes of kitchen range, here used as a generic description as we would use 'Aga'. Invented in the early nineteenth century, these enclosed ranges had flues controlled by dampers which allowed the heat of the fire to be diverted to different parts of the range. For a detailed description, see Asa Briggs, *Victorian Things* (London: Batsford, 1988), 239–40. See also illustration and description on pp. 41–2.

50 *house lamb*: 'when . . . the sheep lambs in mid-winter, or the inclemency of the weather would endanger the lives of mother and young, if exposed to its influence, it is customary to rear the lambs within-doors, and under the shelter of stables or barns, where, foddered on soft hay, and part fed on cow's milk, the little creatures thrive rapidly: to such it is customary to give the name of House Lamb, to distinguish it from that reared in the open air, or grass-fed' (from Ch. XIV; omitted from this edition).

pullets: young domestic fowl, particularly hens, usually from the time they begin to lay until the first moult.

capons: domestic cock birds castrated and fattened for eating.

wild-fowl: game birds.

savoys: hardy winter cabbages with wrinkled leaves.

medlars: fruit resembling a small brown apple, eaten when decayed to a jelly-like consistency. Popularly known by vulgar names such as 'open-arse fruit' because of its curious form. For a fuller account, see Jane Grigson's *Fruit Book* (1983), 235–6

51 *sea-kale*: a perennial herb growing on the sea-shore, with young shoots used as a vegetable.

leverets: young hares.

52 *green geese*: 'geese are called green till they are about four months old, and should not be stuffed' (from Ch. XXI; omitted from this edition).

pease: peas—the older spelling survives in pease-pudding.

plovers: medium-sized wading birds, shot as game.

turkey poults: young turkeys—'poult' refers to the young of any domestic fowl.

wheatears: small birds, distinguished by white bellies and rumps.

salading: salad herbs and vegetables—including lettuces, mustard and cress, endive, etc.

53 *walnuts in high season*: fresh, rather than dried walnuts.

blackcock: the male of the black grouse.

filberts: cultivated hazelnuts.

bullaces: fruit of a species of wild or semi-wild plum tree.

62 *recherché*: devised with care or difficulty—that is, complex or elaborate dishes.

63 *nascitur, non fit*: is born, not made.

EXPLANATION . . . COOKERY: much of the material in this list is an adaptation of the 'Vocabulary of Terms, Principally French, Used in Modern Cookery' given at the end of Eliza Acton's *Modern Cookery for Private Families* (1845), though Beeton does add some terms that Acton does not cover.

64 *a bluish appearance*: this derives from the method of cooking the fish alive. The fish (trout is the classic type for this dish) is knocked on the head to stun it, eviscerated with a sharp knife through the gills, and thrown into a pot of boiling water where it curls in agony (the curl is the mark of this method); the blue colour of the living fish is thus preserved in death. (Elizabeth David has a fuller description in *French Provincial Cooking* (1960), 313.)

kettle: in this case, a wide flat pan (for instance, a fish-kettle), not a tea kettle.

fricassee: a dish in which meat is first fried and then stewed—of French origin, but part of the English culinary tradition since at least the eighteenth century (it is one of the methods Jonathan Swift suggests for cooking the infants of the starving Irish in his satiric *A Modest Proposal* of 1729).

hasty-pudding: neither Beeton nor Eliza Acton, from whom she lifts this description, gives a recipe for hasty-pudding, which is made of wheat or maize flour, stirred to a thick batter in boiling milk or water. It is a traditional English dish with many variations. Dorothy Hartley in *Food in England* (1954) gives an eighteenth-century recipe in which it is enriched with eggs, and nineteenth-century versions where the eggs have been replaced with butter. The surface of the batter is covered with butter, cinnamon, and sugar to serve. The dish is related to both porridge and Italian polenta.

65 ENTRÉES: a term that has undergone significant shifts in meaning over the last century and a half: by the end of the nineteenth century it had come to refer to the whole of the first course (that is, the course served between the soup and/or fish courses and the roast). In America, it has long referred to the main course, and it is in this sense that it is often used in Britain today. Alexis Soyer defined it in his 1846 *Gastronomic*

Regenerator as 'a French culinary term (universally known by the nobility and gentry of Europe) signifying a corner or made dish in which sauce is introduced'.

69 *bread-raspings*: bread-crumbs. A rasp is a grater.

isinglass: a form of gelatin, obtained from the viscera of certain fish, particularly sturgeon.

70 *proverb . . . islanders*: probably referring to the remark of David Garrick (1717–79) in his poem on 'Doctor Goldsmith's Characteristical Cookery' that 'Heaven sends us good meat, but the Devil sends cooks'.

71 *Thus . . . coagulable*: in his fascinating book *On Food and Cooking: The Science and Lore of the Kitchen* (1986), Harold McGee offers another explanation for the proportions of dark meat in different animals, stating that it is not the blood, at least half of which is removed after slaughter, which gives the red colouration to meat, but the oxygen-storing myoglobin, which is located in the muscle cells: 'The muscles that require a lot of oxygen have a greater storage capacity than those that need little, and are consequently darker red. To some extent, oxygen use can be related to the general level of activity: muscles that are exercised frequently and strenuously need more oxygen. Chickens and turkeys do a lot of standing around, but little if any flying, so their breast muscle is white, their legs dark. Game birds, on the other hand, spend more time on the wing, and their breast meat may be as dark as their drumsticks' (p. 92).

lyer: probably meaning lean flesh—*OED* gives 'lyery' as an adjective applied to cattle with a superabundance of lean flesh.

72 *Another . . . man*: despite being to some degree in favour of the increased industrialization of food production (see, for example, her comments on aerated bread in Ch. XXXIV), Mrs Beeton is consistently opposed to the drive for the mechanization and increased efficiency of animal husbandry, and speaks out strongly on the need to treat animals with dignity and care. See, for instance, her remarks on veal production in Ch. XVIII.

osmazome: the name given by the French chemist Jacques Thénard to that part of the aqueous extract of meat which is soluble in alcohol and contains those constituents of the flesh which determine its taste and smell. The first use of the term seems to have been in 1812. Anne Drayton, translator of the Penguin edition of Brillat-Savarin's *The Philosopher in the Kitchen* (1825; 1970) notes that the term (used for what was later discovered to be creatin) was as fashionable in its day as 'vitamin' is in our time.

76 *Above . . . ascertained*: a clear statement of the principles of thoughtful economy underlying the work. Beeton's reputation for extravagance, as discussed in the Introduction, derives from a few anomalous dishes, and from the removal of her most economical dishes in subsequent editions.

77 *RECIPES*: in the original this chapter contains 75 recipes for soups and

stocks, with the largest category (well over half) being fruit and vegetable soups. Meat soups account for almost a third, though almost all of the fruit and vegetable soups are also based on meat stocks. There are only six recipes for fish soups. Among those omitted are almond, barley, cabbage, carrot, cocoa-nut, egg, potato, rice, sago, semolina, turnip, giblet, hare, gravy, ox-tail, partridge, pheasant, rabbit, turkey, crayfish, eel, oyster, and prawn.

it will . . . lessened: Beeton is the first food writer to give the cost of her dishes. It is notoriously difficult to convert the prices of the past into those of the present because of massive changes in social structures, availability of particular goods, and standards of living. Price statistics can, though, give us a very rough mode of comparison: if we conflate the Board of Trade Wholesale Price Indices for 1871–1980 with the more speculative Sauerbeck-Statist Price Indices for 1846–1966, it looks as though today's wholesale food prices are approximately seven times those of the 1860s (see B. R. Mitchell, *British Historical Statistics*, 1988, for statistical tables). See the Introduction for a discussion of Beeton's recipe system.

79 *Apple Soup*: fruit soups are unusual in British cooking, but Eliza Acton also gives a recipe for apple soup. For once, Beeton's recipe does not appear to derive from her predecessor's. Jane Grigson, intrigued by Acton's recipe, claimed to have found its ultimate source in an early fifteenth-century recipe for 'Apple moys' (apple mush, from the French *mol* for soft), reproduced in the collection of the Bodleian Library in Oxford. (See Grigson, *English Food* (1974), 7.)

80 *Artichoke (Jerusalem) Soup*: Jerusalem artichokes were first introduced to Europe from Canada in the early seventeenth century, and called artichokes because of a supposed resemblance in taste to the (unrelated) globe artichoke. The Italian use of the term 'girasole' (sunflower) as a means of distinguishing the new-comer seems to have been corrupted into the English 'Jerusalem'—a place with no connection to the vegetable. Jerusalem artichokes proved a very successful crop—gardeners will know that they grow as easily as weeds—and looked set to provide a staple food for the poor, until ousted by the blander-flavoured and more versatile potato. By the nineteenth century they were grown mainly in the private gardens of the well-to-do, and used largely for soups and purées.

Bread Soup: this is rare as a British recipe and has much in common with the peasant soups of Southern Europe, such as the Spanish gazpacho in its most basic form. As Beeton notes, it is an extremely economical dish: the food of the poor, of a type of subsistence diet for which recipes tend not to be recorded, though Florence White in her 1932 *Good Things in England* gives an even more basic version called 'Brewis' and an instructive historical provenance:

> 'This', writes a Lancashire lady, 'dates from the "Hungry Forties", when we were very poor indeed in Lancashire.'

Pour boiling water on a crust of bread; pour the water off and it is ready; season with salt and pepper. Serve it in a breakfast cup and eat it with a spoon. (p. 106)

The most famous literary account of the Hungry Forties in Lancashire is Elizabeth Gaskell's *Mary Barton* (1848). Beeton's inclusion of such a recipe may indicate the range of readers she was hoping to appeal to, or—more probably, considering the price at which *Household Management* retailed—reflect the encyclopedic impulse underlying the work.

82 *Soup à la Cantatrice*: Eliza Acton gives a similar, though not identical, recipe, which she calls 'Mademoiselle Jenny Lind's Soup', having obtained the recipe, she says, from the Swedish authoress Miss Bremer, who had been given it by the singer. Beeton's biographers tend to claim that Beeton herself had it direct from the singer. Jenny Lind (1820–87), was a very famous figure, celebrated for her remarkable vocal range. Beeton's employment of the French name for this soup is typical of her appeals to middle-class pretensions with her pricier dishes.

colouring it a little: presumably with gravy browning, derived from caramel.

half a drachm: a drachm is an Apothecary's weight of 60 grains, equal to an eighth of an ounce.

83 *When . . . ground*: a telling example of the almost naïve enthusiasm with which Beeton regards scientific knowledge.

Chestnut (Spanish) Soup: this is one of a large number of recipes Beeton lifts directly from Eliza Acton. A word here or there is changed, but the texts are almost identical.

84 *Soup à la Flamande (Flemish)*: a less pretentious use of a foreign name than in the case of Soup à la Cantatrice (p. 82), as the method of stewing vegetables in butter and the addition of egg yolks are clearly French in origin.

Kale Brose (a Scotch recipe): on the whole, *Household Management* reflects English rather than British culinary traditions, but some Scottish and occasional Irish recipes are included. The next recipe is for a better-known Scottish soup.

85 *As . . . desert*: Numbers 11: 5: 'We remember the fish, which we did eat in Egypt freely; the cucumbers, and the melons, and the leeks, and the onions, and the garlick.'

86 *BEETON'S . . . INFORMATION*: one of Sam Beeton's numerous publishing ventures, the *Dictionary of Universal Information* was first published in 1858–62. Sam was compiling it at the time Isabella was writing *Household Management*, and many of the historical notes and anecdotes in the latter were derived from the former.

87 *THE PRINCE OF WALES*: the passage which follows is a striking example of dutiful monarchical sentiments, particularly given the

Republican sentiments of Sam Beeton, who compiled the *Dictionary of Universal Information*.

Soup à la Solferino: the battle of Solferino represented a decisive moment in the Franco–Austrian war: a victory for Napoleon III against Austria over the control of Italy. British liberal public opinion, favouring an independent Italy, was largely on the side of the French, and especially their Italian allies in Piedmont, led by King Victor Emmanuel. The comment that the English gentleman has Anglicized and thus improved the recipe is very revealing of English attitudes to foreign dishes.

88 *Useful Soup . . . Purposes*: most Victorian cookery books had a similar recipe. The 'Lady Bountiful' role was much adopted by middle-class Victorian women, and visits to the poor were a standard item in the weekly activities of wives and unmarried daughters. Soup was considered the best form of food for charitable purposes for reasons of economy, but also, perhaps, because of its ease of digestion for the ill and weak. Alexis Soyer, then chef of the Reform Club, developed a number of recipes for 'Soup for the Poor', and attracted a flurry of publicity when he set up the first soup kitchen in Dublin during the period of the potato famine. It is significant that Beeton attaches one of her relatively few personal asides to this dish, making it clear that she too is aware of her charitable duty. For contemporary literary images of the middle-class woman ministering to the poor we can turn to Elizabeth Gaskell's *North and South* (1854), where the heroine, Margaret Hale, is rebuked by proud Northern factory workers for trying to patronize them with benevolent visits as she had the poor in her rural Southern home. Dickens is similarly scathing in his depiction of the aggressively do-gooding Mrs Pardiggle in *Bleak House* (1853).

89 *Mock Turtle*: because real turtle soup was so expensive, this alternative was a popular dish. The obvious association is with Lewis Carroll's fabulous and lachrymose Mock Turtle in *Alice's Adventures in Wonderland* (1865), illustrated by Tenniel with a calf's head on a turtle's body. It is the Mock Turtle who sings the hymn in praise of turtle soup—whether real or not we are not told—with its haunting refrain 'Soup of the evening, beautiful soup'.

90 *Mullagatawny Soup*: one of a number of Anglo-Indian recipes Beeton gives. See Introduction for a discussion of Anglo-Indian food. Mulligatawny (the modern spelling, and inconsistently spelt by Beeton), a curried meat soup, was one of the most popular Anglo-Indian dishes, and seems to have been introduced early to England.

Turtle Soup: see note to p. 89 for mock turtle soup. Turtle soup was so expensive because of the rarity of and difficulty in obtaining the giant turtles of which it was made. These were transported live from the West Indies. Real turtle soup was not only incredibly extravagant, it also required at least two days' work, as the length and complexity of the recipe indicates. It was the sort of dish that was served at grand functions like the Lord Mayor's Banquet, and it is extremely unlikely that Beeton had ever herself seen, let alone dispatched, a huge live turtle (as her casual remark about cutting off the head perhaps suggests). This is aspirational food *par excellence*.

93 *Hodge-Podge*: a name given to any random-seeming mixture of ingredients: perhaps to suggest left-overs. Beeton also uses it for a dish of minced cold mutton and vegetables.

95 *THE . . . FISHES*: throughout this chapter and the other introductory chapters in the work Beeton employs a startling range of discourses, and moves between them with often jarring effect. Scientific, religious, poetic, industrial, historical, and philosophical discourses are all here applied to the subject of fish.

96 *Experience . . . accessibility*: it is notable how often Beeton employs a discourse of religious awe in discussing questions of natural history. See Introduction for further discussion.

97 *In some . . . employed*: this statement, and the earlier comparison in the previous paragraph of fish to ships, are the insights of an individual who has grown up in a newly industrialized nation, and therefore applies metaphors of industrial design to organic forms and processes (see Introduction).

Innumerable . . . domain: a sentence typifying the heightened poetic discourse Beeton employs in this paragraph.

98 *Fishes . . . Creation*: see note to p. 95 and discussion in the Introduction on Darwinism and religion.

FISH . . . FOOD: the source for all of the discussion of fish in history is Soyer's *Pantropheon*.

99 *With . . . vessel*: note the outrage suggested by the use of italics. See note to p. 71 for a discussion of Beeton's opposition to cruelty in food production.

100 *occasionally . . . dish*: an indication of the relative rarity of fish in the mid-Victorian diet as compared with the present day.

102 *RECIPES*: Beeton gives 129 recipes for fish in this chapter, including 12 for cod, 9 each for salmon, lobster, and soles, 8 for eels, 7 for oysters, and 6 for turbot. Whiting and mackerel have 5 recipes each. This gives a fairly accurate indication of the prevalence of particular dishes on the mid-Victorian middle-class dinner table. Freshwater fish, mostly obtainable only through the activities of sports fishermen, appear in striking variety, but in relatively few forms: pike, tench, trout, barbel, carp, and so on are usually given baked, boiled, or—more rarely—stewed. Beeton appends to her chapter a table, not reproduced here, of the total annual supply of fish to the London market derived from Henry Mayhew's momentous work of sociological journalism, *London Labour and the London Poor* (1851), in which he examines the lives of street sellers and dwellers.

Anchovy . . . Paste: a Victorian classic, especially as a tea-time savoury on toast.

103 *Salt . . . 'Salt-Fish'*: we are inclined to think of salt cod as a Continental food stuff: the centrepiece of the Provençal 'Grand Aïoli' (garlic mayonnaise served with a large array of boiled vegetables, cold meats, and salt cod); the main ingredient of the French 'brandade de morue' and Italian 'baccalà' (virtually identical purees of salt cod served with fried bread). In fact, cod has been salted in Britain since the Middle Ages. By the nineteenth century it was more of a rarity than in Europe, but survived particularly in Catholic communities and more generally as a Lenten dish, as Beeton suggests.

104 *Cod à la Béchamel*: a French method of serving white fish in a masking white sauce that had become thoroughly familiar in England by this date.

Baked Carp: interesting for its suggestion of sewing the fish shut: surely impractical given the delicate nature of the flesh of a fish once cooked.

106 *Eel Pie*: eels, due to the difficulty in killing them, were sold alive. Although Beeton does not acknowledge it directly, the eels in her dishes have to be skinned alive—their heads cut off, and then the skin rolled off from the neck down. As her note on 'Tenacity of Life in the Eel' (p. 107) explains, the pieces would often continue to move even after being skinned and chopped.

108 *Red Herrings, or Yarmouth Bloaters*: Peggotty, the old nurse in Dickens's *David Copperfield* (1850), calls herself a 'Yarmouth Bloater' to indicate her pride in her native town and its most famous food product. Bloaters were smoked whole, so that the flesh remained more moist than with a split herring, and this and the presence of the innards imparted a particular sweet, gamey flavour. Red herrings were saltier and drier, often of a stiff, cardboardy consistency. Bloaters and red herrings were mainly eaten as a dish for breakfast or high tea.

To Boil Lobsters: Beeton gives the method of dispatch thought most humane at the time and until very recently: the RSPCA now recommends putting lobsters in cold water and bringing gradually to the boil to lull them to sleep before they die.

111 *Scalloped Oysters*: the prices of Beeton's oyster dishes seem very expensive given that oysters had been extremely cheap earlier in the nineteenth century—to the extent that Dickens's Sam Weller remarks that 'Poverty and oysters always seem to go together' (*Pickwick Papers*, 1837). According to Elisabeth Ayrton in *The Cookery of England* (1977), 200 oysters cost 4s. in 1700 and in 1840 they were still only about 4d. a dozen. By about 1850, however, they seem to have suddenly become scarce—from a combination of disease and over-fishing. So oysters at Beeton's time of writing were newly luxurious, which perhaps accounts for the number of recipes (seven) she gives for what had until recently been a commonplace street food.

Salmon and Caper Sauce: Beeton gives a recipe for the sauce in Chapter X. Caper sauce is a very old English recipe, traditionally served with both fish and mutton. The caper grows in Southern Europe and was

sometimes replaced in English cooking by pickled nasturtium seeds, for
which Beeton also gives a recipe (not included in this edition).

112 *Potted Shrimps*: another traditional English dish, a speciality of More-
combe Bay since the eighteenth century, they were usually eaten with
bread and butter for tea.

Crimped Skate: crimping is a method Beeton uses frequently for fish
cookery: it involves rolling and tying either whole fish or fillets before
cooking, in order to provide a neat presentation and a greater compact-
ness of flesh.

113 *Soles with Cream Sauce*: soles—Dover, not the cheaper lemon—were the
favourite fish for the nineteenth-century dinner party, almost invariably
served as the fish course in a staggering variety of sauces, and liked for
their delicacy of taste and texture.

114 *Roast Sturgeon*: the sturgeon, the fish whose roe is prepared as caviar, has
been greatly esteemed for centuries and, as Beeton notes, has been considered royal property in many nations. Its firm, meaty flesh allows it to
be roasted, a method that would destroy more delicate fish.

115 *An . . . appendages*: such anecdotes of wise employers and stupid cooks are
a commonplace feature in cookery books through the ages, serving to
unite reader and author in a conspiracy against the iniquities of servants.
They are a clear indication that the primary readership for such books is
not intended to be the servant, however much the author might proclaim
this intention. See Introduction for a discussion of the ambivalence of
tone in *Household Management* in this respect.

Fasten . . . skewer: a traditional mode of serving whiting. Lewis Carroll's
Gryphon offers an explanation in his gloss on the song of the 'Lobster
Quadrille':

> 'The reason is', said the Gryphon, 'that they would go with the
> lobsters to the dance. So they got thrown out to sea. So they had
> to fall a long way. So they got their tails fast in their mouths. So
> they couldn't get them out again. That's all.' *Alice's Adventures in
> Wonderland* (1865)

116 *Water Souchy*: a fishermen's recipe for using up the odd varieties of fish
in a catch. Dorothy Hartley in *Food in England* (1954) records that in the
second half of the nineteenth century it was fashionable for Londoners to
take a day-trip to Greenwich to eat fried whitebait, and that this thin
green fish broth was often eaten while the whitebait was cooking. Bella
and John Harmon celebrate their wedding in Greenwich with just such a
whitebait feast in Dickens's *Our Mutual Friend* (1865).

General . . . Fish: the detail of diagrams and instructions are remarkable,
particularly the etiquette of helping each guest equally to the most valued
portions. The fact that what were considered the choicest morsels were
often the most esoteric portions of the dish—the cheeks and tongue of
cod, for instance, and the fins and skin of turbot—also reveal the extent

to which the Victorian dinner was a very self-conscious exercise in discrimination and ritual for both hosts and guests.

118 *An anecdote*: from Jean-Anthelme Brillat-Savarin's *La Physiologie du goût* (translated in the Penguin edition of 1970 as *The Philosopher in the Kitchen*). M. Brillat-Savarin (1755–1825) was a French judge, famed for his excellent table as well as his treatise on gastronomy. The anecdote Beeton refers to can be found on pp. 54–5 in the 1970 Penguin translation.

119 *milt*: spleen

121 *RECIPES*: the principles of inclusion and arrangement in this chapter, as in a number of others, are geared specifically to the needs of the cook rather than the housewife. This, as discussed in the Introduction, is counter to the tendency for the narrative itself, especially in its anecdotes and asides, to address itself to the housewife. The structure and the main discourse of the book are hence addressed to different readerships. Recipes are grouped together in chapters not in terms of the roles they play at a particular stage of a meal (which would help the mistress in ordering food), but in terms of the sort of cooking they require: so all pies and puddings, sweet and savoury, appear together, and this chapter contains a seemingly heterogeneous collection of items that exist to add flavour to other dishes. The tradition of placing the sauce chapters at or near the start of cookery books is an old one in England and probably derives from France, as sauces are so clearly the basis of French cooking.

Apple . . . Pork: a classic English sauce, dating from at least the Middle Ages.

Aspic . . . Jelly: the French tradition of dishes of meat, fish, and vegetables suspended in clear aspic (a savoury jelly) was much beloved by the Victorians for grand dinners and banquets as the sculptural quality of the moulded jellies and the decorative arrangement of the suspended foods made for dramatic centrepieces.

122 *Béchamel . . . Sauce*: the classic white sauce, used by Beeton as the basis of numerous dishes. It is noteworthy that the primary version she gives is based on a white meat stock. The milk-based version with which we are most familiar today is given by Beeton as 'Béchamel Maigre [that is, meagre, usually denoting dishes for Lent or fasting], or Without Meat' (not included in this edition).

white stock: this recipe was given in the original chapter on soups and involved 4 lb. of veal knuckle stewed with any spare poultry trimmings and 4 slices of lean ham in half a pint of water in a stewpan first rubbed with butter. When the gravy begins to flow, 1 carrot, 1 head of celery, 2 onions, salt, 1 blade of mace, and 12 white peppercorns are added with 8 pints of water, and the whole simmered for 5 hours, skimmed, and strained through a very fine sieve.

123 *'Beeton's Dictionary'*: see note to p. 86.

melted butter: earlier Beeton has given this detailed recipe, not included here, for stabilizing melted butter that is to be served as a sauce. It involves cutting butter into small pieces, dredging with flour in a sauce-pan, adding water and stirring constantly in one direction until blended and just boiling.

124 *Bengal . . . Chetney*: recipes for chutney begin to appear in English cookery books in the eighteenth century, when housewives began to try and reproduce the exotic chutneys and pickles brought home by the merchants of the East India Company. Beeton's recipe is typical in its assertion of authentic derivation from an Indian native via the Anglo-Indian lady. The word 'chutney' derives from the Hindi 'chatní'; Mrs Beeton's spelling does not appear in any dictionary.

Chili Vinegar: although Beeton's biographers claim that she tested every recipe, it is hard to believe that she ever made this vinegar. Handling fifty chilies without gloves or warnings not to rub the eyes would be a hazard-ous enough enterprise, but fifty chilies to one pint of vinegar would surely result in something poisonously intense (though this depends on the strength of the 'English chilies', which I have been unable to identify).

125 *An Excellent . . . Cucumbers*: the Victorians were inclined to treat the cucumber as a vegetable for cooking and preserving as much as one for eating raw. Their recipes are particularly concerned with methods of removing the liquid and seeds from cucumbers—probably because the Victorian cucumber was more bitter than modern varieties (see Beeton's note on the strong flavour of cucumbers attached to the recipe for pickled gherkins on p. 129).

126 *Dutch . . . Fish*: the sauce is a form of Hollandaise—one instance where Beeton does not employ the French name, though she *did* use it in the variation on the recipe which followed (not included here).

127 *melted butter very smoothly*: see note to p. 123 above.

128 *Forcemeat . . . Soups*: possibly derived from European Jewish recipes for Gefilte fish—fish balls poached in fish stock—though Gefilte fish is served cold with the stock reduced and set to a jelly (see Claudia Roden, *The Book of Jewish Food*, 1997).

130 *Either of the stocks*: these were given at the start of the soup chapter (pp. 77–9).

132 *Dr Kitchener*: (usually spelt Kitchiner) William (1775?–1827), author of *Apicius Redivivus, The Cook's Oracle* (1817, enlarged 1831), a cookery book popular for many years after its first publication.

133 *To Pickle Lemons . . . on*: pickled lemons were used mainly as a relish for savoury dishes, but one is reminded of the craze for pickled limes among the schoolmates of Amy in Louisa M. Alcott's *Little Women* (1868). These American girls spent their break-times sucking the bitter limes, and trading them with each other for knick-knacks and favours.

Liver and Lemon . . . Poultry: included in this abridgement for its curi-ously unpleasant sound, though the combination of the rich liver and

sharp citrus fruit might in fact be successful. For 'melted butter', see
note to p. 123 above.

134 *Mayonnaise*: this recipe is very similar to modern versions, except for the
inclusion of stock and cream which are used to thin down the emulsion;
today recipes would tend to suggest milk for this purpose. Mayonnaise is
notoriously difficult to make—perhaps in part because the process is so
awkward to describe. The fact that Beeton waits for the note at the end
before making the crucial point about the need to add the oil drop by
drop until the emulsion has formed may indicate the difficulty of
describing the method logically.

136 *Mushroom Ketchup*: ketchups, like pickles and chutneys, were introduced
to England by the traders of the East India Company. These 'store
sauces' were the forerunners of the modern bottled sauces, and were
beginning to be produced on an industrial scale in the course of the
nineteenth century. Harvey's sauce, one of the most famous (which was
based on anchovies, walnut pickle, soy and shallots, cayenne, and large
quantities of garlic and vinegar), seems to have been commercialized
sometime in the late eighteenth century. Worcestershire sauce was
launched commercially in 1838 (see Elizabeth David, *Spices, Salt and
Aromatics in the English Kitchen* (1973), 11–12). Mushroom, along with
walnut and oyster, was the classic English ketchup, only to be joined by
tomato after 1900 when cheap canned tomatoes began to be imported in
large quantities from North America.

138 *Plum-Pudding Sauce*: little different from the brandy sauces still served
today with Christmas pudding. The Victorians ate steamed suet puddings as an everyday family pudding, but the sweet course at grander
dinners was made up of much more delicate fare: creams, trifles, jellies,
and blancmanges.

139 *Salad Dressing (Excellent)*: the basis for the modern bottled salad cream.
Beeton gives three recipes for this heavily vinegared cream which, used
on salads in place of olive-oil-based dressings, has long been the bug-bear
of those who revile English food. The oft-repeated claim that the English
did not use olive oil for salad dressings until after the Second World War
(the credit for the change is usually awarded to Elizabeth David) is belied,
however, by Beeton's note on the subject.

141 *Sauce Robert*: one of a number of classic French sauces that Beeton gives
without comment, suggesting that they were reasonably well known.

142 *Spinach . . . Dishes*: a reminder of the absence of bottled colouring agents
in most Victorian kitchens—and of the devotion to decorating and
disguising food at this time.

Store . . . Cherokee: a standard store sauce on the lines of Worcestershire
or Harveys, with an interesting name, perhaps deriving from a confusion
of American Indians with the inhabitants of India, though in fact cayenne
pepper comes from either Africa or Nepal.

143 *Pickled Walnuts*: another old English classic, usually eaten with cold meats or cheeses.

145 *Brillat . . . Princes*: *The Philosopher in the Kitchen*, 242–3. Virtually everything in this introductory section is a close paraphrase of Brillat-Savarin's discussion of the 'Philosophy of Cooking' in chapter 21 of that work.

148 *baking . . . roasting*: by baking, Beeton means that method of cooking meats at high heats in an enclosed oven which we now call roasting. Roasting in her day was still carried out on a spit over an open fire.

Boiling . . . removed: a nice example of Beeton's corrective impulses—she is particularly concerned to improve the techniques of the 'ignorant' cooks of the nation.

150 *BROILING*: what we now refer to as grilling, though the older word has been retained in American English.

153 *ROASTING*: the description under this heading gives an acute sense of the sheer complexity of cooking in the Victorian kitchen; reading between the lines we can imagine the vast quantities of smoke, grease, and dirt produced by everyday cooking methods.

155 *Mutton . . . freely*: an interesting corrective to the modern view that traditional English culinary techniques involved habitual overcooking.

156 *GENERAL . . . QUADRUPEDS*: this introductory chapter is paired with one on beef cooking, while each subsequent introductory chapter on meat focuses on a specific animal (so pigs and sheep are assigned separate chapters). It is probable that Beeton altered her intended arrangement of this introductory material without changing the general heading of this section.

157 *Linnaeus*: Carolus Linnaeus, 1707–78, a Swedish naturalist who devised the system of classifying animals and plants by using one Latin or Latinized name to represent genus and another to distinguish the species. Following her general points on classification in this section, Beeton gives a detailed breakdown, omitted from this edition, of all the functions and features that distinguish mammals from other orders and particular mammals from each other, down to the specifics of the toes of rats and squirrels.

158 *THE ALDERNEY*: this is just one of the detailed analyses Beeton gives of the many varieties of cattle bred in Britain, with pictures of the various breeds and information on the prices each customarily fetched. The juxtaposition of the rather sentimentalized pictures of large-eyed cows with the following description of modes of slaughter and diagram of a side of beef marked up for the butcher's cuts is almost certainly unintentionally gruesome.

159 *We hope . . . as possible*: another example of Beeton's humanitarian impulses—in fact rather unusual sentiments in the cookery books of her day (or, for that matter, of our own).

The manner . . . large: interesting social observation, with a tone suggestive of slight distaste for the fashionable world.

161 *RECIPES*: this chapter on beef cooking contains 76 recipes in the original, with a fairly equal division between the main methods of meat cooking of the day—boiling or stewing, baking and roasting. There is also an equal distribution of expensive and cheap dishes, with offal well represented.

Beef à la Mode: a traditional French stew sometimes also referred to as a daube. Such dishes were to become very fashionable in England in the 1920s, mainly as a result of the work done by the famous chef X. Marcel Boulestin in popularizing French peasant and bourgeois cooking. Beeton's earlier recipe is very similar to the description of the Bœuf en Daube at the centre of Virginia Woolf's 1929 novel *To the Lighthouse*, in which the maternal Mrs Ramsay nurtures her guests with this fabulous creation, which has taken three days of preparation to bring to perfection its 'confusion of savoury brown and yellow meats and its bay leaves and its wine'. Although this is an intensely fashionable dish, Woolf attributes it to a French recipe of Mrs Ramsay's grandmother, acknowledging its Victorian antecedents.

162 *Beef-Steak . . . Pudding*: we think of this as one of the most traditionally English of dishes, but in fact Beeton's recipe seems to be the earliest in print. Eliza Acton gives a recipe for a steak pudding called John Bull's pudding which, as Jane Grigson notes in *English Food* (1974) 'suggests a certain national fame which had spread to other countries', but Beeton was the first to add the crucial kidneys. Her detailed reference to the Sussex source of the dish indicates that she did not expect her readers to be familiar with it.

164 *Bubble-and-Squeak*: an extremely cheap dish, designed to use up leftovers. Dr Kitchiner gives a very similar recipe in his 1817 *Kitchen Oracle*, but without the onion. Recipes later than Beeton's invariably omit the onion and add potatoes which are fried with the cabbage. They often serve the vegetable mixture with cold meat, rather than the hot meat of earlier recipes. The name is generally attributed to the sounds made by the dish when cooking: Dr Kitchiner gives a few bars of music as the tune of the dish and a couplet describing the sound:

> When 'midst the frying Pan in accents savage,
> The Beef, so surly, quarrels with the Cabbage.

165 *cook and chemist*: probably Brillat-Savarin, though I have been unable to find the passage.

166 *Boiled Marrow-Bones*: often served as a savoury at the end of the meal. This was a favourite Georgian dish, to the extent that silversmiths produced special long scoops for extracting the marrow. In the Victorian period, marrow-bones tended to be reserved for men as they were considered indelicate fare for ladies; the exception was Queen Victoria, who ate marrow toast for tea or after dinner whenever dining alone.

167 *Fried ... Cow-Heel*: an example of the many forms of offal we no longer consider eating. The Victorians, much more eager meat-eaters than ourselves, were also more economical in their use of the whole animal.

168 *An Excellent ... Small Family*: six people would have been a very small middle-class family in the Victorian period, when a family of ten children was not uncommon, and when servants' meals also had to come out of the remains of the daily joint.

Roast Sirloin of Beef: as Beeton's list of classes of joints of beef on p. 160 indicates, the sirloin was the best piece of beef. We might note that this joint, exorbitantly expensive in our own day, is priced by Beeton at 8½*d.* per lb.—compared with, for example, salmon at 1*s.* 3*d.* per lb.

170 *Toad-in-the-Hole*: today this dish is made with sausages in batter, but Beeton's was the version typical in the nineteenth century, though her use of kidneys is an addition.

171 *To Dress Tripe*: tripe is the stomach of cattle; sold in flat pieces, it is of white, spongy, and cellular construction. It is not much eaten today, but it was strongly traditional in areas of the North, particularly Lancashire, where it was served, as in Beeton's recipe, with onions.

174 *sheep*: Beeton follows this paragraph with eight pages specifying the characteristics of different breeds of sheep and the principles of sheep husbandry.

175 *The ... sheep*: the juxtaposition between this paragraph and the one preceding is as startling as that mentioned in the note to p. 158.

The value ... state: Beeton here displays a highly conventional attitude to the literal historical truth of biblical texts—a perspective which was beginning to be challenged at this time by a number of philosophers and theologians (often referred to as the 'Higher Critics').

178 *RECIPES*: this chapter contains 37 recipes for mutton and 13 for lamb, indicating the relative taste for the former over the latter at this date; today, of course, mutton is rarely sold, though our definition of 'lamb' includes animals considerably older than did the Victorians. Braising (that is, slow cooking in a covered container), stewing, and roasting are the most frequently used methods in the chapter.

179 *China Chilo*: Mrs Acton gives the source recipe for this dish, suggesting the option of adding 'currie-powder', minced mushrooms, or diced cucumber.

Irish Stew: Beeton gives two recipes for this dish, this one having proportionately more potato and onion to meat, and the other involving meat cut smaller and cooked for an hour before the rest of the ingredients are added. There are many debates still raging about the authentic Irish stew, but most authorities agree that it is essentially a *white* stew, so that carrots, for instance, are out of place.

180 *Roast Leg of Mutton*: this is the joint to which Alice is introduced at the Queens' dinner at the end of *Through the Looking Glass* (1872); a dinner which follows the bourgeois convention of soup, fish, joint, pudding, and which is served à la Russe (see note to p. 238), with the waiters bringing each dish in turn (and, indeed, removing them before Alice gets to taste any of them):

> 'You look a little shy; let me introduce you to that leg of mutton', said the Red Queen. 'Alice—Mutton; Mutton—Alice.' The leg of mutton got up in the dish and made a little bow to Alice; and she returned the bow, not knowing whether to be frightened or amused.
>
> 'May I give you a slice?' she said, taking up the knife and fork and looking from one Queen to the other.
>
> 'Certainly not', the Red Queen said, very decidedly: 'it isn't etiquette to cut any one you've been introduced to'.

181 *Roast Saddle of Mutton*: the accompanying picture of this joint, tail rampant, is yet another example of the Victorians' marked lack of squeamishness about meat consumption.

182 *To Dress a Sheep's Head*: the heads of animals were frequently eaten, with much ceremony about the consumption of the best bits: usually agreed to be the brains, tongue and palate, and—by some—the eyes. See also p. 209 for a discussion of the carving of a calf's head.

183 *Lamb Chops*: classic English food, particularly as a luncheon dish. One of the stalwarts of gentlemen's clubs of the Victorian and Edwardian eras.

184 *connoisseurs . . . housekeepers*: another example of Beeton's dismissal of fashionable attitudes in favour of economy and thrifty housewifely virtues. See Introduction for a discussion of her attitudes to class.

Although . . . cooked: Beeton again positions herself firmly on the side of middle-class taste rather than recommending the niceties of fashionable innovation.

188 *instead . . . existence*: yet another example of Beeton's opposition to cruelty in animal husbandry.

191 *RECIPES*: this chapter contains forty recipes, roughly half of which are for pork, with the rest covering ham and bacon.

To Cure . . . Way: Beeton produces a number of recipes for home-cures, reflecting the proportion of her readers who kept pigs, even in the industrialized mid-nineteenth century. She notes in the introductory chapter on pigs (in a section omitted from this edition) that there were an estimated 20 million plus pigs in Great Britain at this date—or almost one pig for each member of the population. Many working-class families, especially in rural areas, still relied on the pig for their main annual meat supply.

saltpetre: potassium nitrate, a white crystalline salty substance used to preserve meat; also a constituent of gunpowder.

192 *LORD BACON*: see note to p. 28.

193　*a common crust*: flour and water paste, usually used to seal in moisture, and not intended to be eaten.

194　*Pig's Pettitoes*: pig's trotters. Notably Beeton has omitted to include the main constituents of the dish in her ingredients list.

195　*Pork Pies*: a very old dish, with the earliest recorded recipes dating from the fourteenth century.

196　*To Scald . . . dates correctly*: the juxtaposition of this note and recipe is remarkable if Beeton does not intend to give the meat-eating reader pause.

200　*GENERAL . . . CALF*: Beeton presumably gives separate chapters on the calf because of the specific qualities of veal—and its ubiquity as a delicate and luxurious meat.

202　*RECIPES*: this chapter in the original contains 51 recipes, with a roughly equal distribution of a number of methods of cooking including baking, roasting, stewing, boiling, fricasseeing, currying, and braising. There are a number of recipes using minced veal and several for cutlets and collops (or escalopes, as we know them).

203　*In France . . . age*: it is notable that this situation is now reversed, in that Britain has more stringent laws on veal production than France.

204　*Veal à la Bourgeoise*: this title denotes the cooking of the French bourgeoisie, traditionally simple methods used on very good ingredients.

206　*When . . . things*: such anti-Puritan or Cromwellian sentiments were highly conventional at this date, though Beeton is not notably conservative in other principles.

207　*Minced . . . Macaroni*: the combination of ingredients is fairly authentically Italian, though the moulding and steaming is clearly an English addition.

208　*Veal and Ham Pie*: a traditional recipe, written versions of which exist at least as far back as the seventeenth century.

209　*phrenologist*: phrenology—the analysis of personality through the study of bumps on the head—was a fashionable neo-science in the eighteenth and nineteenth centuries.

211　*'manifested His handiwork'*: this section is particularly religious in tone.
　　　Each circumstance . . . into life: not traced.

212　*This . . . unlimited*: a typical statement of religious awe produced by the contemplation of nature. See Introduction for a discussion of Beeton's conflation of scientific and religious discourses.

213　*RECIPES*: this chapter contains 71 recipes in the original, with over half on chicken (or fowl) and duck. Goose, turkey, larks, pigeons, and wheatears are also covered, as is rabbit, which Beeton treats as an honorary bird without explanation—presumably because of the meat's resemblance to chicken.
　　　Chicken or Fowl Patties: the chicken, strictly speaking, is the young bird, the fowl (also the generic term for domestic birds in general) is

the adult of either sex, though Beeton usually designates the male as a cock.

215 *Boiled ... Chickens*: boiling was often used as a means of cooking old birds, as it gave tough meat time to soften.

216 *VARIOUS ... circumstances*: an indication of the age of battery farming methods, and also of Beeton's consistency in rejecting all inhumanity in the treatment of farmed animals—on grounds, as here, of quality as well as kindness.

218 *Roast Goose*: the traditional Christmas dish, though at this date in the process of being replaced by the turkey, partly because of the latter's greater size—see Beeton's note on turkey carving on pp. 225–6. It is a goose that the Cratchit family feast off in Scrooge's vision of Christmas Present in Dickens's *A Christmas Carol* (1843):

> There never was such a goose. Bob said he didn't believe there ever was such a goose cooked. Its tenderness and flavour, size and cheapness, were the themes of universal admiration. Eked out by apple-sauce and mashed potatoes, it was a sufficient dinner for the whole family; indeed, as Mrs Cratchit said with great delight (surveying one small atom of a bone upon the dish), they hadn't ate it all at last!

It is a turkey, however, that Scrooge gives the Cratchits when reformed by his ordeal: the prize turkey as big as the boy he sends to buy it from the poulterer's—a bird in no need of any eking out.

220 *Roast Larks*: it is now illegal to eat songbirds in this country, though not on the Continent.

221 *Epsom Grand-Stand Recipe*: see Introduction for discussions of Beeton's childhood on the racecourse. This is a rare reference to her unconventional personal history.

223 *merrythought*: wishbone.

224 *THE GUINEA-PIG*: this and the note that follows are intriguing inclusions in a cookery book as they discuss animals that are not for eating.

226 *A Christmas ... well*: see Introduction for a discussion of this passage.

227 *GENERAL ... GAME*: the attitude to hunting expressed in this chapter is nicely balanced between nostalgia for the nation's rural past and a modern contempt for the bestiality involved.

232 *RECIPES*: the original chapter has 35 recipes for game, covering blackcock, grouse, landrail, leveret, pheasant, plover, ptarmigan, quails, snipes, teal, widgeon, and woodcock; there are several recipes each for wild duck, partridge, hare, and venison. Roasting is the commonest method, with a number of recipes for hashes and pies to cope, presumably, with seasonal gluts of game and mixed bags.

234 *Salmi ... Partridges*: this is not the modern sense of a hash (usually recooked meat, cut up small, and fried with other ingredients), but rather

Beeton's attempt to find an English term for the French *salmis*—a piquant ragout of game characterized by the birds being first lightly roasted and then split or jointed and simmered in a rich brown sauce flavoured with wine.

235 *trail*: entrails.

237 *beak . . . wing*: sometimes this dish is prepared with the beak piercing the breast and legs like a skewer.

238 *The 'Grand Carver' . . . favourite*: the Russian mode of service at grand dinners involved each item of food being circulated on platters by servants who offered it to each diner in turn. In the course of the nineteenth century it gradually replaced the older form of service (à la français), where all the dishes for each stage of the meal were placed on the table at once, and diners helped themselves and their neighbours to those they desired. The introduction of service à la russe to Paris in the 1830s was credited to the Russian Prince Kourakin, and it gained in popularity in both France and Britain, becoming the norm by the 1880s. Mrs Beeton is ambivalent about the new method, as were many of her contemporaries. The advantage was that the food was served hotter, though the wait for all the components of a course to circulate tended to negate this achievement. The very wealthy welcomed the chance to dazzle with large number of attendants and a greater range of dishes, but regretted the lost chance to display their valuable porcelain and plate serving dishes. This passage indicates mild regret at the passing of some of the formalities of service à la français, but perhaps also a hint of the over-elaboration of the old-fashioned mode of dining.

where men-cooks are kept: it is not clear why only men cooks should be capable of removing a hare's backbone, particularly given the heavy labour routinely expected of the Victorian cook (stoking fires, lifting huge joints off spits, and so on). Presumably the art of boning is seen as one belonging to the profession of butchery, and therefore beyond women in a professional rather than a physical sense.

239 *Cowper*: see note to p. 10. The verse is from *The Task* (1785), Bk. 1, ll. 413–21.

Hogg: John Hogg (1800–69), classical scholar and naturalist; brother of Thomas Jefferson Hogg, the friend and biographer of Shelley.

240 *we cannot . . . animals*: it is rather curious to begin a chapter on vegetables by asserting the difficulty of clearly distinguishing them from animals: an example of Beeton's encyclopaedic and academic curiosity overcoming the logic of writing a cookery book.

Whilst . . . ton: a note nice for its abstractly educative qualities: few readers of a chapter of vegetable cooking can really have wanted to know about the natural and economic history of lichens.

242 *Some . . . Conquest*: this note reflects the intense Victorian preoccupation with the past, particularly in the awe it expresses at the mere fact of age (see Introduction).

243 *In the . . . tree*: typical of Beeton's rather unmediated use of scientific discourse: she is inclined simply to reproduce the language of her sources, rather than adjusting it to suit the education or purposes of her likely readers.

244 *RECIPES*: this chapter contains 96 recipes in the original, covering a remarkable range of vegetables. The cooking methods used are less various, with 25 recipes simply involving boiling. This seems to confirm all of the prejudices about Victorian vegetable cookery, but it is significant that the next largest category comprises various forms of foreign recipe, suggesting that Beeton's approach is squarely divided between convention and experimentation. The other popular method in the chapter is stewing. It is certainly true that Beeton recommends longer cooking times than we would use today, but this is perhaps partly to compensate for the fact that vegetables tended to be eaten older and larger than the perfect specimens available all year round in the modern supermarket.

Boiled Artichokes: notably Beeton does not include the usual modern advice about the necessity of removing the choke when eating artichokes. This may be because she expected her readers to be very familiar with the vegetable, which had been used a great deal in English cooking from medieval times until the Victorian period. For some reason they ceased to be much grown in English gardens between the world wars, and therefore became less familiar. (See Elisabeth Ayrton, *The Cookery of England* (1977), 347.)

Asparagus Peas: a curiously fiddly process of making asparagus resemble peas—the sort of fussed-with food typical of that served at the dinner-parties of the upwardly mobile. The technique of cutting asparagus into pea-sized pieces forms the basis also of the recipe that followed this in the original, for an asparagus pudding in which ham and asparagus peas are steamed with a batter of eggs, milk, and flour and then boiled in a pudding basin for two hours. It is this sort of recipe that led to the early twentieth-century conviction that Victorian cooking methods were death to the vitamins in vegetables. Eliza Acton made more sense of the asparagus–pea method by explaining that it 'is a convenient mode of dressing asparagus, when it is too small and green to make a good appearance plainly boiled', and she advises that only the tender points of the stems should be used.

245 *About ¼ hour to boil the beans*: a challenge to the prejudice discussed in the previous note: this method would result in tender but not mushy vegetables.

young and freshly gathered: another contradiction of the idea that the Victorians preferred their vegetables old and boiled to a mush.

246 *Boiled Cabbage*: a vegetable and a mode of cooking that epitomizes, in the popular imagination, all that was worst about the cooking of the Victorian era. In the 1920s, as some attempt was made to leave

this culinary heritage behind, it used to be said that 'the English have only three vegetables and two of them are cabbage'. Today we believe in cooking cabbage very briefly, in the minimum of water, to conserve its vitamins, its bright green colour, and some of its texture. This method also has the advantage of minimizing smells (which are caused by the release of chemicals including hydrogen sulphide—which smells like rotten eggs—as the cell walls of the vegetable break down). The longer-boiled cabbage of Beeton's day produced that powerful aroma with which many of us are familiar from canteens and school dinners: the attempted solution was the small piece of soda added to the water.

247 *Cauliflowers with Parmesan Cheese*: a traditional dish, usually given in eighteenth- and nineteenth-century cookery books with either English cheeses (probably Cheddar) or no particular cheese specified. Parmesan had long been known in England, and was imported in fairly large quantities. (See Beeton's own description on p. 321.)

248 *To Dress Cucumbers*: see note to p. 125.

250 *Boiled Green Peas*: as Beeton's enthusiasm suggests, peas were highly prized in this period, partly as a result of their short natural season. In Elizabeth Gaskell's *Cranford* (1852–3), her elegiac account of life in an old-fashioned small town, there is an amusing scene reflecting both the desirability of peas and the practical difficulties of eating them, when the narrator accompanies two elderly ladies to pay a visit to an old bachelor:

> When the ducks and green peas came, we looked at each other in dismay; we had only two-pronged, black-handled forks. It is true, the steel was as bright as silver; but what were we to do? Miss Matty picked up her peas, one by one, on the point of the prongs, much as Aminé ate her grains after her previous feast with the Ghoul. Miss Pole sighed over her delicate young peas as she left them on one side of her plate untasted; for they *would* drop between the prongs. I looked at my host; the peas were going wholesale into his capacious mouth, shovelled up by his large round-ended knife. I saw, I imitated, I survived! My friends, in spite of my precedent, could not muster up courage enough to do an ungenteel thing; and, if Mr Holbrook had not been so heartily hungry, he would probably have seen that the good peas went away almost untouched. (Penguin edn., pp. 74–5)

251 *In Ireland . . . so*: true, of course, since much of the diet of the ordinary Irish consisted of potatoes, which they developed numerous ingenious ways of cooking, but it is unusual for an English cookery book to give them credit for such culinary achievements.

252 *a silver knife*: a steel knife was thought to brown and bruise the lettuce.

253 *has become . . . art*: despite this assertion, it is worth noting that Beeton gives only three recipes for tomato-based dishes (one baked, two stewed),

and four (not included in this edition) in Chapter X for tomato sauces, out of a total of 135. If we compare this with our own wide culinary usage of tomatoes, the change is marked.

254 *To Dress Truffles with Champagne*: one of the most conspicuously expensive dishes in the book. The fact that Beeton does not give a price for the dish, instead noting that truffles are not often bought in this country, suggests that this is really a fantasy recipe, of the sort that could be enjoyed once the social ladder had been scaled to its acme.

256 *William Cobbett . . . on it*: it was given in *A Treatise of Cobbett's Corn* (1828), one of a number of means Cobbett (1763–1835) used to popularize Indian corn in England (including lending it his own name). Beeton's omissions of any instructions on how to eat a whole ear of corn elegantly suggests that she had not tried the experiment herself.

258 *hasty pudding*: see note to p. 64.

However . . . abundance: a nice summation of the hearty nature of Victorian tastes.

262 *RECIPES*: there are 179 recipes in this chapter, making it the largest single chapter (though, of course, the various meat chapters add up to a greater number of recipes on meat in general). This reflects the Victorian devotion to these hearty, flour-based dishes. It is notable that, as with the chapter on sauces, the arrangement here is dictated by the needs of the cook, rather than the mistress, with sweet and savoury pies and puddings jumbled heterogeneously together.

Very Good Puff-Paste: Beeton also gives recipes for medium and common puff-paste, and for a French puff-paste that is enriched with egg yolks. She also gives a number of shortcrust recipes.

263 *Common . . . Pies*: also known as hot-water paste; the hot water allows the paste to remain malleable so that it can be moulded into elaborate shapes. Its form is more significant than its flavour, as Beeton's comment indicates. The principle of enclosing a meat mixture—often finely chopped—in a paste of this sort goes back to the medieval 'coffyns' of pastry which pre-dated metal or earthenware containers for baking.

Almond Cheesecakes: this is cheesecakes in the old-fashioned British sense—not the American variety made from cream cheese and crumbled cookies. The original cheesecakes were pastry cases containing a mixture of curd cheese, sugar, eggs, and flavourings, but in some cases the curd was replaced by other ingredients, like the almonds in this instance.

264 *Boiled Apple Dumplings*: a very traditional pudding, included in this abridgement for the entertaining notion of knitting cloths in which to boil the puddings. Beeton presumably takes the idea from Acton, who in 1845 called her version of this dish 'Fashionable Apple Dumplings'.

Creamed Apple Tart: in the previous recipe, which she directs the reader to follow up to a certain stage in this case, Beeton has used the words 'pie' and 'tart' as interchangeable, and given directions for producing a covered pie. Here, part of the top is removed after baking to give something resembling the open-faced pastry we call a tart today.

265 *Bakewell Pudding*: now usually known as Bakewell Tart, though Beeton's name is the older.

266 *This . . . favourite*: in *Mr and Mrs Beeton* (1951), H. Montgomery Hyde quotes Isabella's sister Lucy: 'Different people gave their recipes for the book. That for Baroness Pudding (a suet pudding with a plethora of raisins) was given by the Baroness de Tessier who lived in Epsom' (p. 31).

267 *Boiled Bread Pudding*: this is quite a rich recipe; that which preceded it—for 'Very Plain Bread Pudding' was truer to the origins of the dish as an economical way of using up stale bread, but was so plain as to be virtually inedible: it took 'odd pieces of crust or crumb of bread' and soaked them in boiling water before mixing with nutmeg and a small amount of sugar and butter. The only extravagance was the use of ½ lb. of currants. Even Beeton is hesitant about the recipe, remarking that 'boiling milk substituted for the boiling water would very much improve this pudding'.

268 *Canary Pudding*: presumably so called for its yellow colour, this pudding traditionally involves the unusual method of using eggs as weights to measure the rest of the ingredients.

College Puddings: so called because they were traditionally served to the poor scholars of the ancient universities on feast days. They are sometimes baked, but Dorothy Hartley notes in *Food in England* (1954) that the tradition of frying dishes called college puddings (rather like doughnuts) dates back to the Middle Ages. When baked, college puddings are similar to castle puddings, but the latter (intended originally for the aristocracy) are lighter and richer because made with butter rather than suet. (See also Ayrton, *The Cookery of England*, 433.)

Baked Custard Pudding: a dish dating back to medieval times. Jane Grigson notes that a version was served at the coronation of Henry IV (see *English Food*, 237).

270 *Dampfnudeln . . . Puddings*: literally 'steamed noodles', this is a curious dish of baked yeast dumplings, typical in ingredients and approach of much of the food of Northern Europe. This may well be a recipe Beeton acquired during her time in Germany.

271 *Half-Pay Pudding*: an intriguing name. Half-pay was the allowance paid to an army officer when retired or not on active service, so the name presumably suggests an economical pudding to be eaten during periods of temporary financial embarrassment. The treacle, rather than sugar, is a decided economy.

Herodotus Pudding: Beeton borrows this from Acton, who appends the following note to her recipe, which she calls 'a Genuine Classical Receipt':

This recipe is really to be found in Herodotus. The only variations made in it are the substitution of sugar for honey, and sherry for the wine of Ancient Greece. We are indebted for it to an ancient scholar, who had it served at his own table on more than one occasion; and we have given it on his authority, without testing it: but we venture to suggest that *seven* hours would boil it quite sufficiently. (p. 344)

The point on timing refers to the original recipe, which calls for fourteen hours boiling. In her version, Beeton shortens even Acton's 7 hours to 5. Acton had included raisins and figs, which Beeton replaces with a larger quantity of figs alone; Acton also included two wineglasses of sherry: Beeton's wine sauce may be to compensate for this omission.

272 *MACARONI. . . soups*: an intriguingly detailed note, which works to counter our assumption that the British only became knowledgeable about Italian foods after the Second World War.

Mincemeat: the name originated in the Middle Ages, when recipes included finely chopped lean beef or mutton. At this time the distinction between sweet and savoury dishes was not as marked as it later became, and many sweet dishes contained meat (another example is blancmange, twelfth-century recipes for which contain chicken). (See Ayrton, *The Cookery of England*, 23–4.)

273 *Monday's Pudding*: according to Elisabeth Ayrton, this version of the various methods of using up left-over plum-pudding originates from Devon.

274 *Pease Pudding*: an example, as discussed in the note to p. 262, of a savoury dish inserted into a chapter predominantly concerned with sweet dishes.

An Unrivalled Plum-Pudding: the superlative distinguishes this from the previous 'excellent plum-pudding'. This recipe is in fact rather richer than the Christmas plum-pudding recipe Beeton gives slightly later, having more fruit, and nuts and spices not in the Christmas recipe. The most significant difference is that the latter includes no sugar—perhaps a vestige of its origin in the sweet-savoury dishes of the medieval period, when Christmas pudding, like mincemeat, contained meat (see note to p. 272).

275 *Plum Tart*: another traditional dish; perhaps the 'Christmas pie' from which Jack Horner pulled a plum.

276 *Potato Pasty*: a curious inclusion in this chapter as it would have seemed more at home in the meat or vegetable chapters; its position was perhaps suggested by the term 'pasty' which more usually refers to a pastry turnover. The existence of a special mould for the dish indicates that it was quite common, and Eliza Acton also includes it in her chapter on pastry, with the comment that it is a good family dish, and further suggestions for fillings including chicken, veal and oysters, pork chops, salmon and shrimps, salt fish, and so on. It is presumably the forerunner

of our own shepherd's and fish pies. The special dish, which would prevent the mashed potato dissolving into the sauce, appears to be a useful, if fiddly, innovation.

276 *Raised . . . Ham*: different from the recipe given on p. 208: this is the classic filling for a raised pie and a more elaborate and more solid dish than the pie based on puff pastry. The latter is an elegant supportive dish for a large dinner; this, as Beeton notes, is a centrepiece dish for more casual meals.

277 *beef marrow*: the marrow is an unusual addition, added for richness— more conventional recipes use cream.

278 *Boiled . . . Curries &c.*: note the very clear, detailed instructions; also the familiarity with curry that this implies (see the Introduction for a discussion of Anglo-Indian importations).

Lemon . . . Puddings: one of ten sweet-pudding sauces Beeton gives. The sauce was an essential accompaniment to the dense puddings, and many puddings were traditionally paired with a particular sauce.

279 *We . . . dinner*: because of its very economical nature.

282 *Liebig*: Justus, Baron von Liebig (1803–73), was a German chemist who made a major contribution to agricultural chemistry, and discovered chloroform and chloral.

284 *RECIPES*: this chapter contains 97 recipes in the original, covering a wide range of the sort of light sweet dishes that would tend to be selected by ladies at a dinner. Gentlemen would choose the heavier puddings given in the previous chapter or, more stylishly, refrain altogether and instead take the savoury that followed. Savoury dishes—mostly omelettes—are also placed in this chapter, on the basis, it seems, of similar cooking methods. It is notable that many of these dishes, especially the creams, trifles, soufflés, and so on, seem very familiar to us— they have survived because they suit the modern taste for light yet rich foods better than heavy suet puddings. Elisabeth Ayrton comments that such dishes were one of the chief glories of the English culinary tradition; descended from aristocratic tables, 'they were intended for royal and noble feasts where the feasters had already had their fill and more. Only the smoothest, softest cream, the most totteringly delicious jelly could tempt them' (*The Cookery of England*, p. 460).

Flanc . . . Crust: flanc is another word for flan; the raised crust is not the moulded hot-water paste usually known by this name, but a short crust flan case of the type with which we are familiar today. From the complexity of Beeton's description of the lining of the mould, and her offer of a simpler alternative, we can assume that this method was relatively unfamiliar at this date. In fact, the shallow flan tins of today may well have been developed to deal with the difficulties of lining a deep mould as she describes. The flour weighs down the pastry case to prevent it rising as it is 'baked blind' (that is, empty)—today baking beans would be used, with the advantage that, unlike flour, they do not scorch.

285   *Apple Fritters*: one of ten fritter recipes given.

286   *gallipot*: a small pot of earthenware or—as here—metal, used traditionally for ointments and so on. The term probably comes from the ships' galleys in which such pots were originally transported from the Mediterranean. In this recipe the pot serves the same role as the centre of a ring mould—to leave a space in the middle of the cooked rice to be filled with the sauce.

Blanc-mange: another very old dish—clearly originally French, but known in England since the Middle Ages. Beeton also gives a recipe for what she calls 'jaunemange', which is coloured yellow with egg yolks, which replace the cream in the blancmange.

287   *1s. 8d.*: in the brief list of errata included in the first edition, the price was corrected to 3*s.* 3*d.* Similarly, '1*s.* 6*d.*' on p. 291 (Charlotte Russe) was corrected to 2*s.*; '3*s.*' on p. 292 (Chocolate Cream) was corrected to 4*s.* 6*d.*; '2*s.* 3*d.*' on p. 292 (Ginger Cream) was corrected to 3*s.* 6*d.*

Bread-and-Butter: the hyphens are indicative of the significance of buttered bread as a food item in its own right for the Victorians. It was a fixture particularly at tea, when generations of children were required to eat several slices of bread-and-butter before being allowed the more enticing cakes. Lewis Carroll's Bread-and-butter fly is a creature of tea-time: 'its wings are thin slices of bread-and-butter, its body is a crust, and its head is a lump of sugar' and it lives on 'weak tea with cream in it' (*Through the Looking-Glass* (1872)). Because bread was buttered in advance (in fact each slice was usually buttered before being cut from the loaf to prevent the tearing of delicate slices when spreading), too much was often prepared, and bread-and-butter fritters (and bread-and-butter pudding) are designed to deal with the left-overs.

293   *Italian Cream*: this rich jellied custard is a version of that currently fashionable Italian sweet, panna cotta (cooked cream).

Jelly . . . Colours: an elaborate preparation to produce an architecturally spectacular dessert to decorate the dinner table or the supper table at a ball.

294   *To Make . . . Omelet*: the difficulty of describing the act of making an omelette is indicated by the order in which Beeton arranges her points—the crucial information about the size and thickness of the pan and the heat of the fire are added as afterthoughts, rather than placed at the beginning. An amusing scene in Wilkie Collins's sensation novel *No Name* (1863) elaborates on this problem, when the pathetic giantess Mrs Wragge is found weeping over a cookery book as she tries to cook dinner for her demanding husband:

'As sure as ever I sit down to this book, the Buzzing in my head begins again. Who's to make it all out? Sometimes I think I've got it, and it all goes away from me. Sometimes, I think I haven't got it, and it all comes back in a heap. Look here! Here's what he's ordered for his breakfast tomorrow:—"Omelette with Herbs. Beat up two eggs with a little water or milk, salt, pepper, chives, and parsley. Mince small."—There! mince small! How am I to mince small, when it's all mixed up and running? "Put a piece of butter the size of your thumb into the frying pan."—Look at my thumb, and look at yours! Whose size does she mean? "Boil, but not brown."—If it mustn't be brown, what colour must it be? She won't tell me; she expects me to know, and I don't. "Pour in the omelette."—There! I can do that. "Allow it to set, raise it round the edge; when done, turn it over to double it."—Oh, the numbers of times I turned it over and doubled it in my head, before you came in to-night! "Keep it soft; put the dish over the frying-pan, and turn it over." Which am I to turn over—oh mercy, try the cold towel again, and tell me which—the dish or the frying pan?" ... oh, the lots of omelettes all frying together in my head; and all frying wrong.' (Oxford World's Classics edn., pp. 149–50)

296 *Pears à l'Allemande*: in the French lexicon of culinary terms, pears are German if they are stewed.

297 *Snow . . . Neige*: sometimes also called floating islands.

298 *milk into it*: i.e. milk the cow into the bowl. Not a possibility for most nineteenth-century urban dwellers, which is why Beeton offers the alternative of pouring warmed milk from a height to produce the requisite froth.

300 *PRESERVES*: in rural districts, the practice of preserving meats, fruits, and vegetables for use throughout the year was a fundamental element of life. For the new urban middle class who are Beeton's main readership, this tradition was becoming rapidly less significant as more and more food was industrially preserved (see discussion in the Introduction).

302 *DESSERT DISHES*: dessert was served after the meal proper—all dishes and the tablecloths were removed, and the ornamental dessert dishes arranged on the highly polished mahogany table. As Beeton's emphasis in this section suggests, the purpose of the dessert was more display than the gratification of appetites presumably already fully sated.

304 *ice-house*: a covered pit, in which large blocks of ice could be kept cool throughout the summer. Only the grandest houses had ice-houses in their grounds, so these recipes are beyond the reach of most of Beeton's readers.

305 *the instigator . . . St Bartholomew*: Catherine de' Medici plotted to have the Huguenots (a Protestant sect) of Paris killed, leading to the St Bartholomew Massacre, in which, it is believed, 25,000 people were killed between 24 August and 17 September 1572.

306 *RECIPES*: there are 84 recipes in the original chapter, covering jams, jellies, compotes, fruit cheeses, ices, marmalades, toffees, fruits prepared in alchohol, and sundry other fruit and dessert dishes.

Compotes: a compote is a dish of fruits cooked in syrup, but not long enough to preserve them.

307 *Carrot . . . Preserve*: a highly economical 'substitute' recipe, of the type that was to become extremely well-known during the Second World War.

308 *Damson Cheese*: fruit cheeses are boiled until little moisture remains, and the mixture dries to somewhere between the consistency of a jelly and a leather. They have become fashionable again recently, and are often served to accompany actual cheese, as in the Spanish tradition of pairing cheese with quince paste.

311 *Orange Marmalade*: one of three recipes given.

312 *English*: grown in glasshouses.

315 *Zests . . . biscuits*: such savouries were more usually served after the pudding and before the dessert. Beeton gives recipes for a number of such dishes in the 'Milk, Butter, Cheese, and Eggs' chapter which follows.

316 *French Plums*: crystallized: the sugar plums of the Nutcracker Suite's Fairy.

318 *GENERAL . . . EGGS*: this chapter exhibits a tone of nostalgia for a lost rural life, typified by the picture at its head.

320 *red lead*: a compound of lead used as a pigment. Like lead itself, it is poisonous when ingested. The adulteration of food was a scandal in this period, though in fact the practice had been followed by many providers of food since at least Classical times (it continues, of course, today). In the Victorian period alum and chalk were often added to bread to whiten it, and various substances added to milk and beer to render them more palatable or to stretch them further (see Beeton's own note to p. 324). Tobias Smollett's country squire, Matthew Bramble, had famously complained of such outrages in the 1771 novel, *The Expedition of Humphry Clinker*:

> The bread I eat in London, is a deleterious paste, mixed up with chalk, alum, and bone-ashes; insipid to the taste, and destructive to the constitution. The good people are not ignorant of this adulteration; but they prefer it to wholesome bread, because it is whiter then the meal of corn [wheat]: thus they sacrifice their taste and their health, and the lives of their tender infants, to a most absurd gratification of a misjudging eye; and the miller, or the baker, is obliged to poison them and their families, in order to live by his profession. . . . they insist on having the complexion of their pot herbs mended, even at the hazard of their lives. Perhaps you will hardly believe they can be so mad as to boil their greens with a brass halfpence, in order to improve their colour; and yet nothing is more true. . . . [Milk is] the produce of faded cabbage leaves and sour draff, lowered with hot water, frothed with bruised snails, carried through the streets in open pails. . . . the tallowy rancid mass, called butter, is manufactured with candle-grease

and kitchen stuff. . . . Now, all these enormities might be remedied with a very little attention to the article of police, or civil regulation; but the wise patriots of London have taken it into their heads, that all regulation is inconsistent with liberty. (Penguin edn., pp. 152–4)

324 *Curds and Whey*: eaten as a pudding, particularly by children. The milk separates into solids (curds) and liquids (whey). Whey is also known as buttermilk (that is, the milk left over from the butter-making process).

To . . . Butter: butter was salted to preserve it longer. Beeton's lengthy discussion of the treatment of this basic household comestible reminds us of the complications of life before refrigeration.

325 *The woman . . . sauces*: 'leech' presumably means 'medical practitioner', so Beeton's comment refers back to the old tradition of women having a basic knowledge of the medicinal power of herbs, and suggests that the modern doctor can be avoided if rancid or adulterated food is shunned. The connection of women with innocent sauces (and, by implication, with guilty ones) is Old Testament in its associations.

326 *Mode . . . Cheese*: cheese was usually served as a cheese course after luncheon; it was replaced by a savoury (which often involved cooked cheese) after dinner.

carefully scraped: to remove dry portions and surface mould.

327 *celebrated gourmand*: Brillat-Savarin, see note to p. 118.

Cheese Sandwiches: a forerunner of the modern-day toasted cheese sandwich.

CHEESE . . . time: it is unclear why cheese is fit only for the sedentary or the very active: perhaps the sedentary are presumed to be so immobile that the deleterious consequences of eating cheese could hardly affect them more. The passage makes more sense if the comma after 'people' is disregarded.

328 *salamander*: an iron grill, put into the fire to get red hot and then held over cooked dishes to brown their tops. The name derives from the legend that the salamander can survive in fire.

Toasted . . . Rare-bit: before the invention of the overhead grill, bread was toasted on forks held before the fire, and cheese was toasted separately in a dish and then spread on the toasted bread. Food historians now tend to agree that the original name for such ancient dishes of toasted cheese is 'rabbit', later writers, such as Beeton, assumed that this name must be a corruption, and substituted 'rare-bit'. The 'rabbit' is invariably associated with a national identity—usually Welsh—and almost certainly represents an English joke at neighbours who were assumed to be too poor to afford game, and had to substitute cheese instead.

329 *Scotch Woodcock*: a famous English savoury, probably named on the principle of Welsh rabbit (see previous note).

332 *In order . . . success*: yet again, Beeton sets herself against fashion and in

favour of nutrition, advancing just the arguments in favour of wholemeal bread that were again mounted this century.

333 *AËRATED . . . labour*: the method by which the modern pre-packaged loaf is still made today. Although opposed to the adulteration and denaturing of food, Beeton is a child of the industrial age, and is usually impressed by the time-saving its processes afford in the production of food.

334 *Since . . . described*: see previous note.

335 *RECIPES*: there are 63 recipes in the original chapter: 18 for breads, 15 for biscuits, 30 for cakes, and 2 for icings. The breads include rice bread, Indian-corn-flour bread, and soda bread as well as the standard wholemeal loaf and a number of plain buns and rusks. The biscuits are Victorian classics—ratafias, macaroons, rock, and Savoy biscuits—while the cakes are mostly solid 'keeping' cakes—fruit and pound cake mixtures with plenty of butter to stabilize the cakes (the light sponges with which we are more familiar today appear not in this chapter but in the earlier one on creams, whips, and so on). Bread, biscuits, and cakes of this sort were eaten almost exclusively at teatime (except for some breads at breakfast)—a meal that had increasing social significance in the period.

German yeast: a form of compressed yeast that was newly available in England at the time Beeton was writing. It was advertised as more stable than the old barm-type liquid yeast, though Elizabeth David argues (in *English Bread and Yeast Cookery*, 1977), that in the absence of refrigerators its keeping qualities were little better than the barms.

337 *A loaf . . . dish*: modern pop-up toast buttered and laid flat in this way would soon be unpleasantly soggy, but toast made before the fire has a very different consistency. The practice of putting butter on the toast while at its hottest was partly to alleviate the brittleness acquired by such toast as it cools.

Muffins: Beeton's next recipe, not included here, is for crumpets. Muffins and crumpets were invariably associated and were usually served together at teatime. They are made from similar ingredients, but while muffins are formed from a stiff dough, that for crumpets is thinned to a batter, which causes the air bubbles which give the characteristic holes and spongy texture. Elizabeth David notes (in her 1977 *English Bread and Yeast Cookery*) that the contemporary slang meaning of 'crumpet' as a sexually available or attractive girl was in the nineteenth century attached to 'muffin'. Henry Mayhew had a famous account in his *London Labour and the London Poor* (1851) of the muffin men who used to sell muffins and crumpets door to door:

> I did not hear of any street-seller who made the muffins or crumpets he vended. Indeed, he could not make the small quantity required, so as to be remunerative. The muffins are bought off the bakers, and at prices to leave a profit of 4*d.* in 1*s.* . . . . The muffin man carries his delicacies in a basket, well swathed in flannel, to retain the heat: 'People likes them warm, sir', an old man told me, 'to satisfy them

they're fresh, and they almost always *are* fresh; but it can't matter so much about their being warm, as they have to be toasted again. I only wish butter was a sight cheaper, and that would make the muffins go. Butter's half the battle . . . My best customers is genteel houses, 'cause I sells a genteel thing. I like wet days best, 'cause there's werry respectable ladies what don't keep a servant, and they buys to save themselves going out. We're a great convenience to the ladies sir—a great convenience to them as likes a slap-up tea.'

338 *If the cakes . . . ingredients*: she means, add more white of egg to the remaining raw ingredients, not to the cooked biscuits: since the recipe would make a large quantity of biscuits they would be baked in batches, allowing the ingredients to be adjusted to iron out faults in the first batch (more almonds can also be added if the mixture is too soft and so spreads too far). The suggestion, at the end of the recipe, that the reader might as well buy the macaroons from a shop is intriguingly self-defeating.

Rock Biscuits: so called for their appearance, not their texture.

Savoy . . . Cakes: what we know—in their commercially produced form—as sponge fingers.

339 *Rich Bride*: the wedding-cake was known as a bride cake because previously there had also been a groom's cake. This tradition still persists in America, where the groom's cake is usually the rich fruit cake with which we are familiar, and the bride's cake is a lighter sponge.

341 *Sunderland . . . Nuts*: this is one of four gingerbread recipes Beeton gives: gingerbread is one of the earliest-known forms of cake.

Pound Cake: so called because it involves a pound each of butter, sugar, and flour (though Beeton adds a little more flour).

A glass . . . it: if the wine is Madeira, this makes the famous Madeira cake.

342 *A Very . . . Seed-Cake*: seed cake was extremely popular from the sixteenth to the nineteenth centuries, but fell radically out of favour after the First World War. It has a strong scented taste from the caraway seeds which many people dislike—a fact that Mrs Gaskell elaborated on in her portrait of the penny-pinching Mrs Jamieson in *Cranford* (1853):

The tea-tray was abundantly loaded. I was pleased to see it, I was so hungry; but I was afraid the ladies present might think it vulgarly heaped up. I know they would have done at their own houses; but somehow the heaps disappeared here. I saw Mrs Jamieson eating seed-cake, slowly and considerately, as she did everything; and I was rather surprised, for I knew she had told us, on the occasion of her last party, that she never had it in her house, it reminded her so much of scented soap. She always gave us Savoy biscuits. However, Mrs Jamieson was kindly indulgent to Miss Barker's want of knowledge of the customs of high life; and, to spare her feelings, ate three large pieces of seed-cake, with a placid, ruminating expression of countenance, not unlike a cow's. (Penguin edn., p. 111)

344 *To Toast Tea-Cakes*: this sort of large tea-cake, split horizontally, toasted and buttered, then piled up and sliced like a cake, is often known as a Sally Lunn, after an eighteenth-century street-seller (though some authorities think it is a corruption of the French for 'sun and moon' cake: presumably to describe the cutting into spheres and then crescent-like wedges).

349 *RECIPES*: this chapter contains 34 recipes in the original.

351 *To Make Tea*: the tea-making ceremony was a significant one for Victorian ladies, whose delicacy of hand in performing this task was a mark of social distinction. Mary Elizabeth Braddon represents tea-making, with heavy irony, as a form of delicate feminine witchcraft in her enormously popular sensation novel *Lady Audley's Secret* (1862):

> Surely a pretty woman never looks prettier than when making tea. The most feminine and most domestic of all occupations imparts a magic harmony to her every movement, a witchery to her every glance. The floating mists from the boiling liquid in which she infuses the soothing herbs, whose secrets are known to her alone, envelop her in a cloud of scented vapour, through which she seems a social fairy, weaving potent spells with Gunpowder and Bohea. At the tea-table she reigns omnipotent, unapproachable. What do men know of the mysterious beverage? Read how poor Hazlitt made his tea, and shudder at the dreadful barbarism. How clumsily the wretched creatures attempt to assist the witch president of the tea-tray; how hopelessly they hold the kettle, how continually they imperil the frail cups and saucers, or the taper hands of the priestess. To do away with the tea-table is to rob woman of her legitimate empire. To send a couple of hulking men amongst your visitors, distributing a mixture made in the housekeeper's room, is to reduce the most social and friendly of ceremonies to a formal giving out of rations. Better the pretty influence of the tea-cups and saucers gracefully wielded in a woman's hand, than all the inappropriate power snatched at the point of the pen from the unwilling sterner sex. (Oxford World's Classics edn., pp. 222-3)

352 *Cowslip Wine*: another old English classic, probably of only nostalgic value to most of Beeton's urban readership.

Raspberry Vinegar: also an old recipe, despite its brief vogue in the 1980s.

353 *Claret-Cup*: used for drinking toasts.

354 *To Make Hot Punch*: Mr Micawber follows a very similar recipe when he makes punch for the assembled company in David Copperfield's lodging room:

> To divert his thoughts from this melancholy subject, I informed Mr

Micawber that I relied upon him for a bowl of punch, and led him to the lemons. His recent despondency, not to say despair, was gone in a moment. I never saw a man so thoroughly enjoy himself amid the fragrance of lemon-peel and sugar, the odour of burning rum, and the steam of boiling water, as Mr Micawber did that afternoon. It was wonderful to see his face shining at us out of a thin cloud of these delicate fumes, as he stirred, and mixed, and tasted, and looked as if he were making, instead of punch, a fortune for his family down to the latest posterity. (*David Copperfield* (1849–50), Penguin edn., p. 473)

359 *RECIPES*: this is a short chapter, containing 21 recipes, mainly for gruels, broths, and jellies. It is considerably influenced by the ideas of Florence Nightingale, as expressed in her classic *Notes on Nursing* (1859). Nightingale, another iconic Victorian woman, bears comparison with Beeton, since both made their careers and reputations by professionalizing the dominant ideology of female domestic service. Though neither stepped far outside the terms of that ideology, both succeeded in considerably extending the responsibilities and possibilities of women's lives.

360 *Gruel*: basically, a very thin porridge. It is gruel, of course, that Dickens's Oliver Twist begs for more of; it is mutton broth (see next recipe) that revives him when he is taken in by Mr Brownlow.

361 *To Make Toast-and-Water*: a strange dish, in which the toast would turn to a jelly. It is not clear why toast was considered suitable for invalids.

362 *Toast Sandwiches*: a very curious concoction.

363 *M. Brillat Savarin*: see note to p. 118. The account Beeton refers to can be found on pp. 243–4 in the 1970 Penguin translation.

'*Their table . . . on dinner*': from *Don Juan* (1819–24), Canto XIII, stanza 99.

364 '*The mind . . . of nature*': as above, Canto XV, stanza 69.

Thackeray's . . . of hers: *The Book of Snobs* (1846–7), ch. XXXIV: 'Snobs and Marriage'.

'*And Eve . . . and odours*': *Paradise Lost*, v. 303–6, 331–6, 346, 347–8.

365 '*There by the bedside . . . Lebanon*': 'The Eve of St Agnes' (1820), stanza xxix, lines 253–6, stanza xxx, lines 264–70.

'*There . . . injellied*': 'Audley Court' (1842), lines 19–25.

'*feast . . . soul*': Alexander Pope (1688–1744), *Imitations of Horace*, Book II, Satire I (1733), *To Mr Fortescue*, ll. 127–8: 'There St John mingle with my friendly bowl | The feast of reason and the flow of soul.'

General Napier: Charles James Napier (1782–1853), British general who conquered Sind in India (now a province of Pakistan) between 1841 and 1843 with a very small force, and governed it until 1847.

366 *Douglas Jerrold*: (1803–57), playwright, *Punch* contributor, and friend of

Charles Dickens. 'If an earthquake were to engulf England to-morrow, the English would manage to meet and dine somewhere among the rubbish, just to celebrate the event.'

heterae: courtesans or mistresses, who often took the role of society hostesses.

368 *'It has been said . . . liqueurs'*: all the aphorisms in these paragraphs are derived from Brillat-Savarin. They can be found on pp. 13 and 166 in the Penguin translation. See also note to p. 118.

BILLS OF FARE: there are 111 bills in the original, arranged in a month-by month sequence, with dinners for 18, 12, 10, 8, and 6 people, and two weekly sequences of 'Plain Family Dinners' for each month. At the end there are also lavish ball suppers, a game dinner, and dinners à la Russe. This extravagance is countered by the fact that the dinners for six are assumed to be the most useful bills, with at least four given for each month. The menus are not 'balanced' in any way we would understand: ingredients frequently appear several times in the same meal because diners were not expected to partake of every dish. Certain dishes crop up with excessive frequency throughout the year—Nesslerode pudding is particularly ubiquitous. These menus testify to the continuation of a strong seasonal tradition in cooking into this period, despite the increasing availability of tinned, bottled, and hot-house foods: so, the spring menus make the most of seasonal specialities such as salmon, and ducklings and green peas are celebrated by appearing in several courses in menus for June.

369 *Several . . . chapter*: these are relegated to the end—a clear indication that Beeton remains ambivalent about this new mode of service.

Plain . . . January: the interest in these ordinary weekly menus lies in the ingenuity by which ingredients are re-used throughout the week. Although these meals are substantial, they are certainly plain compared to the festal dishes given in the other menus. The standard three courses are presented as the bourgeois norm, and it is notable that on occasions (for instance Thursday in this list) a savoury replaces the pudding (when macaroni is intended as a pudding, Beeton calls it 'sweet macaroni').

390 *BREAKFASTS*: the relative significance of meals to the Victorians is very clearly signalled by the fact that Beeton devotes 109 pages to dinners, and half a page each to breakfasts, and lunches and suppers together. Breakfast is a very substantial, meat-based meal, but Beeton gives no indication of how many of these dishes would be provided for a typical meal.

LUNCHEONS AND SUPPERS: both meals were substantially affected by the shifting time of the dinner. Dinner during the late eighteenth and nineteenth centuries could take place anywhere between 12 noon and late in the evening, but with the tendency towards later dining between six and nine p.m. When dinner was eaten in the early afternoon, luncheon was unnecessary and a late supper would be eaten in the evening; when dinner moved towards the evening, luncheon became more significant, and supper dwindled in importance.

392 *DOMESTIC SERVANTS*: this chapter is long (64 pages in the original), but it has been retained in its entirety because of the many fascinating social details it affords. Much of the material in this chapter was derived from Samuel and Sarah Adams's *The Complete Servant* (1825), and other similar guides. The Adamses are interesting figures as they had both spent their lives in domestic service, and so wrote about it from a position of intimate acquaintance. Their book is directed mainly to the interests of servants themselves, rather than their employers, while Beeton, as discussed in the Introduction, has intriguingly shifting sympathies, with her address oscillating between servant and mistress, sometimes in the course of a single paragraph.

façon dé parler: way of speaking.

393 *This . . . exception*: see Introduction.

394 *slips*: table coverings, usually placed over the main tablecloth and removed for the service of dessert. In the past it had been the practice to remove all table coverings for dessert, so that the fine wood of the dining table could be admired. Beeton remarks on this practice as old fashioned; the keeping of a cloth for dessert tallies with the mid-Victorian preference for covering as much of their furniture as possible.

395 *wine in wood*: wine in casks, where the sediment needs removing before bottling.

397 *finds himself*: supplies for himself.

jean: twilled cotton cloth (from which the modern 'jeans' derives).

Top boots: boots with top portion made of a different colour or material.

398 *rottenstone*: decomposed siliceous limestone used as polishing powder.

sal ammoniac: salts of ammonia.

403 *The footman . . . walks out*: note the repetition of material already covered at the beginning of this section—evidence of hasty editing or transcription from another source.

404 *Caleb Balderstone*: a character in Scott's *The Bride of Lammermoor* (1819), Caleb Balderstone is the old butler comically determined to uphold the dignity of the family he serves.

405 *The writer . . . him*: further evidence that Beeton has failed to disguise her use of source documents.

412 *Carriages*: this section was set in smaller type in the original edition—an error, as it is the start of a new subject which continues in the following paragraphs.

a valuable . . . furniture: to the extent that few middle-class families possessed them. The carriage and horses discussed in this section are the possessions of 'gentlemen's' families, as Beeton explains on p. 393.

414 *The writer*: see note to p. 398.

416 *saith the proverb*: actually Mme Cornuel (1605–94)

419 *one . . . station*: because cheaply manufactured silks and cottons enabled working-class women, and even servants, to wear the same fabrics as the middle and upper classes. Beeton's comment is intriguingly honest about the need to concentrate on points of class-differentiation in dress.

422 *spermaceti*: white, waxy substance found in the head of the sperm whale; used for candles as well as ointments.

424 *hard . . . straight*: this refers to the arrangement of the various straw and feather mattresses.

426 *Crape*: black silk or imitation silk worn for mourning.

443 *Carpets . . . commenced*: an indication of the increasing prevalence of advertising in the period, and Beeton's resistance to it.

444 *The several . . . purchased*: one of a number of examples of plans to occupy every minute of a servant's time—with trivial tasks if necessary ones have been completed.

Breaking . . . family: a curious over-statement, indicating the profundity of housewifely frustration about such accidents.

445 *Floorcloth*: waxed canvas, sometimes painted: this was widely used in the eighteenth century, and still used in the nineteenth for servants' quarters and areas of heavy use.

447 *The general . . . messages*: a very informative passage, both for the sympathy expressed for this most lowly of servants, and also for the underlying class distinctions between 'some small tradesman's wife' and 'some respectable tradesman's house' (see discussion of this passage in Introduction). Such comments make it clear that Beeton imagines her main readership to fall in the 'respectable tradesman', and professional, bands of the middle class, and sees the lower-middle class as, on the whole, outside her remit.

450 *Supposing . . . offices*: an interesting indication of the size of house (reasonably large by today's standards) which Beeton assumes would only employ one servant.

455 *Phyllis's*: a name given to shepherdesses in the literary tradition of pastoral; Beeton's usage is clearly designed to evoke nostalgia for the rural way of life.

465 *cordials . . . known*: these often contained alcohol or drugs such as laudanum; numbers of children died as a result.

474 *When . . . infant*: it is assumed that the normal healthy mother will want to breast-feed her child herself: this represents a significant social change from the eighteenth century, when most women of wealth or social position would hand their infants over to a wet-nurse as a matter of course;

the shift is a function of the greater importance accorded to children and maternity in the nineteenth century.

476   *In all . . . nurse*: a clear example of the attitude that sees incompetent servants as children in need of punishment. This paragraph also reveals the perhaps legitimate paranoia of the mother about her child's treatment at the hands of such servants.

478   *THE REARING . . . CHILDHOOD*: this and the next chapter on 'The Doctor' were compiled, as Beeton tells us in her Preface, by 'an experienced surgeon . . . fully entitled to confidence'.

479   *we see . . . life*: the undertone of repulsion at these examples of squalor is typical of the attitudes of middle-class Victorians whose feelings about the poor were finely balanced between pity on the one hand and fear and loathing on the other.

488   *We must . . . adults*: notably, exactly the opposite of the advice currently offered to parents of small babies.

492   *aperient*: laxative.

496   *As respects . . . readers*: a very consciously tactful statement, paying lip-service to the newly dominant ideology of natural maternal instincts, while also laying down firm modern scientific principles.

       In these . . . halyards: an interesting combination of neo-feminist assertions (albeit directed at 'primitive' cultures), and attitudes to the carrying and dressing of children that tally remarkably with those of the late twentieth century.

497   *Baths*: not, in fact, covered in the following section.

506   *scammony*: a gum-resin from a West Asian plant, used as a drastic purgative.

511   *Cow-pox . . . life*: the cow-pox vaccine was first successfully used to immunize against small-pox in 1796, by the English physician Edward Jenner (1749–1823).

514   *leeches*: it seems incredible that the ancient method of bleeding, through the application of leeches, cups, and so on, was still in use in an age that also understood the significance of vaccination.

515   *jalap*: a purgative derived from the tuberous roots of a Mexican climbing plant.

522   *THE DOCTOR*: see note to p. 478. Many of the drugs given in the following list of domestic remedies are expectorants, emetics, and purgatives. A number are also poisonous if taken in any quantity.

       Antimonial Wine: a mixture of tartrated antimony (a brittle bluish-white metal) and sherry; according to *Beeton's Medical Dictionary* (Ward Lock, 1871) antimonial preparations (including the antimonial powder listed next) are stimulants and expectorants in small doses, and emetic in larger ones. They were used mainly to treat colds and catarrhal infections.

Blue Pill: also known as 'mercurial pill': a mixture of mercury, confection of roses, and liquorice root, used for bilious problems or as a purgative. *Beeton's Medical Dictionary* (see previous note) comments that 'blue pill is very servicable . . . but the frequent or indiscriminate use of this medicine is justly condemned as productive of many evils'.

Carbonate of Potash: derived from the ashes of certain plants, widely used both in surgery and as a purgative.

Colocynth: purgative derived from a gourd plant with bitter-pulped fruit.

Goulard's Extract: triacetate of lead dissolved in water; mainly used as a wash for inflamed surfaces, particularly eyes.

Myrrh and Aloes Pills: used mainly as a laxative.

Nitre: nitrate of potash: used as a refrigerant, diuretic, and diphoretic (to induce perspiration), as a gargle for inflamed throats, and as a sedative.

Oil of Turpentine: used as a liniment for chronic inflammations.

Opium . . . Laudanum: these opiates, particularly laudanum, were widely available and frequently used in this period.

Opodeldoc: a type of liniment made of soap.

523 *sugar of lead*: lead acetate.

527 *under the ground*: somewhat gruesome humour, rather at odds with Beeton's own tone in the rest of the book.

530 *body*: half a page of advice on the treatment of different degrees of burns follows in the original.

531 *CHOLERA*: a bacterial infection transmitted in contaminated water or food. The symptoms include sickness and purging, weakness and cramps; the limbs twist and contort, the patient sinks into a state of apathy and death often follows very rapidly. There were serious epidemics in Britain in 1831–3, 1848, and 1865–6, in which tens of thousands died. Successive measures by local and national governments attempted to improve drainage and sanitation in order to control the disease.

534 *APOPLEXY*: mostly covers the condition we know as stroke.

537 *Fainting Fits*: Victorian women were much given to fainting, almost certainly from the tightness of their corsets, though it is notable that the writer uses the gender neutral 'he' with reference to the patient, in contrast with the assumptions in the following section on hysteria.

538 *Hysterics*: a complaint that much afflicted young Victorian women—and the nervous disorder to which Freud devoted much of his attention. The name derives from the Greek for womb, hysteria being thought to be the result of a disorder of the female reproductive system. Hysterectomies and clitoridectomies were not infrequently performed in the nineteenth century as a cure for the condition. *Beeton's Medical Dictionary* interestingly takes a neo-feminist line on the condition, declaring that 'The great cause of the prevalance of this disorder among our young females is owing to the defective physical and mental training to which they are

subjected. Were their physical frames developed and strengthened, and their mental powers kept in proper subjection, there would be much less of hysteria.'

540 *POISONS*: those mentioned were almost all kept in the average Victorian house, many for medicinal purposes (a number feature on the list of medicines given at the start of the chapter), and others for cleaning, pest extermination, and so on.

544 *ALKALIS . . . mistake*: reveals the fascinating assumption that many of the other poisons are more commonly given, or taken, deliberately.

547 *painters and glaziers*: because lead was present in paint and glass.

551 *linen roller*: bandage.

552 *Carbonic Acid Gas*: carbon monoxide.

556 *WHITLOW*: inflammatory sore on finger.

557 *erysipelas*: local inflammation caused by streptococcus bacteria.

562 *LEGAL MEMORANDA*: this chapter was contributed by a solicitor. The subjects it covers in the original are property law, especially buying, leasing or renting houses; taxes, rates, and insurance; the law affecting apprentices; the legal position governing husbands and wives; and wills. Only those passages have been retained which are notably different from modern law, or shed an interesting light on Victorian social practices.

men . . . too: the solicitor assumes, unlike Beeton, that his address is largely to men.

568 *Divorce . . . Act, 1857*: a significant milestone in the cause of women's rights, this Act allowed an abandoned wife some claim on the money and property she acquired after her husband's desertion: previously he had absolute rights over all such property.

allows his wife: because all of a woman's property automatically became her husband's on marriage (unless a special trust had been established for her beforehand). It was not until the Married Women's Property Acts of 1870 and 1882 that this position was partially adjusted.

INDEX

TROLLOPE IN OXFORD WORLD'S CLASSICS

ANTHONY TROLLOPE

An Autobiography

Ayala's Angel

Barchester Towers

The Belton Estate

The Bertrams

Can You Forgive Her?

The Claverings

Cousin Henry

Doctor Thorne

Doctor Wortle's School

The Duke's Children

Early Short Stories

The Eustace Diamonds

An Eye for an Eye

Framley Parsonage

He Knew He Was Right

Lady Anna

The Last Chronicle of Barset

Later Short Stories

Miss Mackenzie

Mr Scarborough's Family

Orley Farm

Phineas Finn

Phineas Redux

The Prime Minister

Rachel Ray

The Small House at Allington

La Vendée

The Warden

The Way We Live Now

The Oxford World's Classics Website

www.worldsclassics.co.uk

- Information about new titles
- Explore the full range of Oxford World's Classics
- Links to other literary sites and the main OUP webpage
- Imaginative competitions, with bookish prizes
- Peruse *Compass*, the Oxford World's Classics magazine
- Articles by editors
- Extracts from Introductions
- A forum for discussion and feedback on the series
- Special information for teachers and lecturers

www.worldsclassics.co.uk

American Literature

British and Irish Literature

Children's Literature

Classics and Ancient Literature

Colonial Literature

Eastern Literature

European Literature

History

Medieval Literature

Oxford English Drama

Poetry

Philosophy

Politics

Religion

The Oxford Shakespeare

A complete list of Oxford Paperbacks, including Oxford World's Classics, OPUS, Past Masters, Oxford Authors, Oxford Shakespeare, Oxford Drama, and Oxford Paperback Reference, is available in the UK from the Academic Division Publicity Department, Oxford University Press, Great Clarendon Street, Oxford OX2 6DP.

In the USA, complete lists are available from the Paperbacks Marketing Manager, Oxford University Press, 198 Madison Avenue, New York, NY 10016.

Oxford Paperbacks are available from all good bookshops. In case of difficulty, customers in the UK can order direct from Oxford University Press Bookshop, Freepost, 116 High Street, Oxford OX1 4BR, enclosing full payment. Please add 10 per cent of published price for postage and packing.